THE ARDEN SHAKESPEARE

THIRD SERIES

General Editors: Richard Proudfoot, Ann Thompson
and D
Associate Gene
Georg

KING
RICHARD II

THE ARDEN SHAKESPEARE

ALL'S WELL THAT ENDS WELL	edited by G. K. Hunter*
ANTONY AND CLEOPATRA	edited by John Wilders
AS YOU LIKE IT	edited by Agnes Latham*
THE COMEDY OF ERRORS	edited by R. A. Foakes*
CORIOLANUS	edited by Philip Brockbank*
CYMBELINE	edited by J. M. Nosworthy*
HAMLET	edited by Harold Jenkins*
JULIUS CAESAR	edited by David Daniell
KING HENRY IV Parts 1 and 2	edited by A. R. Humphreys*
KING HENRY V	edited by T. W. Craik
KING HENRY VI Part 1	edited by Edward Burns
KING HENRY VI Part 2	edited by Ronald Knowles
KING HENRY VI Part 3	edited by John D. Cox and Eric Rasmussen
KING HENRY VIII	edited by Gordon McMullan
KING JOHN	edited by E. A. J. Honigmann*
KING LEAR	edited by R. A. Foakes
KING RICHARD II	edited by Charles R. Forker
KING RICHARD III	edited by Antony Hammond*
LOVE'S LABOUR'S LOST	edited by H. R. Woudhuysen
MACBETH	edited by Kenneth Muir*
MEASURE FOR MEASURE	edited by J. W. Lever*
THE MERCHANT OF VENICE	edited by John Russell Brown*
THE MERRY WIVES OF WINDSOR	edited by Giorgio Melchiori
A MIDSUMMER NIGHT'S DREAM	edited by Harold F. Brooks*
MUCH ADO ABOUT NOTHING	edited by A. R. Humphreys*
OTHELLO	edited by E. A. J. Honigmann
PERICLES	edited by F. D. Hoeniger*
THE POEMS	edited by F. T. Prince*
ROMEO AND JULIET	edited by Brian Gibbons*
SHAKESPEARE'S SONNETS	edited by Katherine Duncan-Jones
THE TAMING OF THE SHREW	edited by Brian Morris*
THE TEMPEST	edited by Virginia Mason Vaughan and Alden T. Vaughan
TIMON OF ATHENS	edited by H. J. Oliver*
TITUS ANDRONICUS	edited by Jonathan Bate
TROILUS AND CRESSIDA	edited by David Bevington
TWELFTH NIGHT	edited by J. M. Lothian and T. W. Craik*
THE TWO GENTLEMEN OF VERONA	edited by Clifford Leech*
THE TWO NOBLE KINSMEN	edited by Lois Potter
THE WINTER'S TALE	edited by J. H. P. Pafford*

* Second series

KING
RICHARD II

Edited by
CHARLES R. FORKER

SWINDON COLLEGE REGENT CIRCUS	
Cypher	30.01.04
	£7.99

The Arden website is at
http://www.ardenshakespeare.com

The general editors of the Arden Shakespeare have been
W. J. Craig and R. H. Case (first series 1899-1944)
Una Ellis-Fermor, Harold F. Brooks, Harold Jenkins
and Brian Morris (second series 1946-82)

Present general editors (third series)
Richard Proudfoot, Ann Thompson and David Scott Kastan

This edition of *King Richard II,* by Charles R. Forker
published 2002 by The Arden Shakespeare

Arden Shakespeare is an imprint of Thomson Learning

Thomson Learning
High Holborn House
50-51 Bedford Row
London WC1R 4LR

Editorial matter © 2002 Charles R. Forker

Picture Research by Zooid Pictures Ltd

Typeset in Ehrhardt by Multiplex Techniques Ltd
Printed in Croatia

British Library Cataloguing in Publication Data
A catalogue record for this book is available from the British Library

Library of Congress Cataloguing in Publication Data
A catalogue record has been requested

ISBN 1-903436-32-X (hardback)
NPN 9 8 7 6 5 4 3 2 1
ISBN 1-903436-33-8 (paperback)
NPN 9 8 7 6 5 4 3 2

The Editor

Charles R. Forker is Professor of English Emeritus at Indiana University, Bloomington. His many publications include critical editions of Shirley's *The Cardinal* (1964) and Marlowe's *Edward II* (1994), and a major study of the works of Webster, *Skull Beneath the Skin: The Achievement of John Webster* (1986). His most recent work is a study of Shakespeare's Richard II, *Shakespeare: The Critical Tradition: 'Richard II'* (London, 1998).

To
the memory of
Stuart Major Sperry

CONTENTS

List of illustrations   ix

General editors' preface   xii

Preface   xvi

Introduction   1
  Politics   5
    Historical Context and the Issue of Topicality 5
    The Connection with Essex   9
    Ideology: Competing Conceptions of Monarchy   16
    Characterization: Attitudes towards Richard
      and Bolingbroke   23
    Politics in Seventeenth- and Eighteenth-
      Century Stagings   50
  Language   55
    Style   55
    Imagery, Major Themes, Symbolism,
      Patterns of Allusion   64
    Rhetoric   83
  Afterlife   90
  The Date   111
    The Relation to Edward II *and* Woodstock   116
    Richard II *and the Second Tetralogy*   118
  Probable Venues of Early Performance   120
  Sources   123
    Holinshed   124
    Hall   136
    The Mirror for Magistrates   138

Contents

Daniel	140
Woodstock	144
Froissart; Créton; Traïson	152
Edward II	159
Minor Sources	164
Text	165

**THE TRAGEDY OF KING RICHARD
THE SECOND**   171

Longer Notes   485

Appendices   506

1 Textual Analysis   506

2 Doubling Chart   542

3 Genealogical Tables   544

Abbreviations and references   546
  Abbreviations used in notes   546
  Works by and partly by Shakespeare   547
  Editions of Shakespeare collated or referred to 548
  Other works   551
  Modern stage and television productions cited 567

Index   569

LIST OF
ILLUSTRATIONS

1 Richard II in Henry Holland, *Baziliologia*, 1618 (courtesy of
the Huntington Library, San Marino, California)   2

2 Robert Devereux, second Earl of Essex, miniature attributed to
Nicholas Hilliard, *c.* 1587 (courtesy of the National Portrait
Gallery, London)   11

3 Elizabeth I in Parliament, engraving in Robert Glover,
Nobilitas Politica vel Civilis, 1608 (courtesy of the Folger
Shakespeare Library, Washington, D.C.)   20

4 Virtus and Fortuna holding a crown over a king's head, from
Guillaume de la Perrière, *La Morosophie*, Lyons, 1553, emblem
68 (courtesy of the Huntington Library, San Marino, California)   37

5 Anamorphic portrait of Edward VI (two views from front and
side), after Hans Holbein the Younger, 1543 (National Portrait
Gallery, London); reproduced in Jurgis Baltrusaitis,
Anamorphic Art (New York, 1977)   62

6 Emblem of the Pelican, from George Wither, *A Collection of
Emblems, Ancient and Modern*, 1635 (courtesy of the British
Library)   72

7 The badge of Woodstock (Duke of Gloucester), from
C.W. Scott-Giles, *Shakespeare's Heraldry*, 1950   73

8 Death hovering above a crowned king, from Hans Holbein the
Younger, *The Dance of Death*, 1538   84

9 Richard and Bolingbroke (4.1 of the acting version of
Richard II by Richard Wroughton), in an engraving by
G.W. Bonner from a drawing taken in the theatre by
R. Cruikshank (vol. 29 of *Cumberland's British Theatre*,
London, 1823–31)   94

10 Frank Benson as Richard II at the Shakespeare Memorial
    Theatre, 1896 (courtesy of the Shakespeare Centre Library,
    Stratford-upon-Avon)   97

11 John Gielgud as Richard II, Glen Byam Shaw as Mowbray,
    Michael Redgrave as Bolingbroke, Leon Quartermaine as
    Gaunt in Gielgud's production at the Queen's Theatre,
    London, 6 August 1937 (Theatre Museum, London;
    © Kruston Rogers, 23 Golden Square, London WC1)   99

12 John Neville as Richard II with Green (Murray Hayne),
    Bagot (Nicholas Amer) and Aumerle (Anthony White) in
    Michael Benthall's Old Vic production, 1955 (Theatre
    Museum, London)   101

13 Richard (Richard Pasco) is visited by Bolingbroke, disguised
    as the Groom (Ian Richardson), at Pomfret (5.5) in
    John Barton's RSC production, 1973, at Stratford-upon-Avon
    (Joe Cocks Studio Photographic Collection, courtesy of
    the Shakespeare Centre Library, Stratford-upon-Avon)   103

14 Richard Howard as Richard II (3.3), in Howard Jensen's
    Oregon Shakespeare Festival production, Ashland, 1995
    (courtesy of Deborah Elliott, publicist)   107

15 Fiona Shaw as Richard II with Julian Rhind-Tutt as Aumerle,
    in Deborah Warner's National Theatre production, Cottesloe
    Theatre, 1995 (photograph by Neil Libbert, reproduced in
    New York Times, 27 January 1996, Arts Section)   108

16 Richard II's emblem, the white hart, from the back panel of
    the Wilton Diptych (courtesy of the National Gallery, London)   132

17 Q1 title-page (1597), Huntington Library copy (courtesy of
    the Huntington Library, San Marino, California)   530

18 Q4 title-page (1608), second state, Bodleian Library copy
    (courtesy of the Bodleian Library, University of Oxford)   531

19 Uncorrected and corrected pages from Q (sigs D1^v and D3^v) –
    uncorrected P (Petworth; National Trust Photographic Library)
    and corrected TCC (Trinity College Library, Cambridge);
    four pages arranged in parallel, showing how the
    compositor dropped a line in the uncorrected state and then
    restored it in the corrected one   534, 535

GENERAL EDITORS' PREFACE

The Arden Shakespeare is now over one hundred years old. The earliest volume in the first series, Edward Dowden's *Hamlet*, was published in 1899. Since then the Arden Shakespeare has become internationally recognized and respected. It is now widely acknowledged as the pre-eminent Shakespeare series, valued by scholars, students, actors and 'the great variety of readers' alike for its readable and reliable texts, its full annotation and its richly informative introductions.

We have aimed in the third Arden edition to maintain the quality and general character of its predecessors, preserving the commitment to presenting the play as it has been shaped in history. While each individual volume will necessarily have its own emphasis in the light of the unique possibilities and problems posed by the play, the series as a whole, like the earlier Ardens, insists upon the highest standards of scholarship and upon attractive and accessible presentation.

Newly edited from the original quarto and folio editions, the texts are presented in fully modernized form, with a textual apparatus that records all substantial divergences from those early printings. The notes and introductions focus on the conditions and possibilities of meaning that editors, critics and performers (on stage and screen) have discovered in the play. While building upon the rich history of scholarly and theatrical activity that has long shaped our understanding of the texts of Shakespeare's plays, this third series of the Arden Shakespeare is made necessary and possible by a new generation's encounter with Shakespeare, engaging with the plays and their complex relation to the culture in which they were – and continue to be – produced.

THE TEXT

On each page of the play itself, readers will find a passage of text followed by commentary and, finally, textual notes. Act and scene divisions (seldom present in the early editions and often the product of eighteenth-century or later scholarship) have been retained for ease of reference, but have been given less prominence than in the previous series. Editorial indications of location of the action have been removed to the textual notes or commentary.

In the text itself, unfamiliar typographic conventions have been avoided in order to minimize obstacles to the reader. Elided forms in the early texts are spelt out in full in verse lines wherever they indicate a usual late twentieth-century pronunciation that requires no special indication and wherever they occur in prose (except when they indicate non-standard pronunciation). In verse speeches, marks of elision are retained where they are necessary guides to the scansion and pronunciation of the line. Final -ed in past tense and participial forms of verbs is always printed as -ed without accent, never as -'d, but wherever the required pronunciation diverges from modern usage a note in the commentary draws attention to the fact. Where the final -ed should be given syllabic value contrary to modern usage, e.g.

> Doth Silvia know that I am banished?
> (*TGV* 3.1.221)

the note will take the form

> 221 **banished** banishèd

Conventional lineation of divided verse lines shared by two or more speakers has been reconsidered and sometimes rearranged. Except for the familiar *Exit* and *Exeunt*, Latin forms in stage directions and speech prefixes have been translated into English and the original Latin forms recorded in the textual notes.

COMMENTARY AND TEXTUAL NOTES

Notes in the commentary, for which a major source will be the *Oxford English Dictionary*, offer glossarial and other explication of verbal difficulties; they may also include discussion of points of theatrical interpretation and, in relevant cases, substantial extracts from Shakespeare's source material. Editors will not usually offer glossarial notes for words adequately defined in the latest edition of *The Concise Oxford Dictionary* or *Merriam-Webster's Collegiate Dictionary*, but in cases of doubt they will include notes. Attention, however, will be drawn to places where more than one likely interpretation can be proposed and to significant verbal and syntactic complexity. Notes preceded by * discuss editorial emendations or variant readings from the early edition(s) on which the text is based.

Headnotes to acts or scenes discuss, where appropriate, questions of scene location, Shakespeare's handling of his source materials and major difficulties of staging. The list of roles (so headed to emphasize the play's status as a text for performance) is also considered in commentary notes. These may include comment on plausible patterns of casting with the resources of an Elizabethan or Jacobean acting company, and also on any variation in the description of roles in their speech prefixes in the early editions.

The textual notes are designed to let readers know when the edited text diverges from the early edition(s) on which it is based. Wherever this happens the note will record the rejected reading of the early edition(s), in original spelling, and the source of the reading adopted in this edition. Other forms from the early edition(s) recorded in these notes will include some spellings of particular interest or significance and original forms of translated stage directions. Where two early editions are involved, for instance with *Othello*, the notes will also record all important differences between them. The textual notes take a form that has been in use since the nineteenth century. This comprises, first: line reference, reading adopted in the text and closing square bracket; then: abbreviated reference, in italic, to the earliest edition to adopt the accepted reading, italic semicolon and noteworthy alternative reading(s), each with abbreviated italic reference to its source.

Conventions used in these textual notes include the following. The solidus / is used, in notes quoting verse or discussing verse lining, to indicate line endings. Distinctive spellings of the basic text (Q or F) follow the square bracket without indication of source and are enclosed in italic brackets. Names enclosed in italic brackets indicate originators of conjectural emendations when these did not originate in an edition of the text, or when this edition records a conjecture not accepted into its text. Stage directions (SDs) are referred to by the number of the line within or immediately after which they are placed. Line numbers with a decimal point relate to entry SDs and to SDs more than one line long, with the number after the point indicating the line within the SD: e.g. 78.4 refers to the fourth line of the SD following line 78. Lines of SDs at the start of a scene are numbered 0.1, 0.2, etc. Where only a line number and SD precede the square bracket, e.g. 128 SD], the note relates to the whole of a SD within or immediately following the line. Speech prefixes (SPs) follow similar conventions, 203 SP] referring to the speaker's name for line 203. Where a SP reference takes the form e.g. 38 + SP, it relates to all subsequent speeches assigned to that speaker in the scene in question.

Where, as with *King Henry V*, one of the early editions is a so-called 'bad quarto' (that is, a text either heavily adapted, or reconstructed from memory, or both), the divergences from the present edition are too great to be recorded in full in the notes. In these cases the editions will include a reduced photographic facsimile of the 'bad quarto' in an appendix.

INTRODUCTION

Both the introduction and the commentary are designed to present the plays as texts for performance, and make appropriate reference to stage, film and television versions, as well as introducing the reader to the range of critical approaches to the plays. They discuss the history of the reception of the texts within the theatre and scholarship and beyond, investigating the interdependency of the literary text and the surrounding 'cultural text' both at the time of the original production of Shakespeare's works and during their long and rich afterlife.

PREFACE

Richard II has occupied an important place in my literary consciousness since I was introduced to the play as an undergraduate in the late 1940s by Stanley Perkins Chase at Bowdoin College, where I also acted the role of Bolingbroke in a *Mask and Gown* production. H.V.D. Dyson, my tutor at Merton College, Oxford, and Alfred Harbage, my doctoral supervisor at Harvard, further stimulated my interest by prompting me to write essays on topics closely related to the tragedy. The play has figured prominently in my university teaching and research over the years – experience which led eventually to my assembling historical commentary on *Richard II*, published in 1998 as a volume in Brian Vickers's series, *Shakespeare: The Critical Tradition*. That even minor details of the play continue to absorb my attention will be obvious to readers of the commentary, which may be accused, I fear, of threatening at times to overwhelm the text it was written to serve. I would plead in defence that I have devoted much space to extended quotation from the sources (or possible sources), and that it is important to make immediately present to readers as rich a historical context as possible for the understanding and interpretation of a drama that exploits nuanced or conflicting political attitudes and that portrays ambiguities of motive. Because *Richard II* is by design the most lyrical of Shakespeare's histories, I have also thought it useful to suggest ways in which the more problematic and irregular lines may be scanned.

Like all editors of Shakespeare, I am heavily indebted to my predecessors – especially to the deservedly influential editions of *Richard II* by John Dover Wilson (1939), Matthew W. Black (the New Variorum editor, 1955), Peter Ure (1956), Stanley Wells (1969) and Andrew Gurr (1984). Each of these has prepared the ground for my own work and taught me much. Nor could I have read as widely and as profitably in the scholarship and performance history of the play as I have done without the aid of Josephine A. Roberts's indispensable annotated, two-volume Garland bibliography (1988). I owe particular thanks to the reference departments of the research libraries consulted in the preparation of this volume, especially to those at the Bodleian Library, the British Library, the Folger Shakespeare Library, the Henry E. Huntington Library and, far from least, the Indiana University Library and its rare-book adjunct, the Lilly Library. Ann Bristow, David K. Frasier and Jeffrey Graf, my librarian colleagues at Indiana, have been unfailingly resourceful.

Any edition of a work by Shakespeare in the twenty-first century must inevitably be collaborative, often in ways of which the individual contributors may be unaware. Michael J.B. Allen, David M. Bergeron, David Bevington, A.R. Braunmuller, James C. Bulman, Joseph Candido, S.P. Cerasano, T.W. Craik, Katherine Duncan-Jones, R.A. Foakes, Donald Foster, R.D. Fulk, Walter Hodges, Michael Jamieson, Howard Jensen, Frederick Kiefer, F.J. Levy, Trevor Lloyd, Timothy Long, William B. Long, Russ McDonald, Randal McLeod, Gordon McMullan, Giorgio Melchiori, Robert S. Miola, Margaret Loftus Ranald, Peter Slemon, W.E. Slights, Bruce Smith, J.J.M. Tobin, John W. Velz, Brian Vickers, Eugene M. Waith and Stanley Wells have all helped make this edition better than it otherwise would have been – some by giving advice or information on specific points, others by shedding their light more generally. Among innumerable friends who have offered support at moments of frustration or discouragement, sometimes unwittingly, Michael Duff, Denzil Freeth, the Revd John B. Gaskell, John B. Hartley, Lewis J. Overaker, Eric S. Rump, Janet C. Stavropoulos and the Revd James K. Taylor must be singled out.

My greatest debt is to Richard Proudfoot, a general editor of tirelessness, enthusiasm and exemplary tact, who curbed my more flagrant excesses with the irony they merited, made valuable points that had escaped my notice, and guided me with learning, forbearance, and sharp critical intelligence through the shoals and turbulences of the long passage from first draft to final copy. George Walton Williams, associate general editor, was equally assiduous, perceptive and wittily sympathetic in suggesting improvements. I could scarcely have hoped for two scholars as deeply experienced and as personally engaged with *Richard II* as these gentlemen; and although I have dared to disagree with them in a few particulars, their influence on the final product has been pervasive and hugely important – a point which no one who bothers to count the citations of 'RP' and 'GWW' in the commentary will doubt. David Scott Kastan also offered me the benefit of his well-honed critical scrutiny, providing especially helpful counsel on the structuring of the Introduction. These acknowledgements would be seriously remiss if they did not include mention of Jessica Hodge, publisher of the Arden 3 series, whose ability to exert the necessary pressures on authors is expertly leavened by a sense of humour, a genuine respect for her charges and an irresistible capacity for affection. Equally deserving of my homage is Nicola Bennett, my meticulous, self-effacing, eagle-eyed and endlessly diligent copy-editor, who preserved me from many inconsistencies and blunders, who sharpened my logic and clarified cloudy sentences, and who not infrequently bettered the substance as well as the accidents of this book.

Charles R. Forker
Bloomington, Indiana

INTRODUCTION

Richard II marks an exciting advance in the development of Shakespeare's artistry. Its unusual formality of structure and tone as well as the impressive eloquence of its style seem to have been crafted to express the mystique of kingship more emphatically than any of the earlier histories without neglecting a subtle handling of its major action – the dethronement of an unsuitable anointed monarch by an illegitimate but more able one. The power and ordered grandeur of the state as symbolically centred in the throne are brought into tragic conflict with the human weakness and political inadequacy of its incumbent. Thus, audiences are called upon to respond not only to the fall of a particular king (Fig. 1) but also to the disquieting possibility that the institution of hereditary monarchy may itself be unviable. The subject would have been especially magnetic in the waning years of the last Tudor, who was sometimes thought to be dangerously influenced by ambitious favourites, and the identity of whose as yet unspecified successor was stimulating intense partisan speculation. Struggles for a crown were not new. In his plays on the Wars of the Roses Shakespeare had already shown the chaotic horrors of civil war and the displacement of weak kings by stronger ones. What is unique and fresh in *Richard II* is the stress on the divinity that was thought to hedge kings, the abandonment of historical diffuseness and the probing not merely of divine right as a concept but of the unstable personality of a king who puts his whole trust in its theoretical protections.

In the character of Richard, Shakespeare achieved a higher degree of psychological complexity than he had yet managed in tragedy. *Titus Andronicus* with its sanguinary sensationalism, *Romeo and Juliet* with its star-crossed lovers victimized by

1 Richard II in Henry Holland, *Baziliologia*, 1618

circumstance and *Richard III* with its Vice-like, overreaching protagonist offered limited scope for the exploration of tragic personality. In the first play of what was to become his second tetralogy Shakespeare seized the opportunity to dramatize the original mythic cause of the disasters already staged in the *Henry VI–Richard III* sequence. In so doing, he excavated new soil, exposing the roots of the fateful contest for power by showing them to lie not merely in the factionalism of kinship or party but also in contrasts of sensibility, temperament, emotional predisposition and philosophical outlook. Richard, the man of words, postures and ceremonial dignity, is defeated by Bolingbroke, the man of actions and pragmatic realism. A new spirit of assertive individuality seems finally to dissolve the settled harmonies of medieval tradition and hierarchical order. And Shakespeare so arranges the contest that our sympathies are necessarily divided. Depending on one's perspective – an important motif in the play (see especially 2.2.14–27) – Richard is either a tyrant or a martyr, Bolingbroke either a patriot or a ruthless opportunist, York either the reluctant servant of an historical shift or a pusillanimous defector. The ambiguous moral foundations of the action become part of the dramatic experience. Defeat dignifies Richard because the sufferings entailed in the loss of his crown open him to a deeper awareness of his failings and to a less blinkered sense of his dual identity as fallible mortal and God's anointed. But as Alfred Harbage remarks, 'Shakespeare's worst king', judged in terms of competency, 'is never hated, and is often even loved – for his eloquence, his irresponsibility amounting almost to innocence, his deep conviction that he is *deserving* of love' (68). Paradoxically, Henry, the new and unillusioned king, implicates himself in the role-playing and moral compromise (with its attendant guilt) that he had seemed so vigorously to oppose in Richard.

In particular ways *Richard II* adumbrates Shakespeare's maturer tragedies and histories. Hamlet's egotism, self-consciousness and verbal brilliance are all to be found more rudimentarily in Richard's character, as is a pale simulacrum of Lear's growth from

3

arrogance to humility. The sympathy evoked for Richard even at his weakest looks forward to that we feel for the defeated and love-betrayed Antony. The break-up of England that begins under Richard's reign finds a counterpart of sorts in the collapse of the Roman republic in *Julius Caesar*; and Brutus' misguided commitment to political assassination is not wholly unlike Richard's mistake in ridding himself of the troublesome Gloucester. The glowing nationalism of Gaunt's great praise of England anticipates the spirit of Agincourt that so vitally informs *Henry V*.

Finally, *Richard II* is a play for the ear, its balances and symmetries of character and structure finding analogies in the graceful cadences, rhetorical artifices and striking imagery of its language. It is surely significant that the poets Yeats and Masefield were attracted to the vocal charms of its protagonist.[1] Nor is the verbal opulence merely decorative. The play is among Shakespeare's first to utilize patterns of imagery and thematic repetition for dramatic and structural purposes. What both the Duchess of York and Richard refer to as 'set[ting] the word . . . against the word' (5.3.121, 5.5.13–14) marks the play's style, not merely in the narrow sense of juxtaposing one biblical passage with another but in the broader sense of pitting different meanings of words and opposed attitudes against each other. The tragedy's penchant for wordplay and *double entendre* thus becomes an important resource of its characterization and dramaturgy.

This Introduction falls into several subdivisions. 'Politics' seeks to establish the play's ideological and cultural context, its relation to Elizabethan censorship, the ambiguous responses to major characters that its dramatic technique and structure encourage and, finally, the survival of topical significances into the seventeenth and eighteenth centuries. 'Language' discusses the play's complex style, imagery and rhetoric. 'Afterlife' outlines its changing reputation with particular attention to the varied history of twentieth-century stagings. Four final sections take up the 'Date'

---

1 See Forker, 372–8, 463–5.

of the play, 'Venues of Early Performance', Shakespeare's use of 'Sources' and decisions affecting the 'Text' of the present edition.

POLITICS

Historical Context and the Issue of Topicality

As Elizabeth I aged, it became increasingly common to identify her with Richard II. Her remark to William Lambarde in 1601, 'I am Richard II. Know ye not that?', is only the best known of several such comparisons.[1] The reasons were at least two. The first had to do with a perception in some quarters that the Queen was unusually susceptible to flattery and that favourites such as Leicester and Burghley were able to exert dangerous and harmful control over her policies, especially with regard to monopolies and burdensome taxes and, from a Catholic perspective, to religious toleration. The second pertained to the unsettled succession. Both concerns undoubtedly reinforced the parallel with Richard and may have had something to do with the appearance during Shakespeare's career of at least four plays on Richard's reign – *The Life and Death of Jack Straw* (1590–3), *Woodstock* (1591–5), Shakespeare's own tragedy (1595), and an anonymous play, now lost, described by Simon Forman as having been played at the Globe on 30 April 1611.[2]

---

1   For Lambarde, see Chambers, *WS*, 2.326. Sir Francis Knollys, after giving unwelcome advice to the Queen, wrote in 1578 that he refused to 'play the partes of King Richard the Second's men' (a synonym for flatterers), while Lord Hunsdon at some point before 1588 repeated the same phrase. Sir Walter Raleigh in a letter to Robert Cecil (6 July 1597) remarked that Essex was 'wonderfull merry att ye consait [conceit] of Richard the 2', apparently alluding to the same analogy (see Chambers, *WS*, 1.353). On 19 February 1601 at Essex's trial for treason, the prosecutor, Sir Edward Coke, invoked the parallel again: 'Note but the precedents of former ages, how long lived Richard the Second after he was surprised in the same manner [as Elizabeth was surprised by Essex]?' (Black, 581).

2   Chambers, *WS*, 2.339–40. All four plays portray Richard as guilty of tyrannous actions or policies, although the implied condemnation falls heaviest on his counsellors, especially in the case of *Jack Straw* in which the boy king is apparently unaware of how brutally the tax collectors oppress the common people; Straw observes, 'The king God wot knowes not whats done [to] such poore men as we' (l. 61). A fifth play, *Pierce of Exton* (1598) by Chettle, Dekker, Drayton and Wilson, was apparently never completed; see Chambers, *ES*, 2.167.

As to the first point, *Richard II* does indeed dramatize attitudes similar to the complaints against Elizabeth's ministers voiced by opponents of her fiscal policies:

NORTHUMBERLAND

> . . . The King is not himself, but basely led
> By flatterers; and what they will inform
> Merely in hate 'gainst any of us all,
> That will the King severely prosecute
> 'Gainst us, our lives, our children and our heirs.

ROSS

> The commons hath he pilled with grievous taxes,
> And quite lost their hearts. The nobles hath he fined
> For ancient quarrels, and quite lost their hearts.

WILLOUGHBY

> And daily new exactions are devised,
> As blanks, benevolences, and I wot not what.
> But what, i'God's name, doth become of this?

(2.1.241–51)

As Richard Simpson pointed out in 1874, these lines recall the malcontent sentiments of such Catholic controversialists as Thomas Morgan, Richard Rowlands and Robert Parsons.[1] These men wrote tracts with titles such as the following: (1) *The Copy of a Letter Written by a Master of Art of Cambridge . . . about the present state and some proceedings of the Earl of Leicester* (1584); (2) *A Declaration of the True Causes of the Great Troubles, Presupposed to be Intended Against the Realm of England* (1592); and (3) *An Advertisement Written to a Secretary of My Lord Treasurer's of England* (1592). The first of these writings warns Elizabeth to beware of the fates of Edward II, Richard II and Henry VI – 'thre iust and lawful kinges' who came 'to confusion . . . by alienation of their subiectes' and 'to[o] much fauour towardes wicked persons'; for Richard's reign the examples given are Robert de Vere

---

1   See Forker, 240–6, 516–17.

and Thomas Mowbray – 'two moste turbulent and wicked men, that set the kinge againste his owne vncles and the nobilitie' – de Vere being paralleled with Leicester.[1] The second tract contains a philippic against William Cecil, the Lord Treasurer, accusing him of oppressing the people in the Queen's name with all manner of ruinous financial burdens – 'great & grieueous exactions', 'newe *impostes* and *customes*' on merchandise, '*forfaictures*', '*confiscations*', '*forced beneuolences*', 'huge masses of mony raised by *priuy seales*', '*subsidies*' and the like.[2] As Simpson points out (Forker, 242), Shakespeare's use of the terms 'new exactions' and 'benevolences' (2.1.249–50) seems almost to echo the very words of the propagandist (Rowlands?). The third pamphlet, an English translation of a Latin work by Parsons, speaks of the 'fierce & cruell lawes' recently enacted by Elizabeth against Catholics, singling out her chief ministers over the course of the reign 'who haue bin the causes and instrumentes of all miserie to Ingland . . . and of the perdition of the realme by theire especiall authority with her Maiestie', namely Sir Nicholas Bacon, Leicester, Sir Francis Walsingham, Sir Christopher Hatton and especially Lord Burghley.[3] Meanwhile, radical Puritans were as dissatisfied with Elizabeth's government as the Catholics. In 1576, for instance, Peter Wentworth rose in Parliament to attack those royal advisers and politicians who, 'through flattery', sought 'to devour our natural Prince', causing her thereby to commit 'great faults – yea, dangerous faults to herself and the State'.[4] And John Penry, a major force behind the Marprelate pamphlets (executed for sedition in 1593), also attacked members of the Queen's Council, not only for their scandalous leniency to Roman priests and recusants

---

1 Thomas Morgan(?), *Copy of a Letter*, 187–8. The book rapidly became known under the title of *Leicester's Commonwealth* and was so reprinted in 1641 (see Peck).
2 Richard Rowlands(?) (also known as Richard Verstegan), *Declaration*, 60. See also 2.1.250n.
3 John Philopatris (Richard Rowlands?), *Advertisement*, 11. This work is an abridged translation, written under the pseudonym John Philopatris, of a Latin tract, *Elizabethae . . . saevissimum in Catholicas . . . Edictum* (1592).
4 See Neale, 1.320–2. Wentworth was worried about Elizabeth's failure to take forceful action against Mary, Queen of Scots.

but also (on account of their support of the Anglican settlement) for being rebels and conspirators against God.[1]

Concerning the second point, namely the succession, the analogy between Richard II and Elizabeth was even more widely applicable. Both monarchs, after all, were childless. The Queen tried to discourage speculation and debate on the matter just as Richard had done some two centuries earlier;[2] but popular uncertainty about who would succeed was thought to weaken the stability of both reigns. At the time of his deposition, Richard's closest male relative was a child of three, Edmund Mortimer, fifth Earl of March, whose claim descended from Lionel, Duke of Clarence, Edward III's third son, through the female line (see Appendix 3). But claims were also made for Bolingbroke, who descended from the fourth of King Edward's sons, on the grounds that it was customary in the fourteenth century to entail great estates upon the male line.[3] There had also been a bogus legend, created by Lancastrian partisans, that Edmund Crouchback, Earl of Lancaster (an ancestor of John of Gaunt), was the older rather than the younger brother of Edward I and had been passed over for the throne on the grounds of his physical deformity. This story too was used to promote the legitimacy of Bolingbroke as heir presumptive over Mortimer.

Heated debate about Elizabeth's successor arose almost immediately after her accession and continued intermittently throughout the reign. Various names were mentioned, both in and out of Parliament, the possible candidates including (1) Mary, Queen of Scots, descended from Henry VIII's sister Margaret, and, after her execution, her son James VI; (2) Lady Catherine Grey, the younger sister of the tragic Lady Jane Grey, who, however, died in 1568,

1 See Forker, 517, n. 11.
2 See Saul, 397; also 3.3.113n. A law of 1571 (13 Eliz. I c. 1; see *Statutes*, 4.527) prohibiting the promotion of any successor to the throne other than Elizabeth's own issue is a case in point; see also Neale, 1.136, 150. Later when the intemperate Wentworth dared to write *A Pithy Exhortation* urging the Queen to settle the succession (posthumously published in 1598 but circulated earlier in manuscript), he was imprisoned in the Tower.
3 See 1.1.117n., 1.4.35n. and 36n.

leaving her son, Lord Beauchamp, as a possible but weak contender; (3) Lady Margaret Stuart, Countess of Lennox, and, later, her granddaughter, Lady Arabella Stuart; (4) Margaret, Countess of Derby, descended from Mary Tudor, younger sister of Henry VIII, and, after 1593, her son Ferdinando (Lord Strange); (5) Henry Hastings, third Earl of Huntingdon (Leicester's brother-in-law), whose claim would have revived the issues of the Wars of the Roses since his ancestry was Yorkist; and (6) Philip II of Spain, and, after his death, his daughter, the Infanta. Many Catholics, of course, favoured the Scottish queen and, later, the Infanta, while the more extreme Protestants tended to back Catherine Grey or her son Beauchamp, and, later, Huntingdon. James VI, who in strict genealogical terms had the best claim, enjoyed mixed support and was successfully, though clandestinely, promoted after Burghley's death by Sir Robert Cecil, his son and successor as chief minister.

There is no reason to suppose that in *Richard II* Shakespeare intended to allude to the specifics of these controversies, the details of which he would hardly have known since they were the special province of court gossip and intrigue or the stock-in-trade of professional politicians and religious sectarians. Palmer's assertion that in contemporary eyes the tragedy was regarded as 'the most topical . . . of the period' (118) is probably an overstatement. But there can be no doubt that when the play was written and first staged, such questions were in the air and that in some viewers at least the tragedy could have provoked a range of timely political resonances.

The Connection with Essex

Discussion of the play's topicality has centred mainly on events surrounding the Essex rebellion of 1601. This is partly because the dangerous issue of deposition had become entangled in the late 1590s with the other controversies touching the monarchy, the popular but volatile Earl being its chief focus (Fig. 2).[1] At

---

1 The issue of Elizabeth's deposition had arisen in 1570 when Pope Pius V issued his bull of excommunication against her. This document declared her to be no legitimate queen and released her subjects from all fealty and obedience. Most English Catholics, however, do not seem to have taken the papal edict seriously.

Essex's Star Chamber trial for treason in February 1601, Cecil charged that the Earl 'had been devising five or six years to be King of England . . . and meant to slip into Her Majesty's place' by insinuating himself 'into favour' with 'the Puritans', 'the Papists' and 'the people and soldiers' in general.[1] The linking of Shakespeare's tragedy with Essex was obviously after the fact and, from the dramatist's point of view, fortuitous, but it has nevertheless affected interpretation of the play's politics. The relevant facts may be summarized as follows.

On 7 February 1601, the day before Essex staged his abortive rebellion, a group of the Earl's supporters paid Shakespeare's company forty shillings to revive an old play on 'the deposing and killing of King Richard II' at the Globe – generally considered to have been Shakespeare's tragedy. The conspirators apparently believed that the drama would serve as effective propaganda for their treasonable enterprise.[2] When Augustine Phillips, one of the shareholders of the Chamberlain's Men, was summoned to answer for the actors, he pleaded that they had been reluctant to put on the drama, it being 'so old and so long out of use that they should have a small company at it', but had nevertheless been 'content to play it' as requested.[3] That Shakespeare and his fellows were innocent of any seditious design is clear from their having escaped punishment on this occasion and also from the

1   *CSPD*, 554. William Camden in his *History of the . . . Princess Elizabeth* (1630) wrote that when the Catholics despaired of a papist successor to Elizabeth, some of them 'cast their eyes vpon the Earle of *Essex* . . . , feigning a Title from *Thomas* of *Woodstock*, King *Edward* the third's sonne, from whom hee deriued his Pedigree' (4.57). As early as 1594 the Jesuit Robert Parsons, writing under the pseudonym of Doleman, dedicated to Essex his *A Conference about the Next Succession to the Crown of England*; in the dedication Parsons writes, somewhat incriminatingly, 'no man is in more high & eminent place or dignitie at this day in our realme, then your selfe, whether we respect your nobilitie, or calling, or fauour with your prince, or high liking of the people, & consequently no man like to haue a greater part or sway in deciding' the succession '(when tyme shall come for that determination) then your honour.'

2   This performance, if of Shakespeare's play, presumably included the abdication scene absent from the Elizabethan quartos, for without it the play could hardly have been thought to serve the rebels' political ends.

3   *CSPD*, 578.

2 Robert Devereux, second Earl of Essex, attributed to Nicholas Hilliard, *c.* 1587

fact that they were playing at court only days after Essex's trial.[1]

---

1 See Barroll. The treatment of the actors on this occasion contrasts strikingly with the experience of Ben Jonson and two fellow actors of Pembroke's Company (Gabriel Spencer and Robert Shaw), who were imprisoned and probably threatened with torture for performing the 'very seditious' *Isle of Dogs* in the summer of 1597. See Jonson, 1.15–16.

Two years earlier (in February 1599) Sir John Hayward's controversial volume, *The First Part of the Life and Reign of King Henry IV*, had appeared, bearing a dedication to Essex in which the Earl is referred to as 'futuri temporis expectatione' – a phrase that could be interpreted as suggesting him as heir apparent to the throne.[1] The book, despite its misleading title, offers a detailed account of Richard's deposition and death, containing also several passages in which critics have observed similarity to Shakespeare's phrasing.[2] Although Essex himself seems to have repudiated the dedication, the book appeared unhappily at a time when he and the Queen were at odds over his mission in Ireland, and Her Majesty seems to have been infuriated by what she took to be a sign of intolerable presumption and disloyalty on the Earl's part. Accordingly, the dedicatory page was quickly removed from the unsold copies by order of the Archbishop of Canterbury. A revised edition, which included the author's apology for having unwittingly misled readers, was seized and burned by the Bishop of London before any copies could circulate. The book, which was uncommonly popular, continued, however, to cause trouble for the Earl, and its publication was urged as evidence against him in July 1600, when he was being charged with malfeasance in connection with his activities in Ireland. A document in the State Papers, dated 22 July, supports a charge of treason against him in the following language:

> Essex's own actions confirm the intent of this treason. His permitting underhand that treasonable book of Henry IV to be printed and published; it being plainly deciphered, not only by the matter, and by the epistle itself [Hayward's Latin dedication], for what end and for whose behalf it was made, but also the Earl himself being

1 The full phrase that made trouble for both Hayward and Essex, translated from the Latin, reads: 'great thou art in hope, greater in the expectation of future time'.
2 See 2.3.122n., 2.4.9–15n., 4.1.122n., 131–2n., 135n., 208n., 5.2.18–20n., 5.4.2n., 5.5.77–83LN, 5.6.38–40n.

so often present at the playing thereof [i.e. of the book's subject-matter?], and with great applause giving countenance to it.[1]

Already committed to the Tower under suspicion of subversion, the unfortunate Hayward faced interrogation by the authorities at two different trials (on 11 July 1600 and 22 January 1601), Sir Edward Coke having carefully read the suspected book in preparation for his examination of the prisoner. Coke's notes for the first trial list suspicious parallels between Elizabeth's time and Richard II's as depicted by Hayward, including the apparently incriminating coincidences that Bolingbroke, like Essex, was an earl and that Richard, like Elizabeth, was confronted by a rebellion in Ireland. A summary of these notes appears as an abstract in the State Papers:

Interrogatories and notes [by Attorney General Coke] on Dr. Hayward's book, in proof that the Doctor selected a story 200 years old, and published it last year, intending the application of it to this time, the plot being that of a King who is taxed for misgovernment, and his council for corrupt and covetous dealings for private ends; the King is censured for conferring benefits on hated favourites, the nobles become discontented, and the commons groan under continual taxation, whereupon the King is deposed, and in the end murdered. With extracts from various parts of the book.[2]

Although Hayward confessed that he had unhistorically introduced the term 'benevolence' into the reign of Richard II despite his having read about such a device only as early as Richard III, he nevertheless disclaimed any motive of drawing subversive analogies between the earlier king's reign and the present time, citing various precedents and sources, and arguing that historians may legitimately embellish their sources and invent details for literary effect.

1   *CSPD*, 455.
2   *CSPD*, 449.

Essex's further indiscretions, however, victimized Hayward once again and led to the author's second trial of 1601 at which the whole question of his supposed sedition was reopened. Again the biographer of Richard II protested his innocence.[1] But, still not believed, he was kept in prison, apparently until after the Queen's death.[2]

Elizabeth, irritated by the commonly voiced parallel between Richard II and herself, commented wryly on the matter on 4 August 1601 when Lambarde presented to her his digest of historical records kept in the Tower. Glancing at Lambarde's pages, her eye fell upon the reign of King Richard, and the moment elicited her ironic remark about her having become a latter-day re-embodiment of the medieval monarch (see p. 5). In the exchange that followed she and Lambarde alluded specifically to Essex:

> *W.L.* 'Such a wicked imagination was determined and attempted by a most unkind Gent. the most adorned creature that ever your Majestie made.'
>
> *Her Majestie.* 'He that will forget God, will also forget his benefactors; this tragedy was played 40^{tie} times in open streets and houses.'
>
> (Chambers, *WS*, 2.326–7)

Elizabeth's mention of forty performances, presumably of Shakespeare's play, would seem to refer to earlier presentations from about 1595 when *Richard II* was new. And perhaps Cecil's allusion in July 1600 to Essex's 'being so often present at the playing' of Hayward's book is also a loose way of speaking of early stagings of Shakespeare's tragedy – since in Cecil's mind the play, although of earlier date, would constitute merely a dramatized version of the same dangerous matter as that contained

---

1 *CSPD*, 539–40.
2 Dowling gives a detailed account of Hayward's 'troubles' in connection with his ill-fated *Life of Henry IV*. She believes, as I do, that Hayward was a loyal subject but was unjustly suspected of being an accessory to Essex's treason owing to accidents of timing that he could hardly foresee. The letter-writer John Chamberlain could 'finde no buggeswords' (sinister or subversive meanings) in Hayward's dedication (see Chamberlain, *Letters*, 1.70).

in Hayward's prose history. Alternatively, as Heffner (774–5, 780) suggests, Cecil may have been referring to some sort of pageant or recitation founded on Hayward's *Life of Henry IV* and replete with pointed analogies to current affairs. Neither of these references can be logically identified or connected with the special revival of *Richard II* at the Globe on 7 February – a performance from which the Earl was absent. Nor, as Ure (lxi) points out, is it reasonable to suppose that the authorities would have allowed a whole chain of performances after 1599 (when Hayward's book was published) if there was any chance that these were being mounted for the clandestine purpose of exciting popular discontent.

Analogies between Richard and Elizabeth or between Bolingbroke and Essex are clearly available in *Richard II*, but how they are received resides largely in the eye of the beholder. This point becomes clearer if we note two contrasting allusions to Essex in contemporary poetry, both of which seem to have been suggested by Richard's words in Shakespeare's play describing Bolingbroke's 'courtship to the common people' (1.4.24–36). Anonymous verses written about 1603 after the Earl's execution laud 'Renowned Essex' for 'vail[ing] his bonnett to an oyster wife' and behaving humbly in the streets to the 'vulgar sort that did admire his life'; whereas five years earlier in *Skialetheia* the satirist Everard Guilpin had ridiculed the Earl ('great *Foelix*') for the same behaviour – behaviour that he clearly interpreted as evidence of ambitious hypocrisy taught by '*Signor Machiauell*': 'passing through the street', Essex 'Vayleth his cap to each one he doth meet', thus affecting to be the very 'honny-suckle of humilitie'.[1] Even if some viewers of *Richard II* could identify Bolingbroke with Essex, as these poets apparently did, they might respond to the analogy in politically opposite ways. As for the verbal parallels between Hayward's book and Shakespeare's play, these are almost certainly due either to the use of common sources or to Hayward's

---

1 For details, see 1.4.24–36n. and 31LN.

having seen a performance of the tragedy or read one of the three quarto editions that appeared in print before his own work was published. Evelyn Albright, to be sure, tried to make a case for Hayward's *Life of Henry IV* as a source for Shakespeare, arguing that the dramatist had probably read the historical work in an early manuscript and had deliberately set out to construct a political allegory based upon it with a view to commenting upon current affairs. As Heffner showed, however, her argument depends upon false or unlikely assumptions and on a perverse wrenching of dates and time sequences.[1] Contemporary overtones the play certainly contains, but it is hardly possible to maintain that Shakespeare planned it with Richard and Bolingbroke as thinly veiled portraits of Elizabeth and Essex. As Palmer (119) observes, the Queen and her Privy Council knew that the play itself contained no treason. But this did not eliminate the treasonable purposes for which it might be used; Sir Gilly Meyrick, who in 1601 had bespoken the performance of 7 February (see p. 10), paid for confusing a drama of universal scope with a political manifesto by forfeiting his life on the gallows.

Ideology: Competing Conceptions of Monarchy

It would have been impossible for a playwright dramatizing the dethronement of an English king to avoid issues about the locus of ultimate authority in the state, or to suppress entirely the abiding tension between the concept of an anointed monarch (*rex imago Dei*) and a government of laws as incorporated in Parliament. The subject of deposition could not but involve debate, however circumspect or indirect, on the precarious balance between crown and people. Inevitably tied to such questions – especially in the 1590s – was the on-going, though officially silenced, controversy about the succession, accompanied of

---

1 Albright's article, published in *PMLA* in 1927, was answered by Heffner in the same journal in 1930; further debate between the two continued in later issues of *PMLA* in 1931 and 1932.

course by the theory of divine right. The result in *Richard II*, as Clegg phrases it, is 'an uneasy dialectic between alternative views of succession, alternative views of kingship, and alternative views of the actions of both Richard II and Bolingbroke' (442). The dramatist would already have encountered similar tensions in *Woodstock* (see pp. 149–52).

The political theology of the king's two bodies became deeply implicated in the Tudor definition of monarchy. The King's natural body incorporated his humanity and was thus subject to the frailties and mortality of the flesh, but his body politic embodied the state and so set him apart from all others, being ubiquitous and immortal. If the doctrine were applied uncritically, particular actions of a king might be interpreted as possessing a mystical and almost unchallengeable authority.[1] Thus Henry V in Shakespeare's play can speak of himself as double-natured – a 'god' that suffers 'mortal griefs' and so is 'twin-born' (*H5* 4.1.234, 241–2). In her first words to the Privy Councillors after her accession in 1558 Elizabeth adopted the familiar vocabulary, speaking of her sorrow for the death of her sister as a function of her 'bodye naturallye considered' but of her power to govern England as proceeding from her 'bodye politique'.[2]

Kantorowicz (24–41) sensitively interprets *Richard II* as a tragedy of royal christology in which the title figure progressively confronts his peculiar crisis of identity: Richard's dual nature not only defines but magnifies his sufferings, forcing him in stages to come to terms with the fatal disuniting of his human from his mystical body, and pushing him ultimately to self-deposition and self-annihilation. Kantorowicz speaks of the inevitable 'duplications' inherent in kingship and shows how Richard struggles self-consciously, even theatrically, with them: 'Thus play I in one person many people' (5.5.31). That Richard is psychologically

---

1   The historical Sir John Bushy is supposed to have claimed, for instance, that the 'Laws are in the King's mouth, or sometimes in his breast'; quoted by Kantorowicz (28). Holinshed (3.502) makes a version of this comment one of the items (no. 14) charged against Richard in Parliament.

2   Quoted in Axton, 38.

wedded to christological kingship (he believes at one point that God will protect him with a battalion of angels) is obvious in his language – as, for instance, in his reference to himself as the 'deputy elected by the Lord', whom the 'breath of worldly men cannot depose' (3.2.56–7) and in his several comparisons of himself to Christ. But the same idea is also supported by Gaunt, who uses similar terminology ('God's substitute, / His deputy anointed in His sight' (1.2.37–8)), and by Carlisle ('the figure of God's majesty, / His captain, steward, deputy elect, / Anointed, crowned, planted many years' (4.1.126–8)). York refers to Richard as 'the anointed King' (2.3.96) and even after his defection to Bolingbroke can still speak of him as 'sacred' (3.3.9), a word that crops up more often in *Richard II* than in any other work of Shakespeare's. The usurper himself partly endorses Richard's iconic conception of monarchy when he envisages their meeting at Flint as the 'thund'ring shock' of a cataclysmic storm with Richard as the reigning element of 'fire' or lightning and himself as 'the yielding water' (3.3.56–8).[1] But this sacral and absolutist emphasis reflects only one aspect of the play's complex political vision.

As Talbert has pointed out, a more constitutional view of monarchy had steadily evolved through the writings of such men as Sir Thomas Smith, Bishop John Ponet, Richard Hooker, Sir Philip Sidney and others. Although these writers were far from denying divine right, they emphasized a more contractual relationship between ruler and people and viewed the commonwealth as a system of checks and balances rooted in the primacy of law as institutionalized in Parliament. According to this conception, the state was defined less in terms of an opposition between the one and the many than as a corporation in which the King was but the head of a more comprehensive body consisting also of the three estates – clergy, peers and commons. An engraving in Glover's *Nobilitas Politica vel Civilis* (1608) which shows Elizabeth presiding in Parliament on her throne of state (Fig. 3) illustrates this

1   See 3.3.58–60n.

more inclusive understanding of *rex in parliamento*. The so-called Parliament scene of Shakespeare's tragedy (4.1) suggests the same concept, not only by its action but by the use (in both Q and F) of the term '*Parliament*' in the opening stage direction.[1] The coronation oath implied that the King, as distinct from a tyrant, derived his power from the consent of the governed and, as the appointed executive of law and justice (interpreted as the will of God), could be removed from office if he failed to redress grievances or abused his powers. While the *Homilies* stressed the duty of passive obedience even to a wicked prince (as in Gaunt's words to Gloucester's widow in the play),[2] medieval constitutional theorists such as Henry de Bracton and Sir John Fortescue had argued that England was traditionally a limited monarchy, and that passive obedience was therefore repugnant to common law as ordinarily understood. Bracton's famous principle that the King, although not under man, was nevertheless 'under God and under the law because law maketh a king' was quoted in support; and Fortescue's statement to the effect that 'the king exists for the sake of the kingdom, and not the kingdom for the sake of the king' had similar force.[3] Bracton, indeed, had managed a somewhat slippery reconciliation of the seeming contradiction between a king's near-absolutist prerogatives and his theoretically limited powers by suggesting that as God's minister the monarch could only do right, but that if he happened to do wrong he was acting not as a king but as a minister of the devil.[4] Based on such precedents, the concept of a merited as opposed to a merely inherited kingship grew stronger.

This constitutional view of royal power enjoyed wide respect during Elizabeth's reign and seems to have been held by many loyal subjects of humanist and intellectual bent; but the more strident proponents of limited monarchy tended to be either

1 See 4.1.0.1–5n. The altered title-page of Q4 (Fig. 18) refers to 'the Parliament Sceane, and the deposing of King Richard'.
2 See 1.2.37–41n.
3 See Talbert, 216, n. 120; Stubbs, 3.258.
4 See Stubbs, 2.326.

3 Elizabeth I in Parliament, engraving in Robert Glover, *Nobilitas Politica vel Civilis*, 1608

papist or puritan. The Jesuit Parsons in a 1594 treatise supporting the Spanish Infanta as Elizabeth's successor argued that Richard II had been justly and legally deposed, while the Calvinist Wentworth, who favoured James VI, resembled Parsons in being an incendiary defender of parliamentary rights, insisting that though Elizabeth might be God's deputy, her power existed only 'to minister justice according to the good and wholesome laws of the land'.[1]

Reticently, *Richard II* also dramatizes the view of parliamentary supremacy described above, including the power to judge kings. The most obvious instance occurs when Northumberland, acting presumably as Bolingbroke's agent, asks his fellow peers in Westminster Hall 'to grant the commons' suit' that Richard may be brought before Parliament to 'surrender' 'in common view' (4.1.155–7). Later in the scene Northumberland tries at three different points (222–3, 243, 269) to make the captive king read aloud a list of 'accusations' and 'grievous crimes . . . Against the state and profit of this land' so that 'the souls of men / May deem that', 'by confessing them', he is 'worthily deposed' (4.1.223–7). The 'articles' which Richard evades by pleading that his 'eyes are full of tears' (4.1.243–4), and which the play never fully explains, are the '33 solemne articles' which Holinshed says were presented to Parliament as a basis for trying the King – a means of assuring that Richard's power to harm the commonwealth further would be officially nullified. Holinshed prints the document listing Richard's 'heinous points of misgouernance and iniurious dealings' as ruler.[2] When Bolingbroke cautions Northumberland to cease pressing the articles upon Richard, the over-zealous Earl complains that 'The commons will not then be satisfied' (4.1.272). Shakespeare clouds the issue of whether Richard can be legally condemned by Parliament by having the King depose himself, thus removing the matter from their hands, and by prefacing to

---

1   *Conference*, 1.32, 2.61–2. For Wentworth's defence of the liberties guaranteed by Parliament, see Neale, 1.321, 2.262–3.
2   See 4.1.222–3n., 225n. and 227n.

Richard's appearance Carlisle's courageous protestation of divine right. Nevertheless, the playwright suggests the latent power of Parliament to depose its sovereign by converting Richard's private resignation in the Tower (as described by Holinshed) into a public abdication before the highest court of the land.[1] Bolingbroke's adjudication of the quarrels among the 'Lords appellants' with which the scene opens also dramatizes the function of Parliament as a court of law; although not yet installed officially as Henry IV, the Duke presides over these 'differences' as *rex in parliamento*, ordering that they 'shall all rest under gage' until he assigns their 'days of trial' (4.1.105–7).

In addition, the play invites sympathy for nobles and commons both as elements of Parliament and as social classes by having Ross and Willoughby, two choric voices, comment on Richard's tyrannical abuses of power. The King loses his subjects' hearts by governing high-handedly without the participation and consent of his supporting legislators, one of whose functions is to vote subsidies; instead he acts independently – by imposing 'grievous taxes', fines for 'ancient quarrels', 'new exactions', blank charters, 'benevolences' and the like (2.1.246–50). Richard's most criminal act, apart from destroying Gloucester and farming the realm, is the 'robbing of the banished' Bolingbroke (2.1.261), an egregious violation of the cherished law of inheritance on which the royal title itself depends. York laments that 'the commons . . . are cold' to Richard's cause and may 'revolt on Hereford's side' (2.2.88–9), implying thereby that the King has ignored or overridden their interests. Only Bushy and Bagot, the 'caterpillars of the commonwealth' (2.3.166), speak disparagingly of the commons, calling them 'hateful' (2.2.137) and 'wavering' (2.2.128). But Shakespeare complicates our response to the implicit opposition between absolutist and constitutional monarchy by occluding the motives of Richard's antagonist and by deliberately refraining

1   See 4.1 headnote.

from having him defend his usurpation on moral, legal or theoretical grounds.[1] Since he never soliloquizes, we have no access to his private thoughts and must judge him almost exclusively by his actions. Publicly, Bolingbroke claims only to seek what is legally his – his hereditary lands and title. And Richard makes it unnecessary for him to claim more by agreeing to relinquish the crown before it has been formally demanded. Moreover, Bolingbroke is too shrewd politically to contest a concept of divine viceregency so important for his own authority and security in the next reign, even if to do so would serve, in the short term, to justify his occupancy of Richard's place. The closest Bolingbroke comes to acknowledging his ambition for the throne is his response to York's warning at Flint Castle that he and his adherents are under divine judgement: 'the heavens are o'er our heads' (3.3.17). Bolingbroke's answer, 'I know it, uncle, and oppose not myself / Against their will' (3.3.18–19), seems to suggest that the popular Duke regards himself, at least for the moment, as a man of destiny, a figure whom greater powers have singled out to be the deliverer of the nation. If Bolingbroke can ride to power on the crest of some supernatural and foreordained agency, the issues of parliamentary supremacy and rule by legislative assent become moot. A king by virtue of necessity, if not by conquest, may dispense with legalistic niceties.

Characterization: Attitudes towards Richard and Bolingbroke

Shakespeare inherited divergent and competing interpretations of Richard and Bolingbroke (see pp. 129–30, 137–8, 139, 143–4, 147–8, 156–7). In the interests of simplification – indeed oversimplification – these have been referred to conventionally as 'Yorkist' (pro-Richard) or 'Lancastrian' (pro-Henry) according to the dynastic factions that subsequently fostered them for their own political advantage. From the Lancastrian point of view

---

1 Holinshed notes that after Bolingbroke had captured Richard and brought him as prisoner to London, he caused a parliament to be called, 'vsing the name of king Richard in the writs directed forth to the lords' (3.502). The judicial body that the usurper assembled to convict Richard of unfitness to rule had to be called in the name of the figure it was proposing to unseat.

(represented by the majority of English chroniclers), Richard was a weak, incompetent and despotic king, extravagantly self-indulgent, deaf to wise counsel, dominated by corrupt and selfish favourites and altogether ruinous to his country. Bolingbroke, on the other hand, was a justly popular and wronged nobleman, a strong and capable leader, the darling of fortune and destiny, the politically natural successor to Richard, a man who responded boldly to the needs of his time and the saviour of the nation. This essentially is the view of his career that Henry himself voices in *2 Henry IV* when, indulging in the luxury of hindsight, he disclaims any ambition for the throne: 'then, God knows, I had no such intent, / But that necessity so bow'd the state / That I and greatness were compell'd to kiss' (3.2.72–4).[1] But according to the Yorkist writers, who naturally wished to discredit the Lancastrian revolution, the youthful Richard was more victim than villain – a generally devout and well-meaning monarch, misled into wrongful policies and exploited by false and self-seeking friends. Bolingbroke tends to emerge in this interpretation as an ambitious, unscrupulous, opportunistic and dissimulating politician.[2] The French chroniclers, who sympathized with Richard on account of his birthplace and his Gallic wife, promoted the image of a royal martyr betrayed by his own subjects and dethroned by a shrewd and cruel usurper. The complex intersection, assimilation and overlapping of these contradictory traditions in the writings that must have influenced Shakespeare, whether directly or indirectly, have been well described and analysed by Duls.[3]

1   Cf. Holinshed, who remarks on the 'verie notable example . . . that this Henrie duke of Lancaster should be thus called to the kingdome, and haue the helpe and assistance (almost) of all the whole realme, [who] perchance neuer thereof thought or yet dreamed'. Supernatural powers are ultimately responsible for Richard's fall and Bolingbroke's success: 'in this deiecting of the one, & aduancing of the other, the prouidence of God is to be respected, & his secret will to be woondered at' (3.499).

2   Cf. *2H4* 4.5.183–5: 'God knows, my son, / By what by-paths and indirect crook'd ways / I met this crown'. It should be remembered also, as Smidt (98) reminds us, that ambition was considered to be a 'serious . . . vice . . . in the Elizabethan moral system'. Cf. Baldwin's dedication of the *Mirror* (63): 'Well is that realme gouerned, in which the ambicious desyer not to beare office.'

3   See Duls, especially 7–8, 112–90, 196–203.

Even in Holinshed, a chronicle compiled of diverse materials, Shakespeare encountered mixed attitudes to Richard and Bolingbroke. There we read that Richard 'began to rule by will more than by reason, threatning death to each one that obeied not his inordinate desires'; given to 'furious outrage', he was 'a man destitute of sobrietie and wisedome' who wickedly 'abused his authoritie' (3.493). Yet the same chronicler can also refer to him as a 'bountifull and louing souereigne', victimized by 'ingratitude' (3.508) and lied to by the Archbishop of Canterbury, the Pilate-like Arundel, who had promised that he should be safe from 'anie hurt, as touching his person' (3.501). In general Holinshed treats Bolingbroke benignly – as courageous, politically adept, deservedly popular and carefully respectful of the King. Yet it is equally clear that the Duke is ruthless in destroying Richard's friends. Accusing Bolingbroke of 'ambitious' and 'tigerlike crueltie', Holinshed also says that he 'wanted moderation and loialtie in his dooings' for which he was afterwards duly punished: 'What vnnaturalnesse . . . was this, not to be content with [Richard's] principalitie', 'his treasure', 'his depriuation', 'his imprisonment' and 'wooluishlie to lie in wait . . . and rauenouslie to thirst after his bloud, the spilling whereof should have touched his conscience[?]' (3.508). Referring specifically to the scene at Flint Castle where Richard and Bolingbroke have their all-important encounter, Talbert observes that such 'antithetical attitudes . . . are so closely juxtaposed' by Shakespeare 'that for all intents and purposes they fuse with one another, and that fusion accords with the way in which two attitudes toward kingship have been kept alive' throughout the play: 'Even as Richard lacks the vigorous and wise [capacity to govern] . . . , his right by inheritance, by the hand of God, by a simplified world-order, is expressed forcefully' (168–9). What is true of this crucial scene is true in a broader sense of the tragedy as a whole.

Shakespeare partly accomplishes the 'fusion' to which Talbert points by subtly undercutting or rendering ambiguous the roles of Richard and Bolingbroke as divine-right monarch and irresistible challenger. This technique is clearest in the Flint Castle episode where Richard, a figure of 'Controlling majesty' (3.3.70) who dazzles his subjects like the sun, nevertheless descends from his royal eminence into 'the base court' (3.3.176) at the request of a mere vassal and not only grants Bolingbroke's demands but, in his 'doom-eagerness',[1] yields his person to the enemy, all the while indulging in histrionic and unkingly self-pity. Nor does Shakespeare fail to balance the mixed portrayal of Richard with an equally mixed image of Bolingbroke. The Duke approaches the castle with the full force of his army and the sound of 'brazen trumpet' (3.3.33), yet 'without the noise of threat'ning drum' (3.3.51). He protests 'allegiance and true faith of heart' to his sovereign. He offers to lay his 'arms and power' at Richard's 'feet', at the same time issuing an ultimatum to his liege lord that if his demands are not 'freely granted', he will 'use the advantage of [his] power' to create 'showers of blood / Rained from the wounds of slaughtered Englishmen' (3.3.37–44). He kneels before Richard with a show of submission and kisses the royal hand; but the elaborate courtesy and tactful observance of protocol, although minimizing imputations of ambition, in no way alter the military and political facts. And in Northumberland's dropping of Richard's title (3.3.6–9) and failure to kneel (3.3.75–6), Shakespeare subtly conveys a hint of the usurper's ultimate goal. Bolingbroke accomplishes his purpose of regaining the status of Duke of Lancaster and of taking Richard prisoner without creating the impression that he openly seeks the crown. Yet Richard's sarcastic address to him as 'King Bolingbroke' (3.3.173), taken in conjunction with Northumberland's unceremonious behaviour, creates just the opposite impression. Has Richard masochistically delivered up himself and his throne to a hypocritical enemy who would have seized power in any case? Or has Bolingbroke through luck, percipience, a heroic temperament and skilful manoeuvring

---

1   Harold Bloom (2) uses this term: 'Richard is both his own victim, or rather the victim of his own imagination, and the sacrifice that becomes inevitable when the distance between the king as he should be and the actual legitimate monarch becomes too great' (Bloom, 3).

simply placed himself in a position to have greatness thrust upon him? The scene leaves these equivocal issues unresolved.

Shakespeare, indeed, contrives to promote ambiguous impressions of both antagonists throughout the drama and to manipulate audience responses in such a way as to keep approval and disapproval, or sympathy and alienation, in a more or less constant state of flux. According to Rackin, the audience is made to play 'a carefully calculated role' not listed among the cast of characters, 'complete with motivations, actions, errors, and discoveries' (263). Rabkin goes so far as to allege that 'keeping our sympathies in suspense' constitutes the play's 'primary technique' (86). These minor fluctuations, of course, do not disturb the general drift towards increased emotional identification with Richard, as befits a tragic protagonist, or the gradual distancing from Bolingbroke that naturally accompanies it. Nevertheless, the progressive disclosure and complication of character adopted in *Richard II* represents a new and subtler technique than anything observable in earlier plays, especially the histories.

There is space here to touch only on high points by way of illustration. While the opening act presents a generally negative impression of Richard (his weak yielding to subordinates, his apparent responsibility for Gloucester's death, his unjust caprice as judge, his implied jealousy of Bolingbroke, his farming the realm, his callousness towards Gaunt), it simultaneously qualifies the effect by dramatizing his royal demeanour, his shrewd capacity to assess enemies and Gaunt's principled refusal to take vengeance against 'God's substitute' (1.2.37). Although the portrait of Bolingbroke is contrastingly positive, emphasizing courage and patriotism, the action also raises doubts about his loyalty since, while protesting concern for 'the precious safety of my prince' (1.1.32), he seems to threaten Richard by accusing Mowbray and suggesting (in opposition to his father's doctrine) that the duty of avenging Gloucester falls specifically to him. The play promotes further uncertainty by Richard's reference to the opponents' 'sky-aspiring and ambitious thoughts' (1.3.130) and to

Bolingbroke's political craft in wooing commoners 'As were our England in reversion his, / And he our subjects' next degree in hope' (1.4.35–6). An additional ambiguity arises when Gaunt, asserting that Richard has 'caused' Gloucester's death, adds the phrase, 'if wrongfully' (1.2.39), thus blurring the issue of royal guilt.[1] Although Richard later acknowledges his 'weaved-up follies' (4.1.229) and refers to his 'sins' (4.1.275) in general terms, he never expresses the slightest guilt for the killing of his uncle, an action carried out by subordinates. Shakespeare leaves the question of Richard's bad conscience for the death unresolved just as, at the end of the play, he applies a balancing ambiguity to the murder of Richard at the hands of Exton – a deed which King Henry may or may not have secretly authorized despite his combination of relief and guilt after it has been accomplished.[2]

By dramatizing the King's arrogance, his deafness to wise counsel, his heartless response to Gaunt's death and the confiscation of Bolingbroke's inheritance, Act 2 brings Richard to his nadir in the sympathies of the audience; Northumberland's 'Most degenerate King!' (2.1.262) seems justified. Yet our dismay at Richard's tyrannical incompetence is immediately balanced by the news that Bolingbroke has already raised an army and plans to invade England, violating his oath of fealty and delaying only until Richard has left for Ireland.[3] In his phrase, 'Redeem from broking pawn the blemished crown' (2.1.293), Northumberland seems to hint enthusiastically at usurpation. If the 'anointed King' (2.3.96) has demonstrated unfitness to rule, the alternative to the passive obedience which

---

1 Rabkin comments: 'If the unthreatened rule of the King is the principle of the state's survival, there may be some justification for what he [Richard] has caused to be done. At any rate, to take arms against God's minister is to Gaunt an even more egregious crime than Richard's' (83).

2 Morse finds Shakespeare 'specific and explicit on the crisis in 1399, but tacit and inferential about responsibility; he managed to keep interpretation open and to avoid fixing blame' (123).

3 See 2.1.289–90n. As early as 1852 Hudson could speak of Bolingbroke's 'noiseless potency of will', of 'his most silent, all-pervading, inly-working efficacy of thought and purpose' (Forker, 193).

Gaunt had endorsed is the backing, in Bolingbroke's own phrase, of 'a banished traitor' (2.3.60) – what York later calls 'gross rebellion and detested treason' (2.3.109). Moreover, Shakespeare now introduces the Queen, who acknowledges nothing of her husband's misrule, as a means of evoking sympathy for her 'sweet Richard' (2.2.9). In emotional terms, this prepares for York's dilemma, torn, as he is, between his two 'kinsmen' – the one his 'sovereign, whom both my oath / And duty bids defend', the other a nephew 'whom the King hath wronged, / Whom conscience and my kindred bids to right' (2.2.111–15). Worcester's defection and the flight of Bushy, Bagot and Green, who apparently ignore York's order to 'muster up . . . men' (2.2.118), only increase our sense of Richard's vulnerability and further emphasize the King's isolation. Richard's power to command the loyalty of friends now looks significantly weaker than his cousin's.

On his return Bolingbroke conveys mixed impressions – attractive humility in response to Northumberland's fulsomeness but also self-assurance and promises of reward as his 'infant fortune comes to years' (2.3.66); the metaphor suggests his long-range strategy. He speaks also of 'my treasury' (2.3.60) as though he were already a monarch. York's horror of 'braving arms against [the] sovereign' (2.3.112) reincorporates the orthodoxy of passive obedience voiced earlier by Gaunt. Moreover, the speciousness of Bolingbroke's argument that his new title, Duke of Lancaster, has annulled the crime of his early return, since he was banished only as Hereford, has an alienating effect. The situation nevertheless allows him to describe with eloquence the legal injustice of which he has been the victim – an injustice that is seen once more (as in 2.1) to weaken Richard's implied position that inheritance alone is enough to make and protect a king. Then York's futile assertion of authority, his wish to make Bolingbroke 'stoop / Unto the sovereign mercy of the King' (2.3.156–7), proves hollow, as he collapses into a stance of neutrality and offers the rebels whom he has just so roundly scolded the hospitality of his castle.

York's failure of nerve recapitulates Richard's earlier failure (1.1.196–9) to make Bolingbroke and Mowbray obey his will. Although York is 'loath to break our country's laws', he seeks to evade the political untenability of his position by welcoming the invaders as neither 'friends nor foes' (2.3.169–70). Act 2 concludes with Salisbury's gloomy forecast of Richard's setting sun, 'weeping in the lowly west' and the political 'storms' in prospect (2.4.21–2). Up to this point, Shakespeare has so manipulated responses that audiences can hardly be sanguine or approving of either Richard or Bolingbroke.

In Act 3, as Stirling observes, Shakespeare presents Bolingbroke and Richard in two consecutive scenes that individually dramatize their 'utter difference' of 'temperament' (29), finally making them confront each other in the third scene, which settles dispositively the issue of Richard's removal from the throne. All three scenes encourage ambivalent responses to both antagonists. In the first Bolingbroke is shown to be decisive, efficient, brisk and diplomatically prudent, condemning Bushy and Green, sending courteous commendations to the Queen, and setting in motion a military expedition against Glendower and the remaining loyalists. But by executing the favourites, he ruthlessly exceeds his authority, behaving already as though he were king; he also makes them scapegoats, trumping up charges of sexual misconduct and blaming them for Richard's injuries to him personally, just as he had earlier attacked Richard through Mowbray for Gloucester's death.[1] The parallel scene of the King's return from Ireland develops the sentimental side of Richard, showing his histrionic oscillations between unjustified elation and the 'sweet way' of 'despair' (3.2.205). Self-indulgently anticipating total defeat, Richard is the first person after Bolingbroke's return to pronounce the word 'deposed', obsessively repeating it four times (3.2.56, 150, 157, 158). Attraction to the martyrdom of abdication causes him to ritualize the abandonment

1 See 3.1 headnote and 3.1.11–15n.

of his sacred body, the body symbolized by his throne, to sit upon the ground, where he can meditate on death and the common humanity that unites him in his physical body to his subjects and all other mortals:

> Throw away respect,
> Tradition, form and ceremonious duty,
> For you have but mistook me all this while.
> I live with bread like you, feel want,
> Taste grief, need friends. Subjected thus,
> How can you say to me I am a king?
>
> (3.2.172–7)

As a monarch Richard never appears weaker, more self-absorbed or more in love with catastrophe than in this scene, which ends in his renouncing politics altogether: 'Discharge my followers. Let them hence away, / From Richard's night to Bolingbroke's fair day' (3.2.217–18). Clearly the scene functions to contrast the King's emotional instability with the icy and rigorous control of his adversary. Yet tragic sympathy for Richard begins to emerge with the challenge to his authority, and self-knowledge, though incomplete, begins to accompany self-pity. The brittle confidence, arrogant self-possession and careless indifference of the earlier Richard have melted to disclose a richer and more vulnerably complex personality. The 'hollow crown' speech (3.2.160–77) reveals that the speaker's untested faith in the divine protection of his title has been shattered as completely as the mirror he will later break. The new ingredient is Richard's own questioning of the integrity of the king's two bodies – a unity that heretofore he had shallowly assumed. Attack from without has sparked dividedness within. And the result is a protagonist of greater capacity for self-understanding and emotional depth than has yet been disclosed. Meanwhile, Bolingbroke has remained a closed book – a figure whose inner self has been carefully screened from our gaze. Paradoxically, the ineffectual King appears to be a more interesting, interior and multifaceted human being than the figure who threatens him. But most importantly, the scene near the Welsh coast serves as a significant watershed in Shakespeare's dramaturgical scheme, clarifying the lesson that the political conflicts of the play are inseparable from the psychological and moral complexities of the men who contend for dominion. Tragedy, even if its historical subject is a revolution, must concern itself as much with human beings as with political theory.

The pivotal scene at Flint Castle continues to show both figures in a double light. While Bolingbroke presents himself as the loyal proponent of justice ('My gracious lord, I come but for mine own'), thus gaining our approval, Richard's bitter response, 'Your own is yours, and I am yours and all' (3.3.196–7), embraces a more far-reaching truth. Richard becomes a prisoner, knowing that London can mean only dethronement and probable death; and when he adds, 'For do we must what force will have us do' (3.3.207), Bolingbroke revealingly fails to contradict him.[1] Our impression of Richard is equally mixed. While theatricalizing his own humiliation in the 'base court', behaving like a spectator at his own tragedy,[2] Richard nevertheless clings to that exalted conception of royalty that supplies the foundation for his grief in having to forfeit it. Richard's majesty, which impresses even his opponent and causes York, now fully committed to Bolingbroke, to weep for what has been lost, emerges as something more than romantic illusion. At the same time both antagonists are to some extent victims of self-delusion. Richard remains unable or unwilling to confront the flaws of character and policy that have brought him to his unhappy pass, however realistically he may now assess his present

1 Act 4 makes it clear that 'London' means not only Parliament but also 'the Tower' (4.1.316). Stirling notes the 'economy and understatement' as well as the 'taciturnity' of Bolingbroke's 'discursive self-revelation' in the falling action of the play: Bolingbroke's most significant decisions regarding Richard tend to be 'embodied in a terse statement', each time another character having 'either evoked it from him or stated its implications for him' (33–4).

2 Pointing to such moments of self-consciousness as Richard's 'Well, well, I see / I talk but idly, and you laugh at me' (3.3.170–1), Palmer observes that the King is 'possibly the only appreciative witness of his tragedy' (159); he is echoing Chambers, who says of Richard that he 'becomes an interested spectator of his own ruin' (*Survey*, 91).

danger; and Bolingbroke seems equally unable to acknowledge (perhaps even to himself) the thirst for sovereignty that underlies his self-restraint and calculated realism, even though his upward momentum towards the throne is now more obvious than ever.[1]

The garden scene, which immediately follows, confirms objectively what was implicit at Flint Castle – that 'Bolingbroke / Hath seized the wasteful King' (3.4.54–5) and that his deposition at 'London' is imminent (3.4.90). Sympathy for Richard is renewed through the Queen's distressed reaction to the baleful news she has overheard. But at the same time the Gardeners elaborate a patterned explanation of how badly the fallen King had tended his 'sea-walled garden' (3.4.43) and, by implication at least, defend the usurpation of power as a sad necessity. The Queen, moreover, voices the momentous implications of her husband's dethronement by comparing it to the Fall, thus endowing Richard's tragedy, as did the chronicler Hall, with the significance of a mythic and long-lasting national disaster.

Bolingbroke's status as king *de facto* becomes clearer early in Act 4 where the Duke, using the royal 'we', presides impassively over his squabbling nobles and exerts his control by deferring their 'days of trial' (4.1.106–7). By reviving the matter of Gloucester's death, Shakespeare muddies the waters more disturbingly than before. Although Bolingbroke says little, his resolute demeanour contrasts with Richard's inability in the analogous opening scene to make his quarrelling subjects obey him.[2] Yet only when York announces that 'plume-plucked

---

1 Bolingbroke 'never allows himself to know where he is going. Every step in his progress towards the throne is dictated by circumstances and he never permits himself to have a purpose till it is more than half fulfilled' (Palmer, 134). He 'does not attempt to think through his position clearly or persistently' (Baxter, 112). See also the discussion of Daniel (pp. 143–4).

2 Berger ('Perspective', 264–5) argues that the contrast redounds to Richard's credit rather than to Bolingbroke's: sitting 'quietly through most of the scene' Bolingbroke, unlike his counterpart, refuses to 'intervene in the volatile factionalism that bodes ill for future stability'. Although I regard Bolingbroke's silence during the quarrel as evidence of his shrewdness and politic restraint, not of his weakness, Berger's contrary interpretation serves to illustrate the shifting and ambiguous responses that both characters seem designed to elicit.

Richard' has willingly adopted him as 'heir' (4.1.109–10) does Bolingbroke for the first time acknowledge his claim to sovereignty: 'In God's name I'll ascend the regal throne' (4.1.114). This is the dramatic moment in Shakespeare's brilliant recasting of Holinshed that elicits Carlisle's divine-right protest and the prophecy that crowning Bolingbroke will transform England into a Golgotha of national slaughter for generations yet unborn. Carlisle's brave defence of the inviolable sanctity of kingship causes Bolingbroke to hesitate;[1] and although the prelate is instantly arrested for his reactionary loyalty, he nevertheless forces the usurper, most inconveniently, to summon the fallen King into Parliament so that his abdication may be witnessed and Bolingbroke's accession accepted 'Without suspicion' (4.1.158). For once, Bolingbroke has been placed on the defensive. And, once he appears, there Richard manages to keep him for the remainder of the act, dominating the stage in his improvised pageant of self-unkinging. This scene, as Palmer rightly says, 'is the summit of the play' (167).

Thus Shakespeare contrasts two kinds of power – the political and the theatrical. Bolingbroke may hold the reins of sovereignty, but Richard is the master of self-dramatization with its attendant arts – command of rhetoric and metaphor, the power to embarrass enemies, ironic wit and quicksilver fancy, the capacity to evoke both pity and irritation, the posture of associating his own sufferings with the Passion of Jesus, and the histrionic skill to make the narcissistic contemplation of his own identity coterminous with a ceremony of monarchical renunciation that communicates a sense of desecration and the loss of sacred tradition. Richard manages to endow his own fall with cosmic significance – with the fracturing of an ancient and venerable world order in which the king is seen as a vital link in the great chain that connects the celestial with the earthly. The player-king now triumphs theatrically over

---

1   It is debatable whether Bolingbroke actually occupies the throne at this point. See 4.1.114n.

the king of *Realpolitik* but at the cost of half-annihilating both himself and the beautiful principle on which he had believed his royalty to be founded.

Yet again a certain doubleness of perspective, rooted in the sacramental theology of kingship itself, pervades the episode of discrowning; for, paradoxically, Richard contrives to assert the sacred inviolability of his office while simultaneously divesting himself of its symbols and thereby violating it himself. Although Richard has the talents of an actor, inventing 'a great ceremony for his humiliation', as Philip Edwards phrases it, 'kingship is for him no actor's part, put on and put off at will' (102), but rather the defining ground of his being. The man who had grandly claimed that an ocean of sea-water could not 'wash the balm off from an anointed king' (3.2.55) now affects to remove it 'With [his] own tears' (4.1.207). In rituals of the degradation of priests and bishops, only those who have been anointed themselves can presume to officiate in the scraping off of the holy oils and chrism. Yet it is equally clear that in such degradations the subject is prohibited only from lawfully exercising his sacramental powers, since the gifts of the Holy Spirit conferred by anointing at consecrations and ordinations are permanently valid and beyond the power of human beings to annul. 'Ay, no. No, ay', Richard's equivocal answer to Bolingbroke's question of whether he is 'contented to resign the crown' (4.1.200–1), encapsulates concisely his divided attitude. The inverted rite of dispossession to which Pater famously called attention (see Forker, 298), and which Richard languishingly draws out to such liturgical length, expunges in a psychological sense the very identity of the speaker.[1] As Ranald (195) observes, the ceremony 'is infinitely more than mere formality', constituting as it does 'his annihilation as a kingly person, his reduction to the rank of knave, the destruction of his achievements, and, as Richard sees it, his excision from the roster of English kings, since he has become a traitor to the office he had held'. Yet at the same time

---

1 See Ranald, 183–96; also 4.1.203n.

Richard cannot but asseverate the timeless legitimacy of his king-ship – his claim to the body mystical that cannot theoretically be sundered from the body physical until death. He condemns the 'heinous' act of 'deposing . . . a king / And cracking the strong warrant of an oath, / Marked with a blot, damned in the book of heaven' (4.1.233–6); he compares himself twice to Christ, the King of all creation, whose Godhead is sempiternal; and he condemns himself for cooperating in the inversion of an immutable hierarchy – for consenting 'T'undeck the pompous body of a king', for having made 'Glory base and Sovereignty a slave, / Proud Majesty a subject, State a peasant' (4.1.250–2).

Of course the episode exposes also the fallible side of Richard's nature so that a tragic divide opens up between the semi-divine dignity of the rank he once held (and still glorifies) and his own solipsistic exhibitionism. The comparisons to Christ have a dou-ble edge. Looked at from a merely human perspective, Richard's claim that his sufferings exceed those of his Saviour, since Jesus had only one Judas while he has had to cope with 'twelve thou-sand' betrayers (4.1.171–2), reveals a degree of presumption approaching blasphemy. At the same time, however, the analogy between the dethroning of an anointed sovereign and the Passion contains a certain theological validity according to the christology of divine-right doctrine. The windlass image of the two buckets carries something of the same doubleness about it (see 4.1.184n. and Fig. 4). Richard applies it to his own advantage by making the high bucket (Bolingbroke) dance emptily, carelessly and illegiti-mately in the air while the low bucket, representing himself, is heavy with grief and the weight of sacred tradition. The analogy is tactically clever since it apparently exasperates Bolingbroke as intended; but the verbal wit displayed also casts doubt upon the profundity of Richard's grief since the deepest kinds of suffering do not usually accommodate such ostentation. The same point can be made about the emblematic mirror into which Richard gazes before he smashes it in a climactic *coup de théâtre* – an action he himself can refer to as 'this sport' (4.1.290). At one level the

4 Virtus and Fortuna holding a crown over a king's head, from Guillaume de la Perrière, *La Morosophie*, Lyons, 1553, emblem 68

episode can be read as extravagant escapism, a means by which Richard narcissistically evades a reality he himself has invited. The Epistle of James likens a Christian who hears the word of God but, self-deceivingly, fails to translate it into action 'unto a man beholding his natural face in a glass' for 'he beholdeth himself, and goeth his way, and straightway forgetteth what manner of man he was' (1.23–4). It is this self-deception that Bolingbroke imputes to Richard's gesture as he refers with a hint of contempt to 'The shadow of [his] sorrow' (4.1.292). But the mirror, as a reflector of truth (as well as of vanity), also allows the fallen King a moment of deeper insight into his own nature. It becomes for him 'the very book . . . Where all [his] sins are writ' (4.1.274–5) and the means of disclosing, as through a glass darkly, 'the tortured soul' (4.1.298) that lies beneath the youthfully handsome and as yet unwrinkled countenance.[1] The brittleness of the glass symbolizes for Richard the fragility and impermanence of life itself and links up thematically with the 'hollow crown' speech of 3.2 with its effect of expanded consciousness and deepened self-perception.[2] And throughout Richard's quasi-tragic performance, Bolingbroke has been reduced to the role of a 'silent King' (4.1.290), who can only regain a measure of assurance by 'conveying' his rhetorically potent enemy 'to the Tower' (4.1.316). Nor is it other than by masterly design that Shakespeare concludes the scene of Richard's 'woeful pageant' (4.1.321) with the Abbot of Westminster's counter-revolutionary plot. Having permitted Richard to usurp the spotlight emotionally, thereby casting the political usurper into shadow, the dramatist now revives the possibility, perhaps even the distant hope, of an actual reversal in the power structure of the state.

---

1 Nichols quotes a report that in her final illness Queen Elizabeth 'desired to see a true looking-glass, which in twenty years she had not sene, but only such a one as was made of purpose to deceive her sight: which glasse, being brought her, she fell presently into exclayming against those which had so much commended her, and took it so offensively, that some which had flattered her, durst not come into her sight' (3.612).

2 See 4.1.275.1n., 287–8n., 292–3n. and 294n.

Mixed reactions to Richard continue in Act 5. In the largely private farewell of the royal lovers (dramatically, the Guard and the Queen's ladies are non-presences), Richard's devotion to his wife comes over as deep and genuine; yet Richard still acts the player-king, emoting over his own tragedy and transmuting it into literary artifact – 'the lamentable tale of me' (5.1.44). But the self-conscious language of both speakers may be read in part as a psychic effort to control the rawness of grief adopted in the spirit of mutual protectiveness. However we receive Richard's egoism, it contains an element of self-recognition. He can speak of their 'former state' as a 'happy dream' from which present cruelties have awakened them, at the same time acknowledging 'grim Necessity' and hoping for the 'new world's crown' that will deliver them from the 'profane hours' of earthly existence (5.1.18–25). Richard's thoughts of an incorruptible crown probably represent more than a flight to platitude since piety was an aspect of his historical personality well documented in the sources available to Shakespeare. Finding his resigned passivity unroyal, the Queen rebukes him for playing the submissive schoolboy rather than the lion, 'king of beasts' (5.1.26–34), to which Richard wittily responds that he has indeed been overthrown by 'beasts' rather than 'men' (5.1.35–6). In coming to terms with his fall, Richard still lashes out at subjects rather than blaming himself. Northumberland's entrance returns us instantly to Bolingbroke's world of *Realpolitik*, the impingement of the public realm upon the private being a pervasive theme of Shakespeare's histories.[1] And Richard's shrewd forecast of Northumberland's treason under Henry dramatizes the painful truth that the fallen King is a better judge of his enemies than of his friends. The scene shows Richard in defeat as a loving husband and perceptive analyst of the Bolingbroke–Northumberland alliance without diminishing

---

1 Benthall's production starring John Neville emphasized the intimacy of the King's encounter with his wife by having the lovers sit on the ground – a recapitulation of Richard's posture in the 'hollow crown' speech (3.2.160–77). Trewin (*Neville*, 57) comments on the 'heartbreak' in Neville's voice at this point.

our awareness of his self-absorption or his continuing belief in the rightness of his inherited role. The emotional parting between husband and wife also balances the drawn-out leave-taking between Gaunt and his son in 1.3.

York's evocative description of Bolingbroke and Richard in the London streets provides a final contrast between the antagonists. His lingering sympathy for the King he has deserted makes his rigorous commitment to Bolingbroke and, later, his condemnation of his own son in proof of it, doubly ironic. York's finely contrasted vignettes delineate political success and failure, at once underscoring the *de casibus* theme of mutable fortune and the volatility of popular opinion.[1] Bolingbroke, who receives the prayers and accolades of the crowd with gestures of humility, is clearly the master of public relations, nor does the portrait necessarily suggest insincerity despite our memory of what Richard had said about his 'Wooing poor craftsmen with the craft of smiles' (1.4.28). Still, York's metaphor involving the difficulty of following a 'well-graced actor' (Bolingbroke) onstage because the next actor (Richard) will be received as tedious by contrast (5.2.24–6) again suggests political manipulation in the usurper. And in view of Richard's histrionic character, already so thoroughly developed, it is also piercingly ironic, for the contrasting description of the martyr-king, on whose 'sacred head' dust is thrown and who bears his humiliation with 'grief and patience' (5.2.30–3), seems to embody unvarnished authenticity while it is Bolingbroke who has succeeded to the role of player-king. Despite his engaged feelings, York comments gnomically on the providential nature of the power-shift without assigning blame or innocence to either winner or loser: 'heaven hath a hand in these events, / To whose high will we bound our calm contents' (5.2.37–8). Such resignation could be interpreted as York's final evasion of responsibility for pusillanimously capitulating to the stronger of two leaders – to his prizing of a settled order above all else.[2] But the lines are chiefly choric and

1 See 4.1.184–9n.
2 See 5.2.37–8n.

emphasize a theme that undergirds Shakespeare's histories as a group – namely that the tragic currents of political change lie finally outside and beyond the power of men to control.

The eruption of conflict between York and Aumerle dramatizes a tragic effect of revolution – division within nuclear families (staged emblematically in *3 Henry VI*, 2.5). Like Bolingbroke, York also has a rebellious child. The vehement condemnation of a son for treason to one king, by a father who has already committed the same offence to his predecessor, is obviously replete with irony. But the play implies that there is an important difference between Aumerle's immature act of rashness and York's bowing to unalterable circumstance. Moreover, Aumerle, once exposed, is so desperate to save his own skin that he makes no attempt to plead for his confederates whose secrecy he had religiously sworn to protect. Before the dangerous discovery, however, his parents comment tartly on the slippery footing of a courtier's life in a way that would resonate meaningfully with Tudor audiences.[1] When his mother inquires casually about those currently in favour with the new regime (the latest 'violets' of 'the new-come spring'), Aumerle replies suspiciously that he neither knows nor cares, prompting his father to urge caution lest the boy 'be cropped before [he] come to prime' (5.2.46–51). Once Aumerle's secret has been bared, the urgent relevance of these remarks becomes frighteningly clear: in great agitation York calls for his boots to accuse the traitor openly, while his duchess tries to prevent him in a panicky effort to spare her child's life.

Shakespeare complicates our response to the fresh crisis, and to the conflict between family and state that it precipitates, by allowing the parental disagreement to degenerate into farce. Ridiculously trying to cope with contradictory orders, York's servant is baffled, while Aumerle stands impotently mute, transfixed by confusion and despair. Then the son, the father and the mother, each having ridden independently and in sweaty haste to Windsor, successively enter the royal presence, flinging

---

1   It was well known, for instance, that Leicester, Raleigh and Essex, each of them particular favourites of Elizabeth, had several times fallen in and out of her good graces.

themselves down in a contest of kneeling that elicits an amused couplet even from King Henry: 'Our scene is altered from a serious thing, / And now changed to "The Beggar and the King"' (5.3.78–9). The suppliants plead passionately for opposite decisions – the father for his son's death, the mother for his life – and all three embarrass the King by refusing to rise until he has acted on their conflicting petitions. Their begging, couched mostly in a jingling doggerel, cannot but undercut the gravity of the matters in hand – somewhat as the Bastard's unceremonious tone in *King John* undermines the fustian of other characters in that play. The rhetoric becomes absurdly formalistic and antiphonal – a virtual burlesque of court protocol. Henry disposes of the first real threat of his reign with masterful self-possession, implacably executing the most dangerous members of the conspiracy while showing mercy to Aumerle, who no longer poses a security threat. But as Zitner observes, the farcical elements modify the tone and import of the drama in a significant way and therefore, inevitably, of its politics: the scenes of Aumerle's conspiracy parody magniloquence and the courtly ceremoniousness insisted upon elsewhere, even hinting at Shakespeare's growing 'disaffection' with the genre in which he was working and with the 'illusion' that stylized 'historical tragedy' is adequate to its purpose (255).[1] Zitner believes that the Aumerle scenes, often cut in production, 'enrich the play' by introducing a new perspective characteristic of Shakespeare's 'complexity and toughness of mind' (257) and thus anticipate the tension between comedy and tragedy, between high and low, that the *Henry IV* plays were to realize so fruitfully. Perhaps Zitner overstates the revisionary effect of these scenes upon audiences (the comic material passes rather quickly); but there can be no question that the episode encourages a response to political crisis different from that

1 Black disagrees with Zitner, arguing that the near-farcicality of the conspiracy scenes, far from 'undercutting or mocking the seriousness of the play', 'intensif[ies] that seriousness by contrast or counterpoint' as in the relationship between masque and antimasque ('Interlude', 112).

evoked in the more elevated parts of the play. A certain thematic continuity is nevertheless preserved for, to quote Nevo (94), York's 'loss of inner coherence' in his unsuccessful struggle to reconcile his role as a loyal subject with his humanity as a father ironically prefigures the similar problems of identity that beset Richard in his prison soliloquy and that lead up to his confrontation with 'being nothing' (5.5.41).

The small episode (5.4) in which Exton explains what he takes as King Henry's command to murder Richard prepares us for the death scene. It besmirches Henry's character as damagingly as any of the play, still leaving the tiniest doubt as to the precise degree of his culpability because the incriminating words, not themselves fully explicit, are reported rather than heard directly from the King's lips. Like Richard, who never admits to having Gloucester destroyed, Henry clings to a stance of deniability by repudiating and then exiling the agent of his villainy. When Exton later protests that he had acted in response to words from the King's 'own mouth', he is answered with Machiavellian equivocation: 'Though I did wish him dead, / I hate the murderer, love him murdered' (5.6.37–40).[1] A few moments afterwards, of course, King Henry confesses his responsibility in general terms, hoping to 'wash this blood from off my guilty hand' by means of 'a voyage to the Holy Land' (5.6.49–50). But in Shakespeare's handling of the matter, we never know whether King Henry consciously arranged his rival's death or merely encouraged it by innuendo. It is worth noting nevertheless that even in the final episodes, when sympathy flows naturally to Richard as tragic victim, the dramatist gives us reason to identify in certain respects with the private emotions of his destroyer, thereby muting the contrast between them. He slightly mollifies the impression of Henry's cold-hearted ruthlessness and political realism by showing also his concern for his son, his compassion

---

1 See 5.6.40n.; also Berger, 'Perspective' (266–8), where the ambiguities of the Bolingbroke–Exton relationship are explored in detail.

for Aumerle and his bad conscience for the murder he has autho-rized, whether wittingly or no.[1]

Even in the scene at Pomfret, the only episode to stage physical violence, Shakespeare preserves a certain ambivalence of attitude towards Richard. The overall purpose is to create as much sym-pathy as possible, thus muting or helping us to forget his role in Gloucester's death and the other tyrannies. And when Richard manfully strikes down two of Exton's assistants before falling himself to the assassin, Shakespeare leaves us with the impression of a man who finally claims the martial tradition of his royal ancestors from which his uncles had seen him as shamefully defecting.[2] Richard also reasserts his infrangible identity as King, heroically repossessing the sacred title for which his birth had des-tined him.

> That hand shall burn in never-quenching fire
> That staggers thus my person. Exton, thy fierce hand
> Hath with the King's blood stained the King's own land.
> Mount, mount, my soul! Thy seat is up on high,
> Whilst my gross flesh sinks downward here to die.
>
> (5.5.108–12)

These words contain no hint of a guilty conscience nor any sug-gestion of unorthodox doubt about the king's two bodies: Richard's body mystical will rise to rejoin the divine source of its sacramental power, while his body natural will sink down and dissolve to earth like that of other mortals. Regnal flaws notwith-standing, eternal condemnation is for regicides, not for legitimate monarchs. If Cibber had adapted this play instead of *Richard III*, he might have added at this point, 'Richard's himself again' (66). The touching loyalty of the Groom, the mixed humour and pathos of the 'roan Barbary' incident and the surliness of the

---

1 Barton's RSC and Warner's National Theatre productions both stressed the similar-ity, even the symbolic identity, of Richard and Bolingbroke; in the first of these Irving Wardle referred to the two kings as 'fatal twins' (*The Times*, 11 April 1973, 13).
2 Cf. the speeches of Gaunt and York at 2.1.104–8 and 171–83; see also 2.1.172–83n.

Keeper, who, in contrast to the King, treats the visitor badly, combine to bring out Richard's humanity and personal charm. And the Keeper's refusal to taste Richard's food on the orders of Exton, who 'lately / Came from the King' (5.5.100–1), suggests the possibility that instructions from Windsor are being obeyed.

The long meditation on identity, isolation, time and harmony with which the scene opens, Richard's only soliloquy, is, however, less unitary in its effect on audience response. Here uniquely we see Richard without an onstage audience. His island realm has now shrunk to the enclosure of a prison cell, and, psychologically speaking, to the confines of his own fanciful mind. Now he must 'hammer out' the imaginary contours of a new kingdom of introversion, peopling it with a 'generation of still-breeding thoughts', fragmenting himself into a collection of listeners to his own performance, all of them discontented (5.1.5–11). The imaginary roles include the better and worse aspects of himself, the higher and more divine thoughts being 'intermixed / With scruples' and with his consciousness of former pride and worldly luxury. He strains ingenuity to invent analogies for the competing facets of his own personality, exhausting his rhetorical skills in a bewildering confluence of fugitive ideas and speculative associations. See-sawing between opposite conceptions of himself, he must alternately be actor and audience, king and beggar, free spirit and frustrated prisoner. But the competing roles engendered by his fancy tend to obliterate each other, reducing him to nullity:

> Thus play I in one person many people,
> And none contented. Sometimes am I king;
> Then treasons make me wish myself a beggar,
> And so I am. Then crushing penury
> Persuades me I was better when a king;
> Then am I kinged again, and by and by
> Think that I am unkinged by Bolingbroke,
> And straight am nothing. But whate'er I be,
> Nor I nor any man that but man is

    With nothing shall be pleased till he be eased
    With being nothing.

                                              (5.5.31–41)

This, of course, is a reprise of Richard as the 'mockery king of snow' melting himself away 'in water-drops' (4.1.260–2) and of the histrionic narcissist dispersing his identity in the smithereens of a shattered looking-glass.[1] The nothingness on which the King muses is the psychological equivalent of death. But Richard's tragic limitation is that, even in defeat, he cannot break free of his own crippling self-consciousness from which only death will release him.

The intrusion of music awakens him to the disharmony and disproportion that have defined his reign: 'I wasted time, and now doth Time waste me' (5.5.49). Here he acknowledges slackness or self-indulgence as a cause of his fall, but, paradoxically, his confession occurs in a long rumination that, by elaborately pursuing over-strained conceits, constitutes in itself a form of self-indulgence. Yet of this point also Richard seems aware, for, still resentful of his enemy, he contrasts Bolingbroke's world of political activism to his own enforced stasis: the false king in his 'proud joy' has usurped the 'time' that should have been Richard's by right, while the legitimate king must 'stand fooling' in a cell, the puppet or 'jack o'the clock' to an upstart (5.5.58–60). Richard's attempt to come to terms with his own tragedy seems flawed and incomplete, too deeply mired in pain, regret and frustration to allow for full moral self-recognition or access to the larger, more metaphysical significances of his experience. He remains still obsessed with 'this all-hating world' (5.5.66). But at the same time he is able to bless the unidentified musician whose playing offers him 'a sign of love' (5.5.65) and thereby to show that he has shed enough of his egoism to be capable of gratitude.

---

1   The symbolic identification of the mirror with death was enforced visually in Pimlott's RSC production, in which a long wooden casket served as both a coffin and, when turned vertically, a looking-glass.

Summing up the political ambivalences that *Richard II* seems designed to generate, we may note several features of the play's characterization, structure and thematic emphasis that contribute generally to the mixed effect. One such is Shakespeare's technique of making subordinate characters bear the heaviest onus of disapproval – disapproval that would otherwise fall directly upon the chief antagonists. Bushy, Bagot and Green, the 'caterpillars' of Richard's ill-tended garden, are meant to function chiefly as self-aggrandizing parasites and the givers of bad counsel to a youthfully impressionable and emotionally unstable king, although in the action this is merely implied rather than shown.[1] As such, they help to soften and explain, if not wholly excuse, the King's most egregious tyrannies. Yet, even here, there is a measure of ambiguity, for we never see the favourites behave treasonably; Bushy and Green are apparently the victims of scapegoating (see pp. 30, 162–3), and Bagot, who survives the usurper's accession, charges Aumerle with responsibility for Gloucester's death, thus bringing his own loyalty to Richard into question. On the other side, Northumberland serves increasingly as the usurper's hatchet-man, allowing the audience to displace some of its gathering hostility to Bolingbroke onto his more nakedly ambitious second-in-command. York's ambiguously conceived character serves also to complicate our attitude towards the two principals. Early in the play the old Duke stands with Gaunt as a venerable and justified, though fervently loyal, critic of Richard's follies. Then, thrust into an impossible predicament during the King's absence, he collapses into attempted neutrality from which circumstances quickly push

1 Both the play and the principal sources stress Richard's immaturity, influenced by his accession to the throne as a boy of ten and by the earlier domination of his uncles over him. In later ages and even in his own time, writers made much of Richard's minority and the dangers to national security of a child king. When Henry IV succeeded, Archbishop Arundel preached a sermon on 1 Samuel, 9.17, stressing the new king's adulthood and supporting it with a passage from 1 Corinthians, 13.11: 'When I was a child, I spake as a child . . . but when I became a man, I put away childish things.' Arundel was exploiting a Lancastrian myth; in physical age, Bolingbroke was actually junior to Richard by three months. See Aston, 306–7.

him into treason (from a legitimist's perspective) or into acquiescence to necessity and the good order of the realm (from a
Lancastrian point of view). Shakespeare sets York's nostalgic reverence for Richard's sanctity (even after his capitulation to
Bolingbroke) against his almost fanatic condemnation of his own
son for disloyalty to the new king. And the semi-comic elements
in his character make it possible for an actor to portray him as
either a frail, well-meaning old man pathetically driven to choose
between two nephews who both have a valid claim on his loyalty,
or a foolish parcel of self-justifying ineptitude blown hither and
yon by the winds of change. The somewhat featureless portrait of
Aumerle complicates responses further still. In the first three acts
he behaves as one of Richard's most loyal and intimate friends.
Then, with his fierce denial of Bagot's charge that he was
involved in Gloucester's murder and that he had wished for
Bolingbroke's death, we are forced, temporarily at least, to recon-
sider his fidelity to Richard's cause. His rush, later in the scene,
to take part in the plot against the usurper reconfirms his loyalty
to Richard; but he is so quick to seek his own safety, pleading that
his 'heart is not confederate with [his] hand' (5.3.52), that he
seems finally more expedient than even his father. Carlisle, the
Queen and the anonymous Groom emerge as the only supporters
of Richard whose devotion to principle can be counted on.

Certain of the play's 'unconformities', as Smidt terms them,
conduce also to a blurring of the play's politics. Smidt argues that
the tragedy 'underwent . . . major changes of design in the course
of its shaping' (89). Whether or not the text betrays different
phases of composition (as Smidt believes), it is nonetheless true
that curious shifts of thematic emphasis and plot direction are
observable. For the first third of the play we are left with the
impression that Gloucester's death is Richard's most heinous
crime and that the action to follow will surely involve retribution
as well as, perhaps, some depiction of the King's tortured conscience. Bolingbroke, Gaunt and York all refer in turn to
the malicious spilling of Gloucester's blood, and Richard's

banishment of both combatants at Coventry seems motivated, at least in part, by his need to silence Mowbray and to defend himself against revenge at the hands of his threatening cousin. A tragedy of nemesis would appear possible. But even before 2.2.100–2, where York alludes in passing to the victimization of his brother, the theme of crime and punishment is already being supplanted by a heavier emphasis on Richard's more public misrule – his farming the realm, his oppressive tax policies, his ignoring wise counsel and, worst of all, his wanton seizure of Bolingbroke's inheritance. In effect the play drops the murder charge, shelving the unsettled mystery of Gloucester's death until it resurfaces briefly at the beginning of Act 4 where Bagot implicates Aumerle in the murder. But even here, at a point where Richard has already been imprisoned and is facing certain dethronement, the issue of his guilt for murder goes unpursued.[1] As mentioned already, the monarch himself suffers no torment of conscience for the death. At this point Richard's tragedy seems to be defined by a clash between political ineptitude or volatile temperament and hostile circumstance. After the King's return from Ireland, the thematic emphasis shifts again – now to royal martyrdom at the hands of a politically shrewd enemy, who never again charges his adversary directly with any crime whatsoever. And Exton's murder of the fallen ruler, far from being a punishment for past offences, is meant to be received by audiences as a tragical outrage against divine-right legitimacy. To quote Smidt's summing up, 'The misgovernment theme is . . . more and more effaced by the sacrilege theme and the conflict between divine right and mortal frailty'; 'the central issue becomes not the king's guilt or his irresponsibility, but the sacredness of his office' (101–2).

Tomlinson in a shrewd analysis of the dramatist's shaping hand concludes with a statement with which it is hard to disagree:

---

1   Campbell (200) discerns an analogy between Gloucester's death and the execution of Mary Stuart. Perhaps the shedding of royal blood by a legitimate monarch with its implied evil consequences for the perpetrator was too dangerous a subject to carry to its natural conclusion in the theatre.

The pressure of Shakespeare's critical scrutiny does not let up at any point, either in his treatment of authority or of rebellion. He approaches each new situation without rigid ideological preconceptions or pointers. We are used to finding 'contraries' in his work, but this approach has rarely been applied to the great political question of order and rule. Shakespeare's consolidation and development of different attitudes to monarchy leads us to the conclusion that there can be no model kings or adequate model conceptions of kingship, and no univocal doctrines of social allegiance.

(58)

From Rabkin's point of view, the ambivalences of the play are not only vital to its structure but lie also at the heart of its tragedy. 'On one level *Richard II* is a play about political success and the ideal of the commonwealth', a level on which 'Bolingbroke is admirable; on another it is about what it is to be a fully sentient human being', a level on which 'only Richard commands our respect' (92). The tragic conception of politics and history embedded so powerfully in this contrast springs from 'the complementarity of [the] protagonists' virtues' – virtues that are ultimately seen to be irreconcilable or 'incapable of being commingled' (95).

Politics in Seventeenth- and Eighteenth-Century Stagings

Richard II continued to be thought a politically dangerous play long after the Elizabethan quartos had omitted the deposition scene and the stage revival commissioned by Essex's supporters had got the players into hot water. Nahum Tate's altered version of 1680 at Drury Lane and John Rich's Covent Garden production of Shakespeare's text in 1738 show that the tragedy remained topically potent in the reigns of Charles II and George II.[1] Tate wrote during the Exclusion Crisis when Titus Oates's report of a

---

1   For fuller discussion of the seventeenth- and eighteenth-century adaptations and revivals, see Forker (2–5) and Shewring (30–45).

Popish Plot and alarm over the expected succession of Charles's brother had aroused anti-Catholic prejudice to frenzy; Rich mounted his revival when Sir Robert Walpole's Whig government had come in for scathing satire.

Tate foresaw profits in a drama that could be taken to imply analogies between Richard's fabled luxury and the Merry Monarch's well-known licentiousness. However, as Charles II had been restored to the throne as a divine-right monarch, and the adaptation opened only weeks before the fast day established by the Church to commemorate the martyrdom of his father, Charles I, Tate took pains to protect himself. He distorted Shakespeare by exculpating Richard from crimes and weakness, by villainizing Bolingbroke and by making York's support of Henry IV involuntary. In an age when suspicion of subversiveness could be taken for granted, any play on the politics of monarchy was bound to incite parallel-hunting. By retitling his piece *The Sicilian Usurper* and by changing the names of the characters and removing the action to a foreign setting, Tate attempted crudely to disguise its contemporary relevance from the censors. Nevertheless, the play was banned by the Lord Chamberlain after two performances, then prohibited a second time when it appeared under the variant title of *The Tyrant of Sicily*, after which the authorities shut down the Theatre Royal for the rest of the month. The year 1681 saw the publication of Tate's *History of King Richard the Second*, now furnished with a 'Prefatory Epistle in Vindication of the Author' (sigs A1–3ᵛ) in which the poet defends himself from the implied charge of having written 'a Disloyal or Reflecting Play' and from having intended any 'Satyr on present Transactions'. Acknowledging that Richard II lived in a 'dissolute' age and surrounded himself with a 'corrupt' court, Tate explains that he has deliberately portrayed his own character as 'an Active, Prudent Prince', even showing the seizure of Gaunt's estates as a forced loan – property 'Borrow'd onely for the present Exigence'. In aid of reshaping his own Richard as more sympathetic than Shakespeare's, Tate greatly expands the role of the Queen and makes the Duchess of York her confidante. Isabel appears with Richard on his return from Ireland, at Flint Castle and before his abdication, as well as in the street when the King is being conducted under guard to the Tower; and just before the murder he reads letters from his wife – an incident that replaces the visit of the Groom with news of Barbary. Tate also introduces a prose episode of rabble commoners, recalling the Jack Cade scenes of *2 Henry VI*, that, in addition to providing a bit of 'Mirth' to 'help off the heaviness of the Tale', raises the spectre of republicanism and may have been intended to recall the bad old days of Oliver Cromwell. Tate's version ends with an epilogue that hints at the possibility of drawing historical and contemporary inferences from the action while at the same time deflecting that possibility from present circumstances to the past: though audiences might 'see no Sense in this dull Play', 'our abler Judges know' that 'much of it . . . Was famous Sense 'bove Forty Years ago'. Despite his elaborately disclaiming preface, Tate betrays his awareness that well before the deposing and execution of Charles I, Shakespeare's tragedy had been politically cogent and suggestive. Perhaps he had heard about the play's notorious connection with Essex.

Lewis Theobald's even more radical adaptation, *The Tragedy of King Richard the II*, produced at Lincoln's Inn Fields in 1719 under George I and published the following year, went to greater lengths than Tate's to avoid suggestions of political subversion and suspected commentary on present-day affairs that had doomed the earlier play. The Prologue announces, not disingenuously, that the 'Muse', 'Fearful of Censure and offended Law, . . . presumes no *Parallels* to draw' (sig. Bb3). Theobald's assiduously non-political concern was to regularize and classicize Shakespeare's play, bringing it into conformity with eighteenth-century taste. This meant jettisoning the 'rude, Historick Plan' of the original, 'supporting the *Dignity* of the *Characters*', imposing a rigorous 'unity' (everything takes place at the Tower or its precincts) and pruning the language of its Elizabethan conceits and 'Transgressions of Fancy' (sigs Aa1–Bb3). The action commences only after Richard's return from Ireland. Theobald sentimentalizes the drama unblushingly: Richard is parted from the Queen only seconds before his murder; York dies loyally of a broken heart beside his fallen sovereign; and Northumberland's daughter, Lady Percy (an invented character), who is romantically attached to Aumerle, commits suicide after the execution of her beloved, who, unlike his counterpart in Shakespeare, dies for his devotion to Richard. York (in a direct reversal of the original) begs futilely to save his son from the block.

Less than two decades after Theobald's version, however, political topicality prompted a staging of *Richard II* at Covent Garden which adopted Pope's shortened but relatively faithful Shakespearean text – apparently the first production in over a century to use the dramatist's words unaltered. The Shakespeare Ladies Club (organized by anonymous 'Ladies of Quality' according to the playbills) had lately been influential in promoting the revival of the poet's lesser-known plays and seems to have sponsored the production. But Rich, the theatre manager, undoubtedly saw a chance to capitalize on popular discontent with Walpole's government by reviving a drama that had recently figured in the satire of the day directed against the Prime Minister's so-called Playhouse Bill. This legislation established an 'excise office' for the censorship of plays considered politically subversive and was vitriolically attacked in the press as a repressive abridgement of liberty. One such attack, purporting to be by the poet laureate Colley Cibber but actually written by Nicholas Amhurst, appeared in *The Craftsman* of 2 July 1737 in the form of an ironical letter suggesting, among other things, that, in the present climate of seditious disaffection, even passages in Shakespeare and other old plays were too dangerous to be spoken on the stage and should be expunged from playhouse scripts. One of the dramas prominently instanced was *Richard II*, in which speeches critical of Richard's corruption, misgovernment and susceptibility to flattery were cited as examples of the need for censorship, since they could be interpreted as applying to Walpole and his ministry. Amhurst, the editor of the offending journal, and his printer were briefly imprisoned and the publication silenced for a week.

When Rich's production opened about six months later, the text contained all but one of the passages quoted in the mock-serious *Craftsman* letter. Thomas Davies in his *Dramatic Miscellanies* (1784) gives a revealing account of the 'shouts and huzzas' of the audience in response to the topical hits of the play, the spectators applying 'almost every line that was spoken to the occurrences of the time, and to the measures and character of the ministry'. Predictably, Gaunt's censure of Richard's thraldom to wicked counsellors in 2.1 and the dialogue of Northumberland, Ross and Willoughby later in the scene were particular crowd-pleasers. When Northumberland said, 'The King is not himself, but basely led / By flatterers' (2.1.241–2), there was much 'clapping of hands and clattering of sticks', and when Ross reported that 'The Earl of Wiltshire hath the realm in farm' (2.1.256), the speech was instantly referred to Walpole.[1] Many playgoers of the time were itching for a war with Spain, a policy that Walpole vigorously opposed; certain lines in the play mentioning Richard's avoidance of war were received as covert reflections on Walpole's pacifism and loudly hooted from the pit and galleries. As McManaway says, Rich's choice of *Richard II* in 1738 was far from being 'an accident' ('*R2*', 171).

An interesting feature of Rich's production, upon which McManaway comments, was its highly formalized staging of the lists at Coventry (1.3) and the Parliament scene (4.1). The visual effect of these grandly appointed episodes is attested in two sketches by John Roberts that survive from a transcript of the 1738 Covent Garden promptbook, now in the Folger Library, Washington, D.C.[2] Both scenes were dominated by the raised throne or chair of estate situated at the rear centre of the stage,

1   Quoted in McManaway ('*R2*', 171). McManaway gives the most detailed description of the production; my account is much indebted to his.
2   The sketches are reproduced in McManaway, '*R2*', following 174, and in Shewring, 42–3.

with groups of nobles, officials and various ceremonial figures ranged on either side to form two symmetrical arcs extending towards the front. In the combat scene, according to Davies, Bolingbroke and Mowbray 'were dressed in complete armour'. 'Two chairs, finely adorned, were placed on opposite sides of the lists' to which the contestants 'retired after each . . . had stood forth and spoken'. The staging of the abdication scene was perhaps even more spectacular. The arrangement included two cardinals on stools on either side of the throne, a 'long table' extending downstage 'on which rest the Purse and the Mace, symbols of Majesty, with the Chancellor at the upper end, a Secretary at the lower, and a Judge seated on a cushion on either side'. In addition to the speaking characters there were '12 Bishops and 25 Civilians', 'Fryars with crosses' and 'Gentleman Usher and Black Rod'. 'This was such a sight as was familiar to those who had sat in Parliament or had seen the engraving of Queen Elizabeth seated in Parliament' in Glover's volume (see Fig. 3).[1] McManaway goes on to suggest that such ceremonial stagings had long been traditional and would probably have been expected by eighteenth-century audiences, having derived (with modifications to accommodate changes in theatrical architecture) from Elizabethan times.

LANGUAGE

Style

Wilson, following Pater, finds 'a unity of tone and feeling' in *Richard II*, sensing that it was 'composed in a single mood' (xiv–xv). Pater praises the play's 'unity of lyrical effect', its 'sweet-tongued' eloquence, its 'simple continuity' and 'evenness in execution' (Forker, 296–300). Chambers compares the tragedy to opera in its reliance on 'a rhetorical and measured declamation' (*Survey*, 88) while John Gielgud, one of the most successful actors

---

1   The quotations are from McManaway, '*R2*', 170, 173.

of the title role, comments on the danger of monotony in a drama whose 'artificial' and 'tapestried' style is often more musical than revealing of character and can become 'somewhat indigestible' unless the poetry is 'welded imperceptibly into the dramatic action' (28–35). One reason for the widespread impression of tonal unity is Shakespeare's sustained 'attention', in Coleridge's phrase (as redacted by his nephew), to the 'decorum and high feeling of . . . kingly dignity' (Forker, 129). Another is the pervasiveness of lamentation, a theme that draws upon the traditions of late medieval and Renaissance complaint literature. As Wells ('Tale') shows, the speeches often seem to be motivated by hopelessness and frustration or drenched in tears. Gloucester's widow vents anguish for her murdered spouse (1.2); Mowbray and Bolingbroke grieve at their sentences of exile while Gaunt complains that he shall never again see his son (1.3); Gaunt grieves for his country and its reputation, and York, stricken by his brother's death, laments Richard's outrageous action in seizing the dead man's property (2.1); the Queen in her three most important scenes is presented as a living emblem of sorrow (2.2, 3.4, 5.1); Salisbury and the Welsh Captain mournfully presage Richard's fall (2.4); in Wales Richard moans over his political reverses and the death of his friends (3.2), then grieves again during his surrender at Flint Castle (3.3); the abdication scene (4.1) elaborates a cadenza on the theme of grief and loss; the Gardeners comment ruefully on Richard's defeat (3.4); the parting of the royal lovers constitutes a threnody for the end of intimacy (5.1); York laments Richard's humiliation in the London streets (5.2); at Pomfret Richard meditates plaintively on the 'wasted time' of his reign (5.5); and the play ends with Henry IV's guilty lament over the corpse of his rival (5.6). *Richard II* might be described as a staging of Richard's 'lamentable tale' (5.1.44), the theme spreading out to encompass subordinate characters and the nation at large, with *sic transit gloria mundi* as its elegiac motto. Such accumulation of woe seems partly intended to evoke the medieval piety of *contemptus mundi*.

On closer inspection, however, the style of the tragedy proves to be more complex and dramatically discontinuous than the preceding paragraph suggests; Baxter indeed goes so far as to call Pater's unity 'an illusion' (57). Rossiter discerns at least three stylistic modes – rhyme (chiefly couplets) and two kinds of blank verse (an 'earlier' style, 'over-ingenious . . . and obtrusive', and a more mature and flexible style such as 'that of the Deposition'). But the diversity of the play's verse is wider and subtler than Rossiter's confessedly 'crude discrimination' (*Angel*, 26) allows.

Perfect rhyme, more prominent in *Richard II* than in any other play of Shakespeare's except *The Comedy of Errors*, *Love's Labour's Lost* and *A Midsummer Night's Dream*, extends to roughly a quarter of the total line-count, embracing many heroic couplets as well as quatrains and the occasional triplet or sextain. The rhyming is partly conventional, often employed to signal the end or approaching end of a scene or important speech, to lend point to an apothegm or simply to delight hearers with an ornamental flourish of patterned musicality. No doubt Shakespeare's recent experimentation in narrative verse and the sonnets is relevant here. But rhyme can also serve characterization: it may express, for example, Bolingbroke's self-possessed calculation in his quarrel with Mowbray in contrast to his opponent's freer styled, though equally vehement, answer (1.1.41–6); or Richard's callous levity at the news of Gaunt's death (2.1.153–4); or his luxuriance in despair (3.2.209–14); or Scroop's attempt to soften and delay the impact of evil tidings (3.2.194–7). Rhyme seems particularly to characterize Richard, perhaps manifesting his need for a settled order or ironically reflecting his attempt to impose it merely through the harmonies of speech. Rhyme serves to heighten the anger of the stichomythic exchange between Gaunt and the young King (2.1.88–92) and to intensify the jarring effect of the begging and counter-begging at Aumerle's pardoning (5.3.82–135). Unrhymed couplets are sometimes interspersed among the rhyming lines and the more regular blank verse, as for instance in the accusatory speeches of Mowbray and Bolingbroke

(1.1). Shifts from rhyme to blank verse or at least from sections in which one of the two styles predominates can serve to adjust the tone or alter the pace of an episode; the transition between the commutation of Bolingbroke's sentence leading up to the King's exit (1.3.208–52) and the more intimate colloquy between Gaunt and his son (253–309) is a case in point. Within a basic verse structure that is regularly iambic and end-stopped in the manner of Marlowe and Kyd, there is also considerable enjambment as well as a liberal use of feminine endings (about eleven per cent) and some metrical irregularity, sometimes used (as in York's character) to suggest agitation or confusion. Both alexandrines and short lines (dimeters, trimeters and tetrameters) appear from time to time to vary the rhythm and momentum or to introduce interruptions, vocatives, direct questions, dramatic transitions and the like. The play contains a number of lines that can be rationalized uncertainly as uneven hexameters or as hypermetrical pentameters or pentameters by elision; some of these may result from textual corruption, but there are enough of them to suggest a deliberate undertow against the smoothness and regularity that dominate the poetic flow. Such metrical variations add vigour, nervousness and spontaneity and help counteract or constrain the play's tendency to more self-indulgent artifice.

It is a truism that *Richard II* is ritualistic. Wilson (xii) remarks that the play 'stands far closer to the Catholic . . . Mass than to' plays by Ibsen or Shaw. The magniloquent speeches, the stately balances and symmetries, the courtly etiquette and mannered formalities of speech and movement assist this effect, as does the absence of low comedy. For once Shakespeare observes Sidney's stricture against the mingling of kings and clowns (*Apology*, 135); and, unlike his practice in the other histories (except *Henry VIII*), he stages no battles and refrains from making military combat a feature of the offstage action. No subplot diverts attention from the pageantry of Richard's fall, and even the Gardeners speak like gentlemen. Nevertheless, the ritualism is intermittent and sporadic. The two quarrel scenes of Act 1 establish a tone of orotund and ceremonious spectacle; Gaunt's panegyric on England in 2.1 celebrates tradition in a way that supports a sense of national identity and is thus ceremonial in spirit if not in action; York's confrontation with Bolingbroke on the latter's return (2.3) contains an element of ritual since the exile kneels in formal obeisance to the King's official surrogate; the scenes dramatizing Richard on the Welsh coast and his capture at Flint Castle (3.2 and 3.3) allow him to flaunt his sense of royal entitlement, thus stimulating our awareness of both the power and the limits of ritual; Act 4 with its repetition of the earlier gauntlet throwing and the discrowning itself is the heart of the play's ritualism as well as the emotional climax of the tragedy; but nothing genuinely ritualistic occurs thereafter (except possibly the parting of Richard and the Queen in 5.1) until the final scene in which Henry IV presides at court and mourns over Richard's coffin, which he follows in solemn procession.[1] Other scenes produce a formal effect because of their stiffly rhetorical or emblematic style – the Duchess of Gloucester's grief (1.2), the Queen's foreboding (2.2), the choric utterances of Salisbury and the Welsh Captain (2.4), the allegorical reflections of the Gardeners (3.4) – while the pardoning of Aumerle in 5.3 represents ceremony degraded almost to parody. But mixed in with the more formal episodes are scenes of unvarnished realism often dramatized in speech of vernacular directness, serviceable plainness or even jocularity. One thinks of York's explosive call for his boots and his spat with his wife (5.2.74–110), of Northumberland's straightforward news of Bolingbroke's invasion (2.1.277–98) and of the latter's efficient condemnation of Bushy and Green (3.1.1–30); the malicious chat between Richard and Aumerle about Bolingbroke's departure (1.4.1–36) illustrates the collapse of courtly etiquette on a private occasion. Sometimes at moments of stress, royal dignity deserts even Richard: 'I had forgot myself. Am I not king?' (3.2.83);

---

1   Rossiter, somewhat overstating the point, asserts that 'only six scenes out of nineteen can be called "ritualistic" or formalized' (*Angel*, 38). By my count elements of ritualism and formality occur in at least thirteen scenes.

'Whither you will, so I were from your sights' (4.1.315); 'The devil take Henry of Lancaster and thee!' (5.5.102). Such tonal and stylistic shifts make the point that life is more than pageantry; and Barkan suggests, for instance, that variations in verbal texture subliminally communicate a threat of anarchic energy lurking beneath orderly surfaces (6). Thus ceremony exists in tension with its opposite – a traditional and sacrosanct concept of royal authority with its disruption.

The play exploits a range of styles. The combatants' vaunting speeches, Marlovian in their 'high astounding terms', contrast with Richard's more detached loftiness including touches of throw-away lightness ('Our doctors say this is no month to bleed' (1.1.157)). At Coventry the chivalric formulae of the Lord Marshal and heralds provide verbal grandeur of another kind. After the sentencing Mowbray, Bolingbroke and Gaunt become more supple in their speech, reflecting the depth of personal emotion; then in their farewells, father and son reduce rhyme to a minimum. Richard, relaxing with his courtiers (1.4), drops rhyme altogether. Gaunt's set-piece in praise of England (2.1.40–68) returns us to more heightened speech, but in a way that conceals rather than flaunts its art, creating an effect unstrained and natural in comparison with the overstretched bluster of the Coventry contenders. Gaunt's aria contrasts equally with the routine succession of maxims from which it takes flight (2.1.33–9), the proverbial mode being another of the play's many styles. Enraged haughtiness characterizes Richard's response to Gaunt's rebukes and heartless indifference to the news of his death, but after the King's exit, the nobles who remain onstage settle down to a much plainer, lower-keyed blank verse as they assess political realities. Richard, as befits his prominence and volatility, has the greatest range of styles and displays fluctuating shades and levels of poetic eloquence, but he is not alone in the elevated richness of his speeches. His magniloquence contrasts usually with the sparer, more practical style of Bolingbroke and Northumberland, but the future Henry IV is fully capable of florid display:

See, see, King Richard doth himself appear,
As doth the blushing discontented sun
From out the fiery portal of the east,
When he perceives the envious clouds are bent
To dim his glory and to stain the track
Of his bright passage to the Occident.

$(3.3.62-7)^1$

Carlisle's speech on divine right (4.1.115–50), another example of sustained eloquence, though less showy than Richard's characteristic utterance, reveals how theatrically effective declamation can be in a relatively minor character.

Bushy's arduously conceited attempt to console the Queen, the 'metaphysical' passage on 'perspectives' (2.2.14–27; see 2.2.18LN and Fig. 5), reminds us of yet another style that invades the play – that which delights in verbal wit, ingenious fancy, multiple meanings and the strenuous working-out of the details of a comparison. Richard himself is particularly adept at such games, most obviously in the deposition scene where he wittily exploits the *double entendres* of 'Ay, no. No, ay; for I must nothing be' (4.1.201–2) and plays inventively with the significances of the crown (4.1.183–99) and the mirror (4.1.276–302); the style recurs also in the Pomfret episode where, in a heroic assault upon the technique of *discordia concors*, he attempts to 'hammer out' the difficult similitude of his prison and the world (5.5.1–41). In *Richard II* such ingenuity suits the personality of the protagonist, sometimes conveying his escapist psychology, sometimes embodying his delight in the art of self-representation, sometimes becoming the instrument of his performative manipulation; in addition it ties in with the play's metadramatic concern with the power and limitation of words. Conscious verbal artistry and speeches that wrestle intellectually with dissimilars or pursue the

---

1   Hockey cogently challenges the familiar assumption that '*Richard II* is written in two styles' (plain and high) 'to suggest two warring worlds' (189) by showing that nearly all the characters, including those depicted without much complexity, sometimes employ rhetorical artifice.

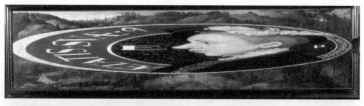

5 Anamorphic portrait of Edward VI (two views from front and side), after
Hans Holbein the Younger, 1543

yoking of heterogeneous ideas through wordplay (Gaunt's punning on his name is a notable example)[1] are means of dramatizing intensity, inner conflict, reflexivity, ironic passion and the need to define one's own situation. This does not mean, of course, that simpler, more direct kinds of expression are any the less powerful. Indeed, they may become more so by reason of the contrast with virtuosity. 'I live with bread like you, feel want, / Taste grief, need friends' (3.2.175–6) shows us that Richard's 'Taffeta phrases' and 'silken terms precise' must sometimes give place to the recognition, as Berowne says, that 'Honest plain words best pierce the ear of grief' (*LLL* 5.2.406, 753).

Renaissance critics distinguished the plain style, best suited to express moral force (*ethos*), from the aureate style, more effective for embodying sweetness and sensuous pleasure or for capturing the psychological dimension of human experience (*pathos*). Sidney in his *Apology* defends both styles, acknowledging that 'a plain sensibleness' often has the force of persuasion to recommend it, but celebrating also the poet's capacity to render Nature's 'brazen' world in 'golden' terms (100). Elizabethan taste endorsed amplitude and variety in verse and regarded 'artificial' as a term of praise. Erasmus writes that there is 'nothing more admirable or more splendid than a speech with a rich copia of thoughts and words overflowing in a golden stream' (11). Baxter (59–66) analyses in detail how *Richard II* effectively contrasts, juxtaposes and combines the two styles, using as an illustration the colloquy between Gaunt and York at the opening of Act 2 (the dialogue that leads up to and includes the much-quoted praise of England) where the verse holds in delicate equipoise the moral force of the plain style with the rhythmic and figurative plenitude of the golden. Such modulations characterize the stylistic texture of the drama as a whole, and, as Baxter (46–55) points out, relate to the

---

1 Coleridge comments incisively on this passage: 'is there not a tendency in the human mind, when suffering under some great affliction, to associate everything around it with the obtrusive feeling, to connect and absorb all into the predominant sensation[?]' (127).

compositional problem of uniting history (whose purpose is chiefly moral) to tragedy (whose desired effect is to excite emotion). In Baxter's estimation *Richard II*'s range of styles reveals Shakespeare in transition between self-declarative forms of artifice and more subtle forms of expression in which art conceals art. The rhetorical exercise in which the Duchess of Gloucester extends for ten lines a parallel between the 'seven vials' of Edward III's 'sacred blood' and the 'seven fair branches' of his family tree (1.2.11–21) belongs to the first category. So does Richard's fantastic variation on his earlier image of making 'dust our paper and with rainy eyes / Writ[ing] sorrow on the bosom of the earth' (3.2.146–7) – making 'some pretty match with shedding tears . . . Till they have fretted us a pair of graves' (3.3.165–6). Another instance of the overwrought style is Richard's attempt to work out the strained parallel between a clock and a human body, the hand of the dial corresponding to the finger wiping away tears and the striking to blows upon the heart (5.5.50–8). In the latter two instances, at least, Shakespeare makes drama out of poetic ingenuity: in the first case Richard becomes self-consciously aware of his own absurdity ('Well, well, I see / I talk but idly, and you laugh at me' (3.3.170–1)); in the second, we see him struggling, somewhat ineffectually, to come to terms with his prison isolation and with the larger issues of time and identity. The finest passages in the play such as Richard's 'hollow crown' speech (3.2.144–77) or York's noble description of the procession into London (5.2.23–40), though golden in their vital particularity, tend to be less blatantly virtuosic and more natural in effect, the dramatist subduing his technique, 'like the dyer's hand' (*Son* 111.7), to the matter in which he works. In these instances elements of both the golden and the plain style modify each other cunningly to create the satisfying result.

Imagery, Major Themes, Symbolism, Patterns of Allusion
Richard II is famous for its profusion of images, elaborately interrelated and woven together like leitmotifs in a musical

composition. Altick's term for the technique is 'symphonic'. The more dominant images tend to take on the status of emblems, radiating a kind of symbolism or iconicity that makes them guideposts to the play's larger meanings. Shakespeare's careful integration of word pictures, his iterative use of them to create patterns and associations of ideas, is evidence of his maturing artistry – of his gradual abandonment of the inorganic and decorative imagery that sometimes characterizes his apprentice style. It has occasionally been asked whether such a complex system of verbal echoes and figurative reverberations observed in the study can ever be fully grasped in the theatre. Conscious recognition of every linkage may indeed elude audiences, but, as Allardyce Nicoll observes, 'the theatre is a strange place, where imaginations are quickened and where more is appreciated than the intellect will allow or acknowledge' (44). As Nicoll (45) points out, it can hardly be fortuitous that when Richard exclaims of Bolingbroke, 'How high a pitch his resolution soars!' (1.1.109), he prepares us through use of an image from falconry for his reference to 'the eagle-winged pride / Of sky-aspiring and ambitious thoughts' (1.3.129–30), words obliquely applied to his cousin. The image patterns of the play seem intended to work, at least in part, like the rhetorical patterns (see pp. 83–90) – subliminally or at a level of receptivity only intermittently alert to the web of repetitions and associations. Nevertheless, the imagery contributes significantly to interpretation.

There is space here only to consider patterns in which the major themes of the play are centred. One of the most pregnant is the matrix of references to language itself – the recurrence of terms such as 'tongue', 'breath', 'throat', 'mouth', 'word', 'name' and 'speech'. This vocabulary reflects the play's abiding concern with the tension between words and reality. As a king by divine right, Richard assumes that his words have an almost supernatural power to enact what they refer to. His judgement against Mowbray, 'The hopeless word of "never to return" / Breathe I against thee, upon pain of life' (1.3.152–3), takes the absolutism and inevitability of its effect for granted; pronouncement of the sentence becomes inseparable from the punishment. And Bolingbroke acknowledges the same painful truth when his own sentence is shortened:

> How long a time lies in one little word!
> Four lagging winters and four wanton springs
> End in a word; such is the breath of kings.
>
> (1.3.213–15)

Richard's essentialist conception of language obliterates the space between signifier and signified, like the priest who transmutes the bread and wine of the Eucharist into the body and blood of Christ by saying the words of institution: 'this is my body . . . this is my blood'. The mystical uniqueness of his voice, an aspect of his 'sacred' status, differentiates it in kind, he believes, from that of ordinary mortals who have no power to annul his divinely conferred authority: 'The breath of worldly men cannot depose / The deputy elected by the Lord' (3.2.56–7). At times, Richard's words take on something of the force of the Word in Saint John's sense of *logos*. Shakespeare, without entirely repudiating this exalted notion, nevertheless undermines it by insisting on Richard's human limitation. When the King tells Gaunt that he has 'many years to live', the old man replies, 'But not a minute, King, that thou canst give' (1.3.225–6). And Richard's hieratic reliance on purely verbal defences to repel his invading enemy – the invocation of spiders, toads, nettles and a troop of angels – is shown to be transparently foolish. His fanciful and impassioned flights of speech have an undeniable power, but they obviously cannot serve to meet political crisis. Finally stripped of his power to rule England, Richard attempts to invent a kingdom of thoughts in his lonely cell, solipsistically germinating his own reality through the only power left him – the mimetic power of words. Moreover, even scripture loses something of its eternal fixity as he 'set[s] the word itself / Against the word' (5.5.13–14). The 'semantics of royalty', to borrow Barber's phrase (35), has devolved from objective and authoritative participation in a cosmic reality to a kind of existential subjectivity. Bolingbroke, in contrast, is presented as possessing a more realistic and utilitarian concept of language, one that instantly perceives the difference between comforting words and harsh actualities: Gaunt's attempt to ease the pain of his son's exile, 'Call it a travel that thou tak'st for pleasure', provokes an instant reply: 'My heart will sigh when I miscall it so, / Which finds it an enforced pilgrimage' (1.3.262–4). Bolingbroke understands, as successful politicians must, that changing the name of a thing does not change its reality. He instinctively recognizes that for most purposes words are but arbitrary instruments of communication, a convenient system of sounds and forms by means of which the business of the world gets transacted. That words should somehow possess a corporeal or mystical substance is, for Bolingbroke, largely illusory.

The two attitudes towards language contrasted in *Richard II* suggest a tragic and more general opposition between the competing value-systems of the play. Richard's essentially feudal world, a world of oaths and codes of honour, of titles and of fixed identities, of ritual solemnity and ceremonial beauty, puts heavy stress on the seriousness and potency of words. Bolingbroke, who challenges and overturns that world, brings to bear a more modern, relativistic, sceptical and less comely understanding of how meaning is generated. Much of the play's pathos has to do with nostalgia for the break-up of traditional coherences and stabilities implied by the older and more beautiful unity of words and things; for the divide between sign and essence that the usurpation opens up wrecks 'the unity and married calm of states' (*TC* 1.3.100). It is in this context that the theme of names becomes a symbolic issue.

As Friedman puts it, 'Richard, like Lear, must assume that his title is indistinguishable from his identity, just as his will is indistinguishable from the act that it wills' (295). Thus the tragedy of his reduction to 'nothing' (4.1.201, 5.5.38, 41) coincides with his loss of title: 'Is not the King's name twenty thousand names? / Arm, arm, my name!' (3.2.85–6); 'O, that I were as great / As is

my grief, or lesser than my name!' (3.3.136–7); 'Must he lose /
The name of King?' (3.3.145–6); 'I have no name, no title – /
No, not that name was given me at the font' (4.1.255–6). For
Richard, ceasing to be king in name is equivalent to non-exis-
tence, a point with which York sympathizes when he rebukes
Northumberland for omitting the royal title (3.3.7–8).
Bolingbroke too is much concerned with titles, especially when,
as a political strategy, he insists to Berkeley on being addressed
by his newly acquired style:

> My lord, my answer is – to 'Lancaster',
> And I am come to seek that name in England;
> And I must find that title in your tongue
> Before I make reply to aught you say.
>
> (2.3.70–3)

Unlike Richard, his adversary is known in the play by a variety of
names – Derby, Hereford, Bolingbroke, Lancaster and finally
Henry IV. The variation suggests his more uncertain and shifting
identity as subject, rebel, usurper and monarch in a way that com-
ports with his more relativistic and pragmatic attitude towards
language. Names are also loaded with significance in the case of
subordinate characters. Mowbray equates his 'fair name' with his
honour in the lists (1.1.167–9); Gaunt bitterly identifies his name
with his illness ('O, how that name befits my composition!'
(2.1.73)); Aumerle's name changes officially to Rutland, his higher
title having been 'lost for being Richard's friend' (5.2.42); the
Duchess of York fears that her son's treason will 'rob [her] of a
happy mother's name' (5.2.93). The names of these characters
reflect their self-estimation and are closely linked to the vicissitudes of their emotional or political circumstances.

The play also ties the theme of language to character in other
ways. The relative volubility or terseness of a speaker's utterance
becomes a register of that character's emotional state or political situation. Gaunt asks his grieving son, 'to what purpose dost thou
hoard thy words . . . ?', and is answered: 'I have too few to take my

leave of you, / When the tongue's office should be prodigal / To breathe the abundant dolour of the heart' (1.3.253–7). Richard's manipulative theatricality in the abdication scene forces the role of 'silent King' (4.1.290) upon his successor. His volatile stream of words partly conveys his narcissistic delight in the aesthetic pleasures of his own eloquence; partly it becomes a means of self-definition, a way of entering into the abyss of his own nature. But the play proves finally that power in the common-sense world lies less in words than in deeds. Mowbray laments for fifteen lines that exile to a foreign land 'robs [his] tongue' of its birthright, his 'native English' (1.3.159–73), without being able to alter his fate. Here the play, in a passage that complements Gaunt's praise of his country, invokes the language theme in celebration of national pride.

Shakespeare roots the motif of patriotism in the pervasive imagery of earth, land and ground ('the three words occur a total of 71 times' (Altick, 341)). Mowbray, Bolingbroke, Gaunt and Richard are all portrayed as feeling a strong emotional bond with England, the country of their spiritual as well as their national identity. Bolingbroke takes leave of 'England's ground', referring to its 'Sweet soil' (1.3.306); Richard salutes his 'Dear earth' by caressing it with his hands (3.2.6–11) and then 'sit[s] upon the ground' to bewail his losses. For Richard a physical connection to the earth becomes an extension of his '*corpus mysticum*' superseding his political and geographical authority and 'transcend[ing] both the king's eternal "body politic" and his personal, natural self' (Nevo, 75). Gaunt's devotion to 'this earth of majesty' (2.1.41), 'this teeming womb of royal kings' (2.1.51), contrasts with Richard's, founded as it is on traditions of chivalric valour, martial prowess, defence against invasion and international respect. For Gaunt the national scandal consists in his nephew's having become 'Landlord of England . . . , not king' (2.1.113), of having 'leased out' the 'blessed plot' of his inheritance and allowing it to degenerate into a 'pelting farm' (2.1.50, 59–60). The garden scene (3.4), strategically placed near the middle of the play, focuses the symbolism of England's earth into a national emblem, projecting an ideal of nurture, fertility, happiness and politico-moral order through the comparison to Eden, yet commenting pointedly on the corruptions of Richard's misrule through the horticultural details. The 'bank of rue' (3.4.105) that the Gardener will plant in the place where the Queen had dropped a tear relates the garden to both personal and national sorrow. Later the Queen speaks of the country that has dethroned her husband as 'this rebellious earth' (5.1.5). The play also links the imagery of earth to human mortality, drawing upon the religious truism that men must ultimately return to the dust of which they are made. Richard thinks of his human body as 'that small model of the barren earth / Which serves as paste and cover to our bones' (3.2.153–4), fantasizes with Aumerle about 'fret[ting]' the ground away with tears to make 'a pair of graves / Within the earth' (3.3.167–8), and imagines himself being consigned to 'an earthy pit' (4.1.219); Mowbray, confronting combat, avers that without honour 'Men are but gilded loam or painted clay' (1.1.179). Carlisle compares an England torn by civil strife to the 'field of Golgotha and dead men's skulls' (4.1.145). In his influential production, Barton introduced a 'little pot of earth' (Page, 59) as a physical emblem to be touched or handled by Bolingbroke, Richard, the Gardener, Carlisle and the Queen at some of the points mentioned above.

Nature imagery suffuses *Richard II*, projecting a landscape of potential fruitfulness and extending the idea of the 'demi-paradise' (2.1.42) introduced into Gaunt's most famous speech. Much of this is idealized and conventional, evoking the golden world of pastoral or England as a pleasance: the 'crystal . . . sky' (1.1.41), 'singing birds' as 'musicians' (1.3.288), 'tuft[s] of trees' (2.3.53), the 'tops of . . . eastern pines' illuminated by dawn (3.2.42), 'silver rivers' (3.2.107), 'dangling apricocks' (3.4.29), 'fairest flowers' (3.4.44), 'fair rose[s]' (5.1.8), 'violets . . . strew[ing] the green lap of the new-come spring' (5.2.46–7), 'immaculate and silver fountain[s]' (5.3.60). But thematically connected with these idyllic images is the marring ugliness of bloodshed and violence. Richard stops the joust at Coventry so that his 'kingdom's earth should not be soiled / With that dear blood which it hath fostered' (1.3.125–6); Bolingbroke threatens to 'lay the summer's dust with showers of blood / Rained from the wounds of slaughtered Englishmen' (3.3.43–4) and speaks of war as a 'crimson tempest . . . bedrench[ing] / The fresh green lap of fair King Richard's land' (3.3.46–7); Richard predicts that the violence of his enemy's revolt will 'ill become the flower of England's face . . . and bedew her pastor's grass with faithful English blood' (3.3.97–100); Carlisle prophesies that 'The blood of English shall manure the ground' (4.1.138); King Henry is consumed with remorse that Richard's 'blood should sprinkle [him] to make [him] grow' (5.6.46). Red versus green becomes the salient colour contrast of the play, to which even the historical names of Bushy and Green contribute incidentally. Richard is accused of having 'drunkenly caroused' Gloucester's blood 'like the pelican' (2.1.126–7; see 2.1.126n. and Fig. 6) and 'the death or fall of kings' (2.4.15) is ominously forecast by a 'pale-faced moon [that] looks bloody on the earth' (2.4.10). The motif of blood, however, signifies more than warfare and murder. Shakespeare makes it also symbolize heredity, family pride, kinship and royal legitimacy. The Duchess of Gloucester pairs the 'vials' of King Edward's 'sacred blood' with the 'fair branches' of the royal family tree (1.2.12–13; see 1.2.15n. and Fig. 7), and Richard addresses Bolingbroke as 'my blood' (1.3.57). Concepts of generation, health, vital energy, high spirits and anger flow into the mix: fruit trees must be bled of their sap to ensure fertility (3.4.58–9); Mowbray speaks of the 'hot' blood of his anger while Richard refers to purging 'choler' in the context of medicinal bleeding (1.1.51, 153); Gaunt's rebuke 'chase[s] the royal blood' from Richard's cheek (2.1.118), setting up a further contrast between ruddiness and pallor when bad news drains 'the blood of twenty thousand men' from the King's face (3.2.76).

The conventional emblem of the sun as a symbol of majesty, historically one of Richard's badges and used similarly by Daniel (see p. 142), is obviously a commanding image of the play, being

Our Pelican, *by bleeding, thus,*
Fulfil'd the Law, *and cured* Vs.

E G R E · P R O L E G E · E T P R O

ILLVSTR. XX.   *Book.*3

6 Emblem of the Pelican, from George Wither, *A Collection of Emblems, Ancient and Modern*, 1635

employed with special effectiveness to accent its *de casibus* structure. Its prominence furnishes the action with a cosmological
dimension identifying the King theoretically with the source of
light and energy. Metaphors of 'the searching eye of heaven'
(3.2.37), of the King 'rising in [his] throne, the east' (3.2.50) and
of Richard on the battlements as 'the blushing discontented sun'
(3.3.63) reinforce the notion of divinely instituted order, just as
counter-images of the setting sun (2.4.21, 3.2.218), the analogy to

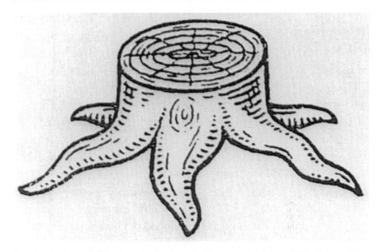

7 The badge of Woodstock (Duke of Gloucester), from C.W. Scott-Giles, *Shakespeare's Heraldry*, 1950

Phaëton, irresponsible driver of the sun–god's chariot (3.3.178), and to the 'mockery king of snow' melting under 'the sun of Bolingbroke' (4.1.260–1) suggest its tragic demise. Barton made it a part of his set at Stratford-upon-Avon, stretching 'a huge golden sun . . . over the center of the "heavens"' and making Richard's coronation costume a 'gleaming pleated golden robe which enable[d] him to look . . . like "glist'ring Phaeton"' (Gilbert, 87, 92). Contrasts between day and night, light and darkness and warmth and cold, stitched into the verbal fabric, extend the symbolism in various ways. Heninger argues that the 'multifaceted image' of the sun functions in three ways: first, as 'the symbol of royal prerogative that passes from Richard to Bolingbroke', second, as an ironic reflector 'that reveals . . . the deficiencies of both Richard and Bolingbroke' by serving to point up the gap between ideal sun-king and human frailty, and, third, as 'an instrument of transition in Richard's personal tragedy' from 'capricious auto-crat' to 'sympathetic victim', from tyrant to sacrificial and 'Christ-like microcosmos' (322–6).

Naturally related to the sun emblem are the earthlier symbols of royalty – the crown, sceptre, jewel, throne and balm images.[1] Richard, with whom these objects are usually associated, functions in the play as an ambiguous icon of divine and human reference. Thus the appurtenances of royalty of which Richard divests himself provide a context for regarding the King as a complex image of cosmic splendour and authority, of inadequate ruler and of suffering humanity (see Brooke, 128). The images of royal ceremony also reinforce the concept of the player-king, combining with the word/speech patterns to emphasize the theme of imagination versus hard fact, or appearance versus reality: 'Thus play I in one person many people' (5.5.31). Lying behind the player-king idea is the Renaissance commonplace, developed by Shakespeare in other places, that life itself is a play – a 'woeful pageant' concluded finally by death. The tradition of the player-king has both its Christian-humanist and Machiavellian thrusts, for the divide between role and self implies a spiritual process of self-discovery, of coming to terms with eternity beneath the superficial vesture of the flesh, as well as the role-playing essential to survival in the political world. Richard and Bolingbroke in their different ways become involved in both processes.[2] In Wales Richard confronts the truth that his reign is but 'a little scene' in which to 'monarchize, be feared and kill with looks' while Death, the 'antic', keeps court within his 'hollow crown' (3.2.160–5). Henry IV comments on a more political aspect of the theme in his amused reference to 'The Beggar and the King' when Aumerle's life is at stake – a 'scene . . . altered from a serious thing' by the exaggerated role-playing of its participants (5.3.78–9). In *2 Henry IV*, Shakespeare would reinforce Henry's association with role-playing by having him admit near death that

1   In addition to specific mention of Richard's jewels (3.3.147), jewel metaphors are surprisingly widespread, being applied to Mowbray's honour (1.1.180), to Bolingbroke's love of home and to his return (1.3.267, 270) and to England as an island (2.1.46).

2   Philip Edwards insightfully explores the tension between person and office in Shakespeare, commenting on the 'autonomous and plastic self' (105) which sometimes, as in the case of Henry V, can conform itself to the definition of its office, and sometimes, as with Richard II, fails through injustice or other unkingly conduct to do so.

'all my reign hath been but as a scene / Acting' out the 'argument' of his disputed right (4.5.197–8).

The multivalent iconography of the mirror[1] relates to play-acting since it ties in with Richard's exploration of his identity and, like Bushy's intricate conceit on the likeness of tears to refracting glasses, raises issues of perception. Bushy's comment, 'Each substance of a grief hath twenty shadows, / Which shows like grief itself, but is not so' (2.2.14–15), becomes relevant. *Richard II* in action, characterization and metaphor toys with epistemological concepts – with the distortions, fragmentation and subjectivity involved in imaging. The mirror and its shattering associate these ideas with Richard's personal tragedy, helping to focus psychic conflicts between vanity and truth, face and mask, role and self, self-construction and dissolution, surface and depth, shadow and substance, illusion and reality. Barton, in his production, gave a fresh twist to the mirror emblem by making Richard Pasco and Ian Richardson exchange the roles of Richard and Bolingbroke on successive evenings and by having each character regard the other as a symbolic double or reflection of himself. He emphasized the interchangeability of the antagonists rather than their differences by introducing the mirror as a prop at points before and after the climactic episode of the deposition (see Gilbert, 90). Shakespeare extends the mirror idea to the dramaturgy. York becomes the political reflector of the play, the character who mirrors the shift in loyalty from Richard to Henry, while the Queen, through commitment to Richard, refracts the emotional changes that accompany this shift. Two 'mirror scenes', the brief colloquy between Salisbury and the Welsh Captain foreshadowing disaster (2.4) and the garden allegory (3.4), present general feelings and political truths as though reflected in a glass.

Another significant pattern in the figurative weave of *Richard II*, analysed by Bryant, is its double set of biblical analogies – on the one hand, references to the linked stories of Adam and Eve

1   See pp. 36–8, 46, 135 and 4.1.275.1n.

and of Cain and Abel from Genesis, and on the other, to the account of Christ's Passion involving allusions to Judas, Pilate and Golgotha.[1] Not surprisingly, the first part of the myth involving Adam and Eve is introduced by Gaunt, who conceives of England as a 'demi-paradise' or second Eden (2.1.42), now, alas, postlapsarian owing to Richard's misgovernment; the garden scene then develops the theme of the Fall in two contrasted ways, first by commenting on Richard's failure to 'Keep law and form and due proportion' in his 'sea-walled garden' (3.4.41–3), second, by making the Queen address the Gardener, whose prophecy of her husband's deposition she has just overheard, as 'old Adam's likeness' and by having her suggest indignantly that his divination of 'a second fall of cursed man' (Richard's expulsion from the garden), must have been prompted by some latter-day 'Eve' or 'serpent' (3.4.72–9). Thus, by implication, the play applies images of the original disobedience to God's command both to the King himself and to those who, by criticizing him, passively cooperate in the treason of his dethronement. The second part of the myth, Cain's killing of his brother Abel (history's first murder), was naturally interpreted as an inevitable consequence of the Fall and therefore part and parcel of the explanation of how death and all our woe came into the world. Shakespeare also utilizes this part of Genesis in a double way: first, Bolingbroke accuses Mowbray of being a latter-day Cain for having 'Sluiced out . . . the innocent soul' of Gloucester, and seems to take upon himself the duty of avenging 'sacrificing Abel's' blood (1.1.103–4); second, Henry IV identifies Exton with Cain (5.6.43). Ironically, of course, the play appears to attach ultimate responsibility for the deaths of Gloucester and Richard to the two kings themselves rather than to the surrogates from whom they distance themselves, with the result that the Cain–Abel story

---

1 Curiously, apart from the significant reference to the myth of Phaëton (3.3.178) and passing references to Julius Caesar (5.1.2) and 'old Troy' (5.1.11), the play contains no corresponding richness of classical allusion. Shakespeare's concentration on a medieval ambience may partly account for the fact.

reflects both positively and negatively upon both. As the putative killer of his uncle, Richard resembles Cain but, as the victim of Exton, is more like Abel, who, according to medieval typology, prefigured Christ; as the accuser of Mowbray-Cain, Bolingbroke aligns himself morally with Abel, yet as the supposed murderer of his royal cousin plays the role of Cain.

Symbolically associated with Cain, whose punishment was to wander as an exile, is also the play's theme of pilgrimage: at Coventry Bolingbroke likens himself and his opponent to 'two men / That vow a long and weary pilgrimage' (1.3.48–9), later referring to banishment as 'an enforced pilgrimage' (1.3.264); Gaunt, dying, speaks of Time's relentless 'pilgrimage' (1.3.230), a word that Richard cruelly echoes when informed of his uncle's death, 'His time is spent; our pilgrimage must be' (2.1.154). The notion of life as a spiritual quest, sounded in these early references, is then ironically unfolded as we learn of 'butcher' Mowbray's service in the crusades and of his death in Venice as a soldier of Christ (4.1.94–101); as we observe Bolingbroke yield to his political ambitions and then contemplate an expiatory 'voyage' to Jerusalem (5.6.49); as we watch Richard sink from all-powerful monarch to defeated subject, exchanging in fancy his 'sceptre for a palmer's walking staff' (3.3.151) and beginning to hope for the 'new world's crown' that eternity may promise (5.1.24). Gurr (4–5) points out that the allusions to pilgrimage and crusading prepare for further expansion of the theme in the later plays of the tetralogy – especially for the King's ironic death in the Jerusalem Chamber at Westminster in *2 Henry IV* (4.5.232–40). As suggested already (see p. 36), similar ironies attend the use of the Passion story. That Richard before Parliament should identify his deposers with Pontius Pilate (4.1.239–42) may be thought a self-serving extravagance; but that Bolingbroke on two occasions (3.1.5–6 and 5.6.50) should allude to his own guilt in terms of Pilate forces us to weigh the implications of the comparison more seriously. A further irony is that Richard in his despair mistakenly identifies Bushy, Green and Wiltshire, three of his most loyal friends, with Christ's betrayer – 'Three Judases, each one thrice worse than Judas!' (3.2.132). Shakespeare raises the concept of Richard as *alter-Christus* only to undermine it by wry equivocations and strategies of scepticism.

Additional image patterns, often thematically related, involve a series of references to blots and stains, to venom or poison, and to tears. The blot–stain sequence applies most saliently to Richard himself: the King's leasing of England is shamefully legitimized by 'inky blots and rotten parchment bonds' (2.1.64); his political reverses 'set a blot upon [his] pride' (3.2.81); his appearance on the walls resembles the sun emerging from 'envious clouds' that 'stain' his 'passage to the Occident' (3.3.65–7), prompting York to lament that 'any harm should stain so fair a show' (3.3.71); the treason of his subjects is 'Marked with a blot, damned in the book of heaven' (4.1.236); Aumerle regards the deposition as a 'pernicious blot' (4.1.325); and Richard accuses his murderer of having 'stained the King's own land' with royal blood (5.5.110). The last example echoes the King's excuse for interrupting the combat at Coventry – that 'our kingdom's earth should not be soiled' with blood (1.3.125–6). The stain imagery is extended also to other characters – to Mowbray (1.3.202), to Bushy and Green (3.1.14–15), to Bagot (4.1.29–30) and to Aumerle (5.3.65). Nearly all of these are associated in some way with shame, dishonour, guilt and desecration and connect with the related imagery of Pilate's hand-washing and of Richard's references to the washing off of the sacramental balm. Venom imagery is another component of the same matrix, relating to the themes of disloyalty, betrayal and the corruption of a disordered kingdom: Richard wishes that 'a lurking adder' might 'Throw death upon' his enemies (3.2.20–2); he calls his former favourites 'vipers', 'Snakes' warmed 'in [his] heart-blood' that 'sting [his] heart' (3.2.129–31); and the Queen relates the news of her husband's deposition to the biblical Fall with its treacherous 'serpent' (3.4.75). References to venom, poison, pestilence, plague, infection, festering, rankling, rotting and wounds convey the sense of a realm weakened by disease and threatened by civil war. The imagery of weeping is too obvious and too frequent to need much illustration (see 3.2.4–5n.), but the range of ideas and emotions with which tears are associated is impressive. Tenderness, grief, self-indulgence, despair and weakness of will figure naturally enough; but the dramatist also associates tears more surprisingly with concepts of perception and dissolution: Bushy, for instance, invokes the notion of tears as blinders of vision or as prisms that distort, falsify or multiply images (2.2.16–27), thus providing a link with the mirror; Richard not only repeats the blinding motif by refusing to read Northumberland's list of 'grievous crimes' ('Mine eyes are full of tears; I cannot see' (4.1.223, 244)), but imagines himself 'melt[ing] . . . away in water-drops' under the annihilating heat of the new sun-king (4.1.260–2). Tear imagery also links up with the play's emotional and physical weather: Richard imagines 'rainy eyes' writing 'sorrow on the bosom of the earth' (3.2.146–7) and suggests that he and Aumerle 'make foul weather with despised tears' (3.3.161). Harris has explored the elemental and symbolic contrasts between 'fire and water' (3.3.56), between the sun and the sea, noting the several mentions of storms and flooding of which the grief and tear imagery is a functional part.

Another antithesis that runs through the play is that between sweet and sour, often in a way that stresses their paradoxical or ironic interdependence. Gaunt sadly acknowledges consenting to his son's exile with the proverb, 'Things sweet to taste prove in digestion sour' (1.3.236); Richard, about to receive ill news from Scroop, orders him to 'Speak sweetly . . . although [his] looks be sour' (3.2.193), then moans of being diverted from his 'sweet way . . . to despair' (3.2.205); Scroop, noting Richard's mistaken hostility towards his executed favourites, remarks, 'Sweet love, I see, changing his property, / Turns to the sourest and most deadly hate' (3.2.135–6); the Duchess of York addresses her spouse as both 'sweet husband' (5.2.107) and 'sour husband' (5.3.120) in pleading for Aumerle; and the music that Richard hears at Pomfret is at once pleasant and disturbing: 'How sour sweet music is / When time is broke and no proportion kept!' (5.5.42–3). Occasionally one of the two terms merely implies its antonym, as in speeches by York (2.1.169), Northumberland (2.3.7) and the Gardener (3.4.105). 'Sweet', a common term of endearment (it is applied to Richard, York and the Queen as well as to England's soil, Grief, Peace and the word 'pardon'), balances such phrases as 'sour cross' (4.1.241) and 'sour melancholy' (5.6.20).

Additional antitheses, supporting the traditional concept of Fortune's wheel and connected with the myth of the Fall, are the many images contrasting up and down, ascent and descent. Shakespeare fortifies the figure of the two buckets (4.1.184–9), thematically and structurally central, by means of allusions to heaven and hell, to the rising and setting sun, to 'a shooting star / Fall[ing] to . . . earth' (2.4.19–20), to Phaëton's crash (3.3.178), to castle walls and 'base court' (3.3.176, 180, 182), to a pair of scales in which the fortunes of Richard and his enemies are weighed (3.4.85–9), and to Northumberland as the 'ladder' by which Bolingbroke mounts Richard's throne (5.1.55–6). What McGuire has called the choreography of the play, its non-verbal language, strongly reinforces concepts of verticality through necessary stage movements. Kneeling, rising, failing to kneel, the casting down and taking up of gages, descending from and mounting the throne, throwing down the warder and the mirror, sitting on the ground, touching the earth, Richard's descent from the walls and sinking down to die while his soul mounts – all are actions that buttress the theme of rising and falling. They lend a physical dimension to a tragedy played out against the cosmic backdrop of heaven and earth and help to ritualize as well as to disturb through restless undulation contrasts between hierarchical stability and disruption, idealism and baseness, political ambition and dejection, success and failure. Barton's set at Stratford featured two parallel ladder-like staircases at stage right and left 'suggesting ascent and descent as the key to the drama' (Page, 59). Gurr, elaborating upon Harris, believes that 'the images of the play are organized in relation to the four elements' (23), implying thereby that their various combinations and permutations can be located on a vertical scale, from those that involve the lower elements (earth and water) to those that make use of the higher (air and fire). If discerning so conscious a pattern seems forced, at least we may acknowledge that elemental imagery pervades the play and that it contributes in a general way to the symbolism of height and depth.

Three final themes woven into the fabric of the play are time, birth and death. The first emerges in the seasonal motif which conveys a sense of cyclical change and relates to the relentless turning of Fortune's wheel and the workings of providence or destiny. The 'summer leaves' of Gloucester's flourishing life are 'all faded' (1.2.20); Bolingbroke's exile consists of 'Four lagging winters and four wanton springs' (1.3.214); Richard's sighs and tears will 'lodge the summer's corn' (3.3.162); the Gardener speaks of the King's 'disordered spring' and of his having 'met with the fall of leaf' (3.4.48–9); Richard associates the winter of his discontent with a melting snowman (4.1.260–2) and the narration of his story in 'winter's tedious nights' (5.1.40); York characterizes the accession of Henry IV as 'this new spring of time' (5.2.50). The garden allegory accentuates the orderly changes associated with the disciplines of cultivation as opposed to the 'waste of idle hours' (3.4.66) that bring 'noisome weeds' (3.4.38) and 'caterpillars' (3.4.47). Later, 'I wasted time, and now doth Time waste me' becomes the linchpin of Richard's tortured reverie on the disharmony and disproportion of his 'state and time' (5.5.45–9) during which he must measure out his 'minutes, times, and hours' in 'sighs, and tears, and groans'; now he must accept that his 'time / Runs posting on in Bolingbroke's proud joy' (5.5.57–9). An important irony of the tragedy is that a divine-right king who conceives of himself as existing in some sense beyond temporality must confront in the end his own time-boundedness and finitude. The sense of lagging time conveyed in the prison speech contrasts with an earlier sense of its tragic rapidity, when Mowbray at Coventry predicts that 'all too soon . . . the King shall rue' (1.3.205), when Richard returns from Ireland

'One day too late' and Salisbury laments, 'O, call back yesterday, bid Time return . . . Today, today, unhappy day too late' (3.2.67–71). Ironically, Richard had departed for his campaign abroad with the words, 'Be merry, for our time of stay is short' (2.1.223). And the fatal rush of time has already been suggested in the radical compression that crowds Gaunt's death, the seizing of his lands and the news of Bolingbroke's return into a single scene. A contrast between age and youth defines another aspect of the time theme: Gaunt remarks that Richard can 'help Time to furrow [him] with age, / But stop no wrinkle' from appearing in his face (1.3.229–30), an effective adumbration of Richard's mirror speech, 'No deeper wrinkles yet?' (4.1.277). Also, as is usual in the chronicle plays, references to time set Richard's tragedy in the context of what is past, or passing, or to come: allusions to Edward III, the Black Prince and Gloucester nostalgically recall a bygone age of heroism while Carlisle's prediction of civil war, Richard's forecast of Northumberland's discontent and Henry IV's plans for a penitential journey offer a baleful vision of what lies ahead. Our awareness of passage from a glorious past to a clouded future carries with it a sense of tragic entropy.

The play counterpoints images of birth, parenthood and generation with those of death. Gaunt calls England a 'teeming womb' of kings (2.1.51); the Queen elaborates her inchoate sorrow by likening it to an 'unborn' child, 'ripe in Fortune's womb', to which Green becomes 'the midwife' and she 'a gasping new-delivered mother' (2.2.10, 62–5); Richard regreets his realm 'As a long-parted mother with her child' (3.2.8) and warns that 'children, yet unborn and unbegot' (3.3.88) will suffer pestilence if the rebels persist; Carlisle reiterates the warning in his reference to 'children yet unborn' (4.1.322); the Duchess of York, trying to protect her son, argues that her 'teeming date' is 'drunk up with time' (5.2.91); and Richard in prison begets a 'generation of still-breeding thoughts' engendered by the union of his male soul with his female brain (5.5.6–8). Virtually all these allusions occur in contexts of suffering or incipient disaster and therefore carry ironic force.

Gaunt's mention of the 'hollow womb' of the grave that inherits 'naught but bones' (2.1.83) illustrates the thematic connection to mortality, an idea that presides over the tragedy from first to last and is emblematized in the *memento mori* image of Death 'the antic' sitting within 'the hollow crown' to 'scoff' and 'grin' at royal pomp and state (3.2.160–3; see LN and Fig. 8). Shakespeare extends the word 'hollow', applied significantly to the crown, to Aumerle's 'hollow parting' from Bolingbroke (1.4.9), to Northumberland's mention of 'the hollow eyes of Death' (2.1.270) and to Scroop's reference to Bushy and Green 'graved in the hollow ground' (3.2.140). Further reinforcement of the *memento mori* symbolism appears in references to 'the barren earth / Which serves as paste and cover to our bones' (3.2.153–4), to Edward III's 'bones' (3.3.106), to Fitzwater's 'father's skull' (4.1.70) and to Golgotha, the 'field of . . . dead men's skulls' (4.1.145). The play, in which the words 'death', 'dead' and 'deadly' are heard nearly sixty times, opens with a quarrel about Gloucester's death and ends with a funeral procession. Perhaps the overarching significance of a tragedy about the contention for a throne is the ultimate supremacy of Death. Barton made this point visually in 1973 by presenting the Duchess of Gloucester as a ghost who emerged from a grave 'carrying a skull' (Page, 61) and by having both Richard and Bolingbroke at the conclusion (now merely actors) stand subject to the robed figure of a king whose face was suddenly revealed as the grinning mask of Death (Page, 64).

Rhetoric

Elizabethan poets and theorists delighted in tropes and figures, not only in their use but also in their definition, taxonomy and classification. Studying the established formulae and techniques of rhetoric was recognized as an obvious avenue to the enrichment of style. The practice usually involved the selection of topoi or received patterns which the writer inventively combined, varied and repeated in multiple permutations to achieve an interlacing of related themes and ideas. Trousdale fruitfully examines *Richard II*

8 Death hovering above a crowned king, from Hans Holbein the Younger, *The Dance of Death*, 1538

as 'a rhetorical exercise' (65) – as a way of organizing the story of a king's deposition by choosing plot elements from Holinshed together with the ideas implicit in them, and then developing these into a series of scenes held together less by causality than by the verbal and structural patterns they can be made to explore. In such a concept physical action becomes less important than the competing perspectives or points of view that the subject releases for consideration. The play emerges as a fabric of thematic or perspectival interconnections woven together by verbal or rhetorical techniques that view reality from different angles, thus providing for the sophisticated audience 'the intellectual pleasure' of exercising 'different modes of understanding' (79). As the first part of the play concentrates on the 'doing' (Richard's tyrannies), so the second part dramatizes his 'suffering', the compositional techniques required for rendering the two emphases being distinct yet related. Contending attitudes towards weak legitimate kings and strong illegitimate rulers call for differing rhetorical modes. Richard's courage and despair in the face of adversity draw upon similarly divergent techniques. As Trousdale explains, Shakespeare's method is to 'open up the history' of a famous monarch by considering its possibilities from varied standpoints and with different modes of perception – the King as judge, the King as tyrant, the King as a man deposed, the King as loving spouse, for instance – to 'unfold it' by 'suggesting some of the topics that lie within' (79).

To write in such a manner poets and dramatists had obviously to master the various decorums and forms of discourse appropriate to their subjects[1] as well as the formidable array of rhetorical figures and linguistic devices systematically catalogued and illustrated by rhetoricians such as Thomas Wilson, George Puttenham and Henry Peacham. Shakespeare assimilated these from the start and in *Richard II* composed a play from which a full anthology of examples might be readily extracted. By using Lanham's modern *Handlist*, which divides the traditional figures of speech into

---

1 Carlisle's protest, for instance, is couched in the form of a sermon and follows the structure of a classical oration; see 4.1.115–50n.

categories according to function, it is possible to find illustrations in the play for roughly a third of the nearly four hundred terms listed, although there is a fair amount of duplication and overlap in the terminology since Renaissance writers did not always agree on definitions and labels.[1] The astonishing copiousness of these rhetorical devices contributes to the play's conscious artistry, often serving to canalize feelings expressed at particular moments and to give actors the means of speaking their lines in character and with conviction. Often the figures help in subterranean ways to reinforce dominant themes and ideas, as, for instance, when the repeated use of privatives ('undeaf', 'unkinged', 'unkiss', etc.)[2] subtly communicates a pervasive sense of loss.

Among the most prominent groups of rhetorical figures are those that involve amplification, repetition, balance and symmetry. The heaping up of details (*accumulatio*) clearly suits a play about a luxury-loving and spendthrift monarch, as when the widowed Duchess imagines Pleshy's desolation (1.2.68–9), when Boling-broke accumulates analogies to show that fantasy cannot alter facts (1.3.294–303), when Northumberland multiplies images of the kingdom's reform (2.1.291–6) and when one of the Gardener's men describes the effects of horticultural neglect (3.4.43–7). Other figures of dilation are *divisio*, the breaking-up of a subject into sub-categories (as in Richard's 'stories of the death of kings' (3.2.156–60) or his 'thoughts' in prison (5.5.9–30)); *auxesis*, the arrangement of syntactic elements in climactic order:'This blessed plot, this earth, this realm, this England' (2.1.50); and *asyndeton*, the packing of words together in series without conjunctions to suggest content too full for the space it occupies: 'so heinous, black, obscene a deed' (4.1.132), 'Lest child, child's children, cry against you, "Woe!"' (4.1.150), 'my manors, rents, revenues I forgo' (4.1.212). Various devices of repetition furnish the poetry with

---

1 Sister Miriam Joseph lists some two hundred figures of speech that Shakespeare used over the course of his career; Vickers points out that for working purposes 'a central corpus of about the forty most frequently used figures' suffices for study of the dramatist's rhetorical practice ('Rhetoric', 86).
2 See 2.1.16n.

effects of pleasing ornamentation and redundancy. The play delights in substitutions (*synonymia*): 'first head and spring' (1.1.97), 'conclude and be agreed' (1.1.156), 'plot, contrive or complot any ill' (1.3.189), 'Bereft and gelded of his patrimony' (2.1.237); in the use of the same word with a different ending (*polyptoton*): 'the accuser and the accused' (1.1.17), 'doubly redoubled' (1.3.80), 'A beggar begs that never begged before' (5.3.77); and in the repetition of words without separation to convey intensity of feeling (*epizeuxis*): 'My dear dear lord' (1.1.176), 'Desolate, desolate, will I hence and die!' (1.2.73), 'this dear dear land' (2.1.57), 'Today, today, unhappy day too late' (3.2.71), 'Too well, too well, thou tell'st a tale so ill' (3.2.121), 'a little grave, / A little, little grave' (3.3.153–4). Elaborate patterning such as using the last word in a clause to begin the next (*anadiplosis*) or repetition of the same word at the end of clauses or lines (*epistrophe*) gives a sense of conscious artifice. In one particularly contrived passage, the same that plays punningly on Gaunt's name, the dramatist combines *anadiplosis* with *epistrophe*: 'And therein fasting hast thou made me gaunt. / Gaunt am I for the grave, gaunt as a grave' (2.1.81–2); here 'gaunt' ends one line and commences the next, while 'grave' concludes both clauses of the following verse. The most popular of the schemes of repetition was *anaphora* (the obverse of *epistrophe*) in which successive lines, clauses or sentences begin with the same words. Shakespeare uses this device with consummate power in two of Richard's most emotional speeches – in his self-divestiture ('With mine own tears . . . With mine own hands . . . With mine own tongue' etc. (4.1.207–10)) and in the mirror episode ('Was this . . . the face . . . Was this the face . . . Is this the face . . . at last outfaced by Bolingbroke?' (4.1.281–6)). All these devices, whatever their specific use or dramatic context, are designed in the aggregate to enhance the hearer's sense of unity in variety and to create pleasure in the play's copia of linguistic patterns and inventions. It is as if the drama had been conceived of as a mille-fleur tapestry, its varied rhetorical schemes substituting for the profusion of plants and blossoms.

Figures of balance and antithesis accord with a world ordered by symmetry or support themes of opposition and contrast (between Mowbray and Bolingbroke, Richard and Gaunt, Bolingbroke and Richard, York and his duchess). *Parison*, or *iso-colon*, juxtaposes phrases of equal length or corresponding structure: 'Too good to be so, and too bad to live' (1.1.40); 'His time is spent; our pilgrimage must be' (2.1.154); 'On this side my hand, and on that side thine' (4.1.183); 'My care is loss of care, by old care done; / Your care is gain of care, by new care won' (4.1.196–7); 'The traitor lives, the true man's put to death' (5.3.72). *Antimetabole* (inverting the order of repeated words in equilibrium) utilizes a structure that imitates on a small scale the tragedy's inversion of political order: 'Ay, no. No, ay' (4.1.201). Perhaps even more noticeable is the use of *chiasmus*, a related crisscross figure in which a whole phrase or clause is reversed – reflected, as it were, in mirror: 'Think not the King did banish thee, / But thou the King' (1.3.279–80); 'I speak to subjects, and a subject speaks' (4.1.133); 'I wasted time, and now doth Time waste me' (5.5.49). Here we get something like the rhetorical equivalent of Hazlitt's observation that 'The steps by which Bolingbroke mounts the throne are those by which Richard sinks into the grave' (Forker, 115).

Numerous other figures to be found in the rhetorical manuals of Shakespeare's age appear in *Richard II*. Some of these such as punning (*paronomasia*), strained metaphors or conceits (*catachresis*) and the use of proverbs (*aphorismus*) have already been mentioned in the general discussion of the play's style. The first two are intended to flatter hearers by appealing to their intellectual agility. *Paronomasia*, one of the most dominant and characteristic devices of the play on which Mahood comments importantly, exploits by wit the divergent meanings of a single word: 'I brought high Hereford . . . But to the next highway' (1.4.3–4); 'Subjected thus, / How can you say to me I am a king?' (3.2.176–7); 'O, good – "Convey"! Conveyors are you all' (4.1.317). Much of the quibbling serves to express grief or anxiety (see

Black, 535) and, as Coleridge recognized, is not intended merely as levity. Also, as McDonald notes, Shakespeare's extensive *polysemy*, in addition to its intellectual delights, obstructs 'semantic transparency or certainty of meaning', thus fostering a certain scepticism about the possibility of simple or ultimate truth: the pun becomes 'a subversive agent', requiring the 'listener to hesitate, to look in two directions at once' and so enforces 'a momentary shift into another context' (141). In a play that exploits competing ideological perspectives and ambiguities of motive, wordplay becomes richly functional. *Catachresis* often calls attention to the uncomfortable gap between the tenor of a metaphor and its vehicle: 'Thine eye begins to speak, set thy tongue there; / Or in thy piteous heart plant thou thine ear' (5.3.124–5); here the figure well conveys the Duchess of York's absurdly overstrained urgency. *Aphorismus* is usually employed to lend the weight of tradition, received wisdom or authority to a speech: 'Truth hath a quiet breast' (1.3.96); 'There is no virtue like necessity (1.3.278); 'He tires betimes that spurs too fast betimes' (2.1.36); 'pride must have a fall' (5.5.88).

Shakespeare's habit of converting nouns into verbs usually energizes the verse in notable ways. Technically speaking, the device of functional shift was known as *anthimeria* and in *Richard II* can convey impatience, as when the speaker picks up a word from his interlocutor and throws it back at him as a mock: 'Grace me no grace, nor uncle me no uncle' (2.3.87); different uses of the same figure occur at 3.4.13–18, where the Queen turns an initial adjective ('wanting') into both a noun and a verb ('want'), at 5.3.84–5, where York plays on the word 'rest' in a similarly contrived manner, and at 5.3.94, where the Duchess in another example of overwrought pleading uses 'joy' as both a noun and a verb in the same line. Another rhetorical strategy used to enhance the drama of an encounter is a speaker's purposeful ambiguity, sometimes labelled *significatio*. The play provides an effective example of this figure when Richard falsely assumes that his favourites 'have made peace with Bolingbroke' and is then informed by Scroop, 'Peace have they made with him indeed, my lord' (3.2.127–8). Ironically, the King has just threatened to behead them for their supposed treachery, only to be told opaquely, as a means of softening the blow, that they have already lost their heads in his service. Shakespeare allows eight and a half lines to elapse before Scroop makes fully explicit to the King the true significance of his words: 'Their peace is made / With heads, and not with hands' (3.2.137–8). A final rhetorical device worth mentioning is *prosopopoeia*, the practice of treating abstractions such as Death, Shame, Envy, Time and Grief as human beings. *Richard II* contains numerous personifications of this kind, one overall effect being to evoke a sense of experience as enfleshed, animistic, corporeal in every dimension of its reality. The technique partly suggests an older concept of the world not as inert, bloodless or impersonal but as *anima mundi*.

More than a collection of decorative or individually pleasurable effects, the rhetoric of *Richard II* constitutes by inference a practical discourse on verbal power, an illustration of the means of persuasion that operates not only among characters onstage but between the stage and the audience. Rebhorn points out that the treatises and handbooks of Shakespeare's age stressed the capacity of rhetoric, masterfully used, 'to control the will and desire of the audience' – 'to subjugate' them through the force of words (15). In a play whose subject is a contest for power, which indeed explores divergent concepts of power, the techniques of rhetoric become central to politics.

AFTERLIFE

Richard II is now regarded as one of the greatest of Shakespeare's histories, second in popularity only to *1 Henry IV*. The number of books, articles and editions treating every aspect of the play, most post-dating World War II, now approaches 3000, and the twentieth century saw a steady increase in the number of successful stagings in Europe and North America. As early as 1948 the theatre critic

Harold Hobson pronounced it 'almost the favourite of Shakespeare's plays' (140–1), and it has continued since then to be highly esteemed onstage and in the study. This was not always so. After its initial popularity in the later 1590s and early 1600s (six quartos appeared within the first four decades and Meres in *Palladis Tamia* (1598) listed it first among the tragedies), *Richard II* fell into general disfavour as an actable drama and seems to have been valued chiefly by miscellanists and later poets and dramatists for detachable wisdom and figurative language to be quoted or imitated. Robert Allot's *England's Parnassus* (1600), John Bodenham's *Belvedere, or the Garden of the Muses* (1600) and John Cotgrave's *English Treasury of Wit and Language* (1655) all reprint memorable passages: Bodenham quotes *Richard II* forty-seven times, more often than any other play; *The Shakespeare Allusion-Book* shows that it remained more quotable than the other histories except *Richard III* and *Henry IV* until the end of the seventeenth century. Webster, Dekker, Heywood, Fletcher, Massinger, Day and probably the anonymous dramatist of *Caesar's Revenge* imitate verbal details, as do Everard Guilpin, Robert Baron, George Herbert, Sir John Hayward and Thomas Walkington.[1] Three years before the Restoration William London listed *Richard II* and *King Lear* as the two most vendible of Shakespeare's plays apart from the Folio collection – a politically revealing datum since both dramas concern dispossessed monarchs.[2] It was York's 'passionate description' of Richard as Bolingbroke's captive that prompted Dryden's famous admiration in his Preface to *Troilus and Cressida* (1679).[3]

The last recorded performance by the King's Men took place at the Globe in 1631. Thereafter, for the better part of two and a

---

1 For details, see Forker, 1–2; also 1.1.109n., 160n., 177–9n., 196n., 1.3.292–3n., 302–3n., 1.4.31LN, 2.1.5–14n., 40–64LN, 2.2.141–2n., 3.1.21n., 3.2.54–7n., 61–2n., 156LN, 165n., 3.3.194–5n., 203n., 3.4 headnote, 38LN, 4.1.138n., 184–9n., 185n., 5.1.13–15LN, 55–6LN, 5.2.18–20n., 103n., 5.5.111–12n., and 5.6.38–40n.

2 William London, *A Catalogue of the Most Vendible Books in England* (1657). The book is unpaginated, but the Shakespeare titles are listed under the heading 'Romances, Poems, Playes' (sig. F1ᵛ).

3 See 5.2.23–36n.

half centuries, stagings of the play were infrequent and usually produced in radically adapted or heavily cut versions. For Tate's and Theobald's transformations of 1680 and 1719 and Rich's 1738 revival, see pp. 50–5. A new but now lost adaptation by Francis Gentleman was acted at Bath in 1755; still another alteration by James Goodhall was published in 1772 but never acted, although Goodhall attempted to interest Garrick in the title role (Forker, 10). The waspish George Steevens, who opposed revivals of the play, remarked in 1780 that 'the successive audiences of more than a century have respectively slumbered over it, as often as it has appeared on the stage' (Sprague, 30). Nor was Dr Johnson a great admirer. He thought the tragedy possessed little 'unity of action' on account of its mere 'chronological succession' and pronounced the characterization of Richard defective since he showed 'only passive fortitude, the virtue of a confessor rather than of a king' (Forker, 8). Generally speaking, Restoration and eighteenth–century critics objected to the play's quibbling and rhyming style, to its unclassical structure and violations of decorum (such as onstage murder), to its paucity of stage action and to the unheroic weakness of its protagonist.

Romanticism, particularly in the writings of Charles Lamb, Hazlitt, A.W. von Schlegel and Coleridge, brought sympathetic revaluation, not only of Richard's character as a subtle combination of feebleness and dignity but also of the play's secondary characters, its poetic splendours, its chiastic structure, its blend of epic and tragic elements and its sense of dynastic politics as cyclical. Coleridge noted in 1813 without regret that the play was 'not much acted', the 'enormous' theatres of his day being unsuited to Shakespeare's nuances (126). Two years later Edmund Kean assayed the title role at Drury Lane, the first star actor to do so in London for nearly a century. But Hazlitt was disappointed in the portrayal of Richard as 'a character of *passion*' rather than of '*pathos*', 'of feeling combined with energy' rather than 'of feeling combined with weakness' (Forker, 104). Kean was using a text drastically altered by Richard Wroughton (1815) which attempted to 'rescue' the tragedy from its long neglect by cutting more than a third of the lines and by adding many others from a range of Shakespearean plays as well as new speeches and a pastiche Elizabethan song by the adapter; the play ends with Lear's words over the corpse of Cordelia, spoken by the Queen over her dead husband. Wroughton's version, which now became the standard acting text and continued to be reprinted in *Cumberland's British Theatre* until about the mid-ninteenth century (Fig. 9), omits the lists and the Aumerle conspiracy, expands the Queen's role and coarsens the tragedy by heavy moralization and by making Richard more heroically forceful than in Shakespeare. Some critics approved of the conceptual change, characterizing Shakespeare's Richard, for instance, as 'a spoilt child reluctantly yielding up its playthings' or 'so pusillanimous a monarch' as to appear 'dreadfully insipid' without some dramaturgical rewriting.[1] Earlier than Kean, William Charles Macready, using a version closer to Shakespeare, had revived *Richard II* in the provinces between 1812 and 1815 without much success; he did not try the experiment again until 1850–1 when he appeared as Richard in two performances at the Haymarket, London.

Undoubtedly the most spectacular and popular production until the end of the century, indeed since Elizabethan times (it ran for eighty-five nights), was that of Edmund Kean's son Charles, which opened at the Princess's Theatre, London, in March 1857. The younger Kean may possibly have responded to the observation by William Watkiss Lloyd the year before that 'The best commentator on the character of Richard would be a great actor' (Forker, 208). Kean emphasized the King's pathos at the expense of the play's political content, eschewing Wroughton but cutting the authentic text so savagely that almost a third of the play disappeared: entirely gone were 1.4, 2.4, 3.1, 5.2 and 5.3 as well as most of Gaunt's praise of England and York's remonstrance against the seizure of property in 2.1, the quarrel episode of 4.1,

---

1 See Sprague, 31. The critics cited are from *The New Monthly Magazine*, vol. 3, no. 17 (1 June 1815), 459, and *The Drama; or, Theatrical Pocket Magazine*, 5 (1824), 404–5.

R. *Cruikshank, Del.*   G. *W. Bonner, Sc.*

King Richard the Second.

King Richard. Up, cousin, up : your heart is up, I know,
Thus high at least, altho' your knee be low.

9 Richard and Bolingbroke (4.1 of the acting version of *Richard II* by Richard
Wroughton), in an engraving by G.W. Bonner from a drawing taken in the
theatre by R. Cruikshank

Carlisle's protest, Richard's speeches comparing himself to Christ and much of the prison soliloquy. To compensate for the omissions, Kean introduced expensive scenery, costumes and music of the late fourteenth century (archaeologically researched), dummy horses and a triumphal procession of Bolingbroke leading Richard into London thronged with scores of extras – visual spectacle on a scale never witnessed before. This was the production that inspired Pater's famous essay on the aesthetic unity of the play, becoming in Kean's hands 'like an exquisite performance on the violin' (Forker, 297).

Meanwhile, *Richard II* was being tried out before American audiences. Junius Brutus Booth performed the title role in Baltimore in 1831–2, apparently without attracting much interest. In New York in 1865 Charles Kean played the part that had won him such praise in London; and Edwin Booth, the elder Booth's son, gave four performances in New York a decade afterwards in an acting version later edited by William Winter. In what would be the last American performance of the nineteenth century, Booth played Richard in Chicago on 23 April 1879, when a crazed member of the audience tried to shoot him. The tragedy would not be seen again in the United States until 1930 when the Stratford Players under William Bridges-Adams performed it in Boston and Philadelphia with George Hayes (who had already made his name in the role at the Old Vic five years earlier) as the King – perhaps because, as Winter summed up American opinion in 1893, the tragedy 'has never flourished on the stage', being regarded as 'a pageant rather than [a] drama' (Forker, 26).

By the end of the Victorian era opinions about Richard's character had settled into two antithetical camps. The moralistic school, typified by H.N. Hudson, Edward Dowden and F.S. Boas, tended to stress Richard's contemptible weakness and want of virility. Hudson spoke of 'a wordy whimperer', a 'pampered and emasculated voluptuary', Dowden of a 'dilettante', 'an amateur in living' who voiced a 'pseudo-poetic pathos', and Boas of the King's 'puerile' fancy and 'diseased' will (Forker, 19, 248, 252,

354). In contrast, the aesthetic school, represented by Pater, Yeats and C.E. Montague, celebrated Richard's refinement of sensibility: Yeats delighted in Richard's 'capricious fancy' and 'dreamy dignity', elevating him as a 'vessel of porcelain' above Henry V, the more philistine 'vessel of clay', while Montague saw in Richard the quintessential artist, possessing the 'gift of exquisite responsiveness' and forever questing for the 'completion' of his 'inward vision' through perfect 'expression' (Forker, 375–7, 367). Yeats and Montague were both reacting to performances in 1901 and 1899 respectively by the actor-manager Sir Frank Benson, who excelled in the part of Richard (initially at Stratford-upon-Avon in 1896), skilfully contriving to endow the character with mingled strength, sensitivity and weakness in a way that commanded great sympathy, even in contrast to the manliness and pragmatism of Bolingbroke (Fig. 10). Finely spoken, minimally cut and visually impressive (the King wore a furred robe of lime-green velvet and stroked his hounds while Mowbray and Bolingbroke accused each other), the production remained in Benson's company 'for almost twenty years' (Shewring, 68). Benson's interpretation was to set an important trend for future actors and helped establish the tragedy, temporarily at least, as a staple of the Shakespearean repertoire.

William Poel, famous for reviving Elizabethan plays as he thought they had originally been staged, produced *Richard II* without scenery in a lecture hall at the University of London in 1899 with the twenty-two-year-old Harley Granville-Barker in the lead. The venue made entrances and exits awkward, and the virtually uncut text is said to have consumed four hours (Cam[1], xc). Unlike his sixteenth-century predecessors, Poel based his groupings and stage movements on medieval documents and illustrations in the spirit of Charles Kean. He dressed the Duchess of Gloucester as a nun and at one point had Richard disguise himself as a friar. A contrasting production from the same period was Beerbohm Tree's sumptuous mounting in 1903. Divided into three sections in a manner that clarified logical progression, this staging featured the

10 Frank Benson as Richard II at the Shakespeare Memorial Theatre, 1896

coronation of Henry IV as well as a fresh version of Kean's spectacular entry into London using real horses. Speeches were
displaced and reassigned, the cutting fairly extensive and the tone
declamatory. In the title role Tree stressed Richard's self-dramatizing and sacramental aspects and was congratulated by a fellow actor
on having transformed Shakespeare's king from 'a worm' into 'a
man' (Sprague, 34–5). Nevertheless, faith in the theatrical viability
of *Richard II* remained shaky. In 1907, the Harvard professor
George Pierce Baker could speak of the tragedy as being 'without a
hero', noting also 'how little the actors care for this play' (Forker,
428), and no productions after Tree's garnered significant enthusiasm until John Gielgud and Maurice Evans assumed the title role at
the Old Vic in 1929 (H. Williams) and 1934 (Cass) respectively.

The initial success of these stagings encouraged both actors to
return to the play, Gielgud in 1937 and Evans the same year in
New York (Webster), both for extended runs. The latter production also toured extensively and after closing in 1938 was revived
two years later, bringing the total number of performances up to
400 by 1940. Gordon Daviot's costume drama, *Richard of
Bordeaux* (1933), in which Gielgud also starred, shows the rising
interest in the subject matter of Shakespeare's play, undoubtedly
stimulated by recent revivals. After Gielgud and Evans, actors no
longer shied away from the drama, and the remainder of the century saw a steady succession of leading men and one leading
woman in the part, including players as diverse as Alec Guinness
(Richardson, 1947), Michael Redgrave (Quayle, 1951), Paul
Scofield (Gielgud, 1953), John Neville (Benthall, 1955), David
Warner (Hall, 1964), Ian McKellen (Cottrell, 1968), Ronald
Pickup (D. Williams, 1972), Ian Richardson and Richard Pasco
(Barton, 1973), Derek Jacobi (Giles, 1978), Alan Howard (Hands,
1980), Brian Bedford (Cottrell, 1983), Jeremy Irons (Kyle, 1986),
Fiona Shaw (Warner, 1995) and Ralph Fiennes (Kent, 2000).

Gielgud, influenced to some degree by the practices of Poel
and later advised by Granville-Barker, concentrated on a natural,
lucid, but subtly nuanced and musical speaking of the verse that

11 John Gielgud as Richard II, Glen Byam Shaw as Mowbray, Michael
   Redgrave as Bolingbroke, Leon Quartermaine as Gaunt in Gielgud's production at the Queen's Theatre, London, 6 August 1937

enthralled audiences. In Gielgud's initial 1929 portrayal the elaborate scenery of the Victorian stage was jettisoned in favour of
simpler and more flexible sets that facilitated continuity and made
radical cutting less requisite. The Aumerle conspiracy scenes
could for once be accommodated. In Gielgud's 1937 revival (Fig.
11), which was more lavishly dressed and designed, Michael
Redgrave played Bolingbroke in a cast that included Glen Byam
Shaw, Anthony Quayle, Alec Guinness and Peggy Ashcroft. Apart
from Gielgud's dignified and minutely controlled portrayal of the
King, by turns conveying petulance, charm, frailty and despair,
critics admired the admirable ensemble acting of the company
which resulted in an 'extraordinarily complete performance'
(Shewring, 81). In Webster's New York production, Evans's portrayal secured the play's reputation in America, according to one
critic 'making stage history' (Shewring, 139), just as Gielgud's

reappearance as Richard did in Britain. Richly costumed in
Plantagenet style but played against a relatively uncluttered set,
this production again focused on the poetry and the presentation
of a broad range of emotional tones and colours, being especially
memorable for the different shades of anguish expressed by the
protagonist; William Hawkins found the enunciation 'faultless'
(Leiter, 575). Evans once more revived what became his most
famous role in 1951, and was chosen to play Richard yet again in
a Hallmark television performance (Schaefer) shown on NBC in
1954; this latter marked the debut of the play on TV and catered
to its popular audience by including an interpolated scene that
showed Exton receiving payment from Bolingbroke to murder
Richard.

  Variety and innovation have naturally marked productions since
Gielgud and Evans proved that by balancing the formality of the
verse against the humanity of the character Richard can triumph
onstage. Guinness, according to Kenneth Tynan, was the 'sad
neurotic . . . seething and sorrowful at his own impotence', while
Redgrave emphasized Richard's supposed homosexuality, playing
him, in the words of Laurence Olivier, as 'an out-and-out pussy
queer, with mincing gestures to match' at the expense of kingli-
ness. Richard Findlater believed that Redgrave, perhaps
deliberately, contravened Gielgud's kindly portrait by presenting
Richard as 'sharp with cruelty, spite and envy' (Page, 49). Neither
portrayal suggested a king who could have suppressed a rebellion.
Scofield played Richard as a chilly, cerebral depressive, 'abstract
and remote', giving no evidence of the 'rash fierce blaze of riot'
(2.1.33) of which Gaunt complains (Page, 51). Neville (Fig. 12),
like Gielgud before him, was praised for his modulating voice
which allowed him to project cold imperiousness at first and passionate heartbreak later – intellectual strength as well as melting
grief; his development from foppish dandy to dignified sufferer
was visually supported by effective costume changes. The opening
night earned him thunderous applause and 'twenty-three curtain
calls' (Trewin, *Neville*, 58). McKellen, who played Richard

12 John Neville as Richard II with Green (Murray Hayne), Bagot (Nicholas Amer) and Aumerle (Anthony White) in Michael Benthall's Old Vic production, 1955

together with Marlowe's Edward II in paired Prospect Theatre productions, gave audiences the rare opportunity to compare two plays that critics as far back as Lamb had discussed in conjunction. Muting the possible homosexuality of Richard in contrast to his overt emphasis on it in Edward, McKellen centred his interpretation on Richard's conviction of semi-divine status. To quote Michael Billington:

> Richard is steeped in ceremony and . . . through the years . . . has come to accept it as proof of his physical inviolability. . . . There is comparatively little here of Montague's artist-king. . . . Rather, this Richard is a man engaged in the process of discovering his own

vulnerability and genuinely appalled at the collapse of his unquestioning belief in the divine right of kings.

(78–9)

McKellen conveyed Richard's sense of his own uniqueness by using special ritual gestures derived in part from studying the Dalai Lama (Shewring, 83). In what Frank Cox judged an 'intensely original reading', Pickup played Richard as 'coldly regal' and superficially unemotional, emphasizing 'dangerous calmness, the tranquility which often cloaks potential violence' (45). The memorably symbolic set featured a contoured model of England. In all of these stagings Bolingbroke was relegated to the status of a subordinate character so that Richard's personality could dominate. Productions, however, were beginning to redress this imbalance, giving more weight to the political opposition without necessarily slighting the personality of Richard. Littlewood's Theatre Workshop production consciously uglified the play by making Bolingbroke into a Marxist revolutionary who overthrows a psychopath, a monarch whom one critic described as 'a weak, treacherous, decadent pervert' (Page, 51). In Hall's staging of the cycle of histories from *Richard II* to *Richard III* at Stratford, a staging less concerned with personal tragedy than with political issues, David Warner (who played the fallen King) stressed the symbolism of Christ-like martyrdom, pitting his weakness against the 'considerable strength and theatrical presence' of Eric Porter as Bolingbroke (Shewring, 100–1). But the most audaciously revisionary balancing of Richard against Bolingbroke was to be realized in Barton's celebrated RSC production in which Pasco and Richardson interchanged the two roles on successive evenings (Fig. 13).

Barton's influential staging, a prime example of what has come to be known as 'Director's Shakespeare', has received so much attention from scholars that only brief discussion is necessary here.[1]

---

1   See, for instance, O'Brien, Stredder, Wells, *Productions* (65–81), David, *Theatre* (164–73), Gilbert, Page (57–68) and Shewring (117–37).

13 Richard (Richard Pasco) is visited by Bolingbroke, disguised as the Groom
(Ian Richardson), at Pomfret (5.5) in John Barton's RSC production, 1973,
at Stratford-upon-Avon

A big box-office success, it played not only in Stratford but also in New York and London for a total of nearly two hundred performances. Hobson's statement that the production necessitated 'a total re-orientation of our conventional attitude' (Stredder, 24) crystalizes Barton's achievement. Central to the conception was the two-natured idea of kingship itself with its fusing of divine and human aspects so that the struggle between the two contenders for the throne became less a matter of contrasted personalities than of 'a conflict of roles – the roles of man becoming king and king becoming man' (Stredder, 26). The mirror-like reversal of the two positions thus became the fulcrum on which the action was balanced. Barton stressed the similarities of the two antagonists as well as the metadramatic concept of player-king, which affected them both. At each performance Pasco and Richardson were seen being arbitrarily assigned their roles by a figure representing Shakespeare, and their common involvement with regality was emphasized by a coronation at both beginning and end. Barton's most radical but symbolically significant departure from Shakespeare's text was to introduce Bolingbroke disguised as the Groom. This device allowed the two men, one of whom transferred the frame of the shattered mirror from his own shoulders to those of his opposite, to share a moment of common rapport as human beings who understand each other's plight. Thus Barton dissolved the traditional notion of implacable irreconcilability between Richard and his deposer, replacing it with a less psychological image of symbolic commonality. Inevitably, the two actors gave different emphases to their portrayals of Richard and Bolingbroke. Pasco tended to bring out the humanity of the two, allowing audiences to identify more closely with each, while Richardson gave a more distanced and enigmatic interpretation of both characters; but writers who returned to later performances have noted that each actor continued to refine and develop his conception of the twin roles, subtly introducing new facets and changing original emphases so that the interaction remained dynamically provisional and unfixed. Techniques of staging were consciously anti-naturalistic: symmetrical blocking and ritualized movement, speeches often being spoken directly to the audience, enhanced an effect of choric statement and intellectual serious-ness. Symbolic properties, physical realizations of the play's imagery, complemented the emblematic set of parallel staircases with a rising and falling platform hung between them; in addition to the mirror (used motivically), these included a glistering coro-nation robe, hobby-horses for the tournament, a chalice of earth, a snowman, a toy 'roan Barbary' presented to Richard and a skull-mask. Richard was spectacularly hoisted by the wrists on ropes to be shot with a crossbow, an image of quasi-crucifixion. Barton reduced the number of minor characters, slimmed down the more decorative speeches, cut others altogether, added a few of his own composition and built up Bolingbroke's part by adding material from *2 Henry IV* (including parts of Henry's great insomnia solil-oquy at 3.1.4–31). He also fleshed out the role of Exton by introducing him repeatedly as a figure associated with death and treachery.

In 1978 Derek Jacobi as the King brought the play to a world-wide television audience as part of Cedric Messina's ambitious project of broadcasting all thirty-seven of Shakespeare's plays. Wishing to record 'classic' versions for posterity, the BBC approach was visually conservative, generally naturalistic in costume, settings and sound effects, and involved comparatively minor cutting; but Giles, the director, took advantage of the medium to reflect psychological and motivational nuances through close-ups and angled camera shots, a device that worked effectively for Mowbray's surprised reaction to his banishment and for Richard's long prison soliloquy, where greater variety than is pos-sible onstage became an advantage. Gielgud lent his famous voice to the part of Gaunt and Wendy Hiller her dignity (with comic touches) to York's duchess. Jacobi was perhaps most successful in conveying Richard's gift for personal intimacy. The production included a homoerotically relaxed bathing scene in which Richard and his favourites conversed dressed only in towelling or sitting in a tub. Once more the play became Richard's personal tragedy rather than a political contest between antagonists.

A 1979 production directed by Zoe Caldwell in Canada went one better than Barton by presenting three different pairs of actors as Richard and Bolingbroke without, however, any interchange of roles, the intention being to make varied interpretations of the major parts available to audiences in the same season. Under such conditions, a certain loss of focus was unavoidable. According to Page, the issue raised by these contrasting performances was the perennial one of 'whether Bolingbroke ruthlessly seizes the throne or whether an ineffective Richard gives it up' (68).[1] An RSC staging by Terry Hands in 1980–1 starring Alan Howard as the King fastened on analogies to the Mass and Christian martyrdom, underlining the theme of desecration by having Bolingbroke (David Suchet) stand upon a huge portrait of Richard, lowered from its position as a backdrop to make a sloping floor. Playing Richard III concurrently, Howard made much of the contrast between the crude aggression of the later Richard and the divine right of the earlier one, remarking, according to Lucy Hughes-Hallett, that '*Richard II* is a writer's play' while '*Richard III* is an actor's play' (Page, 74). His comment shows that George Pierce Baker's old prejudice about the play's actor-unfriendliness persists still in some quarters. The key to Howard's interpretation of the title role was apparently a contrast between supreme outward confidence and inward insecurity. Benedict Nightingale noted that the total effect of the production was of watching 'the Middle Ages wane before our eyes' to be replaced by 'Expediency and pragmatism' (Page, 78). A fine, well-balanced production directed by Howard Jensen at the Oregon Shakespeare Festival presented Richard Howard as the tragic King (Fig. 14). Karl Barron of the *Ashland Daily Tidings* (20 June 1995) reported that the American Howard successfully caught 'the almost schizophrenic aspect' of a character who at

1 The three Richards were Stephen Russell, Nicholas Pennell and Frank Maradan; their respective Bolingbrokes were Craig Dudley, Rod Beattie and Jim McQueen.

14 Richard Howard as Richard II (3.3), in Howard Jensen's Oregon Shakespeare Festival production, Ashland, 1995

15　Fiona Shaw as Richard II with Julian Rhind-Tutt as Aumerle, in Deborah
　　Warner's National Theatre production, Cottesloe Theatre, 1995

one moment is 'belligerently ready to ride out and conquer the
Irish, courting national bankruptcy in the attempt' while in the
next 'vacillat[ing] about whether he should hand over the crown
without a battle' (3).

　　The mention of two highly experimental and controversial
productions must conclude this selective survey of later
twentieth-century stagings. The first is Mnouchkine's kabuki-
style, five-hour-long rendering by her Théâtre du Soleil
company near Paris in 1981. The second is Warner's National
Theatre production in 1995 with the Irish actress Fiona Shaw
as the King (Fig. 15), of which a modified version was broadcast

on BBC television in 1997. Both productions sought to discover new significances by radically defamiliarizing the play. Mnouchkine's method was to efface all semblance of psychology and realism by costuming the actors in colourful Samurai-like costumes, some with Elizabethan ruffs, and by employing a combination of stylized, balletic movements, anti-naturalistic gestures, masks, white-face make-up and percussive music on a geometrically patterned stage with changing silk backdrops to reflect alterations of mood. Speeches (in Mnouchkine's own French verse translation) were articulately but unemotionally declaimed at high volume directly to the audience. Stiff ritualism united with acrobatic energy to produce striking visual excitement. Actors externalized the dominant emotion of a particular utterance by inventing a specific movement or gesture to encode it. The Gardeners were depicted as clowns. Props and stage furniture were minimal, but a structure of poles allowed Georges Bigot, as Richard, to tower over his subjects at Flint Castle, poles that were later reconfigured as a cage for the almost naked King at Pomfret. Lavish colour, chiefly in the costuming, suggested political power, while its sudden absence expressed deprivation or loss. Although semiotics were intended to generalize the meanings of the play and to displace any sense of historical specificity (less accessible to French than to English audiences), critics divided strongly over the success of Mnouchkine's intercultural experiment. Many found the directness of her theatrical communication daringly original and imaginative, while others thought that the attempt to combine the traditions of feudal Japan with medieval England (including Tudor overtones) resulted only in obfuscation and confusion, distorting Shakespeare almost beyond recognition. Mnouchkine's production nevertheless illustrates the fact that *Richard II*, the Shakespearean history play most often performed outside Britain and North America, belongs not only to the English-speaking world but to global culture; it is worth noting that the play has been seen, especially since World War II, in Athens, Avignon, Berlin, Bonn, Bratislava, Braunschweig, Bucharest, Dublin, Hamburg, Kampala (Uganda), Marseilles, Milan, Munich, Verona and Zurich, not infrequently in productions that have deliberately distanced the play from its English context, occasionally using foreign settings, in the service of more modern and universal kinds of relevance.[1]

Despite the casting of Fiona Shaw as Richard, Warner's production was more notable for its postmodernist, superficially apolitical approach than for feminism. The intention was to convey Richard's gift for female-style intimacy (a trait noticed by Coleridge) without suggesting homosexuality, a difficult task for a male actor. Shaw played the King as genuinely adoring of Bolingbroke (David Threlfall), running his fingers through his hair and kissing him on the lips as if to apologize for exiling him, possibly taking her cue from the symbolic identity between the two men suggested in Barton's extra-textual prison meeting. When Richard received devastating news in 3.2, he not only sat upon the ground but sucked his thumb, a gesture of infantile terror and hopelessness that many critics loathed. Pomp and pageantry were entirely eliminated, Richard being costumed mostly in white sheet-like garments that, as Shewring remarks, 'seem to have been brought together almost at random, as by a child dressing up'; mummy-like linen bands in the death scene suggested 'a shroud' (182–4). Kingship as charade lay at the heart of Shaw's interpretation, a recognition that the player-king is mysteriously involved in problems of psychic doubleness of which androgyny and a close emotional relationship with his cousin-destroyer could be made the vehicles. Richard's everpresent tears became a mark of the gender-ambiguity, and gave the breakdown of good relations with Bolingbroke the semblance

---

1   See Black (573–5), Leiter (569–92) and Shewring (154–79). It should be noted that the report of a 1949 South African production, recorded in *SQ*, 2 (1951), 372, and again in Black, 574, is an error. This staging at Makerere University took place in Kampala, Uganda; see Alastair MacPherson, '*Richard II* performed by the Students of Makerere', *East African Annual 1950–51*, 123–7.

of a 'wrecked love affair' (Rutter, 318). The steeply raked seats on either side of the stage, suggesting grandstands at a joust, accommodated part of the paying audience, thus enhancing both the theme of doubleness and of politics as sport. The avant-garde reduction of monarchy to child's play and mischievous clowning outraged traditionalist critics, but Warner's production also provoked spirited defence, especially among academics and the more literary journalists.[1]

The obvious proof of the continuing vitality of *Richard II* is the steady record of changing interpretations it has inspired. Distortion and partiality have inevitably been part of the process. The revisionist and culturally dissident liberties taken by directors such as Mnouchkine, Warner and to a lesser extent Barton have in fact been no more extreme than those of Tate, Theobald and Wroughton in the two centuries following Shakespeare. The Victorian fashion of elaborate archaizing represented by the likes of Charles Kean was no truer to the historical conditions of the Elizabethan theatre than the ahistorical violence done the play by actresses such as Fiona Shaw. Each age remakes the drama according to its own lights and will undoubtedly continue to do so.

THE DATE

Although there is wide scholarly consensus that *Richard II* was composed in 1595 or thereabouts, the evidence for this date is problematic. The obvious *terminus a quo* is the second edition of Holinshed's *Chronicles* (1587), Shakespeare's major source, while the *terminus ad quem* is clearly the first quarto of 1597. By this time the play had undoubtedly had its initial run by the Chamberlain's Men, who then, apparently, released it for publication. That the quarto sold out quickly is proved by the issuing of two reprints the following year – the only instance apart from *1 Henry IV* in which

---

1   See especially Paul Taylor, *The Independent* (14 June 1995), 23, Rutter, and Shewring, 180–4.

a play by Shakespeare was able to provoke three separate editions within a two-year span. The style of the play, unusual among the histories, constitutes the most reliable way of narrowing its time limits, for its distinctive features group it obviously with *Love's Labour's Lost*, *Romeo and Juliet* and *A Midsummer Night's Dream*, dramas that almost all scholars agree fall within the period 1594–5. The tell-tale characteristics include the high number of rhymed lines; the penchant for elaborate punning, conceits and rhetorical patterning; the avoidance of colloquialism; and the high degree of metrical regularity. The absence of prose is a feature shared only with *1* and *3 Henry VI* (1592 or earlier) and with *King John* (1594–6?). Students of rare vocabulary in Shakespeare have shown that *Richard II* is most strongly linked to *Richard III* (1591–3) and *Titus Andronicus* (1592), to a lesser extent to the three parts of *Henry VI*, and still less to *King John*, while, apart from *John*, no such affinities to any play conventionally dated later than 1594 have been demonstrated.[1]

External evidence is bedevilled by various kinds and degrees of uncertainty. That there is a close relationship between *Richard II* and Daniel's epic poem, *The First Four Books of the Civil Wars* (1595), has been clear to most scholars since Knight in his *Pictorial Edition* (1839) proposed Daniel as a source. Unconvincing attempts to argue that Daniel, not Shakespeare, was the debtor were made by Hudson (in 1852), and by White (in 1859), who confused his bibliographical facts.[2] Though this view

---

1 See *TxC*, 118; also Anne Barton's introduction to *LLL* (*Riv*, 174–5).
2 See Hudson, 5.6–7. White (6.138–45) and, later, Chambers (*WS*, 1.351) believed incorrectly that there were two separate editions of *The Civil Wars* in 1595, the second containing the changes, as White regarded them, that show the closest resemblance to *Richard II*. In fact there were two different issues of the same edition, the second involving only a change in title-page. Daniel revised his poem in 1601, 1609 and 1623, but the important alterations – those, for instance, concerning the quarrel between Bolingbroke and Mowbray and the Exton story, which convinced White that Daniel had levied upon Shakespeare – occur in the 1609 edition, indicating that by this point Daniel had probably consulted the text of *Richard II* or had come to know it from performance. Given Daniel's indebtedness to Shakespeare in his 1609 revision, it seems unlikely that the poet had already borrowed from the same play before its publication. Wells and Taylor record their 'suspicion that, in this period of their respective careers, Shakespeare was more likely to borrow from a prestigious courtly poet like Daniel than

continued to find adherents, and although Shakespeare's play almost certainly did influence Daniel's later revision of his poem, enough links remain between the tragedy and Daniel's first edition – similarities of action, language, mood, characterization, situation and historical outlook – to convince most modern investigators that Shakespeare was the debtor and that he read Daniel during his composition of *Richard II*, though perhaps not until he was well advanced in the writing. The most telling influence seems to be concentrated in the final act where Queen Isabel's deepest grief, her final meeting with Richard, York's description of Bolingbroke's entry into London and the King's prison soliloquy all occur. Only in Daniel, for instance, could Shakespeare have encountered a conception of the Queen as a mature woman rather than as a child of eleven (Daniel, 2.71–98)[1] and of Harry Percy as a youth (Daniel, 3.97). In addition, Logan demonstrates that Daniel used Lucan's *Pharsalia* as his model whereas Shakespeare, who appears to have been little interested in Lucan, is close to the latter only in places where Daniel also shows indebtedness; Carlisle's speech (4.1.137–50), for instance, is far more likely to have been influenced verbally by the opening two stanzas of Daniel's poem than by the passage in Lucan of which Daniel's lines are an idiosyncratic paraphrase. The initial instalment of *The Civil Wars*, the section of the poem relevant to Richard II, was entered in the Stationers' Register on 11 October 1594 and was probably published fairly early the following year; a second issue also appeared in 1595, and a letter from Rowland Whyte to Sir Robert Sidney (3 November 1595)[2] makes it obvious that the

---

Daniel to borrow from a public playwright' (*TxC*, 117–18). Michel (8–11) gives a full account of the textual history of Daniel's poem including an explanation of how the phantom edition got perpetuated in the scholarship after White and Chambers.

1 In his dedication (1609 edn), Daniel apologizes for having '*erred somewhat in the draught of the young* Q. Isabel . . . *in not suting her passions to her yeares*'. Daniel writes in this passage as though his portraying her as an adult were a conscious artistic decision, not a conception derived in error from Shakespeare or some other source. Logan strengthens this likelihood by suggesting that 'Daniel raised the age of Isabel' (128) in response to elements in Lucan, his classical model.

2 Printed in Collins, 1.357.

volume was by this time attracting some attention. If, in accord with most recent opinion, we accept Daniel's first edition as a valid Shakespearean source,[1] the play could not have been composed earlier than the latter part of 1595.[2]

Apart from the probable influence of Daniel, a letter from Sir Edward Hoby to Sir Robert Cecil (7 December 1595), inviting him to dine and be entertained, is often adduced as confirmatory evidence that *Richard II* was being publicly acted at this time:

> Sir, findinge that you wer not convenientlie to be at London to morrow night I am bold to send to knowe whether Teusdaie [9 Dec.] may be anie more in your grace to visit poore Channon rowe where as late as it shal please you a gate for your supper shal be open: & K. Richard present him self to your vewe. Pardon my boldnes that ever love to be honored with your presence nether do I importune more then your occasions may willingly assent unto, in the meanetime & ever restinge
>
> At your command
> Edw. Hoby

[Endorsed] 7 Dec. 1595 [and] readile.[3]

---

1 Minority voices are several. Kittredge[2] thinks that the so-called parallels with Daniel 'prove nothing' (viii), and Harrison that there 'is no definite evidence' (430). Greer and Lambrechts are also sceptical: the first insists that 'There is not . . . a single sure verbal parallel' (Greer, 'Daniel', 53); the second concludes that in the few places where a relationship seems likeliest, Daniel is the probable debtor (Lambrechts, 128–38).

2 Tobin (6–7) argues that the garden scene is indebted for two phrases to Nashe's *Have With You to Saffron Walden*, not published until early 1596 but apparently circulating in manuscript at least three months earlier: 'presse a man to death' (Nashe, 3.57) and 'one slip . . . of herb of grace' (Nashe, 3.62); cf. *R2* 'pressed to death' (3.4.71) and 'sour herb of grace' (3.4.105). Although the phrases are common and their contexts diverse, their proximity to each other in both Nashe and Shakespeare is suggestive, besides which Shakespeare seems to have borrowed language from a variety of Nashe's writings (including *Have With You to Saffron Walden*) in *1* and *2 Henry IV*; Wilson collects the later Nashe parallels in his Cambridge edition of *1 Henry IV* (1946), 191–6. If the verbal links between Nashe and *Richard II* are evidence of Shakespeare's indebtedness rather than mere coincidences or borrowings in the opposite direction, at least the garden scene must have been composed fairly late in 1595.

3 Printed in Chambers, 'Gleanings', 75–6.

If 'K. Richard' refers to a private performance of Shakespeare's tragedy, as many think, Hoby's letter would confirm late 1595 as its probable date, for Hoby would be sponsoring a drama that was recent, newsworthy and already in production on a public stage. As the son of Lord Burghley, Elizabeth's chief minister, Cecil was an important guest who would be interested in seeing a play that dealt with so politically sensitive and controversial a subject as the deposition of a king often regarded as a prototype of his own royal mistress.[1] The endorsement of the letter by Cecil's secretary and the word 'readile', written in a different hand, suggest that Cecil accepted the invitation. Although a broad spectrum of scholars tentatively accepts the Hoby letter as valid evidence of the play's date,[2] dissent has been vocal. Kittredge (1941; viii) questions whether Hoby was referring to a drama at all, or perhaps to some non-Shakespearean play, or even *Richard III*. Shapiro argues that Hoby was alluding perhaps to a painting (he is known to have been a collector of historical portraits), or to something that Hoby himself had written. Kincaid, who points out that Hoby and Cecil were first cousins who enjoyed 'a relationship of easy intimacy', proposes that Hoby was inviting Cecil to examine a lost tract in Latin about Richard III, which had served as the basis for Sir Thomas More's *History of Richard III*; Kincaid thinks that the occasion for which Cecil's presence was being sought (he stresses that the guest was to come to a town house, not a great estate, and as late in the evening as he pleased) was an 'informal supper' rather than a banquet and therefore inappropriate for theatrical entertainment.[3] Clearly the 'K. Richard' of Hoby's letter is open to various interpretations; but Cecil's political prominence and the apparently heightened interest in Richard II as a subject in 1595 and earlier (see p. 5) have seemed

1 See pp. 5–9.
2 These include Lothian (7), Wilson (vii–x), O.J. Campbell (182), Hardin Craig[2] (643), Feuillerat (224–6), Petersson (155), Muir (xxiii), Herschel Baker (*Riv*, 800), Gurr (1–3) and Bevington[2] (114).
3 See also Greer, 402–3. The most thorough account of believers and non-believers in the Hoby letter as evidence for the dating of *Richard II* is that by Bergeron ('Hoby Letter').

to most scholars to make the offer of a recent and probably controversial play more likely than a painting or a book.

Two further considerations relate to dating. The first concerns earlier plays that seem to have influenced or prompted Shakespeare in some way. The second takes into account the sequence of Shakespearean histories that *Richard II* initiated.

The Relation to Edward II *and* Woodstock

That Marlowe's *Edward II* and the anonymous *Woodstock* served in their different ways as models for *Richard II* is virtually certain. More verbal and conceptual links, as well as similarities of characterization, occur between Shakespeare's tragedy and these two plays than can be explained as fortuitous.[1] Marlowe's powerful drama on the subject of a weak king fatally dominated by favourites, indebted in its turn to Shakespeare's own first tetralogy (see *E2*, 17–41), was published in 1594 but may have been staged in London as early as 1592. *Woodstock*, which unhistorically idealizes the character of Gloucester in a way that probably influenced Shakespeare's portrayal of Gaunt, which depicts the widowed Duchess of Gloucester as thirsting for revenge and which offers details about Richard's flatterers and 'blank charters' to which Shakespeare makes only cryptic reference, was almost certainly composed between 1591 and 1595.[2] The play survives in a single manuscript (British Library Egerton MS 1994, fols 161–85) copied in a hand dating from the late sixteenth or early seventeenth century. The manuscript has also been marked up for use in the theatre and contains various additions, insertions, deletions and other changes, bearing evidence, as Long (96), following Frijlinck, points out, of eight hands besides that of the transcriber. A few scholars have queried the priority of *Woodstock* to *Richard II*, noting that the play's verse contains a higher

---

1 For further discussion of these links, see pp. 145–52, 158–64.
2 See Hunter (*History*, 204). Long, the most recent and authoritative analyst of the *Woodstock* MS, dates the earliest performances of the play 'in the season of 1594–95' (96, 109), a conclusion which agrees with findings by both Chambers in 1923 and Greg in 1931 (Long, 116, n. 17).

percentage of feminine endings (slightly more than one fifth of the lines) than one would expect in a drama composed in the early 1590s. Timberlake, seeking an explanation for the discrepancy between *Woodstock*'s metrical anomalies and its relatively early date, suggests, however, that it is quite possible that other revisions not shown in the manuscript might have taken place during the play's theatrical lifetime after its original composition but before the transcript was made.[1] Less speculative, perhaps, is the way in which *Woodstock* mangles historical chronology in its confusion of the two separate groups of Richard's favourites, associating the fall of Tresilian (a member of the first group overthrown in 1388) with the 'blank charters' and abuses of the second group (Bushy, Bagot, Green and Wiltshire) whose downfall in 1399 accompanied the King's own tragedy. As Bullough points out, 'It is hard to believe that any play written after Shakespeare's would set chronology at such defiance or separate the destruction of Bushy, Bagot and Greene from the downfall of the King' (3.360).

It is clear also that *Woodstock* is closely related conceptually and verbally to both *2 Henry VI* and *Edward II*; Rossiter (62–3) constructs a complex argument to suggest that *Woodstock* borrowed from *2 Henry VI* and then in turn influenced *Edward II*.[2] As Hunter observes, the indebtedness of both dramas to *2 Henry VI* 'is probable enough' even if 'the priority between the two debtors seems impossible to determine' (*History*, 204–5). Thematic and verbal ties nevertheless suggest strongly that all three plays belong to the same period of composition and were

1 See Timberlake, 71–2, and Wilson, xlviii–xlix. Frijlinck also stresses 'the monotonous end-stopped verse and the considerable proportion of rhyme which point to an early date' and also believes some of the chief scribe's spellings, his use of double long *s* and 'the appearance of rare verbal forms' to be 'old-fashioned' (xxiii–xxiv). J.R. Weeks, in 'The Use of the Rhymed Couplet in Elizabethan and Jacobean Drama' (Oxford University B.Litt. thesis, 1970), speculates that the pattern of rhyming in the play may point to a date of composition later than 1592 (42), but nevertheless accepts the conventional dating (1591–5). Lambrechts, building on the work of Boas and Frijlinck, argues on various grounds that *Woodstock* is 'postérieur' (120) to Shakespeare's tragedy, but Long (109) convincingly refutes him.
2 F.N. Lees comments on Rossiter's position in his revision of Charlton & Waller, 219.

originally staged within a few years of each other. Scholarly consensus on the dates of *Edward II* and *Woodstock*, both of them dramatic forerunners of our play, tends to strengthen the case for 1595 as the probable date of *Richard II*.

Richard II *and the Second Tetralogy*

Scholars have often noted the significant links between *Richard II* and the later plays of the tetralogy written between 1596 and 1599 – links that suggest that Shakespeare in 1595 was already planning ahead. The introduction of Harry Percy as a character of fictive youthfulness and Bolingbroke's worried speeches about his son's licentiousness and possible reformation (5.3.1–12, 20–2) are hardly intrinsic to *Richard II* as a self-contained tragedy, though both of course add colour and enrich the characterization of the youths' two fathers. The chief purpose, clearly, was to lay down a foundation for the next play of the sequence in which Hotspur and Prince Hal are presented as rivals – rivals whose historical ages have both been altered to afford a dramatic balance between figures who were, on the one hand, a soldier senior to the King and, on the other, a boy of twelve.[1] Other preparatory details also stand out such as the character of the Welsh Captain, an early version, perhaps, of Glendower; the emphasis on Bolingbroke's self-ingratiation with the common people (cf. *1H4* 3.2.50–4); and King Henry's intention to make a 'voyage to the Holy Land' or to undertake a crusade, repeatedly alluded to in both parts of *Henry IV* and ironically consummated by his death in the Jerusalem Chamber (*2H4* 4.5.231–40).[2] The crusading idea recurs again at the end of *Henry V*, when the young monarch envisions the begetting of 'a boy, half French, half English, that shall go to Constantinople and take the Turk by the beard' (5.2.207–9).

---

1 Daniel perhaps contributed to this unhistorical equalization of ages, for *The Civil Wars* treats Prince Hal at seventeen as a contemporary of Hotspur whom, in the chivalric act of saving his father's life, he encounters at the Battle of Shrewsbury.

2 Glendower is also mentioned by name in *Richard II* (see 3.1.43n.). See also 1.4.24–36n., 5.2.18–20n. and 5.6.49n.

Richard II is also notable for incidents and speeches remembered or quoted in the later plays, often with ironic bias or revisionary perspective. Thus Westmoreland in *2 Henry IV* (4.1.129–37) recalls the quarrel between Bolingbroke and Mowbray that opens *Richard II*, casting a more negative light upon Mowbray's reputation than was clear in the first play. Richard's casting down his warder with its long-range consequences is dramatically recalled by Mowbray's son in *2 Henry IV* (4.1.123–7), as is Worcester's breaking his rod of stewardship in *1 Henry IV* (5.1.34–5). Hotspur in *1 Henry IV* (1.3.251–5) derisively misquotes Bolingbroke's words of diplomatic courtesy at their first meeting in the earlier play (2.3.45–50) and indignantly remembers (*1H4* 4.3.60–1) that the Duke of Lancaster had promised that 'his coming is / But for his own' (*R2* 2.3.148–9). Hotspur refers to the king he had earlier betrayed as 'that sweet lovely rose' (*1H4* 1.3.175), an ironic echo of the Queen's epithet for Richard ('My fair rose') in their scene of parting (*R2* 5.1.8). York's detail about the throwing of dust on Richard's head as he is led through the London streets (*R2* 5.2.6) is repeated by the Archbishop of *2 Henry IV* (1.3.103–7). And Richard's prophecy that Northumberland will forsake his new master as he has forsaken his old (5.1.55–61) appears almost verbatim in a speech by Henry IV, who now knows only too well how truly his predecessor had spoken (*2H4* 3.1.65–79). Even in *Henry V* before Agincourt the young King's consciousness of his father's 'fault . . . in compassing the crown', of Richard's murder and of the debilitating guilt inherited on account of it (*H5* 4.1.289–305) jog the audience's memory back to the initial play in the series. It is hardly likely that any of these reminiscences and backward glances could have taken full shape in Shakespeare's mind as early as 1595; but the sheer extent of the cross-referencing suggests that the entire tetralogy developed rapidly in the playwright's creative imagination, and that he could count on Elizabethan audiences to respond to the dramatic subtleties and ironic shifts of attitude that the cross-references would enable him to realize onstage. It goes without saying that each of the four plays of the so-called Henriad has a dramatic structure, style and independence of its own, continuing now, as originally, to be performed separately. But their obvious proximity to each other in matter and sequence helps us to set an upper boundary for the date of *Richard II* just as the earlier histories help to fix the lower limit.[1]

PROBABLE VENUES OF
EARLY PERFORMANCE

We cannot be certain at which playhouse *Richard II* was first performed, probably in the autumn of 1595, but it was very likely James Burbage's Theatre, built in 1576 and located north of the city of London, in Shoreditch. This was the main playhouse used by the Lord Chamberlain's Men after Shakespeare joined the company in 1594, doubtless available to them because their leading tragedian, Richard Burbage, was son to the owner.[2] In 1596–7, after *Richard II*

1 The plays of the first tetralogy (*1, 2* and *3 Henry VI* and *Richard III*) all appear to have been composed and originally mounted between 1590 and 1593. But they 'were probably never performed as a sequence' until the dramatist was established 'with the Chamberlain's Men, the company he joined when it was formed in mid 1594' (Cam², 3–4). In the unsettled and plague-burdened period before this date, the plays of the Yorkist sequence were apparently staged under different auspices at different theatres in somewhat piecemeal fashion. Their fresh success and popularity as revived by the new company which Shakespeare served until the end of his career may well have prompted him to conceive a group of Lancastrian plays as a way of profitably dramatizing the roots of the dynastic struggles he had already addressed. His putative part in *Edward III* (1592–3?), an apparently successful play about the heroic grandfather of Richard II and Bolingbroke, may also have contributed to the decision. *King John*, the other chronicle history written very close to *Richard II*, deals with the problems of a weak king (like Henry VI and Richard), who (like Bolingbroke) was also a usurper. If this drama was written between the two tetralogies, as many think probable (there is no external evidence to fix the date either pre- or post-*Richard II*), Shakespeare would then have been free to pursue his exploration of the Lancastrian cycle chronologically as an interrelated group without the distraction of dramatizing events that occurred nearly two centuries earlier. For the view that *King John* postdates *Richard II*, see *TxC*, 119, and Williams, 'Notes', 49–50.
2 A possible alternative might be the Cross Keys in Gracechurch Street, an inn near Falstaff's Eastcheap used as a theatre, which Lord Chamberlain Hunsdon requested the Mayor of London on 8 October 1594 to let his company occupy as a 'winter' house (Chambers, *ES*, 2.383). Unfortunately we do not know whether the Cross Keys was still available a year later when *Richard II* was presumably written.

had made its debut, a dispute over renewing the lease forced the company to play elsewhere – either at the nearby Curtain, built in 1577, or at the Swan, which by 1595 had been newly constructed by Francis Langley on the south bank of the Thames. It was not until 1599 that the Globe, which was to become the company's permanent residence, was erected on the bankside using timbers from the old Theatre now dismantled and transported south. We know that a *Richard II*, probably Shakespeare's play, was revived at the Globe on 7 February 1601 at the behest of Meyrick, one of Essex's followers (see pp. 10, 16). Even after the company had become the King's Men at the change of reign, the play apparently remained in the repertory, for a performance at the second Globe is recorded as late as 12 June 1631.[1] *Richard II* could have been acted in all four of these early theatres, which were undoubtedly similar in design. They all must have featured a thrust stage, an upper level over the main playing space for episodes requiring an 'above' such as the action at Flint Castle, and at least two doors in the tiring-house wall wide enough for processional entries and the passage of the raised throne or 'sacred state' (4.1.209, 5.6.6).[2] This latter is a symbolic centre of the play's action and the only cumbersome property needed. Gurr and Hodges have assumed, not unreasonably, that the play was designed for production on a stage like that shown in Johannes de Witt's well-known drawing of the Swan, and Hodges has produced several drawings of his own that illustrate how crucial scenes such as the Coventry lists (1.3) and the Flint Castle episode (3.3) could be effectively presented on such a stage.[3] The Swan drawing shows no central opening or curtained recess between the

1 See Black, 567, 568.
2 See also 1.3.190n., 2.1.120n., 3.2.72n., 163n., 4.1.114n., 180n., 192n. and 5.2.40n.
3 Hodges (31); Gurr (38–9). In the de Witt illustration the upper level of the stage is occupied by spectators or, possibly, musicians. Because of the row of posts along its front, some scholars interpret this area as a series of discrete boxes rather than an undivided space that could be utilized by actors. Ingram (143–50) believes that Shakespeare's company were performing at the Swan between October 1596 and January 1597, mentioning *Richard II*, *Romeo and Juliet* and *The Merchant of Venice* as possible offerings (148) – all plays that require actors to appear 'aloft', i.e. at a window or balcony above the main stage. *King John*, written within a year of *Richard II*, also requires the upper level, e.g. for the scene with Prince Arthur '*on the walls*'.

left and right doors such as the Globe possessed, but nothing in *Richard II* requires this feature, and indeed, if the throne was not trundled or carried off and on through one of the side doors at the Theatre or the Swan, it might, as Hodges (32–3) suggests, have remained onstage throughout the entire performance as a dominant emblem of the play's theme. Nor were performances limited to the public theatres: the possibility of a 1595 private showing for Cecil in Canon Row has already been mentioned (see pp. 114–16); and on 30 September 1607 the shipmaster William Keeling in the presence of Captain William Hawkins sponsored an amateur performance on board his ship the *Dragon*, lying off the coast of Sierra Leone, before setting sail for the East Indies. On 4 August 1601 Queen Elizabeth, apparently referring to Shakespeare's play, told William Lambarde, her keeper of records at the Tower, that 'this tragedy was played 40^{tie} times in open streets and houses'.[1] Even if Her Majesty was exaggerating or speaking in round numbers, it is clear that *Richard II* was popular enough to be widely acted (see p. 91).

The actors would have been among the most accomplished in the land. Richard Burbage, the company's leading man in tragedy, probably took the title role as he did in *Richard III*, *Hamlet*, *King Lear* and *Othello*; Baldwin conjectures that Augustine Phillips, who was later examined by the authorities in connection with Essex's abortive coup, acted Bolingbroke.[2] According to the computer-based findings of Donald Foster, Shakespeare himself played Gaunt and the head Gardener in addition to doubling as the anonymous Lord of 4.1 and perhaps also the Groom.[3]

---

1   Black, 567–8; Chambers, *WS*, 2.326–7. The Chamberlain's Men performed at court on 24 February 1601, the eve of Essex's execution (Chambers, *ES*, 4.113). Although the nature of the entertainment is unknown, Robert Sharpe speculated in 1935 that the play might have been *Richard II*, acted at the Queen's command as an act of 'bravado to conceal her real feelings' and as 'a gesture of contempt, triumph, and warning', since Shakespeare's drama was believed by many to expose her weaknesses covertly and to hint at her deposition. Sharpe also suggests that *Richard II* could have been procured by Essex's enemies at court to prevent Elizabeth from reprieving her former favourite at the last minute; see Black, 585–6.

2   See Black, 565, 581.

3   Foster's findings rest on the theory that 'the rare-words in Shakespearean texts are not randomly distributed . . . but are in fact "mnemonically structured".

SOURCES

Chambers observes that *Richard II* is 'carefully written'; Saintsbury calls it 'the most *carefully* written of all Shakespeare's plays', a work aiming uncharacteristically at 'correctness'; Hibbard says that it 'has every appearance of having been studied'.[1] Its ritualistic language, ceremonial staging and formal settings (a jousting arena, throne rooms, castle battlements and courtyard, a walled garden, Parliament) seem deliberately conceived to evoke an ethos of archaic stylization and decorum. Shakespeare could hardly have approached his subject casually. Rather he appears to have taken uncommon pains to read as widely as possible about the reign whose tragic end he was about to dramatize, and there is good reason to suppose that for the first play of a connected series he researched more strenuously than for any other chronicle play. This is not to suggest that he felt less free to alter chronology, events and emphases, or to reinvent character than was his normal practice in handling historical material, but only to point out that he seems to have saturated himself as much as possible in all that was available. This included earlier drama, narrative verse, homiletic, *de casibus* and *memento mori* literature as well as the chronicles (possibly foreign as well as domestic) – in addition to works by such ancients and moderns as Ovid, Livy, Cicero, Lyly, Marlowe, Du Bartas and Lodge, levied upon for incidental ideas and rhetorical adornment. A possible reason for the surprising diversity of source material is the play's innovative reduction of historical narrative as compared with the other histories. It is as though Shakespeare for once preferred ideas, motivational complexities and modulations of feeling to facts as a stimulus to his creative dramaturgy. Some editors have contended that Shakespeare

Shakespeare's active lexicon as a writer was systematically influenced by his reading, and by his apparent activities as a stage-player' (25). Foster's data seem to confirm the long-standing tradition that Shakespeare characteristically enacted old men and secondary roles such as Adam in *As You Like It* and the Ghost in *Hamlet*.

1 Chambers, 151; Forker, 438; Hibbard, 117.

drew upon no fewer than eight principal sources: (1) Holinshed's *Chronicles of England, Scotland, and Ireland* (1587); (2) Hall's *Union of the Two Noble and Illustrate Families of Lancaster and York* (1548); (3) *The Mirror for Magistrates* (1559); (4) Daniel's *First Four Books of the Civil Wars* (1595); (5) the anonymous play *Woodstock* (1591–5?), not published until modern times; (6) Froissart's *Chronicle*, in the translation by Lord Berners (1523–5); (7) an anonymous French manuscript chronicle entitled *Chronicque de la Traïson et Mort de Richart Deux Roy Dengleterre* (*c*. 1400), also extant in a variant redaction by Jean Le Beau (see Buchon); and (8) Créton's metrical *Histoire du Roy d'Angleterre Richard* (1399?). To these should probably be added Marlowe's *Edward II* (1591–2, published 1594) which clearly served Shakespeare as a dramatic model.

Holinshed

For incidents, names and the overall sequence of events Shakespeare relied on Holinshed's twenty-four densely packed, double-column pages (3.493–517) covering the end of Richard's reign and the start of Henry's, sometimes echoing their phrasing or vocabulary (full discussion of significant details will be found throughout the commentary). In *Richard II*, in fact, he deviated less from Holinshed than in the other histories. But simplifications, compressions, changes of chronology, omissions and shifts of emphasis were all necessary to provide focus, clarity of outline, deeper characterization and dramatic impact, as were important additions, sometimes suggested by collateral sources or often simply invented.

In the handling of Holinshed calculated telescoping becomes a major technique – notably in the treatment of the opening quarrel (which allows for greater ceremoniousness); in the rapid decision to banish the combatants (which suggests greater arbitrariness and instability in the King); in the early timing of Bolingbroke's return (which complicates our initial estimate of his motives); in the fusing of the Duke's triumphant entry into

London with Richard's conveyance to the Tower (which contrasts the one's popularity with the other's humiliation, thus shifting Holinshed's stress on jubilation to an effect of sadness); and in making Richard's transfer to Pomfret coincide with the Queen's departure for France (which enhances the pathos of their final parting). The most radical streamlining of Holinshed occurs in Act 4. Here three separate parliaments, the challenges and recriminations resulting from Gloucester's murder, the legal pressures upon Richard, his renunciation of the crown and Bolingbroke's claiming of it, Carlisle's protest, the announcement of Mowbray's death and the launching of the Abbot's counterplot are all compassed in a scene of 334 lines. These actions are spread over some fourteen pages in the chronicle, many of which are devoted to transcripts of documents concerning the deposition – among others, thirty-three articles detailing Richard's unworthiness to rule and his own formal instrument of resignation. Shakespeare subordinates everything here to the great emotional climax of Richard's appearance before Parliament to depose himself, whereas in the chronicle the act of resignation took place privately in the Tower. The articles, whose specifics Shakespeare purposefully omits in mitigation of Richard's tyrannies, are reduced to a stage property with which Northumberland torments the King, while all the other documents disappear entirely except for a few verbal traces of the formal abdication worked into one of Richard's more histrionic speeches.[1]

Other reorderings of Holinshed also signify. In contrast to the chronicle, Shakespeare allows Richard to dominate more directly at Coventry by having him enter before either of the duelists and by eliminating the participation of Aumerle, Surrey and Bushy as spokesmen for the King. Shakespeare gives Surrey's role to the Lord Marshal (historically, Surrey served as Lord Marshal, but Shakespeare makes them separate characters; see 1.3.251–2n.).

1   See 4.1.204–15n.

Moreover, Bolingbroke's entrance, like Richard's, is heralded by trumpets and delayed until after Mowbray's – an obvious violation of the protocol by which appellants were to precede and speak before defendants. The reversal is subtly disturbing, perhaps intentionally suggesting suppressed disorder beneath the ceremonial facade.[1] But it is also astute to reserve the entry of the more politically important character until last – the man who is to become the principal antagonist of the play. Such alterations may seem minor, but they illustrate how the dramatist shapes his material from the outset in almost unnoticed ways to lend prominence to the central figures. Shakespeare pointedly antedates the Duchess of Gloucester's death, introducing it just after the King has left for Ireland as a means of exacerbating York's 'tide of woes' (2.2.98). The same kind of antedating applies also to Worcester's dispersal of the royal household and defection to Bolingbroke, reported to the Queen while Richard is still abroad and greatly magnifying her distress. In Holinshed Worcester does not break his staff of office until Richard's military situation at Flint Castle looks hopeless. Placing Worcester's disloyalty earlier has the effect of weakening Richard's position even more disastrously than the facts of history warranted. Shakespeare also alters the thrust of Carlisle's speech of protest by bringing it forward to just after Bolingbroke has proclaimed his accession and by making it an eloquent appeal to the doctrine of divine right. Holinshed gives us nothing about royal indefeasibility. Moreover, the bishop of the chronicle is silent until the new king has already been crowned; even then, he speaks out not so much to protest against the accession as to object to trying Richard in absentia. Perhaps the subtlest of all Shakespeare's chronological shifts concerns Richard's self-torturing consciousness of his own impending deposition and death well in advance of any realistic confirmation that dethronement is inevitable. In Holinshed, although the King's early fear and despair are mentioned, it is not

---

1   For the awryness, compare the opening of *Hamlet* in which the ordinary roles of the two sentinels are strangely transposed, the relieving guard (Barnardo) giving the challenge while the guard being relieved (Francisco) answers him.

clear that Richard must lose his crown until he reaches London as a prisoner; even then, he agrees to resign partly as a means of saving his life. Shakespeare, in contrast, has Richard already talking of deposition and death in Wales before he has confronted his enemy: 'Our lands, our lives and all are Bolingbroke's' (3.2.151).

Shakespeare significantly alters the characters of York, Mowbray and Gaunt. The colourless York of the chronicle becomes a serio-comic figure caught up pathetically in a conflict of loyalties – a far feebler man than his historical counterpart, who actually assembled an army to defend Richard, albeit vainly. The nobleman's naive attempt to 'remain as neuter' (2.3.159) is Shakespeare's invention – an effective way of marking the turning point in his descent to apostasy. In Holinshed the degree of Mowbray's culpability for Gloucester's death is already unclear, but Shakespeare beclouds matters further by having Mowbray deny Bolingbroke's charge with a suspiciously unexplained reference to his having 'Neglected my sworn duty' (1.1.134), whereas in Holinshed his evasion simply takes the form of silence. In the play as in the chronicle Mowbray seems to be protecting the King. Then in 4.1, when Bagot is questioned before Parliament about Gloucester's murder, he responds by accusing Aumerle but, in a further departure from Holinshed, omitting entirely to implicate Richard or Mowbray.[1] Moreover, the Mowbray of the play reacts with such passionate eloquence to the patent injustice of perpetual banishment, together with the royal ingratitude it reflects, that it is difficult to regard him as either criminal or insincere.[2] In Shakespeare, the King sees 'Virtue' in Mowbray's 'eye' (1.3.98) and claims to exile him 'with some unwillingness' (1.3.149). In Holinshed, Richard justifies his banishment of Mowbray by

---

1 Holinshed (3.511) mentions 'a bill . . . which he [Bagot] had made, conteining certeine euill practises of king Richard'; this document went on to describe how Bagot had heard Mowbray defend himself to the effect that he had reluctantly complied with the order to have the Duke made away 'onelie for feare of the king, and sauing of his owne life' (3.512).
2 Bolingbroke's speech in similar circumstances is contrastingly cooler; see 1.3.154–73n.

127

charging that he 'had sowen sedition in the relme', and in addition Richard garnishes the revenues from Mowbray's estates to pay for his supposedly unauthorized expenditure of royal funds (3.495). When we learn late in the play that Mowbray has died in Venice as a devout Christian (4.1.93–101), presumably now absolved of his gravest sins, it is harder yet to cast him in the role of tool villain or murderer. As for Mowbray's connection with the crusades, Shakespeare's introduction of this note entirely lacks historical foundation and could not have come from Holinshed.[1]

One of the most telling changes from Holinshed is the new prominence accorded Gaunt. In the section of the chronicle from which Shakespeare drew his facts, Richard's uncle is scarcely a presence at all. Indeed he enters Holinshed's narrative briefly at only two points: first, in a sentence recounting his death (3.496) and, second, in Carlisle's speech reminding Parliament that Bolingbroke, now King, had been banished partly on the advice 'of his owne father' (3.512). On this slender foundation Shakespeare constructs one of the most memorable personalities of the tragedy, a character who appears saliently in four of the first five scenes. The dramatist makes Gaunt an important figure in the quarrel scenes, inventing his grief as Richard's motive for commuting Bolingbroke's sentence, and constructing an entire episode out of the leave-taking of father and son in which the significant theme of fantasy versus realism can be introduced. Another innovation, Gaunt's visit to the widowed Duchess of Gloucester, which could have been prompted by a scene in *Woodstock* (see 1.2 headnote), allows Shakespeare to present the aged statesman as a defender of the Tudor doctrine of non-resistance to tyranny and a wise proponent of Christian patience. In his death scene Gaunt is presented as the one man in Richard's court whose venerable status as wise counsellor permits him to condemn Richard to his face for headstrong follies and selfish abuses, and to reaffirm the traditional standards of patriotism and

---

1   See 4.1.92–101LN.

chivalry which his nephew's rule has shockingly repudiated. Shakespeare's deliberate idealization of Gaunt, a powerful means of exposing Richard's self-destructiveness, constitutes a bold reconceptualization of the historical Duke, who, even in the earlier pages of Holinshed, emerges as an arrogant, quarrelsome, ambitious, devious and self-aggrandizing noble, who was accused of plotting to 'destroie the king, and to vsurpe the crowne' (3.445), and who inspired much popular enmity.[1]

Shakespeare complicates the relationship between Richard and Bolingbroke as found in the chronicle by muting Richard's initial hostility to his cousin (it emerges only gradually in the play) and by making him confiscate his inheritance on the pretext of military necessity; no such excuse appears in Holinshed, who reports merely that the seizure made it 'euident, that the king meant his vtter vndooing' (3.496). The tragedy also complicates Bolingbroke's character by eliminating all mention of how the English nobles begged him to return from exile to 'take vpon him the scepter, rule, and diademe of his natiue land' (3.497). Shakespeare thus deprives Bolingbroke of any opportunity to claim that he re-entered England in response to popular demand. Rather he places the initiative for the invasion entirely upon the Duke himself, at the same time shortening the interval between his exile and return in such a way as to suggest that he had been planning his enterprise even before he could have known about the loss of his estates and, in fact, almost as soon as he could be sure that Richard had embarked for Ireland. It is notable too that when Holinshed gives his readers a choice about the size of the invading army owing to a prodigious discrepancy in his authorities, Shakespeare opts for the larger number (eight ships and three thousand men as against three ships and fifteen men) so as to make the threat against Richard as formidable as possible. Shakespeare's strategy is to veil the deeper motivations of both Richard and Bolingbroke from the beginning, allowing suggestions of darker or ulterior motives to

---

1 Daniel (1.30) describes Gaunt as 'Too great a subiect growne for such a state'.

occur from time to time without either completely confirming or dismissing them.

Significant omissions from Holinshed are revealing as well. Shakespeare keeps his focus on England by skipping over Richard's campaign in Ireland and (except for the detail of the blocked marriage)[1] Bolingbroke's activities in exile. Any emphasis on Richard as a stalwart general or on Bolingbroke as an international politician would obviously undermine the desired impression of the one's abjectness and of the other's cloudy motivation. The knighting of the future Prince Hal for his battle services in Ireland and Richard's holding him hostage as a weapon against Bolingbroke had to be rejected as working against reports of Hal's youthful laxity and King Henry's disappointment in his heir. Another significant omission is the mention of Edmund Mortimer's status as Richard's designated successor (3.511), which leaves the usurper in Shakespeare's play without any rival contender for the throne. The deliberate exclusion of Mortimer's claim has the effect of making Henry IV's accession seem historically more inevitable; and it has the further advantage of reserving Mortimer's political resentment for the rebellious coalition of *1 Henry IV.* Shakespeare also omits an important reason for Richard's calamitous delay in returning to defend his realm – namely Aumerle's bad advice to wait until 'he might haue all his ships, and other prouision, fullie readie for his passage' (3.499). This item, if included, might have forced Shakespeare to alter the relationship of trust and dependency between the King and his closest ally after Bushy, Bagot and Green have disappeared. The dramatist prefers to attribute Richard's return 'One day too late' (3.2.67) entirely to misfortune and bad weather rather than to his faulty judgement as a strategist.

Shakespeare's innovative concept of Richard's defeatist psychology accounts for one of the most striking omissions – Holinshed's account of how the King through the treachery of Northumberland

1   See 2.1.167–8LN.

was lured from Conway Castle under false pretences, trapped, captured and taken to Flint under guard. In the play, Richard despairingly discharges all his forces as soon as he hears the bad news of York's defection, then voluntarily chooses Flint Castle as a refuge (3.2.204–14); no betrayal or capture by Northumberland is involved. By shifting focus from the Machiavellian strategy of the King's enemies to his own passive emotionalism, the dramatist makes Richard himself almost as much the architect of his own defeat as was Bolingbroke. As Gaunt had warned, he is 'possessed now to depose [him]self' (2.1.108). Moreover, in Shakespeare, Bolingbroke is already so powerful militarily that he has no need of such underhand tactics as Holinshed ascribes to his deputy.

Of course, the coronation of Henry IV on which Holinshed dilates vanishes from the play, obviously because Shakespeare's subject is tragic failure and deposition, not conquest. And naturally the playwright suppresses the two less dramatic versions of Richard's death (the first by enforced famine, the second by self-starvation), preferring the more heroic account of Richard's assassination at the hands of Exton. The Exton story, though historically less reliable, was patently selected because it allowed for more exciting stage action and because it afforded the protagonist a kind of dignity lacking in the alternative accounts. By omission Shakespeare also greatly simplifies the Abbot's plot to murder Henry IV and reinstate Richard. The Earl of Huntingdon, ringleader of the conspiracy, is glancingly mentioned as Richard's 'trusty brother-in-law' (5.3.136), but Richard Maudelyn, the chaplain who was to impersonate Richard in a plan to deliver the King from prison (3.515), is entirely missing. Unlike Holinshed, the play leaps over the scattering of the conspirators, their capture and the bloodbath of their deaths.[1] Shakespeare opts only for a brief list of executed rebels, delivered to King Henry in the final scene, the object being to conclude the action with Henry's stringent justice, meant to balance the clemency granted Aumerle and

---

1   King Henry does allude to Cirencester, the town in Gloucestershire which 'the rebels have consumed with fire' (5.6.2); see 5.6.1–4n. and 7–16n.

16 Richard II's emblem, the white hart, from the back panel of the Wilton Diptych

Carlisle. Shakespeare also suppresses the Abbot of Westminster's original motive as given in Holinshed (3.514), namely his fear that Henry IV would diminish the power and wealth of the Church. To have introduced such self-interest as the engine behind the attempt to restore Richard would have soiled what the dramatist wished to present as the passionate, if misguided, idealism of the legitimists and thus to lessen the symbolic magnitude of Richard's dethronement. Other Holinshed matter omitted includes Gloucester's past as a fractious troublemaker, the main reason for his being eliminated (contradicted by Gaunt in the play, who refers to his dead brother as a 'plain well-meaning soul' (2.1.128)); Bolingbroke's cautious waiting offshore until he can be certain of his reception in England (a detail that might reinforce too strongly earlier suggestions of the Duke's sinister motives); the refusal of Richard's loyal Gascon adherent, Jenico d'Artois, to put off his master's emblem, the white hart, after Richard's capture (replaced by the invented episode of the Groom – see 5.5.66n. and Fig. 16); the role of the Archbishop of Canterbury (an ally of Bolingbroke whom Richard had banished but who returned to England with the usurper) in persuading Richard to renounce his throne while the King was still in Wales (an episode that would rob Richard's self-deposition before Parliament of its climax); Richard's giving of his signet-ring to Bolingbroke (replaced in the play by his offering up the crown and sceptre); the foray into England by the Scots shortly after Henry's accession (an irrelevant distraction from Shakespeare's purposes); and the preparations in France for a military incursion to save Richard's life but aborted when the French loyalists learned of the King's death (another irrelevancy).

Although Holinshed was his principal resource, Shakespeare's inventions bulk surprisingly large in the final result. Of the nineteen scenes that make up the tragedy, four have no parallel in Holinshed at all: Gaunt's interview with Gloucester's widow (1.2), Aumerle's conversation with Richard about Bolingbroke's departure (1.4), the garden scene (3.4) and the dolorous separation of Richard from his queen (5.1). The same can be claimed for substantial portions of nine others: Bolingbroke's farewell to his father (1.3.253–309); Richard's visit to the dying Gaunt including the famous aria on England (2.1.1–146); the Queen's colloquy with Bushy concerning her premonitions of disaster (2.2.1–40); the 'woeful pageant' of Richard's self-martyrdom before Parliament and his shattering of the mirror (4.1.163–318); York's sad retrospective of Richard's humiliation in the London streets (5.2.1–40);[1] Henry IV's worries about his wayward son (5.3.1–22); the semi-farcical pleading contest between York and his duchess over Aumerle's fate (5.3.73–135); the vignette of the Groom and 'roan Barbary' (5.5.67–94); and Exton's presentation of Richard's corpse to Henry IV together with the latter's repudiation of the murderer (5.6.30–44).[2] These episodes put flesh on Holinshed's bones.

A handful of examples will illustrate the artistic magnitude of Shakespeare's additions. His introduction of three female characters, mere shadows or names in the chronicle, tends to humanize the political environment of the play and circumscribe its harshness. In terms of statecraft, all three are marginal, but they enrich the tragedy by reflecting personal and family concerns, thereby helping to establish an important tension of the drama. In their anguish and grief, the women soften the tone of the play (Gloucester's widow is partly an exception) and help to shape audience responses in the direction of greater pathos and away from judgemental severity. Gaunt's early scene with his sister-in-law sheds new light on Richard's guilt in the matter of Gloucester's death and establishes the motif of vengeance, a value

1 The image of 'dust thrown upon his [Richard's] sacred head' (5.2.30) is a typically Shakespearean heightening. Holinshed (3.501) says only that when Richard, who was accustomed to 'sumptuous' dress, was conducted to London as Bolingbroke's prisoner, he was not 'permitted all this while to change his apparell, but rode still through all these townes simplie clothed in one sute of raiment'.

2 R.M. Smith (153) claims erroneously that Henry's disavowment of Exton derives from Daniel. The passage on which Smith bases his contention does not, however, appear in the 1595 edition of the *Civil Wars*; rather it was added in the 1609 revision of the poem and is probably the best evidence we possess that by then Daniel had been sufficiently impressed by Shakespeare's play, either in print or in performance, to imitate several of its details.

rejected by the venerable patriot but partly taken up (in the guise of political necessity) by his ambitious son.

The garden scene, choric in function, objectifies the failures of Richard's reign by casting them allegorically into the mode of pastoral, by means of which the green world reflects disorder in the state. The fruitful processes of horticulture are made to comment from below on great affairs at court, while implying that violations in the proper ordering of a kingdom must be viewed as breaches of natural law and ultimately therefore of divine imperatives. The verdant setting creates associations with Gaunt's vision of England as 'This other Eden, demi-paradise' (2.1.42) and with the play's matrix of blood and growth imagery; also its placement near the centre of the action creates a kind of temporary stasis or pause for reflection that allows for an expansion and development of the play's thematic ideas – ideas expressed earlier or in prospect.

The invented episode with the mirror taps into a complex iconography of medieval and Renaissance ideas, brilliantly dramatizing the title figure as at once narcissist, self-deceiver, victim of flattery, seeker after self-knowledge, escapist from reality and destroyer of his own identity, while associating these personal roles with the literary traditions of *de casibus* tragedy (*The Mirror for Magistrates*) and historical or moral truth itself as exemplified in such titles as Richard of Cirencester's *Speculum Historiale de Gestis Regum Angliae* (*c.* 1385–1400), Gascoigne's *Glass of Government* (1575) and Lodge and Greene's *A Looking Glass for London and England* (1587–91).

Shakespeare's decision to have Exton present Richard's corpse to Henry IV has the clear advantage of closing the tragedy with a stately procession of mourning, as in *Edward II*. But it also implicates the new king directly in the guilt of Richard's murder and effectively underscores the burden of his illegitimacy, even though he tries to compensate by disavowing Exton as a latter-day Cain and by promising to purge his crime by a voyage to the Holy Land. In the open-ended way that characterizes history plays as a genre, Shakespeare suggests through this innovation that one

135

unhappy king has been succeeded by a monarch as potentially tragic as the man he has displaced.

Hall

Hall's chronicle, much of which Holinshed absorbed, had already served Shakespeare in the first tetralogy, so that its general influence on *Richard II* can hardly be doubted. Commencing with the quarrel between Bolingbroke and Mowbray, this narrative shares a point of departure with the play. And Hall entitles his account of Richard's fall 'An Introduccion into the History of Kyng Henry the Fourthe', thus treating it, like Shakespeare, as the necessary prelude to the 'Vnquiete Tyme' of the successor. Hall embeds his events in a teleological context absent from Holinshed, who was more interested in year-by-year details than in any grand historical design or providential pattern. His opening paragraph sets the historiographical agenda by stressing the 'miserie', the 'murder' and 'execrable plagues' England 'suffered by the deuision and discension of the . . . houses of Lancastre and Yorke' (fol. i) – a passage that sounds very like Carlisle's vision of doom in Shakespeare's play (4.1.138–9). Hall indeed seems to have been the dramatist's principal authority for the idea that the deposition and murder of Richard were the seeds from which sprang the internecine bloodshed of the following century – a 'second fall of cursed man' (3.4.76) as the Queen phrases it. Hall's theological outlook, derived to some extent from Polydore Vergil, is apparent in his generalizations on the virtues of union over division: as manhood and Godhead were joined in the Incarnation, thus repairing the separation caused by Adam and Eve, so the union of Henry of Richmond and Elizabeth of York finally restored the harmony breached by the quarrels of Richard II's reign and his dethronement – 'the originall cause and fountain' of the divisions that beset the nation afterwards (fol. iᵛ). The so-called Tudor myth, drawn from Hall's work by commentators such as Tillyard and Lily B. Campbell, undoubtedly represents a gross oversimplification. But since aspects of this viewpoint influenced

Shakespeare in *Henry VI* and *Richard III*, and since he specifically linked the two tetralogies in his epilogue to *Henry V*, it is reasonable to assume that his memory of Hall carried over in general terms to the first play of the later group. And the symbolism of Eden, of Cain and Abel, and of Christ's Passion that Shakespeare introduces into *Richard II* are consistent with Hall's emphasis even if these specific details do not explicitly originate in his chronicle.

Whereas Holinshed tends to take a somewhat constitutional view of government, Hall is more interested in personality. Mowbray and Bolingbroke, for instance, are portrayed more colourfully by the earlier historian and with a somewhat different bias. Hall refers to the first as 'bothe a depe dissimuler and a pleasaunte flaterer' (fol. ii^v) and to the second as 'a prudente and politike persone, but not more politike then welbeloued, and yet not so welbeloued of all, as of some highly disdayned' (fol. ii). Hall stresses Bolingbroke's deviousness more strongly than Holinshed. Only in the former, for instance, does the Duke dissemble his reason for leaving Paris for Brittany, knowing that Charles VI would prevent him from unseating his son-in-law, were he aware of his true intention. But Hall is also balder than Holinshed in asserting that, once assured of popular support in England, Bolingbroke 'was clerely determyned to depose kynge Rycharde from his rule and dignitie' (fol. vi); Hall also speaks of Richard as Henry's 'longe desyred praye' (fol. vi^v) and reports that, once the King was in his power, he 'gaped and thrusted' for the crown (fol. viii). Shakespeare's characterization of both men is more subtle and ambiguous than Hall's, but the less attractive aspects of each as suggested in the play could have taken their inception from Hall's chronicle. An additional point to be considered is Hall's account of how the quarrel between Mowbray and Bolingbroke came about. Hall differs from Holinshed in making Bolingbroke criticize Richard confidentially to Mowbray and then having Mowbray betray his confidence to the King; Holinshed has Bolingbroke accusing Mowbray directly for uttering treasonous statements.[1] Although Shakespeare is closer in detail to Holinshed than to Hall at this point, the climate of ambiguity and intrigue in the opening scene may well owe something to Hall's version. It is worth noting too that, unlike Holinshed, Hall omits Richard's activities in Ireland, protesting that these are 'no parte of my processe' (fol. iiii^v).

Despite some evidence of Hall's ideological colouration of the play, it seems unlikely that Shakespeare had this chronicle open before him as he wrote. Very few verbal links between it and Shakespeare have been discovered, and those that can be or have been adduced involve words whose commonness or special contexts make them easy to explain as coincidences or virtual necessities.[2] It seems fairly clear, then, that Hall's contribution to *Richard II* was general rather than specific.

The Mirror for Magistrates

The issue of Shakespeare's indebtedness to the *Mirror* can be similarly resolved. Its general influence is obvious enough in the *de casibus* concept and structure of *Richard II*, in the 'sad stories of the death of kings' (3.2.156) with which Richard associates his own tragedy and in the invented episode of the mirror, which may be taken in part as a glancing allusion to the most popular of the many sixteenth-century works whose titles contain the emblematic word. In addition to the first five poems of the collection (on Tresilian, an earlier favourite of Richard; on Mortimer, Richard's designated heir; on Gloucester, Richard's troublesome uncle; on Mowbray; and on the deposed monarch himself), two others on Northumberland and Salisbury (the seventh and ninth poems in Baldwin's sequence) describe the falls of men who figure prominently as characters

---

1 See also *Mirror* (110) where Baldwin, in one of his prose links, says that for 'Lord Mowbray' he has followed Hall in making Mowbray the accuser, whereas Fabyan 'reporteth the matter quite contrary . . . makyng Boleynbroke the accuser', although the 'matter . . . is harde to desise [decide]'. On this point Holinshed is in line with Fabyan rather than Hall.

2 See 2.1.4n., 267n., 3.3.12–14n., 4.1.99n., 5.2.41–117n. and 62–3n.

in the drama.[1] The famous anthology of notable unfortunates
was a regular source for the writers of chronicle plays (almost
certainly including Shakespeare himself in 3 *Henry VI* and
Richard III)[2] for, its subject matter apart, the volume struck an
uneasy balance between two concepts useful to dramatists – on
the one hand, the medieval fatalism of inscrutable chance and the
inherent instability of the human lot, and, on the other, the more
didactic idea of Fortune as the instrument of God's retribution
in a moral universe. Also Baldwin's preachy dedication implicitly
endorses the divine right of kings, the principle to which
Shakespeare's title figure clings so tenaciously.[3] It would be
astonishing if Shakespeare had not made himself familiar with
these poems in at least a cursory way, especially since, like Hall's
chronicle, they offer a moral framework for the fall-of-princes
theme and provide a starting point for future disasters in much
the same way as *Richard II* lays a foundation for the later histories. But, as in the case of Hall, it is difficult to establish specific
indebtedness. Generally speaking, the *Mirror* is much more hostile to Richard than is Shakespeare, at one place characterizing
him as 'dispising god and all good lawes' (134; 'Henry, Earl of
Northumberland', l. 52). The treatment of Mowbray is equally
condemnatory and much less ambiguously nuanced than
Shakespeare's. These differences, of course, can be largely
explained by the heavily didactic and essentially undramatic
nature of Baldwin's genre. As the few verbal similarities between

---

1 The Salisbury of the *Mirror* (143–53) is Thomas de Montacute, fourth Earl and son
of Richard II's loyal ally in Shakespeare's play; he died by gunshot at the siege of
Orleans in the reign of Henry VI (see List of Roles, 20n.). Baldwin's ninth tragedy
nevertheless includes the story of the abortive plot to 'restore kyng Richard' (l. 49),
mentioning Aumerle's betrayal of the conspirators' plans and the third Earl's execution 'in iust pursute' (l. 19) of an honourable cause. The poem also alludes to Henry
IV's attempt 'to starve' Richard in prison (l. 39) and to the 'tiranny and wrong' of
Gloucester's murder (ll. 34–5).
2 See Campbell, 308–9, 319–20; Bullough, 3.159, 211–17, 232–3, 301–5.
3 'For it is Gods owne office, yea his chiefe office, whych they [rulers] beare & abuse.
For as Iustice is the chief vertue, so is the ministracion therof, the chiefest office: &
therfore hath God established it with the chiefest name, honoring & calling Kinges
. . . by his owne name, Gods' (*Mirror*, 65).

139

Shakespeare and the *Mirror* are equally uncompelling, it seems safest to conclude that, like Hall, the anthology served the dramatist more as an influence than a direct source.

Daniel

Daniel's *Civil Wars*, his epic on the Wars of the Roses, stands as a source of the play second in importance only to Holinshed. Preparing for his long narrative in *ottava rima*, Daniel seems to have read widely, consulting Froissart, Polydore Vergil, Walsingham, Fabyan, Grafton, Hall, Holinshed, Stow and other historians. Indeed, by drawing his materials from a broad spectrum of sources and freely imagining incidents and aspects of character as Sidney had recommended in his *Apology* (111), he may have set Shakespeare an example. Although Daniel's effort is unfinished (it extends only into the reign of Edward IV), its intended coverage and perspective are like Hall's, beginning (after a survey of previous kings) with the reign of Richard II and continuing, had the plan been fulfilled, to the death of Richard III. This is the time span of Shakespeare's two tetralogies. The outlook is equally like Hall's and probably derived therefrom. Daniel's controlling theme is the 'tumultuous broyles / And bloudy factions' (1.1) that followed the deposition of Richard II, whose 'reign began this fatal strife' (1.28) – horrors that did not run their full course until the Tudors came to power. Daniel incorporates the idea of a chain of crimes issuing from the initial crimes of Richard's reign, underscoring, like Shakespeare (if the individual plays are taken as a panorama), a sense of history as repetitive and cyclical. The same attitude can be discerned in *Richard II*, not only in Carlisle's prophecy but also in Richard's prediction of Northumberland's treason and in Henry IV's guilty beginning of what is obviously to be a troubled reign. Like the contributors to the *Mirror*, Daniel conceives of his purpose as didactic: ''tis good to learn by others' woes' (1.28). Hence we get lengthy meditative and moralistic passages that impede the forward momentum of the action. Like Sidney's *Arcadia* and the first three books of Spenser's *Faerie*

Queene, both published in 1590, the first instalment of the *Civil Wars* was an important literary event – an attempt to do for England what Lucan's *Pharsalia* had done for civil war in Rome. It would be remarkable if Shakespeare had not taken a lively interest in the poem, especially as he had previously used Daniel's *Complaint of Rosamond* as a model for his *Rape of Lucrece*.

The numerous similarities of thought, situation and wording that link Shakespeare's play to Daniel, although distributed throughout the play, tend to increase in frequency in the final two acts.[1] Act 5 contains the heaviest concentration, since it is here that Shakespeare dramatizes the parting of the royal lovers, makes York contrast the demeanours of Bolingbroke and Richard in the London streets, portrays Exton's decision to murder the King and stages Richard's meditation in prison. All these elements, or particular details connected with them, seem to derive largely from the *Civil Wars*. Daniel's protracted section (2.71–98) describing the Queen's grief before and during her final meeting with Richard is sheer invention but constitutes a major set-piece of evocative pathos in the tradition of the complaint. The same can be said in lesser degree of Daniel's portrayal of Richard's thoughts at Pomfret (3.63–71). Such salient aspects of the poem would be difficult to ignore, and although Shakespeare contributes his own very different tone and content to the stage version of these episodes, it is fairly clear that Daniel sparked his imagination. Some of the parallels of word and thought could have come to Shakespeare and Daniel independently; and others may simply represent the fortuitous appearance of ideas or images that would be common or expected in similar contexts. But there are too many parallels of thought and language in cognate situations to be explained as mere coincidence. Full details appear in the commentary notes; here it is enough to mention several of the more suggestive links by way of illustration.

---

1   The scenes that seem most clearly indebted to Daniel are 2.1, 3.2, 3.3, 4.1 and all six scenes of Act 5. Although Shakespeare must have read all four books of the *Civil Wars* in the 1595 edition, Books 1 and 2 appear to have been the most influential.

Gaunt's praise of England connects insularity with the notion of protection from foreign diseases and corrupting influences (2.1.43–9), a point also in Daniel (4.90), where it is suggestively associated with the 'contagion' of civil strife (4.43, 90), another of Gaunt's complaints (2.1.65–6). Both Daniel and *Richard II* invoke the power of rivers as a natural force, the first to describe the rush of defectors to Bolingbroke's cause (2.7–8), the second to make vivid the 'rage' of the usurper and his army (3.2.109–11). Both passages wittily exploit the pun on Bolingbroke's name, the last syllable of which must be pronounced 'brook'.[1] Images of the rising and setting sun appear in both Daniel (2.1) and Shakespeare as emblems of the shift from 'Richard's night to Bolingbroke's fair day' (3.2.218), and both also employ the idea of civil war besmirching peaceful landscapes with slaughter (1.121; 3.3.96–7). Carlisle's self-deprecating rhetoric as invented by Daniel (3.22) seems to have influenced Shakespeare's corresponding speech (4.1.116), which contains additional verbal echoes from the same context. Three further parallels make Daniel's influence upon *Richard II* virtually undeniable: Richard's projection of the Queen listening to sad stories in France and responding with his own 'lamentable tale' (5.1.40–4; cf. Daniel, 3.65); Richard's prophecy that Northumberland will betray King Henry, including the idea of the Earl as Henry's 'ladder' (5.1.55–6, 59–68; cf. Daniel, 2.3, 15); and the concept of the parting lovers combining their grief to 'make one woe' (5.1.86; cf. Daniel, 2.91). That all three should occur in the same Shakespearean scene, and are also fairly close to each other in Daniel (within thirty-four pages), is probably more than mere coincidence. Although the most striking links with Daniel are often more conceptual than linguistic, a scattering of purely verbal echoes appears as well; see, for example, 2.3.148–9n., 4.1.142n., 208n., 328n., 5.3.10n., 5.4.2n. and 7n.

---

1   Earlier in his poem Daniel also compares the warlike faction of the English nobility, frustrated by Richard's new-made peace with France, to a river overrunning its banks (1.84); Daniel identifies this unrest as one of the causes of the 'Home broiles' that prepared the ground for Bolingbroke's 'Soueraintie' (1.85).

Apart from his significant thematic and stylistic influence, Daniel contributed also to characterization in the play. Here the most obvious indebtedness appears in the Queen, whom Hall and Holinshed marginalize but who in the poem becomes the emotional centre of Book 2. Daniel appears to have taken his cue for her prominence as well as her womanliness from Froissart, who, without giving an exact age, reports that 'for all that she was but yonge, ryght plesauntly she bare the porte of a quene' (6.190). Shakespeare was clearly impressed by Daniel's artful elaboration of her grief, not only adopting the poem's unhistorical occasion for a final meeting, but also preparing for the intensity of its pathos by inventing two earlier scenes (2.2 and 3.4) in which she figures as a heavy-hearted commentator on her husband's plight. In Daniel, then, Shakespeare found a means of reflecting Richard's suffering through a loyal and non-political adjunct to the action. But, even without the Queen, Shakespeare would have discovered in Daniel a treatment of Richard more sympathetic than he could have found in the English chroniclers. By mentioning York's 'milde sprite' and preference for 'quiet and safe delight' (1.30), Daniel may have provided Shakespeare with a hint of York's passivity. But, apart from the characters already mentioned, the most influential for the playwright's purposes was probably Bolingbroke. Daniel makes the Duke's 'Belou'd' standing with the people the reason for his exile (1.64), then launches into a complex analysis of his true motives in returning to seize power, couched in the form of a debate. In a dream the Genius of England warns him of the dire consequences of his actions: 'The babes vnborne, shall ô be borne to bleed / In this thy quarrell if thou doe proceede' (1.90).[1] But the dreamer counters that he has come as his country's 'Champion' (1.91), to seek justice not only for himself but for others. The Genius responds that he is a self-deceiver who disguises his ambition even from himself. Once

---

1   Cf. Richard's reference to 'Your children, yet unborn and unbegot' (3.3.88) and Carlisle's warning, 'The children yet unborn / Shall feel this day as sharp to them as thorn' (4.1.322–3).

awake, Bolingbroke dismisses the dream and gets on with the aggressive politics to which both Fortune and his own pride have impelled him. Daniel takes the position that 'the heauens, fate and fortune' brought Henry 'to [his] scepter easily' (1.85), but leaves open the question of whether he did 'meane as [he did] swere' (1.95) in claiming that his sole purpose was the recovery of his lands and family title. By preserving the same fruitful ambiguity, the dramatist treads in Daniel's footsteps.

Woodstock

After Holinshed and Daniel, the anonymous untitled play known today as *Woodstock* stands third in importance as a source for *Richard II*. We know nothing of the theatrical auspices under which this manuscript drama on Richard II's murdered uncle came into being; but that Shakespeare attended a performance, or acted in the play, or somehow became familiar with the promptbook seems more than probable.[1] Possibly, as Chambers suggests, it was acquired by the Chamberlain's Men and became part of their repertory, although there is no evidence of this.[2] The drama is a neo-morality in which the conflict between good and evil is chiefly generational. Virtue resides with the old nobility represented by the King's uncles (Lancaster (Gaunt), York and, principally, Woodstock (Gloucester)), while corruption, vice and irresponsibility are represented by the young (King Richard and his parasitical favourites – Bushy, Bagot, Greene, Scroope and the arch-villain Tresilian). The older men, who espouse venerable native traditions, wear beards and favour simplicity of dress. The more youthful courtiers, who embody recklessness, extravagance, extortion and disregard of national welfare, are (except for Tresilian) clean-shaven and go in for foppish and newfangled foreign

---

1 Ure is cautious, owing largely to the question of *Woodstock*'s priority to *Richard II* (see my discussion, pp. 116–7); he admits that 'there is a relation of some kind between' the two plays (xxxviii).

2 See Chambers, *ES*, 4.43. Elson (187–8), who discerns parallels of character, situation and language between *Woodstock* and *1 Henry IV*, thinks it likely that *Woodstock* belonged to Shakespeare's company.

clothing. Richard, far from being evil incarnate, is on the wrong side of this balance throughout most of the play, having been led into vicious policies by the flatterers who surround him. Near the end, however, the death of his beloved queen, Anne of Bohemia, awakens him to a sense of his impious folly, and he tries unsuccessfully to prevent the murder of Woodstock that he had earlier authorized.[1] Possibly Richard's remorse and conversion to rectitude marked the conclusion of the play more emphatically than is true of the text we possess; but the final page of the manuscript in which alone it survives is missing. Still, it would have been difficult to dramatize a totally reformed Richard who casts off his corruptors, for if audiences knew nothing else about this king, they surely knew of his deposition and death – historical facts that even this liberty-taking dramatist could scarcely have circumvented. Woodstock's murder provokes an unhistorical rebellion led by his brothers, Lancaster and York, unorthodoxly condoned by the ghosts of Edward III and the Black Prince, who appear to Woodstock in a dream just before he is killed. After the evil forces have been defeated in battle, are facing execution or have been driven into flight, the last we hear of Richard is that he will retire to the Tower for security, although Tresilian alleges that he has been 'taken prisoner by the peers' (5.5.9).

Woodstock has occasionally been regarded as a play to which Shakespeare's drama formed a continuation and conclusion.[2] This view is obviously mistaken since the plots of the two dramas do not mesh. In the earlier piece, the fictional Lapoole, rather than Mowbray (as in Shakespeare), organizes Woodstock's

---

1   An earlier pang of guilt has already struck Richard as he is about to 'Rent out our kingdom like a pelting farm' (4.1.147) – a twinge of conscience quickly suppressed.

2   F.S. Boas in 1902 argued that the play was 'an indispensable fore-piece' to *Richard II* (Forker, 382). Wolfgang Keller, in an edition of 1899 printed in the *Shakespeare Jahrbuch* (35.3–121), adopted the title, *Richard II, Erster Teil*; Wilhelmina Frijlinck entitled her 1929 Malone Society edition *The First Part of the Reign of King Richard the Second, or Thomas of Woodstock*; and E.K. Chambers's label in 1923 (*ES*, 4.42–3) was *I Richard the Second*. Hardin Craig, pointing out the puzzlingly incomplete background information about Gloucester's murder in Shakespeare's *Richard II* (1.1), averred that it must be 'part two of a two-part play' (Craig, *Interpretation*, 126), whether or not we regard *Woodstock* as constituting part one.

murder, which is accomplished not by beheading but by strangling and stifling with a feather bed; and Lancaster promises the widow that he will avenge the death of her husband, whereas in Shakespeare he refuses the same request. Moreover, Bushy, Bagot and Green, who ride high in Richard's favour during the early acts of *Richard II*, are already dead, captured or fugitive by the end of the anonymous play. *Woodstock* is chronologically inconsistent with Shakespeare's tragedy, fancifully introducing Bushy, Bagot and Green as characters contemporary with Tresilian and Queen Anne. These latter, as Holinshed makes clear, actually belonged to an earlier phase of Richard's reign before the abduction of Gloucester.[1] Bolingbroke is entirely absent from the action, an oddity for 'Part 1' of a theoretically two-part drama, since, historically, the political careers of Bolingbroke and Gloucester had been much entangled. Any spectator who tried to follow the action of *Richard II* after seeing *Woodstock* would be hopelessly confused.

Nevertheless, the impact of the earlier play upon *Richard II* is profound and pervasive, especially in the first two acts. Both plays introduce the Duchess of Gloucester seeking vengeance for her husband at the hands of Gaunt, an incident missing from the chronicles. Shakespeare's Gaunt refers to his murdered brother as 'plain well-meaning soul' (2.1.128), an almost certain allusion to the Gloucester of *Woodstock*, who repeatedly calls himself 'Plain Thomas' on account of his forthright speech and homely dress. Beyond this, however, Gaunt himself seems to be modelled on the plain-spoken Woodstock of the earlier drama and is most unlike the treacherous, ambitious and quarrelsome noble whom Shakespeare would have met in Holinshed.[2] Indeed Shakespeare's character, in

---

1 See also Bullough, 3.360.
2 Dr Simon Forman reported seeing a different drama on the reign of Richard II at the Globe on 30 April 1611. The play is lost, but it apparently included a plot devised by Lancaster (Gaunt) to stir up hatred against Richard and replace him with his own son (Bolingbroke) as king. The Gaunt of this play was uncommonly cruel and Machiavellian: after encouraging 'a wise man' to speak his mind, he had him hanged for predicting that Bolingbroke would one day be king, merely to suppress rumours of the family's secret ambition. See Chambers, *WS*, 2.339–40.

his function as spokesman for the highest values of English monarchy, as champion of the common people and as outspoken critic of Richard, fulfils precisely the role of statesmanlike counsellor that Woodstock plays in the anonymous drama.[1]

Apart from the Woodstock–Gaunt parallel, suggestions for other characters of *Richard II* may have come from *Woodstock*. Whereas the Lancaster of the anonymous play is entirely different from Shakespeare's Gaunt, being hot-headed and irascible, York, whom Richard in *Woodstock* calls 'relenting' (2.1.49) and later 'gentle' and 'mild and generous' (2.1.126), conforms more closely to Shakespeare's portrait. Queen Anne, like Queen Isabel, is shown sorrowing in distress (2.3). And even King Richard in *Woodstock*, although possessing none of the psychological complexity or verbal brilliance of Shakespeare's monarch, shows touches of the vanity, petulance and childish perversity that mark the Richard of the later drama before his return from Ireland; since he takes part in a masque (4.2), he may even foreshadow the player-king of *Richard II*. Other similarities between the two plays, though less exclusive to them alone, are worth noting. A long passage in *Woodstock* on fashions including the mention of 'Italian cloaks' (2.3.88–95) might have suggested Richard's 'base imitation' of 'fashions in proud Italy' (2.1.21–3); 'flakes of fire' in the sky and other portents of Queen Anne's impending death (4.2.67–8) are similar in tone to those mentioned by the Welsh Captain as foreboding 'the death or fall of kings' (2.4.7–15); the two murderers (Lapoole in *Woodstock*, Exton in *Richard II*) both experience qualms of conscience (*Woodstock*, 5.1.32–44; *R2* 5.5.113–16); and both murder scenes feature the use of off-stage music as a means of establishing a mood of relaxation before the violence (*Woodstock*, 5.1.51–3; *R2* 5.5.41–61), though the contexts are utterly different.

---

1 A contributing influence may have been the character of good Duke Humphrey in Shakespeare's own *2 Henry VI*. In both plays the analogous figures (Humphrey and Woodstock) are styled 'Lord Protector'. Wilson (xlv, n. 1) argues that Shakespeare's Gaunt is based mainly on Froissart.

Also *Richard II* is mysteriously unclear about the details of Gloucester's murder as well as vague about how the blank charters and the farming of the realm actually operated. *Woodstock* makes these matters unmistakably clear. Whether or not Shakespeare counted on audience familiarity with the money-raising abuses, assuming that they had been amply explained in the earlier play, it seems probable that he relied on the explanations himself (even though the main outlines were available in Holinshed).

The most telling evidence of Shakespeare's reliance on *Woodstock*, however, lies in the verbal echoes, which are far too prominent to be coincidental. Some could be unconscious borrowings while others may involve the use of common phrases or conventional images such as the epithets for the favourites: 'caterpillars of the commonwealth' (2.3.166), 'vipers' (3.2.129) and 'noisome weeds' (3.4.38); compare *Woodstock*, 1.3.158, 5.3.30 and 5.6.4. Several, at least, would appear to be direct appropriations: Gaunt's complaint that Richard has become 'Landlord of England . . . not king' (2.1.113)[1] and that his realm is 'now leased out . . . Like to a tenement or pelting farm' (2.1.59–60);[2] also Ross's statement, 'The commons hath he pilled with grievous taxes' (2.1.246; cf. *Woodstock*, 1.3.112), and Bagot's farewell to his fellows, 'We three here part that ne'er shall meet again' (2.2.142; cf. *Woodstock*, 3.2.102–5). At least sixteen additional verbal parallels between the two plays must be mentioned (see 1.2.38n., 1.3.140n., 153n., 2.1.69n., 77n., 205n., 241–2n., 247, 248n., 262n., 2.2.98n., 100n., 3.2.79n., 126n., 4.1.283n. and 5.2.75n.). It can hardly be an accident that seven of these echoes are concentrated in a single scene of *Richard II* and that almost all the others fall within the first half of the play. Two of them, moreover – 'upon pain of life' (1.3.140, 153) and 'God for His mercy' (2.2.98 and

---

1   See *Woodstock*, 4.1.146, 210, 244, 5.1.90 and 5.3.106–7. As Ure (xxxviii) points out, 'There is no parallel in Holinshed or elsewhere to this five-times repeated reproach' (except in Hayward's 1599 work on Henry IV).

2   The word 'pelting' in the *Woodstock* manuscript (4.1.147) is smudged and has been overwritten; the original may read 'peltry', which means the same thing. Even so, the similarity of the two speeches is unlikely to be accidental.

5.2.75) – occur nowhere else in Shakespeare; admittedly, the first appears in Froissart, but not in contexts likely to have influenced Shakespeare.

In addition to the verbal links, we may note several parallels of idea or situation. In Shakespeare Gaunt concludes his great speech on England with, 'Ah, would the scandal vanish with my life, / How happy then were my ensuing death!' (2.1.67–8). Woodstock's words in the earlier play express the same idea: 'I would my death might end the misery' (3.2.108), and, ironically, he repeats the sentiment just before he is killed: 'I wish my death might ease my country's grief' (5.1.128). Within a few lines of his wish for death Shakespeare's Gaunt is also appalled that his realm, 'Dear for her reputation through the world', 'that was wont to conquer others', has 'made a shameful conquest of itself' (2.1.58, 65–6). The momentarily remorseful Richard of *Woodstock* says something similar, accusing himself of having become the mere renter-out of a nation 'That erst was held . . . The maiden conqueress to all the world' (4.1.148–9). Continuing to lament the sorry state of Richard's rule, Shakespeare's dying Gaunt comments on the shameful irony that the grandson of Edward III 'should destroy his sons' (2.1.105), presumably Gloucester and his brothers. Again Shakespeare's meaning is clarified by reference to *Woodstock*, to the phrase 'my accursed grandchild' uttered by the ghost of Edward III, who speaks of Richard's 'ruinat[ing]' the 'lives' of Woodstock and the other royal dukes (5.1.86–9). In Shakespeare Northumberland represents Bolingbroke as swearing 'by the honourable tomb' of Edward III (3.3.105–6), an idea the dramatist probably picked up from York's similar gesture in *Woodstock*: 'even by my birth I swear, / My father's tomb' (2.1.142–3). Once more it should be observed that three of these four parallels cluster in the scene of *Richard II* (2.1) that contains so many of the verbal echoes.

Despite the many details, linguistic and otherwise, that link Shakespeare's tragedy to *Woodstock*, differences between the two plays remain more significant than the likenesses, for they appear, superficially at least, to embody opposed theories of monarchy – contractual versus sacramental. Marie Axton, who has analysed the politics of *Woodstock*, calls the anonymous author 'unconventional and audacious' (97) in defending by implication the treasonous proposition that, to quote Stavropoulos, 'subjects oppressed by tyrannical rule may understandably rebel against their king'(1). Two royal dukes, Lancaster and York, seditiously take up arms against their sovereign, intending to 'call [him] to a strict account', not only for Woodstock's death but 'for his realm's misgovernment' (5.3.20–1). The peers take the view that, having violated his coronation oath, Richard has broken faith with his realm and is therefore no longer worthy of the crown. Even Woodstock, who remains loyal to Richard unto death, gives utterance in a moment of frustration to a position that the *Homilies* would certainly condemn: 'Let me be chronicled Apostata, / Rebellious to my king and country both!' (3.2.77–8). In contrast, Shakespeare's play with its stress on the mystique of kingship, which contains Gaunt's policy of non-resistance to God's anointed as well as Carlisle's horror of rebellion, would appear to steer well to the right of the *Woodstock* dramatist.

Politically, however, *Woodstock* is less univocal than might at first appear. If the shade of Edward III urges Woodstock to 'join' the rebellion against Richard in order to avoid being murdered (5.1.100–3), he stops short of endorsing tyrannicide. Moreover, Woodstock retreats from the supposed reality of the ghost's injunction and the dream-vision by which it had reached him: 'Twas but my fancy: / All's whist [hushed] and still, and nothing here appears / But the vast circuit of this empty room' (5.1.112–14). In other places also *Woodstock* undercuts its apparent heterodoxy by putting into the mouths of sympathetic characters speeches that recognize and support the conventional tenets of divine-right conservatism. Queen Anne, for instance, opines that although Richard 'Neglects, and throws his sceptre carelessly', misled as he is by flatterers, 'Yet none dares rob him of his kingly rule' (2.3.41–2). Woodstock himself is the most vocal defender of orthodoxy. Fearing rebellion from the oppressed commons, he nevertheless will 'tell them plain / We all are struck – but must not strike again' (3.2.112–13). When he entertains the masquers at Plashey (Pleshy), he is fearlessly critical of Richard, yet he nevertheless adds:

> But he's our king: and God's great deputy;
> And if ye hunt to have me second ye
> In any rash attempt against his state,
> Afore my God, I'll ne'er consent unto it.
>
> (4.2.144–7)

Even as the murderers enter under royal sanction to dispatch him, he is able to say of Richard, 'though here I spend my blood – / I wish his safety . . . and all England's good' (5.1.211–12).

As Axton (97) observes, by presenting such contradictory views in the same play, the *Woodstock* author 'questioned axioms of the theory of the king's two bodies'. In a much subtler way, by manipulating audience sympathies both towards and away from Richard and Bolingbroke, Shakespeare dramatized something of the same ambivalence. It is possible then that, apart from debts of characterization and verbal indebtedness to *Woodstock*, Shakespeare found already available in the anonymous play a dramatically fruitful dubiety that could serve his own purposes as a maker of tragedy. A single illustration may help to make the point. In *Woodstock*, where we see Richard actually renting out the kingdom to his four favourites, the scene shows us a king who, by quartering his realm, actually shatters the unity of his political body by an act of self-alienation and self-dispersion. As Lancaster wryly puts it, 'we have four kings more, are equalled with him: / There's Bagot, Bushy, wanton Greene, and Scroope / In state and fashion without difference' (3.2.40–2). In effect, Richard has destroyed his identity as king by sharing out and thereby obliterating his uniqueness. Later on, when he disguises himself in the masque (the device by which Woodstock is kidnapped) and then refuses to reveal himself, he symbolically confirms this loss of identity.[1] As Edgar Schell puts it, 'the author of *Woodstock* imagined Richard's fall as the loss of his likeness to himself' (88). Shakespeare's Richard is much occupied with the nature of his own identity and its destruction, claiming that even his 'name' has been 'usurped' (4.1.255–7), imagining himself 'a mockery king of snow' melting himself away 'in water-drops' (4.1.260–2), and fracturing the glass that reflects his intolerably diminished self. Could not this psychological and emotively charged conception of political self-destruction have germinated in Shakespeare's imagination through familiarity with a much more external dramatization of the same conflict in *Woodstock*?

Froissart; Créton; Traïson

Although we cannot be certain that Shakespeare consulted any of the French chronicles in composing *Richard II* (the verbal evidence is inconclusive), their influence, if perhaps only indirect, was probably important. Holinshed made use of Froissart, Créton and *Traïson*, referring to all three in his marginal notes; Hall took his account of Carlisle's protest and Richard's murder from *Traïson*; and Daniel admits that he drew upon Froissart. There can therefore be no doubt that the dramatist was aware of these narratives. The dominantly sympathetic attitude of the French historians to Richard and his queen contrasts strikingly with that expressed by the English chroniclers, so that the tradition which they embody, if not the texts themselves, could well have contributed significantly to the tone of the tragedy, especially in its falling action. If Shakespeare had detailed knowledge of any of the French writers, Froissart seems the likeliest candidate. In *1 Henry VI* (1.2.29) he mentions Froissart, apparently alluding to a specific passage in Lord Berners's translation (4.429). Berners's version is also a

---

1   As Schell (102) points out, 'Richard obscures both the *imago regis* and his own natural image, the "counterfeit" [2.1.93] of his father', the Black Prince. I am indebted here also to Janet Stavropoulos (6–12), who analyses the symbolism of the masque in *Woodstock* and relates it to the larger political issues of the play.

major source for *Edward III*, a play of which Shakespeare was probably part-author. Froissart had visited England in 1395 and was a close observer of the final years of Richard's reign – the period that concludes his chronicle. And the medieval splendour and charming courtliness of his account, especially in Berners's energetic English version, would have been a strong attraction to any dramatist and a counterweight to the unrelenting moralism of the *Mirror*. It is therefore hard to disagree with Tillyard, who thought it 'scarcely conceivable that Shakespeare should not have read so famous a book' (253), or with Bullough: 'It would be strange if Shakespeare did not look into' a work that conveys a 'sense . . . of being *in* the situations described' (3.367).

The portrayal of Gaunt seems to owe most to Froissart, who, like the *Woodstock* dramatist, presents him as a wise and sympathetic counsellor whose advice Richard rejects. Little warrant for such a conception appears in either Holinshed or Hall. Froissart's Gaunt, like Shakespeare's, resists pressure to avenge Gloucester's murder, 'lyke a sage and a prudent prince . . . wisely and amiably . . . appeas[ing] all these maters' (6.338). Since Froissart is the only source to give a detailed account of Gaunt's death, he may well lie behind Shakespeare's dramatization of this event, including some of the dying man's sentiments and warnings. Froissart says, for instance, that Gaunt 'lyved in great dyspleasure . . . bycause the kynge had banysshed his sonne out of the realme for so litell a cause, and also bycause of the yvell governynge of the realme by his nephewe'; a partial cause of the old man's demise was his painful awareness that if Richard 'longe perceyvered and were suffred to contynewe' his foolish policies, 'the realme was lykely to be utterly loste' (6.335–6). Shakespeare's Gaunt sees the abandonment of foreign conquest for internal strife as a great national scandal (2.1.65–6); Froissart's counterpart expresses similar feelings (6.311). And Froissart also mentions that Richard outwardly 'toke no great care for' Gaunt's 'dethe' and later transmitted the news by letter to the French king 'in maner of joye' (6.336–7). This detail could have suggested the callous attitude of

Shakespeare's Richard to his uncle's illness and death. Muir's view that Froissart probably contributed to Shakespeare's 'idea of Gaunt' (Muir, *Sources*, 52) seems justified, but we must weigh Rossiter's contrary view (*Woodstock*, 52) that most of what Shakespeare needed for his conceptualization of the character could have been found in *Woodstock*.

Froissart may have suggested a few additional touches in the play including the prominence of the Percys as supporters of Bolingbroke (6.347–52), the importance of Northumberland and York in London at the time of the deposition (6.372, 378), York's political ineffectuality as well as his distress at the conflict between Richard and Bolingbroke (6.371), the Queen's isolation from news of her husband's capture (6.370–1), the image of Bolingbroke on horseback bowing to the people (6.361), the allusion to Richard's baptismal name – possibly suggested by the rumour that Richard was illegitimate (6.377), the reference to street hangings in York's description of the procession into the capital (6.380) and roan Barbary's disloyalty to Richard (conceivably modified from the anecdote of Richard's favourite greyhound in Froissart, 6.369).[1] Not all of these, however, are exclusive to Froissart: Hall mentions Henry IV's reliance on York in the abdication proceedings; Daniel contains the detail of Bolingbroke's bowing to crowds; and *Traïson* repeats the bogus story about Richard's bastardy. On balance, we must conclude that Froissart was a probable source for *Richard II* or at least one that cannot be discounted. Tillyard's suggestion that the play may represent the dramatist's 'intuitive rendering of Froissart's medievalism' (253) therefore has its attractions.

The major difficulty in deciding whether Shakespeare read Jean Créton's mostly metrical *Histoire* and/or the anonymous *Traïson* while composing *Richard II* lies in assessing the availability of these texts in 1595 or thereabouts. Neither of these pro-Ricardian

1   See 2.2.58–61n., 2.3 headnote, 3.4.94n., 4.1.107.1LN, 151–5n., 256–7LN, 5.2LN, 18–20n. and 5.5.83–9LN.

manuscripts, written close to the events they narrate,[1] had reached print by the late sixteenth-century. Both, however, seem to have circulated widely on the continent – the latter in more than one version including a recension by Jean Le Beau that claims uniquely that Gloucester was beheaded.[2] Copies are rare in England, probably because Henry IV and his successors suppressed accounts that treated Richard's deposition as a heinous crime and his death as a martyrdom. Shakespeare's attention would have been directed to these documents by Holinshed, who refers three times to Créton and four times to *Traïson* in marginal notes. The first he calls 'a French pamphlet that belongeth to master Iohn Dee'; the second he refers to as 'an old French pamphlet belonging to Iohn Stow'.[3] Dee's copy of Créton (bearing his signature and the date 1575) survives at Lambeth Palace; another, the copy translated by Webb and cited in this edition, is in the British Library. Stow's copy of *Traïson*, now also in the British Library (Harleian MS 6219 fols 9–12b), turns out to be only a fragment – a translation into English of roughly the first fifth of the text, which breaks off at the point where Richard throws down his warder. As Ure shows, Holinshed probably knew no more of *Traïson* than the early section covered by this fragment, relying on Créton for anything after Richard's action at Coventry, whereas Hall possessed (or had access to) a complete text in 1548.[4] No French manuscript of *Traïson* is known

1 Créton visited England in 1399, was with Richard in Ireland and Wales, but returned to France after his capture, being merely informed of the deposition and its aftermath. Créton's poem begins with Richard's departure for Ireland and extends through his death and burial. The author of *Traïson* appears to have been attached to Queen Isabel's entourage. His account commences in mid-1397 with Richard's cession of Brest to the French and the events leading up to Gloucester's arrest; it ends with the display of the King's corpse in St Paul's.

2 Cf. Bolingbroke's line: 'Sluiced out his innocent soul through streams of blood' (1.1.103; and see n.). *Traïson* (9/133) says merely that 'the King sent his uncle to Calais, and there caused him to be put to death'. Strangling and smothering are the means of death in Holinshed, *Woodstock* and Froissart.

3 For the seven marginal references, see Holinshed, 3.497, 499, 500 (Créton); 3.487, 488, 489, 494 (*Traïson*).

4 Ure, 'Sources', 427–9. Where Hall obtained his full copy of *Traïson* is unknown. It is theoretically possible, of course, that Stow, in addition to the translated fragment, possessed the French text entire. If so, however, he seems to have made little use of it.

to exist in England now, and Williams's edition (with translation), cited here and throughout, is based on the so-called St Victor manuscript, located in Paris at the Bibliothèque du Roi. Although Wilson (xlvi) claims that 'Daniel knew *Traïson*', he furnishes no evidence for the statement, and Ure argues that Daniel follows neither of the French manuscripts but rather Stow's *Chronicles of England* (1580) for the one detail about Richard's being 'meanely mounted on a simple steed' (Daniel, 2.66) where Stow is translating Créton (Ure, 'Sources', 429). Nevertheless, as Bullough (3.372–3) observes, 'the attitudes of Créton and of the *Traïson*' seem to have had 'a considerable influence' on Daniel, so that whether or not the texts themselves were consulted, the tradition of pity for King Richard which they enshrine had to some extent made itself felt in Elizabethan England. Opinions vary as to how well Shakespeare would have read fifteenth-century French, although the fact that he had some working knowledge of the language is obvious from several scenes in *Henry V*. We cannot rule out the possibility that he consulted Créton and perhaps even *Traïson* (as Hall had done), but the likelihood of his having done so remains questionable.

The most obvious parallels between *Richard II* and the French manuscripts lie in the conception of Richard's character, especially in the final two acts. Both Créton and *Traïson* emphasize the analogy between the betrayal of Richard and Christ's Passion. Three such allusions can be found in *Traïson*, one of them comparing Northumberland to Judas, while a particularly extended passage, in which Bolingbroke's delivery of Richard to the hostile Londoners is paralleled to Pilate's release of Jesus for crucifixion, appears in Créton.[1] Although Holinshed contains a glancing reference to Pilate in the context of Archbishop Arundel's hypocrisy to Richard at Flint,[2] the French works treat the religious correspondence much more emphatically; nor does Holinshed show open hostility to Bolingbroke in more than one or two isolated passages. Shakespeare,

1 See 4.1.171–2LN.
2 See 3.3.53–61.3n. and 4.1.239n.

of course, has Bolingbroke refer twice to washing his hands of guilt (3.1.5–6, 5.6.49–50). Even more central is Richard's outburst at the abdication: 'some of you, with Pilate, wash your hands . . . yet you Pilates / Have here delivered me to my sour cross, / And water cannot wash away your sin' (4.1.239–42). It may be argued that the doctrine of divine right as embodied in the *Homilies* implies the analogy between Christ and the monarch, and that Shakespeare would have no need of an explicit source for such ideas. In Richard's own day the correspondence was commonplace, having been iconographically embodied, for instance, in the pageantry that greeted the King on his ceremonial entry into London in 1392.[1] Also over a half century after *Richard II* had appeared, Charles I on the morning of his execution could apply the story of the Passion in Matthew, 27, the Gospel appointed for the Eucharist at which he received the Blessed Sacrament, 'to his own present condition' (Coit, 357); and when the Martyr-King's writings were published at the Restoration, an anonymous elegy invoked the same parallels to Judas, Pilate and Golgotha that figure in Shakespeare's tragedy (Charles I, 1.419). Nevertheless, the salience of these elements in the French writers together with their near-absence in the English sources is striking.

Both French texts, like Shakespeare's play, make much of Richard's weeping, despair and humiliation. Créton (116/340), shocked by Richard's treatment in Wales, is moved to 'shed many a tear for him' – a passage that could have prompted York's words about the 'hearts of men . . . melt[ing]' (5.2.35).[2] Such an emphasis could have contributed to the more sentimental aspects of Shakespeare's protagonist, especially in 3.2 where he receives successive onslaughts of bad news – 'one after another' in Créton's phrase (113/337)[3] – and in the deposition scene. Also, like Daniel, the French authors give no indication that the Queen was a mere child. They likewise stress the strong emotional bond between Richard and his wife: when the King leaves for Ireland, for

1 Kipling, 89–90, and Saul, 343–4.
2 See 5.2.35–6n.
3 See 3.2LN.

instance, the author of *Traïson* (27/166–8) says that he 'never saw so great a lord make so much of, nor shew such affection to, a lady', adding that the King 'kissed her more than forty times' and that it was 'Great pity . . . that they separated, for never saw they each other more'.[1] If Shakespeare read or recalled this passage, he transferred the passionate leave-taking to a later point (5.1). But again the corresponding episode in Daniel (2.71–98) together with Shakespeare's imagination may be enough to explain the scene of parting, entirely absent from Hall and Holinshed. In *Traïson*, Bolingbroke, referring to hidden 'traitors', vows that he 'will gather up the weeds and will clear [his] garden of them' (92–3/247), a speech that has been invoked as the source of the extended horticultural allegory in 3.4; but the association of corrupt politicians and courtiers with weeds is proverbial, and Gaunt's image of England as an 'other Eden, demi-paradise' (2.1.42) has already established the appropriate context.

Assessing the evidence, we may concur with Muir, who concludes guardedly that 'a slight balance of probability' weighs in favour of Shakespeare's having been 'acquainted, directly or indirectly, with Créton's poem and *Traïson*'.[2] Finally, however, we should stress the value of the French works as analogues to particular elements in *Richard II*, for as Bullough rightly observes, 'quite apart from any question of influence, . . . they show the existence of a tradition more favourable to Richard than that found in the Tudor chroniclers' (3.370). Examining the French chronicles in conjunction with the English ones therefore helps to illustrate the complexity and ambivalence of Shakespeare's conception of his subject, allowing us to observe his combining and fusing of Lancastrian and anti-Lancastrian prejudices such as those reflected respectively in the early chronicles of Thomas Walsingham and John Hardyng.[3]

---

1   Créton (117/340) also emphasizes Richard's pain in being separated from the Queen; see 5.1.71–3LN.
2   Muir, *Sources*, 51. Black ('Sources', 214) believes that Shakespeare 'read the French accounts himself'.
3   See Kelly, 36, 39–40.

Edward II

It would be astonishing if Marlowe's grim tragedy of failed king-ship had not influenced Shakespeare's play on a similar subject. As I have argued elsewhere, the evolution of the chronicle drama from *Tamburlaine* and *Henry VI* to *Edward II* and *Richard II* involved a creative synergy between the two playwrights almost from the start (*E2*, 17–41). Going back as far as Lamb and extending through Swinburne, A.W. Verity, Havelock Ellis, C.H. Herford, Barrett Wendell, Georg Brandes, Morton Luce, Saintsbury, Ashley Thorndike, Tucker Brooke, Ivor John and beyond, a long tradition of comparing *Richard II* to its Marlovian predecessor has established itself (not invariably to Shakespeare's credit).[1] This is hardly surprising, given the obvious resemblances of theme and outline and the numerous parallels of plot and char-acter. Shakespeare could hardly have avoided facing what Harold Bloom has famously called 'the anxiety of influence'.

Both plays concern the same dynasty, Edward III being both the successor of Marlowe's king and the predecessor of Shakespeare's.[2] Berkeley Castle figures in the geography of both.[3] Each presents a weak and youthfully wilful monarch dominated by self-serving, upstart favourites and opposed by senior nobles who represent tradition, stability and, mostly, wise counsel. The king in each case has a trio of flatterers, Gaveston, Spencer and Baldock anticipating in some respects Bushy, Bagot and Green. Each drama features a weeping queen,[4] a maltreated and imprisoned bishop and a character who is banished only to return. In both plays the protagonist's folly and irresponsibility lead to rebellion and civil strife, these in turn bringing on dethronement, humiliation, imprisonment

1 See Forker, 94, 255–7, 281–5, 288, 324–7, 336, 349–51, 360–1, 396–8, 421, 423–5, 436–9, 444–5, 458–61, 480.
2 The Mortimer of Marlowe's play is also the ancestor of the Mortimer whom Richard II designated as his heir, though this latter character had to wait until *1 Henry IV* to make his appearance.
3 See 2.2.119n.
4 Both were historically named Isabelle, although Shakespeare used no Christian name for Richard's wife.

and murder by assassins who are then either eliminated or repudiated themselves. A regicide in each play (Matrevis in
Marlowe, Exton in Shakespeare) suffers qualms of conscience.
In both plays the king's closest friends are summarily but ille-
gally executed and meet their deaths with aplomb. Neither play
introduces clowns or scenes of low comedy, each rather incorporating sparse elements of levity into the largely aristocratic
fabric of the political action. Both plays are chiastic in structure
and utilize the *de casibus* trope of Fortune's wheel or its equivalent,[1] the descent of the tragic character being coterminous
with the rise of his antagonist. In both also, sympathy initially
drains away from the title figure, who by rejecting reason and
arrogantly abusing his powers, demonstrates his unfitness to
rule. Meanwhile, his wronged subjects and vocal critics claim
the higher moral ground. Then with his defeat, capture and
impending death, sympathy flows back again to the title figure,
while those who gain power at his expense become increasingly
ruthless, cynical, self-aggrandizing and morally compromised.
Both plays end with the solemnity of the dead king's funeral
procession.

The superficial parallels, some of which were perhaps dictated
as much by accidents of history as by authorial choice, serve only,
of course, to expose more profound differences of emphasis, tone,
style, emotional climate and overall effect. Marlowe's play
embraces events from an entire reign, extending from Edward's
accession to his death; Shakespeare's focuses only on the final two
years of Richard's kingship. Shakespeare deliberately avoids the
spiteful bickering, gritty realism and sexual obsessiveness of court
life as presented by Marlowe – as well as the degradation and
extremes of cruelty and terror of Marlowe's death scene. Violence
and physical suffering play almost no part in Shakespeare's drama,
and, with few exceptions, the formalities of royal protocol mark

---

1   See *E2*, 5.2.51–2 and 5.6.58–62. In *Richard II* Shakespeare transmutes the image of
    Fortune's wheel into that of a scale's balances (3.4.84–9) and the two buckets of a
    well (4.1.184–9). But see also, for instance, 2.3.48 and 66.

Richard's relations with his courtiers even at their most contentious and condemnatory. Edward's infatuation with Gaveston and afterwards with the younger Spencer is shown to be the direct cause of his doom, while Bushy, Bagot and Green are treated as mere adjuncts of Richard's collapse and seem to share but little of their master's intimate or interior life. Edward's queen, harshly rejected by her husband, becomes an adulteress and takes part actively in the plan for his destruction; Richard's spouse is both loved and loving, plays no political role and exists in Shakespeare's play only to evoke the charm of the King's personality, his devotedness and the pathos of his ruin. Mortimer, Edward's antagonist, metamorphoses from an irascible baron with understandable grievances into an ambitious Machiavel whose criminal overreaching topples him at the zenith of his success. Bolingbroke, Shakespeare's parallel antagonist, is an enigmatic combination of acumen, opportunism, ambition and political realism not unmixed with patriotism and guilt for the elimination of a legitimate predecessor; unlike Mortimer, he lives on to punish those who would unseat him. Marlowe's homosexual king, a man of limited insight and abject dependency, is defined by his emotional needs; Shakespeare's monarch is endowed with wit, imagination, eloquence and theatrical flair, and, despite his sentimentality, struggles to define himself in terms of his exalted calling rather than relying solely on lesser persons. Marlowe has no interest in the sanctity of kingship or in the religious symbolism and traditions that undergird it. Shakespeare fastens upon the sacramental violation implicit in the theme of deposition, making it central to the human tragedy of Richard himself and replete with gloomy import for the disasters it will unleash. Also absent from Marlowe is Shakespeare's association of governmental harmony with the green world and the processes of nature. *Edward II*, with its more nihilistic outlook and restless tempo, could have contained no garden scene. With Shakespeare's new emphasis goes a change in poetic style characterized by ceremonial stateliness, metaphoric opulence and a lyric sweetness entirely foreign to Marlowe's drama. With Herford, then, it is fair to say that '*Richard II* is the work of a man who has broken decisively with Marlowesque influence, but yet betrays its recent hold upon him, partly by violent reaction and partly by involuntary reminiscence' (Forker, 326).

That Shakespeare knew Marlowe's play well enough to absorb certain of its verbal and situational details is obvious. Some of the most noticeable imitations cluster in Act 4. Bolingbroke impatiently asks Richard whether he is 'contented to resign the crown' (4.1.200) in the same way that Leicester questions Edward (*E2*, 5.1.49–50). Richard's angry interruption of Northumberland reproduces a nearly identical exchange in Marlowe (*R2* 4.1.253–4; *E2*, 5.1.112–13). Richard's bitter pun on 'convey', when Bolingbroke orders Richard to prison, is almost certainly based on the same pun in Marlowe's drama when the Bishop of Coventry is similarly taken into confinement (*R2* 4.1.316–17; *E2*, 1.1.199). Both plays contain the imagery of assaulting the ears of adversaries (*R2* 4.1.54–5; *E2*, 2.2.127–8). And Richard's mention of 'sunshine days' (4.1.221) repeats Edward's words at 5.1.27.[1] Act 4 by no means exhausts the echoes: at least two phrases, 'high disgrace' and 'the worst is death', appear verbatim in both plays (*R2* 1.1.194, 3.2.103; *E2*, 2.2.187–8, 3.2.59–60). Richard's desire to 'forget what I have been' (3.3.138) imitates Edward's 'let me forget myself' (5.1.111). The Queen's attempt to strengthen Richard's resolve by reminding him that kings, like lions, are strong and superior and must not act with the 'base humility' of schoolboys (*R2* 5.1.29–34) combines imagery from three different passages in *Edward II* (2.2.202–3, 3.1.28–31, 5.1.11–14). Richard's parting from his queen picks up the idea of silent grief ('dumbly part', 5.1.95) from Edward's similar parting from Gaveston ('dumb embracement', 1.4.134).[2]

Other ideas in *Richard II*, though verbally less indebted to Marlowe's tragedy, seem nevertheless to have been suggested by it. The most obvious is Bolingbroke's fraudulent charge at

1   See 4.1.55n., 200n., 221n., 253–4n. and 317n.
2   See 1.1.194n., 3.2.103n., 3.3.138–9n., 5.1.29n., 31–2n. and 95n.

162

3.1.11–15 that Bushy and Green have been homosexually involved with Richard, thus bringing grief to the Queen. Since no historical warrant for such a claim exists, Shakespeare almost certainly borrowed the idea from Marlowe's play where Edward's passion for Gaveston does indeed inspire jealousy and grief in his queen.[1] Other possible links between the two plays involve the use of vine imagery to refer to royal lineage (*R2* 1.2.13–15; *E2*, 5.1.47–8); the possible consolation through fantasy for those facing hardship – in one case Bolingbroke, in the other Edward (*R2* 1.3.275–93; *E2*, 5.1.2–4); the King's desire for the death of an enemy – Gaunt in Shakespeare, Mortimer and Lancaster in Marlowe (*R2* 1.4.59–60; *E2*, 2.2.236–7); the taste of both monarchs for wanton music and Italian fashions and entertainment (*R2* 2.1.19–23; *E2*, 1.1.50–5); complaints that men of 'base' origin rise through unjustified royal preferment (*R2* 2.3.139; *E2*, 1.1.100); the striking anomaly of the two kings sitting on the ground at moments of stress (*R2* 3.2.155; *E2*, 4.7.14–18); unrealistic self-encouragement on the part of both monarchs in situations of impending danger or defeat (*R2* 3.3.127–30; *E2*, 4.5.4–7); the paradox that kings who theoretically command all subjects should themselves be commanded (*R2* 3.3.143–6; *E2*, 1.1.134, 4.7.83); the invocation in both plays of the Phaëton myth (*R2* 3.3.178–9; *E2*, 1.4.16–17); both kings' desire for death as an anodyne to grief (*R2* 4.1.219; *E2*, 5.1.110); guilt incurred by a king who consents to his own deposition (*R2* 4.1.247–52; *E2*, 5.1.97–9); the idea of suffering as the cause of premature aging in both kings (*R2* 4.1.277–9; *E2*, 5.2.119, 5.3.23); the conception of kings and their sufferings as mere shadows or reflections (*R2* 4.1.292–9; *E2*, 5.1.26–7); the implied contrast between earthly and celestial coronation (*R2* 5.1.24–5; *E2*, 5.1.107–9); a king's poignant reminiscence of happier days with his queen-to-be (*R2* 5.1.78–9; *E2*, 5.5.67–9); and the sensitivity of the two kings to the art of stringed instruments (*R2*

1 See 3.1.11–15n. and LN.

5.5.45–6; *E2*, 1.1.50–3).[1] Some of these may be coincidental, but scarcely all of them.

As has often been observed, Shakespeare's most famous debt to Marlowe in *Richard II* comes not from *Edward II* but from *Doctor Faustus*. Surely some of Shakespeare's audience would have recognized the allusion to Marlowe's doomed scholar when Richard confronts his own image in the glass and asks rhetorically, 'Was this the face . . . That . . . Did keep ten thousand men?' (4.1.281–3). Faustus's address to the apparition of Helen of Troy, 'Was this the face that launched a thousand ships?' (5.1.91), would have special resonance in the new context, since the implied identification of Richard with the woman whose beauty wrought the destruction of a great and ancient civilization deepens and extends the meaning of the King's tragedy in a peculiarly poignant way.[2] Additional debts to the same play probably show up in the Duchess of Gloucester's reference to the 'branches' of her husband's family, 'by the Destinies cut' (1.2.15); in Richard's image of himself 'melt[ing] . . . away in water-drops' (4.1.262); and in his characterization of Northumberland as a 'Fiend' who 'torments me ere I come to hell' (4.1.270).[3] Precedents for Richard's swearing 'by my seat's right royal majesty' (2.1.120) and for York's '*Pardonne-moi*' (5.3.118) occur in *1 Tamburlaine* and *The Jew of Malta* respectively.[4]

Minor Sources

Among his minor sources, Ovid's *Fasti*, Cicero's *Tusculan Disputations* (translated by John Dolman) and Lyly's *Euphues* seem to have been especially prominent in Shakespeare's mind, particularly in elaborating Gaunt's consolation of Bolingbroke after Richard has banished him.[5] Gaunt's oft-quoted speech on

1   For details, see 1.2.12–13n., 1.3.275–80n., 1.4.59–60n., 2.1.19n., 21–3n., 2.3.139n., 3.2.155n., 3.3.127–30n., 143–6n., 204n., 4.1.219n., 248–50n., 292–3LN, 5.1.24n., 78–9n. and 5.5.45n.
2   See 4.1.281–6n.
3   See 1.2.15n., 4.1.260–2n. and 270n.
4   See 2.1.120n. and 5.3.118n.
5   For details of these and other minor sources, see 1.3.275–80n., 288n., 294–301n., 295n., 309n., 3.4.33n. and 5.3.60–2n.

England was probably derived in part from Du Bartas's encomium of France, either in a version translated by John Eliot (1593) or in Sylvester's adaptation, applying the praises to England.[1] Gaunt's lines lauding England as an island-fortress were possibly influenced by Thomas Lodge's 'Truth's Complaint over England'.[2] As Muir (*Sources*, 54–66) has shown, some of Shakespeare's minor sources seem to have mingled in his mind, so that it is often difficult to specify the exact origin of a specific idea or image.

TEXT

I defer detailed analysis of the text to Appendix 1. Here it is sufficient to note that Q (1597) serves as the basic text for this edition except for the deposition scene (4.1.155–318), which was evidently marked for deletion in the manuscript from which Q was printed, and which appeared in a reliable text for the first time in the 1623 Folio (F). Q4 (1608) printed a different version of the missing lines, perhaps derived in some way from a theatrical performance, and not entirely negligible. Q is apparently the text closest to Shakespeare's holograph and many scholars believe that it may even have been printed directly from it. F appears to have been set from a copy of Q3 (1598) that had been extensively annotated by reference to the theatre promptbook and augmented from the same source by a manuscript insertion of the missing abdication episode. It seems probable that the 'woeful pageant' (4.1.321) of Richard's dethronement was considered too dangerous to print in 1597 (see pp. 515–17) but that the episode was nevertheless performed onstage from its inception in 1595.

---

1   See 2.1.40-64LN, 42n. and 48LN. Sylvester's lines were published only in 1605 but possibly existed in an earlier version that Shakespeare conceivably knew; see Ure, 50. The most reasonable conclusion seems to be Muir's – 'that Shakespeare was echoing Eliot, and that Sylvester, in translating Du Bartas, blended the original with memories of Shakespeare's lines which he might have heard on the stage, or read in one of the first three quartos, or in *England's Parnassus*' (Muir, *Sources*, 62).

2   For indebtedness to Lodge, see 2.1.43–4n., 70n. and 3.4.38LN.

The theatre promptbook, including the lines missing from Q, was presumably a transcript of Shakespeare's fair copy as originally composed but modified in minor respects over time owing to the practical exigencies of production.

Richard II is one of Shakespeare's few plays to be written exclusively in verse – for the most part in rather formal pentameter with a prominent element of rhyme. In the matter of emendation, therefore, editors have been more than usually concerned with disturbances of metre. This edition is no exception to that tradition, and, accordingly, I have been somewhat more hospitable to readings that repair metre than I might otherwise be. Readers will find Theobald, Pope, Capell and other eighteenth-century editors mentioned more frequently in the textual apparatus than might perhaps be expected in an early twenty-first-century edition. In Shakespearean verse regularity is never absolute. Sometimes lines only appear to be unmetrical on the page and can be rendered tolerably metrical in delivery by rapid or slowed down pronunciation of syllables or by elision of articles and connectives. When particular pronunciation seems to be required, I have tried to suggest it in the commentary. Occasionally, as in the case of York's agitation at 2.2.109–22, metrical irregularity seems to be a deliberate feature of the characterization. Here, metrical emendation (although it has been attempted by others) might seem to defeat the dramatist's purpose. In cases where I have adopted emendations that improve Q's metre, however, I have tried, unlike Pope, to justify them on textual principles that transcend mere aesthetic preference.

In modernizing spelling and punctuation, I have generally followed the ground rules of Arden 3 as set out in the General Editors' Preface, retaining archaisms only in the few instances where they serve the metre or where some aspect of Shakespearean usage or context appears to justify them. Thus F's 'parle' (1.1.192) and Q's 'noblesse' (4.1.120) retain their older spellings for the sake of the iambic pentameter, while F's 'moe' (2.1.239), Q's 'Cotshall' (2.3.9) and F's 'apricocks' (3.4.29) also remain unmodernized because the first is an Elizabethan plural collective form of 'more', the second reflects a contextually appropriate pronunciation of 'Cotswold' in Gloucestershire dialect and the third is Shakespeare's invariable form of 'apricots' deriving from the Portuguese rather than the French. My most unusual departure from ordinary modernizing practice consists in the capitalizing of a number of abstract nouns such as Death, Grief, Fortune and Sorrow where personification or quasi-personification seems to be intended. Q and F are inconsistent in this respect, but enough examples appear in both texts to warrant capitalizations in numerous passages, *prosopopoeia* being a favourite rhetorical device in this highly rhetorical play (see p. 90).

A word must be added about stage directions and speech prefixes. My general policy in the case of the former has been to follow the wording of Q's directions (except, of course, for the deposition scene which Q lacks) and almost invariably to supplement these with the fuller and often more specific information contained in the Folio directions. Stage directions (and other passages) unique to the Folio, i.e. those that have no verbal equivalent in Q, are highlighted in the text by being preceded and followed by superscript[F], in the manner of R.A. Foakes's Arden 3 edition of *King Lear* (1997). Except for '*Exit*' and '*Exeunt*', I have translated Latin forms. Additional stage directions, whether taken over from previous editors or introduced here for the first time, have also been liberally adopted, enclosed in square brackets and credited to their source in the collation notes. *Richard II* is a highly ceremonial play, and much of its special effectiveness onstage lies in the movements and gestures that supplement its ritualistic tone or, contrastingly, disrupt its normative order. Shakespeare embeds much of this movement, both explicitly and by implication, in his dialogue, but it seems important in an edition intended to be useful in the theatre to make such movement both prominent and clear without closing off the possibility of alternative stagings and gestures that properly belong to the prerogative of a director.

As in all modern editions of Shakespeare, I have normalized the speech prefixes, which in the case of Richard and Bolingbroke take on significant and politically debatable implications (see McLeod, 137–67). My solution is to designate the title character 'King Richard' throughout the play, for although he ceases to be king politically after his forced abdication in Act 4 and although his psychic struggle to define himself as man and king is integral to his tragedy, he never fully relinquishes his title and, in dying, heroically asseverates it. Richard's antagonist is labelled 'Bolingbroke' until 5.3, where he enters for the first time with his nobles as a crowned sovereign, at which point he becomes officially 'King Henry' in the speech prefixes and is treated by everyone onstage as king. To be sure, York has proclaimed Henry king at 4.1.110–13, and Bolingbroke has announced his imminent coronation at 4.1.319–20, yet the protest and arrest of Carlisle have intervened to cast doubt on his actual title during this scene. Admittedly, there is a certain illogicality in suggesting an overlap in reigns, for Bolingbroke becomes a king *de facto* before Richard is dead; yet to preserve this ambiguity symbolically and dramatically is surely part of the play's tragic power and import.[1] Aumerle retains his ducal title in speech prefixes throughout the action even though he has been demoted to Rutland (an earldom) by the time he abortively rebels in Act 5. Here the avoidance of confusion rather than political bias becomes paramount, and in the matter of this naming I have simply followed Q and F. As the text never mentions Queen Isabel by her Christian name (possibly to avoid calling attention to the fact that, historically, she was still a child), she is

---

1   A similar overlap occurs in *3 Henry VI* where Edward IV and Henry VI both claim the throne simultaneously. The issue arose provocatively in 1974 when Pasco and Richardson, the actors who exchanged the roles of Richard and Bolingbroke in Barton's production, gave a public reading of speeches from *Richard II* at King's College, London, followed by discussion. On this occasion (the University of London's annual John Coffin Literary Reading), the two actors were asked to say at what point in the drama they thought Richard ceased to see himself as king. Pasco identified a point in 4.1 when Richard formally relinquishes the crown; but Richardson said 'Never'. I owe this information to RP, who was present at the reading.

designated in this edition merely 'Queen' as in Q and F. I follow Q in referring to Northumberland's son as 'Harry Percy', as he is called 'Harry' in speeches by both Northumberland (2.3.21, 23) and Bolingbroke (3.3.20); QF abbreviate the name in most speech prefixes to '*H. Per.*', '*Per.*' or '*L. Per.*' and F once substitutes '*Henrie Percie*' (2.2.53), but it would seem appropriate to normalize to the more informal name by which the future Hotspur is regularly known in this play and in *1 Henry IV*, and, further, to distinguish him from his father, who was also called Henry. For reasons of enhanced dramatic variety, I follow Stanley Wells in differentiating the speeches of the Queen's attendants and the Gardener's assistants in 3.4. Mahood in her discussion of bit parts offers warrant for the practice (*Parts*, 3, 264–5). In Q and F these speeches are marked simply '*Lady*' (or '*La.*') and '*Man.*' (or '*Ser.*'); I divide them between 1 and 2 Lady, and between 1 and 2 Man. Following the Oxford editors, I adopt the same principle in the brief scene (5.4) in which Exton confers with his fellow assassins. Q and F assign the two short lines of the assistants to '*Man*' (or '*Ser.*'); in this edition the servants become 1 and 2 Servant.

For the most part, my collation notes record only substantive departures from the copy-text or rejected readings that have some reasonable claim to be considered legitimate. Variants that involve only differences in spelling or punctuation are not recorded unless they express some genuine ambiguity or affect interpretation or pronunciation significantly. Selected spellings from Q and F are collated, within italic parentheses, where they may have phonetic or metrical significance, and changes of hyphenation, which can affect meaning, are also collated. Alterations in lineation and metre are regularly included since, as noted in Appendix 1, these often figure importantly in the consideration of larger textual issues.

THE TRAGEDY
OF
KING RICHARD
THE SECOND

LIST OF ROLES

KING RICHARD the Second

QUEEN Isabel — *wife to King Richard*

John of GAUNT, Duke of Lancaster
Edmund of Langley, Duke of YORK } *uncles to King Richard*

DUCHESS OF YORK — *wife to Edmund of Langley* 5

Henry BOLINGBROKE, Earl of Derby,
Duke of Hereford; *afterwards*
KING HENRY the Fourth — *son to John of Gaunt*

Duke of AUMERLE, Earl of Rutland — *son to Duke of York*

DUCHESS OF GLOUCESTER — *widow of Thomas of Woodstock, Duke of Gloucester (uncle to King Richard)* 10

Thomas MOWBRAY, Duke of Norfolk

BAGOT
BUSHY } *favourites of King Richard*
GREEN

Henry Percy, Earl of NORTHUMBERLAND
HARRY PERCY (his son, *later surnamed* Hotspur)
Lord ROSS } *followers of Bolingbroke*
Lord WILLOUGHBY 15

Earl of SALISBURY
Bishop of CARLISLE } *friends of King Richard* 20
Sir Stephen SCROOP
ABBOT of Westminster

Duke of SURREY

Lord BERKELEY 25

Lord FITZWATER

Another LORD

LORD MARSHAL

Two HERALDS

Sir Piers of EXTON   30

CAPTAIN *of the Welsh army*

Two LADIES *attending upon
Queen Isabel*

Two SERVANTS *to Exton*

A SERVINGMAN *to York*

GARDENER   35

Two Gardener's MEN

KEEPER *of the prison at
Pomfret Castle*

GROOM *of the Stable to
King Richard*

Lords, Officers, Soldiers, Servants and other Attendants

LIST OF ROLES Rowe supplied a partial list of roles, absent from Q and F. Subsequent editors added Berkeley, the Lord Marshal and the Welsh Captain, plus Lords, Heralds, Officers, Soldiers and the Groom. Most of the characters are historical and are mentioned in Holinshed. The full text (Q plus the revised SDs and added abdication scene from F) contains thirty-nine speaking roles and a number of mute parts such as attendants, soldiers, servants, guards, lords and the like – a few not mentioned in the SDs but merely implied by the action. The number of mutes will vary depending on the relative simplicity or elaborateness of the staging. The play can be performed by twenty-one actors (seventeen men and four boys). If men take the two older women's parts (the Duchesses of Gloucester and York), as might have occurred in Shakespeare's theatre, three boys are still needed for the Queen and her ladies. A doubling chart (see Appendix 2) shows a possible distribution of parts plus the number of lines for each actor according to Spevack's line-count for every speaking role in F; no allowance is made for the almost insignificant number of lines reassigned by editors. King's analysis of the casting shows that the major roles, playable by thirteen actors (ten men and three boys), comprise some 94 per cent of the entire play; in Q (lacking the deposition scene) the percentage is slightly lower – 93 per cent (King, 83, 177–9). Bradley (45–9) proposes a slightly different casting.

1 KING RICHARD 1367–1400, reigned 1377–99, known as Richard of Bordeaux, his birthplace; a grandson of Edward III and second son of Edward, the Black Prince (Edward III's eldest son), who died before his father and therefore never became king; Edward of Angoulême, Richard's elder brother, next in succession, died in early childhood. Richard's private army wore a white

hart as the emblem of their service (see Fig. 16). The action of the play, which concerns the final two years of the reign, is true in essentials, although Richard's ceremonial abdication (as Shakespeare dramatizes it) and the circumstances of his murder are largely imaginary. In SDs and SPs, F tends progressively to normalize the name from 'King Richard' or 'King' to 'Richard', whereas Q hovers more uncertainly between the two designations. This variation between the two texts carries potential interpretive and political implications. For details and further discussion, see Appendix 1, pp. 510–11, and Introduction, pp. 67–8, 168. Since Richard never fully sheds his royal identity and title, this edn names him King Richard in SDs and SPs throughout.

2 QUEEN Isabel (or Isabelle) of Valois (1389–1410), Richard II's second wife, daughter of Charles VI of France, was a child of hardly eight years at the time of her marriage in 1396 (Holinshed, 3.486), but Shakespeare depicts her as an adult, possibly following Daniel (2.71–98), who had similarly augmented her age. The devotion between husband and wife dramatized in the play seems to be partly based on Richard's first marriage to Anne of Bohemia (1366–94), which became legendary for its romantic happiness (cf. Holinshed, 3.481, and *Woodstock*, 4.3.109–16, 141–66; see also Saul, 456–7). The maturity of the first queen would have been an additional reason for altering Isabel's age and for never referring to the Queen by her Christian name in the dialogue.

3 GAUNT John of Gaunt, i.e. Ghent, in Flanders (1340–99), Duke of Lancaster, fourth son of Edward III and younger brother of the Black Prince; the richest and most powerful of the royal dukes. As Williams (195, n. 23) points out, the historical figure did not use the toponym Gaunt 'after the age of three. Shakespeare found the name in his

sources and utilized it for its theatrical and metaphoric significance [cf. 2.1.73–84]; it is a mark of Shakespeare's popular appeal as a historian that "John of Gaunt" is now the common name for this Duke of Lancaster.' Shakespeare mentions him with the other six sons of Edward III at *2H6* 2.2.14. Gaunt is consistently idealized in the play, whereas the historical figure was of more dubious character – ambitious, contentious and, in the eyes of some writers at least, autocratic, feared and much hated by the nobility and commons alike. Fighting for three years in Spain (1386–9), he failed to make good a questionable claim to the throne of Castile. Inasmuch as Kyd (*Spanish Tragedy*, 1.4.162–7) and Shakespeare (*3H6* 3.3.81–2) had referred glowingly to Gaunt's Spanish campaign, Elizabethan audiences would have been familiar with his heroic reputation among Englishmen. Although suspected at one point of planning to usurp his nephew's throne, he was probably loyal. He was the progenitor of the House of Lancaster, one of the two factions (symbolized by the red rose) in the Wars of the Roses; see *1H6* 2.4.33.

4 YORK Edmund of Langley (1341–1402), so called from his place of birth near St Albans in Hertfordshire; Duke of York and fifth son of Edward III (see 2.1.171n. and *2H6* 2.2.15). Historically, he was much given to hunting and uninterested in politics (see 2.2.100n.). The House of York (symbolized by the white rose in the Wars of the Roses) traced its origin to him; see *1H6* 2.4.30.

5 DUCHESS OF YORK Joan Holland (*c.* 1366–1434), second wife of York and Aumerle's stepmother, though presented in the play as his birth mother (5.2.90–3); also sister to the Duke of Surrey. She later married Lord Willoughby.

6 BOLINGBROKE Henry Plantagenet (1367–1413), eldest son of Gaunt by his first wife, Blanche; created Earl of Derby as a young man and Duke of Hereford (1397) from the estate of Mary de Bohun, his first wife and

daughter of the last Earl of Hereford; he became Duke of Lancaster on his father's death. Bolingbroke (or 'Bullingbrooke' as spelled in Q and Holinshed, apparently reflecting Elizabethan pronunciation; cf. the rhyme at 3.4.98–9) refers to his birthplace, Gaunt's castle near Spilsby in Lincolnshire. The meaning may be 'boiling brook' since 'bull' and 'boll' are recorded spellings of 'boil', and 'broke' and 'brooke' are early forms of 'brook' (see *OED*); the castle had 'watery associations' (Cam², 11), being located in fen country. (For the form of the name adopted in this edn, see Appendix 1, p. 511, n. 1; pronunciation in modern productions should probably be 'Bullingbrook'; see Introduction, p. 142.) In a detail of which the play makes nothing, Shakespeare mentions Bolingbroke's thwarted attempt while in exile to marry a cousin of the King of France (see 2.1.167–8LN.). In SDs and SPs (as in the case of Richard) Q names this character inconsistently: 'Bullingbrooke', 'Hereford' and 'King' (or 'King Henry'); F, with a few exceptions, regularizes to 'Bullingbrooke' throughout. In the present edn, the character is called Bolingbroke until 5.3 where he appears for the first time as a crowned monarch, at which point he becomes King Henry. For textual details and further discussion of their political-interpretive implications, see Appendix 1, p. 511, and Introduction, pp. 67–8.

9 AUMERLE Edward of York (1373?–1415), eldest son of the Duke of York, created Earl of Rutland (1390) and Duke of Aumerle (or Albemarle, in Normandy) after Gloucester's arrest (1397); Holinshed and occasionally Q spell the name 'Aumarle', showing the probable Elizabethan pronunciation. For a time he was one of King Richard's most loyal adherents; some historians (see Black, 4) believe that, contrary to Holinshed, Aumerle deserted Richard's cause after his return from Ireland and probably was not involved in the Abbot of

Westminster's conspiracy (but see Saul, 424–5). He figures later in *H5* (4.8.103) as the heroic Duke of York slain at Agincourt.

10 DUCHESS OF GLOUCESTER Eleanor de Bohun (1365–99), widow of Edward III's sixth son, Thomas of Woodstock, Duke of Gloucester (probably murdered at Calais in 1397); sister of the Mary de Bohun who married Bolingbroke. She died at the Minories in London (see Black, 8 and 2.2.97n.) – according to Holinshed, of grief for the loss of Humphrey, her son and heir. Shakespeare glances at her husband's murder, as well as that of Humphrey of Gloucester, in *3H6* when the future Richard III remarks that 'Gloucester's dukedom is too ominous' (2.6.107).

11 MOWBRAY Thomas (1366?–99), twelfth Baron Mowbray and second Earl of Nottingham; of the blood royal through his mother (a descendant of Edward I) and therefore a distant relative of King Richard. He became Duke of Norfolk in 1397 at the time of Gloucester's death, for which he was blamed, since the Duke had been his prisoner at Calais while he was governor there. Although the precise circumstances of Gloucester's death remain cloudy, Holinshed makes Mowbray responsible, whether directly or indirectly, for the murder of Richard's uncle, implying that the crime was instigated by the King himself. Generally speaking, Elizabethan writers concur; in *Woodstock* 'Lapoole' (with two assistants) becomes Gloucester's murderer, though again the ultimate responsibility is Richard's. Dying in exile, Mowbray was buried in St Mark's, Venice. According to Shallow in *2H4* (3.2.24–6), young Jack Falstaff served as Mowbray's page. The adult Falstaff maintains his opposition to Bolingbroke in *1H4*, befriending the latter's recalcitrant heir, Prince Hal. Mowbray's eldest son (Thomas Mowbray, the Earl Marshal) appears as a character in *2H4* (see 1.3LN).

12 BAGOT Sir William (d. 1407), Sheriff of Leicester, adherent of Mowbray; MP, finally king's minister and councillor (1397), then, during Richard's absence, a member of the Regency Council. He escaped to Ireland after Bolingbroke's invasion and, although later arrested, was released.

13 BUSHY Sir John (d. 1399), Sheriff of Lincoln, Speaker of the House of Commons and Richard's chief agent in that body; like Bagot, a Regency Councillor during the King's absence in Ireland. Having fled to Bristol after Bolingbroke's landing, he was captured when the castle fell and beheaded.

14 GREEN Sir Henry (d. 1399), MP for Northamptonshire, royal councillor and member of the Regency Council. Like Bushy, he fled to Bristol, was captured and executed.

15 NORTHUMBERLAND Sir Henry Percy (1342–1408), created first Earl of Northumberland at Richard's coronation at the behest of Gaunt and therefore, for much of his life, a loyal Lancastrian. Having joined Bolingbroke's forces upon the latter's return from exile (cf. *1H4* 4.3.56–77), he guilefully engineered Richard's capture, although he seems to have been less than enthusiastic about Bolingbroke's usurpation of the throne; cf. Hotspur's account of how the Percys received Bolingbroke. Under the new king, he became Constable of England. Ultimately as disloyal to Henry as he had been to Richard, he was slain in battle at Branham Moor, Yorkshire, and his head displayed in London as a penalty for his treason. Compressing history, Shakespeare represents his final capture as occurring three years earlier (1405), at the same time as the rebellion crushed at Gaultree forest (cf. *2H4* 4.4.97–101).

16 HARRY PERCY Sir Henry (1364–1403), the Hotspur of *1H4*, so called for his energetic campaigns against the Scottish border clans. As son and heir of the Earl of Northumberland, he was also known by the courtesy title of Lord Percy. He was killed at the battle

of Shrewsbury, although not (as in Shakespeare) by Prince Hal. The dramatist makes him a youth; historically, he was senior to Bolingbroke by two years and to Bolingbroke's son by twenty-two years. Significantly, he is the first to give us an account of the prodigal (5.3.13–19).

18 ROSS Sir William, sixth Baron de Ros (or Roos) of Helmsley (*c.* 1369–1414), a Yorkshireman; MP, Knight of the Garter, and Lord Treasurer under Henry IV

19 WILLOUGHBY Sir William, fifth Baron, of Eresby (*c.* 1370–1409); MP, Knight of the Garter; like Ross and Bolingbroke's other original supporters, a northerner. Later he married York's widow.

20 SALISBURY John de Montacute (or Montague), third Earl (1350?–1400); a loyal supporter of King Richard, who accompanied him to Ireland but returned to Wales to raise an army in resistance to Bolingbroke. After Richard's deposition, he entered into a conspiracy against Henry IV (with the Abbot of Westminster), was captured and beheaded (see 5.6.8). His son appears as a character in *H5* and *1H6*; his great uncle (the first Earl) has a role in *E3*. The Salisbury of *2H6*, fifth Earl by marriage and father of Warwick, was his grandson-in-law.

21 CARLISLE Thomas Merke, or Merkes (d. 1409), mistakenly called 'Iohn' by Holinshed (see 4.1.324n.), monk of Westminster, Oxford doctor and one of Richard's intimates; consecrated in 1397 at the King's request the Pope, he became a 'courtier bishop', spending little or no time in his diocese, and accompanied his sovereign to Ireland. Protesting at the treatment of Richard after his deposition (see 4.1 headnote), he was arrested in 1399, placed in the custody of the Abbot of Westminster and deprived of his bishopric; finally pardoned, he was made rector of Todenham in Gloucestershire.

22 SCROOP or Lescrope, Sir Stephen (d. 1408), third son of Richard, first Baron Scrope of Bolton, and younger

brother to the Earl of Wiltshire beheaded with Bushy and Green at Bristol (see 3.2.141) – like them, a loyal friend of Richard II, whom, according to Créton and Holinshed (see 3.2 headnote), he attended at Conway Castle when the King surrendered himself to Northumberland. A renowned soldier, he served as deputy-lieutenant of Ireland under Henry IV, fought successfully there and died of the plague. His widow (*née* Milicent Tibetot) married Sir John Fastolfe (1378–1459), the minor figure of *1H6* and the chronicles, from whose name the name of the largely fictional Falstaff is thought to derive. The Richard Scroop, Archbishop of York, of *1H4* and *2H4* and the Henry, Lord Scroop of Masham, of *H5* are relatives in a collateral branch of the family. A different Sir Stephen (*c.* 1345–1406), second Baron Scrope of Masham and father of the treasonous Lord Scroop of *H5* (third Baron), is sometimes confused with this Sir Stephen. In *Woodstock* (2.2.130), Richard, unhistorically, appoints as Lord Admiral a favourite named Sir Thomas Scroope – possibly another member of the same family.

23 ABBOT of Westminster Scholars are in doubt as to the historical name of this cleric, sometimes identified as William of Colchester, Abbot from 1386 to 1420, despite dates which fit neither the play nor Shakespeare's major source. Holinshed, who records the Abbot's death as having occurred in 1400, gives no name but merely reports that the monk who sheltered the conspirators against Henry IV in his house died of a 'sudden palsie' (3.516).

24 SURREY Thomas Holland (1374–1400), third Earl of Kent, son of Richard's half-brother, Sir Thomas Holland (d. 1397); created Duke of Surrey in 1397 at the same time that Bolingbroke, Mowbray and Aumerle were given dukedoms. He acted as Lord Marshal at the Coventry lists and later sided with Aumerle in the latter's quarrel

with Fitzwater (see 4.1.61–71n.). He joined the plot against Henry IV and was beheaded with Salisbury at Cirencester.

25 BERKELEY Thomas (1353–1417), fifth Baron Berkeley, in Holinshed referred to simply as 'lord Berkelie' (3.498). He fought against Owen Glendower, introduced as a character in *1H4*, and was a parliamentary commissioner in Richard's deposition.

26 FITZWATER Walter Fitzwalter, fifth Baron (1368–1406), MP; one of the lords who assented to the secret imprisonment of Richard. He was later captured by the Saracens, imprisoned at Tunis, ransomed, and (like Mowbray) died in Venice. Q spells the name Fitzwaters, which may reflect Shakespeare's orthography; Holinshed uses the alternative spelling, Fitzwater, which probably indicates Elizabethan pronunciation (Sir Walter Raleigh punned on his Christian name as 'Water'). See also *2H6* 4.1.31–5, where the same double meaning is exploited dramatically.

28 LORD MARSHAL Historically, Mowbray was Earl Marshal, an office to which he was entitled for life; the Duke of Surrey was granted the office temporarily so that he could officiate at a duel in which Mowbray was a combatant. Surrey then succeeded Mowbray after the latter's banishment. Shakespeare, interested only in the dramatic function of the Earl Marshal, ignores his historical identity. Chambers, however, in his edn, makes Surrey and the Lord Marshal the same character – a theoretical possibility since the two never appear together onstage. See, however, 1.3.251–2n.

30 EXTON We know nothing of the historical Sir Piers except what Holinshed relates concerning his role in Richard's murder (Shakespeare bases the character wholly on this source). A play, now lost (1598), entitled *Pierce of Exton* (by Drayton, Chettle, Dekker and Wilson; see Chambers, *ES*, 2.167) suggests his legendary status as a regicide. Piers was very likely a close relation of Sir

Nicholas Exton, Sheriff of London, also Lord Mayor (1386–7), named 'Richard' in Holinshed (3.452), who fiercely opposed King Richard in Parliament. A Lord Mayor Exton appears as a character in *Woodstock* (1.1). A modern biographer of Henry IV suggests that 'it is not unlikely that the name could have arisen from a misreading of that of Peter or Piers Bukton, a Yorkshire knight and a lifelong follower of Henry, who was now his standard-bearer' (Kirby, 94).

31 CAPTAIN the commander of Richard's Welsh forces. Shakespeare gives him no name because his only function in the single scene in which he appears (2.4) is to serve as a kind of chorus, adding a sense of cosmic fatality to Richard's tragedy by means of his gloomy portents. It has sometimes been suggested that he is an early sketch of Owen Glendower (or Owain Glyn Dwr in modern Welsh), mentioned at 3.1.43, who figures prominently in *1H4*, and whom Holinshed refers to as 'capteine' of the Welsh (3.518). The Captain's belief in supernatural phenomena and inclination to superstition fit nicely the later portrait of Glendower in *1H4* (3.1.13–17, 23), but the portents themselves come from Holinshed, and perhaps Daniel, and have no specific connection with Glendower.

35 GARDENER a choric, quasi-allegorical figure who uses horticulture as a vehicle for political wisdom and whose speech is not intended to represent his humble station naturalistically. Apart from York's servant in 2.2, however, he and his two assistants are the first genuine commoners to speak in the play and, for this reason alone, are symbolically important; as Gurr (56) notes, they are 'visually distinct' by reason of their rustic dress. The twentieth-century theatrical innovation of playing the gardeners as clowns (see Sprague, 40–1) has no textual warrant and should be rejected out of hand. Barton costumed the gardeners as monks by way of reconciling their literate speech with their humble activity.

THE TRAGEDY
OF
KING RICHARD
THE SECOND

[1.1]   *Enter* KING RICHARD, John of GAUNT, [Lord Marshal,]
         with other Nobles and Attendants.

KING RICHARD
   Old John of Gaunt, time-honoured Lancaster,

TITLE Q's title is obviously more appropriate than F's for a play whose action is confined to the final years of Richard's reign and that belongs so unmistakably to the *de casibus* tradition of tragic fall from high estate. F's formula 'The Life and Death of' seems to be taken over from *The life and death of King Iohn*, the drama which immediately precedes *Richard II* in the Folio and was also printed before it. The standing type of the first five words of the head-title of F *R2* are apparently taken over from the analogous head-title of F *KJ*.

1.1 For act and scene divisions, see Appendix 1, p. 512. This scene is mainly a compression and adaptation of Holinshed (3.493–4). The charges, counter-charges and denials of Bolingbroke and Mowbray continue the political climate of calculated ambiguity and obfuscation already present in the sources. Hall's account contrasts with Holinshed's in making Mowbray rather than his rival the first accuser, Mowbray having betrayed to the King Bolingbroke's criticism of Richard spoken in confidence. ('Lord Mowbray' in *Mirror* follows Hall.) The private censure of Richard

apparently had to do with his ill-treatment of the high nobility (including his uncles). According to Holinshed, Bolingbroke accused Mowbray of treason at a Parliament in Shrewsbury, the charge being hotly denied by Mowbray, and the matter was then referred to a court of chivalry six weeks later at Windsor. The play opens at this point. Richard enters processionally with his nobles, and presumably takes his place on a centrally placed (probably raised) throne to hear Bolingbroke's formal appeal. Holinshed mentions 'a great scaffold erected within the castell . . . for the king to sit with the lords and prelats of his realme' (3.492). Wilson (118, 129) believes that the upper level represented this scaffold in Shakespeare's theatre, but the more limited space of the 'above' would probably have made such a staging awkward or impractical – for instance, by complicating the King's descent from his state.

1   **time-honoured** Gaunt was fifty-eight in 1398, an age that would probably strike Richard as 'old'; Shakespeare depicts him as a venerable figure (cf. 1.2.44) who evokes nostalgia for the chivalric ideals of the lost world of

TITLE] *Qq (title page and running titles);* The life and death of King Richard the Second *F (heading and running titles subst.)*   1.1] *F (Actus Primus, Scaena Prima.); act and scene divisions not in Q*
0.1 Lord Marshal] *Wells (subst.)*   1 SP] *King Richard. QF*   time-honoured] *F;* time honoured *Q*

179

Hast thou according to thy oath and band
Brought hither Henry Hereford, thy bold son,
Here to make good the boist'rous late appeal –
Which then our leisure would not let us hear –   5
Against the Duke of Norfolk, Thomas Mowbray?

GAUNT

I have, my liege.

KING RICHARD

Tell me, moreover, hast thou sounded him
If he appeal the Duke on ancient malice,
Or worthily, as a good subject should,   10
On some known ground of treachery in him?

GAUNT

As near as I could sift him on that argument,

Edward III and the Black Prince, in
contrast to the youth of Richard (cf.
2.1.69) and his luxury-loving favourites.
Richard was just over thirty years old.
The same contrast occurs in *Woodstock*.

2   **oath and band** According to Froissart,
Gaunt, York, Northumberland 'and
dyuerse other lordes' were 'pledges'
(guarantors) of Bolingbroke's appearance (6.309); Holinshed adds Aumerle's
name to the list of pledges (3.493).
'Band' is an alternative spelling of
'bond' (cf. 2.2.71, 4.1.77, 5.2.65); Q and
F use both spellings indifferently.

3   **Hereford** spelled inconsistently as
'Herford' or 'Hereford' in Q and F.
Holinshed, unlike Hall, prefers 'Hereford', which is also the modern spelling
adopted in this edn. Metre indicates
that the name is usually pronounced
dissyllabically ('Herford' or 'Harford').
However, occasionally the modern trisyllabic form may be required (see
2.1.232n., 279n., 2.3.69n.).

4   **boist'rous late appeal** 'recent violent
criminal indictment' (i.e. six weeks
earlier at the Shrewsbury Parliament;
see Holinshed 3.493). An *appeal* was a
formal charge requiring both *appellant*

and *defendant* to give surety for their
appearance at a specific time and place
(see 2n. and cf. 4.1.80).

5   **our leisure** our convenience (i.e. our
want of leisure; cf. *R3* 5.3.97); Richard
uses the royal plural, signalling the
official character of the occasion.

7   **liege** Gaunt uses the ancient feudal
term appropriate to the values for
which he stands (cf. 5.3.38).

8   **me** Richard's use of the more personal
form of the pronoun where we might
expect 'us' is perhaps a subtle indication of the volatile personality that
underlies his carefully preserved royal
demeanour (cf. 116n.); it may also hint
for the first time at the family intimacy
that underlies the public roles.
sounded enquired of

9   **appeal** accuse
on ancient malice on the basis of long-
standing personal hatred or grudge

12   an alexandrine; shorter and longer
lines are occasionally introduced into
the normal pentameter system of the
play for variety or emphasis.
sift him discover from him by questioning; cf. *Ham* 2.2.58.
argument subject

6 Mowbray] *(Moubray)*, F   8 SP] *King. QF*

On some apparent danger seen in him
Aimed at your highness; no inveterate malice.

KING RICHARD

Then call them to our presence.   [*Exeunt Attendants.*]
                          Face to face,   15
And frowning brow to brow, ourselves will hear
The accuser and the accused freely speak.
High-stomached are they both and full of ire,
In rage, deaf as the sea, hasty as fire.

Enter BOLINGBROKE *and* MOWBRAY [*with Attendants*].

BOLINGBROKE

Many years of happy days befall   20
My gracious sovereign, my most loving liege!

---

13 **apparent** manifest
  him Mowbray
15 **our presence** A formal hearing before
the sovereign as judge entailed special
protocols such as standing, removing
headgear and not turning one's back on
the throne. Bolingbroke alludes to the
legal aspect of *this princely presence* at 34.
***presence . . . face** The punctuation
of both Q and F makes *face to face* part
of the preceding sentence. An alternative, though unlikely, interpretation
would be: 'Then call them to our presence face to face, and – [they] frowning
brow to brow – ourselves' (Wells, 163).
16 **ourselves** we ourself (royal plural)
18–19 sometimes spoken as an aside to
register Richard's private apprehension. The use of a rhymed couplet
tends to set the comment apart.
18 **High-stomached** haughty; full of
resentment; stubbornly courageous.
Traditionally, the stomach was the seat
of courage, anger, arrogance; cf. *1H6*
1.3.88; *Tit* 3.1.233; *2H4* 1.1.129.
19 **deaf . . . fire** 'as deaf (to moderating

counsel) as the sea, as quick (to take
offence) as (spreading) fire'; cf. *KJ*
2.1.451: 'The sea enraged is not half so
deaf'. Both expressions are proverbial
(see Dent, S169.2, F246.1).
19.1 Possibly Bolingbroke and Mowbray
with their attendants enter 'at several
doors', which would lend their formal
opposition visual emphasis. See
1.4.0.1–2 for a different use of opposed
entrances.
20 **Many . . . days** The half-foot pause at
the beginning of this line led early
editors to emend, but no change is
needed. GWW, however, would defend
Pope's emendation (see t.n.) as a case of
'compositorial fusion by which "May
many" becomes "Many"'. Bolingbroke's elaborate politesse here,
although conforming to the expected
formality of the occasion, creates an
effective anticipatory irony, for he will
cut short Richard's reign by usurpation, an event already familiar to most
of the audience. Shakespeare reinforces
the irony later (see 4.1.220–1).

---

15 SP] *King. Q; Kin. F*   presence. Face] *Johnson¹ (subst.);* presence face *QF*   SD] *White² (subst.)*
18 High-stomached] *Pope;* High stomackt *QF*   19.1 *with Attendants*] *Capell (subst.)*   20 SP]
(Bulling.), F (Bul.)   Many] May many *Pope*

181

MOWBRAY

> Each day still better other's happiness
> Until the heavens, envying earth's good hap,
> Add an immortal title to your crown!

KING RICHARD

> We thank you both. Yet one but flatters us,   25
> As well appeareth by the cause you come,
> Namely, to appeal each other of high treason.
> Cousin of Hereford, what dost thou object
> Against the Duke of Norfolk, Thomas Mowbray?

BOLINGBROKE

> First – heaven be the record to my speech! –   30
> In the devotion of a subject's love,
> Tend'ring the precious safety of my prince,
> And free from other misbegotten hate,
> Come I appellant to this princely presence.
> Now, Thomas Mowbray, do I turn to thee,   35

---

22 'May every succeeding day always be happier than its predecessor' (*better* = make better).

23 **envying** probably pronounced with emphasis on the second syllable, if *heavens* is taken as a monosyllable; cf. *TS* 2.1.18; see also Cercignani, 39.
hap fortune

24 'add a heavenly crown to your earthly one'; cf. *Woodstock*, 1.1.37–8: 'But heaven forestalled his diadem on earth / To place him with a royal crown in heaven' (said of Richard's father, the Black Prince). The notion of exchanging an earthly for a heavenly crown was a religious commonplace; cf. 'Our holy lives must win a new world's crown' (5.1.24). Here the idea of immortality is fused with the royal theology implicit in the standard acclamation used at coronations: 'Long live the King! May the King live forever!'

25 **flatters** deceives through flattery

26 **you come** for which you come

28 **thou** the less formal pronoun, here used to Bolingbroke as a member of Richard's family; cf. *you* (186), where Richard shows displeasure, and also 35n.
object charge

30 **First** Cf. 54. As Gurr (58) notes, both antagonists begin by enumerating points but in their ardour never get past number one. Both may use the number only to signal the preliminary nature of their early words.
record witness

32 **Tend'ring** out of regard for, solicitous about

34 **appellant** as appellant (accuser); see 4n.
presence See 15n.

35 **thee** In quarrelling, both Bolingbroke and Mowbray tend to use the familiar form of the pronoun. This may be a rhetorical expression of their contempt for each other (see Abbott, 233), but it is also possible that Shakespeare employs the more archaic form (which was gradually disappearing) simply as a

25+ SP] *King. QF*   30+ SP] *(Bul[l].)*

And mark my greeting well; for what I speak
My body shall make good upon this earth,
Or my divine soul answer it in heaven.
Thou art a traitor and a miscreant,
Too good to be so, and too bad to live,   40
Since the more fair and crystal is the sky,
The uglier seem the clouds that in it fly.
Once more, the more to aggravate the note,
With a foul traitor's name stuff I thy throat,
And wish – so please my sovereign – ere I move,   45
What my tongue speaks my right-drawn sword may
    prove.

MOWBRAY

Let not my cold words here accuse my zeal.
'Tis not the trial of a woman's war,
The bitter clamour of two eager tongues,
Can arbitrate this cause betwixt us twain;   50

means of enhancing the intended effect of medieval stiffness and ritual legality.
36 **greeting** form of speech (i.e. precise accusation)
38 **answer** answer for
40 **Too good** of too high a rank
41–6 The three couplets lend additional weight and finality to Bolingbroke's charge, and convey the speaker's rage constrained by the artificial formalities of his situation. The technique reappears throughout the scene. Coleridge remarks of these verses that they 'well express the *preconcertedness* of Bolingbroke's scheme, so beautifully contrasted with the vehemence and sincere irritation of Mowbray' (132). Wilson thinks, however, that the only 'scheme' Bolingbroke envisions at this early point is to take vengeance on the enemies of his family (120).
41 **crystal** i.e. clear as crystal, bright; Ptolemaic cosmology held that the

earth formed the centre of the universe and was surrounded by a series of concentric crystal spheres whose revolutions defined the planetary orbits.
43 **aggravate the note** increase the reproach or stigma (by reiterating the charge); Latin *nota* = official censure.
44 **stuff . . . throat** 'keep you from replying by forcing you to swallow the insult' (cf. *Tit* 2.1.55)
45 **so please** if it please (impersonal construction)
46 **right-drawn** drawn in a just cause
47 'Let not the calmness of my language impugn the ardour of my feelings (and loyalty).'
48 **trial . . . war** test of a woman's combat (i.e. mere scolding). *Trial* = trial by combat; legal process of judgement.
49 **eager** biting, sharp (cf. *3H6* 2.6.68)
50 **Can arbitrate** 'which can decide judicially' (a common ellipsis of the relative pronoun)

46 right-drawn] *Theobald;* right drawen *QF*

The blood is hot that must be cooled for this.
Yet can I not of such tame patience boast
As to be hushed and naught at all to say.
First, the fair reverence of your highness curbs me
From giving reins and spurs to my free speech,   55
Which else would post until it had returned
These terms of treason doubled down his throat.
Setting aside his high blood's royalty,
And let him be no kinsman to my liege,
I do defy him, and I spit at him,   60
Call him a slanderous coward and a villain;
Which to maintain, I would allow him odds
And meet him, were I tied to run afoot
Even to the frozen ridges of the Alps,
Or any other ground inhabitable   65
Wherever Englishman durst set his foot.
Meantime let this defend my loyalty:
By all my hopes most falsely doth he lie.

BOLINGBROKE
    Pale trembling coward, there I throw my gage,

---

51 **cooled** i.e. by death in battle (also alluding, perhaps, to bleeding, a medical practice believed to reduce fever)

53 **hushed** Q's spelling ('huisht'), usually considered a misprint, may reflect Elizabethan pronunciation (Cam², 59).

54 **First** See 30n.
fair reverence of proper respect for; cf. 'fair sequence and succession' (2.1.199). Mowbray initiates his apology for opposing Bolingbroke, who is Richard's blood relation (cf. 58–9).

56 **post** ride fast like a messenger on horseback (continuing the imagery of *curbs*, *reins* and *spurs*)

57 **These . . . doubled** i.e. *traitor* and *miscreant* (39), reiterated to make them twice as insulting; cf. *Woodstock*, 5.3.122.
down his throat echoes 44 (see n.)

58 **high blood's royalty** his high rank as a

member of the royal family (with a pun on *high blood* = enflamed anger); cf. *TC* Prologue, 2: 'their high blood chaf'd'.

59 **let him be** assuming that he were

62 **odds** an advantage

63 **tied** bound, obliged

64–6 Cf. Fitzwater's similar defiance at 4.1.75; also *Mac* 3.4.103 and *Cym* 1.1.165–9. Daring one's opponent to meet at some remote, uncivilized place implied mortal combat since there would be no one present to separate the duellists or assist the wounded. The idea was not uncommon.

65 **inhabitable** uninhabitable; cf. *in*human.

67 **this** i.e. this statement (what follows in the next line); or possibly 'this sword'

69 **gage** pledge, token of security (usually a glove or gauntlet; cf. *H5* 4.1.208–11). Flinging it down was an act of challenge

---

53 hushed] *(*huisht), Q2, F *(*husht)   57 doubled] doubly *F*

[*Throws down his gage.*]
Disclaiming here the kindred of the King,   70
And lay aside my high blood's royalty,
Which fear, not reverence, makes thee to except.
If guilty dread have left thee so much strength
As to take up mine honour's pawn, then stoop.
By that and all the rites of knighthood else,   75
Will I make good against thee, arm to arm,
What I have spoke or thou canst worse devise.
MOWBRAY
I take it up;   [*Takes up gage.*]
            and by that sword I swear
Which gently laid my knighthood on my shoulder,
I'll answer thee in any fair degree   80
Or chivalrous design of knightly trial.

and taking it up signified acceptance. As Wells notes, however, hoods were sometimes thrown down, as in Holinshed's account of Fitzwater accusing Aumerle of Gloucester's murder (3.512; cf. 4.1.38); but the phrase *manual seal* (4.1.26) suggests that Shakespeare 'thought of the gage as a glove' (Wells, 165). The taker-up of the challenge would probably tuck the glove into his belt.

70–1 Cf. 58–9 and 58n.
70 **kindred** kinship
71 **lay aside** laying aside
72 **reverence** respect (cf. 54 and n.)
   except set aside (cf. 58)
74 **honour's pawn** i.e. the gage; the phrase is formulaic (cf. 4.1.56, 71).
   stoop bend down (to pick up the gage). Cf. 3.3.48n.
75 **rites** customary usages (possibly with a play on 'rights' = just claims); cf. F2's emendation, adopted by Q6, Rowe, Theobald and others. According to *OED*, 'rite' was an available spelling

of 'right' (*sb.*).
77 **or . . . devise** a crux. Probably this phrase means 'or anything you can invent against me worse than what I have already charged you with', or perhaps 'anything worse you can imagine my having said about you'. The t.n. indicates the progressive attempts of early reprints to emend the line; see Appendix 1, p. 507. Chambers (79) interprets *or* (a variant of 'ere') to mean 'before' (cf. *Ham* 5.2.30); if he is right, the sense would be 'before you can invent anything worse to my discredit'. See also 108n.
78 **that sword** i.e. Richard's sword (by which Mowbray had been dubbed a Knight of the Garter in 1383)
79 **gently** 'Perhaps "conferring nobility" rather than "with a light touch" or "in friendly fashion"' (Wells, 165)
80–1 **answer . . . trial** 'give you satisfaction to any honourable extent or in any manner sanctioned by the rules of chivalry'

69 SD] *Irving (subst.)*   70 the King] a King *Q2–F*   73 have] hath *F*   75 rites] rights *F2*
77 spoke . . . devise] spoke, or thou canst deuise *Q2;* spoke, or what thou canst deuise *Q3–5;* spoken, or thou canst deuise *F*   78 SD] *Irving (subst.)*

And when I mount, alive may I not light
If I be traitor or unjustly fight!

KING RICHARD [*to Bolingbroke*]

What doth our cousin lay to Mowbray's charge?
It must be great that can inherit us   85
So much as of a thought of ill in him.

BOLINGBROKE

Look what I speak, my life shall prove it true:
That Mowbray hath received eight thousand nobles
In name of lendings for your highness' soldiers,
The which he hath detained for lewd employments,   90

82 **mount . . . light** mount my horse . . .
dismount (alight)
83 **unjustly** in an unjust cause
85 **inherit us** put me in possession
87 **Look what** whatever, that which (a
common Shakespearean idiom; cf.
1.3.286)
88–103 The cloudy charges that
Bolingbroke levels at Mowbray in this
passage (embezzlement, treasonable
counsel and the compassing of
Gloucester's death) allude to scandals
that grew out of hostilities almost ten
years earlier in the reign (1387–8).
When Richard was still relatively
untried in rule, the lords appellant (led
by Gloucester, and including the earls
of Arundel and Warwick as well as
Mowbray and Bolingbroke) succeeded
in displacing and condemning his
favourites and, by their high-handed
tactics in Parliament and council,
reducing him to a mere figurehead. By
1389 Richard had gained enough maturity to assert his own authority and rid
himself of the lords appellant.
Mowbray, formerly an adversary, now
became one of his inner circle, and
Bolingbroke also had regained a measure of royal favour. The King continued to resent the senior appellants'
humiliation of him, and in 1397 he settled accounts by arresting Gloucester,

Arundel and Warwick and having them
tried in Parliament for treason;
Warwick was exiled, Arundel beheaded
and Gloucester, Mowbray's prisoner at
the time, mysteriously disappeared at
Calais (probably at Richard's bidding;
see 100n.). As *Woodstock* had already
dramatized these events, Shakespeare
may have assumed some knowledge of
them in his audience. But the absence
of clarifying detail, the obscure motivation and the careful refusal to resolve
the truth or falsity of the antagonists'
statements in this scene constitute a
deliberate dramatic strategy (see
Introduction, pp. 27–8, 127–8, 137–8).
88 **nobles** gold coins worth twenty groats
(6s 8d, or one third of a pound); cf.
5.5.67–8n.
89 **In . . . for** 'for the purpose of advancing
money to'. When ordinary pay for soldiers was not available, they were
sometimes given advances (*lendings*) to
improve their morale; see *OED sb.* 2b.
In Holinshed the implication is that
Mowbray kept or diverted money
intended for the soldiers: 'Norfolke
hath receiued eight thousand nobles to
pay the souldiers that keepe your
towne of Calis, which he hath not
doone as he ought' (3.494).
90 **The which** i.e. the *nobles* (88)
lewd vile, base, improper

84 SD] *Oxf* 87 speak] said *Q2–F*

Like a false traitor and injurious villain.
Besides I say, and will in battle prove,
Or here or elsewhere to the furthest verge
That ever was surveyed by English eye,
That all the treasons for these eighteen years   95
Complotted and contrived in this land
Fetch from false Mowbray their first head and spring.
Further I say, and further will maintain
Upon his bad life to make all this good,
That he did plot the Duke of Gloucester's death,   100

91 **injurious** malicious, pernicious
93 **Or ... or** either ... or
93–4 **furthest ... eye** Cf. 64–6n. Bolingbroke echoes Mowbray's challenge to
fight at some remote location.
95 **eighteen years** i.e. ever since 1381, the
year of the Peasants' Revolt. Holinshed
also mentions the time period without
explaining its significance: 'all the treason that hath beene contriued . . . for
the space of these eighteene yeares'
(3.494). The Cade scenes in *2H6* use
additional material from the accounts in
Holinshed and Hall of the 1381 revolt
led by Wat Tyler and Jack Straw.
96 **Complotted** plotted in conspiracy
with others
97 **head** source; cf. 3.3.108.
100 **plot . . . death** Cf. Holinshed: 'he
hath caused to die and to be murdered
. . . the duke of Glocester' (3.494).
Bolingbroke strategically ignores
Richard's supposed complicity. The
precise circumstances of the death of
Thomas of Woodstock (Gloucester) in
September 1397 are still unknown to
historians, and Mowbray's responsibility
in the matter is no less doubtful. In
Shakespeare's age, however, it was generally believed that Richard ordered his
uncle's murder – or private execution
(since in one version of the story
Gloucester had confessed his treason).
Holinshed (3.488–9) reports that
Gloucester had entered into a conspiracy

to imprison the King together with the
dukes of Lancaster and York and to
have the other members of his council
executed, which, when Richard learned
of it, caused him to have Gloucester
seized and dispatched to Calais.
'Thomas, Duke of Gloucester' in
Mirror takes it for granted that Richard
committed an act 'odious to God' (98).
Woodstock portrays the King as similarly criminal. But later *Mirror* (144)
reveals how popular attitudes to the
death quickly changed: 'Duke Thomas
death was Iustice two yeres long, / And
euer sence sore tiranny and wrong'
('Thomas, Earl of Salisbury', ll. 34–5).
According to Holinshed, who speaks of
'some variance' in the different
accounts, 'The king sent vnto Thomas
Mowbraie . . . to make the duke
secretlie awaie [at Calais]. The erle prolonged time for the executing of the
kings commandement, though the king
would haue had it doone with all expedition, wherby the king conceiued no
small displeasure, and sware that it
should cost the earle his life if he quickly obeied not his commandement. The
earle thus as it seemed in maner
inforced, called out the duke at mid-
night, as if he should haue taken ship to
passe ouer into England, and there . . .
he caused his seruants to cast feath-
erbeds vpon him, and so smoother him
to death, or otherwise to strangle him

97 Fetch] Fetcht *Q2–F*

Suggest his soon-believing adversaries,
And consequently, like a traitor coward,
Sluiced out his innocent soul through streams of
  blood –
Which blood, like sacrificing Abel's, cries

with towels (as some write). This was
the end of that noble man, fierce of
nature, hastie, wilfull, and giuen more
to war than to peace: and in this greatlie
to be discommended, that he was euer
repining against the king in all things,
whatsoeuer he wished to haue forward.
He was thus made awaie not so soone as
the brute [rumour] ran of his death.
But (as it should appeare by some
authors) he remained aliue till the parlement that next insued, and then about
the same time that the earle of Arundell
suffered, he was dispatched (as before
ye haue heard)' (3.489). Summing up
the disastrous conflict between Richard
and his nobles and the deposition which
it finally precipitated, Holinshed
blames dissoluteness and 'the frailtie of
youth' in the King, his unpopular
favourites and the machinations of
Gloucester, 'cheefe instrument of this
mischeefe' (3.508). See LN.

101 'prompt the Duke's overcredulous
    opponents to believe him guilty of
    treason'. Indirectly Bolingbroke seems
    to implicate Richard, since the King
    was chief among the *adversaries*.

102 **consequently** afterwards, subse-
    quently
    *traitor RP suggests that Q's 'taitour'
    might conceivably be an error for 'fai-
    tour' (impostor) rather than for 'traitor'.

103 The imagery here obviously suggests
    beheading rather than smothering or
    strangling (as in Holinshed, Froissart
    and *Woodstock*); cf. also 1.2.21 and
    2.2.102. Perhaps the detail derives from
    Traïson, which reports that 'Le roi
    envoya son oncle à Calais, et là fut décollé'
    ('The King sent his uncle to Calais and
    he was beheaded there') (Buchon, 10).

The anonymous play on Richard II
which Simon Forman describes having
seen at the Globe on 30 April 1611 also
apparently represented Gloucester as
beheaded (Chambers, *WS*, 2.340). But
Shakespeare may have invented the
beheading (the customary Elizabethan
penalty for noblemen) not only to allow
for the motif of sacrificial blood (e.g. at
104 and 1.2.17) but also to preserve the
uncertainty as to whether Gloucester
had been murdered or unofficially executed; see 100n.

104 **blood . . . cries** Possibly Shakespeare
    recalled *Woodstock*: 'Blood cries for
    blood' (5.4.49); but the phrase is a
    commonplace.
    sacrificing Abel's See Genesis, 4.4,
    8–10. Abel, a shepherd, sacrificed the
    firstlings of his flock to God; his broth-
    er Cain, a tiller of the soil, having no
    sacrifice to offer other than fruit of the
    ground, became jealous of Abel and
    committed the first murder. His blood
    cried out from the earth for retribution,
    unlike that of Christ whose blood
    promised salvation (Hebrews, 12.24).
    Ironically, it is Richard rather than
    Mowbray who has shed the blood of a
    close kinsman, although Shakespeare
    keeps this aspect veiled until 1.2. If we
    assume   audience   awareness   of
    Richard's putative guilt at this point,
    Bolingbroke's allusion to the Abel–Cain
    story may be taken as a covert threat to
    the King. Proleptically, we have an
    additional irony, for as God punished
    Cain with exile, so Bolingbroke will
    punish   Gloucester's   slayer   with
    dethronement.   But   the   exile   of
    Bolingbroke-Cain precedes the murder
    of Richard, whereas the punishment of

101 soon–believing] *Pope;* soone beleeuing *QF*   102 traitor] *Q2–F;* taitour *Q*   103 Sluiced] *(Slucte),*
*F (*Slucʼd*)*   104 Abel's, cries] *Q4–5;* Abels cries *Q1–3, F*

Even from the tongueless caverns of the earth   105
To me for justice and rough chastisement.
And by the glorious worth of my descent,
This arm shall do it, or this life be spent!

KING RICHARD

How high a pitch his resolution soars!
Thomas of Norfolk, what sayst thou to this?   110

MOWBRAY

O, let my sovereign turn away his face

Richard-Cain follows the murder of Gloucester. Bolingbroke invokes the story again at 5.6.43–4, where, with a further ironic twist, Exton rather than the King is identified with the first murderer. In both cases, interestingly, Bolingbroke associates the agent of murder (Mowbray, Exton) with Cain rather than the monarch (Richard, Henry IV) who is ultimately responsible. For the significance of the Genesis motif, see Maveety, 175–93, and Introduction, pp. 75–8.

106 **To me** Bolingbroke implies that, since Gloucester has no son of his own, the duty of avenging Gloucester's death falls to him as the eldest son of Gaunt, Gloucester's brother. Kittredge[2] notes that 'Bolingbroke seems to arrogate to himself an office which, if it belongs to anybody, belongs to the King' (103). Ironically, of course, Richard is equally a nephew of the murdered man, so that Bolingbroke may intend a covert rebuke to his sovereign.

107 **glorious . . . descent** As a grandson of Edward III (like Richard himself), Bolingbroke insists on his own royal pedigree in a way that suggests his potential rivalry with the King.
worth dignity, nobility, worthiness (cf. 3.3.110)

108 **or** This is usually taken to express an alternative, but Chambers (81) reads it as an equivalent of 'ere'; see 77n.

109 Cf. the anonymous *Caesar's Revenge* (1592–6?), l. 210: 'To what a pitch would this mans vertues sore'.

Conceivably Shakespeare knew this tragedy, performed by the students of Trinity College, Oxford (see also notes on 1.1.196, 2.2.141–2, 3.2.165, 4.1.138); but it is uncertain whether *R2* is earlier or later than the revenge drama. Given the anonymous author's habit of borrowing from such writers as Marlowe, Kyd, Spenser and Sidney, however, it seems likelier that the academic playwright was the debtor.
pitch the highest point of a falcon's flight before it dives upon its prey (cf. 1.3.129–30) – an allusion, perhaps, to the royal badge or emblem used by Bolingbroke's grandfather, Edward III, by Gaunt, and probably by Bolingbroke himself (see Scott-Giles, 70, 73; Cam[2], 60). In addition to which the image could suggest Bolingbroke's latent ambition for the crown, since the falcon (like the lion) was often associated in the hierarchy of nature with the monarch. For a more extended example of the falcon motif and its relevance to political conflict, see *2H6* 2.1.1–20. Actors sometimes deliver this line airily, with a touch of derision, to indicate Richard's foolish lack of concern; alternatively, it can be spoken as an aside to dramatize private alarm. Either way, Richard expresses resentment of Bolingbroke's presumption and lays the groundwork for his decision to banish him in 1.3, although at this point he may not yet definitely suspect him of aspiring to the throne. But cf. 116n.

189

And bid his ears a little while be deaf
Till I have told this slander of his blood
How God and good men hate so foul a liar!

KING RICHARD

Mowbray, impartial are our eyes and ears.   115
Were he my brother, nay, my kingdom's heir,
As he is but my father's brother's son,
Now, by ^Fmy^F sceptre's awe, I make a vow
Such neighbour nearness to our sacred blood
Should nothing privilege him nor partialize   120
The unstooping firmness of my upright soul.

---

113 **slander . . . blood** disgrace to the royal family (cf. 5.6.35)
114 **God . . . men** a common expression (cf. *R3* 3.7.109–10)
115 **eyes and ears** responding to Mowbray's *face* and *ears* (111–12)
116 **my kingdom's heir** a clear instance of ironic foreshadowing. Shakespeare's audience would have known that Bolingbroke became Henry IV. F's emendation ('our') normalizes to the royal plural, but Shakespeare may have intended an occasional reversion to the more personal form as a means of suggesting the private Richard behind his public facade; cf. 8n.
117 **my . . . son** a deliberate slur on Bolingbroke's supposedly distant place in the succession, in contrast to *my kingdom's heir* (116). Inasmuch as Richard had sired no children, Parliament in 1385 designated Roger Mortimer, fourth Earl of March (grandson of Lionel, Duke of Clarence, third of Edward III's sons), as heir presumptive to the throne. When Roger was killed in Ireland in 1398, one motive for Richard's campaign there, Richard designated Roger's son Edmund, fifth Earl of March (then three years old), as heir presumptive. If Mortimer's line should expire, however, Bolingbroke (as male

child of Edward III's fourth son) would indeed be the legal successor after his father, Gaunt; see Appendix 3. After the death of the adult Earl of March, Bolingbroke was already beginning to think of himself as a possible heir to the crown (see Saul, 396–7). In *1H4* Edmund Mortimer (whom Holinshed and Shakespeare confused with his uncle Sir Edmund Mortimer) becomes pretender to the throne and takes part in the unsuccessful rebellion against Bolingbroke; cf. *1H4* 1.3.145–50.
118 ***my sceptre's awe** 'the reverence owed to my sceptre'. F supplies the missing *my*, omitted by Q (see Appendix 1, p. 525); Q6 normalizes unnecessarily to 'our' (see 116n.).
119 **neighbour** neighbouring; cf. *LLL* 5.2.94.
    sacred blood the first of numerous explicit references to divine right in kingship. Bolingbroke's mention of 'my high blood's royalty' (71), however, has already made the concept implicit.
120 **partialize** make partial in judgement (a unique use in Shakespeare)
121 **unstooping . . . upright** Kings kneel only to God. *Upright* implies both erect posture and righteous judgement.

---

116 my kingdom's] our kingdomes *F*   118 my] our *Q6*

He is our subject, Mowbray; so art thou.
Free speech and fearless I to thee allow.

MOWBRAY

Then, Bolingbroke, as low as to thy heart
Through the false passage of thy throat, thou liest.   125
Three parts of that receipt I had for Calais
Disbursed I duly to his highness' soldiers;
The other part reserved I by consent,
For that my sovereign liege was in my debt
Upon remainder of a dear account   130
Since last I went to France to fetch his queen.
Now swallow down that lie. For Gloucester's death,
I slew him not, but to my own disgrace

---

122 *subject, Mowbray; so** The punctuation of both Q and F is ambiguous. We might also read: 'subject. Mowbray, so' (Wells, 167). Meaning is little affected either way.

124 **Bolingbroke** For pronunciation, see List of Roles, 6n.

124–5 **as low . . . throat** an elaborated version of the proverbial expression 'to lie in the throat' (also continuing the imagery of 44 and 57). Bolingbroke's lie is worse than mere verbal deceit since it comes from a false heart. For a negative estimate of Mowbray's reputation in this quarrel, see *2H4* 4.1.129–37.

126 **Three . . . receipt** three-fourths of the money
     Calais pronounced as spelled in the early editions (Callice) – the usual Elizabethan pronunciation

128 **by consent** i.e. with the King's permission. Shakespeare gives Mowbray a better excuse for withholding funds than Holinshed, who reports merely that he retained money owed him by the King, apparently without prior approval: travelling to France to nego-

tiate Richard's marriage to Charles VI's daughter in 1395, he and Aumerle had 'spent great treasure' (some 300,000 marks), yet 'neuer receiued either gold or siluer' in recompense (3.493).

130 **for** the balance of a large (*dear*) amount; see 128n. Cf. also 'dear account', *MA* 4.1.333.

131 **fetch** perhaps meaning 'arrange for her to come to England'; see 128n. Richard himself, not Mowbray, actually escorted her (see Saul, 229–30).

132 **swallow** See 44n. and 57n.
     For as regards (Abbott, 149)

133–4 Mowbray is deliberately obscure (probably to protect himself as well as to shield the King from embarrassment), but most of all because Shakespeare wished for dramatic reasons to becloud not only the physical but also the ethical circumstances of Gloucester's death. In Holinshed (3.494), Mowbray makes no response at all to Bolingbroke's charge, thus protecting the King by his silence. In a different context, however, the chronicler does say that Mowbray delayed

---

122 subject, Mowbray; so] *Ard²*; subiect Mowbray so *Q;* subiect Mowbray, so *Q2;* subiect (*Mowbray*) so *F*   124 heart] heart, *F*   125 throat,] *F (*throat;*);* throate *Q*   126 Calais] *(*Callice*)*   127 duly] *om. Q2–F*   130 account] *Q2 (*account,*);* account: *Q;* Accompt, *F*   133 my] mine *Q2–F*

Neglected my sworn duty in that case.
For you, my noble Lord of Lancaster,   135
The honourable father to my foe,
Once did I lay an ambush for your life –
A trespass that doth vex my grieved soul;
But ere I last received the sacrament
I did confess it and exactly begged   140
Your grace's pardon, and I hope I had it.

having the Duke put to death at Calais, only carrying out the King's order under threat of death (see 100n.). Was Gloucester's execution for treason the *sworn duty* that Mowbray *neglected*? Or does Mowbray mean that his duty was to save Gloucester's life and that in this he failed? Rossiter (48) thinks that Mowbray's *sworn duty* was 'to make anything threatening [Gloucester's] life known to him'. Muir suggests that Mowbray's *duty* may have been 'to reveal the murder' (45), but to whom other than God would he have *sworn* such a vow? In a later passage implicating Aumerle in the murder, Holinshed (3.511) says that Mowbray told Bagot he had spared the Duke 'contrarie to the will of the king . . . by the space of three weeks, and more; affirming withall, that he was neuer in all his life time more affraid of death, than he was at his comming home againe from Calis . . . to the kings presence, by reason he had not put the duke to death. And then (said he) the king appointed one of his owne seruants and certein other . . . to go with him to see the said duke of Glocester put to death, swearing that as he should answer afore God, it was neuer his mind that he should haue died in the fort, but onelie for feare of the king, and sauing his owne life' (cf. 4.1.2–13). The phrase *slew him not* may also be taken as an equivocation – a way of saying that Mowbray's

servants rather than Mowbray personally carried out the killing. Although we cannot know Mowbray's veracity when he denies that he slew Gloucester, it seems clear that he is signalling Richard to come to his rescue; Mowbray implies that he cannot honourably defend himself unless the King restores his dignity by admitting his own role in the death of his uncle. Champion (3–7) argues that Mowbray deliberately implicates the King by his indiscreet reference to Gloucester's death at 132–4, thereby angering Richard and causing his own banishment.

137–41 almost verbatim from Holinshed: 'Marie true it is, that once I laid an ambush to haue slaine the duke of Lancaster . . . but neuerthelesse he hath pardoned me thereof, and there was good peace made betwixt us, for the which I yeeld him hartie thankes. This is that which I haue to answer' (3.494). No details about this puzzling incident have survived, but the mention of it in this context seems intended to complicate our estimate of Mowbray's character yet further. Smidt (185) suggests that the confession of an intended crime against Gaunt, for which he has already been forgiven, 'adds to the impression of sincerity' in Mowbray, thus helping to contrast him in this respect with Bolingbroke.

139 **But** See LN.

140 **exactly** in full detail, precisely

137 did I] I did *F*   139 But] *Qc, F;* Ah but *Qu*

This is my fault. As for the rest appealed,
It issues from the rancour of a villain,
A recreant and most degenerate traitor,
Which in myself I boldly will defend,   145
And interchangeably hurl down my gage
Upon this overweening traitor's foot,
To prove myself a loyal gentleman
Even in the best blood chambered in his bosom. –
        [*Throws down his gage. Bolingbroke takes it up.*]
In haste whereof most heartily I pray   150
Your highness to assign our trial day.

KING RICHARD
Wrath-kindled gentlemen, be ruled by me:
Let's purge this choler without letting blood.
This we prescribe, though no physician;

142 **rest appealed** other things charged against me (see 4n.)
144 **recreant** faithless (to both his religion and his king); sometimes taken as a noun (= coward, traitor)
    degenerate false to his own royal blood (cf. 58)
145 The syntax is ambiguous: either 'which I in my own person will boldly defend against, repel' (the antecedent of *Which* being *rest*); or 'And I will myself boldy defend this statement' (i.e. that Bolingbroke is a traitor). In the latter case the antecedent of *Which* is the entire preceding clause (cf. *Which to maintain* at 62).
146 **interchangeably** reciprocally, in exchange
148–9 'to demonstrate that I am a loyal gentleman by shedding the best blood lodged in his heart'. Mowbray suggests that the blood near the heart is *best* because it is the most vital.
150 **In haste whereof** to hasten which (i.e. in order to bring my innocence to immediate demonstration)

152 *****gentlemen** For F's pluralization of Q's 'gentleman', see Appendix 1, p. 525.
153 **purge . . . blood** expel this wrath medically without bleeding (quibbling on the sense of shedding blood in battle). Biliousness was generally remedied by administering a purgative or cleansing medicine, as opposed to bleeding the patient. Richard plays on the idea of two related bodily humours – one dry and hot (choler or yellow bile), associated with anger; the other moist and hot (blood), associated with passion and physical courage.
154 **though no physician** Monarchs were traditionally supposed to be healers of the body politic. Ure (12–13) cites Tyndale's *Obedience of a Christian Man* (1528) and James I's *A Counterblast to Tobacco* (1604), in which this idea is expressed. Shakespeare develops the theme of the sickly commonweal in *2H4* (e.g. 4.1.54–66) and *Mac* (e.g. 5.2.27–9).

149 SD] *Irving (subst.)*   152 Wrath-kindled] *F;* Wrath kindled *Q*   gentlemen] *F;* gentleman *Q*

Deep malice makes too deep incision.   155
Forget, forgive, conclude and be agreed;
Our doctors say this is no month to bleed.
Good uncle, let this end where it begun;
We'll calm the Duke of Norfolk, you your son.

GAUNT
To be a make-peace shall become my age.   160
Throw down, my son, the Duke of Norfolk's gage.

KING RICHARD
And Norfolk, throw down his.

GAUNT   When, Harry, when?

155 **too deep incision** Medicinal bleeding involved only superficial opening
of the veins or the use of leeches.
156 **Forget, forgive** proverbial (Dent,
F597)
conclude come to terms
157 **doctors** astrologers; learned authorities
this . . . bleed Much ink has been
spilled over the possible superiority of
F's emendation ('time' for *month*), one
of the numerous 'indifferent' substitutions in the later text perhaps derived
from the MS promptbook (see
Appendix 1, pp. 513–14, 529). Jowett
& Taylor, for instance, argue unconvincingly that the change was made 'to
remove the unfortunate suggestion of
menstruation' (191–2). Medieval
almanacs, phlebotomies and other so-
called authorities differed as to the
particular seasons recommended for
the periodic blood-letting regarded as
salutary for bodily health; but the old-
fashioned avoidance of specific
months or times was probably thought
of as superstitious by Shakespeare's
age. The somewhat flippant tone of
Richard's remark, enhanced by the use
of rhymed couplets and the need to
pronounce with four syllables the
rhyme words in 154–5, lends force to
this latter interpretation and indeed

brings the whole passage close to a
kind of unwise levity on Richard's
part, levity at odds with the inflamed
passions of the two contestants. See
109n. on *pitch*. Historically, this confrontation occurred on 29 April 1398.
159 'Richard is not entirely detached and
impartial. Mowbray is his man on the
evidence of the Gloucester murder, and
Bullingbrook is implicitly attacking
Richard through his agent' (Cam², 64).
160 **make-peace** peacemaker (a nonce
word in Shakespeare). Cf. Heywood, *2
If You Know Not Me* (1606), l. 292: 'To
be a make-peace doth become me
well'; for Heywood's pervasive indebtedness to *R2*, see Forker, 'Heywood'.
161–2 **Throw . . . his**. *Throw down* = give
up, relinquish; Bolingbroke and
Mowbray are being urged to renounce
(or *resign*; cf. 176n.) their acceptance of
each other's challenges by throwing
down the gages they have previously
picked up at 78 and 149.
162–3 ***when? / Obedience bids** Pope's
emendation (which follows the punctuation of Q2 and F but omits Q's repetition of 'obedience bids' at 162)
probably restores what Shakespeare
intended. H.F. Brooks plausibly conjectured that 'When . . . againe' must
have appeared in the MS as a single
line and that the compositor belatedly

157 month] time *F*   162–3 When . . . bids] *Pope* (bids,)*;* When Harry? when obedience bids, /
Obedience bids *Q;* When Harry, when? obedience bids, / Obedience bids *Q2–F*

Obedience bids I should not bid again.

KING RICHARD

Norfolk, throw down, we bid; there is no boot.

MOWBRAY

Myself I throw, dread sovereign, at thy foot.   [*Kneels.*]   165

My life thou shalt command, but not my shame.

The one my duty owes; but my fair name,

Despite of death that lives upon my grave,

To dark dishonour's use thou shalt not have.

I am disgraced, impeached and baffled here,   170

Pierced to the soul with Slander's venomed spear,

The which no balm can cure but his heart-blood

Which breathed this poison.

KING RICHARD   Rage must be withstood.

recognized the metrical need to divide but did not go back to delete the words already set in error (Ard², 13).

163 **Obedience** the obedience you owe to me as your father

164 **we** royal plural
   boot alternative, remedy (i.e. you must obey)

165 **Myself I throw** (as an alternative to throwing down Bolingbroke's gage); an exaggerated expression for kneeling in supplication. It is not clear when Mowbray rises again. Perhaps he stands at the end of his last speech (185) or when Gaunt leaves (195).

167 **The . . . owes** my allegiance as a subject may compel me to risk my life at your command

168 **that . . . grave** 'that survives in the epitaph on my grave' (the antecedent of *that* is *fair name*, not *death*; see Abbott, 262). The inversion here seems to be caused by the use of a rhymed couplet.

170 **impeached** accused
   baffled publicly disgraced for cowardice or perjury. To baffle was to degrade a knight ceremonially from his rank by stripping him of his armour

and shield. Traditionally, the knight's image (or even the man himself) was hung upside down from the heels. A description of the procedure appears in Hall (fol. xl); cf. also *FQ*, 6.7.27, where Turpine is baffled. A form of baffling occurs in *1H6* 4.1.15, where Fastolfe is punished for cowardice by having his garter torn off. Some commentators have regarded 'disgraced, impeached and baffled' as chivalric terms arranged in an ascending order of ignomity.

171 **Slander's** *R2* employs many personifications, a technique known to sixteenth-century rhetoricians as *prosopopoeia*. See LN and Introduction, pp. 90, 167.

172 **The which** which wound, i.e. that made by *Slander's venomed spear* (171), the antecedent being implied only. Abbott (270) explains that the addition of *the* to *which*, a common usage in Shakespeare, makes *which* more definite, often in cases where more than one possible antecedent or a similar ambiguity might cause confusion; cf. 90n.

172–3 **his . . . breathed** the heart-blood of him who uttered (see Abbott, 218, 265)

173 **poison** slander, venomous falsity

165 SD] *Bevington (subst.)*   172 heart-blood] *Pope;* heart bloud *QF*

Give me his gage. Lions make leopards tame.

MOWBRAY

Yea, but not change his spots. Take but my shame,   175
And I resign my gage. My dear dear lord,
The purest treasure mortal times afford
Is spotless reputation; that away,
Men are but gilded loam or painted clay.
A jewel in a ten-times-barred-up chest   180
Is a bold spirit in a loyal breast.
Mine honour is my life; both grow in one.

---

174 **his gage** See 78 SD.
  Lions . . . tame The lion, king of beasts, is a traditional emblem of the monarch (cf. 5.1.29), having appeared on the British royal coat of arms from early Plantagenet times as *three lions passant guardant*; the crest of Norfolk's family arms was a *lion léopardé* (an alternative heraldic term for a lion) – in Mowbray's crest shown *statant* rather than *rampant* or *passant guardant* (see Scott-Giles, 74–5). In the precise terminology of heraldry a *lion léopardé* is any lion in a stylized attitude other than *rampant* and has no connection with the spotted leopard of zoology; if Shakespeare knew the heraldic phrase, he could have suggested the conflict between lions and leopards (see Chambers, 83). There is no indication of Mowbray's actually wearing his family arms in this scene, although he might do so in the tournament episode (1.3) for which this scene is obviously a preparation. In Giles's production, Mowbray at Coventry wore an inauthentic spotted leopard clearly emblazoned on his chest. The main point of Richard's remark, of course, is that in nature the greater animal forces the lesser to acknowledge his subordinate position.

175 **change his spots** proverbial expression (Dent, L206; cf. Jeremiah, 13.23, Geneva Bible: 'Can the blacke More change his skin? or the leopard his spots?'). There is a quibble on *spots* = stains on one's reputation (cf. *shame*, 175; *spotless reputation*, 178).
  Take . . . shame Mowbray suggests obliquely that Richard could cure his subject's *shame* by owning up to the *spots* in his own past (i.e. his responsibility for Gloucester's death).
176 **resign** give up (cf. 161–2n.)
  ***gage. My** F's punctuation seems to render the best sense, although Q's ambiguous 'gage, my deare deare Lord,' could be read as indicating a stop after *lord* rather than after *gage* as in Q2.
177–9 excerpted in *Parnassus* (1600), no. 605, under the heading 'Good name'
177 **mortal times afford** that can be experienced in earthly life
179 **gilded . . . clay** alluding to the biblical tradition that God created mankind from the dust of the earth (Genesis, 2.7, 3.19)
180 **ten-times-barred-up chest** i.e. a heavily barricaded strong box (with a possible pun on the sense of 'heavily armoured upper body', anticipating *loyal breast* in 181). The rhyme makes the *double entendre* slightly more likely.
182 **in one** i.e. inseparably

---

176 gage. My . . . lord,] *F;* gage, my . . . Lord, *Q;* gage my . . . Lord. *Q2*   178 reputation;] *F (*reputation:*);* Reputation *Q*   179 gilded] *(*guilded*), F*   180 ten-times-barred-up] *Capell;* ten times bard vp *QF*

Take honour from me, and my life is done.
Then, dear my liege, mine honour let me try;
In that I live, and for that will I die.   185

KING RICHARD [*to Bolingbroke*]
Cousin, throw up your gage; do you begin.

BOLINGBROKE
O, God defend my soul from such deep sin!
Shall I seem crest-fallen in my father's sight?
Or with pale beggar-fear impeach my height
Before this outdared dastard? Ere my tongue   190
Shall wound my honour with such feeble wrong
Or sound so base a parle, my teeth shall tear

---

184 **try** put to the test, prove (by combat)
186 **Cousin** Richard's stress at this juncture on his blood kinship to Bolingbroke seems deliberate and pointed, as though he were trying to use it as leverage in persuasion.
throw up probably 'surrender, relinquish', although *OED* (*v.* 48g) lists no such usage before 1678. Wilson (129) believes that the King occupies the upper level in this scene and that Bolingbroke is here being directed literally to 'throw up' the glove to him. Richard is more likely enthroned on a raised chair (see headnote) and therefore physically higher than the antagonists. F's emendation ('throw downe'), if it comes from the MS promptbook, may reflect a different staging adopted for a later production; alternatively it may represent an attempt in F or its copy to bring the line into conformity with the similar commands at 161–2.
187 **God defend** may God protect. F's change to 'heauen' here and elsewhere is the result of censorship – the Act to Restrain Abuses (1606); see Appendix 1, p. 513.

deep F's 'foule' is an indifferent variant; see Appendix 1, pp. 513–14, 529.
188 **crest-fallen** humbled (literally, 'having a drooping head', with a possible quibble on Bolingbroke's heraldic crest, i.e. 'lowered in rank'). In contrast to Mowbray (165 SD), Bolingbroke refuses to kneel – another sign, perhaps, of his assertion of royal status. RP suggests that this line might be used to motivate Gaunt's awkward exit at 195 (see n.).
189 **impeach my height** discredit my exalted rank; stoop
190 **outdared dastard** outbraved coward; terrified wretch
191 **feeble wrong** the wrong of speaking so cravenly
192 ***parle** truce (literally, a trumpet call to enter upon negotiations at a battle; cf. 3.3.61.1). F's monosyllabic form suits the metre better than Q's 'parlee'; the two words were interchangeable and Shakespeare uses both. See Appendix 1, p. 525.
192–4 **my . . . bleeding** The idea of biting off one's tongue to ensure silence (originally to prevent a torturer from compelling revelation) is common (cf. *3H6* 1.4.47). It is also ancient. Lyly,

---

186 SD] *this edn* up] downe *F*   187 God] heauen *F*   deep] foule *F*   189 beggar-fear] *QF;* beggar-face *Q2*   height] *Qc* (height,), *F;* height? *Qu*   190 dastard?] *Qc, F;* Dastard, *Qu*   191 my] mine *F*   192 parle] *F;* parlee *Q*

The slavish motive of recanting fear
And spit it bleeding, in his high disgrace,
Where Shame doth harbour, even in Mowbray's face.   195
                                                          ᶠ*Exit Gaunt.*ᶠ
KING RICHARD
We were not born to sue but to command;
Which since we cannot do to make you friends,

quoting Plutarch's *De Garrulitate* (chap. 8) in *Euphues* (1578), relates that the philosopher Zeno, 'bicause hee woulde not be enforced to reueale any thinge agaynst his will by torments, bitte of his tongue and spit it in the face of the Tyraunt' (1.279). The extravagantly sanguinary rhetoric of Bolingbroke's speech reflects an aspect of Elizabethan taste. The popular tragedies of blood sometimes staged such gory details: Hieronimo bites out his tongue to forestall forced confession (*Spanish Tragedy*, 4.4.191–4); and Titus Andronicus threatens to imitate his daughter Lavinia, whose tongue has been brutally cut out to keep her mute, with 'shall we bite our tongues, and in dumb shows / Pass the remainder of our hateful days?' (*Tit* 3.1.131–2).

193 **motive** moving organ (i.e. Mowbray's tongue); cf. *TC* 4.5.57.

194 **his** its (i.e. the tongue's, since it would have spoken out of cowardice); see Abbott, 228. This interpretation entails the adding of a comma after *bleeding*. Some commentators think *his* refers to Mowbray, which is possible though unlikely, since it produces a more contorted sense.

high disgrace Cf. *E2*, 2.2.187–8: 'the fleering Scots, / To England's high disgrace, have made this jig'.

195 **Where** in the place where (Mowbray's face)

harbour abide, dwell (intransitive)

SD *F supplies the necessary (if somewhat abrupt) SD so that Gaunt can re-enter at the beginning of the following scene. It probably derives

from the MS promptbook (see Appendix 1, p. 509), although conceivably it was omitted from Q in error. Wilson thinks the exit too unmotivated dramatically to have been part of Shakespeare's original intention (129). The exit is problematic, as it occurs just as Richard is about to announce his decision, in which Gaunt would have every interest, besides which it would normally be a violation of court etiquette for a noble to leave the royal presence without being formally excused or dismissed; but if F is wrong, it would be the sole instance of a mistakenly interpolated SD in the Folio text, which partly explains why most editors accept it. If the exit was an afterthought, as GWW suggests (see Appendix 1, p. 509, n. 1), it might perhaps have been motivated onstage by some explanatory gesture on the part of Gaunt, Richard or both. Gaunt, for instance, might express his mounting impatience or frustration at his son's refusal to yield to his entreaty to 'throw down' Norfolk's gage at 161–3, and Richard might motion him offstage with a nod or even an extended hand to be kissed. See LN.

196 Cf. *Caesar's Revenge*, l. 179: 'And sue and bow, where earst I did command', presumably echoing *R2*; see 109n.

sue entreat, beg

197 **Which . . . do** Having made a sweeping assertion of royal authority in 196, Richard immediately discloses his weakness by yielding to circumstance – an early and revealing example of the

Be ready as your lives shall answer it
At Coventry upon Saint Lambert's Day.
There shall your swords and lances arbitrate   200
The swelling difference of your settled hate.
Since we cannot atone you, we shall see
Justice design the victor's chivalry.
Lord Marshal, command our officers at arms   204
Be ready to direct these home alarms.   *Exeunt.*

discrepancy which the play develops between the regal posturing of the King and his actual power to command allegiance.

199 **Saint Lambert's Day** 17 September. The date comes from Holinshed, who says that historians disagree: 'some saie, it was vpon a mondaie in August; other vpon saint Lamberts daie, . . . other on the eleuenth of September' (3.494). See LN.

200 **lances** long weapons used in tilting (with perhaps a glancing reference to the instruments used in surgery to relieve *swelling* (201), thus extending the medical motif of bleeding from 153–7)

201 **swelling** increasing; puffed up by pride

202 **atone** reconcile (literally to make 'at one')

we shall There would seem to be no justification for Q2's emendation (or misremembering), 'you shall', followed by Q3 and F.

203 **design . . . chivalry** designate the champion through chivalric contest. In theory, trials by combat were decided by God, who would award victory to the righteous contestant in cases where lack of evidence made proof by other means impossible; in practice, however, duelling became a matter more of aristocratic honour (associated with Italianate ruthlessness) than of

religious justice. Elizabethans, who debated the morality of trials by combat, tended to disapprove of them – especially the Christian humanists (see Bornstein, 131–41); but Shakespeare invokes an archaic (medieval) ethos. Fortune rather than Justice was sometimes regarded as the arbiter of victory in such combats (cf. Westmoreland's account in *2H4* 4.1.131–3).

204 **Lord Marshal** Capell, followed by other editors, emends to 'Marshal' on metrical grounds, but this is hardly necessary. *Lord Marshal, command* may be spoken either as an iamb followed by an anapaest (with the final syllable in *Marshal* given very light value; see Abbott, 468); or as three iambic feet in an alexandrine, if *Marshal* were pronounced trisyllabically as in French ('Lord Màr- | e-shàl, | commànd'; cf. Q's spelling 'Martiall' at 1.3.44, 46, 99, and see Cercignani, 347). Since the line is part of a rhymed couplet, the first solution seems preferable. The Lord Marshal's official responsibility was to enforce the rules of the combat and ensure orderly procedure. See List of Roles, 28n.

205 **home alarms** domestic (as opposed to foreign, possibly Irish; cf. 1.4.38) troubles. Originally 'alarm' meant a call to arms.

198 lives] *QF;* life *Q2*   202 we shall] you shall *Q2–F*   204 Lord Marshal] Marshal *Capell*
205 SD] *F; Exit. Q*

[1.2]   *Enter* John of GAUNT *with the*
                        DUCHESS OF GLOUCESTER.

GAUNT

Alas, the part I had in Woodstock's blood
Doth more solicit me than your exclaims
To stir against the butchers of his life.
But since correction lieth in those hands
Which made the fault that we cannot correct,   5

1.2 The chroniclers provide no source for this scene (set probably in Gaunt's London residence or at Ely House in Holborn, where he dies; cf. 1.4.58). The Duchess of Gloucester, who never reappears after this episode, is, however, a character in *Woodstock*, where (as here) she is characterized as grief-stricken and craving vengeance for her husband (5.3.1–18). Rossiter (234) believes that Shakespeare 'assumed' audience familiarity with her situation as presented in *Woodstock*. The Duchess seems to be portrayed as an elderly woman (see 73–4; 2.2.97) and is usually played as old, although in fact she was still in her thirties. Her wailfulness introduces a tone of desolation and woe that will later dominate Richard's speeches and indeed the play as a whole. Apart from allowing the actors who play Bolingbroke and Mowbray an opportunity to armour themselves for the lists in 1.3, and to convey the sense of lapsed time (the historical interval between the first and third scenes was from April to September), this scene also reinforces the gravity of Gloucester's death and to some degree clarifies Richard's role therein, thereby temporarily alienating him from the audience's sympathy. It also establishes an important concern of the play by setting up a conflict between private and public concepts of order, between personal duty to family (in this case, vengeance) and the larger duty of

obedience to God (as vested in the anointed sovereignty of the king). The older generation (Gaunt and Gloucester's widow) also contrasts meaningfully with the younger generation (Richard and Bolingbroke).

1   **part** share (as his brother); see List of Roles, 3n.
    Woodstock's the only use of this name (Thomas of Woodstock's) in the play. F's regularization to 'Glousters' may represent a clarification in the theatre promptbook (possibly authorial), adopted in production to make audience recognition of the character easier (see Appendix 1, p. 529 and n. 1).
    blood blood kinship (not a reference to murder, despite the fact that Gaunt knew his brother had been charged with treason)

2   **solicit** arouse, stir
    exclaims outcries

3   **stir** take action
    butchers continues the imagery of blood developed in the preceding scene (see especially 1.1.103n.). Note also the plural – another indication of diffused responsibility for the death (cf. *offenders'* at 8).

4   **correction** punishment
    those hands i.e. the King's

5   **we cannot correct** 'We, as subjects, cannot punish the King (who holds all power).' Gaunt plays on the double meaning of *correct*: to punish; to set right.

1.2] *F (Scaena Secunda.)*   0.1–2] *Enter Gaunt, and Dutchesse of Gloucester. F*   1 Woodstock's] Glousters *F*

Put we our quarrel to the will of heaven,
Who, when they see the hours ripe on earth,
Will rain hot vengeance on offenders' heads.
DUCHESS OF GLOUCESTER
Finds brotherhood in thee no sharper spur?
Hath love in thy old blood no living fire?   10
Edward's seven sons, whereof thyself art one,
Were as seven vials of his sacred blood,

6 unlike the antagonists of 1.1
   Put we let us submit (hortatory subjunctive)
7 **they** The antecedent is *heaven* (6)
   understood as a plural (perhaps implying heavenly powers, God and His
   angels).
   hours a dissyllable (often spelled
   'howers'; see 1.3.261t.n.); cf. 5.1.25n.,
   5.5.58n.
8 **rain hot vengeance** a common biblical image; cf. Genesis, 19.24–5, where
   God so punishes Sodom and
   Gomorrah; see also Luke, 17.28–9 and
   Psalms, 11.6, 140.10.
   offenders' See 3n. on *butchers*.
9 **brotherhood** the circumstance of
   your being brothers
10 **old blood** blood of an old man; blood
   of an ancient family. See 1.1.1n.
11 **Edward's seven sons** Edward III's
   sons; Shakespeare catalogues them in
   2H6 2.2.10–17, and they are referred
   to twice in *Woodstock* (5.1.84, 161).
   Most were dead by 1398 (the year in
   which this conversation would have
   occurred; cf. 14–15): William of
   Hatfield and William of Windsor
   expired as children; Lionel, Duke of
   Clarence, died in Italy in 1368;
   Edward, the Black Prince, the heir
   apparent, predeceased his father in
   1376; Thomas of Woodstock, Duke of
   Gloucester, was killed at Calais in
   1397. The two surviving sons were
   John of Gaunt, Duke of Lancaster,
   who died in 1399 (cf. 2.1.149–50), and
   Edmund of Langley, Duke of York,
   who died in 1402. See Appendix 3.
12–13 a perfectly balanced pair of lines to

which 14–15 (see n.) respond in an
equally balanced way
seven . . . branches Shakespeare
extends these two similes for Edward
III's progeny in parallel, alternating
between and combining them in the
passage that follows with a calculated
artificiality typical of his early, conceited
manner. The genealogical tree with its
seven branches probably derives from
the Tree of Jesse, a common emblem of
religious iconography in medieval
stained-glass windows showing the
symbolic ancestry of Christ; Jesse (the
root of the tree) was the father of seven
sons (the branches), one of whom was
King David – hence the royal analogy.
Stow's *Annals* has a similar tree illustrating Elizabeth I's forebears on its title-
page. Ure (18) cites the parable of the
vine signifying Christ and the members
of his body (John, 15.5) as perhaps lying
behind the root and branch imagery; cf.
E2, 5.1.47–8: 'So shall not England's
vine be perishèd, / But Edward's name
survive though Edward dies'.
Throughout the play Shakespeare richly interweaves the various connotations
and symbolism of blood – the source of
vitality or essence of life, family kinship,
violent bloodshed, royal descent, religious sacrifice – all of which come
together in this speech. The imagery of
branches and vegetation is equally significant, being a pervasive motif of the
play, especially important in the garden
scene (3.4).
12 **sacred blood** a stock phrase for 'royal
   blood', reflecting belief in the divine
   right of kings (cf. 17 and 1.1.119n.)

Or seven fair branches springing from one root.
Some of those seven are dried by nature's course,
Some of those branches by the Destinies cut;   15
But Thomas, my dear lord, my life, my Gloucester,
One vial full of Edward's sacred blood,
One flourishing branch of his most royal root,
Is cracked, and all the precious liquor spilt,
Is hacked down, and his summer leaves all faded   20
By Envy's hand and Murder's bloody axe.
Ah, Gaunt, his blood was thine! That bed, that womb,
That mettle, that self mould that fashioned thee

14–15 These lines balance 12–13: some of the *seven vials* (12) are *dried*, and some of the *seven fair branches* (13) are *cut*; *dried* = dried up, withered by age (like Gaunt and York), while *cut* = cut off from life, dead (like Gloucester).

15–21 The Duchess contrasts the four sons who died of natural causes (see 11n.) with her husband, who died violently.

15 **Destinies** the mythological fates – Clotho, Lachesis and Atropos – the last of whom carried shears to cut the thread of life; *Destinies* is pronounced as a quasi-dissyllable ('Dest'nies'; see Abbott, 468). Shakespeare may have recalled the epilogue of *Doctor Faustus*, written shortly before *R2*: 'Cut is the branch that might have grown full straight' (cf. 4.1.283n.). The reference to cut branches probably alludes to one of Thomas of Woodstock's badges, 'a gold stock of a tree, uprooted and cut short' (Scott-Giles, 58; see Fig. 7); if the Duchess were appropriately costumed to display the family impresa on her mourning dress, the connection between her verbal imagery and the particularity of her widowhood would be greatly strengthened.

20 **summer . . . faded** Gloucester, being in his early forties at the time of his

death, was in the *summer* of his life. Q's 'faded' and F's 'vaded' are the same word, the latter being a weaker form (see *OED*); cf. *PP* 10.1: 'Sweet rose, fair flower, untimely pluck'd, soon vaded'.

21 **Envy's hand** Spite's or Malice's hand (much stronger than today). For the personification, see 1.1.171n. Possibly Shakespeare remembered the description of Invidia in Ovid, *Met.* (2.760–85). Here the warrior-goddess Pallas visits Envy's loathsome, poisonous and infertile cave and is touched by the creature's 'festering hand' ('*manu ferrugine tincta*', l. 798). In Golding, Envy with 'a crooked staffe in hand' tramples and burns 'both grasse and corne' making 'all the fresh and fragrant fieldes seeme utterly forlorne' (2.985–9).
axe. Cf. 1.1.103n.

23 *****mettle** substance, material. F's spelling; originally the same word as 'metal' (cf. Q's 'mettall'), although here used figuratively. Gradually 'mettle' came to signify 'composition, spirit', while 'metal' retained the more specific, concrete sense. The two spellings were used indifferently in the early editions of Shakespeare.
self mould selfsame mould (as in casting metal), i.e. the womb

20 faded] vaded *F*   23 mettle] (mettall), *F*

Made him a man; and though thou livest and breathest,
Yet art thou slain in him. Thou dost consent   25
In some large measure to thy father's death,
In that thou seest thy wretched brother die,
Who was the model of thy father's life.
Call it not patience, Gaunt; it is despair.
In suff'ring thus thy brother to be slaughtered,   30
Thou show'st the naked pathway to thy life,
Teaching stern Murder how to butcher thee.
That which in mean men we entitle patience
Is pale cold cowardice in noble breasts.
What shall I say? To safeguard thine own life   35
The best way is to venge my Gloucester's death.

GAUNT

God's is the quarrel, for God's substitute,
His deputy anointed in His sight,

24 **livest and breathest** perhaps pronounced with elided suffixes: 'liv'st', 'breath'st'

25 **consent** assent (i.e. by acquiescing to injury). The meaning approaches 'approve of' or 'become accessory to'.

28 **model** perfect copy, image

29 **patience** self-control; a specifically Christian virtue implying the willingness in humility to accept and wait upon the will of God (cf. 6–8)
despair loss of hope (the worst of sins from a theological perspective, being the inverse of pride)

30 **suff'ring** tamely permitting, enduring

31 **naked** i.e. defenceless, unprotected from assault

33–4 'These lines give point to the emphasis on cowardice by the quarrelling nobles in 1.1' (Cam², 67).

33 **mean** of humble station, low born

36 **venge** avenge (an archaic form)

37–41 Gaunt voices the orthodox doctrine of obedience to the sovereign (*God's substitute* or the representative of His authority on earth) as articulated in the tenth *Homily* (1547) appointed to be read in Elizabethan churches: even in the case of a wicked prince 'wee may not in any wise withstand violently, or rebell against rulers, or make any insurrection, sedition, or tumults, either by force of armes (or otherwise) against the annointed of the Lord, or any of his officers: But wee must in such case patiently suffer all wrongs, and iniuries, referring the iudgement of our cause onely to God' (*Homilies*, 1.74–5); *A Homily against Disobedience and Wilful Rebellion* (1570) amplifies the same lesson. York (2.3.96, 108–12) and Carlisle (4.1.122–34) express a similar attitude. Cf. also Gloucester's sentiments in *Woodstock* (4.2.144–50).

38 **deputy** 'Richard is twice called God's deputy in *Woodstock* (4.2.144, 5.3.58)' (Ard², 19).
anointed . . . sight i.e. at the coronation in Westminster Abbey, God's

31 show'st] *F;* shewest *Q*   35 thine] *QF;* thy *Q2*   37 God's . . . God's] Heauens . . . heauens *F*

Hath caused his death, the which if wrongfully,
Let heaven revenge, for I may never lift   40
An angry arm against His minister.

DUCHESS OF GLOUCESTER

Where then, alas, may I complain myself?

GAUNT

To God, the widow's champion and defence.

DUCHESS OF GLOUCESTER

Why then, I will. Farewell, old Gaunt.
Thou goest to Coventry, there to behold   45
Our cousin Hereford and fell Mowbray fight.
O, sit my husband's wrongs on Hereford's spear,

house; anointing with holy oil was (and is) the liturgical sign of the monarch's consecration to his unique office. Cf. 1 Samuel, 24.6. See 3.2.55n.

39 **his** Gloucester's
if wrongfully if it was done wrongfully. The *if* is important: Gaunt, who clearly believes in Richard's guilt (cf. 2.1.126–31), nevertheless leaves room for the theoretical possibility that the killing of Gloucester might be defended. Historically, Gaunt and Gloucester were sometimes at odds (see Holinshed, 3.488; Froissart, 6.260): in foreign policy Gloucester opposed his brother's more pacific attitude to France, and Gaunt formally assented to Gloucester's arrest for treason in 1397.

40 **heaven** God; here the substitution seems to be authorial and probably has nothing to do with the official censorship of blasphemy reflected in the similar substitutions that characterize F (see Appendix 1, p. 513).

41 **His** *God's* (37). Some editors take *His* to be a variant of 'its' (see Abbott, 228), making *heaven* (40) the antecedent.

42 **Where** to whom
may . . . myself can I lodge a complaint on my own behalf (reflexive

construction; cf. French *me plaindre*). See Abbott, 296.

43 **God . . . defence** a common biblical idea; cf. Psalms, 68.5, 146.9; Ecclesiasticus, 35.14. Cf. also *KJ* 3.1.107–8; Wilson notes the 'strong resemblance between Constance [in *KJ*] and the Duchess' (132).

44 a tetrameter line probably introduced for variety (see 1.1.12n.), although attempts have been made to scan it as a pentameter by prolonging *will* and interpreting *Farewell* as a trisyllable. An obvious pause occurs before *Farewell*.

46 **cousin** kinsman (as often in Shakespeare); Bolingbroke is the Duchess's nephew by marriage and also her brother-in-law (see List of Roles, 10n.); he is Gaunt's son.
fell cruel, ruthless (as the putative murderer of her husband)

47 ****sit . . . wrongs** 'may the wrongs done to my husband sit' (optative subjunctive); F's apparent emendation could be an alternative spelling of Q's 'set' (cf. 5.5.27n.); the two words tended to fall together in Elizabethan usage (see *OED*). See Appendix 1, p. 525.

42 then, alas, may] *Qc* (then alas may), *F* (then (alas may); then may *Qu*   43 God] heauen *F*   and] to *F*   47 sit] *F*; set *Q*

That it may enter butcher Mowbray's breast!
Or if misfortune miss the first career,
Be Mowbray's sins so heavy in his bosom   50
That they may break his foaming courser's back
And throw the rider headlong in the lists,
A caitiff recreant to my cousin Hereford!
Farewell, old Gaunt. Thy sometimes brother's wife,
With her companion, Grief, must end her life.   55
    [*Starts to leave.*]

GAUNT
Sister, farewell; I must to Coventry.
As much good stay with thee as go with me!
    [*Starts to leave.*]

DUCHESS OF GLOUCESTER
Yet one word more. Grief boundeth where it falls,
Not with the empty hollowness, but weight.

---

48 **butcher** Cf. 3n.

49 **if . . . career** 'if the first encounter of the horses in combat does not result in Mowbray's death'. In tourneying a 'career' was a gallop at full speed ending in a sudden stop, a manoeuvre that could 'throw the rider headlong' (52) from his saddle. F's 'carreere' is probably only a variant spelling of the Q ('carier') and Q3 ('carriere') forms of the word.

50–1 Wilson (132) cites *Woodstock*, 5.3.16–17: 'And may their sins sit heavy on their souls / That they in death, this day, may perish all'; cf. 4.1.67–70.

50 **Be . . . sins** let Mowbray's sins be (subjunctive)

52 **lists** Originally lists were the barriers built to enclose a tournament; later they came to signify the entire arena.

53 **A . . . cousin** 'thus proving him a cowardly wretch, faithless (in chivalry)

to my nephew' (see 46n.); literally, *caitiff* = 'cowardly captive'; *recreant* = apostate, faith-breaking, recanting. Some editors interpret *caitiff* as an adjective (cowardly, base) modifying *recreant* (faithless wretch).

54 **Thy sometimes** formerly thy (*sometimes* is a variant form of 'sometime'); cf. 5.1.37, 5.5.75. Pope's emendation is needless.

55 'must die as a result of grief'; a dramatic preparation for the news that York receives at 2.2.97 (see n.)

58 **boundeth** rebounds (like a ball). She explains her reason for continuing to vent her sorrow by comparing it to a ball that bounces back.

59 'not with the lightness (of a bouncing tennis ball) but with the heaviness of grief'. Having let out some of her grief, she feels paradoxically heavier now than before, and so has more to say.

---

48 butcher] *Qc, F;* butchers *Qu*   49 career] *(carier), F*   54 sometimes] sometime *Pope*   55 SD] *this edn*   57 SD] *this edn*   58 it] *Q2, F;* is *Q*   59 empty] *Qc, F;* emptines, *Qu*

I take my leave before I have begun,   60
For sorrow ends not when it seemeth done.
Commend me to thy brother, Edmund York.
Lo, this is all. Nay, yet depart not so!
Though this be all, do not so quickly go;
I shall remember more. Bid him – ah, what? –   65
With all good speed at Pleshy visit me.
Alack, and what shall good old York there see
But empty lodgings and unfurnished walls,
Unpeopled offices, untrodden stones?
And what hear there for welcome but my groans?   70
Therefore commend me; let him not come there
To seek out sorrow that dwells everywhere.
Desolate, desolate, will I hence and die!
The last leave of thee takes my weeping eye.   *Exeunt.*

60–1 As Gurr (32) notes perceptively, this couplet by its formality would seem to signal the conclusion of the scene (Gaunt and the Duchess have already begun their exits); yet she cannot break off so easily, continuing for thirteen more lines to elaborate her desolation in a speech that employs both rhyme and blank verse. The combination of styles produces the subtle effect of struggle between incipient breakdown and emotional control.

60 **before . . . begun** before I have scarcely begun my lamentations

62 **Commend me** give my affectionate greetings (an Elizabethan formula)

66 **Pleshy** (or Plashy); the Duke of Gloucester's country estate near Dunmow in Essex (mentioned in Holinshed; also the *locus* of several scenes in *Woodstock*). Gloucester was arrested there. The name occurs also

in 'Thomas, Duke of Gloucester' in *Mirror* (98). Q's spelling indicates probable pronunciation.

68 **lodgings** apartments, living quarters
   unfurnished walls walls without adornment (tapestries, armour, weaponry, etc.). Wall hangings were usually taken down during family absences.

69 **offices** rooms or outhouses where servants perform their duties (the kitchen, pantry, wine cellar, etc.)

74 **last leave** This phrase may embody a double presentiment of both the speaker's and Gaunt's impending death, particularly if the actor playing Gaunt characterizes him as showing signs of ill health (see 1.1.195LN).

74 SD Gaunt and the Duchess, who are taking leave of each other, probably exit by separate doors.

60 begun] *(begone), Q2, F*   62 thy] my *Q2–F*   65 ah] Oh *F*   66 Pleshy] *Q6 (Pleshie);* Plashie *QF*   70 hear] *Qc, F;* cheere *Qu*

[1.3]   *Enter* Lord Marshal *and the* Duke [of] AUMERLE.

LORD MARSHAL

My Lord Aumerle, is Harry Hereford armed?

AUMERLE

Yea, at all points, and longs to enter in.

LORD MARSHAL

The Duke of Norfolk, sprightfully and bold,

Stays but the summons of the appellant's trumpet.

1.3 Basically a condensation and rearrangement of Holinshed (3.494–5), who describes the lists at Coventry in colourful detail but says that the events occupied four different days: on the first two Bolingbroke and Mowbray visited the King; on the third the abortive combat and sentencing took place; on the fourth day Bolingbroke's exile was reduced. In Froissart, Richard banishes the dukes before they can confront each other at the tournament. Froissart alone explains the reduction of Bolingbroke's sentence (recommended in advance by the King's advisers 'to please the people') and makes it clearer than the other sources that Gaunt assented to the exile (6.315). Shakespeare invents Gaunt's sorrow as a pretext for shortening the banishment as well as the emotional parting between father and son. He also omits Bushy as official spokesman for the King (cf. 121–2n.). Within the limits of Elizabethan staging (which probably would have omitted horses despite the use of one in *Woodstock*, 3.2) the formal pageantry and spectacle so insisted upon in the sources are preserved. Hodges (31), envisioning the Swan as an early venue (see Introduction, p. 121), suggests in a drawing that Mowbray and Bolingbroke may have occupied facing chairs placed with their backs against the left and right pillars. See LN.

1 **Aumerle** For pronunciation, see List of Roles, 9n. According to Holinshed, Aumerle officiated 'that daie' as 'high constable of England, and the duke of Surrie' as 'marshall' (3.494); see List of Roles, 28n.

2 **at all points** completely, wearing all the pieces of his armour; cf. *Mirror*'s description of Mowbray, 'At all poyntes armde' (106, l. 135).
   in into the lists

3 **bold** boldly; adverb (Abbott, 397)

4 **Stays** awaits
   summons of might be emended to 'summons to' (as such substitutions are common in the work of the Q compositor designated 'A'; see Appendix 1, pp. 537–9). *Summons of* apparently means 'summons comprising' whereas 'summons to' would imply that Mowbray is being summoned more threateningly to answer a specific charge symbolized by Bolingbroke's trumpet.
   appellant's accuser's. Technically, Mowbray should be waiting for the Herald's trumpet, not Bolingbroke's. Shakespeare violates the correct chivalric procedure; the appellant was supposed to enter the lists first, as occurs in Hall and Holinshed. The play reverses the order, perhaps to heighten dramatic effect, saving the appearance of the more popular of the contestants (Bolingbroke) until last; see Introduction, p. 126.

1.3] *F (Scena Tertia.)*   0.1] *Enter Marshall, and Aumerle. F*   4 of] to *(this edn)*

AUMERLE

Why then, the champions are prepared and stay   5
For nothing but his majesty's approach.

The trumpets sound and KING [RICHARD] *enters with his nobles,*
[F]GAUNT, BUSHY, BAGOT, GREEN *and others*[F] [*with Attendants*].
When they are set, [*the trumpets sound, and*] *enter* [F]MOWBRAY,[F]
Duke of Norfolk, *in arms, defendant,* [F]*with* [1] Herald[F].

KING RICHARD

Marshal, demand of yonder champion
The cause of his arrival here in arms.
Ask him his name, and orderly proceed
To swear him in the justice of his cause.   10

LORD MARSHAL [*to Mowbray*]

In God's name and the King's, say who thou art

---

5   **champions** combatants
6.3   *set* As in 1.1, the King is seated, probably on a raised chair (cf. 54), to serve
as umpire; his nobles are also seated.
the trumpets sound After the King's
entrance, a separate fanfare should
announce Mowbray (cf. Bolingbroke's
entrance at 25.1). The two combatants
probably enter by separate doors, since
in the sources they dismount from
their horses and occupy chairs at
opposite ends of the field. In Hall and
Holinshed the two chairs are richly
appointed and curtained about with
green and blue velvet (for Bolingbroke) and red and white damask (for
Mowbray).
6.4   *with* 1 Herald Both Mowbray and
Bolingbroke's heralds would have had
their masters' arms emblazoned on
their tabards; cf. *2H6* 4.10.70–1. See
also 1.1.174n.
7   **demand** ask (not peremptory); cf. 26.
9   **orderly** in accordance with the proper

regulations
10   to swear him in (as in a legal proceeding). Before being admitted to the lists,
knights were obliged to swear before
the Lord Marshal and the Constable
that their cause was just; presumably
one of them would thus perjure himself and so invite defeat.
11–13   Formal identification of the champions was part of the ritual, originally,
perhaps, because full armour with the
visor closed made a man's face unrec-
ognizable and his coat of arms might
not be known; cf. *KL* 5.3.142–6. Verity
observes that 'a knight was not bound
to fight with one of inferior rank'
(109). Cf. *Traïson*: 'the Marshal . . .
asked him who he was, what he wanted,
and for what purpose he was come
hither' (18–19/151–2).
11   **In God's name** For F's anomalous
retention of 'God' in parts of this scene
rather than substituting 'Heaven', see
Appendix 1, p. 513.

6.1–4] *Flourish. Enter King, Gaunt, Bushy, Bagot, Greene, & others: Then Mowbray in Armor, and*
Harrold. F   6.1   KING RICHARD] *the King Q*   6.2   *with Attendants*] *this edn*   6.3   *the trumpets . . . and*]
this edn   6.4   Duke] *the Duke Q*   arms, defendant] *Cam;*   armes defendant *Q*   1 Herald] *this edn;*
Harrold F   7+   SP] *King Q;   Rich. F*   11   SD] *Wells*

And why thou com'st thus knightly clad in arms,
Against what man thou com'st, and what thy quarrel.
Speak truly, on thy knighthood and thy oath,
As so defend thee heaven and thy valour.   15

MOWBRAY

My name is Thomas Mowbray, Duke of Norfolk,
Who hither come engaged by my oath –
Which God defend a knight should violate –
Both to defend my loyalty and truth
To God, my king and my succeeding issue   20
Against the Duke of Hereford that appeals me,
And, by the grace of God and this mine arm,
To prove him, in defending of myself,
A traitor to my God, my king and me;
And as I truly fight, defend me heaven.   25

The trumpets sound. Enter [BOLINGBROKE,] *Duke of Hereford,*
appellant, in armour, ^F*with* [2] *Herald*^F.

13 **quarrel** cause
15 'as heaven and your valour may truly protect you' (inverted word order; cf. 25, 34, 41); *so* probably refers to *truly* (14).
17 **engaged** engagèd; pledged
18 **defend** forbid
20 **my succeeding issue** my heirs. Johnson defends Q's *my* on the grounds that Mowbray's children, on account of the charge of treason, were 'in danger of an attainder': the Duke 'might come among other reasons for their sake'. Mowbray is concerned for the honour of his family and title as well as for his own honour as an individual. F's 'his' (referring to the King's heirs) also makes sense, however, despite the fact that Richard had no children and that past and present fidelity to the sovereign would be more

likely to occupy Mowbray's thoughts at this moment than loyalty to his successors. Johnson, despite his defence of Q, regarded F as 'more just and grammatical' (1.430). That *my* also occurs in close proximity in the same speech (at 16, 17, 19 and 24) makes the possibility of compositorial error plausible. Nevertheless, Q's reading seems the safer choice. Note that 24 repeats the same sequence as 20.
21 **appeals** accuses; cf. 1.1.9.
25 **truly** in a righteous cause
    defend me heaven See 15n. According to Holinshed, each champion, after formally presenting himself, 'sate him downe in his chaire' (3.495); see 6.3n.
25.1 *trumpets sound* F's '*Tucket*' (trumpet flourish) is equivalent.

12 com'st] *F;* comest *Q*   13 what thy] what's thy *Q2–F*   14 thy oath] thine oath *F*   15 thee]
(the), Q2–F   17 come] comes *F*   18 God] heauen *F*   20 my succeeding] his succeeding *F*
25.1–2] *Tucket. Enter Hereford, and Harold. F*   Hereford, *appellant,*] *Irving; Hereford appellant Q*
25.2 2 Herald] *this edn; Harold F*

KING RICHARD

Marshal, ask of yonder knight in arms
Both who he is and why he cometh hither
Thus plated in habiliments of war,
And formally, according to our law,
Depose him in the justice of his cause.   30

LORD MARSHAL [*to Bolingbroke*]

What is thy name? And wherefore com'st thou hither
Before King Richard in his royal lists?
Against whom comest thou? And what's thy quarrel?
Speak like a true knight, so defend thee heaven.

BOLINGBROKE

Harry of Hereford, Lancaster and Derby   35
Am I, who ready here do stand in arms
To prove, by God's grace and my body's valour,

---

26 *tetrameter line in both Q and F (or
possibly a failed pentameter).
Keightley smoothed the metre by
emending to 'Lord Marshal, ask of' (cf.
46), but since *Marshal* is consistent
with Richard's earlier vocative in a parallel situation at 7, this solution seems
unsatisfactory. Some editors follow
Irving, adopting Ritson's conjecture,
'demand of' (for *ask*), thus regularizing
the metre and restoring what they take
to be a formulaic expression given correctly at 7. Gurr argues that Q's compositor perhaps 'associated the *demand
of* in 7 with the *Ask* of 9, and the memory confused him at 26' (70). Although
this is possible, the separation between
9 and 26 is more than half a page in Q
(sig. B2) – too great to make memorial
substitution likely. GWW conjectures
that Shakespeare may have written
'Marshall, now aske'. In any case
Shakespeare occasionally introduces

short lines for variety (see 1.1.12n.).
27 **who . . . hither** See 11–13n.
28 **plated** armoured (in plate armour
rather than chain mail). F's 'placed' is
probably a misreading, *c* for *t*, rather
than a genuine variant.
29 **formally** For the significance of
Q5–F's variant, 'formerly', see
Appendix 1, p. 507, n. 3.
30 **Depose him** administer his oath and
take his sworn statement
32 **royal lists** royal because of the King's
presence. Holinshed reports: 'The
king caused a sumptuous scaffold or
theater, and roiall listes . . . to be erected and prepared' (3.494).
33 *comest The metre requires two syllables. F's 'com'st' can be accepted as a
variant spelling of 'comest'; Q seems
to have dropped the final *t* in error.
34 **so . . . heaven** 'on that condition may
heaven defend you'; see 15n.

---

26 Marshal] Lord Marshal *Keightley*   ask of] *Keightley*; aske *QF*; demand of *Irving (Ritson)*
28 plated] placed *F*   29 formally] formerly *Q5–F*   31 SD] *Wells*   31–2 hither . . . lists?] *Q4*
(hither,), *Q5, F*; hither? . . . lists, *Q1–2*; hither? . . . lists? *Q3*   33 comest] *Q5*; comes *Q*; com'st *F*
35+ SP] *(Bul[l].)*   37 God's] heauens *F*

210

In lists, on Thomas Mowbray, Duke of Norfolk,
That he is a traitor, foul and dangerous,
To God of heaven, King Richard and to me;   40
And as I truly fight, defend me heaven.

LORD MARSHAL

On pain of death, no person be so bold
Or daring-hardy as to touch the lists
Except the Marshal and such officers
Appointed to direct these fair designs.   45

BOLINGBROKE

Lord Marshal, let me kiss my sovereign's hand
And bow my knee before his majesty.
For Mowbray and myself are like two men
That vow a long and weary pilgrimage;
Then let us take a ceremonious leave   50
And loving farewell of our several friends.

LORD MARSHAL

The appellant in all duty greets your highness

---

39 **he is** probably elided (as in F)
42–5 Cf. Holinshed (3.495): 'a king at armes [a chief herald] made open proclamation, prohibiting all men in the name of the king, and of the high constable and marshall, to enterprise or attempt to approch or touch any part of the lists vpon paine of death, except such as were appointed to order or marshall the field'.
43 **daring-hardy* recklessly bold. Theobald's emendation merely clarifies F. Q's reading may represent the occasional compositorial practice of substituting a comma for a hyphen. Compound adjectives are not uncommon in Shakespeare (Abbott, 2). *Traïson* (20/154) uses French '*hardie*' in precisely the same context: 'that no

person . . . be so daring ['*hardie*'] as to put his hand upon the lists'.
touch interfere in
45 **these fair designs** the proper conduct of the tournament; cf. *fair degree* (1.1.80–1n.).
49 Perhaps an unconscious but ironic presage of 5.6.49–50, where Bolingbroke (now Henry IV) vows to 'make a voyage to the Holy Land'. The prophecy that Henry would die in Jerusalem was legendary and is mentioned by Holinshed in the context of his death (3.541); cf. *2H4* 4.5.232–40. Consciously, of course, Bolingbroke refers conventionally to the *pilgrimage* of life (cf. 230), or perhaps even of life after death.
51 **several** respective; various

39 he is] he's *F*   43 daring-hardy] *Theobald;* daring, hardy *Q;* daring hardie *F*   44, 46, 99 Marshal] *(Martiall), Q5–F*

211

And craves to kiss your hand and take his leave.
KING RICHARD
We will descend and fold him in our arms.
Cousin of Hereford, as thy cause is right,   55
So be thy fortune in this royal fight.
Farewell, my blood, which if today thou shed,
Lament we may, but not revenge thee dead.
BOLINGBROKE
O, let no noble eye profane a tear
For me, if I be gored with Mowbray's spear.   60

54 Richard's embrace of his cousin, particularly as a response to Bolingbroke's
more formal hand-kissing, seems to
carry paternal – perhaps even maternal
– overtones; cf., for instance, 3.2.8–11.
The gesture here is an early display of
Richard's characteristic emotionalism,
though in this case there may be an element of unctuousness or hypocrisy.
His descent from the raised throne or
dais also represents a symbolic condes-
cension to a person of lower rank.
Adams (70) takes the action as an ironic prolepsis of Richard's abdication.
The couplets which follow, however,
instantly alter the tone, seeming
clipped and chilly by comparison, and
artfully express the King's volatility.
Note that Richard fails to embrace
Mowbray (see 97–8n.), who, though
not a near kinsman, might be thought a
closer companion. But, as RP suggests,
the King's omission serves partly to
prepare the audience for a loss of interest in Mowbray as a character, who
never reappears after his banishment;
after this scene the play seems deliberately to forget Richard's possible complicity with Mowbray. See 148n.
55 right F's substitution ('iust') destroys
the rhymed couplet completed in 56
with *fight*. *TxC* suggests unconvincingly that 'Shakespeare may have
emended to avoid the rhyme' (308)

since *flight*/*fight* (61–2) occurs a little
later.
56 **royal fight** See 32n.
57 **my . . . shed** Richard alludes playful-
ly to the two different senses of *blood*:
kinship; the blood Bolingbroke might
lose (*shed*) if wounded in the tourney;
shed is intransitive in force. See
1.2.12–13n.
58 **not revenge** As umpire at a trial of
truth, Richard cannot legitimately
avenge the loser, a proved liar by reason of vanquishment. A covert allusion to Bolingbroke's supposed desire
to avenge Gloucester's murder may
lurk behind the King's words.
*thee Q1–2's 'the' seems likely to be
merely an alternative spelling ('the'
was a frequent spelling of 'thee'; see
OED pers. pron.). Rhetorical balance
and rhyme with *thou shed* (57) support
thee dead. However, Gurr (71) defends
Q on the grounds that 'the dead'
includes both combatants, a supposedly more appropriate sentiment for
Richard to voice; but the speech is
clearly aimed at one person only:
Cousin of Hereford (55). See also
5.1.41n. and 5.2.17n.
59 **profane a tear** 'weep for one proved
by his defeat to be treasonous and a liar'
60 **gored** If the word carries animal connotations here, it would suggest an
additional slur on Mowbray.

55 right] iust *F*   58 thee] *Q3–F*; the *Q*

As confident as is the falcon's flight
Against a bird do I with Mowbray fight.
[*to Lord Marshal*]
My loving lord, I take my leave of you.
[*to Aumerle*]
Of you, my noble cousin, Lord Aumerle;
Not sick, although I have to do with death,   65
But lusty, young and cheerly drawing breath. –
Lo, as at English feasts, so I regreet
The daintiest last, to make the end most sweet.
[*to Gaunt*]
O thou, the earthly author of my blood,
Whose youthful spirit, in me regenerate,   70
Doth with a twofold vigour lift me up
To reach at victory above my head,
Add proof unto mine armour with thy prayers
And with thy blessings steel my lance's point,

61 **falcon's flight** perhaps proverbial (Dent, F34.1); see 1.1.109n.
63 SD *Although a few editors make *loving lord* apply to Richard, Malone is surely right to assume that it is spoken to the Marshal. Bolingbroke has already taken leave of the King at 52–4; the Marshal is apparently among Bolingbroke's *several friends* (51). See also 251–2.
64 **cousin** Since their fathers are brothers, Bolingbroke and Aumerle are first cousins.
65 **have . . . with** have dealings with
66 **young** Bolingbroke was thirty-one.
   cheerly cheerfully
67–8 It was customary for the English, unlike many continental foreigners, to end feasts with elaborate sweets or confectionary ('bankets'). Bacon (*Letters*, 3.215) alludes to the custom.
67 **regreet** salute, greet (with no suggestion of repetition); contrast 142n.

and 186n.
68 **daintiest** the most delicious (the best)
69 **earthly author** as opposed to his heavenly author (God). F's variant, 'earthy', although perhaps deliberate, could be merely compositorial missetting of *earthly*.
70 **spirit** perhaps pronounced monosyllabically ('sprite') or else with the final syllable elided
   regenerate reborn. Cf. *E3* 1.1.105, where the word is misused in the sense of 'degenerate'.
71 **twofold vigour** i.e. the vigour of Gaunt when he was young as well as Bolingbroke's present strength
   lift me up Gurr interprets the phrase, 'As a parent lifts up a child' (72); the image, however, may be intended more abstractly, i.e.'inspire me'.
73 **proof** impenetrability; cf. *Mac* 1.2.54: 'lapp'd in proof' (i.e. in armour of proof).

63 SD] *Malone (subst.)*   64 SD] *Wells*   Aumerle] *(Aumarle)*, F   66 cheerly] *(cheerely)*   69 SD] *Collier*   earthly] earthy F   71 vigour] rigor F   72 at] *QF;* a *Q3–5*

That it may enter Mowbray's waxen coat   75
And furbish new the name of John o'Gaunt
Even in the lusty haviour of his son.

GAUNT

God in thy good cause make thee prosperous.
Be swift like lightning in the execution,
And let thy blows, doubly redoubled,   80
Fall like amazing thunder on the casque
Of thy adverse pernicious enemy.
Rouse up thy youthful blood, be valiant and live.

BOLINGBROKE

Mine innocence and Saint George to thrive!

MOWBRAY

However God or Fortune cast my lot,   85

---

75 **enter . . . coat** penetrate Mowbray's
armour as though it were wax
76 **furbish new** add new lustre to (literally,
'scour' or 'polish', as with armour)
77 **haviour** actions, carriage, behaviour
(an archaic form)
78 **make thee prosperous** make you
succeed
79 **swift like lightning** proverbial
(Dent, L279)
execution performance (of the action)
80 **redoubled** probably pronounced
quadrisyllabically – 're-dòub-el-èd';
alternatively, but less likely, *doubly* may
be given three syllables. Cf. *Mac* 1.2.38:
'Doubly redoubled strokes upon the
foe'. RP suggests that an adjective may
have dropped out before *blows*.
81 **amazing** stupefying, terrifying (the
sixteenth-century sense is almost
'paralyzing')
thunder a thunderbolt (a fiery or
stone missile thrown down from the
heavens, originally conceived of as
hurled by Jupiter; cf. *JC* 1.3.49)
casque helmet
82 **adverse** advèrse; opposing. F's 'amaz'd'
is probably a compositorial mis-setting,

influenced by *amazing* in 81.
83 **valiant** a trisyllable. The line is an
alexandrine. But see Craven's conjecture (t.n.) and Appendix 1, pp. 537–9.
84 **innocence** Many editors adopt
Capell's 'innocency' for the sake of
smoother metre (a mis-setting of
'innocencie' in Q would indeed be
plausible); but the line can be made to
scan satisfactorily by pausing slightly
after *innocence* or by assuming a
nine-syllable line with two strong
stresses at the start: Mìne ìnnocence.
Saint George a metonymy for
'England' of which Saint George was
the patron; cf. *H5* 3.1.34. The line is a
prayer: 'May my innocence with the
aid of Saint George bring me victory!'
Bolingbroke implies that his motives
are patriotic, not merely personal. In
Traison Bolingbroke carries a shield
with a red cross 'like unto the arms of
St. George' (19/152–3).
85–96 Lothian (147) suggests that
Mowbray's farewell speech 'sounds
more sincere and less boastful' than
Bolingbroke's. Wilson observes further
that the effect is to establish Mowbray

---

76 furbish] furnish *F*   78 God] Heauen *F*   82 adverse] amaz'd *F*   83 youthful blood] blood
(*Craven³*)   84 innocence] innocency *Capell*   85 God] heauen *F*

There lives or dies, true to King Richard's throne,
A loyal, just and upright gentleman.
Never did captive with a freer heart
Cast off his chains of bondage and embrace
His golden uncontrolled enfranchisement   90
More than my dancing soul doth celebrate
This feast of battle with mine adversary.
Most mighty liege, and my companion peers,
Take from my mouth the wish of happy years.
As gentle and as jocund as to jest   95
Go I to fight. Truth hath a quiet breast.

KING RICHARD

Farewell, my lord. Securely I espy
Virtue with Valour couched in thine eye.
Order the trial, Marshal, and begin.

LORD MARSHAL

Harry of Hereford, Lancaster and Derby,   100
Receive thy lance; and God defend the right.

as 'a staunch friend' of the King 'in order that we may more fully appreciate' Richard's 'folly and treachery towards him later' (138).

88 **freer** more liberated (as opposed to *captive*); less guilty

90 **golden . . . enfranchisement** precious freedom without limits; Ure (26) cites *Edward I*, l. 995: 'golden libertie' (Peele, 2.105).

91 **dancing soul** beating heart? Cf. *WT* 1.2.110: 'my heart dances'.

92 **feast** festivity (with connotations of joy)

95 **gentle** unperturbed in spirit
jest take part in a game or court masque; as a noun, 'jest' often referred to theatrical entertainment (cf. *Spanish Tragedy*, 1.4.137). The line uses alliteration effectively.

96 **Truth . . . breast.** Cf. the proverb, 'Truth fears no trial' (Dent, T583).
quiet calm, untroubled by bad conscience

97–8 Richard's curt farewell to Mowbray contrasts with his more elaborate leave-taking of Bolingbroke (cf. 54n.).

97 **Securely** confidently, surely (modifying *couched*, 98)

98 **couched** couchèd; lodged

99 **Order** set in order, i.e. carry out
trial a dissyllable

100 **Lancaster** i.e. heir to the dukedom of Lancaster

101–3 Cf. Holinshed (3.495): 'The lord marshall viewed their speares, to see that they were of equall length, and deliuered the one speare himselfe to the duke of Hereford, and sent the other vnto the duke of Norfolke by a knight.'

101 **the right** Q's use of the definite article expresses the impartiality essential to the Marshal's role; Q2's 'thy' is probably a mis-setting, influenced by *thy* earlier in the same line.

99 trial,] *Rowe;* triall *QF*   101 God] heauen *F*   the] thy *Q2–F*

[*Attendant gives lance to Bolingbroke.*]

BOLINGBROKE

Strong as a tower in hope, I cry 'Amen'!

LORD MARSHAL [*to Attendant*]

Go bear this lance to Thomas, Duke of Norfolk.

[*Attendant gives lance to Mowbray.*]

2 HERALD

Harry of Hereford, Lancaster and Derby

Stands here for God, his sovereign and himself   105

On pain to be found false and recreant,

To prove the Duke of Norfolk, Thomas Mowbray,

A traitor to his God, his king and him,

And dares him to set forward to the fight.

1 HERALD

Here standeth Thomas Mowbray, Duke of Norfolk,   110

On pain to be found false and recreant,

Both to defend himself and to approve

Henry of Hereford, Lancaster and Derby

To God, his sovereign and to him disloyal,

Courageously, and with a free desire,   115

Attending but the signal to begin.

LORD MARSHAL

Sound trumpets, and set forward, combatants.

^F*A charge* [*is*] *sounded;*^F [*King Richard throws down
his warder.*]

102 **Strong . . . hope** biblical echo
  (Psalms, 61.3)
106 **On . . . be** at the risk of being
  false and recreant synonymous
  terms; cf. 1.1.144n., 1.2.53n.
108 **him** Bolingbroke (cf. *himself*, 105),
  echoing Mowbray at 24
112 **approve** prove (an archaic form)
115 **free** unconstrained, free of guilt

(cf. 88n.)
116 **Attending** awaiting, listening for
117 SD *charge is sounded* A trumpet
  signals the moment for attack; cf. the
  description in *2H4* 4.1.120: 'And the
  loud trumpet blowing them together'.
  warder truncheon, baton (the symbol
  of Richard's supreme authority as
  judge of the combat)

101 SD] *Bevington (subst.)*   103 SD1] *Capell (subst.)* SD2] *Bevington (subst.)*   104 SP] *this
edn; Herald Q; 1 Har. F*   108 his God] *Qc, F;* God *Qu*   109 forward] forwards *Q2–F*   110 SP] *this
edn; Herald 2 Q; 2. Har. F* Duke] *(D.), F*   117 SD *A . . . sounded*] *as Rann; opp. 116 F* King . . .
warder] *Cam¹ (subst.)*

Stay! The King hath thrown his warder down.

KING RICHARD

Let them lay by their helmets and their spears

And both return back to their chairs again.   120

Withdraw with us, and let the trumpets sound

While we return these Dukes what we decree.

^{F}*A long flourish.*^{F} [*King Richard confers apart with
Gaunt and other Nobles, then addresses Combatants.*]

Draw near,

118–22 Cf. Holinshed (3.395): 'The duke of Norfolke was not fullie set forward, when the king cast downe his warder, and the heralds cried, Ho, ho. Then the king caused their speares to be taken from them, and commanded them to repaire againe to their chaires, where they remained two long houres, while the king and his councell deliberatlie consulted what order was best to be had in so weightie a cause'; also Daniel (1.63): 'lo the king changd sudenly his mind, / Casts downe his warder and so staies them there'. See also headnote.

118 **Stay!** An obvious dramatic pause occurs after this word. Some earlier editors, beginning with Pope, added an additional, but unnecessary, word (e.g. 'But stay') to regularize the metre.

119–20 Perhaps Richard speaks only to the Marshal here, but these lines, like the rest of the speech, could as easily be spoken to his council as a body.

120 **chairs** See 1.3.6.3n.

121–2 In Holinshed this council takes two hours (see 118–22n.), after which Bushy, acting as the King's secretary, reads the sentence from 'a long roll' (3.495). Shakespeare reduces the time to a few moments – long enough only for a symbolic dumb show or pantomime. Then Richard himself delivers the judgement. The dramatic effect of

such radical condensation is to make Richard's change of mind seem more personal and whimsically irresponsible. In Froissart, the King calls off the battle beforehand to avoid being accused by his subjects of secretly aiming at Bolingbroke's destruction (6.314). Shakespeare leaves Richard's motivation for stopping the combat unclear; equally ambiguous is the question of whether his action in throwing down the warder is premeditated or spontaneous. Historically, there is every reason to suppose that the King acted in accordance with *Realpolitik*, not impulsively or arbitrarily (Saul, 401–2). See headnote.

121 **us** royal plural

122 **While we return** until I inform

122 SD* Richard probably throws down the warder while still in his raised chair, then descends to confer with his council, who cluster around him at the back of the stage (cf. *Withdraw*, 121), and finally mounts the throne again to announce his decision. Other stagings, however, would be possible.
flourish a fanfare of trumpets; such fanfares were normally reserved for kings.

123–4 *Theobald's relining not only helps to regularize the metre but also allows for an effective dramatic pause after the part-line, *Draw near*.

122 SD *King . . . Combatants*] Wells (subst.)   123–4] *as Theobald; QF line* list / done: /

217

And list what with our council we have done.
For that our kingdom's earth should not be soiled   125
With that dear blood which it hath fostered;
And for our eyes do hate the dire aspect
Of civil wounds ploughed up with neighbours' sword;
And for we think the eagle-winged pride
Of sky-aspiring and ambitious thoughts,   130
With rival-hating envy, set on you
To wake our peace, which in our country's cradle
Draws the sweet infant breath of gentle sleep,
Which so roused up with boist'rous untuned drums,
With harsh-resounding trumpets' dreadful bray   135

---

124 **list** listen to
  *council Q's 'counsell' and F's 'Councell' are alternative spellings of the same word. Elizabethan orthography did not distinguish the body of lords from the advice they gave.
125 **For that** so that
126 **dear** beloved; costly, if spilled
  fostered fosterèd
127 **for** because
  aspect aspèct
128 **sword** common use of the singular with plural force; F's 'swords' is unnecessary. Cf. *RJ* 1.1.82: 'this neighbor-stained steel'.
129–33 F omits these lines, perhaps because they were struck out in the theatre promptbook. The entire sentence from which they were excised is awkwardly tangled, and the actor playing Richard may have had difficulty with it. Unfortunately, the omission fails to improve the sense because the metaphors of the cut passage extend confusingly into what follows. The main problem is that grammatically *Which* in 134 seems to refer to *peace* (132) while at the same time serving as the subject of the clause, 'Which . . . Might . . . fright

fair peace'. Therefore *peace* is conceived of as an infant roused from sleep by the drums, trumpets and *grating shock* of civil strife (134–6) and then later goes on to *fright fair peace* (137); cf. the similarly confusing passage in *Mac* 1.7.21–4, where the image of infancy is also associated with trumpets. Although there may be textual corruption, it is likely, as Wells suggests, that the dramatist simply 'lost control of his metaphors' (178). *Which* could, however, refer to *ambitious thoughts* or *rival-hating envy*, which are so *roused* (stirred) *up* by the sounds of war, that they will *fright fair peace* and contribute to further discord and shedding of *kindred's blood* (138); therefore the King has banished them. As Ure (29) points out, *Mirror* (106, 'Lord Mowbray', ll. 141–4) 'is the only source that mentions this reason for stopping the fight'. In any case omission can hardly be justified since 129–38 comprise a syntactical unit.
129 **eagle-winged** eagle-wingèd; cf. 1.1.109n., on *pitch*, and 1.3.61.
131 **envy** hostility, enmity
  set on you set you on, incited you
134 **boist'rous** Cf. 1.1.4n.

---

124 council] *(counsell)*, F *(Councell)*   128 civil] *Qc, F;* cruell *Qu*   sword] swords *F*   129–33] *om.*
F   131 rival-hating] *Qc;* riuall hating *Qu*   133 Draws] *Qc;* Draw *Qu*   sleep,] *Qu;* sleepe *Qc*
135 harsh-resounding] *Theobald;* harsh resounding *QF*

And grating shock of wrathful iron arms,
Might from our quiet confines fright fair peace,
And make us wade even in our kindred's blood:
Therefore, we banish you our territories.
You, cousin Hereford, upon pain of life,   140
Till twice five summers have enriched our fields,
Shall not regreet our fair dominions,
But tread the stranger paths of banishment.

BOLINGBROKE

Your will be done. This must my comfort be:
That sun that warms you here shall shine on me,   145
And those his golden beams to you here lent
Shall point on me and gild my banishment.

KING RICHARD

Norfolk, for thee remains a heavier doom,

---

136 **shock** the impact of horses and armour colliding
wrathful iron The uncorrected reading in Q ('harsh resounding') obviously repeats the phrase from 135; Pollard (16) suggests that the error resulted from dictation; but it could just as well have been the result of eyeskip or memorial confusion, since compositors normally held more than one line in memory while setting. *Wrathful* applies to the soldiers, not to the *arms* they would carry (a synecdoche).

137–43 an instance of effective dramatic irony; by banishing Bolingbroke, Richard brings on the very danger he seeks to avoid.

139 **you** both of you

140 **You** Contrast 55–8 and see 1.1.28n. Here the King speaks officially as judge.
of life i.e. of losing your life; F's substitution ('death') is unnecessary. Froissart uses the phrase often; it also appears in *Woodstock*, 4.3.171.

142 **regreet** return to, see again (contrast

67 and n.)

143 **stranger** alien, foreign (a noun used adjectivally, not a comparative)

144–7 Bolingbroke's rhymed response to the sentence of exile may express steely self-control. Cf. Coleridge: 'Bolingbroke's ambitious hope, not yet shaped into definite plan, beautifully contrasted with Mowbray's desolation' (133).

144 **Your . . . done.** possibly an ironic echo of the Lord's Prayer (Smidt, 185)

145–7 proverbial idea (cf. Dent, S985)

147 **point on** focus on, aim themselves at; cf. *Oth* 5.2.46.

148 **thee** an indication of Richard's intimacy with Mowbray (see 149n.)
heavier doom harsher punishment, heavier sentence. Hayward notes the ironic timing and symbolic justice of Richard's punishment: 'This sentence of banishment was giuen against him [Mowbray] the same day of the yeere wherein the Duke of Gloucester by his wicked meanes was strangled to death at Calice' (50).

---

136 wrathful iron] *Qc, F;* harsh resounding *Qu*   140 life] death *F*   141 fields] *QF;* field *Q2*

Which I with some unwillingness pronounce:
The sly slow hours shall not determinate   150
The dateless limit of thy dear exile.
The hopeless word of 'never to return'
Breathe I against thee, upon pain of life.

MOWBRAY

A heavy sentence, my most sovereign liege,
And all unlooked for from your highness' mouth.   155
A dearer merit, not so deep a maim
As to be cast forth in the common air,
Have I deserved at your highness' hands.
The language I have learnt these forty years,
My native English, now I must forgo,   160
And now my tongue's use is to me no more

---

149 **with some unwillingness** Gurr
notes: 'Richard here seems to make his
only concession to the debt which
Mowbray has been hinting he owes'
(75). Cf. *2H4* 4.1.113–14, where
Mowbray's son recalls his father's sentence of exile: 'The King that lov'd
him, as the state stood then, / Was force
perforce compell'd to banish him.'

150 **sly slow** creeping along stealthily
determinate bring to an end, termi-
nate (a legal term); cf. *Woodstock*, 5.3.32.

151 **dateless limit** unlimited term (cf.
Son 30.6: 'death's dateless night')
dear heartfelt, grievous, severe
exile exile (Cercignani, 38)

152 **word** 'utterance', or possibly 'verdict, sentence'

153 **Breathe** pronounce
of life See 140n.

154–73 Mowbray's unrhymed and obviously heartfelt response to his *sentence*
contrasts with Bolingbroke's (see
144–7n.). Not only is the effect more
spontaneous, it also reinforces our
awareness of Richard's defensiveness
and vulnerability (since Mowbray's
punishment comes as such a nasty and
unjust surprise).

154 **sentence** playing on *word*, 152

155 **unlooked for** Holinshed says that
Mowbray 'was in hope . . . that he
should haue beene borne out in the
matter by the king, which when it fell
out otherwise, it greeued him not a little' (3.495).

156 **dearer merit** better reward (for past
services); a veiled allusion to Mowbray's
loyalty – possibly as the King's agent in
the matter of Gloucester's death or as
the reporter of Bolingbroke's disloyal
sentiments (see 1.1 headnote)
maim wound

158 **deserved** deservèd

159 **these forty years** Historically,
Mowbray was thirty-two or thirty-
three. Metrical requirements may
account for the rounding up of numbers. Cf. Richard's *twenty thousand*
(3.2.76; see n.), an exaggeration of
Salisbury's *twelve thousand* (3.2.70; see
n.), and also 2.4.1n. Such changes are
common in Shakespeare's histories.

161–5 As Clark & Wright (96) point out,
'This speech is entirely Shakespeare's
own invention. It is not probable that
Norfolk was ignorant of French and
Latin, as he had been sent on an embassy
to France and Germany.' GWW notes,
'Here begins the metaphor of language,

Than an unstringed viol or a harp,
Or like a cunning instrument cased up –
Or, being open, put into his hands
That knows no touch to tune the harmony.   165
Within my mouth you have engaoled my tongue,
Doubly portcullised with my teeth and lips,
And dull unfeeling barren Ignorance
Is made my gaoler to attend on me.
I am too old to fawn upon a nurse,   170
Too far in years to be a pupil now.
What is thy sentence ^Fthen^F but speechless death,
Which robs my tongue from breathing native breath?

brought to conclusion in *H5* 3.4 (the language lesson), and in the frequent reference to language in that play. It contrasts with the metaphor of the garden, which has its glorious presentation in 3.4 of this play and finishes in the fair garden of France in *H5*.' See also Introduction, pp. 65–9.

162 **unstringed** unstringèd; the word applies to both *viol* (played with a bow) and *harp* (played with the fingers).
viol a dissyllable; cf. 2.1.149.

163 **cunning** skilfully fashioned, requiring skill to play

164 **open** uncased

164–5 **his hands / That** the hands of someone who (see Abbott, 218)

165 **touch** skill, fingering

166 **engaoled my tongue** Although the surface meaning of Mowbray's lament is that banishment to a foreign country will deprive him of the use of his mother tongue, there may also be a hint of his enforced silence in the matter of Gloucester's death. The play never explains why Mowbray, once in exile and beyond Richard's power to constrain him further, did not speak out (see 4.1.81–103).

167 **portcullised** fenced off (as with a

grating dropped within a doorway to prevent entrance); see Appendix 1, p. 521, n. 1. Kittredge[2] (116) cites Lyly, *Euphues*: 'We maye see the cunning and curious work of Nature, which hath barred and hedged nothing in so stronglye as the tongue, with two rowes of teeth, therewith two lyppes' (1.279).

168 **Ignorance** standard character in the moral interludes, as, for instance, in *Interlude of the Four Elements* (1517–18), *The Longer Thou Livest the More Fool Thou Art* (*c*. 1559–68) and *New Custom* (1559–73)

170 **nurse** who, among her other duties, would teach children to speak; cf. 307. See also 161–5n.

172 **sentence** legal sentence; element of speech. Mowbray plays on the paradox of a *sentence* that results in speechlessness, the equivalent of *death*, extending his earlier wordplay from 154.
*then F's emendation mends the metre; see Appendix 1, p. 525.

173 **breathing native breath** speaking native language (implying also, 'breathing the air of my native country'). Poetically, words were often considered to be made of breath (cf. *Ham* 3.4.197–9).

167 portcullised] *Qc (*portcullist*)*; portculist *Qu*; percullist *Q4–F*   168 Ignorance] *this edn*; ignorance *QF*

221

KING RICHARD

It boots thee not to be compassionate.

After our sentence, plaining comes too late.   175

MOWBRAY

Then thus I turn me from my country's light

To dwell in solemn shades of endless night.

[*Starts to leave.*]

KING RICHARD [*to Mowbray*]

Return again, and take an oath with thee.

[*to Bolingbroke and Mowbray*]

Lay on our royal sword your banished hands.

[*They place their hands on King Richard's sword.*]

Swear by the duty that you owe to God –   180

Our part therein we banish with yourselves –

To keep the oath that we administer:

You never shall, so help you truth and God,

Embrace each other's love in banishment;

Nor never look upon each other's face;   185

Nor never write, regreet, nor reconcile

This louring tempest of your home-bred hate;

174 **boots** avails (cf. 1.1.164 where Richard uses the word as a noun)
be compassionate appeal for sympathy; an ironic rebuke, as Lothian (147) points out, coming from a character as self-indulgently emotional as Richard

175 **plaining** lamenting (a form of 'complaining')

176 **me** myself

177 **shades . . . night** Cf. 5.6.43n.

179 **on . . . sword** i.e. on the hilt and guard which together form a cross; cf. *Ham* 1.5.147.

180 *****you owe** F's emendation restores the metre; see Appendix 1, p. 525. RP

suggests that the appropriate expansion could be 'ye owe'.

181 **Our part therein** i.e. your loyalty to me, your anointed sovereign (God's deputy). The question of whether or not banishment released a subject from allegiance to his king was a moot point in international law. Richard seems to concede that during terms of exile he can enforce no such claim.

185, 186, 188 **Nor never** The double negative used for emphasis is common in Shakespeare; cf. 4.1.255, 5.5.70.

186 **regreet** meet again; cf. 67n.

177 SD] *Bevington*   178 SP] *King. Q; Ric. F*   SD] *this edn*   179 SD1] *Wells (before 178)*   SD2] *Bevington*   180 you owe] *F;* y'owe *Q*   God] heauen *F*   183 God] Heauen *F*   185, 186, 188 never] euer *F*   186 nor] or *F*

Nor never by advised purpose meet
To plot, contrive or complot any ill
'Gainst us, our state, our subjects or our land.   190
BOLINGBROKE
    I swear.
MOWBRAY
    And I, to keep all this.
BOLINGBROKE
    Norfolk, so far as to mine enemy:
    By this time, had the King permitted us,
    One of our souls had wandered in the air,   195
    Banished this frail sepulchre of our flesh,
    As now our flesh is banished from this land.
    Confess thy treasons ere thou fly the realm.
    Since thou hast far to go, bear not along
    The clogging burden of a guilty soul.   200
MOWBRAY
    No, Bolingbroke. If ever I were traitor,
    My name be blotted from the book of life,

188 **by advised purpose** advisèd; by prearrangement, with deliberate intent
189 **complot any ill** plot together any evil; the entire line, in the manner of legal formulae, is tautological. Some critics take Richard's lack of trust in the two enemies as reflecting his own insecurity, even guilt, in the affair of Gloucester's death.
190 **our state** our high rank (cf. 3.2.117, 163; 5.6.6); our government (symbolized by the regal chair, or *state*, from which he has just risen); royal plural
193 ***so . . . enemy** 'This much I have to say to you, my enemy (since the oath we have just taken forbids us ever to be friends).' Both Q and F read 'fare' (a sixteenth-century spelling of 'far'), which F2 modernized for clarity. Some editors, however, interpret Q's 'fare' as a different word (as in 'farewell') with the

meaning, 'So go your way as I would wish to mine enemy' (see Cam[1], 144). Although possible, this reading seems strained. Now that the legal formalities have been concluded, Bolingbroke and Mowbray are free to speak to each other in more personal terms.
196 **sepulchre** here pronounced 'sepùlchre'; but contrast 2.1.55. See Cercignani, 41.
200 **clogging burden** Cf. *clog of conscience* (5.6.20). Clogs were wooden blocks tied to prisoners' ankles or hung on animals to restrict movement.
202 **book of life** echoes Revelation, 3.5: 'He that overcometh shall be thus clothed in white array, and I will not blot out his name out of the book of life'; see also 4.1.236n. The biblical solemnity of Mowbray's denial of guilt is striking; and since he has

193 far] *(fare)*, F *(fare,)*, F2   195 wandered] *(wandred)*   198 the] this *F*

223

And I from heaven banished as from hence!
But what thou art, God, thou and I do know;
And all too soon, I fear, the King shall rue.   205
Farewell, my liege. Now no way can I stray;
Save back to England, all the world's my way.   *Exit.*

KING RICHARD [*to Gaunt*]
Uncle, even in the glasses of thine eyes
I see thy grieved heart. Thy sad aspect
Hath from the number of his banished years   210
Plucked four away. [*to Bolingbroke*] Six frozen winters
     spent,
Return with welcome home from banishment.

BOLINGBROKE
How long a time lies in one little word!
Four lagging winters and four wanton springs
End in a word; such is the breath of kings.   215

---

little to lose but face at this point, his permanent exile having been sealed already, his apparent sincerity seems further to obfuscate both his and Richard's morality in the matter of Gloucester's death.

205 **shall rue** 'will learn to his sorrow' (perhaps with the further sense of 'must learn'); the verb is transitive, *what thou art* (204) being its object. Mowbray seems to anticipate Bolingbroke's future action against Richard. The King's remission of part of Bolingbroke's sentence at 209–11 may be partly motivated by the threat implied in Mowbray's statement. Wilson remarks that the juxtaposition of Mowbray's prophecy with Richard's curtailment of Bolingbroke's banishment 'conveys the effect of spineless timidity' in the King (144).

206–8 Cf. the similar conjunction of images in *KL* 4.1.18: 'I have no way, and therefore want no eyes.'

206–7 This couplet puts a stamp of bitter finality on Mowbray's exit speech.

208 **glasses** windows. The notion of eyes being the windows of the heart was a proverbial conceit (Dent, E231).

209–12 Shakespeare invents this sentimental cause of the shortened sentence; see headnote. In Holinshed the commutation occurred some weeks later: 'The duke of Hereford tooke his leaue of the king at Eltham, who there released foure yeares of his banishment' (3.495). At this time Richard also granted Bolingbroke the *letters patents* of 2.1.202 (see 2.1.202–4n.).

209 **grieved** grievèd
     aspect aspèct

211 **spent** having passed (absolute construction; Abbott, 378)

214 **wanton** luxuriant, profuse in growth

215 **breath** language; cf. 173n. Bolingbroke seems to imply scornfully that Richard's words are mere 'air' in contrast to the heavy reality of his

---

204 God] heauen *F*   206 stray;] *Capell (Roderick)*; stray, *QF*   208+ SP] *King. Q; Rich. F*
208 SD] *Wells*   211 SD] *Johnson¹*

GAUNT

I thank my liege that in regard of me
He shortens four years of my son's exile.
But little vantage shall I reap thereby,
For ere the six years that he hath to spend
Can change their moons and bring their times about,   220
My oil-dried lamp and time-bewasted light
Shall be extinct with age and endless night.
My inch of taper will be burnt and done,
And blindfold Death not let me see my son.

KING RICHARD

Why uncle, thou hast many years to live.   225

GAUNT

But not a minute, King, that thou canst give.
Shorten my days thou canst with sullen sorrow,
And pluck nights from me, but not lend a morrow.
Thou canst help Time to furrow me with age,

punishment. Or perhaps, as RP suggests, Bolingbroke comments on the power that lies in a single royal word. See Introduction, pp. 65–6.

217 **exile** exile (Cercignani, 38)

218 **vantage** advantage

220 **bring . . . about** produce the cycles of their seasons

221 **oil-dried lamp** proverbial (Dent, O29); cf. *1H6* 2.5.8.
time-bewasted Cf. *time-honoured* (1.1.1).

222 **extinct** extinguished; cf. *Ham* 1.3.118.
***night** Q4's emendation restores the rhyme with *light* (see Appendix 1, p. 525). Gaunt may unconsciously echo Mowbray's *endless night* (177).

223 Cf. 221 and *Mac* 5.5.23: 'Out, out, brief candle'.

224 **blindfold Death** Death was traditionally represented as a skull (and therefore eyeless), but Gaunt may also image *Death* as blindfolding his eyes by

removing the power to see his son. Wilson (145) suggests that the dramatist fuses the image of *Death* (who is often hooded and who extinguishes the taper of life; cf. 223) with the hood of an implement for snuffing candles. An allusion to Atropos, the blind Fate who cuts the thread of life, may also be intended; cf. Milton, *Lycidas* (l.75): 'the blind Fury with th' abhorred shears'.

226 **King** Gaunt's unceremonious address underlines both his own impatience and the limits of Richard's power; contrast 5.3.54, 86, 115, 118.

227 **sullen** dismal, gloomy (a recurring word in the play; cf. 1.3.265, 2.1.139, 5.6.48). *TxC* defends F's 'sudden' as an authorial revision resulting in part from F's omission of 239–42, which brings the *sullen* of 265 uncomfortably close (i.e. within thirty-four lines).

221 time-bewasted] *F;* time bewasted *Q*   222 night] *Q4–F;* nightes *Q*   227 sullen] sudden *F*
229 Time] *this edn;* time *QF*

But stop no wrinkle in his pilgrimage;   230
Thy word is current with him for my death,
But dead, thy kingdom cannot buy my breath.

KING RICHARD

Thy son is banished upon good advice,
Whereto thy tongue a party-verdict gave.
Why at our justice seem'st thou then to lour?   235

GAUNT

Things sweet to taste prove in digestion sour.
You urged me as a judge, but I had rather
You would have bid me argue like a father.
O, had it been a stranger, not my child,
To smooth his fault I should have been more mild.   240
A partial slander sought I to avoid,
And in the sentence my own life destroyed.
Alas, I looked when some of you should say

---

230 **his pilgrimage** 'time's journey' (the pilgrimage of life)
231 **current** authoritative, valid (cf. 4.1.264: 'if my word be sterling')
232 **dead** when I am dead (absolute construction = 'I being dead'; Abbott, 380)
   breath life
234 **party-verdict** i.e. one vote in a joint decision to banish. Holinshed's authority for Gaunt's consent to his son's exile occurs in the account of Carlisle's speech at the deposition (3.512): 'it is manifest & well knowne, that the duke [of Hereford] was banished the realme by K. Richard and his councell, and by the iudgement of his owne father, for the space of ten yeares' (for the fuller context see 4.1.115–50LN). Créton (106/330) likewise mentions Gaunt's agreement, and Froissart implies it in his state-

ment that the 'sentence greatly contented the lordes' of the council (6.317) and in the words of Bolingbroke's adherents: 'sithe the duke of Lancastre his father suffreth it, wee must nedes suffre it' (6.319).
236 proverbial (Dent, M1265); cf. Revelation, 10.10.
237 **urged me** requested an opinion of me (not 'incited me')
239–42 Various editors defend F's excision of these couplets as unnecessarily repeating ideas already expressed.
239 ****had it** Theobald's emendation repairs the metre; Q's 'had't' may simply reproduce an authorial abbreviation in the MS.
240 **smooth** palliate, gloss over
241 **partial slander** accusation of bias (on behalf of my son)
243 **looked when** expected that, looked forward to the time when

233 SP] *King. Q; Ric. F*   upon] *QF;* with *Q2–5*   advice] *(aduise), F*   234 party-verdict] *F;* party verdict *Q*   237 urged] *(vrgde), F* (vrg'd); vrge *Q2*   239–42] *om. F*   239 had it] *Theobald;* had't *Q*
240 should] would *Q2*   241 sought] *Qc;* ought *Qu*

I was too strict to make mine own away;
But you gave leave to my unwilling tongue,   245
Against my will, to do myself this wrong.

KING RICHARD

Cousin, farewell, and uncle, bid him so.
Six years we banish him, and he shall go.

^F*Flourish.*^F *Exit [King Richard with his train].*
[*Aumerle, Lord Marshal, Gaunt and Bolingbroke remain.*]

AUMERLE [*to Bolingbroke*]

Cousin, farewell. What presence must not know,   249
From where you do remain let paper show.   [*Exit.*]

LORD MARSHAL [*to Bolingbroke*]

My lord, no leave take I, for I will ride

---

244 **too . . . away** 'too conscientiously
severe in destroying my own son (by
exiling him)'
246 **wrong** injury (not 'injustice')
248 SD *Flourish* See 1.3.122 SDn.
249 **What . . . know** what I cannot learn
from you in person (i.e. by your *presence*); alternatively, *presence* could
mean 'presence chamber at court' (cf.
289).
250 **paper** letters. Because Bolingbroke, as an exile, will no longer have
official contact with the court,
Aumerle seeks to keep in private
touch with him on the grounds of
kinship (cf. *Cousin, farewell*). But
Aumerle is Richard's man, and the
farewell is somewhat curt; the implication is that he wishes prudently to
keep tabs on the location and activities of a potential enemy. As Wells
(180) observes, it is a little odd that
Aumerle should take such formal
leave of a man whom he accompanies
'to the next highway' (1.4.4); but the
decision to escort Bolingbroke may
have been taken later and, again,
the motive could be intelligence-

gathering. RP points to audience
interest in, and engagement with,
Aumerle as a character, which commence at this point; the slight oddity
which Wells notices could thus be
explained as the dramatist's means of
starting to raise questions about a
deliberately enigmatic figure.
250 SD *Aumerle's exit is dramatically
natural at this point; but it is also necessary, since he enters fifty-nine lines
later at the beginning of the following
scene (cf. Gaunt's exit at 1.1.195). See
LN.
251–2 The Lord Marshal's extraordinary
gesture of comradeship to Bolingbroke
(the offer to accompany him from
Coventry to Dover) may be an early
indication of the exile's popularity;
other lords (Northumberland, Ross,
Willoughby, etc.) similarly join
Bolingbroke immediately after his
return to England in 2.3. The speech
shows that Shakespeare did not identify
the Marshal with Surrey, who was a
strong supporter of Richard (see List
of Roles, 28n.).

---

247 SP] *King. Q; Rich.* F   248 SD *Exit*] *Qc, F; not in Qu   King . . . train*] *Capell (subst.)   Aumerle
. . . remain*] *this edn*   249 SD] *Bevington*   250 SD] *Cam²*   251 SD] *Bevington*

As far as land will let me by your side.
[*Bolingbroke fails to respond. Lord Marshal stands apart.*]

GAUNT

O, to what purpose dost thou hoard thy words
That thou return'st no greeting to thy friends?

BOLINGBROKE

I have too few to take my leave of you,   255
When the tongue's office should be prodigal
To breathe the abundant dolour of the heart.

GAUNT

Thy grief is but thy absence for a time.

BOLINGBROKE

Joy absent, grief is present for that time.

GAUNT

What is six winters? They are quickly gone.   260

BOLINGBROKE

To men in joy; but grief makes one hour ten.

GAUNT

Call it a travel that thou tak'st for pleasure.

---

252 SD *Some such stage action seems necessary to explain Bolingbroke's failure to respond to the Marshal's generosity and the latter's apparent non-inclusion in the private conversation that ensues. It would appear that Bolingbroke is too absorbed emotionally in parting from his father (whom he will never see again) to pay attention to the Marshal. Note that he can barely speak even to Gaunt (253–4). The ignoring of the lesser figure in favour of the greater is subtly poignant – a little like Lear's ignoring Kent in his overwhelming concern with Cordelia (*KL* 5.3.268–75).

256 **office** function

257 **To breathe** in uttering
   dolour grief (with a possible pun on 'dollar', referring back to *hoard* (253) and *prodigal* (256))

258–64 Wilson remarks on the use of stichomythia (dialogue in alternating lines) as a trait of Shakespeare's earlier style: here it 'gives a light, almost flippant, tone, to cover the deeper feelings of the speakers, which is very English' (146).

258 **Thy** perhaps emphatic (as contrasted with the *grief* Gaunt must suffer); 'Gaunt knows he is ill' (Lothian, 148). See also 1.1.195LN.
   grief the cause of your grief; grievance. The exchange that follows extends *dolour* (257).

259 **Joy absent** joy being absent (see Abbott, 380)

262 **travel** journey; labour. Shakespeare develops both senses in the imagery that follows; cf. *pilgrimage* (264), *tedious stride* (268), *apprenticehood*

252 SD *Bolingbroke . . . respond*] *Bevington (subst.)   Lord . . . apart*] *this edn*   254 return'st] *F;* returnest *Q*   261 hour] *(hower), F*   262 travel] *(trauaile), F*

BOLINGBROKE

My heart will sigh when I miscall it so,
Which finds it an enforced pilgrimage.

GAUNT

The sullen passage of thy weary steps   265
Esteem as foil wherein thou art to set
The precious jewel of thy home return.

BOLINGBROKE

Nay, rather, every tedious stride I make
Will but remember me what a deal of world
I wander from the jewels that I love.   270
Must I not serve a long apprenticehood
To foreign passages, and in the end,
Having my freedom, boast of nothing else

(271), *foreign passages* (272), *freedom* (273) and *journeyman* (274). Mahood (78) comments, 'When Gaunt bids him call his exile "a *trauaile* that thou takst for pleasure" and a "*foyle* wherein thou art to set, The pretious Iewell of thy home returne", Bolingbroke takes up *travel* in its harsher sense of "travail" and *foil* in the meaning "frustration, obstacle" to fashion the bitter wordplay of his reply.'

263 **miscall it so** Bolingbroke contrasts *for pleasure* (262) with *enforced* (264); also, perhaps, *travel* with 'travail' (see 262n.).

264 **enforced** enforcèd

265 **sullen** Cf. 227n.

266 **Esteem** regard
    as foil as a setting for a gem (technically a metal leaf placed behind a jewel to enhance its brilliance); see also 262n.

268–93 F omits this exchange, an elaborate amplification of ideas already presented. Feuillerat judges it 'more ingenious than dramatic' (227); the cut, however, makes the transition between Gaunt's jewel imagery (267) and Bolingbroke's fire imagery (294)

awkwardly abrupt.

269 Editors have emended for metre but the line can be rendered tolerably metrical by treating *-ber me whàt* (or perhaps *what a dèal*) as an anapaestic foot in an otherwise regular iambic pentameter.
    remember me remind me
    deal of world distance (literally, 'quantity of earth')

271–4 a difficult passage. Bolingbroke anticipates serving a long apprenticeship to *foreign passages*, i.e. not merely to wanderings abroad but also to events in general (cf. *1H4* 3.2.8: 'thy passages of life'). Apprentices were normally bound to serve their masters for a term of seven years, at which point they obtained their freedom and became journeymen (literally, 'workers for daily wages') or fully-fledged tradesmen in a craft. Bolingbroke imagines that, having earned his freedom to return home, his only reward for long years of servitude, paradoxically, will be proficiency in grief. The logical difficulty lies in the tense of the verb (*was*), since the years of

266 as foil] a foyle *Q2;* a soyle *Q3–F*   268–93] *om. F*   269 remember me] remind me *(Cam²);* remember *Oxf*   a deal] deale *Q4*   world] *Q2;* world: *Q*

229

But that I was a journeyman to Grief?

GAUNT

All places that the eye of heaven visits   275
Are to a wise man ports and happy havens.
Teach thy necessity to reason thus:
There is no virtue like necessity.
Think not the King did banish thee,
But thou the King. Woe doth the heavier sit   280
Where it perceives it is but faintly borne.
Go, say I sent thee forth to purchase honour,

banishment are metaphorically equivalent to his apprenticehood, not to his freedom as a journeyman. The preterite, *was*, does of course fit Bolingbroke's literal sense of *journeyman* as traveller or exile.

274 **journeyman** See 271–4n.; Bolingbroke puns on 'journey' (travel, exile).

275–80 **All . . . King**. Editors cite Lyly's *Euphues* (1.314) as a probable source for these lines: '*Plato* would neuer accompt him banished that had the Sunne, Fire, Aire, Water, & Earth, that he had before; where he felt the Winter's blast and the Summers blaze; where the same Sunne & the same Moone shined: whereby he noted that euery place was a countrey to a wise man, and all partes a pallaice to a quiet minde. . . . When it was cast in *Diogenes* teeth that the *Synoponetes* had banished hym *Pontus*, yea, sayde hee, I them of Diogenes'; see 288n. and 294–301n. In the first part of this quotation, Lyly is translating Plutarch's *De Exilio*. Cf. also a stock *sententia* from Ovid, *Fasti*, 1.493 ('Omne solum forti patria est'; 'to a brave man every place is his country'), found in the quotation books under *patria*. The sentiment became proverbial (Dent, M426); Shakespeare may have encountered it in Arthur Brooke's *Romeus and Juliet* (ll. 1443–6; Bullough, 1.323), his source for *RJ*. Cf. also

Tusculan Disputations: 'For in what soeuer place we haue such thynges [as exile and banishment], there we may liue well and happelye. And therfore, hereunto, that saying of Teucer may well be applyed. My countrey (quod he) is, wheresoeuer I liue well' (V: Dolman, sigs Ei^v–ii; Loeb edn, 533). In *E2*, a model for Shakespeare, Leicester tries to console Marlowe's desolate king with an invitation to fantasy: 'Imagine Killingworth Castle were your court, / And that you lay for pleasure here a space, / Not of compulsion or necessity' (5.1.2–4). Muir (*Sources*, 54–8) discusses the sources of Gaunt's speech in detail.

275 **eye of heaven** a common periphrasis for the sun (cf. 3.2.37). Gaunt may imply a submerged pun on 'sun' and 'son'.

278 proverbial (Dent, V73). Cf. Chaucer, *Knight's Tale*, ll. 3041–2; *TGV* 4.1.60.

279–80 **Think . . . King**. Cf. *Cor* 3.3.120–3: 'You common cry of curs . . . I banish you!'

279 a tetrameter line. See 1.1.12n. RP suggests that the line might originally have begun, 'Think not that the King', and that the successive words beginning with *th* (probably written 'y^t' and 'y^e' in the MS) confused the compositor.

281 **faintly** faintheartedly, weakly

282 **purchase** win

274 Grief] *this edn*; griefe *Q*   280 King. Woe] King, who *Q4*

230

And not the King exiled thee; or suppose
Devouring pestilence hangs in our air,
And thou art flying to a fresher clime.   285
Look what thy soul holds dear, imagine it
To lie that way thou goest, not whence thou com'st.
Suppose the singing birds musicians,
The grass whereon thou tread'st the presence strewed,
The flowers fair ladies, and thy steps no more   290
Than a delightful measure or a dance;
For gnarling Sorrow hath less power to bite
The man that mocks at it and sets it light.

BOLINGBROKE

O, who can hold a fire in his hand

---

283 **exiled** exiled; cf. 151n.
284 **Devouring pestilence** mortal plague
   hangs . . . air It was believed that
   bubonic plague was transmitted
   through putrescent air; cf. *Summer's
   Last Will and Testament*: 'Brightnesse
   falls from the ayre, / Queenes haue
   died yong and faire . . . I am sick, I
   must dye' (*Nashe*, 3.283); also *Tim*
   4.3.110–11: 'poison / In the sick air'.
286 **Look what** whatever
287 **goest** probably monosyllabic: 'go'st'
288 **singing birds** Muir (*Sources*, 57)
   cites Lyly's *Euphues* (1.316): 'the
   Nightingale singeth as sweetly in the
   desarts as in the woodes of *Crete*'; cf.
   275–80n.
   musicians four syllables (see
   Cercignani, 309)
289 **the presence strewed** i.e. the
   King's presence chamber strewn with
   rushes; cf. *TS* 4.1.46. Q's spelling
   ('strowd') shows the Elizabethan pronunciation.
291 **measure** stately dance; cf. 3.4.7–8.
292–3 excerpted in *Parnassus* (no. 1560)
   but ascribed mistakenly to Edmund
   Spenser
292 **gnarling** snarling, growling

293 **sets it light** regards it lightly
294–301 Again Lyly's *Euphues* is probably Shakespeare's source: 'hee that is
   colde doth not couer himselfe wyth
   care, but with clothes, he that is
   washed in the rayne dryeth himselfe
   by the fire not by his fancie, and thou
   which art bannished oughtest not with
   teares to bewaile thy hap, but with
   wisedome to heale thy hurt'
   (1.313–14). This quotation comes
   from the same passage as that quoted
   at 275–80n. Cf. also *Tusculan
   Disputations*: 'But he sayeth, he is contented onely with the remembraunce
   of his former pleasures. As if, a man
   well nye parched with heate, so that,
   he is no longer able to abide the sonne
   should comfort him selfe with the
   remembraunce, that once heretofore,
   he had bathed himselfe in the cold
   ryuers of Arpynas. For truly, I see not,
   howe the pleasures that are past, may
   ease the gryeues that are present' (V:
   Dolman, sigs Cv–v^v; Loeb edn,
   501–3).
294 **fire** dissyllabic; 'fier', or 'fyer', was a
   common spelling.

---

289 strewed] *(strowd)*   292 Sorrow] *this edn;* sorrow *Q*

By thinking on the frosty Caucasus?   295
Or cloy the hungry edge of appetite
By bare imagination of a feast?
Or wallow naked in December snow
By thinking on fantastic summer's heat?
O no, the apprehension of the good   300
Gives but the greater feeling to the worse.
Fell Sorrow's tooth doth never rankle more
Than when he bites but lanceth not the sore.

GAUNT

Come, come, my son, I'll bring thee on thy way.
Had I thy youth and cause, I would not stay.   305

BOLINGBROKE

Then England's ground, farewell! Sweet soil, adieu –

295 **frosty Caucasus** the mountain range separating Europe from Asia, considered by Elizabethans to be unusually cold. Wells (182) cites Lyly, *Euphues*: 'If thou be as hot as the mount *Aetna*, faine thy self as colde as the hil *Caucasus*' (1.255). Cf. also *Tusculan Disputations*: 'What parte of Barbary is there, more wylde or rude, then India? Yet neuerthlesse, emonges theim those which are counted wyse men, are fyrst bred vp, bare and naked. And yet suffer both the colde of the hil Caucasus, and also, the sharpenes of the winter, without any paine. And when they come to the fyer, they are able to abide the heate, well nie, till they rost' (V: Dolman, sig. Cviᵛ; Loeb edn, 505). Coghill (95) adduces the collocation of *fire* (294) and the frosty mountains in Chaucer's *Wife of Bath's Tale* (ll. 1139–40): 'Taak fyr, and ber it in the derkeste hous / Bitwix this and the mount of Kaukasous'.

296 **cloy . . . appetite** mixed metaphor. As applied to *appetite*, *cloy* means 'glut', 'satiate' or perhaps merely 'satisfy'; as applied to *edge*, it apparently means 'clog, obstruct, hamper' (*OED v.* 6) with the implication of blunting a

knife. The general idea of counteracting sharp hunger is obvious enough.
298 **wallow . . . snow** Cf. 295n.
299 **fantastic** imagined
300–3 Bolingbroke argues that facing up to sorrow at its worst is finally less painful than trying unrealistically to evade it; the wound that grief inflicts may fester if not manfully lanced.
300 **apprehension** conception
302–3 quoted in *Parnassus* (no. 1557), but misattributed to 'S. Daniell'
302 **Fell** fierce
rankle irritate and cause festering
303 **when he bites** Gaunt's reference to *gnarling Sorrow* (292).
lanceth not does not open surgically (so as to relieve infection)
304 **bring** escort (cf. 1.4.2)
305 **not stay** not linger. Some editors interpret *not stay* to mean 'not remain abroad' (i.e. refuse to accept exile); but Gaunt has earlier voted for banishment (234) and would hardly counsel such rebellion.
306 **Sweet soil, adieu** Cf. 3.2.6 and n. In Giles's production, Jon Finch (Bolingbroke) touched the ground, anticipating Richard's later gesture.

302 Sorrow's] *this edn;* sorrowes *QF*   never] euer *F*   303 he] it *Q2–F*

My mother and my nurse that bears me yet!
Where'er I wander, boast of this I can,
Though banished, yet a true-born Englishman.   309
Exeunt [Gaunt and Bolingbroke, followed by Lord Marshal].

[1.4]   *Enter* KING [RICHARD,] *with* GREEN *and* BAGOT
at one door, and the Lord AUMERLE *at another.*

KING RICHARD
We did observe. – Cousin Aumerle,
How far brought you high Hereford on his way?

---

307 **nurse** wet nurse (one that provides
vital nourishment); cf. 170. Ordinarily,
aristocratic infants were not suckled by
their own mothers.
bears me yet because Bolingbroke
still stands on English soil (with a possible quibble on *bears* = 'gives birth
to')
309 Muir (*Sources*, 56) thinks Lyly's
Euphues (1.313) may have suggested
Bolingbroke's last line: 'I thincke thee
happy to be so well rydde of the courte
and to bee so voyde of crime. Thou
sayest banishment is bitter to the free
borne'.
1.4 Shakespeare invents Richard's
relaxed interview with Aumerle in the
presence of Green and Bagot. Nor
does the chilly leave-taking between
Aumerle and Bolingbroke have any
counterpart in the sources; see 1.3.250
SDn. and LN. Because this scene also
refers for the first time in the play to
the Irish insurrection, to Richard's
strategies for raising funds to meet the
emergency and to Gaunt's illness, it
serves to prepare the audience for
impending events – Gaunt's death,
Richard's confiscation of Bolingbroke's
inheritance, the King's departure for

Ireland, Bolingbroke's return from
exile and Richard's loss of support at
home.
0.1 *F's omission of Bushy is unavoidable, since he must enter later at 52.1.
Q specifies the manner of entry while
F specifies the characters. Some confusion in Q seems to have resulted
from a change of mind about
who should bring the news of
Gaunt's illness to the King at 54. For
fuller discussion, see Appendix 1,
pp. 509–10, 510, n. 1, 525; also 23LN
and 52.1–53n.
1   short line, with missing foot supplied
by the pause. The King, who has
apparently been discussing Bolingbroke's departure with Green
and Bagot (cf. 24), enters in mid-
conversation. As Gurr (81) points out,
Richard shows interest only in
Bolingbroke, not in Mowbray. This
disregard of Mowbray reinforces our
disquiet at the unjust inequality of the
punishments assigned in 1.3.
2   **brought** Cf. 1.3.304.
high high in rank; proud (with
perhaps the added senses of 'aspiring'
and 'haughty'); cf. 3.3.195, 4.1.189.

---

307 that] which *F*   309 true-born] *F*; true borne *Q*   SD *Exeunt*] *om. F   Gaunt . . . Marshal*] *this edn*
1.4] *F (Scoena Quarta.)*   0.1–2] *Enter the King with Bushie, &c at one dore, and the Lord Aumarle at
another. Q; Enter King, Aumerle, Greene, and Bagot. F*   0.1 GREEN *and* BAGOT] *F; Bushie, &c Q*
1+ SP] *King Q; Rich. F*   1 Aumerle] *(Aumarle), F*

AUMERLE

> I brought high Hereford, if you call him so,
> But to the next highway, and there I left him.

KING RICHARD

> And say, what store of parting tears were shed?   5

AUMERLE

> Faith, none for me, except the northeast wind,
> Which then blew bitterly against our faces,
> Awaked the sleeping rheum and so by chance
> Did grace our hollow parting with a tear.

KING RICHARD

> What said our cousin when you parted with him?   10

AUMERLE

> 'Farewell' –
> And, for my heart disdained that my tongue
> Should so profane the word, that taught me craft
> To counterfeit oppression of such grief
> That words seemed buried in my sorrow's grave.   15

3–4 **high . . . highway** Aumerle puns flippantly in court style.
4 **next** nearest
5 **store** quantity, abundance. Grammatically, *store* is either collective with plural force (hence *were*), or else *were* agrees with *tears* by attraction; cf. 5.5.55–6n. See also Abbott, 302, 425.
  parting tears perhaps a bit of self-projection. Tears are more characteristic of Richard's sensibility than of Bolingbroke's; cf. 3.2.4–10, 3.3.161–5, 4.1.244, 5.1.44–8, 86–7, 5.2.32, 5.5.51–8. Again the tone is flippant; cf. 3–4n.
6 **for me** on my part
  except unless
8 **Awaked . . . rheum** 'made our eyes moist' (*rheum* = watery discharge). A few editors have preferred F's 'sleepie', but as this reading originates in Q3 rather than deriving from the

promptbook, it lacks authority.
9 **hollow** insincere, empty of genuine affection
11 **Farewell** under the circumstances, the most laconic, unemotional word possible; as Gurr notices, 'Its extrametrical position emphasises the baldness' (82).
12 **for** because
  disdained disdainèd
13 **that** i.e. my disdain (emphatic)
  craft skill
14 'to feign being so weighed down with grief'. Aumerle's disingenuousness to Bolingbroke 'prepares us to some extent for his conspiratorial role towards the end of the play' (Smidt, 97).
15 **words** i.e. words apart from *Farewell*
  my sorrow's grave i.e. the grave made by (or for?) my sorrow

7 blew] grew *F*   faces] face *Q3–F*   8 sleeping] sleepie *Q3–F*   10 our] *QF;* your *Q2*   11–12] *as Pope; one line QF*   13 word, . . . craft] *F;* word . . . craft, *Q*   15 words] word *F*

234

Marry, would the word 'farewell' have lengthened hours
And added years to his short banishment
He should have had a volume of farewells,
But since it would not, he had none of me.

KING RICHARD

He is our cousin, cousin, but 'tis doubt,   20
When time shall call him home from banishment,
Whether our kinsman come to see his friends.
Ourself and Bushy, Bagot here and Green
Observed his courtship to the common people –
How he did seem to dive into their hearts   25

16 **Marry** indeed (a mild oath derived
from the name of Our Lady)
17 **short** shortened (cf. 1.3.210–11)
18 **should** would certainly
a volume an entire book; a great
quantity
19 **of** from. At 1.3.249, Aumerle did say
farewell to Bolingbroke, who did not
reciprocate. Aumerle may exaggerate
his report of unfriendliness to please
Richard.
20 **our** royal plural
***cousin, cousin** Tonally, F's emenda-
tion seems natural, according nicely
with Richard's airy delight in wordplay
and with his notable fondness for
Aumerle, which emerges gradually in
the play; he has already addressed the
latter as his cousin at line 1 and
referred to Bolingbroke in the same
way at 10. See Appendix 1, p. 525. But
Q's 'Coosens Coosin' (= 'cousin's
cousin', i.e. Aumerle's cousin) may be
correct, and several editors follow
Pollard (83–4): 'Aumerle is reminded
with a touch of formality that
Hereford is his own cousin, and there
is an ironical suggestion of regret that
in spite of this he may not be recalled'.
GWW, however, regards the terminal *s*

in Q's 'Coosens' as a compositorial
misreading of a comma, properly corrected by F. Cf. notes on 2.2.57, 2.3.36,
3.2.32, 44, 3.3.31, 119. As the sons of
three brothers, Richard, Aumerle and
Bolingbroke were first cousins.
20–2 **'tis . . . friends** *doubt* = doubtful;
friends refers with or without irony to
Bolingbroke's close associates and
kinsmen (including his two cousins).
Richard may hint that he will have to
find some means (reluctantly?) to prevent Bolingbroke's return at the expiration of his exile. He implies that
Bolingbroke already constitutes a
potential threat – but not a threat that
needs to be taken too seriously.
22 **come** will come (subjunctive; see
Abbott, 368)
23 *a problematic line, undoubtedly
affected by the crux mentioned in connection with the opening SD (see 0.1n.
and 52.1–53n.). See LN.
24–36 probably based chiefly on
Holinshed: 'A wonder it was to see
what number of people ran after him
[Bolingbroke] in euerie towne and
street where he came, before he tooke
the sea, lamenting and bewailing his
departure, as who would saie, that

16 hours] *(*howers*), F*   20 cousin, cousin] *F (*Cosin (Cosin)*);* Coosens Coosin *Q;* cousin's cousin
Cam¹ (Pollard); cousins' cousin *(Vaughan)*   22 come] *QF;* comes *Q2*   22–3 friends. . . . Bushy,]
friends, . . . *Bushy: F*   23 Bushy . . . Green] *Q6;* Bushie, *Q; Bushy:* heere *Bagot* and *Greene F*

With humble and familiar courtesy,
What reverence he did throw away on slaves,
Wooing poor craftsmen with the craft of smiles
And patient underbearing of his fortune,
As 'twere to banish their affects with him.   30
Off goes his bonnet to an oyster-wench.
A brace of draymen bid God speed him well,
And had the tribute of his supple knee

when he departed, the onelie shield, defense and comfort of the commonwealth was vaded and gone' (3.495). See also LN. In *1H4* 3.2.50–4 Shakespeare again describes Bolingbroke's ingratiating himself with the populace, though now from the usurper's angle of vision. In the present context Richard's carping speech betrays a new note of jealousy, his imputation of disingenuousness perhaps implying a secret dislike of Bolingbroke from the start. We cannot ignore Richard's bias in construing Bolingbroke's supposed *craft* (28), since subsequent events prove popular support for the Earl to be spontaneous and more than could have been achieved by political manipulation alone. Nevertheless, this passage stresses the theme of *Realpolitik* (cf. Hotspur's characterization of Bolingbroke as 'this vile politician', *1H4* 1.3.241) in a way that compels us to re-evaluate both Richard and his rival, and to be more alert for evidence of hidden motives, retrospectively as well as in what lies ahead. Harrison (*TLS*) sees in Richard's description an image of the ambitious Essex in 1597; see also 31LN for Essex as the target of Elizabethan satire. The speech's careful ambiguities, like those of 1.1, are probably part of the dramatist's larger pattern. See also the acute comments on the

double meanings of this passage in Mahood, 78–9.

27 **What** Q's initial error ('With') probably represents a misunderstanding of the ambiguous contraction 'w^t' in the MS from which Q was set; see 52.1–53n.
reverence respect
slaves Richard contemptuously stresses the distance between his own exalted rank and the mere nobodies at the opposite social extreme; cf. *oyster-wench* (31), *brace of draymen* (32).

28 **craftsmen . . . craft** Richard's wordplay on *craft* (implying both 'trade' and 'deceit') typifies his sardonic wit.

29 **underbearing** endurance; rare in Shakespeare (cf. 'underbear', *KJ* 3.1.65)

30 **banish . . . him** 'carry their affections (*affects*) into exile with him'

31 See LN.
bonnet fashionable soft cap, often brimless

32 **brace of draymen** pair of carters

33 **supple** readily bending (implying flattery). Cf. *Ham* 3.2.61–2: 'crook the pregnant hinges of the knee / Where thrift may follow fawning'; *Oth* 1.1.45: 'a duteous and knee-crooking knave'. Men as well as women expressed reverence by curtsying ('courtesying'); cf. *make a leg* (3.3.175). Cf. also Bolingbroke's behaviour on horseback (5.2.18–20).

27 What] *Qc, F;* With *Qu*   28 smiles] *Q3* (smiles,); smiles. *Q;* soules, *F*   31 oyster-wench] *F;* oysterwench *Q*   32 bid] *Qu, F;* bid, *Qc*   well] *Qu, F;* wel *Qc*

With 'Thanks, my countrymen, my loving friends',
As were our England in reversion his,   35
And he our subjects' next degree in hope.

GREEN

Well, he is gone, and with him go these thoughts.
Now for the rebels which stand out in Ireland,
Expedient manage must be made, my liege,
Ere further leisure yield them further means   40
For their advantage and your highness' loss.

KING RICHARD

We will ourself in person to this war,
And, for our coffers with too great a court
And liberal largesse are grown somewhat light,

---

35 **As . . . England** 'as if England, which is mine, were'; *our* is either general in reference or royal plural, probably the latter.
in reversion by right of future inheritance – technically, by the reverting of property to its true owner after the expiration of a tenancy or lease (legal terminology); cf. 2.2.38, 38–40n., 62–6n. Richard's sarcasm creates a deeper irony since audiences would be aware that the exile would soon become Henry IV. Froissart reports that when Bolingbroke left England some Londoners were already in a mood 'to ryse agaynst the kyng' (6.319); see also 24–36n.

36 **next . . . hope** heir presumptive to the throne (*degree* = step). See 1.1.117n.

37 **go these thoughts** let these thoughts go (hortatory subjunctive)

38 **for** as for
which stand out who are making a stand, resisting; see 42n.

39 **Expedient . . . made** Swift measures must be taken.

40 **leisure** delay

42 **to** go to. Holinshed (3.496–7) writes: 'the king being aduertised that the

wild Irish dailie wasted and destroied the townes and villages within the English pale [the small territory surrounding Dublin still controlled by England], and had slaine manie of the souldiers which laie there in garison for defense of that countrie, determined to make eftsoones a voiage thither, & prepared all things necessarie for his passage now against the spring . . . and so in the moneth of Aprill, as diuerse authors write, he set forward from Windesor, and finallie tooke shipping at Milford, and from thence with two hundred ships, and a puissant power of men of armes and archers he sailed into Ireland'.

43 **for** because
too . . . court Later Richard reveals that he kept 'under his household roof . . . ten thousand men' (4.1.282–3).

44 The line scans if *liberal* is elided ('lib'ral') and *largesse* is accented on the first syllable ('làrgesse').
liberal largesse lavish generosity (mainly to his courtiers). Richard was notorious for extravagant gifts, banquets and entertainments, and for luxurious clothing (cf. 2.1.255).

42+ SP] *King. Q; Ric. F*   44 grown] *(growen), Q2, F*

We are enforced to farm our royal realm,   45
The revenue whereof shall furnish us
For our affairs in hand. If that come short,
Our substitutes at home shall have blank charters

Holinshed notes that 'he was . . . exceeding sumptuous in apparell, in so much as he had one cote, which he caused to be made for him of gold and stone, valued at 30,000 marks' (3.501); and 'He kept the greatest port, and maintained the most plentifull house that euer any king in England did either before his time or since' (3.508). *Woodstock* also stresses Richard's reckless spending, and *Traïson*, as Wilson (151) points out, actually uses the words 'grant [grand] Court' and 'largesce' (11/140). See also Saul, 336–7. As Gurr notes, however, Elizabeth herself was 'conspicuously parsimonious', thereby making her subjects 'acutely sensitive to the moral and even institutional requirements that monarchs should make generous grants to their subjects' (83).

45 **farm . . . realm** 'lease my land to tenants' (who have the right to collect revenues for their own use); cf. 2.1.110: 'let this land by lease'. Holinshed writes, 'The common brute [report] ran, that the king had set to farme the realme of England, vnto sir William Scroope earle of Wiltshire, and then treasuror of England, to sir Iohn Bushie, sir Iohn Bagot, and sir Henrie Greene knights'; a marginal note, 'The realme let to farme', highlights the practice (3.496). See also LN. Shakespeare's innovation is to connect these exactions as well as the *blank charters* (48) specifically with the Irish emergency; none of the sources does so, although Holinshed had earlier mentioned a 'new and strange subsidie' levied on Richard's subjects 'towards the

charges of this armie that went ouer into France' in 1381 under the command of Thomas of Woodstock, then Earl of Buckingham (3.428). Cf. also the charge brought against Richard by the bishops at the time of his deposition that 'he at his going into Ireland exacted manie notable summes of monie, beside plate and iewels, without law or custome, contrarie to his oth taken at his coronation' (Holinshed, 3.502).

48 **substitutes at home** 'those appointed to exercise authority during my absence abroad, deputies'. Just before departing for Ireland, Richard makes York 'Lord Governor of England' (2.1.220).

blank charters writs authorizing agents of the crown to extort revenues in unspecified amounts from the affluent – forced loans; cf. 2.1.250. Holinshed explains (again with an emphatic note in the margin) that when the City of London fell into Richard's disfavour, such instruments were used to assuage his vexation: 'manie blanke charters were deuised, and brought into the citie, which manie of the substantiall and wealthie citizens were faine to seale, to their great charge, as in the end appeared. And the like charters were sent abroad into all shires within the realme, whereby great grudge and murmuring arose among the people: for when they were so sealed, the kings officers wrote in the same what liked them, as well for charging the parties with paiment of monie, as otherwise' (3.496). Cf. also *Woodstock*, 3.3.78–83; *Mirror*, 114 ('King Richard the Second', l. 43). Modern

47 hand. If] *F* *(*hand: if*)*; hand if *Q*

238

Whereto, when they shall know what men are rich,
They shall subscribe them for large sums of gold,   50
And send them after to supply our wants;
For we will make for Ireland presently.

Enter BUSHY.

^FBushy,^F what news?

BUSHY

Old John of Gaunt is grievous sick, my lord,
Suddenly taken, and hath sent post-haste   55
To entreat your majesty to visit him.

KING RICHARD

Where lies he?

historians have questioned whether such charters were actually used since, among the well-preserved financial records of the reign, no examples have survived.

50 **subscribe them** enter their names (with the amounts to be collected) in the blank spaces of the charters

51 **them** the sums of gold or, possibly, the charters themselves; not the *rich men*

52 **presently** immediately

52.1–53 *F's abbreviated SD and the continuation of Richard's speech, which follows, undoubtedly represent a correction of Q derived from the promptbook; see Appendix 1, pp. 509–10, 510, n. 1, 525. Q's awkwardly wordy '*Enter Bushie with newes*' probably resulted from misreading of an alteration in copy. Wilson (151–2), amplified by Ure (44), conjectures that when it was decided to make Bushy deliver tidings of Gaunt's illness (see 0.1n. and 23LN), the MS from which Q was set was corrected to read 'Enter Bushie Ric. Bushie, w^t newes?' or words to this effect. Then the compositor (or editor), believing that the correction

applied to the SD alone, mistakenly dropped the second 'Bushie' as redundant and misunderstood the 'w^t' as a contracted form of 'with' (rather than 'what') as in 27 (see n.). See LN. Ure points out that the second 'Bushie' (a direct address in dialogue) would be essential as a means of identifying the new character immediately before his first speech of the play. Gurr (84) suggests that, apart from economy in casting, an additional reason for giving Bushy rather than an anonymous stranger the role of messenger would be Shakespeare's wish to keep Richard more tightly encircled by his own clique of flatterers and adherents.

54 Of all the possible sources, Froissart alone mentions Gaunt's illness: 'the physicions and surgyons in Englande sayd surely, howe that the duke his [Bolingbroke's] father had on hym a paryllous sycknesse, whiche shulde be his dethe' (6.335); see also 2.1 headnote. But, as Ure (44) observes, Shakespeare would need no authority for such a dramatically requisite detail.

53 what news?] *F; with newes Q, as part of 52.1*   54 grievous] verie *F*   55 post-haste] *Rolfe;* post haste *QF*   57–8] *one line / Cam²*

BUSHY
    At Ely House.
KING RICHARD
    Now put it, God, in the physician's mind
    To help him to his grave immediately!   60
    The lining of his coffers shall make coats
    To deck our soldiers for these Irish wars.
    Come, gentlemen, let's all go visit him.
    Pray God we may make haste and come too late!   64
ALL
    Amen!   *Exeunt.*

58 **Ely House** the Bishop of Ely's palace in Holborn at the edge of London, then set in the midst of gardens and open land (cf. *R3* 3.4.31–2); Holinshed (3.496) reports that Gaunt died there. It was often rented to noblemen as a town residence.

59–60 As Herford (156) notes, Richard's callous wish for Gaunt's death may be indebted to Edward's similar sentiment in *E2*, 2.2.236–7: 'Would Lancaster and he [Mortimer] had both caroused / A bowl of poison to each other's health'.

59 **put** probably imperative, though conceivably, as Wells (187) suggests, subjunctive ('Now if God should put it'), in which case a comma would be needed for the exclamation mark after *immediately* (60)

61 **lining** contents (possibly with a quibble on the cloth lining of *coats*)
   coats probably 'coats of mail, armour', but perhaps 'uniforms'

62 **deck** dress (perhaps with the secondary meaning, 'adorn')

65 ***ALL Amen!** Staunton's emendation plausibly corrects Q's unsatisfactory ascription of *Amen* to Richard, making it instead a general response to his prayer of 64. Anglican liturgy prescribed that the priest alone recited most of the prayers, after each of which the clerk and congregation would respond in unison; cf. 4.1.173–4. The indentation of *Amen* in Q1–5 suggests that the line was intended as a separate speech whose SP has somehow dropped out. F omits the line, maybe, as *TxC* (309) suggests, because it had been deleted in the promptbook at the same time that *God* was changed to 'heauen' (59, 64) and '*Exeunt*' to '*Exit*' (65). GWW suggests that when the change to 'heauen' occurred in F, the speech ceased to be a prayer and *Amen* therefore became redundant.

59 God] heauen *F*   in the] into the *Q2;* in his *F*   64 God] heauen *F*   65 SP] *Staunton; not in QF* Amen] *om. F*   SD] *Exit. F*

240

[2.1] *Enter* John of GAUNT *sick, [carried in a chair,] with the* Duke of YORK, *and Servants.*

GAUNT

Will the King come that I may breathe my last
In wholesome counsel to his unstaid youth?

YORK

Vex not yourself, nor strive not with your breath,

2.1 Shakespeare invents Richard's visit to Gaunt in his final illness, although for the death itself he may have consulted Froissart (cf. 1.4.54n.) and remembered *Woodstock* which, especially in its title character, 'Plain Thomas' (1.1.199), anticipates many of Gaunt's dying sentiments and opinions. Froissart writes: 'duke Johan of Lancastre, who lyved in great dysplesure, what bycause the kynge had banysshed his sonne out of the realme for so litell a cause, and also bycause of the yvell governynge of the realme by his nephewe kynge Rycharde: for he sawe well that if he longe perceyvered and were suffred to contynewe, the realme was lykely to be utterly loste: with these ymagynacyons and other, the duke fell sycke wheron he dyed, whose dethe was greatly sorowed of all his frendes and lovers. The kyng, by that he shewed, toke no great care for his dethe, but sone he was forgotten' (6.335–6). Richard's seizure of Gaunt's property and York's protest derive from Holinshed (see 160–2n., 202–4n., 205–8n.), as does the treasonable talk of the disaffected nobles at the end of the scene and their secret decision to back Bolingbroke (see 277–88n.).

0.1–2 *Gaunt is probably borne onstage in a chair. Cf. *1H6* 2.5.0.1: '*Enter* Mortimer, *brought in a chair*' and *KL* 4.7.23.1: '*Enter* Lear *in a chair carried by* Servants'; also Tamburlaine, who

dies in his 'fatal chair' (*2 Tamburlaine*, 5.3.211). Gaunt is later conveyed offstage to his bed (138 SD) where he dies. As Gurr (85) points out, Gaunt's sitting posture sets up a telling reversal of the usual decorum when the King enters at 68.1: in 1.1 the King presumably sat while the court stood (1.3 is an exception; see 1.3.6.3n.), and in 4.1, 5.3 and 5.6 the same protocol will perhaps obtain after Bolingbroke becomes king; but Gaunt, near death, can be accorded the symbolic status of a privileged elder statesman, who in terms of wisdom outranks his royal nephew. Wells (188) suggests that Northumberland should enter with Gaunt and York although he remains silent until 147; see 146.1n.

1 **breathe my last** gasp out my final breath, expire; utter my final words (*breathe* = speak; cf. 8). Mahood (79) points to the rich irony of Gaunt's dying words as potentially life-giving to the King and his kingdom 'if only Richard would heed them'.

2, 4 **counsel** advice. Richard's council included both Gaunt and York.

2 **unstaid** unrestrained, unregulated; Mahood (80) suggests a pun on 'unstayed' with the meanings 'giddy' and 'unpropped'.

3 **strive . . . breath** 'Don't exert yourself to speak when breathing itself is so difficult' (cf. 1n.). Gaunt's breath is laboured because of illness.

2.1] F (*Actus Secundus. Scena Prima.*)   0.1–2] Enter Gaunt, sicke with Yorke. F   0.1 *carried in a chair*] Cam[1] (subst.)   0.2 *and Servants*] Wells (subst.); *&c. Q*

For all in vain comes counsel to his ear.

GAUNT

O, but they say the tongues of dying men   5
Enforce attention like deep harmony.
Where words are scarce, they are seldom spent in vain,
For they breathe truth that breathe their words in pain.
He that no more must say is listened more
Than they whom youth and ease have taught to glose.   10
More are men's ends marked than their lives before.
The setting sun and music at the close,
As the last taste of sweets, is sweetest last,
Writ in remembrance more than things long past.
Though Richard my life's counsel would not hear,   15
My death's sad tale may yet undeaf his ear.

---

4 Cf. Hall: 'kyng Richarde . . . was nowe brought to that trade of liuyng that he litle or nothyng regarded the counsaill of his vncles, nor of other graue and sadde persones, but did all thyng at his pleasure, settyng his will and appetite in stede of lawe and reason' (fol. ii).

5–16 The weighty sententiousness of these lines, slowed down by three couplets and a quatrain, not only suggests old age but also Gaunt's laboured utterance. Gurr (85) notes that the lines 'augment . . . the imagery of words, tongues, and breath'; cf. 1.3.161–5n. Bolingbroke and Mowbray introduce the motif at 1.1.44 and 57.

5–14 excerpted in *Parnassus* (no. 311) under the heading 'Death'

5–8 a proverbial idea; cf. 'Dying men speak true' (Dent, M514).

7 **they are** probably elided to 'they're'

9 **that . . . say** who is about to be silenced by death
listened heeded, listened to; cf. *JC* 4.1.41.

10 **glose** speak smoothly, emptily or speciously (literally, 'flatter')

11 **marked** paid attention to

12 **close** cadence; cf. *H5* 1.2.181–3.

13 **last . . . sweets** the final taste of sweet things (before the sweetness dies on the palate)
is sweetest last is longest remembered as sweet

14 **Writ in remembrance** recorded in the memory

15 **my life's counsel** advice given during my life

16 **death's sad tale** solemn words spoken on my deathbed; *sad* = 'solemn, grave', not 'sorrowful'.
undeaf unstop, free from deafness; a Shakespeare coinage (see *OED v.*). As observed in *Riv* (813), such words characterize the play's style: cf. *unhappied* (3.1.10), *uncurse* (3.2.137), *unsay* (4.1.9), *undo* (203), *unkinged* (220), *undeck* (250), *unkiss* (5.1.74). A vocabulary of negation is appropriate to a tragedy about psychic annihilation and ties in with the motif of 'nothing' (see 2.2.12n.).

12 at] *is F*

YORK

> No, it is stopped with other, flatt'ring sounds,
> As praises, of whose taste the wise are fond;
> Lascivious metres, to whose venom sound
> The open ear of youth doth always listen;   20
> Report of fashions in proud Italy,

17 ***other, flatt'ring sounds** other voices, which, unlike yours, flatter him

18 ***of . . . fond** 'by whose taste even the wise are delighted' (probably with a quibble on *fond*, 'made foolish by'). Collier's conjecture (*fond*), adopted by Cam and most other editors, makes acceptable sense (if *the wise* is understood to mean 'even the wise') and, of the solutions proposed, involves the least alteration of Q. Q's compositor may have erred by adding a *u* to *fond* in order to create a rhyme with *sound* in 19, since there is a great deal of rhyme in the immediate vicinity (see 7–16n.); or he may have been unconsciously attracted to 'soundes' in 17. Progressive corruption continued in Q2, Q3 and F. (It is clear that F's reading cannot have derived from the promptbook but was based on Q3. See Appendix 1, pp. 537–8, 537 n. 2). The weakness of the traditional solution, as *TxC* (309) notes, is that *fond* gives a sense nearly opposite to the word one would expect (such as 'loath' or 'ware') and therefore requires us to understand the syntax in a less than obvious way, i.e. ' Even the wise are fond of praises, not to mention Richard, who is anything but wise'. This necessary straining of the sense may point to some flaw in the text beyond our mending.

19 **Lascivious metres** salacious verses, lewd poems. Cf. Gaveston's seductive programme for Edward II in Marlowe's play: 'I must have wanton poets, pleasant wits, / Musicians that,

with touching of a string, / May draw the pliant king which way I please' (*E2*, 1.1.50–2); cf. also *R3* 1.1.13: 'the lascivious pleasing of a lute'. Holinshed (3.502) refers to Richard's 'lasciuious liuing'.

venom poisonous

21–3 Italy was regarded as the quintessential source of folly and wickedness; cf. the famous assault on the 'Italianated Englishman' in *The Schoolmaster* (Ascham, 222–37). Cf. also *E2*, 1.1.53–5: 'Music and poetry is his delight; / Therefore I'll have Italian masques by night, / Sweet speeches, comedies, and pleasing shows'; also *Woodstock*, 2.3.88–95, where Richard and his flatterers 'sit in council to devise strange fashions, / And suit themselves in wild and antic habits / Such as this kingdom never yet beheld: / French hose, Italian cloaks, and Spanish hats, / Polonian shoes with peaks a hand full long, / Tied to their knees with chains of pearl and gold. / Their plumèd tops fly waving in the air / A cubit high above their wanton heads'. Holinshed reports that 'euerie daie there was deuising of new fashions' (3.508). The foreign (especially Italian) styles mainly reflect sixteenth- rather than fourteenth-century tastes.

21 **fashions** mainly 'clothing' but also, perhaps, manners, customs and behaviour

proud arrogant; lavish, gorgeous (cf. *KL* 3.4.83: 'proud array')

17 other,] *Staunton;* other *QF*   flatt'ring] *F;* flattering *Q*   18 of . . . fond] *Cam (Collier);* of whose taste the wise are found *Q;* of whose state the wise are found *Q2;* of his state: then there are found *Q3;* of his state: then there are sound *F;* of whose taste th' unwise are fond *(Lettsom);* of whose taste the wise are feared *Oxf*

Whose manners still our tardy-apish nation
Limps after in base imitation.
Where doth the world thrust forth a vanity –
So it be new, there's no respect how vile –   25
That is not quickly buzzed into his ears?
Then all too late comes Counsel to be heard,
Where Will doth mutiny with Wit's regard.
Direct not him whose way himself will choose.
'Tis breath thou lack'st, and that breath wilt thou lose.   30

GAUNT
Methinks I am a prophet new inspired,
And thus, expiring, do foretell of him.
His rash fierce blaze of riot cannot last,

22 **still** ever, always
   tardy-apish i.e. copying foreign fashions after they are outmoded
23 **imitation** If pronounced 'im-i-tà-
   ti-on' (five syllables), the line scans
   nicely as a regular pentameter; but
   such a pronunciation implies that the
   rhyme word (*nation*) in 22 must be
   pronounced trisyllabically, making
   that line (22) an alexandrine. *VA*
   rhymes 'posterity' (758) with 'obscurity' (760) in a metrically analogous way;
   cf. also *Luc* 352, 354–5, where a similar
   conflict between regular metre and
   rhyme occurs.
24 **vanity** frivolous pursuit, trivial idea or
   fad
25 **there's no respect** it matters not
   vile contemptible
26 **buzzed** whispered, reported (by his
   sycophantic courtiers); a contemptuous word
27 **Counsel** probably another personification since Q capitalizes the word; see
   28n. and 1.1.171n.
28 'where desire rebels against considerations of good sense and prudence'.

Gurr (86) cites Sidney's *Apology for
Poetry*, which contrasts 'our infected
will' with 'our erected wit'; cf. also *Luc*
1299. *Will* and *Wit* are treated here as
personifications so as to be consistent
with *Counsel* (27); both appear prominently as characters in *The Marriage of
Wit and Science* (1568).
29 **whose . . . choose** 'who insists on
   choosing his own path'
30 **breath . . . breath** continuing the serious wordplay on *breath* (words) introduced earlier; cf. 1, 3 and 8. The metre
   requires a stress on *that*.
   lose waste
31 The concept of the dying man as
   prophet extends the meaning of 5–6.
   Cf. also *lean-looked prophets* (2.4.11).
   Methinks literally, 'it seems to me'
32 **expiring** dying (literally, 'breathing
   my last'; cf. 1n.); note also the wordplay on *new inspired* (literally, 'having
   had new breath breathed into me')
   from 31.
33 **rash** sudden, quickly kindled; cf. *1H4*
   3.2.61: 'rash bavin wits'.
   riot dissolute revelling, profligacy

22 tardy-apish] *Dyce;* tardy apish *QF*   27 Then] That *F*   28 Will] *this edn;* will *QF*   Wit's] *this edn;* wits *QF*

For violent fires soon burn out themselves;
Small showers last long but sudden storms are short;   35
He tires betimes that spurs too fast betimes;
With eager feeding food doth choke the feeder.
Light vanity, insatiate cormorant,
Consuming means, soon preys upon itself.
This royal throne of kings, this sceptred isle,   40
This earth of majesty, this seat of Mars,
This other Eden, demi-paradise,

34–7 This piling up of proverbial maxims or apothegms (*sententiae*), a habit of rhetoric for which there was greater Elizabethan than current tolerance, is meant to establish Gaunt as a figure of long experience and seasoned wisdom; cf. Friar Lawrence: 'These violent delights have violent ends' (*RJ* 2.6.9) and 'Wisely and slow, they stumble that run fast' (*RJ* 2.3.94); also Dent, N321. Warwick's speeches in *E3* (2.1.386–409, 433–54) provide a parallel to *sententiae* used, as here, in series. No comic effect is intended. The imagery of fire, storms, riding and eating extends thematically well beyond the immediate context.

34 **fires** dissyllabic; see 1.3.294n.

35 **Small** light, composed of tiny drops
showers monosyllabic (see t.n.); as Wells notes, the first two feet of the line contain four accented syllables, an example of 'Shakespeare matching the sound to the sense' (189).

36 **betimes . . . betimes** soon . . . early in the day

38 **Light vanity** reckless extravagance, frivolity
insatiate cormorant voracious glutton (literally, a seabird notable for swallowing prey in one gulp)

39 **means** i.e. means of sustenance, resources

40–64 See LN.

40 **royal . . . kings** Cf. *R3* 3.1.164: 'the seat royal of this famous isle'; also

Peele, *Arraignment of Paris*, l. 1153: 'An auncient seat of kinges, a seconde Troie, / Ycompast rounde with a commodious sea', and *Edward I*, l. 11: 'Illustrious England, auncient seat of kings' (Peele, 3.111 and 2.72).

41 **earth of majesty** i.e. domain for kings to rule over (amplifying the images of 40)
seat of Mars home of the god of war. Note that the line paradoxically combines ideas of England as a natural place (*earth*), anticipating the paradisal metaphor to follow, and as heroically warlike. Both images suggest traditional ideals from which the shameful reign of Richard is a falling off.

42 **other Eden, demi-paradise** i.e. second or local Paradise (*demi* = 'half' or 'quasi'). Ure (51, 206–7) points out that both John Eliot and Sylvester (translating Du Bartas) refer to the 'earthly paradise' or '*Earths rare Paradice*'; cf. also *Tem* 4.1.124 and Greene, *Spanish Masquerado* (1598): 'the Lord our mercifull God maketh England like Eden, a second Paradise' (sig. E3ᵛ). Shakespeare carefully prepares us for the garden imagery to be developed later (cf. 3.4.43: *our sea-walled garden*), already anticipated by implication, as Gurr (86) notes, in the references to the *earth* at 1.1.23 and 37. Cf. also *H5* 5.2.36, where France is imaged as 'this best garden of the world'.

35 showers] *(shoures)*   36 betimes;] *Q2 (*betimes,*), F;* betimes *Q*   42 demi-paradise] *Steevens;* demy Paradice *QF*

This fortress built by Nature for herself
Against infection and the hand of war,
This happy breed of men, this little world,   45
This precious stone set in the silver sea,
Which serves it in the office of a wall
Or as a moat defensive to a house
Against the envy of less happier lands,
This blessed plot, this earth, this realm, this England,   50
This nurse, this teeming womb of royal kings,

43–4 As an island Britain was naturally fortified against invasion, the encircling sea
forming her *moat* (48). *Infection* (as
Kittredge² believes) may simply mean
'pestilence' or 'plague', but the likely
association of the word with foreign hostility may be partly based on memories
of the Spanish Armada (1588) with its
pestilential threat of Catholic domination. *Infection* may also suggest continental vices and fashions (cf. 21–6). Ure
(51) points out that Daniel identifies civil
war in both France and England with
'contagion' (4.43, 90). If Shakespeare's
audience shared Daniel's linkage of
infection with civil strife, Gaunt's words
at this point would carry an additional
proleptic irony. Muir comments on the
relevance of this passage to Lodge's
'Truth's Complaint': 'Here the sequence
of ideas is very close to that of Gaunt's
speech: Island (Isle) – defence (defensive) – England – seate – Paradise (demi-
paradise) – sacred plot (blessed plot) –
peace (war)' (*Sources*, 63).
45 **happy breed** fortunate race
   little world England as a microcosm
   was a common idea; cf. *Friar Bacon*, sc.
   4.6–7: 'England's . . . promontory
   cliffs / Show Albion is another little
   world'; also *Cym* 3.1.12–13: 'Britain's a
   world / By itself'.
46 **precious . . . sea** Cf. *precious jewel*
   (1.3.267); Sylvester refers to 'Albion'
   as 'Europes *Pearle of price*' (see Ard²,
   207). See also LN (and *passim*).

47 **office** function
48 ***a moat defensive** Q4's 'a moate'
   mends Q's metre by adding the necessary article, probably omitted in error; F
   seems to have restored the correct reading independently, probably responding
   to the annotator of Q3, who was correcting from the promptbook (see Appendix
   1, p. 525), although so obvious an emendation might easily be introduced (as in
   Q4) by the F editor or compositor on his
   own authority. See LN.
49 **envy** enmity, malice
   less happier less fortunate (Abbott, 11)
50, 56 **blessed** blessèd
50 **plot** arable ground, land fit for culti-
   vating
   earth country (cf. 41)
51–6 Gaunt invokes the heroic past of
   such crusader monarchs as Richard
   Coeur de Lion and Edward I with whose
   chivalry and military achievements
   abroad Richard II's self-indulgence
   contrasts tellingly. The play ends ironically with Henry IV's (unfulfilled) vow
   to make a penitential 'voyage to the
   Holy Land' (5.6.49) in atonement for
   the death of his predecessor. Sylvester
   (462–3) celebrates English chivalry:
   'Albion' is a '*Thrice-happy Mother,
   which aye bringest-forth / Such Chiualry
   as daunteth all the Earth, / (Planting the
   Trophies of thy glorious Armes / By Sea
   and Land, where euer* Titan *warmes)*';
   see also 48LN.
51 **teeming** productive of offspring, fertile

48 a moat] *Q4–F; moate Q*

Feared by their breed and famous by their birth,
Renowned for their deeds as far from home,
For Christian service and true chivalry,
As is the sepulchre in stubborn Jewry   55
Of the world's ransom, blessed Mary's son,
This land of such dear souls, this dear dear land,
Dear for her reputation through the world,
Is now leased out – I die pronouncing it –
Like to a tenement or pelting farm.   60
England, bound in with the triumphant sea,
Whose rocky shore beats back the envious siege
Of wat'ry Neptune, is now bound in with shame,

52 **Feared . . . breed** held in awe by reason of their ancestral prowess; *by*, used twice in the line, is equivalent to 'on account of'. F's emendation is unnecessary.
53 **Renowned** renownèd
55 **stubborn Jewry** i.e. the stony-hearted inhabitants of Judea who resisted Christianity and fought the crusaders. *Homily* refers to the Jews as 'a stubborne people' (2.289).
56 **the world's ransom** Christ, the Saviour of the world (Matthew, 20.28; 1 Timothy, 2.5–6)
57, 58 **dear** playing on the related senses of 'beloved', 'costly' and 'priceless'; the repetition (cf. Mowbray's *dear dear lord* at 1.1.176) underscores Gaunt's horror of such inestimable value being debased to the status of a commodity – being *leased out* (59).
59 **leased out** Cf. 1.4.45n. Daniel employs the same term: 'who as let in lease doe farme the crowne' (2.19).
pronouncing proclaiming
60 **tenement** property rented to a tenant (buildings with the surrounding land)
pelting paltry, of trivial importance (cf. *KL* 2.3.18). *Woodstock* (4.1.145–7) may be Shakespeare's direct source here: 'And we . . . Become a landlord to

this warlike realm, / Rent out our kingdom like a pelting farm'; although the surviving MS possibly reads 'peltry' rather than 'pelting', the meaning is synonymous (see Rossiter, 198–9).
61–3 **bound . . . Neptune** Cf. 48LN. Neptune was the Roman god of the sea. Muir suggests that *siege* may contain 'a partial pun on "surge"' (67).
61 **with** by
62 **envious** hostile
63 a rough line metrically. The third foot of the pentameter is probably anapaestic: 'Of wàt- | 'ry Nèp- | tune, is nòw'; or perhaps *Neptune, is now* is elided to 'Neptune's now'.
63–4 **bound . . . bonds** Cf. *Woodstock*, 4.1.180–93, where Tresilian specifies the supposed particulars of the legal instruments Gaunt seems to have in mind at this point, and Rossiter's note (227); see also 1.4.45n. Holinshed (3.496) is warrant enough for these lines, although Shakespeare may also have recalled *Woodstock*. 'Bound in with shame' (legally confined by the shameful fetters of mere paper agreements) plays bitterly on 'bound in with the triumphant sea' (surrounded by the overpowering ocean) in 61; *inky blots* (ink stains and stains on

With inky blots and rotten parchment bonds.
That England that was wont to conquer others   65
Hath made a shameful conquest of itself.
Ah, would the scandal vanish with my life,
How happy then were my ensuing death!

[Flourish.] Enter KING [RICHARD] *and* QUEEN,
^FAUMERLE, BUSHY, GREEN, BAGOT, ROSS *and*
WILLOUGHBY^F, *with Attendants.*

England's reputation) and *rotten parchment bonds* (physically perishable documents and papers that signify the
decay of England's former grandeur)
further complicate the wordplay,
which effectively intensifies Gaunt's
pain at the national disgrace. Imagery
of legal bonding (1.1.2, 4.1.77, 5.2.65),
blots and stains (1.3.202, 3.2.81,
3.3.66, 71, 4.1.30, 236, 325, 5.3.65)
suffuses the play; see Introduction,
p. 78.

64–5 *bonds. / That* Q's colon after
bonds is ambiguous since *That* could be
interpreted as a conjunction ('so that')
rather than a demonstrative adjective.
In the former case, the colon would
have to be equivalent to a comma
rather than, as is more likely, a full stop
(see F).

65–6 The notion of England conquered
by internal quarrels when foreign
invasion would otherwise fail was
common in Elizabethan propaganda:
Froissart, elaborating on Gaunt's displeasure with Richard, writes, 'The
Frenchemen . . . canne nat recover
their dommages, nor come to their
ententes, but by our owne meanes and
dyscorde bytwene ourselfe' (6.311);
Daniel opens *Civil Wars* by announc-
ing that his subject is the English, a
'people hauty, proud with forain
spoyles' who 'Vpon themselues, turne
back their conquering hand' (1.1);

and the Bastard in *KJ* 5.7.112–14,
probably imitating *2 Troublesome
Reign*, ll. 1187–8, 1195–6, boasts,
'This England never did, nor never
shall / Lie at the proud foot of a conqueror, / But when it first did help to
wound itself'. See also Sylvester in
48LN. Ure (54) gives additional
examples.

65 **wont** accustomed

67–8 Cf. *2H6* 3.1.148–50: 'if my death
might make this island happy, / And
prove the period of their tyranny, / I
would expend it with all willingness';
also *Woodstock*, 3.2.108–9: 'I would my
death might end the misery / My fear
presageth to my wretched country.'

68 **ensuing** approaching

68.1 *Inasmuch as F specifies a flourish
(see 1.3.122 SDn.) for the King's exit
at 223, it seems appropriate, as Wells
suggests (190), that his entrance
should likewise be so accompanied,
even though the King is visiting the
private house of a sick man; a trumpet
announcement at this point would suit
the King's callousness. York's line,
immediately following, probably indicates that the speaker has already
heard the trumpets, which might vali-
date Q's placing of the King's entry
after 70. F's placing of the entrance
two lines earlier, however, probably
derives from the promptbook and, if
so, shows how it was handled in the

64 bonds.] *(*bonds:*), F*   68.1–3 *Enter king and Queene, &c. Q, after 70; Enter King, Queene, Aumerle,*
Bushy, Greene, Bagot, Ros, and Willoughby. F   68.1 *Flourish] Wells*   68.3 *with Attendants] this edn; &c. Q*

YORK

The King is come. Deal mildly with his youth,
For young hot colts, being raged, do rage the more.   70

QUEEN

How fares our noble uncle Lancaster?

KING RICHARD

What comfort, man? How is't with aged Gaunt?

GAUNT

O, how that name befits my composition!
Old Gaunt indeed, and gaunt in being old.

theatre. Note the abrupt shift of tone from the sombre colloquy between Gaunt and York (two old men) to the colour, brightness and careless energy of the youthful King and his court. GWW interprets the King's entrance differently, believing that a trumpet blast would be inappropriate in approaching a sick man and that York's words, 'The King is come' (69), indicate that Richard has entered so quietly that Gaunt, who is deaf, must be informed of the royal arrival.

69 **mildly . . . youth** Cf. *Woodstock*, 1.1.186: Richard's marriage, Gloucester hopes, will 'mildly calm his headstrong youth'. Aston (306–10) shows how Tudor historians exaggerated Richard's extreme youth, attributing many of his faults to immaturity, at the same time stressing Bolingbroke's developed manhood by contrast (cf. 1.1.100n.). In fact, Bolingbroke was three months younger than Richard.

70 **raged** probably 'enraged' (by chafing or rough handling), although *OED* (*v.* 8) gives no other examples of this transitive use; but cf. 173. Kittredge[2] (127) notes 'the frequent rhetorical trick of repetition' in classical tradition, and such repetitions within the line are common in this scene (cf. 36, 82, 105, 112, 114, 135, 157, 180, 187,

200, 252). It is also suggestive that the annotator of Q3, preparing copy for F (see Appendix 1, p. 520), apparently saw no need to alter. Some editors, unhappy with the repetition, have nevertheless emended. Ritson's 'rein'd' is plausible enough if we suppose, as Gurr (88) suggests, compositorial error in anticipating the later *rage* two words earlier in his copy; or else, as GWW proposes, Q's 'ragde' could be a compositorial misreading of MS 'raȳde' ('raynde' = reined) since *y* with a tilde above it could look very like *g*. The proverb-like force of the line might be used to argue either for or against the emendation. Additional support for the emendation may appear in *Mirror* (78), a conceivable source for the passage: 'The king . . . Not raygning but raging by youthfull insolence' ('Robert Tresilian', ll. 92–3). Wilson's 'ragged' (shaggy, unruly, not broken-in) is less convincing (158–9). The line could have been influenced by a stanza in Lodge's 'Truth's Complaint' (Muir, *Sources*, 63).

72 **comfort** encouragement, consolation; Richard enquires routinely about Gaunt's health.
   aged agèd

73 **composition** bodily and mental condition, state of health

70 raged] *(ragde), F (rag'd); rein'd Singer (Ritson); ragged Cam¹*   72 SP] *King Q; Ri. F*

Within me Grief hath kept a tedious fast,   75
And who abstains from meat that is not gaunt?
For sleeping England long time have I watched;
Watching breeds leanness, leanness is all gaunt.
The pleasure that some fathers feed upon
Is my strict fast – I mean my children's looks,   80
And therein fasting hast thou made me gaunt.
Gaunt am I for the grave, gaunt as a grave,
Whose hollow womb inherits naught but bones.

KING RICHARD
Can sick men play so nicely with their names?

GAUNT
No, misery makes sport to mock itself.   85

---

75 **Grief . . . fast** Apart from religious observance, fasting was sometimes occasioned by mourning; cf. *R3* 4.4.118, *Ham* 5.1.275.
76 **meat** food
77 **watched** forgone sleep, kept awake (punning on the sense of 'kept guard'). Gaunt implies that he has been watchful for the nation's good in contrast to the irresponsible parasites who have ignored or exacerbated danger. Cf. *Woodstock*, where York complains that while among Richard's favourites he 'ne'er slept soundly' (3.2.8). See also Gloucester's statement: 'bear record, / righteous heaven, / How I have nightly waked for England's good' (5.1.124–5); although, as Ure (55) notes, the latter quotation probably derives from *2H6* 3.1.110–11: 'So help me God, as I have watch'd the night, / Ay, night by night, in studying good for England'. Gurr (88) suggests that *sleeping England* refers to Richard himself in addition to the nation, carelessly unaware of the disasters already incubating.
78 **Watching** lack of sleep (from worrying) **gaunt** lean; Gaunt
80 **my strict fast** 'what I have been

forced to abstain from'
my children's looks i.e. because his son Bolingbroke has been exiled. Although Gaunt had other sons besides Bolingbroke (who could presumably still look at their father), Shakespeare ignores this fact. Gaunt's looks at his sons could be implied but the plural *children* may be merely generic.
81 **therein fasting** modifying *me* later in the line
83 **womb** a more imaginative word than the 'tomb' we might expect, suggesting the catastrophe and grief to which Gaunt's death will give birth as well as the macabre relatedness of birth and death; Gurr (88) notes the similar image at 2.2.10 where the Queen presages 'Some unborn sorrow, ripe in Fortune's womb'; cf. also 2.2.62–6.
inherits receives by due right, possesses
84 **so nicely** with such witty precision and subtlety, so triflingly
85 'No, misery (rather than sickness) prompts the wordplay by mocking itself' – an interesting confirmation that punning in the play can frequently be a symptom of genuine pain; cf. 1.3.262n., 274n. The trait is a prominent feature of

84, 88 SP] *King Q; Ric. F*

Since thou dost seek to kill my name in me,
I mock my name, great King, to flatter thee.

KING RICHARD
Should dying men flatter with those that live?

GAUNT
No, no, men living flatter those that die.

KING RICHARD
Thou, now a-dying, sayest thou flatterest me.   90

GAUNT
O no, thou diest, though I the sicker be.

KING RICHARD
I am in health, I breathe, and see thee ill.

GAUNT
Now He that made me knows I see thee ill –
Ill in myself to see, and in thee seeing ill.
Thy death-bed is no lesser than thy land,   95

Gaunt's character, the psychological validity of which Coleridge defended (see Introduction, pp. 68, 88–9).

86 **kill . . . me** 'blot out my name (and therefore my family reputation) by banishing my heir' (cf. 80n.). Gurr (88) observes that the 'loss of names' is one of the themes of the play; cf. especially 1.3.202, 2.3.71, 3.3.145–6, 4.1.255–6, 5.2.41–3, 93, and see Introduction, pp. 67–8. Baxter (91) suggests that in this context Gaunt's *name* embraces three aspects of his identity – brother to the murdered Gloucester, father to the banished Bolingbroke, and counsellor to the English throne: Richard has killed all three 'in so far as Gaunt's essence subsists' in each of them.

86–7 The introduction of rhymed couplets (cf. 90–1) as well as patterned repetition (cf. 92–4) into this stichomythic exchange obviously heightens the effect of sarcasm and bitterness on both sides.

87 Gaunt implies that mocking the name 'Gaunt' should please the King since by exiling Bolingbroke he has already tried to wreck the whole family.

88 **flatter with** try to please, fawn upon (cf. *TGV* 4.4.188, *TN* 1.5.303)

89 **flatter** attempt (insincerely?) to cheer up (slightly varying the sense from 88)

90 **sayest . . . flatterest** pronounced 'say'st . . . flatter'st' (as in F; see t.n.)

91 **diest** monosyllabic ('dy'st') and meant figuratively, as explained in Gaunt's next speech.

93 **see thee ill** *Thee* receives the stress. Gaunt puns on Richard's phrase (92): see you imperfectly (because of failing eyesight); see you sick (i.e. sinful and incapable). The dual sense becomes clearer in 94.

94 **in thee . . . ill** seeing illness (evil, abuse of royal power) in you
thee stressed so as to contrast with *myself*. The line is an alexandrine.

---

87 I] *QF;* O *Q2*   88 flatter with] flatter *Q2–F*   90+ SP] *King. Q; Rich. F*   90 a-dying] *Collier;* a dying *QF*   sayest] sayst *F*   flatterest] flatter'st *F*   92 and see] I see *Q2–F*   95 thy land] the land *Q2–F*

Wherein thou liest in reputation sick;
And thou, too careless patient as thou art,
Committ'st thy anointed body to the cure
Of those physicians that first wounded thee.
A thousand flatterers sit within thy crown,   100
Whose compass is no bigger than thy head;
And yet, encaged in so small a verge,
The waste is no whit lesser than thy land.
O, had thy grandsire with a prophet's eye

96 **liest** perhaps monosyllabic
97 **too careless patient** Richard, being sick in reputation, takes too little care of his own malady (by choosing his favourites as doctors)
98 **anointed body** See 1.2.38n. Cf. also 3.2.54–5. Probably, as Wells (191) suggests, the line is a pentameter in which the first two syllables of *thy anointed* are elided (see F's 'thy'anointed'), although it may be an alexandrine if *Committ'st* (elided in QF) is expanded to 'Committest'.
99 **those physicians** Richard's corrupt favourites
100 **sit . . . crown** 'exercise authority as though they wore your crown'. Cf. 3.2.160–2, where Richard himself elaborates upon this image by imagining Death as the ironic occupier of the same space. Wilson (159) suggests that *crown* is 'used quibblingly and implies the King's head as well as his diadem'.
101 **compass** circumference, rim (playing on the idea that, technically, the boundary of supreme authority is no larger than the monarch's head)
102 *****encaged** encagèd. F's correction of Q3's 'inraged' probably represents the annotator's consultation of the theatre promptbook; see Appendix 1, pp. 525–7. **verge** limit, demarcation, border; cf. *R3* 4.1.58–9: 'the inclusive verge / Of golden metal that must round my brow'. Wordplay on two more technical terms is perhaps also intended: the

twelve-mile sphere of jurisdiction around the King's court assigned to the Lord Marshal; a measure of land of some fifteen to thirty acres.
103 **waste** Gaunt's punning continues. The word has at least four possible senses: foolishly extravagant expenditure (owing to the misgovernment of favourites); wasteland, infertile ground; waist (playing on *head* in 101); damage done to a rented property by a tenant, either deliberately or through neglect (a legal term probably extending the reference to *tenement* in 60). For an illuminating discussion of the legal implications of *waste* in the play, see Klinck (cf. 3.4.55: *the wasteful King*). Klinck explores the paradox of Gaunt's charging Richard with an offence associated with tenants when, as king and *Landlord of England* (113), he 'is the one person in the kingdom who cannot be a tenant' (22); the apparent contradiction, Klinck suggests, is resolvable by considering the doctrine of 'the king's two bodies' – a conception that distinguishes the 'body natural' (which allows the monarch to be a kind of tenant of the kingship) from the 'body politic' (which makes him symbolically the permanent embodiment of supreme ownership and national law).
104 **thy grandsire** Edward III; cf. 121, 124–5, 1.2.11. See also 105n.
prophet's eye Cf. 31.

Seen how his son's son should destroy his sons,   105
From forth thy reach he would have laid thy shame,
Deposing thee before thou wert possessed,
Which art possessed now to depose thyself.
Why, cousin, wert thou regent of the world,
It were a shame to let this land by lease;   110
But for thy world enjoying but this land,
Is it not more than shame to shame it so?
Landlord of England art thou now, not king.
Thy state of law is bondslave to the law,

105 **sons** probably alluding to the murder of Gloucester and the death of Gaunt, but perhaps (or even also) referring to Richard's own sons, as yet unborn, with the implication that his misrule is destroying his patrimony. Cf. *Woodstock*, 5.1.86–9, where the ghost of Edward III warns his son Gloucester: 'Richard of Bordeaux, my accursed grandchild, / Cut off your titles to the kingly state / And now your lives and all would ruinate: / Murders his grandsire's sons: his father's brothers'. Rossiter (232) regards this passage as Shakespeare's source for the line.
106 **forth** beyond
107 **Deposing** disinheriting
107–8 **possessed . . . possessed** 'possessed of the crown' and 'possessed by the devil, insane'
108 **depose thyself** by ceding authority to unworthy favourites and by leasing the realm
109 **cousin** nephew (cf. 1.2.46n.)
   regent ruler
110 **let . . . lease** Cf. 60n.
111 **for . . . land** 'inasmuch as this land constitutes your entire domain', i.e. since you are not 'regent of the world'; *thy world* = your *little world* (45). Gaunt wittily contrasts the macrocosm (*the world*, 109) with the microcosm (England).

113 **Landlord of England** probably an echo of *Woodstock*, 5.3.106: 'And thou no king, but landlord now become'; see also 60n. Nothing similar appears in Holinshed.
***now, not king** Theobald's emendation is attractive metrically and makes good sense, whereas Q5 improves sense but not metre, while F smoothes metre at the expense of forcefulness. F's reading looks like an editorial or compositorial guess. Q's compositor probably interpolated the first 'not' in error, perhaps because of the juxtaposition of 'now' and 'not' in his copy; alternatively, there may have been some unclarity in the MS.
114 'Your legal status, rather than that of a monarch by divine right, has now been reduced to that of a subject bound to obey the law (a *bondslave*).' The divine right of kings, accepted by Elizabeth I and explicitly endorsed by the early Stuarts, held that kings were subject only to God. Rossiter believes that only the audience's familiarity with *Woodstock*, which actually shows Richard signing away his rights to favourites, would keep this line from being 'hopelessly obscure' (48); but, as Ure (57) observes, 110 and 113 make Gaunt's meaning sufficiently clear.

107, 108 possessed] *(*possest*)*   109 wert] *were F*   110 this] his *F*   113 thou . . . king] *Theobald (also MS correction in HN copy of Q);* thou now not, not King *Q1–4;* thou now not, nor King *Q5;* thou, and not King *F*

And thou –

KING RICHARD   A lunatic lean-witted fool,   115
Presuming on an ague's privilege!
Darest with thy frozen admonition
Make pale our cheek, chasing the royal blood
With fury from his native residence?
Now, by my seat's right royal majesty,   120
Wert thou not brother to great Edward's son,
This tongue that runs so roundly in thy head

---

115 *And thou – Capell's dash after *thou* clarifies the dramatic interruption specified by Q. Richard's retort twists Gaunt's *thou* into a reference to Gaunt himself. Although F's reading conceivably derives from the promptbook, it seems to weaken the theatrical explosiveness of Q's arrangement; nor are all of F's departures from Q necessarily authoritative (see Appendix 1, pp. 528–9). H.F. Brooks cited the similar interruption in *R3* 1.3.232–3 when Gloucester turns back Queen Margaret's curse upon herself (Ard², 57).
lunatic Ironically Gaunt has just referred to Richard as *possessed* (mad) at 108.
lean-witted Richard cruelly suggests through wordplay that Gaunt's mind is now as gaunt, weak and sickly as his body.
116 **Presuming on** taking advantage of
ague's privilege The dying are traditionally allowed to speak plainly; but see 117n.
117 **Darest** do you dare; the line is probably scanned by pronouncing *Darest* as one syllable ('Dar'st') and *admonition* as five ('àd-mon-ì-ti-on')
frozen cold, hostile; chilled by illness. Kittredge² (129) suggests that there is scornful wordplay on the meaning, 'frigid in style'. The usual

symptoms of *ague* are alternating fever and shivering, but this customarily non-fatal ailment seems too slight for Gaunt's mortal illness. Although Richard has already anticipated his uncle's death (see 1.4.64), he may subconsciously – or even callously – minimize the seriousness of his uncle's plight.
118–19 Richard's facial changes (paleness vs. ruddiness, youthfulness vs. signs of aging) approach the status of a motif in the play and become a significant register of emotion; cf. 3.2.75–9, 3.3.63–4. The theme of narcissistic self-consciousness reaches its climax in the mirror episode of 4.1.276–98; see also 4.1.291LN. F's 'chafing' may be a compositorial error – the substitution of *f* for long *s* – rather than an intentional emendation (see t.n.).
119 **his** its (Abbott, 228)
120 **seat's . . . majesty** Richard swears by his throne, a symbol of his authority as king; cf. *state of law* (114); also *1 Tamburlaine*, 1.1.97: 'I swear by this my royal seat –'.
121 **great Edward's son** the Black Prince, Richard's father and eldest son of Edward III
122 **roundly** unceremoniously, bluntly (here 'rudely'), possibly quibbling on the two senses

---

115 And thou –] *Capell;* And thou *Q;* And thou. *Q3;* And – *F*   A lunatic] Ah lunatick *Q3;* And thou, a lunaticke *F*   116 privilege!] *this edn;* priuiledge, *QF*   118 chasing] chafing *F*   119 residence?] *F;* residence. *Q*

Should run thy head from thy unreverent shoulders!
GAUNT
O, spare me not, my brother Edward's son,
For that I was his father Edward's son.   125
That blood already, like the pelican,
Hast thou tapped out and drunkenly caroused.
My brother Gloucester, plain well-meaning soul –

123 **unreverent** disrespectful (see 5.6.25n.). Gurr (90) suggests that the word alludes to Gaunt's posture, his failure to bow in awe of the monarch when he is already 'bowed with age and sickness' and 'might have to bow under the executioner's axe'; see 0.1–2n. The threat to behead Gaunt also evokes Gloucester's 'execution' (cf. 1.1.100n., 2.2.102).

124–5 possibly a memory of *Woodstock*, 4.2.180–3: 'Villains, touch me not! / I am descended of the royal blood, / King Richard's uncle, / His grandsire's son; his princely father's brother' (see Rossiter's note, 229). Gaunt's meaning, however, is almost the opposite of Woodstock's lines.

124 *brother** Q2's correction of Q's 'brothers' seems warranted; but it is hard to account for F's restoration of Q's error since there is no other evidence that the editor of F consulted Q. The mistaken QF agreement is probably mere coincidence – perhaps the result of compositorial confusion of multiple *s* sounds (cf. Q's 'Edwards sonne') resulting in the improper anticipation ('brothers') of the correct possessive (GWW; but see *TxC*, 309). RP raises the remote possibility that Q's 'my brothers Edwards sonne' means 'my brother's – Edward's – son'.

125 **For that** because (cf. 1.3.125)

126 **pelican** Here the legendary image of the bird whose offspring fed on her lifeblood (cf. *Ham* 4.5.147–8) connotes ingratitude; cf. *KL* 3.4.75 and *Mirror*,

448. Gaunt's point is that Richard has sucked the blood of an elder (Gloucester) who had nurtured him. The image became a favourite with the compilers of emblem books, who often turned the symbolism around to stress the idea of sacrifice on the part of the nurturer, since the bird was thought to wound her own breast in order to provide nourishment for her young. Sometimes the sacrificial idea was applied specifically to Christ (see Fig. 6) or to self-sacrifice in general; cf. *E3* 3.4.122–6 and Melchiori's note, 133). In *Euphues* Lyly applied it to Elizabeth, 'the good pelican that to feed her people spareth not to rend her own person' (2.215). In view of Richard's later comparison of himself to Christ, a martyr betrayed by all his subjects (4.1.171–2), Gaunt's negatively charged image of Richard as bloody predator is replete with irony.

127 **tapped out** drawn as from a cask of wine (referring to Gloucester's murder) **caroused** drunk greedily, quaffed, drained in great draughts. Despite ambiguity elsewhere, Gaunt here clearly accuses Richard of being Gloucester's murderer (cf. 165); see also 1.2.39n.

128 **plain well-meaning soul** This unhistorical conception of Gloucester's character probably derives from *Woodstock* in which the frequent epithet 'Plain Thomas' (e.g. 1.1.99) sums up his humble dress and outspoken honesty; cf. also 'Homely and plain: both free from pride and envy' (1.1.107).

124 brother] *Q2*; brothers *QF*   127 Hast . . . out] Hast thou tapt *Q2*; Thou hast tapt out *F*
128 well-meaning] *Pope*; well meaning *QF*

Whom fair befall in heaven 'mongst happy souls! –
May be a precedent and witness good   130
That thou respect'st not spilling Edward's blood.
Join with the present sickness that I have,
And thy unkindness be like crooked Age
To crop at once a too long withered flower.
Live in thy shame, but die not shame with thee!   135
These words hereafter thy tormentors be.
Convey me to my bed, then to my grave.
Love they to live that love and honour have.

        Exit [borne off by Servants].

KING RICHARD
And let them die that age and sullens have,

Holinshed, Froissart, Daniel and *Traïson* treat Gloucester unsympathetically (see 1.1.100n.). *Mirror*, although more favourable, does not emphasize his plainness. Ure, nevertheless, suggests that the tradition of 'plain Thomas' – a kind of antithesis to Richard – could have had 'an existence independent of' the author of *Woodstock* 'which did not get much admission to the history-books', and to which 'Shakespeare may have had access without going through' the anonymous play (58).

129 **Whom fair befall** to whom may good happen

130 **precedent** example, instance, proof. QF 'president' was a common spelling (see *OED*).

131 **respect'st not spilling** do not scruple to shed. As Wells (192) notes, Q's word ('respectst') could be an elliptical form of 'respectedest' (past tense).
 Edward's blood i.e. the blood of Edward III's son (cf. 124–5n.)

133 **thy unkindness be** let your unnaturalness serve (subjunctive)
 crooked Age probably referring both to Gaunt's crooked body (deformed by illness and long years) and to Time itself (often personified as a bent figure

carrying a crooked scythe or sickle); cf. *Son* 100.14: 'his scythe and crooked knife', and Shirley, *The Contention of Ajax and Ulysses*: 'the poor crooked scythe and spade' (6.397). 'Crooked age' was a common phrase.

134 **crop** cut down (continuing the image of the reaper from 133)

135 **die . . . thee** 'may your bad reputation survive you'

137 **Convey** escort, help (here probably 'carry'; see 0.1–2n.). Richard puns bitterly on the same verb at 4.1.317.

138 The syntax is slightly ambiguous. Gaunt, probably speaking declaratively, means that, having lost both the love and respect (honour) of his king and nephew, he would rather die than live. Kittredge[2] (130) glosses 'Love they to live' as a subjunctive ('Let those love to live'), which does not much alter the general sense.

139–40 As Gurr (91) observes, 'Richard reverses the rhymes of Gaunt's final couplet'; the effect is to underscore Richard's arrogance and his contempt for the old man's speech.

139 **sullens** sulks, moroseness (nonce usage as noun in Shakespeare); cf. 1.3.227n.

130 precedent] *(president)* 133 Age] *this edn;* age *QF* 138 SD *borne . . . Servants*] *Capell (subst.)*

For both hast thou, and both become the grave.　　140

YORK

I do beseech your majesty, impute his words
To wayward sickliness and age in him.
He loves you, on my life, and holds you dear
As Harry, Duke of Hereford, were he here.

KING RICHARD

Right, you say true. As Hereford's love, so his;　　145
As theirs, so mine; and all be as it is.

^F*Enter* NORTHUMBERLAND.^F

NORTHUMBERLAND

My liege, old Gaunt commends him to your majesty.

KING RICHARD

What says he?

NORTHUMBERLAND　　Nay, nothing; all is said.
His tongue is now a stringless instrument;

---

140 **become** suit, are fit for
141 probably an alexandrine; but possibly
an irregular pentameter with an elided
majesty (dissyllabic): 'I dò | besèech |
your màj- | 'sty, impùte | his wòrds';
or else with three unstressed syllables
before the first heavy stress in *besèech.*
143–4 i.e. Gaunt loves Richard as much as
he loves his own son
145 Richard twists York's meaning to
assert that Gaunt's love of the King is
no more dependable than Bolingbroke's – another early sign of
Richard's hostility to his cousin.
146 'as Gaunt's and Bolingbroke's love to
me, so mine to them'; 'all be as it is' (so
be it, let it be what it will) is proverbial
(Dent, B112.1).
146.1 *Wells, who believes that Northumberland has been present from the
beginning of the scene (see 0.1–2n.),
makes him exit with Gaunt and the

attendants at 138 and then re-enter at
this point. So long a silence on the part
of a major character, however, seems
unlikely. Since F appears to be fairly
reliable in clarifying SDs (see
Appendix 1, pp. 509–10), there is little
warrant to emend. RP, however, compares the long silences of Aaron in *Tit*
1.1 and (possibly) of Edmund in *KL*
1.1, pointing out that Shakespeare
occasionally introduces characters
onstage as a way of raising audience
questions about their silent presence
before revealing them more fully.
147 **commends him** commends himself, sends his respectful greetings.
The line may be an alexandrine to
mark the seriousness of the message;
alternatively *My liege* is an extra-
metrical vocative.
149 **stringless instrument** Cf.
1.3.161–2, 5.5.46.

145 his;] *Q2 (* his.*), F; his *Q

Words, life and all old Lancaster hath spent.   150

YORK

Be York the next that must be bankrupt so!
Though death be poor, it ends a mortal woe.

KING RICHARD

The ripest fruit first falls, and so doth he.
His time is spent; our pilgrimage must be.
So much for that. Now for our Irish wars: 155
We must supplant those rough rug-headed kerns,
Which live like venom where no venom else
But only they have privilege to live.
And, for these great affairs do ask some charge,

150 **spent** used up, exhausted
151 **bankrupt so** likewise dead (having *spent* all his 'Words, life and all')
152 **death** the state of being dead
poor a biblical commonplace; Kittredge[2] (130) cites 1 Timothy, 6.7: 'We brought nothing into this world, and it is certain we can carry nothing out' (continuing the figure of death as bankruptcy from 151).
mortal deadly; human, experienced by mortals
153 **ripest . . . falls** proverbial (Dent, R133); cf. also *MV* 4.1.115–16.
154 **pilgrimage** Life as a pilgrimage was a commonplace; cf. 1.3.49n., 230n. and *AYL* 3.2.129–30: 'how brief the life of man / Runs his erring pilgrimage'.
must be is yet to be completed. Richard's couplet here assists the effect of flippancy, the exact opposite of the gravity of Gaunt's couplets at 135–8. Muir (71) suggests that Bolingbroke receives the news of Mowbray's death at 4.1.104–5 with equal callousness, also changing the subject in mid-line (cf. 155). GWW doubts the supposed parallel.
155 **Irish wars** See 1.4.42n., 61–2.
156 **supplant** drive out, rid ourselves of, oust

rug-headed shaggy-haired (cf. *2H6* 3.1.367 'shag-hair'd crafty kern'). According to *A View of the Present State of Ireland* (1596), the Irish often wore 'longe glibbes which is a thicke Curled bushe of haire hanginge downe over theire eyes and monstrouslye disguisinge them' (Spenser, 9.99). 'Rug' was a coarse woollen material, here applied metaphorically to human hair.
kerns lightly armed Irish footsoldiers. Q's uncorrected reading 'kerne' (retained in Q2) has been regarded by some editors as an alternative plural (collective); Spenser (9.103) uses it in his *View of . . . Ireland*. But after proof-reading, Q corrected it to 'kernes', the usual spelling elsewhere in Shakespeare: cf. *2H6* 3.1.310, 361, 4.9.26; and *Mac* 1.2.13, 30, 5.7.17. Q3 normalized independently to 'kernes' which F took over.
157 **venom** reptiles (a synecdoche), alluding to the familiar legend that Saint Patrick cleansed Ireland of snakes; cf. *2 Honest Whore*, 3.1.202–3: 'a Country where no venom prospers / But in the Nations blood' (Dekker, 2.171).
159 **for** because
ask some charge require some outlay

156 rug-headed] *F;* rugheaded *Q*   kerns] *Qc, Q3–F (* kernes*);* kerne *Qu*

Towards our assistance we do seize to us   160
The plate, coin, revenues and moveables
Whereof our uncle Gaunt did stand possessed.

YORK

How long shall I be patient? Ah, how long
Shall tender duty make me suffer wrong?
Not Gloucester's death, nor Hereford's banishment,   165
Nor Gaunt's rebukes, nor England's private wrongs,
Nor the prevention of poor Bolingbroke
About his marriage, nor my own disgrace

160–2 Holinshed emphasizes the general enmity that Richard's confiscation provoked: 'The death of this duke gaue occasion of increasing more hatred in the people of this realme toward the king, for he seized into his hands all the goods that belonged to him, and also receiued all the rents and reuenues of his lands which ought to haue descended vnto the duke of Hereford by lawfull inheritance' (3.496). See also 202–4n., 205–8n.

160 **seize** the legal term for appropriating property. But a predatory connotation seems present as well (cf. *MA* 5.4.53: 'Which is the lady I must seize upon?'); see 160–2n.

161 **moveables** portable property (such as furnishings, clothing, jewellery, etc.); cf. *R3* 3.1.195.

162 **stand possessed** more legal terminology; cf. *R3* 3.1.196: 'stood possest' (Q1–6).

163 **patient** signifying Christian patience; see 1.2.29n. Shakespeare echoes Holinshed's word (see 205–8n.).

164 **tender duty** scrupulous regard (for the King; *tender* suggests York's moral sensitivity to the obligation of loyalty (as in the expression 'tender conscience'; cf. 207) as well as his personal

affection for Richard.
suffer endure, tolerate

165 **Gloucester's death** York implies that Gloucester's murder (or execution) was the direct result of Richard's command. See 127n. and 1.1.100n.

166 **Gaunt's rebukes** the King's rebuking of Gaunt (115–23)
private wrongs wrongs by which private individuals have been injured; cf. 246–50.

167–8 **prevention . . . marriage** See LN.

168 **my own disgrace** No historical explanation for this phrase has been found. Rossiter (221) believes that the source is *Woodstock*, where Gloucester, speaking to York and Lancaster (i.e. Gaunt), complains that 'Richard with a false, and mind corrupt / Disgraced our names and thrust us from his court' (3.2.3–4); later in the same play, Lancaster charges Richard with having 'made us infamous' (5.3.64), the 'us' apparently including York along with Gloucester and the speaker. Q's uncorrected reading ('his owne') would apparently make the *disgrace* refer to Bolingbroke's exile; but this reading seems ruled out by York's having mentioned *Hereford's banishment* (165) among his grievances.

---

161 coin] *Qc, F (*coine*); coines *Qu*   168 my] *Qc, F;* his *Qu*

259

Have ever made me sour my patient cheek,
Or bend one wrinkle on my sovereign's face.   170
I am the last of noble Edward's sons,
Of whom thy father, Prince of Wales, was first.
In war was never lion raged more fierce,
In peace was never gentle lamb more mild
Than was that young and princely gentleman.   175
His face thou hast, for even so looked he,
Accomplished with the number of thy hours;
But when he frowned, it was against the French

169 **sour . . . cheek** 'lose my self-restrained countenance' (scowl or glower); cf. *VA* 185. For *patient*, see 163n.; for the motif of facial change, see 118–19n.

170 **bend . . . on** 'direct one little frown at', or possibly 'cause one little frown to appear on'; *bend* probably refers to arching or knitting the brows (cf. *KJ* 4.2.90).

171 **last** last surviving (not youngest). See Appendix 3.

172–83 Negative comparison of Richard to his heroic progenitors (Edward III and the Black Prince) constitutes an important theme of the play (cf. 2.3.99–102n.). Editors commonly point to a similar speech in *Woodstock* (1.1.29–45) contrasting Richard with his famous father. The mention in the earlier play of the Black Prince's 'sweet and lovely . . . countenance', of his not having 'a swart and melancholy brow' (1.1.31–2), somewhat increases the likelihood that Shakespeare recalled these lines (cf. 176 where York alludes to Richard's handsomeness). The germ of York's speech, however, may have been prompted by Froissart: 'He [Richard] sheweth nat that the prince of Wales shulde be his father, for if he had, he wolde have folowed his condicions, and have taken great pleasure in his prowes, and nat to lyve in reste and

ease as he dothe: for he loveth nothynge but sporte and ydelnesse . . . and to beleve men of small reputacion, and to gather great rychesse, and distroy the realme, whiche thynges ought nat to be suffred' (6.352). It is also worth noting that *Edward III* (1592–3), a play in which Shakespeare almost certainly had a hand, dramatizes the Black Prince's heroic exploits in France.

173 **was . . . raged** syntactically ambiguous: either '(there) was never a lion (which) raged' (elliptical) or 'never was a lion enraged'. The second interpretation provides a parallel to the transitive use of *rage* at 70 (see n.). Gurr (92–3) detects the possibility of an allusion to Richard the Lion-hearted, another chivalric ancestor (cf. 51–6n.); but lions, being emblazoned on the royal coat of arms, are commonly associated with English kings in general (cf. 1.1.174 and 5.1.34 where Richard himself is referred to as a lion).
   fierce fiercely (Abbott, 1)

177 **at your age* (*Accomplished* = furnished, completely equipped). Richard was thirty-two at the time of Gaunt's death. F's correction of Q's error ('a number') probably derives from the MS promptbook; see Appendix 1, p. 525. But a compositor might himself correct this kind of idiomatic mistake.

169 sour] *(sower),* F   172 first.] *Q2–F (*first,*);* first *Q*   177 the] *F;* a *Q*   hours] *(howers)*

And not against his friends. His noble hand
Did win what he did spend, and spent not that   180
Which his triumphant father's hand had won.
His hands were guilty of no kindred blood,
But bloody with the enemies of his kin.
O Richard! York is too far gone with grief,
Or else he never would compare between –   185

KING RICHARD

Why, uncle, what's the matter?

YORK   O my liege,
Pardon me, if you please; if not, I, pleased
Not to be pardoned, am content withal.
Seek you to seize and gripe into your hands
The royalties and rights of banished Hereford?   190
Is not Gaunt dead? And doth not Hereford live?
Was not Gaunt just? And is not Harry true?

180 **win** earn
182 another allusion to the death of Gloucester
185 *****compare between** – York apparently breaks down, unable to finish his sentence (Pollard, 66). Perhaps, as some editors suggest, the phrase is syntactically complete and means 'make comparisons'; but *OED* (*v.* 1c) cites only this instance, and if York's sentence is complete, the King has no need to ask further about it (see 186n.).
186–8 *****Theobald's relineation is usually adopted. For detailed discussion of the textual transmission of these lines, see Appendix 1, p. 533, and Jowett & Taylor, 171.
186 **Why . . . matter?** 'Richard may be callously detached or genuinely bewildered' (Wells, 195). In view of his attitude elsewhere in this scene, indifference seems the likelier reaction. See Appendix 1, p. 533, and Fig. 19.

187 **pleased** satisfied
188 **withal** i.e. with not being pardoned
189–94 York's series of pointed rhetorical questions amounts to a statement that Richard is about to commit political suicide.
189 **gripe** grasp, clutch
190 **royalties** rights and prerogatives granted by a king to a subject through *letters patent*; these are specified at 202–4. Bolingbroke himself mentions his *rights and royalties* at 2.3.120; cf. also *lineal royalties* (3.3.113).
192 **just** honourable, truthful
Harry Henry Bolingbroke, Duke of Hereford
true a possible *double entendre*: legitimate (and therefore worthy to inherit); loyal (both to his father and the crown). The second meaning contains an obvious irony since Elizabethan audiences knew that Bolingbroke did usurp.

182 kindred] kindreds *F*   185 between –] *Hanmer*; betweene. *QF*   186–8] *as Theobald; Q lines* matter? / please, / with all, / ; *F lines* Vncle, / matter? / if not / with all: /   186 KING RICHARD . . . O] *Qc, F; not in Qu*   my] *Qc, F;* My *Qu*   188 withall] *Q2;* with all *QF*

Did not the one deserve to have an heir?
Is not his heir a well-deserving son?
Take Hereford's rights away, and take from Time   195
His charters and his customary rights;
Let not tomorrow then ensue today;
Be not thyself, for how art thou a king
But by fair sequence and succession?
Now, afore God – God forbid I say true –   200
If you do wrongfully seize Hereford's rights,
Call in the letters patents that he hath
By his attorneys-general to sue

195–6 Richard will be depriving *Time* himself of his rights since the *customary rights* of inheritance (primogeniture) only apply in the course of time.
195 Take . . . take if you take . . . you will take
197 ensue follow upon
199 succession four syllables: pronounced 'suc-cèss-i-on'
200 God – God One of the few instances in which F leaves Q's word for the deity unaltered; see Appendix 1, p. 513.
I say true that my predictions come to pass
201 Note the wordplay on *wrongfully* and *rights*.
202–4 York describes Bolingbroke's rights of inheritance in technical language, which even an Elizabethan audience might have had difficulty understanding fully. *Letters patents* (the double plural is a survival of law French) is a document, literally 'a letter open to inspection', signed by the King granting rights, titles, lands, etc. The particular right which Richard is accused of revoking (*calling in*) is the right of Bolingbroke to *sue / His livery*, that is, to claim the lands held by his father as a tenant of the crown through his

attorneys-general – his legal representatives who would petition the crown on his behalf for delivery (*livery*) of the said lands. This procedure established that the heir to an estate was of age and so capable of inheriting legally. The heir would also do ceremonial *homage* to his sovereign as part of the formal process of receiving his inheritance, and it is this *offered homage* of Bolingbroke which Richard is on the point of refusing (*denying*). By revoking Bolingbroke's right to claim his inheritance in the legal way and by refusing to accept his feudal homage, Richard, in effect, is arranging for Gaunt's lands and revenues to revert to the crown. The passage is based closely on Holinshed (see 160–2n.), who specifically mentions 'reuoking his [Bolingbroke's] letters patents, which he [the King] had granted to him before, by vertue wherof he might make his attorneis generall to sue liuerie for him, of any maner of inheritances or possessions that might from thencefoorth fall vnto him, and that his homage might be respited, with making reasonable fine: whereby it was euident, that the king meant his vtter vndooing' (3.496).

194 well-deserving] *F;* well deseruing *Q*   195 Time] *this edn;* time *QF*   200 say] *Qc, F;* lay *Qu (variable inking?)*   201 rights] right *Q2–F*   202 the] his *F*   203 attorneys-general] *Rowe;* attourneies generall *QF*

His livery and deny his offered homage,
You pluck a thousand dangers on your head,   205
You lose a thousand well-disposed hearts
And prick my tender patience to those thoughts
Which honour and allegiance cannot think.

KING RICHARD

Think what you will, we seize into our hands
His plate, his goods, his money and his lands.   210

YORK

I'll not be by the while. My liege, farewell.
What will ensue hereof there's none can tell;
But by bad courses may be understood
That their events can never fall out good.   *Exit.*

205–8 appropriated from Holinshed, who, however, says nothing about a personal protest by York to the King: 'This hard dealing was much misliked of all the nobilitie, and cried out against the meaner sort: but namelie the duke of Yorke was therewith sore mooued, who before this time, had borne things with so patient a mind as he could, though the same touched him verie neere, as the death of his brother the duke of Glocester, the banishment of his nephue the said duke of Hereford, and other mo iniuries in great number, which for the slipperie youth of the king, he passed ouer for the time, and did forget aswell as he might. But now perceiuing that neither law, iustice nor equitie could take place, where the kings wilfull will was bent vpon any wrongfull purpose, he considered that the glorie of the publike wealth of his countrie must needs decaie, by reason of the king his lacke of wit, and want of such as would (without flatterie) admonish him of his dutie: and therefore he thought it the part of a wise man to get him in time to a resting place, and

to leaue the following of such an unaduised capteine, as with a leden sword would cut his owne throat' (3.496).

205 Cf. *Woodstock* (4.3.136): 'A thousand dangers round enclose our state'.
pluck pull down
206 **well-disposed** well-disposèd
207 **prick . . . patience** spur my vulnerable self-restraint
208 **think** contemplate; tolerate
209–14 The couplets signal the approaching end of an episode; they express both Richard's high-handed deafness to wise counsel and York's gnomic prophecy of disastrous consequences. York replicates the role of prophet that Gaunt had played earlier.
211 **by** near by, present. Holinshed reports that York 'with the duke of Aumarle his sonne went to his house at Langlie' (3.496).
212 **ensue hereof** come of this
213–14 'good consequences (*events*) cannot be expected to issue from bad courses of action'; literally, 'concerning bad courses, it may be understood that their outcomes can never turn out well'

206 well-disposed] *F;* well disposed *Q*   209 SP] *King Q; Ric. F*   seize] *(cease), F (*seise*)*

KING RICHARD

Go, Bushy, to the Earl of Wiltshire straight.   215
Bid him repair to us to Ely House
To see this business. – Tomorrow next
We will for Ireland, and 'tis time, I trow.
And we create, in absence of ourself,
Our uncle York Lord Governor of England,   220
For he is just and always loved us well.
Come on, our queen. Tomorrow must we part.

215 **Earl of Wiltshire** Richard's fourth favourite (with Bushy, Bagot and Green) who never appears onstage; he was Lord Treasurer and older brother of the Sir Stephen Scroop who enters at 3.2.90 SD. See List of Roles, 22n., and 1.4.45n.
straight immediately
216 **repair** come
Ely House Richard's present location; see 1.4.58n.
217 **see** attend to (see to)
business the confiscation of Gaunt's estate (three syllables: 'bus-i-ness')
Tomorrow next apparently tautological, but originally 'morrow' meant simply 'morning' (Chambers, 107). Possibly 'a week from tomorrow', as in Scottish or US Southern usage, where 'Friday next' = 'the Friday of next week' as distinct from 'this Friday' (see *OED* next *a.* 10a). Shakespeare has Richard leave the country either immediately or very soon after Gaunt's death; see 289–90n. Holinshed merely mentions April as the month when Richard left Windsor: 'the king being aduertised that the wild Irish dailie wasted and destroied the townes and villages within the English pale, and had slaine manie of the souldiers which laie there in garison for defense of that countrie, determined to make eftsoones a voiage thither, & prepared all things necessarie for his passage now against the spring. [After holding jousts at Windsor] . . . the king departed toward

Bristow, from thence to passe into Ireland, leauing the queene with hir traine still at Windesor: he appointed for his lieutenant generall in his absence his vncle the duke of Yorke: and so in the moneth of Aprill, as diuerse authors write, he set forward from Windesor, and finallie tooke shipping at Milford, and from thence with two hundred ships, and a puissant power of men of armes and archers he sailed into Ireland' (3.496–7).
218 **We will** I will leave
'tis . . . trow it is high time, I think (*trow* = believe)
219–21 based on Holinshed; see 217n. The jarring effect of Richard's high valuation of the uncle who has just been so critical of royal policy results partly from Shakespeare's telescoping of the source material (Wells, 196); as York was Richard's only surviving uncle, 'he was to some extent the king's natural representative' (Chambers, 107). York's rank is his major qualification, but the King seems to appreciate his uncle's sincerity (*just* = honest).
222–3 a couplet (*part* rhymes with *short*) used to give point to Richard's exit; cf. Richard's departure at the end of 1.4, where he also refers to the pressure of time. *We* (222) is probably not the royal plural but refers to the speaker and his queen; earlier in the speech Richard mixes the personal *I* with the royal *we* (218–19).

Be merry, for our time of stay is short.

^F*Flourish.*^F *Exeunt all but Northumberland,*
^F*Willoughby and Ross.*^F

NORTHUMBERLAND

Well, lords, the Duke of Lancaster is dead.

ROSS

And living, too, for now his son is duke.   225

WILLOUGHBY

Barely in title, not in revenues.

NORTHUMBERLAND

Richly in both, if Justice had her right.

ROSS

My heart is great, but it must break with silence
Ere't be disburdened with a liberal tongue.

NORTHUMBERLAND

Nay, speak thy mind, and let him ne'er speak more   230
That speaks thy words again to do thee harm.

224–300 The remainder of the scene is based chiefly on Holinshed's description of national discontent during Richard's absence in Ireland: 'diuerse of the nobilitie, aswell prelats as other, and likewise manie of the magistrats and rulers of the cities, townes, and communaltie, here in England, perceiuing dailie how the realme drew to vtter ruine, not like to be recouered to the former state of wealth, whilest king Richard liued and reigned (as they tooke it) deuised with great deliberation, and considerate aduise, to send and signifie by letters vnto duke Henrie, whome they now called (as he was in deed) duke of Lancaster and Hereford, requiring him with all conuenient speed to conueie himselfe into England, promising him all their aid, power and assistance, if he expelling

K. Richard, as a man not meet for the office he bare, would take vpon him the scepter, rule, and diademe of his natiue land and region' (3.497). See also 277–88n.

226 **Barely** merely; scarcely (as an exile cannot legally take possession). Kittredge[2] (134) notes that Willoughby refers to Bolingbroke not as Lancaster but as *Duke of Hereford* (232) and that Green calls him *The banished Bolingbroke* (2.2.49).

228 **great** pregnant with sorrow (and perhaps indignation)
   break with silence (*with* = by reason of keeping). Anticipates *Ham* 1.2.159: 'But break my heart, for I must hold my tongue'.

229 **liberal** freely-speaking (perhaps dis-syllabic: 'lib'ral')

230 **ne'er speak more** die

---

223 SD] *Exeunt King and Queene: Manet North. Q; Flourish. / Manet North. Willoughby, & Ross. F*
all but] *this edn; Manet QF*   225 too] *(to), F*   226 revenues] reuennew *F*   227 Justice] *this edn;*
iustice *QF*   229 Ere't] *(Eart), F (*Er't*)*

WILLOUGHBY

Tends that thou wouldst speak to the Duke of Hereford?
If it be so, out with it boldly, man.
Quick is mine ear to hear of good towards him.

ROSS

No good at all that I can do for him,   235
Unless you call it good to pity him,
Bereft and gelded of his patrimony.

NORTHUMBERLAND

Now, afore God, 'tis shame such wrongs are borne
In him, a royal prince, and many moe
Of noble blood in this declining land.   240
The King is not himself, but basely led

232 The line can be pronounced accept-
ably by retaining Q's wording and
adopting F's implied pronunciation of
Hereford: 'Tends thàt | thou wouldst
spèak | to the Dùke | of Hèr- | e-fòrd'.
Keightley's addition of a second 'that'
(which), which several editors accept,
smoothes the metre without requiring
Hereford to be trisyllabic, but would
have to be justified as a Q omission
uncorrected in Q3 and F. F's elision
('thou'dst') could also have been influenced by the need to crowd text within
the measure, as evidenced by the abbreviated form, 'th'Du.' (see *TxC*, 309).
   Tends . . . to 'does what (*that*) you are
about to say concern'

237 **gelded** deprived (literally, 'castrat-
ed'; 'gelt' could also mean 'money',
therefore perhaps specifically 'stripped
of his gold')

238–9 **wrongs . . . him** The syntax is
ambiguous: either 'wrongs in his case
(i.e. against him) are countenanced' by
others (cf. 2.3.10n.); or 'wrongs are
endured by him'. The first interpretation seems likelier (see Abbott, 162).

239 **moe** Rowe's 'emendation' is merely a
modernization of Q's 'mo', the plural

collective form of 'more' (see Abbott,
17).

241 **is not himself** i.e. forgets the duties
and responsibilities of his office; cf.
198 and 3.2.82. The statement has
proverbial overtones (Dent, FF9).

241–2 **basely . . . flatterers** This charge is
the chief emphasis of *Woodstock* (cf.
4.2.143: 'His youth is led by flatterers
much astray'), and appears also in
Mirror (113): 'I . . . alway put false
Flatterers most in trust' ('King Richard
the Second', ll. 31–3). It was also a regular feature of indirect attacks on
Elizabeth for being misled by favourites
(especially Leicester and Burghley) and
a main cause of the popular parallel
between her and Richard (Cam², 95; see
Introduction, pp. 5–9). The anonymous
*Copy of a Letter Written by a Master of
Art of Cambridge* (1584) warns the
Queen against the influence of 'wicked
persons' (187), citing the precedent of
Richard II. *Copy of a Letter* (later
reprinted as *Leicester's Commonwealth*,
1641) has been variously attributed to
Thomas Morgan, Robert Parsons,
Charles Arundell and other Catholics
(see Peck, 25–32).

232 that thou wouldst] that thou'dst *F;* that, that thou would'st *Keightley*   the Duke] th'Du. *F*
238 God] heauen *F*   239 moe] *(mo), F;* more *Rowe*

By flatterers; and what they will inform
Merely in hate 'gainst any of us all,
That will the King severely prosecute
'Gainst us, our lives, our children and our heirs.   245

ROSS

The commons hath he pilled with grievous taxes,
And quite lost their hearts. The nobles hath he fined
For ancient quarrels, and quite lost their hearts.

WILLOUGHBY

And daily new exactions are devised,

242 **inform** say (implying falsely)
243 **Merely in hate** out of sheer hatred
244 **prosecute** take vengeance on the basis of accusatory statements (a quasi-legal term)
246 **pilled** stripped bare, despoiled (literally, 'peeled'); cf. *Woodstock*, 1.3.112: 'tax and pill the Commons'; also *R3* 1.3.158. The word is cognate with modern 'pillage' and was associated through false etymology with 'caterpillars' (Cam², 95; cf. 2.3.166); see *OED* pill *v.* 9. Holinshed describes the 'new and strange subsidie' levied upon clergy and lay people alike in 1380 to pay for Richard's army in France: 'Great grudging & manie a bitter cursse followed about the leuieng of this monie, & much mischeefe rose thereof, as after it appeared' (3.428). See also 249n., 250n.
247, 248 **quite . . . hearts** perhaps an echo of *Woodstock*, 5.3.94: 'Thou well may'st doubt their loves that lost their hearts'; but see also 2.2.130n. Wilson (165) suggests that the duplication of this phrase may represent a printer's blunder and that, if so, line 248 'is hopelessly corrupt'. F's failure to correct, however, could mean perhaps that the repetition stood in the MS promptbook and was therefore intended. Kittredge² believes that the repeated phrase 'is in accordance with Elizabethan style' (135), while Ure (65) points out that it is applied to two different groups – to the *commons* first, then the *nobles*.

247–8 **fined . . . quarrels** Richard in 1399 'borrowed great summes of monie of manie of the great lords and peeres of his realme, both spirituall and temporall, and likewise of other meane persons . . . which notwithstanding [his promise to make good] he neuer paid. Moreouer, this yeare he caused seuenteene shires of the realme by waie of putting them to their fines to paie no small summes of monie, for redeeming their offenses, that they had aided the duke of Glocester, the earles of Arundell, and Warwike, when they rose in armor against him. The nobles, gentlemen, and commons of those shires were inforced also to receiue a new oth to assure the king of their fidelitie in time to come; and withall certeine prelats and other honorable personages, were sent into the same shires to persuade men to this paiment, and to see things ordered at the pleasure of the prince: and suerlie the fines which the nobles, and other the meaner estates of those shires were constreined to paie, were not small, but exceeding great, to the offense of manie' (Holinshed, 3.496).

249 **new exactions** This phrase echoes Holinshed's marginal note, 'New exactions' (3.496). Cf. also *Mirror* (113–14): 'Subsidies, sore fines, loanes, many a prest, / Blanke charters, othes, & shiftes not knowen of olde' ('King Richard the Second', ll. 42–3). See Introduction, p. 7.

246 pilled] *(pild)*   247 And quite] And *Pope*

As blanks, benevolences, and I wot not what.   250
But what, i'God's name, doth become of this?
NORTHUMBERLAND
Wars hath not wasted it, for warred he hath not,
But basely yielded upon compromise
That which his ancestors achieved with blows.
More hath he spent in peace than they in wars.   255
ROSS
The Earl of Wiltshire hath the realm in farm.
WILLOUGHBY
The King's grown bankrupt like a broken man.

250 **blanks** blank charters (see 249n.; also 1.4.48n.)
   benevolences forced loans (see LN). Editors sometimes insist that the final *s* in *benevolences* should be silent (see Abbott, 471); pronounced in the usual way, however, the word fits easily into the rhythm of an alexandrine.
   I . . . what stock phrase (*wot* = know). A quibble on *what* may be embedded here (cf. the rhyme at 2.2.39–40).
251 **i'God's name** Again F failed to alter to 'heaven' (see 200n.).
   this the money thus raised
252–4 Gloucester's disapproval of Richard's pacific policy in France was one of the causes of the bad blood between them; when the fortified town of Brest was surrendered to the Duke of Brittany in 1397 (in fulfillment of a treaty with Charles VI), Gloucester infuriated Richard by saying, 'Sir, your grace ought to put your bodie in paine to win a strong hold or towne by feats of war, yer [ere] you take vpon you to sell or deliuer anie towne or strong hold gotten with great aduenture by the manhood and policie of your noble progenitours' (Holinshed, 3.487). *Mirror* (114) likewise emphasizes Richard's 'fault' in ceding the territory:

'I also made away the towne of Brest' ('King Richard the Second', ll. 45–6).
252 **Wars hath** a common sixteenth-century form of the third-person plural verb (here ending in *th*; see Abbott, 334, and 2.2.16–17n.); cf. 2.3.4–5, where Northumberland again uses it (*ways / Draws*). 'It may possibly be a northern dialectal form especially appropriate to Northumberland' (Wells, 197).
253 **basely** in cowardly fashion
254 *Despite Holinshed's use of the phrase, 'noble progenitours' (see 252–4n.), F's omission of Q's extra-metrical 'noble' is almost certainly correct, since inadvertent interpolation, by scribe (Ard[2], 65–6) or compositor (Craven[3], 59), is made likelier by the use of the same adjective twice more in close proximity (*noble blood*, 240; *noble kinsman*, 262). The corrected reading in F probably derives from the promptbook (see Werstine, '*Lear*', 271), and the measure here is not tight. See Appendix 1, p. 525.
   achieved won
255 See 1.4.44n.
256 Cf. 59n., 60n., 110n.; also 1.4.45n.
257 *Q3's 'King's', followed by F, supplies the missing verb (see Pollard, 59).
   broken financially ruined, bankrupt

251 But] *QF; North.* But *Q4* i'God's] *Mowat & Werstine;* a Gods *Q;* o'Gods *F*   252 SP] *QF; Willo. Q2* Wars hath] Wars have *Rowe*   254 ancestors] *F;* noble auncestors *Q*   257 King's] *Q3, F (*Kings*);* King *Q* grown] (growen*), Q2, F*

NORTHUMBERLAND

Reproach and dissolution hangeth over him.

ROSS

He hath not money for these Irish wars,

His burdenous taxations notwithstanding,   260

But by the robbing of the banished Duke.

NORTHUMBERLAND

His noble kinsman! Most degenerate King!

But, lords, we hear this fearful tempest sing,

Yet seek no shelter to avoid the storm.

We see the wind sit sore upon our sails,   265

And yet we strike not, but securely perish.

ROSS

We see the very wrack that we must suffer,

And unavoided is the danger now

For suffering so the causes of our wrack.

---

258 another alexandrine

   dissolution ruin, destruction (also suggests 'dissoluteness', dissipation)

   hangeth over him Cf. *Woodstock*, 2.2.47: 'Confusion hangeth o'er thy wretched head'; also Hall, who speaks of 'the darke clowde . . . dependying ouer his [Richard's] hed' (fol. iiii). The phrase and idea, however, are not uncommon.

260 **burdenous** burdensome

261 **But by** except through

262 **degenerate** i.e. lacking the strength and stature of his heroic progenitors (such as Edward III and the Black Prince); cf. 254 and *Woodstock*, 1.1.28–9: 'so wild a prince / So far degenerate from his noble father'.

263 **sing** Cf. *Tem* 2.2.19–20: 'another storm brewing, I hear it sing i'th' wind'.

265 **sit sore** weigh heavily, blow threateningly

266 **strike** furl, haul in (a nautical term); take up arms against (strike blows)

   securely overconfidently, heedlessly; cf. 3.2.34, 5.3.42 and *Mac* 3.5.32–3.

267 **wrack** ruin (fused with 'wreck', as in 'shipwreck', possibly playing on 'rack',

the instrument of torture). Hall uses kindred images in Archbishop Arundel's speech to Bolingbroke, persuading him to return to England: Arundel mentions 'this tempesteous world and ceason', Richard's outrages which have brought England 'almoste to wrecke', and the nobles looking to Bolingbroke as 'their last ankerholde' (fol. iiii and see Reyher, 57–8); cf. also Daniel, 1.113: 'Calme these tempestuous spirits O mighty Lord, / This threatning storme that ouer hangs the land'. Ure, pointing out the commonness of such imagery, thinks the 'analogies in Hall and Daniel . . . prove very little' (66).

268 **unavoided** not to be avoided, unavoidable (see Abbott, 375, for the customary use of passive participles with active force; cf. 2.3.109n. and 3.2.44n.)

269 'because we have permitted the causes of our disaster (i.e. Richard's misgovernment) to go unresisted'. Ross plays on his earlier use of *suffer* (267), changing the sense to 'allow' (269). *Suffering* is probably dissyllabic: 'suff'ring'.

NORTHUMBERLAND

Not so. Even through the hollow eyes of Death   270
I spy life peering, but I dare not say
How near the tidings of our comfort is.

WILLOUGHBY

Nay, let us share thy thoughts as thou dost ours.

ROSS

Be confident to speak, Northumberland.
We three are but thyself, and, speaking so,   275
Thy words are but as thoughts. Therefore, be bold.

NORTHUMBERLAND

Then thus: I have from Le Port Blanc, a bay

---

270 **hollow eyes** eye sockets; Northumberland imagines mortality as a
skull, a common *memento mori* emblem
(cf. 1.3.224n.). Personifications or
quasi-personifications of death constitute a notable motif of the tragedy; cf.
1.3.224, 2.2.70, 3.2.103, 162, 184–5,
5.5.105. See also 1.1.171n. and 4.1.26n.

272 **tidings . . . is** 'Tidings' (like 'news')
was used as both singular and plural;
cf. 3.4.80.

275 **are but thyself** are as one with you,
totally share your sentiments; proverbial idea (Dent, F696)

277–88 closely based on Holinshed:
'there were certeine ships rigged, and
made readie for him, at a place in base
Britaine [lower Brittany], called Le
port blanc, as we find in the chronicles
of Britaine: and when all his prouision
was made readie, he tooke the sea, togither with the said archbishop of
Canturburie, and his nephue Thomas
Arundell, sonne and heire to the late
earle of Arundell, beheaded at the
Tower hill, as you haue heard. There
were also with him, Reginald lord
Cobham, sir Thomas Erpingham, and
sir Thomas Ramston knights, Iohn
Norburie, Robert Waterton, & Francis

Coint esquires: few else were there, for
(as some write) he had not past fifteene
lances, as they tearmed them in those
daies, that is to saie, men of armes, furnished and appointed as the vse then
was. Yet other write, that the duke of
Britaine [John IV, Duke of Brittany]
deliuered vnto him three thousand
men of warre, to attend him, and that
he had eight ships well furnished for
the warre, where *Froissard* yet speaketh
but of three' (3.498). For the apparent
contradiction in timing, see 289–90n.
In Shakespeare Northumberland plays
a greater part in the rebellion against
Richard than 'Holinshed allows', being
made privy to Bolingbroke's strategy
'before the other conspirators' (Ard²,
46); in Holinshed (3.397–8) and Hall
(see 267n.), Archbishop Arundel is the
principal instigator.

277 *****Le Port Blanc** from Holinshed (see
277–88n.) although Shakespeare or Q
dropped the final *c*; F's 'Port *le Blan*'
changes the word order but, since the
spelling remains uncorrected, probably
represents a compositorial guess. There
may have been some confusion with Le
Blanc, a medieval fortified town on the
river Creuse in central France not far

---

270 Death] *this edn;* death *QF*   277–8] *as Capell; QF line* Blan / intelligence, /   277 Le Port Blanc]
Wright (after Holinshed); le Port Blan *Q;* Port *le Blan* F

In Brittany, received intelligence
That Harry, Duke of Hereford, Rainold Lord Cobham,
Thomas, son and heir to th'Earl of Arundel,   280

from Châteauraux and Poitiers. The
modern name is simply Port Blanc, a
small port on the north coast of
Brittany near Tréguier. Holinshed's
mistaken designation, 'a place in base
Britaine' (i.e. lower Brittany, the south
coast), contributes to the geographical
perplexity; but 'base Britaine' might
simply mean Little Britain (GWW) –
the Britain that is lower than we are (i.e.
south of England).

278 ***Brittany** Q2's spelling, 'Brittanie',
together with Capell's relineation, regularizes the metre, although F's
'Britaine' comes close to restoring Q's
spelling. The apparent metrical problem could be illusory: Q's 'Brittaine'
may have been pronounced trisyllabically ('Brìt-tain-e', an approximation
of modern 'Bretagne'). 'Brittany',
'Brittanie' and 'Britanie' occur in *3H6*
(2.6.97, 4.6.97, 101) and *Cym* (1.4.72),
although the name is clearly dissyllabic in other places, e.g. *KJ* (2.1.156, 301,
311). *E3* (1596) seems to contain both
dissyllabic and trisyllabic forms of the
word: 'Brittayne' (1.1.133) and
'Brittaines' (4.1.4) are dissyllabic; but
'Brittayne' (2.2.93) is almost certainly
trisyllabic and 'Brittaine' (5.1.97) may
be. Shakespeare could simply have
copied Holinshed (see 277–88n.).
  intelligence information, reports
279 a rough line metrically: if *Hereford* is
pronounced 'Herford' (as spelled in
QF) and *Rainold* (spelled 'Reginald' in
Holinshed) is elided, a shaky pentameter emerges. Other proper names in
this passage cause further 'metrical
disturbances' (Ard[2], 67); cf. especially
284. Shakespeare, transcribing from
Holinshed, may have taken less than
his usual care with versification. See
also 5.5.100–1n.
280 *Qq and F lack a line, supplied from

Holinshed by Malone (1790), Ritson
(1793) and, in the version adopted here,
Evans (*Riv*). Without some such interpolation Northumberland's account
makes historical nonsense, for it was not
Lord Cobham who 'broke from the
Duke of Exeter' but 'Thomas Arundell,
sonne and heire to the late earle of
Arundell, beheaded at the Tower hill'
(Holinshed, 3.498); this latter 'was kept
in the duke of Exeters house, escaped
out of the realme, . . . and went to his
vncle Thomas Arundell late archbishop
of Canturburie' (3.496). Shakespeare
depends so heavily on Holinshed in this
speech that it is unlikely that he omitted
the reference to Thomas Arundel carelessly or ignorantly. Q may simply have
missed a line, but F's failure to restore it
in a section of the text showing evidence
of fairly careful correction with reference to the theatre promptbook is suspicious. A likelier reason for the omission
is censorship, perhaps in both the printed and acting texts. The Elizabethan
Earl of Arundel, Philip Howard
(1557–95), a Catholic, who was executed in October 1595, near the time *R2*
was first performed, had sometimes
been mentioned (especially by
Catholics) as a possible successor to the
throne; Philip's son and heir (also
named Thomas, like his ancestor in
Holinshed) was therefore in great disfavour with the Queen, who strove
assiduously to deprive him of his title
and estates. If the missing line mentioned 'Thomas, son and heir to th'Earl
of Arundel' – wording very close to
Holinshed's – what could readily be
taken as an inflammatory allusion to the
Elizabethan Thomas in a context of
rebellion against a reigning monarch
would be difficult for the authorities to
overlook.

278 Brittany] *Q2 (*Brittanie*); Brittaine *QF*   279 Lord] *(L..), F*   280] *Riv (after Holinshed); not in QF*

271

That late broke from the Duke of Exeter,
His brother, Archbishop late of Canterbury,
Sir Thomas Erpingham, Sir Thomas Ramston,
Sir John Norberry, Sir Robert Waterton and Francis
    Coint,
All these well furnished by the Duke of Brittany   285
With eight tall ships, three thousand men of war,

281 **broke** escaped
   Duke of Exeter John Holland, also
   Earl of Huntingdon, married to
   Bolingbroke's sister, Elizabeth. He was
   also uncle to the second Duchess of
   York (see Appendix 3). Bolingbroke, on
   becoming king, took away Holland's
   ducal title (see 5.2.41–3n.) and later had
   him executed for his part in the Abbot
   of Westminster's conspiracy. He is
   referred to at 5.3.136 (see n.). His ward,
   Thomas Arundel the younger, was kept
   against his will as a virtual prisoner.
282 Thomas Arundel, Archbishop of
   Canterbury, brother to Richard, Earl
   of Arundel (one of the lords appellant,
   beheaded in 1397; see 1.1.88–103n.),
   and uncle to the Thomas Arundel
   mentioned in 280, was deprived of his
   see and exiled to the continent at the
   time of his brother's execution
   (Holinshed, 3.496).
283 **Sir Thomas Erpingham** In his
   younger days an active adversary of
   Richard II and part of the deputation
   that demanded his abdication; later a
   distinguished veteran of Agincourt
   and a venerable character in *H5* (4.1).
   ***Sir Thomas Ramston** Q's 'Iohn
   Ramston', uncorrected in F, is an historical mistake; Holinshed gives the name
   correctly (see 277–88n.), so that the
   error is unlikely to have been authorial.
   Muir's emendation can be defended not
   only on metrical grounds but also on the
   likelihood that the MS abbreviation
   'Tho.' might easily be mistaken for 'Iho'

(at *H5* 4.1.94 the same compositorial
misreading occurs in F for the same
Christian name – Sir Thomas
Erpingham). An alternative explanation
is that Q's 'Iohn' anticipates 'Sir Iohn
Norberry' in 284 (see *TxC*, 309). Like
Erpingham, Ramston became an opponent of Richard II and was Warden of
the Tower of London when the King
was confined there after his capture.
284 possibly a very rough alexandrine but
   more likely unmetrical; see 279n.
   Norberry and Waterton were both given
   royal appointments at the accession of
   Henry IV – the first as Governor of
   Guînes and Treasurer of the Exchequer,
   the second as Master of the Horse.
   ***Coint** For F's correction of Q
   'Coines' ('Quoint' is apparently a variant spelling of Holinshed's 'Coint'),
   see Appendix 1, p. 525. Nothing is
   known of the figure historically.
285 ***Duke of Brittany** John IV (John de
   Montfort), who died in 1399, and
   whose widow, Joan of Navarre, became
   Henry IV's queen and second wife. For
   pronunciation of Q's 'Brittaine' and for
   varying forms of the word, see 278n.
286 **eight** Shakespeare follows Holinshed
   for the number of ships, but see
   277–88n. and Froissart, 6.359.
   tall large, stout, fine (cf. *MV* 3.1.6,
   Oth 2.1.79)
   men of war fighting men, soldiers.
   Holinshed reports a vast disagreement
   among historians as to the size of
   Bolingbroke's invasion forces – only

281 Exeter,] *F;* Exeter *Q*   283 Thomas Ramston] *Muir;* Iohn Ramston *Q; Iohn Rainston F*
284 Coint] *Halliwell (after Holinshed);* Coines *Q; Quoint F*   285 Brittany] *Mowat & Werstine;*
Brittaine *QF*

Are making hither with all due expedience,
And shortly mean to touch our northern shore.
Perhaps they had ere this, but that they stay
The first departing of the King for Ireland.   290
If, then, we shall shake off our slavish yoke,

fifteen men by some accounts and as many as three thousand by others (see 277–88n.). Shakespeare chooses the larger number, thus maximizing the threat to Richard.

287 **expedience** speed
288 **our northern shore** Bolingbroke landed at *Ravenspurgh* (or Ravenspur), modern Spurn Head, a haven in Yorkshire formed by a 'sliver of land that curves in a great hook into the mouth of the Humber' (Monsarrat, 317; cf. 296). Holinshed again reports a major dispute among historians: 'where *Froissard* and also the chronicles of Britaine [Brittany] auouch, that he should land at Plimmouth, by our English writers it seemeth otherwise: for it appeareth by their assured report, that he approching to the shore, did not streight take land, but lay houering aloofe, and shewed himselfe now in this place, and now in that, to see what countenance was made by the people, whether they meant enuiouslie to resist him, or freendlie to receiue him. . . . The duke of Lancaster, after he had coasted alongst the shore a certeine time, & had got some intelligence how the peoples minds were affected towards him, landed about the beginning of Iulie in Yorkshire, at a place sometime called Rauenspur, betwixt Hull and Bridlington, and with him not past threescore persons, as some write' (3.498).
289–90 Through radical telescoping, Shakespeare annihilates historical time in this scene (see 217n.), for Richard's visit to his dying uncle (1.4.63–4) seems to take place shortly after Aumerle has accompanied Bolingbroke 'to the next highway' (1.4.4) and reported his leave-

taking to the King, and also shortly after Green has spoken of Bolingbroke as having left the country (1.4.37). Now we learn that Bolingbroke is already on his way back (287–8). Gaunt died on 3 February 1399, and his estates were confiscated on 18 March; Richard crossed from England to Ireland on 1 June and, although Bolingbroke's forces were being assembled in France as early as 28 June, the landing at Ravenspurgh did not occur until early July. Holinshed, while explaining that Bolingbroke delayed landing until he could be sure of his reception (see 288n.), makes it unmistakable that Richard had already departed for Ireland before the disaffected nobles sent letters to Bolingbroke, 'requiring him with all conuenient speed to conueie himselfe into England' (3.497). Northumberland's suggestion that Bolingbroke may be postponing his invasion until Richard is safely out of the country is Shakespeare's invention and, dramaturgically speaking, strengthens the impression that the invader has already embarked upon his enterprise before he could have known about Richard's expropriation of his inheritance – an act dramatized only eighty lines earlier (209–10). Whether by design or otherwise, Shakespeare's handling of the historical compression significantly affects our interpretation of Bolingbroke's character and motives. Bradley (29, 32–3) explores the fluidity of time and space in this scene, especially as implied by Q; see Introduction, pp. 28, 82, 124, 129.

289 **had** would have
stay await
291 **shall** mean to

291 our] *QF;* our countries *Q2*

Imp out our drooping country's broken wing,
Redeem from broking pawn the blemished crown,
Wipe off the dust that hides our sceptre's gilt
And make high majesty look like itself,   295
Away with me in post to Ravenspurgh.
But if you faint, as fearing to do so,
Stay and be secret, and myself will go.

ROSS

To horse, to horse! Urge doubts to them that fear.   299

WILLOUGHBY

Hold out my horse and I will first be there.   *Exeunt.*

[2.2]   *Enter the* QUEEN, BUSHY ᶠ*and*ᶠ BAGOT.

BUSHY

Madam, your majesty is too much sad.

292 **Imp out** repair by grafting on new feathers (a technical term from falconry)
293 **from broking pawn** from being pledged to pawnbrokers (a 'broker' was a go-between or pander); cf. Gaunt's charge that Richard has become *Landlord of England* (113) and Willoughby's characterization of him as *a broken man* (257).
294 **gilt** golden lustre (with a probable quibble on 'guilt', Q's spelling; cf. *2H4* 4.5.128, *Mac* 2.2.53–4)
295 **high majesty** Cf. *high Hereford* (1.4.2). Northumberland's unconscious echo of Richard's adjective from the preceding scene (he was not present) creates a certain dramatic irony. The King's semi-contemptuous use and Aumerle's punning response (1.4.3–4) would make the word emphatic and memorable.
296 **in post** at full speed (riding northward with exchange of horses along the way)
297 **faint** lack courage, are faint-hearted
298 **myself** See Abbott, 20.

299 **Urge . . . fear.** Speak of doubts only to the fearful.
300 **Hold . . . and** if my horse holds out (subjunctive; Abbott, 102)
2.2 Apart from the movement of characters in reaction to Bolingbroke's landing, taken from scattered places in Holinshed but reconfigured to produce the sense of a rapidly escalating crisis, this scene is mainly fictitious. The location is presumably Windsor Castle, where Richard left 'the queene with hir traine' (Holinshed, 3.497) before departing from Bristol for Ireland. By making the Queen an adult (as did Daniel), Shakespeare can use her to draw sympathy to the King as well as to sound an effective voice of tragic foreboding. Gradually, also, the play forges a kind of symbolic identity between the two; cf. 5.1.86. As in Act 1, the pattern of following a public with a private scene continues.
0.1 Gurr (98) notes that, as in 1.4, two of Richard's flatterers enter at the

292 drooping] *(drowping),* F   293 broking] *QF;* broken *Q3*   294 gilt] *(guilt),* F
2.2] F *(Scena Secunda.)*   0.1] *Enter Queene, Bushy, and Bagot.* F

You promised, when you parted with the King,
To lay aside life-harming heaviness
And entertain a cheerful disposition.

QUEEN

To please the King I did; to please myself   5
I cannot do it. Yet I know no cause
Why I should welcome such a guest as Grief,
Save bidding farewell to so sweet a guest
As my sweet Richard. Yet again, methinks,
Some unborn sorrow, ripe in Fortune's womb,   10
Is coming towards me, and my inward soul
With nothing trembles. At something it grieves

---

beginning of the scene, the third being reserved for a later entrance (at 40.1) with the function of messenger; now, however, Green replaces Bushy as the bringer of bad news. Bagot, the third parasite, is given a function of his own in 4.1 by becoming the only one of the trio to escape death. Although, like Rosencrantz and Guildenstern in *Ham*, the three figures are politically interchangeable, Shakespeare does his best to keep them individual in the minds of his audience.

3 **life-harming** Melancholy was popularly believed to threaten health, each sigh supposedly consuming a drop of blood (cf. 4.1.92–101LN, 5.6.20n.; also *RJ* 3.5.59: 'Dry sorrow drinks our blood'). Cf. also Ecclesiasticus, 30.23: 'heauinesse hath slayne many a man'.

4 **entertain** assume, take on; receive, harbour
disposition mood

7–8 **guest . . . guest** extending the metaphor of entertainment from 4. The Queen uses several images of hospitality; she later refers to Richard as a *beauteous inn* in which *Grief* is the guest (5.1.13–14).

10–12 **Some . . . trembles** In *Woodstock*,

4.2.5–14, the Duchess of Gloucester, 'full of fear and heaviness', dreams prophetically of her lord's murder; absent, however, is Shakespeare's distinctive image of pregnancy. Wilson (170) compares similar misgivings in *RJ* 1.4.106 ff. and *MV* 1.1.1 ff.

10 **unborn** probably pronounced 'ùnborn'
ripe mature, ready to be born

11, 28 **inward soul** inmost self, heart of hearts

12 **With nothing** at nothing (for no ostensible reason). 'Nothing', one of the play's prominent motifs (the word occurs twenty-five times), is often associated with absence, vacancy or loss and, especially in Acts 4 and 5, with the problem of Richard's identity as a deposed monarch; the Queen's usage here is therefore effectively proleptic.
something some unknown thing (stressed on the second syllable as if it were a separate word). Clark & Wright (110) compare the Queen's apparently causeless melancholy with that of Antonio in *MV* 1.1.1–7: 'In both cases the poet wishes to convey a presentiment of approaching disaster.'

---

3 life-harming] halfe-harming *Q3;* selfe-harming *F*   11 me, . . . soul] *F;* me . . . soule, *Q*   12 With]
Qc, F; At *Qu*

More than with parting from my lord the King.
BUSHY
Each substance of a grief hath twenty shadows,
Which shows like grief itself, but is not so;   15
For Sorrow's eyes, glazed with blinding tears,
Divides one thing entire to many objects,
Like perspectives, which, rightly gazed upon,
Show nothing but confusion; eyed awry,
Distinguish form. So your sweet majesty,   20
Looking awry upon your lord's departure,
Find shapes of grief more than himself to wail,
Which, looked on as it is, is naught but shadows

13 **More than with** greater than, beyond
14 'For each actual cause of sorrow twenty
   illusory ones appear.' The shadow–
   substance contrast becomes a significant
   idea of the play at 4.1.292–3, 294, 296–8
   (see notes); a favourite with Shakespeare,
   it figures also in *3H6* 4.3.50, *Tit* 3.2.80,
   MV 3.2.127, *Ham* 2.2.258 and *AW*
   5.3.307–8.
15 **Which shows** each of which shows
   (the antecedent is *shadows*)
16–17 **eyes . . . Divides** For the third
   person plural ending in *s*, see Abbott,
   333, 2.3.4–5, 5.1.77 and cf. 2.1.252n.).
   F's emendation is superfluous. See also
   18LN.
16 **glazed** glazèd
17 **entire** self-contained, complete in itself
18 **perspectives** pèrspectives; deliberately
   distorted images in works of art. See
   LN.
   rightly directly, straight on, from the
   front (as opposed to obliquely).
   Bushy's usage is paradoxical because
   looking at a perspective painting *rightly*
   (i.e. directly) is in fact the wrong way to
   perceive its true but hidden content.
19 **awry** obliquely, from the edge (see
   18LN)
20 **Distinguish form** reveal a distinct
   shape, resolve into a comprehensible

image
21–4 **Looking . . . not** These lines are
   somewhat obscure, combining, as they
   do, the different types of perspectives
   explained in 18LN. The Queen, looking directly at Richard's departure,
   would see only a single true image; but,
   viewing the same departure in a many-
   faceted refracting glass, i.e. through
   tears (the second kind of perspective),
   she would see deceptively multiple
   images of grief, mere 'shadows / Of
   what it is not'. Bushy here reverses the
   image of the anamorphic picture by
   suggesting that the Queen, *Looking
   awry* on a simple image, is imagining or
   inventing complexity. Now *Looking
   awry* (21) means 'looking through distorting eyes', whereas *eyed awry* (19)
   relates to the correct oblique position
   for viewing an anamorphic picture.
22 **Find** Modern grammar would require
   'Finds', but the understood subject is
   'you' (from *your sweet majesty*).
   shapes images, semblances, reflections
   (cf. *shadows*, 14, 23)
   himself Richard or (if *himself* = itself)
   Richard's departure
22–3 **wail, / Which** bemoan, which.
   Which refers to *shapes of grief*.
23 **it** Richard's *departure* (21)

16 Sorrow's eyes] sorrowes eye *F*   19 Show] *Qc (Shew)*, *F*; Shews *Qu*

Of what it is not. Then, thrice-gracious Queen,
More than your lord's departure weep not. More is
    not seen,   25
Or if it be, 'tis with false Sorrow's eye,
Which for things true weeps things imaginary.

QUEEN

It may be so; but yet my inward soul
Persuades me it is otherwise. Howe'er it be,
I cannot but be sad – so heavy sad   30
As thought, on thinking on no thought I think,
Makes me with heavy nothing faint and shrink.

BUSHY

'Tis nothing but conceit, my gracious lady.

---

25 **More . . . not** Weep for nothing other than your lord's departure.
   More is probably elided (cf. F's 'more's'); the line is an alexandrine.
26 **false Sorrow's eye** i.e. the eye 'glazed with blinding tears' (16) that perceives mistakenly (see 18LN)
27 **weeps** weeps for, laments
29 probably an alexandrine, although the line may be delivered as a pentameter by eliding *it is* to ''tis': 'Persuàdes | me 'tis òth- | erwìse'.
30–2 **so . . . shrink** unusually tortured word-play, turning on *heavy*, *thought* and *nothing*. The Queen means: I am 'so heavily depressed that my very thought process – my attempt not to think about what comes into my mind (or, perhaps, when I think about the insubstantial *nothing* I keep thinking about – "thinking on no thought I think") – depresses me further ("Makes me . . . faint [lose heart] and shrink") because of the burdensome absence of thought (*heavy nothing*)'. *Nothing* represents a further development of 12 (see n.) and, in *heavy*, probably includes the notion of pregnancy from the *unborn sorrow* of 10. For Elizabethans

thought was often associated with melancholy; cf. 5.5.11, and *Ham* 3.1.84: 'sicklied o'er with the pale cast of thought'. See also 3n. and 5.6.20n. The Queen's inexplicable sadness touched a sensitive chord in Johnson: 'The involuntary and unaccountable depression of the mind, which everyone has sometime felt, is here very forcibly described' (1.436). Although most editors adopt Q2's 'though' for Q's 'thought' in 31, Oxf's insertion of a comma allows us to retain Q's word, at the same time making clearer sense of the syntax: the first *thought* (31) thus becomes the subject of *Makes* (32).
30 **heavy** heavily (see Abbott, 2)
33 To save space (owing to inaccurate cast-off of his copy) Q's compositor omitted Bushy's speech and 34 SP; Q's corrected state restored the speech, necessitating an additional line on the page (sig. D3'); see Appendix 1, p. 533, 2.1.186n. and Fig. 19.
   nothing Bushy extends the Queen's wordplay by echoing her word from 32; the echoing continues in 34, 36 and 37 (cf. 12n.).
   conceit fanciful thinking

---

24 thrice-gracious Queen,] *F*; thrice (gracious Queene) *Q*   25 More is] more's *F*   26 Sorrow's eye]
sorrowes eie *F*; sorrowes eyes *Q2*   27 weeps] weepe *F*   31 thought,] *Oxf*; thought *Q*; though *Q2–F*
33 BUSHY . . . lady] *Qc, F; not in Qu*

277

QUEEN

'Tis nothing less. Conceit is still derived

From some forefather grief. Mine is not so,   35

For nothing hath begot my something grief,

Or something hath the nothing that I grieve.

'Tis in reversion that I do possess –

But what it is, that is not yet known what,

I cannot name. 'Tis nameless woe, I wot.   40

^F*Enter* GREEN.^F

GREEN

God save your majesty! And well met, gentlemen.

I hope the King is not yet shipped for Ireland.

QUEEN

Why hop'st thou so? 'Tis better hope he is,

For his designs crave haste, his haste good hope.

Then wherefore dost thou hope he is not shipped?   45

34 **nothing less** anything but that (fancy)
   Conceit thinking
   still always, constantly
36–7 The Queen extends the paradox already voiced at 30–2, adding the birth imagery begun at 10.
36 **something** substantial, real (adjectival)
37 The syntax and meaning are both ambiguous: either 'something has *begot* (understood from 36) the nothing for which I grieve' or 'the nothing that I grieve about has something in it, i.e. some substance'.
38–40 'I possess my grief as though it were a legacy (coming to me *in reversion* (cf. 1.4.35) at the death of the present owner); and because it is still undefined, I cannot name it and must therefore, I know (*wot*), call it *nameless woe.*' In 39 the second *what* is the object of *known*; Q2, followed by the later quartos and F, tried to improve the syntax by inserting a comma after *known*, interpreting 'what / I cannot name' as in apposition to the preceding clause. For rhyming *wot* with *what*, cf. 2.1.250–1.
40.1 *Q's missing, but obviously necessary, entry for Green may have been squeezed out by the space problems that led to omission of 33 on the same page (see n.). But Q has a habit of omitting entry SDs; cf. 85.1, 2.1.146.1, 2.3.56.1, 67 SD, 80.1, 5.2.40.1, 74 SD, 5.3.44.1, 81.1.
44 **crave** urgently require, greatly need
   good hope favourable expectation
45 **wherefore** why

34 SP] *Qc, F; not in Qu*   39 is, that] *Q2–F;* is that *Q*   known what,] knowne, what *Q2–F*
40 name. 'Tis] *(name, tis)*   41 God] Heauen *F*   43 hop'st] *F;* hopest *Q*

278

GREEN

That he, our hope, might have retired his power
And driven into despair an enemy's hope,
Who strongly hath set footing in this land.
The banished Bolingbroke repeals himself,
And with uplifted arms is safe arrived   50
At Ravenspurgh.

QUEEN   Now God in heaven forbid!

GREEN

Ah, madam, 'tis too true; and, that is worse,
The lord Northumberland, his son, young Harry
    Percy,
The lords of Ross, Beaumont and Willoughby,

46–7 Green plays on the Queen's use of *hope* (44). Richard is *our hope* because the fortunes of the speakers are bound up with his; *enemy's hope* refers proleptically to Bolingbroke's designs – a reference that becomes clear only in the following lines. Green also unwittingly anticipates the Queen's *cozening Hope* (69).

46 **retired his power** pulled back his forces (not committed them to fight in Ireland)

48 **Who strongly** who with formidable military support; *Who* refers to *enemy's*.

49 **repeals himself** 'recalls himself from exile' (cf. 4.1.86) or 'repeals his sentence of banishment'

50–1 *And . . . Ravenspurgh* Jowett & Taylor (171–2) plausibly attribute F's relineation of Q to consultation of the MS promptbook.

50 **uplifted arms** 'brandished weapons' or 'arms raised in prayer' (in gratitude for *safe* arrival); the first interpretation seems likelier.

51 **Ravenspurgh** See 2.1.288n.

52 **that** what (Abbott, 244)

53–5 based on Holinshed (3.498): at Ravenspurgh Bolingbroke 'was so ioifullie receiued of the lords, knights, and gentlemen of those parts, that he found means (by their helpe) forthwith to assemble a great number of people, that were willing to take his part. The first that came to him, were the lords of Lincolnshire, and other countries adioining, as the lords Willoughbie, Ros, Darcie, and Beaumont. At his comming vnto Doncaster, the earle of Northumberland, and his sonne sir Henrie Persie, wardens of the marches against Scotland, with the earle of Westmerland, came vnto him.'

53 probably an alexandrine (see 2.1.279n.) *Harry* Q's 'H.' might stand for 'Henry' (cf. F), but Harry is the name used by both his father (2.3.21, 23) and Bolingbroke (3.3.20). Northumberland later repeats Green's phrase (see 2.3.21n.).

54 **Beaumont** Henry, fifth Baron Beaumont (*c.* 1378–1413), a Yorkshireman

---

50–1 And . . . Ravenspurgh] *as F; one line Q*   52 Ah] O *F*   worse,] *F;* worse: *Q*   53 son, young] *(*son yong*);* yong sonne *Q2–F*   Harry] *Riv;* H. *Q; Henrie F*   54 lords] *Qc, F;* lord *Qu*   Beaumont] *Halliwell;* Beaumond *QF*

With all their powerful friends are fled to him.   55

BUSHY

Why have you not proclaimed Northumberland
And all the rest revolted faction, traitors?

GREEN

We have, whereupon the Earl of Worcester

---

55 **powerful** pòw'rful (two syllables; see
t.n.)
57 **all . . . traitors** Q's syntax, which
clearly gave trouble to later compositors and editors, has been much disputed; several interpretations are possible:
'all the rest (of the) revolted faction,
traitors'; 'all the rest (that are) revolted,
faction-traitors'; 'all the rest, revolted
faction, traitors'. The first ellipsis,
seeming more natural, is adopted in
this edn; but none of the three possibilities differs greatly from the others in
substance. Bushy asks simply why the
members of Bolingbroke's treasonous
clique (Northumberland and the others) have not been publicly denounced.
The 'improvements' of the later quartos and F apparently lack independent
authority. RP suggests that Q's 'faction,' might be a mis-setting of 'fac-
tious' – the *n* being a misreading of MS
u and the comma a misreading of MS *s*.
Both errors are common; cf. 1.4.20n.
58–61 Cf. Holinshed, 3.499–500: 'Sir
Thomas Persie earle of Worcester, lord
steward of the kings house, either being
so commanded by the king, or else vpon
displeasure (as some write) for that the
king had proclaimed his brother the
earle of Northumberland traitor, brake
his white staffe, which is the representing signe and token of his office, and
without delaie went to duke Henrie.
When the kings seruants of houshold
saw this (for it was doone before them
all) they dispersed themselues, some
into one countrie, and some into an
other.' Shakespeare assumes that
Worcester's motive was displeasure (see

2.3.30). *Mirror* also makes much of
Northumberland's being 'openly pro-
claymed trayterous knight' (133) and of
Worcester's 'in sight of least and moste
/ Bebreake[ing] his staffe' (115).
Froissart, although he elaborates at
length on the disloyalty of the Percys
(6.347–52), omits Worcester's resignation as steward. In *1H4* 5.1.34–8
Worcester himself, addressing Bolingbroke, recalls his defection: 'For you my
staff of office did I break / In Richard's
time, and posted day and night / To
meet you on the way, and kiss your
hand, / When yet you were in place
and in account / Nothing so strong
and fortunate as I'. In Holinshed
Worcester's defection occurs after
Richard's return from Ireland; by
antedating it, Shakespeare magnifies
the peril and urgency of the dramatic
situation.
58 a metrically rough line, necessitating a
pause (or beat) between *have* and
whereupon; the five stresses then fall on
have, *whèreupòn*, *Earl* and *Wòrcester*. A
less likely alternative would be to
regard *whereupon* as a regular iambic
foot (by eliding the second syllable:
'where'pòn') and to pronounce
Worcester trisyllabically ('Wòr-ce-
stèr').
Earl of Worcester Thomas Percy
(1343–1403), younger brother of
Northumberland and Lord High
Steward of the King's household, who
accompanied Richard to Ireland but
deserted him on his return to Wales.
As steward, he held one of the most
important and honorific offices in the

---

55 powerful] *(powrefull) F* 57 all . . . revolted] the rest of the reuolted *Q2–3, F;* the rest of the
reuolting *Q4–5;* all the rest, revolted *Wells* faction, traitors] faction-traitors *Oxf (Abbott 22, 246)*

Hath broken his staff, resigned his stewardship,
And all the household servants fled with him   60
To Bolingbroke.

QUEEN

So, Green, thou art the midwife to my woe,
And Bolingbroke my sorrow's dismal heir.
Now hath my soul brought forth her prodigy,
And I, a gasping new-delivered mother,   65
Have woe to woe, sorrow to sorrow joined.

BUSHY

Despair not, madam.

QUEEN   Who shall hinder me?

I will despair and be at enmity
With cozening Hope. He is a flatterer,
A parasite, a keeper-back of Death   70
Who gently would dissolve the bands of life,

---

kingdom. Worcester figures prominently in *1H4*, where he also rebels
against Richard's successor.

59 **broken** brok'n; Q2's 'broke', followed
by F, is unnecessary.

60 **household** Richard's extensive royal
establishment, consisting of nobles
and men of rank as well as humbler
servants; cf. 4.1.282–3 where Richard
claims that 'under his household roof'
he did 'keep ten thousand men'.

61 The short line creates a dramatic
pause, perhaps an effective means of
letting the shock register (Cam², 101).

62–6 The Queen elaborates her conceit
of pregnancy and childbirth begun at
10 and continued in 36–7 (see notes).
Bolingbroke becomes the ill-omened
offspring (*dismal heir*) of her sorrow,
the monstrous creature (*prodigy*)
born of her soul's pangs of apprehension (cf. 11–12). Having delivered
such a monster and added new suffering to her condition on account of

its unnaturalness, she has exacerbated
her birth pains rather than relieved
them, that is, she has *joined . . . woe to
woe* and *sorrow to sorrow*. The word
heir picks up the earlier metaphor of
inheritance from 38 (*reversion*); see
38–40n. It also recalls Richard's 'As
were our England in reversion his'
(see 1.4.35n.). Daniel's description of
the final parting of Richard and his
Queen might have planted the germ
of the natal imagery: 'both stood
silent . . . Their eies relating how
their harts did morne / Both bigge
with sorrow, and both great with woe
/ In labour with what was not to be
borne: / This mightie burthen
wherewithall they goe / Dies vndeli-
uered, perishes vnborne' (2.97).

65 **gasping** exhausted

69 **cozening** deceitful, cheating; see also
46–7n.

71 **Who** *Death*
bands bonds (cf. 1.1.2n.)

---

59 broken] broke *Q2–F*   60–1] *as Pope; one line QF*   62 to] of *Q2–F*   65 new-delivered] *Pope*;
new deliuerd *QF*   69 cozening] *QF*; couetous *Q4*   70 keeper-back] *Capell*; keeper backe *QF*

Which false Hope lingers in extremity.

^F*Enter* YORK.^F

GREEN

Here comes the Duke of York.

QUEEN

With signs of war about his aged neck.
O, full of careful business are his looks!   75
Uncle, for God's sake, speak comfortable words.

YORK

Should I do so, I should belie my thoughts.
Comfort's in heaven, and we are on the earth,
Where nothing lives but crosses, cares and grief.
Your husband, he is gone to save far off,   80
Whilst others come to make him lose at home.

---

72 'which at the point of death (*in extremity*) *false Hope* postpones (lingers)',
thus delaying the relief death would
bring

73 a half line, perhaps indicating a brief
pause as York enters

74 **signs of war** York is wearing a gorget,
a piece of armour to protect the throat,
sometimes worn over civilian garb as
an emblem of military status. The so-
called Zucchero portrait of Sir Philip
Sidney (National Portrait Gallery,
London) shows the subject so attired
(reproduced in M. Wilson, 167). Cf. *TC*
1.3.174; also *Perkin Warbeck*, 3.1.0.1:
'*Enter King Henry, his gorget on.*'
aged agèd. Historically, York was fifty-
eight, an advanced age by medieval and
Renaissance standards; cf. 83 and 1.1.1
where Gaunt, also fifty-eight at the
time, is addressed as *old* and *time-
honoured*. See also 5.2.114–15n.

75 **careful business** worried preoccupa-
tion, distressful concern (*careful* = full

of care)

76 difficult to scan; a possible pattern
would be: 'Ùncle, for | Gòd's sàke, |
speak còm- | fortà- | ble wòrds'. The
Queen's agitated appeal to York makes
the irregularity dramatically natural.
comfortable words encouraging
news, words of hope. Probably an echo
of the Anglican liturgy for Holy
Communion: 'Hear what comfortable
words our Savior Christ saith' or, less
likely, of Zachariah, 1.13 (Geneva
Bible). Cf. 3.2.36n. The phrase became
common, e.g. *White Devil*, 3.3.12.

77 F may have dropped this line inadvertently or in order to make a 'more
pointed antithesis' (Pollard, 93)
between *comfortable words* (76) and
Comfort's in heaven (78).

79 **crosses** troubles, obstructions

80 **save far off** i.e. keep Ireland under
English sovereignty (*save* = protect,
preserve)

81 **lose** lose sovereignty

---

72 Hope lingers] hopes linger *F*   76 God's] heauens *F*   77] *om. F*   78 on the] *Qc, F;* in the *Qu*
79 cares] care *Q2–F*   81 lose] *(*loose*)*

Here am I left to underprop his land,
Who, weak with age, cannot support myself.
Now comes the sick hour that his surfeit made;
Now shall he try his friends that flattered him.   85

^F*Enter a* Servingman.^F

SERVINGMAN [*to York*]
My lord, your son was gone before I came.
YORK
He was? Why, so! Go all which way it will!
The nobles they are fled, the commons they are cold

83 **weak with age** See 74n.
   cannot support myself 'can barely
   support myself'
84 **sick . . . made** the illness brought on
   by his excesses (literally, overeating; cf.
   2.1.37–9 and *KL* 1.2.119–20). In substance, York says that Gaunt's prediction has come to pass.
85 **try** put to the test (test the worth of).
   Undoubtedly York expresses justifiable scorn of the favourites onstage
   with him (*friends* is heavily ironic). We
   learn shortly, in fact, that they are
   interested chiefly in saving their own
   skins (see 124–40).
85.1 *apparently the same character who
   enters again at 5.2.74; see Mahood,
   Parts, 265.
86–8 In desperation York has sent to his
   son Aumerle for assistance, and his
   servant now returns to report that he
   has left the country. The implication
   is that Aumerle, alarmed by
   Bolingbroke's return to England and
   without York's knowledge, has
   already rushed to join Richard in
   Ireland and therefore cannot come to
   his father's rescue; in 3.2 Aumerle
   accompanies the King, who has just
   landed in Wales. Shakespeare departs

here from Holinshed, who reports
that Aumerle sailed to Ireland at the
same time as Richard (3.497). There
is no suggestion in 88 ('The nobles
they are fled') that York suspects his
son of defection to Bolingbroke. The
French chroniclers depict Aumerle as
behaving treacherously from the
start. The news about Aumerle's
departure simply lays heavier stress
on York's political feebleness and isolation. Holinshed (3.498) reports that
York, when he learned of Bolingbroke's impending arrival on English
soil, sent for certain members of
Richard's privy council (including
Bushy, Bagot and Green), asking
'what they thought good to be doone
in this matter'.
87 **so** so be it (let matters fall out however
   they will)
88 Pope's emendation can be defended
   as the elimination of a mistakenly
   repeated phrase (*they are*) of a kind
   found elsewhere in Q. But an alexandrine, created by the echoed words,
   may be deliberate – a metrical effect
   to assist the impression of York's
   laboured defeatism. That another
   hypermetrical line occurs two lines

85.1 Servingman] *Q (86 SP); seruant F*   86 SD] *this edn*   87 was?] *Capell; was; Q; was: F*   so!] *F
(so:); so Q*   88 commons . . . cold] commons cold *Pope*

And will, I fear, revolt on Hereford's side.
Sirrah, get thee to Pleshy to my sister Gloucester;   90
Bid her send me presently a thousand pound.
Hold, take my ring.

SERVINGMAN

My lord, I had forgot to tell your lordship:
Today, as I came by, I called there –
But I shall grieve you to report the rest.   95

YORK

What is't, knave?

SERVINGMAN

An hour before I came, the Duchess died.

later (90) would seem to confirm the
point that metrical irregularity is a
feature of York's characterization (cf.
2.2.109–22 and see Introduction,
pp. 165–6).
   commons probably the House of
Commons (the third estate in
Parliament) rather than the common
people in general; see 128n., 132n.
   cold unenthusiastic (given the likely
success of Bolingbroke's revolt)
90 **Sirrah** used to address inferiors, here
probably an extra-metrical vocative.
Wilson suggests a dramatic pause after
89: 'the old man has fallen into gloomy
silence, from which he rouses himself
by turning abruptly to the servingman'
(173–4).
90, 120 **Pleshy** See 1.2.66n.
90 **sister** sister-in-law
91 another metrically anomalous line, the
first two feet being trochaic and the
third dactylic (with stresses on *Bid*,
send and *prèsently*). See 88n.
91, 119 **presently** without delay, immediately
92 **my ring** a signet ring – proof to the
receiver of the genuineness of the

sender's request
94 **called** callèd
96 **knave** fellow (literally 'boy', here
impatient rather than deprecatory)
97 **the Duchess died** Historically, the
Duchess died some three months later
than the events of this scene (October
1399 rather than July) and at the
Minories (see List of Roles, 10n.), not
Pleshy. Holinshed specifies neither
date nor place: 'The same yeare
deceassed the duchesse of Glocester,
thorough sorrow (as was thought)
which she conceiued for the losse of
hir sonne and heire the lord Humfrie,
who being sent for foorth to Ireland . . .
was taken with the pestilence, and
died by the waie' (3.514). Shakespeare's transfer of her death to the
new context magnifies the *tide of woes*
(98); it also frees a boy actor for other
roles later in the play (see Appendix
2). GWW assumes, however, that old
women such as the Duchesses of
Gloucester and York were played by
men rather than boys (see List of
Roles headnote).

90 Pleshy] *Wells (*Pleshey*); Plashie QF   93–4] F *lines* forgot / there, /   94 as I . . . called] I came
by and call'd *Q2–F*

YORK

God for His mercy, what a tide of woes
Comes rushing on this woeful land at once!
I know not what to do. I would to God –   100
So my untruth had not provoked him to it –
The King had cut off my head with my brother's.
What, are there no posts dispatched for Ireland?
How shall we do for money for these wars?

98 **God . . . mercy** a prayerful oath (literally, 'I pray God for mercy'); cf. 5.2.75. York uses the expression twice in *Woodstock* (1.1.8, 1.3.208). Shakespeare employs this locution, 'an exclamation peculiarly characteristic of the feeble York' (Brereton, 'Notes', 104), only in *R2*. Since the phrase appears twice in *Woodstock* and twice in Shakespeare (both in *R2*), and since all four instances occur in speeches by York, the case for Shakespeare's indebtedness to the anonymous play is strong. See Introduction, pp. 148–9.
tide of woes This figure anticipates Scroop's description of Bolingbroke as a river overflowing its banks at 3.2.109–11 (Cam², 103).

100 **I . . . do** York's political frailty is probably indebted to Holinshed (3.485): 'The duke of Yorke was a man rather coueting to liue in pleasure, than to deale with much businesse, and the weightie affaires of the realme'. Cf. *Woodstock*, where Gloucester, likewise flustered in a crisis, says, 'Afore my God / I know not which way to bestow myself / The time's so busy and so dangerous too' (1.1.126–8); later in the same play he repeats 'I know not which way to bestow myself!' (1.3.240), and exclaims, 'Afore my God I know not what to do' (1.3.246).

101 **So my untruth** 'provided that my disloyalty'; a suggestion that York *has* been disloyal is not intended.

102 **cut . . . brother's** an indication, perhaps, that York thought of Gloucester's death as an extra-legal execution (beheading) rather than a murder; see 1.1.100n. Conceivably, York refers to Richard's threat to behead Gaunt at 2.1.123, but this interpretation seems strained.

103 Again York's agitation is conveyed by an abruptness in the metre – the exclamation *What*, probably extrametrical, followed by a beat or brief pause. The word was often used to hail or summon a servant as well as to express astonishment. *Ireland* is trisyllabic.
no posts possibly influenced by Holinshed, who says that bad weather prevented Richard from gaining intelligence (*posts* = messengers) about Bolingbroke's movements in England: 'the seas were so troubled by tempests, and the winds blew so contrarie for anie passage, to come ouer foorth of England to the king, remaining still in Ireland, that for the space of six weeks, he receiued no aduertisements from thence' (3.499). At 123, Bushy announces that conditions have altered.

104 **do for** provide

98 God] Heau'n *F*   99 Comes] Come *F*   100 God] heauen *F*   103 there no posts] there two posts
Q2; there postes *F*

[*to Queen*]
Come, sister – cousin, I would say – pray pardon me.   105
[*to Servingman*]
Go, fellow, get thee home; provide some carts
And bring away the armour that is there.   [*Exit Servingman.*]
[*to Bushy, Bagot and Green*]
Gentlemen, will you go muster men?
If I know how or which way to order these affairs
Thus disorderly thrust into my hands,   110
Never believe me. Both are my kinsmen.
Th'one is my sovereign, whom both my oath

---

105 In his distraction York is preoccu-
pied with his sister-in-law, Duchess of
Gloucester, whose death has just been
reported to him (97); he alludes to her
again by mentioning Pleshy at 120.
Steevens in 1793 was the first to
notice this detail as 'one of
Shakespeare's touches of nature'
(Forker, 84).

106 **home** perhaps referring to the
royal household, just abandoned by
Worcester and the servants (cf. 58–61
and 2.3.26–8), but, more likely, one
of York's homes in or near London,
possibly Langley (see List of Roles,
4n.)

108–9 Possibly the line break should
come after *how* rather than *men*,
Gentlemen being explained as an extra-
metrical vocative; *or which way*, all
three words receiving full stress, would
then constitute the slow start of 109.
But see 109–22n.

108 **muster men** based, probably, on
Holinshed (3.498), where York is advised
by privy councillors 'to depart from
London, vnto S. Albons, and there to
gather an armie to resist the duke in his
landing'. The soldiers to be mustered

would probably be retainers and tenants.

109–22 York's speech contains a number
of metrically irregular lines. Attempts
have been made to improve them (see,
for instance, 109t.n. and 110t.n.; also
Craven³, 60), but no rearrangement
can make all of them scan normally.
The irregularities are probably a
deliberate means of conveying York's
dithering distraction. See 88n.; also
Introduction, pp. 166. York's concluding couplet (121–2; see 120–2n.) scans
normally.

109–10 Brereton ('Notes', 105) compares
Woodstock, 1.1.126–8. See 100n.

109 **order** bring order to, regulate

110 **disorderly** in a state of disorder

111–15 **Both . . . right.** This dramatization of York's dilemma, the first step
in his gradual shift to the support of
Bolingbroke, lays the groundwork for
his decision to *remain as neuter* at
2.3.159. His indecision – a conscious
attempt to avoid choice – effectually
signals an unconscious decision in
favour of Richard's enemy (Cam²,
103).

112 **sovereign** probably three syllables
('sòv-e-rèign')

---

105 SD] *this edn* 106 SD] *this edn* 107 SD] *Capell (subst.)* 108 SD] *this edn* go muster]
muster *F* 109 how . . . way] how *Pope* 110 Thus disorderly thrust] Disorderly thus thrust *Pope;*
Thus thrust disorderly *Steevens* 112 Th'one] *F;* Tone *Q;* T'one *Q3*

And duty bids defend; th'other again
Is my kinsman, whom the King hath wronged,
Whom conscience and my kindred bids to right.   115
Well, somewhat we must do. [*to Queen*] Come, cousin,
     I'll
Dispose of you. –
Gentlemen, go muster up your men,
And meet me presently at Berkeley ᶠCastleᶠ.
I should to Pleshy too,   120
But time will not permit. All is uneven,
And everything is left at six and seven.

                              Exeunt Duke [of York and] Queen.

BUSHY
     The wind sits fair for news to go for Ireland,

---

oath oath of allegiance (formalized at Richard's coronation). *Homily* stresses the heinousness of breaking such oaths; see 4.1.235n.

115 **kindred** family relationship, kinship

117 **Dispose of** make safe arrangements for. The royal household having been dispersed, the Queen requires alternative accommodation. Possibly she is housed at Langley; see 106n. and 3.1.36n.

118 **Gentlemen** pronounced trisyllabically in the line arrangement here adopted (see 116–18t.n.); if QF's lining is retained (as a few editors prefer), *Gentlemen* becomes an extra-metrical vocative in an alexandrine.

119 *****Berkeley Castle** Q and F spellings ('Barkly', 'Barkley') indicate the pronunciation. F's addition of the word 'Castle' seems to derive from the MS promptbook (see Appendix 1, p. 525) and could have been introduced by the actors, for reasons of historical clarity (Holinshed, 3.498, specifies 'the

castell of Berkelie' rather than the adjoining town) as well as smoother metre. Mention of the castle in Gloucestershire where Edward II was gruesomely murdered (1327), referred to also at 2.3.53, adds an ominous note (the grisly historical association would undoubtedly register with an Elizabethan audience); it also reminds us that *E2* was one of Shakespeare's models (see Introduction, pp. 116, 124, 159–64).

120–2 *****Pope's rearrangement of QF lineation clarifies the rhyme on *uneven* (= in disorder) and *seven*.

120 **should** ought to go

122 **at . . . seven** at hazard (in total chaos). Proverbial (Dent, A208); cf. also Nicholas Udall's translation of Erasmus, *Apophthegmata* (1542): 'to sette all on sixe and seuen' (fol. 267ᵛ). See LN.

123 See 103n.
     sits fair blows favourably (in a westerly direction); cf. 2.1.265n.

---

113 th'other] *F;* tother *Q*   116–18] *as Cam¹; QF line* cousin, / men, /   116 SD] *Irving*
119 Berkeley] *(Barkly), F (Barkley)*   120–2] *as Pope; QF line* permit: / seauen. /   120 Pleshy] *Wells (Pleshey);* Plashie *QF*   122 SD] *Exeunt Duke. Qu man. Bush. Green. Q; Exit. F*   123 go for] go to *F*

287

But none returns. For us to levy power
Proportionable to the enemy is all unpossible.   125

GREEN

Besides, our nearness to the King in love
Is near the hate of those love not the King.

BAGOT

And that's the wavering commons, for their love
Lies in their purses; and whoso empties them,
By so much fills their hearts with deadly hate.   130

BUSHY

Wherein the King stands generally condemned.

BAGOT

If judgement lie in them, then so do we,
Because we ever have been near the King.

---

124 **none returns** because the wind is
not favourable for return sailings
power troops, forces (cf. 46)
125 Metrically rough, reflecting Bagot's
demoralization. The line may be
best scanned with full stresses on
Propòrtionable, ènemy, àll, unpòssible.
See t.n.
Proportionable to sufficient for,
equal to (literally, 'proportional to')
all wholly
126–7 **our . . . King** 'Our intimacy with
the King makes us vulnerable to the
hatred of his enemies.' Bushy plays on
two different senses of *near*: emotionally close to, possessing affection for;
conceptually proximate to, within a
short distance of (*Is near* = implies,
means).
127 **those love** those who love (Abbott,
244)
128 **that's** F's contracted form, smoothing the metre, probably derives from
the MS promptbook; see Appendix 1,
p. 526).
wavering commons probably the
House of Commons, as at 88 (see n.);
wavering = fickle.

129 **whoso empties them** 'whoever
makes them empty (through heavy
taxation)'. *Them* is emphatic.
130 Ross has already mentioned
Richard's loss of the commons' *hearts*
because of *grievous taxes* (2.1.246–7)
and *burdenous taxations* (2.1.260).
Bagot echoes *hearts*. Here and at
2.1.247 (but see n.) Shakespeare may
have been influenced by a marginal
note in Holinshed, 3.498: 'The harts
of the commons wholie bent to the
duke of Lancaster'. Cf. also
Holinshed, 3.492: 'the commons
vndoubtedlie bare great and priuie
hatred' against Bushy, Bagot and
Green.
131 **Wherein** 'in which matter' (the emp-
tying of their purses)
generally by everyone
132 'If the King's fate depends on *the
wavering commons* (or *their hearts*), we
too stand condemned.' Parliament
functioned as a high court as well as a
legislature.
133 **ever** constantly
near politically and emotionally close
to (cf. 126–7n.)

125] *Pope lines* enemy / impossible. /   unpossible] impossible *F*   126 Besides,] *Q4*; Besides *QF*
128 that's] *F;* that is *Q*   133 ever have been] haue beene euer *F*

GREEN

Well, I will for refuge straight to Bristol Castle.
The Earl of Wiltshire is already there.   135

BUSHY

Thither will I with you, for little office
Will the hateful commons perform for us
Except like curs to tear us all to pieces.
[*to Bagot*] Will you go along with us?

BAGOT

No, I will to Ireland to his majesty.   140
Farewell. If heart's presages be not vain,

134–40 The escape plans of the favourites
as stated here are based on Holinshed,
3.498: 'The lord treasuror [the Earl of
Wiltshire], Bushie, Bagot, and Greene,
perceiuing that the commons would
cleaue vnto, and take part with the
duke, slipped awaie, leauing the lord
gouernour of the realme [York], and
the lord chancellor [Edmund Stafford,
Bishop of Exeter] to make what shift
they could for themselues: Bagot got
him to Chester, and so escaped into
Ireland; the other [Wiltshire, Bushy
and Green] fled to the castell of
Bristow, in hope there to be in safetie.'
Later in the play a seeming contradiction occurs. Bagot (rather than Green)
is said to be at Bristol with Bushy at
2.3.164–5, although Bushy and Green
are executed there in 3.1 (but see LN).
At 3.2.122 Richard is ignorant of
Bagot's whereabouts, suggesting that
he never succeeded in joining the King
abroad (see 3.2.122LN). In 4.1, Bagot,
having survived, is brought on, under
arrest, to give evidence in the matter of
Gloucester's death. Shakespeare may
simply have forgotten or been careless
about these details (which, in any case,
would probably not have been noticed
in performance). Apart from reporting
that Bagot did reach Ireland, Holinshed
says that he was later held 'prisoner in

the Tower' and 'disclosed many secrets'
concerning Richard and Aumerle
(3.511). Ultimately Parliament pardoned the historical figure.
134, 140 **I will** probably elided to 'I'll'
134 *Bristol** Q's 'Brist.' probably stands
for 'Bristow', the spelling at 2.3.164; F
modernizes to 'Bristoll'.
135 **Earl of Wiltshire** See 134–40n. and
2.1.215. Shakespeare economizes by
eliminating the fourth of Richard's
favourites from the stage action.
136 **office** service
137 **hateful** malignant, hostile (literally,
'full of hate')
commons here probably 'common
people'
141–2, 147–8 In *Woodstock*, 3.2.102–5,
Gloucester takes leave of his brothers
in similar language: 'Adieu, good York
and Gaunt, farewell for ever. / I have a
sad presage come suddenly / That I
shall never see these brothers more: /
On earth, I fear, we never more shall
meet'. Rossiter (48) finds Shakespeare's lines 'a clear echo' of the earlier play. Cf. also *JC* 5.1.114–21. Line
142 is repeated almost verbatim in
Caesar's Revenge, l. 183: 'Heere three
do part that ne're shall meet againe';
see 1.1.109n.
141 **If . . . vain** 'if I can trust the fore-
bodings of my heart' (*vain* = in vain,

---

134 Bristol] *(Brist.), F*   137 Will . . . commons] The hateful commons will *Pope*   commons] commoners *Oxf*   138 to pieces] in pieces *Q2–F*   139 SD] *this edn*   141 Farewell.] *Q3, F (*Farewell,*)*;
Farewell *Q*

We three here part that ne'er shall meet again.

BUSHY

That's as York thrives to beat back Bolingbroke.

GREEN

Alas, poor Duke! The task he undertakes

Is numbering sands and drinking oceans dry.   145

Where one on his side fights, thousands will fly.

BAGOT

Farewell at once – for once, for all and ever.

BUSHY

Well, we may meet again.

BAGOT   I fear me, never.   ᶠ*Exeunt.*ᶠ

worthless). *Presages* (presentiments) is
stressed on the second syllable. The
line gains force from the gloomy news
presented earlier in the scene (52–61,
88–9, 97–104).

143 'That depends on how well York suc-
ceeds in driving back Bolingbroke (in
battle).'

145 proverbial expressions of attempting
the impossible (see Dent, S91 and O9)

147 SP *Grant White's emendation, giving this line to Bagot rather than treating it as a continuation of Green's
speech (as in Q) or making it the
beginning of Bushy's speech (as in F)
renders the dialogue more dramatic; as
TxC notes, the alteration preserves a
psychological distinction between
Bagot and his two friends, he being
more insistent on taking leave than
they, who 'are inclined to delay the
moment' (310); see 0.1n. F's awkward

emendation does not fit logically with
Bushy's 'Well, we may meete againe',
clearly a response to the words that
have just preceded, not an expansion
of them. F's SP '*Bush.*' presumably
results from misreading of MS '*Ba.*' as
'*Bu.*', either by F's compositor or by
the annotator of Q3 (see Appendix 1,
pp. 522, 540). If it was compositorial
misreading, it may have arisen because
the compositor expected to see '*Bu.*' in
his copy, having just set Bushy's SP at
143.

148 SD *The exits here are probably 'at
several doors' to emphasize the finality
of the separation; cf. 1.2.74 SDn.
Adams (128) notes the ironic contrast
between the 'energetic determination'
of three of Richard's enemies at the
end of the preceding scene and the
supineness and 'selfish gloom' of three
of his 'friends' here.

145 numbering] *(numbring)*   147 SP] *White; not in Q; Bush. F*   148 SD] *F (Exit.), Rowe*

[2.3] *Enter* [BOLINGBROKE,] ᶠDuke ofᶠ Hereford, ᶠandᶠ
NORTHUMBERLAND [*with Soldiers*].

BOLINGBROKE
How far is it, my lord, to Berkeley now?
NORTHUMBERLAND
Believe me, noble lord,
I am a stranger here in Gloucestershire.
These high wild hills and rough uneven ways
Draws out our miles and makes them wearisome.   5

2.3 This scene, which shifts from the confusion and pessimism of Richard's friends to the assured optimism and resoluteness of Bolingbroke's party, well illustrates the flexibility of the Elizabethan stage: it begins on a road somewhere in Gloucestershire where Bolingbroke, Northumberland and their men are travelling toward Berkeley Castle, unaware that they are already near it; then it settles down (at 53) to a definite site just outside the castle itself. The particulars of Bolingbroke's return are largely invented, although the basic movements of the characters come from Holinshed, who reports that Willoughby and Ross joined Bolingbroke at Ravenspurgh, that Northumberland and his son Harry joined him at Doncaster (where Bolingbroke en route to Berkeley paused to gather forces), and that York stayed at Berkeley Castle on his way to meet the King returning from Ireland. The successive entrances of Harry Percy, Ross and Willoughby, Lord Berkeley and, finally, York dramatize Bolingbroke's gathering strength, giving point to Holinshed's statement that after his landing 'what for loue, and what for feare of losse, they came flocking vnto him from euerie part' (3.498; see also

2.2.53–5n). York's fatally significant attempt to remain *as neuter* (159) is Shakespeare's important addition – a way of dramatizing York's incipient defection (see 2.2.111n.), and therefore a turning point which already, in effect, marks the irreversible direction of the play's political action. Froissart too, however, may have influenced the conception of York's character in this scene: 'the duke of Yorke laye styll in his castell, and medled with nothynge of the busynesse of Englande: no more he dyde before, he toke ever the tyme aworthe as it came. Howbeit, he was sore displeased in his mynde, to se suche difference within the realme, and bytwene his nephues and blode' (6.371).

4   **high wild hills** the Cotswolds, whose northern extremity is not far from Shakespeare's own Stratford; see 9n. Northumberland, a northerner, would know his own more rugged Pennines better. Ure (80) suggests that Daniel's account of Richard at Conway may partly account for the emphasis on wildness here; cf. 'deserts, rockes and hils . . . Where desolation and no comforts are' (Daniel, 2.33). Note also the contrast with Richard's much softer response to landscape at 3.2.6–25.

4–5 **ways / Draws** See 2.2.16–17n.

2.3] *F (Scaena Tertia.)*   0.1–2] *Enter the Duke of Hereford, and Northumberland. F*   0.2 *with Soldiers*]
Capell (subst.)   1+ SP] *(Bul[l].)*   1 Berkeley] *(Barckly), F (Berkley)*   3 here] *QF; om. Q2–5*

291

And yet your fair discourse hath been as sugar,
Making the hard way sweet and delectable.
But I bethink me what a weary way
From Ravenspurgh to Cotshall will be found
In Ross and Willoughby, wanting your company,   10
Which I protest hath very much beguiled
The tediousness and process of my travel.
But theirs is sweetened with the hope to have
The present benefit which I possess;
And hope to joy is little less in joy   15
Than hope enjoyed. By this the weary lords
Shall make their way seem short as mine hath done
By sight of what I have, your noble company.
BOLINGBROKE
Of much less value is my company
Than your good words.

Enter HARRY PERCY.

But who comes here?   20

6–7 **fair . . . delectable** Northumberland
lays on his flattery very thickly (it continues for eleven more lines); the idea is
proverbial (Dent, C566); cf. *King Leir*
(*c.* 1594), sc. 4.48: 'Thy pleasant company will make the way seem short'. The
effect of ironic insincerity is heightened
if we recall that Northumberland condemned Richard for being 'basely led /
By flatterers' at 2.1.241–2. In contrast,
Bolingbroke's language is 'practical and
almost monosyllabic' (Cam², 105).
7   **delectable** stressed on the first and
third syllables
9   **Cotshall** the Cotswolds, hills in
Gloucestershire (a local spelling); for
similar forms, cf. *MW* 1.1.90 and *2H4*
3.2.21. F modernizes slightly, while
preserving an element of Gloucestershire dialect.
10 possibly an alexandrine, or else *Willoughby* may be elided to a dissyllable

('Will'by'), leaving an unstressed syllable hanging before the caesura
In in the case of (see Abbott, 162)
wanting lacking
11 **protest** declare
beguiled diverted, made pleasant (literally, 'agreeably deceived')
12 **tediousness and process** tedious
course (hendiadys)
15–16 **And . . . enjoyed** Northumberland
effusively decorates his fawning with
wordplay: the hope of enjoying (*to joy*)
Bolingbroke's companionship is little
less enjoyable (*in joy*) than the actual
fulfilment of the hope (*hope enjoyed*).
16 **this** this hope (of enjoying Bolingbroke's company)
17 **hath done** has seemed short
20–1 tetrameter lines for the entrance of a
new character who brings news; the
excited questions (23, 25) evoked by
his arrival are also short lines.

6 your] our *F*   9 Cotshall] Cottshold *F;* Cotswold *Hanmer*   14 which] that *Q2–F*   20 SD] *Oxf;
after* here? *QF*   HARRY] *H. F*

NORTHUMBERLAND

    It is my son, young Harry Percy,

    Sent from my brother Worcester whencesoever.

    Harry, how fares your uncle?

HARRY PERCY

    I had thought, my lord, to have learned his health of

        you.

NORTHUMBERLAND

    Why, is he not with the Queen?   25

HARRY PERCY

    No, my good lord. He hath forsook the court,

    Broken his staff of office, and dispersed

    The household of the King.

NORTHUMBERLAND   What was his reason?

    He was not so resolved when last we spake together.

HARRY PERCY

    Because your lordship was proclaimed traitor.   30

    But he, my lord, is gone to Ravenspurgh

---

21 **son . . . Percy** Shakespeare emphasizes Harry's youth by repeating the same phrase from 2.2.53 (see n.) and by having his father address him as *boy* at 36. The historical Harry (called 'Hotspur' in *1H4*) was actually older than Bolingbroke (see List of Roles, 16n.). By presenting Harry as a youth, Shakespeare may already have been anticipating the rivalry with Prince Hal, Bolingbroke's *unthrifty son* (cf. 5.3.1–22).

22 **whencesoever** 'from wherever he may be'. Holinshed (3.498) says merely that together Northumberland and Harry Percy 'came vnto' Bolingbroke when the latter reached Doncaster. Shakespeare invents Harry Percy's mission from Worcester and separate joining up with Bolingbroke near

Berkeley.

23 **your uncle** Earl of Worcester

24 Young Percy's response is metrically hurried, requiring the elision of syllables in the first and third feet of his line: 'I'd thought', 'to've learned'. **of** from

26–30 Cf. 2.2.58–61.

28–9 *F relines, probably owing to the editor's consultation of the prompt-book; see Jowett & Taylor, 171. F's transposition in 29, however, appears to be a compositorial blunder. RP suggests relining: *He was / together /*. In this arrangement, the stresses in 28 would fall on *hòusehold, Kíng, Whát, rèason* and *wás*; in 29 on *so, resòlved, lást, spáke* and *togèther*.

30 **proclaimed** proclaimèd. See 2.2.58–61n.

24+ SP] *Oxf; H. Per. Q; Percie. F*   25 Why,] *Q3 (*Why?*), F;* Why *Q*   28–9 What . . . together] *as F; Q lines* resolude, / togither? /   29 last we] we last *F*   30 lordship] *(*Lo:*), Q2, F*   31 lord] *(*Lo:*), Q2, F*

To offer service to the Duke of Hereford,
And sent me over by Berkeley to discover
What power the Duke of York had levied there,
Then with directions to repair to Ravenspurgh.   35

NORTHUMBERLAND

Have you forgot the Duke of Hereford, boy?

HARRY PERCY

No, my good lord; for that is not forgot
Which ne'er I did remember. To my knowledge
I never in my life did look on him.

NORTHUMBERLAND

Then learn to know him now. This is the Duke.   40

HARRY PERCY [*to Bolingbroke*]

My gracious lord, I tender you my service,
Such as it is, being tender, raw and young,
Which elder days shall ripen and confirm
To more approved service and desert.

33–5 See 22n.

33 **over** probably monosyllablic ('o'er')

34 **power** troops

35 **repair** travel, go. Percy, on his way to rejoin Worcester at Ravenspurgh, has clearly gathered at Berkeley the information he imparts to his father; see 53–6.

36 *Hereford, boy See 21n. North-umberland chides his son for failing to greet Bolingbroke. Q3's correction of Q1–2 (adopted, in substance, by F) is merely compositorial; but the sense obviously requires the suppression of the possessive *s* in Q's 'Herefords' (see Craven[1], 53) and the treatment of *boy* as a vocative. Perhaps, as RP suggests, Q's compositor merely misread MS comma as *s* (cf. 1.4.20n.), the reverse of the error postulated at 2.2.57 (see n.).

38 **To my knowledge** so far as I know

41 **tender** respectfully offer (cf. 1.1.32n.). We might expect Harry to kneel at this point, but since the two men later shake

hands (50), in recognition, perhaps, of conspiratorial equality, the more formal gesture seems improbable (Cam[2], 106).

42 **tender** juvenile, untested (punning on *tender* in 41; cf. *Ham* 1.3.99–109, and see *Cym* 3.4.11–12)
   raw inexperienced, untrained

43–4 In view of Hotspur's impetuosity and later disloyalty as dramatized in *1H4*, these lines are replete with irony. Although young Percy intends nothing but deferential politeness, they also hint at the egotism, self-assurance and blindness to self that become features of the character in the later play.

43 **confirm** strengthen

44 **approved** approvèd; put to the proof, demonstrated
   service The repetition of *service* here (from 41) may hint at some disturbance of the text, though it in no way impairs sense. See, however, further repetitions noted in 48n. and 62n.

33 Berkeley] *(Barckly)*, F *(Barkely)*   35 directions] direction *F*   36 Hereford,] *Q3, F;* Herefords *Q*
37, 41 lord] *(Lo:)*, *Q3, F*   41 SD] *Mowat & Werstine*

BOLINGBROKE

I thank thee, gentle Percy; and be sure,   45
I count myself in nothing else so happy
As in a soul rememb'ring my good friends;
And as my fortune ripens with thy love,
It shall be still thy true love's recompense.
My heart this covenant makes; my hand thus seals it.   50
    [*Clasps Harry Percy's hand.*]

NORTHUMBERLAND [*to Harry Percy*]

How far is it to Berkeley, and what stir
Keeps good old York there with his men of war?

HARRY PERCY

There stands the castle by yon tuft of trees,
Manned with three hundred men, as I have heard.
And in it are the lords of York, Berkeley and Seymour –   55

45–50 Hotspur recalls Bolingbroke's words here with revulsion in *1H4* 1.3.251–5: 'Why, what a candy deal of courtesy / This fawning greyhound then did proffer me! / "Look when his infant fortune came to age" / And "gentle Harry Percy" and "kind cousin" – / O, the devil take such cozeners!'; the word 'candy' in the later play may distantly reflect Northumberland's *sugar* at 6 (see also 65–7). But Hotspur, who remembers Bolingbroke's expressions imprecisely, also misrepresents the situation: 'It is Northumberland who fawns, Bolingbroke being merely diplomatic with his supporters' (Cam[1], 177).

45 **gentle** of gentlemanly rank, noble (not 'mild-mannered')

47 **soul rememb'ring** heart that remembers

48 **fortune** political advantage; financial enrichment
    ripens Bolingbroke (consciously?) echoes Percy's word from 43.

48–9 **love . . . recompense** As GWW points out, Bolingbroke emphasizes

Harry's *love* whereas the lad had offered only *service* (41); and, in the later passage from *1H4* (see 45–50n.), Percy fails to remember *love*. The political irony implied by this contrast seems deliberate on Shakespeare's part; cf. *KL* 1.4.5–6, 88, where 'love' and 'service' are also linked.

49 'It (*my fortune*) will continually (*still*) be your reward for loyalty to me (*thy true love's recompense*).' Black notes 'a touch of politic vagueness in the phrasing' (159). Cf. the similar vagueness in Gertrude's promise to Rosencrantz and Guildenstern: 'such thanks / As fits a king's remembrance' (*Ham* 2.2.25–6).

50 **covenant** dissyllabic ('còv'nant')

51–2 **what . . . York** 'What commotion detains . . . York?' or possibly 'What keeps . . . York busy?'

52 **men of war** soldiers (cf. 2.1.286)

53–6 See headnote.

53 **tuft** cluster, small group

55 **Berkeley and Seymour** Thomas, Lord Berkeley (see List of Roles, 25n.)

---

50 SD] *Oxf (subst.)*   51 SD] *Mowat & Werstine (subst.)*   Berkeley] *(Barckly)*, F *(Barkely)*
55, 68 Berkeley] *(Barkly)*, F *(Barkely)*   55 Seymour] *(Seymer)*, F *(Seymor)*

None else of name and noble estimate.

^F*Enter* ROSS *and* WILLOUGHBY.^F

NORTHUMBERLAND
Here come the lords of Ross and Willoughby,
Bloody with spurring, fiery-red with haste.
BOLINGBROKE
Welcome, my lords. I wot your love pursues
A banished traitor. All my treasury   60
Is yet but unfelt thanks, which, more enriched,
Shall be your love and labour's recompense.
ROSS
Your presence makes us rich, most noble lord.
WILLOUGHBY
And far surmounts our labour to attain it.

---

and Richard Seymour, fourth Baron de
Saint Maur (d. 1401). Cf. Holinshed
(3.498): 'With the duke of Yorke were
the bishop of Norwich, the lord
Berkelie, the lord Seimour, and other.'
56 **estimate** repute (here almost 'rank')
57 **Ross and Willoughby** According to
Holinshed, they joined Bolingbroke at
Ravenspurgh, not Berkeley Castle (see
2.2.53–5n.).
58 **Bloody with spurring** spattered with
the blood of their spurred horses
59–61 Coleridge (124, 129) compared
what he took to be Bolingbroke's pre-
tended humility here to that of Marius
in Plutarch's *Lives* (9.501), 'when on
his arrival from exile in his mean robes,
the consular investments were brought
him'; when the robes were presented,
Marius said (according to Coleridge),
' "do these befit 'a banished traitor' "',
concealing . . . the implacable ambition
that haunted him'.
59 **wot** believe, know
love Cf. 48–9n. Bolingbroke repeats
the word again at 62; whereas Percy

had offered him *service* (41), Ross and
Willoughby have apparently expended
their *labour* (62) on his behalf.
60 **All my treasury** 'Bolingbroke speaks
as if he were already king' (Watt, 120);
cf. the second meaning of *fortune* at 48.
61 **unfelt** intangible (expressed only in
promises)
which referring to *treasury* and perhaps also to *thanks*
more enriched with additional
thanks and (at a later time) tangible
gifts
62 **love** love's (Abbott, 397)
recompense repeated from 49.
Bolingbroke is careful to stress that his
supporters will not lack rewards.
63 **presence** state of being present here
(perhaps with overtones of 'royal presence' as at court, which would suggest
that the lords flocking to Bolingbroke's
standard may think of him already as
their future monarch); cf. 60n.
64 **far . . . it** '(Your presence) is worth
more than our efforts to come into it.'

58 fiery-red] *Theobald;* fiery red *QF*   62 labour's] *(*labours*)*

BOLINGBROKE

    Evermore thanks – the exchequer of the poor,   65

    Which, till my infant fortune comes to years,

    Stands for my bounty.

^F*Enter* BERKELEY.^F

                But who comes here?

NORTHUMBERLAND

    It is my lord of Berkeley, as I guess.

BERKELEY

    My lord of Hereford, my message is to you –

BOLINGBROKE

    My lord, my answer is – to 'Lancaster',   70

---

65 **Evermore** always, continually
*thanks – the exchequer Although
Q's reading is possible (= ' "thank you
is", i.e. gratitude is, the exchequer'),
F's reinterpretation, putting 'thankes'
in apposition to 'th'Exchequer', is less
awkward and may derive from the theatre promptbook (see Appendix 1, pp.
526–7). Q5's anticipation of F, however, is probably independent. *Exchequer*
= 'treasury' (see 60n.).

66 **Which** referring to *thanks*
infant . . . years Child heirs were
legally prevented from taking possession of their property. Bolingbroke
speaks metaphorically, referring not to
his physical youth but to the infancy of
his changed circumstances (cf. 48n.);
years = years of discretion, maturity.
For Hotspur's derisory quotation of
this line in *1H4*, see 45–50n. Wilson
(177) cites Daniel, 3.13, which refers
to Henry IV newly crowned: 'Nor was
it time now in his tender raigne / And
infant-young-beginning gouernment,
/ To striue with bloud'; cf. also *KJ*
2.1.97: 'Outfaced infant state'.

67 **Stands for** does duty for, represents

68 **lord of Berkeley** See List of Roles,
25n. Shakespeare departs from
Holinshed by having Berkeley act as
York's messenger, thereby allowing his
confrontation with Bolingbroke to
precede the regent's; see 80.1n.

69 **Hereford** trisyllabic if the line is an
alexandrine; but dissyllabic pronunciation as 'Herford' would produce an
irregular pentameter with anapaestic
third foot ('of Hèr- | ford my mèss- |
age'); see 1.1.3n. Stevens (accepting
trisyllabic *Hereford*) conjectured that
the line is interrupted after *is* (see t.n.),
which would regularize the metre as
well as set up Bolingbroke's response;
but the emendation would be hard to
justify bibliographically.
*to you – This edition follows Irving
in supposing that Bolingbroke aggres-
sively interrupts Berkeley here.

70 ***my . . . Lancaster** 'I reply only to the
proper title, Duke of Lancaster (inherited from my father Gaunt), rather than to
my old title, Duke of Hereford, by
which you have just addressed me.'
Bolingbroke, however, was far from
frosty to Northumberland (an ally) when

---

65 thanks –] *Q5–F* (thankes,*); thanke's *Q* 67 SD] *Oxf; after* here? *F* BERKELEY] *(Barkley)*
69 SP] *(Barkly), F (Bark.)* is to you –] *Irving* (is / To you –*); is to you. *QF;* is – *(Steevens)*
70 is – to] *Var 1785;* is to *QF*

And I am come to seek that name in England;
And I must find that title in your tongue
Before I make reply to aught you say.

BERKELEY

Mistake me not, my lord, 'tis not my meaning
To rase one title of your honour out.   75
To you, my lord, I come, what lord you will,
From the most gracious regent of this land,
The Duke of York, to know what pricks you on
To take advantage of the absent time
And fright our native peace with self-borne arms.   80

^F*Enter* YORK [*with Attendants*].^F

he too used the older style at 36. Political
calculation, including the need to establish his negotiating position firmly, is
apparent: 'Bolingbroke is about to reply,
but in the middle of the sentence he
changes his mind [or merely pauses?], to
say that he will answer only in the name
of Lancaster' (Muir, 85).

75 **rase . . . out** scrape . . . away, expunge
(as with an inscription or impresa on a
building or monument; cf. 3.1.25); Q's
spelling ('race') is a variant of the same
word; 'erase' is a later variant.
title probably with a slightly mocking
quibble on 'tittle' (particle, trifling
component); cf. *LLL* 4.1.83, and
Gabriel Harvey's letter to Spenser:
'But to let Titles and Tittles passe'
(Spenser, 9.444).

76 **what . . . will** 'whatever title you may
prefer to be known by' (again with
mild sarcasm)

78 **pricks** incites (literally, 'spurs'); cf.
2.1.207.

79 **absent time** i.e. the time of (King
Richard's) absence

80 **fright . . . peace** 'disturb the peace
characteristic of our island'. Berkeley
implies that Bolingbroke is behaving

like a foreign invader, stirring up civil
war in order to divide and conquer (see
2.1.43–4n.). Cf. also 92–5.
self-borne 'carried in your own interest (or cause) rather than for defence of
the realm', perhaps quibbling on 'self-
born' = 'originating with yourself,
indigenous', and glancing at *native*
earlier in the line. The latter meaning
emphasizes Bolingbroke's fomenting
of civil war. F3's spelling ('born') may
imply the second meaning, but the two
senses were not orthographically distinct in Shakespeare's age.

80.1 *based on Holinshed (3.498): 'The
duke of Yorke therefore passing foorth
towards Wales to meet the king, at his
comming foorth of Ireland, was
receiued into the castell of Berkelie,
and there remained, till the comming
thither of the duke of Lancaster
(whom when he perceiued that he was
not able to resist) on the sundaie, after
the feast of saint Iames, which as that
yeare came about, fell vpon the fridaie,
he came foorth into the church that
stood without the castell, and there
communed with the duke of
Lancaster. With the duke of Yorke

74 SP] *(Bar.)*, F *(Bark.)*   75 rase] *(race)*, F *(raze)*   76 lord . . . lord] *(Lo: . . . Lo:)*, *Q3*, F   77
gracious regent] ghorious *Q2;* glorious *Q3–F*   80 self-borne] F; selfeborne *Q;* self-born *F3*
80.1 *with Attendants*] Capell *(subst.)*

BOLINGBROKE

I shall not need transport my words by you.
Here comes his grace in person. My noble uncle!
[*Kneels.*]

YORK

Show me thy humble heart, and not thy knee,
Whose duty is deceivable and false.

BOLINGBROKE

My gracious uncle –   85

YORK

Tut, tut!
Grace me no grace, nor uncle me no uncle.
I am no traitor's uncle, and that word 'grace'
In an ungracious mouth is but profane.
Why have those banished and forbidden legs   90

were . . . the lord Berkelie . . . and
other.' In his anxiety and confusion,
York has not waited for Berkeley to
return to him with a reasoned assess-
ment of Bolingbroke's intentions.
81 **need . . . words** need to send my message
83 Bolingbroke kneels in formal acknowledgement of the King's authority (as
represented in the person of his
regent) as well as in respectful obeisance to an elder kinsman. York seems
to doubt the sincerity of both motives.
84 **Whose duty** the reverence of which
(*Whose* refers to *knee*)
deceivable deceitful, deceptive (not
'readily deceived'); used by
Shakespeare only here and in *TN*
4.3.21
86 **Tut, tut!** probably authorial since it
appears in Q
87 For the mocking use of another character's noun or adjective as a verb, cf.
RJ 3.5.152: 'Thank me no thankings,
nor proud me no prouds', where
Capulet rebukes his daughter's disobedience in a similar vein. See also

3.4.18n., 5.2.81n., 5.3.84n., 94n.
These are mostly comic uses of what
the classical rhetoricians called *figura
etymologica* (a species of *derivatio*), in
which the speaker 'derives', or in
Shakespeare's case coins, a word from
one already used previously. Defined
in terms of functional shift, the figure
is *anthimeria*. See Introduction, p. 89.
89 **ungracious** lacking divine grace,
wicked (with much stronger force than
today); synonymous with *profane* in
the same line. The exchange exploits
various connotations of *grace*:
Bolingbroke addresses York as *gracious*
(benevolent, kind), which York picks
up in the double sense of the courtesy
due a duke ('your grace'; cf. 115) and
grace from God (being 'in a state of
grace'), the latter implying both truth-
fulness and submission to duly consti-
tuted authority. Then York says that
his nephew's words are *ungracious*
because they violate normal standards
of honesty, virtue and respect. Falstaff
plays comically with the same word in
1H4 1.2.17–21.

82 SD] *Rowe (subst.)*   86–7] *as Rolfe; one line QF*   87 no uncle] *om. F*   90 those] these *F*

Dared once to touch a dust of England's ground?
But then, more why – why have they dared to march
So many miles upon her peaceful bosom,
Frighting her pale-faced villages with war
And ostentation of despised arms?   95
Com'st thou because the anointed King is hence?
Why, foolish boy, the King is left behind,
And in my loyal bosom lies his power.
Were I but now ᶠtheᶠ lord of such hot youth
As when brave Gaunt, thy father, and myself   100
Rescued the Black Prince, that young Mars of men,
From forth the ranks of many thousand French,
O, then how quickly should this arm of mine,
Now prisoner to the palsy, chastise thee
And minister correction to thy fault!   105

BOLINGBROKE
My gracious uncle, let me know my fault.

---

91 **a dust** a grain of dust (cf. *KJ* 4.1.92)
92 **more why** additional questions follow
93–4 **peaceful . . . Frighting** an echo of Berkeley's language at 80
94 **pale-faced villages** whole villages of people with faces made pale by fear
95 **ostentation** display
   despised despisèd; despicable (because borne in support of a traitor; cf. 109)
96–7 **anointed . . . behind** See 1.2.38n. York alludes to the doctrine of 'the king's two bodies'; the monarch's mortal body may be absent, but his authoritative and political body is present in York, his regent (98).
99–102 The youthful valour of York and Gaunt in rescuing the Black Prince (their brother and Richard's father) is fictitious; the chronicles record no instance in which York fought beside the Black Prince in France. York's

words recall his earlier encomium of the Black Prince at 2.1.172–83 (see n.) in which Richard was contrasted with his father. See LN.
99 *****now the lord** F's addition of 'the' to Q's line improves the metre and may reflect the authority of the prompt-book (see Appendix 1, p. 526).
101 **Mars** Cf. 2.1.41n.
104 **palsy** paralysis (here perhaps meaning no more than old-age weakness); cf. the description of Nestor 'with a palsy fumbling on his gorget' (*TC* 1.3.174). Some historians have claimed, however, that York actually was paralytic (see Black, 165).
   chastise chàstise
105 **minister** administer
106 **My gracious uncle** Bolingbroke repeats the tactful address he had used at 85 (cf. 82 and 89n.).

---

92 then, more] *(then more);* more than *Q2;* more then *Q5–F*   94 pale-faced] *F;* pale fac't *Q*
101 Black Prince] *F;* blacke prince *Q*   men,] *Q3, F;* men. *Q*

On what condition stands it and wherein?

YORK

Even in condition of the worst degree,
In gross rebellion and detested treason.
Thou art a banished man, and here art come,   110
Before the expiration of thy time,
In braving arms against thy sovereign.

BOLINGBROKE

As I was banished, I was banished Hereford;
But as I come, I come for Lancaster.
And noble uncle, I beseech your grace,   115
Look on my wrongs with an indifferent eye.
You are my father, for methinks in you
I see old Gaunt alive. O then, my father,
Will you permit that I shall stand condemned
A wandering vagabond, my rights and royalties   120
Plucked from my arms perforce and given away
To upstart unthrifts? Wherefore was I born?

---

107 'What provision of the law have I infringed and in what specific way?' 'Condition' is a legal term meaning 'provision of a contract' or 'point of law'; but 'condition' also meant simply 'personal quality' (cf. *Oth* 2.1.250), in which case the sense would be, 'From what aspect of my character does the fault arise and in what does it consist?'
108 'even in a circumstance of the worst kind' (namely, rebellion); York plays on Bolingbroke's *condition*.
109 **detested** detestable (cf. 2.1.268n.)
112, 143 **braving** defiant, flaunting (adjectival). 'To brave' meant 'to display threateningly, to make an outward show of bravery'.
114 **for Lancaster** 'as a claimant for the title and rights of Duke of Lancaster'. According to Holinshed (3.498), Bolingbroke swore at Doncaster 'vnto those lords, that he would demand no

more, but the lands that were to him descended by inheritance from his father, and in right of his wife [Mary de Bohun, co-heiress of Hereford]'. See also 148–9n.
116 **indifferent** impartial
120 **A** as a
    royalties See 2.1.190n.
121 **arms** coat of arms; perhaps punning on 'arms' (= limbs)
    perforce forcibly, without my consent
122 **unthrifts** profligates, spendthrifts (undoubtedly referring to favourites such as Bushy, Bagot, Green and Wiltshire); Hall reports that Richard 'defrauded his [Gaunt's] heire of his laufull inheritaunce, reccauying the rentes and reuenues of all his patrimony, & geuyng to other that whiche was not his, distributed the dukes landes to his paresites and flatterering foloers' (fol. iiii). Both *Woodstock* and *Mirror* stress

---

112 thy] *QF;* my *Q2*   117 for] *QF;* or *Q3*   118 my] *QF; om. Q2–5*

If that my cousin king be King in England,
It must be granted I am Duke of Lancaster.
You have a son, Aumerle, my noble cousin.   125
Had you first died and he been thus trod down,
He should have found his uncle Gaunt a father
To rouse his wrongs and chase them to the bay.
I am denied to sue my livery here,
And yet my letters patents give me leave.   130
My father's goods are all distrained and sold,
And these, and all, are all amiss employed.
What would you have me do? I am a subject,

the idea of Richard's flatterers profiting from the displacement of the established nobility and from wealth extorted from the gentry. Ure (85) suggests that Hayward may echo Shakespeare here: 'great summes of money are pulled and pilled from good subiects to be throwne away amongst vnprofitable vnthrifts' (63). Bolingbroke uses the cognate word, *unthrifty*, to characterize his own son (5.3.1), thus perhaps subliminally linking him with his political enemies; cf. *1H4* 3.2.94–5 where Henry IV rebukes Prince Hal: 'As thou art to this hour was Richard then / When I from France set foot at Ravenspurgh'.
Wherefore why
123–4 Bolingbroke restates York's argument at 2.1.195–9, invoking the principle of 'fair sequence and succession' – a principle that must apply as infrangibly to a subject as to a king.
123 **cousin king** king who is also a cousin
125–8 Bolingbroke's clever appeal to York's sympathy by invoking the hypothetical parallel of Aumerle is a masterful stroke of persuasive psychology designed to move his uncle beyond being merely *indifferent* (116) to genuine partisanship. His tactic anticipates 163 (see n.).
126 **first died** before your brother Gaunt
   thus like me
128 **rouse** expose (literally, 'startle from

the lair'; a term from hunting); *wrongs* (wrongdoers?) are figuratively conceived of as the quarry.
bay last stand of a trapped animal (another hunting term, derived from the baying of hounds when the quarry is cornered)
129 **denied . . . livery** 'refused the right to claim my ancestral properties held in tenancy from the crown' (legal terminology). See 2.1.202–4n.
130 **letters patents** See 1.3.209–12n. and 2.1.202–4n.
131 **distrained** seized by the crown, confiscated
132 **and all** and everything else
   all amiss employed 'unjustly misused' (apparently another reference to the squandering of Bolingbroke's inheritance on unworthy parasites); cf. 122n.
133–4 ***subject . . . law** This edn follows Q4's punctuation (in substance), placing a stop after *law*; Q puts the stop after *subject*, making it necessary to interpret *And* in 134 as 'An' (if; see 4.1.50n.). Q3, the copy for F, is ambiguous since it uses a comma in both places, although F (like Q4) printed the second comma as a stop. Since both readings make logical sense, editors are divided. The more assertive effect of Q4/F seems dramatically preferable.

123 in] of *Q2–F*   125 cousin] Kinsman *F*   133–4 subject, . . . law.] *Q4 (*law;*)*, *F (*Law:*)*; subiect; . . . law, *Q*

And I challenge law. Attorneys are denied me,
And therefore personally I lay my claim   135
To my inheritance of free descent.

NORTHUMBERLAND

The noble Duke hath been too much abused.

ROSS

It stands your grace upon to do him right.

WILLOUGHBY

Base men by his endowments are made great.

YORK

My lords of England, let me tell you this: 140
I have had feeling of my cousin's wrongs
And laboured all I could to do him right.
But in this kind to come – in braving arms
Be his own carver, and cut out his way
To find out right with wrong – it may not be.   145

---

134 Ure (85–6) suggests that the extra-metrical *And* at the beginning of this line 'may be intrusive, caught by the compositor from the *And* which opens the line immediately following' (see Craven[2], 189–90). The connective, however, is very natural in context and does not noticeably disturb the flow of the speech. Moreover, 'I am a subject; I challenge law' is unsatisfactorily abrupt.

    challenge law demand my legal rights. Gurr (110) cites Daniel (1.91), where Bolingbroke reponds to the plea of a grieving Genius of England in a dream not to invade his country: 'I am thy Champion and I seeke my right'; the Genius interprets his decision as 'ambitious' self-deception.

    Attorneys attorneys-general (the legal representatives who would petition the crown on Bolingbroke's behalf); see 2.1.202–4n.

136 **of free descent** through legitimate succession (*free* from impediments or flaws); see 114n.

137 **abused** ill-used, unfairly treated

138 **stands . . . upon** is incumbent upon, is the duty of

139 **Base** of low birth; morally inferior. In *E2*, 1.1.100, the Earl of Lancaster scorns Gaveston as 'base and obscure'.
    endowments properties and revenues

141 **cousin's** nephew's (cf. 1.2.46n.)

142 **laboured . . . could** See 2.1.189–208.

143 **kind** fashion, manner

144 **Be . . . carver** take the law into his own hands, i.e. greedily help himself to food which he should properly wait to be served to him (literally, 'carve his own portion of meat at table'; cf. *Ham* 1.3.19–20). The phrase has proverbial associations (Dent, C110). Here the metaphor carries overtones of using a sword as well as a table knife (cf. 'cut out his way', which suggests battle). Cf. also *Mac* 1.2.19, *Oth* 2.3.173.

145 **find . . . wrong** win his rights by means of wrongful actions
    may not be cannot be allowed

---

134 I] *om. F*   145 wrong –] *Kittredge;* Wrongs, *F;* wrong *Q*

And you that do abet him in this kind
Cherish rebellion and are rebels all.

NORTHUMBERLAND

The noble Duke hath sworn his coming is
But for his own; and for the right of that
We all have strongly sworn to give him aid.   150
And let him never see joy that breaks that oath!

YORK

Well, well, I see the issue of these arms.
I cannot mend it, I must needs confess,
Because my power is weak and all ill-left;
But if I could, by Him that gave me life,   155
I would attach you all and make you stoop
Unto the sovereign mercy of the King.
But since I cannot, be it known unto you
I do remain as neuter. So fare you well –
Unless you please to enter in the castle   160

---

147 **Cherish** promote, nurture
148–9 **The . . . own** See 114n.; cf. also *mine own* at 3.3.196 and Daniel's 'Sought but his owne, and did no more expect' (1.94). In *1H4* 4.3.60–1, Hotspur indignantly recalls how Bolingbroke did 'swear and vow to God / He came but to be Duke of Lancaster'.
149 **right** legal right; moral rightness
150 **strongly** Cf. similar use at 2.2.48.
151 **never** probably a monosyllable ('ne'er'); see t.n.
152 **issue . . . arms** result of this resort to military force
154 Holinshed (3.498) gives a different reason for York's failure to resist: York 'assembled a puissant power of men of armes and archers . . . but all was in vaine, for there was not a man that willinglie would thrust out one arrow against the duke of Lancaster, or his partakers, or in anie wise offend him or his freends'.
power army

ill-left left in disarray (or, possibly, 'ill provided')
156 **attach** arrest
stoop kneel (for mercy)
157 **sovereign** probably dissyllabic ('sòv'reign')
158 **unto you** Q2's emendation ('to you'), followed by F and some modern editors (see t.n.), somewhat smoothes the metre but lacks external authority. Q's compositor may have misread his copy, influenced in his haste by 'Vnto' in 157 (see Craven[3], 49–50 and Appendix 1, pp. 537–8, 537 n. 1). However, as RP argues, Q serves the sense better as the final stress falls on *untò* rather than on *you*.
159 **as neuter** neutral (perhaps with the added connotation – ironically, of course – of 'impotent' or 'sterile'); cf. 'Nor friends, nor foes' (170), also 2.2.111n. Used only here in Shakespeare.
160–1 York's offer of hospitality, although humane, is further evidence of

---

151 never] ne're *Q3;* neu'r *F*   154 ill-left] *Hanmer;* ill left *QF*   158 known] *(*knowen*), F*   unto] to *Q2–F*

And there repose you for this night.

BOLINGBROKE

An offer, uncle, that we will accept;
But we must win your grace to go with us
To Bristol Castle, which, they say, is held
By Bushy, Bagot and their complices,   165
The caterpillars of the commonwealth,
Which I have sworn to weed and pluck away.

YORK

It may be I will go with you; but yet I'll pause,
For I am loath to break our country's laws.
Nor friends nor foes to me welcome you are.   170
Things past redress are now with me past care.   *Exeunt.*

his malleability and failure to resist;
Bolingbroke's supposed enemy has
suddenly become his host (cf. 170–1).

163 **win** persuade. Bolingbroke 'does not
hesitate to push York further once he
has begun to weaken' (Cam², 111); cf.
125–8n. Herford (174) comments,
'Under a show of deference York is
virtually arrested.'

165 **Bagot** Bagot has earlier spoken of his
intention to join Richard in Ireland;
see 2.2.134–40n.
complices accomplices. These include the Earl of Wiltshire (see
2.1.215n., 2.2.134–5).

166 **caterpillars** parasites, rapacious
hangers-on (a much-used epithet in
the sixteenth and seventeenth centuries for different categories of persons considered to be dangerous to
social, governmental and economic
health). Shakespeare had already used
the term in political contexts in *2H6*
(3.1.90, 4.4.37), but he may also have
remembered *Woodstock*; see LN.

167 **weed and pluck** *weed* = remove, get
rid of; cf. 3.4.50–2, where the Gardener
speaks of Wiltshire, Bushy and Green as
weeds which Bolingbroke has 'plucked
up root and all'. In *Traison*, after the con-

spirators associated with the Abbot of
Westminster have been punished, Henry
IV addresses the prelacy in London: 'By
St. George! 'twere a fine sight to see us
all here assembled, provided we were all
true and faithful . . . for certainly there
are some traitors amongst us; but I vow
to God that I will gather up the weeds
and will clear my garden of them, and
will sow good plants, until my garden
shall be clean within my ditches and
walls, unless some of you repent'
(92–3/247). See also 3.4 headnote.

168–71 Couplets are used conventionally
here as a formal means of concluding
the scene. They also retard York's exit
lines and give effect to his divided allegiance – the *pause* (168) to which he
refers. *Are* and *care* (170–1) rhyme.

168 an alexandrine
pause put off deciding. But see
2.2.111n. and 2.3 headnote.

170 'I welcome you neutrally – as neither
friends nor foes.' RP suggests that *welcome* may perhaps be stressed *welcòme*.

171 **past redress . . . past care** Cf. the
proverb, 'Past cure, past care' (Dent,
C921); also *LLL* 5.2.28, *Mac*
3.2.11–12.

164 Bristol] *(Bristow)*   170 foes] foes, *Q2–F*

[2.4]   *Enter* Earl of SALISBURY *and a Welsh* Captain.

CAPTAIN

My lord of Salisbury, we have stayed ten days
And hardly kept our countrymen together,
And yet we hear no tidings from the King.
Therefore we will disperse ourselves. Farewell.

2.4 This brief scene, set somewhere in Wales, marks an interval between Bolingbroke's stated intention to advance to Bristol Castle (2.3.163–4) and his arrival there (3.1). The basis is Holinshed (3.499), who writes that when King Richard in Ireland, prevented by bad weather, learned belatedly of Bolingbroke's landing, 'he meant foorthwith to haue returned ouer into England, to make resistance against the duke: but through persuasion of the duke of Aumarle (as was thought) he staied, till he might haue all his ships, and other prouision, fullie readie for his passage. In the meane time, he sent the earle of Salisburie ouer into England, to gather a power togither, by helpe of the kings freends in Wales, and Cheshire, with all speed possible, that they might be readie to assist him against the duke, vpon his arriuall, for he meant himselfe to follow the earle, within six daies after. The earle passing ouer into Wales, landed at Conwaie, and sent foorth letters to the kings freends, both in Wales and Cheshire, to leauie their people, & to come with all speed to assist the K. whose request, with great desire, & very willing minds they fulfilled, hoping to haue found the king himselfe at Conwaie, insomuch that within foure daies space, there were to the number of fortie thousand men assembled, readie to march with the king against his enimies, if he had beene there himselfe in person. But when they missed the king, there was a brute [rumour] spred amongst them, that the king was suerlie dead, which wrought such an impression, and euill disposition in the minds of the Welshmen and others, that for anie persuasion which the earle of Salisburie might vse, they would not go foorth with him, till they saw the king: onelie they were contented to staie foureteene daies to see if he should come or not; but when he came not within that tearme, they would no longer abide, but scaled [flaked off] & departed awaie; wheras if the king had come before their breaking vp, no doubt, but they would haue put the duke of Hereford in aduenture of a field: so that the kings lingering of time before his comming ouer, gaue opportunitie to the duke to bring things to passe as he could haue wished, and tooke from the king all occasion to recouer afterwards anie forces sufficient to resist him.' For the view that this scene is out of proper sequence, see 3.2LN.

0.1 **Captain** See List of Roles, 31n.

1   **Salisbury** elided to two syllables, the first of which is stressed; see List of Roles, 20n.

     stayed waited

     ten days Cf. Holinshed's 'foureteene daies' (see headnote). Shakespeare often rounds out numbers in the history

---

2.4] F *(Scoena Quarta.)*   0.1] *Enter Salisbury, and a Captaine.* F   1, 7 SP] F *(Capt.);* Welch. Q

SALISBURY

Stay yet another day, thou trusty Welshman.   5

The King reposeth all his confidence in thee.

CAPTAIN

'Tis thought the King is dead. We will not stay.

The bay trees in our country are all withered,

And meteors fright the fixed stars of heaven;

---

plays (cf. 1.3.159n.).

2 **hardly** with difficulty

3 **yet** as yet, still

6 **all his confidence** Holinshed (3.499) reports that Richard 'had . . . no small affiance [trust] in the Welshmen, and Cheshire men'. The line is an alexandrine.

8 Shakespeare imports this detail from an earlier passage in Holinshed (3.496) where the chronicler is describing England, not Wales, at a time before Richard's departure for Ireland: 'In this yeare [1399] in a manner throughout all the realme of England, old baie trees withered, and afterwards, contrarie to all mens thinking, grew greene againe, a strange sight, and supposed to import some vnknowne euent.' The re-greening of the trees is omitted – a touch of hope at odds with the gloominess intended (cf. 3.4.101), although, as Mahood (*Parts*, 78–9) notes, the regenerative theme reasserts itself in the garden scene when the Gardener resolves to plant 'a bank of rue' (3.4.105) in memory of the Queen. Bay trees and evergreens in general were often taken to symbolize the soul's immortality; the bay (or laurel) was also associated with victory, which in the present context makes its withering a particularly dolorous sign. Since this sentence is missing from the first edn of Holinshed (1577), we can be sure that the dramatist used the

second (1587).

9–15 The Captain's other omens may derive in part from Daniel, 1.114–17 (see LN), but such 'unnatural' signs as bloody moons, meteors, shooting stars and the like are the common currency of superstition; the similarities to Daniel may therefore be coincidental. Cf. also *Woodstock*, 4.2.66–70, where 'flakes of fire' which 'run tilting through the sky' are taken as 'dim ostents to some great tragedy', i.e. Anne a' Beame's impending death. It is worth noting that the omens in *JC* (1.3, 2.2) and *Ham* (1.1) are quite different. Hayward, in a passage that includes the withered laurels and may reflect knowledge of the present scene, elaborates upon additional omens that were interpreted to 'presage the reuolt of the people' (51).

9 **meteors** fireballs, comets, shooting stars (seen only intermittently and thought to be portentous); cf. *KJ* 3.4.157: 'meteors, prodigies, and signs'. Ptolemaic astronomy held that ordinary stars (as distinguished from planets and meteors) were 'fixed' within the crystalline sphere that revolved around the earth; the Captain imagines *meteors*, which are unfixed, as a threat to *the fixed stars* which symbolize the established order of the heavens and of the universe in general.

fixed fixèd

8 are all] all are *Q2–F*

307

The pale-faced moon looks bloody on the earth,   10
And lean-looked prophets whisper fearful change;
Rich men look sad, and ruffians dance and leap,
The one in fear to lose what they enjoy,
The other to enjoy by rage and war.
These signs forerun the death or fall of kings.   15
Farewell. Our countrymen are gone and fled,
As well assured Richard their king is dead.   ^F*Exit.*^F

SALISBURY

Ah, Richard, with the eyes of heavy mind
I see thy glory like a shooting star
Fall to the base earth from the firmament.   20
Thy sun sets weeping in the lowly west,
Witnessing storms to come, woe and unrest.
Thy friends are fled to wait upon thy foes,
And crossly to thy good all fortune goes.   ^F*Exit.*^F

---

10 **looks bloody on** looks bloodily on (has a bloody appearance); perhaps also 'influences in a bloody way'

11 **lean-looked** lean-faced, emaciated (perhaps because of anxiety), ascetic **prophets** soothsayers, prognosticators. As Ure (88–9) points out, the prophets in Daniel (1.110) – his 'graue religious fathers' – resemble biblical figures, i.e. 'divines and divine spokesmen', rather than Shakespeare's more secular foretellers of disaster. Ure also mentions prophecies concerning Richard's fall in the French materials that Shakespeare could perhaps have known: Froissart, 6.341; *Traïson*, 62/213; and Créton, 169/374. None of these latter, however, is at all close to the prophecies of the Welsh Captain.

13 **The one** the *Rich men*, 12
enjoy possess

14 **rage** rioting, tumult

18 **heavy** sad, grieved

19–21 The *shooting star* falling to earth (see 9–15n.) and the setting sun are obvious metaphors of tragic fall. See LN, 3.3.62–7LN and Mahood, *Parts*, 71–2.

20 **base earth** The earth is *base* (low in position) as compared with the *firmament*. Note the subtle anticipation of Richard's descent into the *base court* (see 3.3.176 and n.).

22 **Witnessing** betokening, portending

23 **wait upon** offer allegiance to

24 **crossly** adversely

15 or fall] *om. Q2–F*   18 the eyes] eies *Q2–F*

[**3.1**]   *Enter* ^FBOLINGBROKE,^F Duke of Hereford, YORK, NORTHUMBERLAND, ^FROSS, [HARRY] PERCY, WILLOUGHBY, *with*^F BUSHY *and* GREEN [*as*] *prisoners*[*, and Soldiers*].

BOLINGBROKE

Bring forth these men.   [*Bushy and Green stand forth.*]
Bushy and Green, I will not vex your souls –

3.1 By dramatizing the capture and summary execution of Bushy and Green, two of Richard's closest friends, Shakespeare makes it unmistakable that Bolingbroke, despite Northumberland's earlier assurances (2.3.148–9), is now in total control of England and has in fact already assumed the powers, if not the ceremonial appurtenances, of kingship. For the first time we see Bolingbroke with a show of legality ruthlessly eliminating his enemies and even charging them with crimes for which there is no support, either historically or in terms of actions elsewhere revealed in the play. York's silent presence is theatrically powerful, probably indicating that the Duke has already privately acquiesced, albeit with painful reluctance, to Bolingbroke's ascendancy (cf. 2.2.111n., 2.3 headnote and 2.3.159n.); Saul writes that 'York's presence at the executions could only have been seen as publicly committing him to Duke Henry's cause' (411). The scene at Bristol Castle thus functions as a significant peripety in the dramatic trajectory of Bolingbroke – a perceptible shifting of sympathy away from a figure who, at the surface level at least, had earlier been characterized more as a victim of injustice than its agent. The basis of the scene is almost wholly Holinshed (3.498): Bolingbroke and his army marched 'towards

Bristow, where (at their comming) they shewed themselues before the towne & castell, being an huge multitude of people. There were inclosed within the castell, the lord William Scroope earle of Wiltshire and treasuror of England, Sir Henrie Greene, and sir Iohn Bushie knights, who prepared to make resistance: but when it would not preuaile, they were taken and brought foorth bound as prisoners into the campe, before the duke of Lancaster. On the morow next insuing, they were arraigned before the constable and marshall, and found giltie of treason, for misgouerning the king and realme, and foorthwith had their heads smit off.' Bolingbroke's solicitude for the Queen, his account of how Bushy and Green have wronged him personally, and his specific responsibility for their deaths as self-appointed judge have no known source other than the dramatist's imagination.

0.2 *F's addition of Ross, Percy and Willoughby to the other adherents of Bolingbroke in this scene strengthens the impression of the usurper's might, although the three have no dramatic function apart from swelling his numbers. The additions probably derive from the promptbook and reflect the original staging.

1 This curt opening, an anomalous two-foot line, appropriately sets the tone of dictatorial dispatch.

3.1] F *(Actus Tertius. Scena Prima.)*   0.1–3] *Enter Bullingbrooke, Yorke, Northumberland, Rosse, Percie, Willoughby, with Bushie and Greene Prisoners.* F   0.3 *and Soldiers*] Capell *(subst.)*   1+ SP] *(Bul[l].)*
1 SD] *Collier*

Since presently your souls must part your bodies –
With too much urging your pernicious lives,
For 'twere no charity; yet to wash your blood   5
From off my hands, here in the view of men
I will unfold some causes of your deaths:
You have misled a prince, a royal king,
A happy gentleman in blood and lineaments,
By you unhappied and disfigured clean.   10
You have in manner with your sinful hours
Made a divorce betwixt his queen and him,
Broke the possession of a royal bed

---

3   **presently** immediately
    part depart, be separated from
4   **urging** dwelling on, emphasizing, going into detail about (in order to justify your condemnation)
5   **charity** kindness (probably elided to a dissyllable: 'char'ty')
5–6 **wash . . . men** an interesting anticipation of Bolingbroke's final speech in which he vows to make a religious pilgrimage 'To wash this blood off from my guilty hand' (5.6.50), i.e. to do penance for Richard's death. Both speeches glance at the biblical story of the Passion in which Pontius Pilate washed his hands before releasing Christ to be crucified (Matthew, 27.24); cf. also Richard's characterization of his deposers as being latter-day Pilates who 'wash your hands' (see 4.1.239–42n.). Bolingbroke wishes to demonstrate publicly ('in the view of men') that the executions are required for the sake of justice rather than acts of vengeance. GWW notes that 'two parallel systems of scriptural allusion' run through the play – 'the Eden complex and the Passion' (see Introduction, pp. 36, 75–8, 156–7).
7   **unfold** disclose, explain
    causes of legal reasons for
9   a gentleman fortunate in his birth and natural gifts (*lineaments* probably includes abilities as well as handsome personal appearance). Holinshed (3.507) notes that Richard 'was seemelie of shape and fauor, & of nature good inough, if the wickednesse & naughtie demeanor of such as were about him had not altered it'.
10 **unhappied** made unfortunate; see 2.1.16n.
    disfigured clean marred totally (utterly ruined in reputation)
11–15 This implication of homosexual attachments between Richard and his flatterers – attachments that have brought grief to the Queen and destroyed her marriage – has no historical validity and disturbingly contradicts the impression of devoted fidelity between the King and his consort that the play otherwise builds up. *R2* dramatizes no hostility on the Queen's part towards Richard's friends. See LN.
11 **in manner** so to speak, as it were (literally, 'in a manner' (of speaking), modifying *Made a divorce*)
12 **divorce** estrangement, breach, separation (metaphorical only)
13 violated the marriage covenant (involving rights shared equally by husband and wife)

7 deaths] *QF;* death *Q2*

And stained the beauty of a fair queen's cheeks
With tears drawn from her eyes by your foul wrongs.   15
Myself, a prince by fortune of my birth,
Near to the King in blood, and near in love
Till you did make him misinterpret me,
Have stooped my neck under your injuries
And sighed my English breath in foreign clouds,   20
Eating the bitter bread of banishment,
Whilst you have fed upon my signories,
Disparked my parks and felled my forest woods,

16–17 **prince . . . blood** Bolingbroke is careful to underline a certain likeness between himself and the King by repeating ideas used earlier to describe Richard: as Richard is 'a prince, a royal king' (8), so Bolingbroke also is *a prince*; as Richard is *happy . . . in blood* (9), so Bolingbroke is royal, 'by fortune of my birth' and 'Near to the King in blood'.

17–27 The notion that Bushy and Green were specifically responsible for Bolingbroke's banishment and the confiscation of his properties is fictitious; it is also inconsistent with what we have already seen and heard onstage. Bolingbroke was exiled on the advice of Richard's *council* (1.3.124) including Gaunt (1.3.233–4); and the stated motive for the King's appropriation of Bolingbroke's property was to finance the campaign in Ireland (1.4.61–2, 2.1.155–62, 209–10). The play undoubtedly implies that Bushy and Green have been guilty of giving evil and self-interested advice and of prejudicing Richard against his cousin (cf. 1.4.12–19, where Aumerle's attitude seems to typify that of all the favourites), but the impression of scapegoating on Bolingbroke's part in this speech is difficult to overlook.

18 **misinterpret me** misconstrue my conduct (see 17–27n.)

19 **stooped . . . injuries** 'submitted unresistingly to your harms' (cf. 2.3.156). Possibly Bolingbroke alludes to the Roman manner of subjugating enemy captives by making them pass under the yoke: in *Cym* 3.3.91–2 this extends to a mythical Britain culturally influenced by Rome: 'Thus mine enemy fell, / And thus I set my foot on's neck'.

20 **foreign clouds** probably referring to Bolingbroke's *breath*, exhaled (*sighed*) into the *clouds* of foreign climes and so augmenting them; cf. *RJ* 1.1.133: 'Adding to clouds more clouds with his deep sighs'; but the phrase could mean simply 'the atmosphere (or air) of places abroad'.

21 biblical overtones (cf. 1 Kings, 22.27: 'bread of affliction'; Isaiah, 30.20: 'bread of aduersitie', Geneva Bible); the alliteration lends additional force. Cf. also Holinshed's 'cup of affliction' (see 5.2.37n.). *The Lovers' Progress* (1623?), 5.1.81, echoes the line verbatim (Fletcher, 10.512).

22 **signories** manors, estates; cf. 4.1.90.

23 **Disparked my parks** 'converted my parklands to uses other than keeping game and hunting'. Less aristocratic uses such as timbering and farming seem to be implied as well as destruction of the walls or fences that traditionally enclose game parks.

15 by] with *Q2–F*   18 you] *QF*; they *Q2*   20 sighed] *(*sigh't*), F*   22 Whilst] While *Q2–F*

From my own windows torn my household coat,
Rased out my imprese, leaving me no sign   25
Save men's opinions and my living blood
To show the world I am a gentleman.
This and much more, much more than twice all this,
Condemns you to the death. See them delivered over
To execution and the hand of death.   30

BUSHY
More welcome is the stroke of death to me
Than Bolingbroke to England. Lords, farewell.

GREEN
My comfort is that heaven will take our souls
And plague injustice with the pains of hell.

---

24 'destroyed the windows in which my family coat of arms was emblazoned in stained or painted glass' (*torn* = broken). Cf. *2H6* 4.1.42: 'my arms torn and defac'd'; defacing family arms was thought to be especially heinous and insulting.

25 **Rased . . . imprese** expunged my family emblem (usually including a small allegorical picture and motto); cf. 2.3.75n. Metre here requires dissyllabic pronunciation of *imprese* (though Italian *imprese* (plural) has three syllables); cf. the spellings in Q and F (see t.n.). *OED* lists '*impresa*' (Italian singular) and '*imprese*' (Italian plural) as singular forms in English (plural 'impresas'). Men of rank adopted such emblems 'in addition to their regular coat of arms' and Bolingbroke 'used several', including a silver swan, an antelope, a red rose and a fox's brush (Chambers, 120). His motto was 'Souveraine'. Shakespeare himself devised an *impresa* (a shield with an emblem and motto), painted by Richard Burbage, for Francis, Earl of Rutland, to display on 24 March 1613

at the annual Accession Day tilt; see Chambers, *WS* (1.87; 2.153). Cf. also the shields or *imprese* of the knights in *Per* 2.2.

26 **my living blood** myself, my physical life (as long as it lasts)

27 **gentleman** nobleman

29 **the death** the death penalty (legal phraseology)
over probably monosyllabic ('o'er'); the line seems to be an alexandrine, but 'Condèmns | you to the dèath' could be the irregular start of a pentameter.

30 **hand of death** virtually a stock phrase in Shakespeare (cf. *1H4* 4.1.136, 5.4.84)

31–4 H. Craig (129) compares the 'plucky deaths' of Edward's favourites, Gaveston, Baldock and Spencer Junior, in *E2*, 2.5.44–6, 2.6.15, 3.1.118–20, 4.7.105–12.

32 **Lords, farewell.** *TxC* (310) suggests unconvincingly that F's omission (see t.n.) represents 'an authorial revision' undertaken to avoid the 'jingle' of the rhyme of *farewell* with *hell* two lines later.

33 **heaven** monosyllabic

24 my own] mine own *Q3–F*   25 Rased] *(Rac't)*, F *(Raz'd)*   imprese] *Q6;* impreese *Q;* Impresse *F*   32 Lords, farewell] *om. F*

BOLINGBROKE

My Lord Northumberland, see them dispatched.   35

[*Exeunt Northumberland and Soldiers
with Bushy and Green.*]

[*to York*] Uncle, you say the Queen is at your house.
For God's sake, fairly let her be entreated.
Tell her I send to her my kind commends;
Take special care my greetings be delivered.

YORK

A gentleman of mine I have dispatched   40
With letters of your love to her at large.

BOLINGBROKE

Thanks, gentle uncle. Come, lords, away,
To fight with Glendower and his complices.
A while to work, and after holiday.   *Exeunt.*

---

35 **dispatched** taken away; beheaded (literally, 'sent out of this world')

36 **at your house** This is the first mention of the Queen's residing at one of York's houses outside London, possibly Langley (see List of Roles, 4n.). It is Shakespeare's invention; Froissart reports that the Queen remained at Windsor after Richard left for Ireland (6.346) and that later, after he was taken, she resided 'at Ledes [Leeds] in Kent' (6.370); later still she lived at 'Haveringe of the Bowre' (6.388).

37 **entreated** treated

38 **commends** regards, compliments (cf. 3.3.126). The 'references to Isabel are perhaps partly in preparation for' 3.4 and 'partly to soften the rigour of the scene and Bolingbroke's behaviour' (Ard², 93).

40–1 It is not entirely clear whether the *letters* (= a letter?; cf. 3.4.69–70n.) have been written by Bolingbroke or

by York himself; but in any case Bolingbroke controls their content. Bolingbroke, aware of York's fondness for the Queen, has apparently acted to dispel any possibility of politically damaging communication between them by speaking on York's behalf.

41 **at large** in full, at length

42 a nine-syllable line, requiring a pause (or beat) at the caesura after *uncle*. Pope's emendation is unnecessary.

43 **Glendower** dissyllabic ('Glendow'r'; cf. Q's spelling). Although Holinshed reports that in 1400 Henry IV launched a campaign against Owen Glendower 'and his vnrulie complices' (3.519), nothing of the sort actually happened at the time represented by this scene. See LN.
complices Cf. 2.3.165n. Shakespeare probably took the word from Holinshed (see previous n.).

44 **after** afterwards

---

35 SD] *Capell (subst.)*   36 SD] *Mowat & Werstine*   37 God's] Heauens *F*   42 lords] my lords *Pope*   43 Glendower] *(Glendor), F (Glendoure)*

[3.2] ^F*Drums. Flourish and Colours.*^F *Enter* KING ^FRICHARD,^F
AUMERLE, [Bishop of] CARLISLE *and Soldiers.*

3.2 One crowded page of Holinshed (3.499) supplies the basic material for this important scene in which Richard's character is extensively developed. This includes the landing of the King's party from Ireland at 'Barclowlie' (Barkloughly) Castle in Wales; his dismay at the extent of Bolingbroke's military and political success; his learning that his favourites have been beheaded; his falling into despair; his meeting with Salisbury (whom he had dispatched from Ireland to prepare the way for his arrival home); his discovery that the Welsh army have abandoned him; and his licensing of his own soldiers to disperse. According to the chronicle (3.499–500), Richard (with Sir Stephen Scroop and others) left Barkloughly for Conway Castle where he conferred with Salisbury and from which place he was decoyed by Northumberland on a false promise of safe conduct, captured by Bolingbroke's forces, and then conducted forcibly to Flint Castle. Omitting the Conway episode altogether, Shakespeare condenses events by setting the scene on the Welsh coast near Barkloughly and having the gloomy news delivered in waves of mounting catastrophe by Salisbury and Scroop, thus preparing for a climactic confrontation between Richard and Bolingbroke at Flint for the first time since the latter's exile – to be dramatized in the following scene (see 209n.).

In Holinshed (3.499) Aumerle, Exeter, Surrey, Carlisle with other nobles and bishops 'landed neere the castell of Barclowlie in Wales, . . . being aduertised of the great forces which the duke of Lancaster had got togither against him [Richard], wherewith he

was maruellouslie amazed, knowing certeinelie that those which were thus in armes with the duke of Lancaster against him, would rather die than giue place, as well for the hatred as feare which they had conceiued at him. Neuerthelesse he departing from Barclowlie, hasted with all speed towards Conwaie, where he vnderstood the earle of Salisburie to be still remaining. He therefore taking with him such Cheshire men as he had with him at that present (in whom all his trust was reposed) he doubted not to reuenge himselfe of his aduersaries, & so at the first he passed with good courage: but when he vnderstood as he went thus forward, that all the castels, euen from the borders of Scotland vnto Bristow were deliuered vnto the duke of Lancaster, and that likewise the nobles and commons, as well of the south parts, as the north, were fullie bent to take part with the same duke against him; and further, hearing how his trustie councellors had lost their heads at Bristow, he became so greatlie discomforted, that sorrowfullie lamenting his miserable state, he vtterlie despaired of his owne safetie, and calling his armie togither, which was not small, licenced euerie man to depart to his home. The souldiers being well bent to fight in his defense, besought him to be of good cheere, promising with an oth to stand with him against the duke, and all his partakers[,] vnto death: but this could not incourage him at all, so that in the next night insuing, he stole from his armie, and with the dukes of Excester and Surrie, the bishop of Carleill, and sir Stephan Scroope, and about halfe a score others, he got him to the castell of Conwaie, where he found the earle of Salisburie, determining there to hold

3.2] *F (Scena Secunda.)*   0.1–2] *Enter the King Aumerle, Carleil, &c. Q; Drums: Flourish, and Colours. Enter Richard, Aumerle, Carlile, and Souldiers. F*   0.2 *and Soldiers*] *F; &c. Q*

KING RICHARD

Barkloughly Castle call they this at hand?

AUMERLE

Yea, my lord. How brooks your grace the air
After your late tossing on the breaking seas?

---

himselfe, till he might see the world at
some better staie; for what counsell to
take to remedie the mischeefe thus
pressing vpon him he wist not. On the
one part he knew his title iust, true, and
infallible; and his conscience cleane,
pure, and without spot of enuie or malice: he had also no small affiance in the
Welshmen, and Cheshire men. On the
other side, he saw the puissance of his
aduersaries, the sudden departing of
them whom he most trusted, and all
things turned vpside downe: he
euidentlie saw, and manifestly perceiued, that he was forsaken of them,
by whom in time he might haue beene
aided and relieued, where now it was
too late, and too farre ouer-passed.'
After a paragraph of sympathetic commentary on Richard's plight (see
218n.), Holinshed continues with the
desertion of Worcester (see
2.2.58–61n.). See LN.

0.1 *Flourish* See 1.3.122 SDn.
Colours flag carried by a bearer

0.2 AUMERLE The shifting of Aumerle's
political allegiances (see List of Roles,
9n.) seems to have puzzled Holinshed.
The chronicler reports that Aumerle
accompanied Richard on his return
from Ireland (see headnote) but does
not make clear, when Aumerle arrives at
Flint Castle (3.501), whether at this
point he remained loyal or had perhaps
defected to Bolingbroke with Worcester
(who is mentioned in the same sentence). Shakespeare keeps him loyal to
Richard in obvious preparation for his
involvement in the Abbot of
Westminster's plot (4.1.324–5, 5.2, 5.3),
an episode also based in part on
Holinshed.

1 **Barkloughly** probably pronounced
'Barklòwly', thus approximating
Holinshed's spelling; Shakespeare's
word is a respelling of Holinshed's
'Barclowlie' (see headnote). The cor-
rect name was 'Hertlowlie' (modern
Harlech), a castle in northern Wales
built by Edward I (cf. Oxf's
'Harlechly', modernized 'Hertloughly';
see t.n.). Some confusion with
Berkeley (spelled 'Barkley') is possible.
Historically Richard landed at Milford
Haven in southern Wales, not in the
north (Stow, 407).

2 nine-syllable line lacking first,
unstressed syllable
brooks usually 'endures, suffers, puts
up with' but here seems closer to 'likes'
your grace an honorific address ordinarily reserved for dukes and bishops
but sometimes used also for kings
(along with 'your majesty', 'your highness' and 'my lord'); cf. *R3* 4.2.110,
2H4 4.5.49.

3 Cf. *1H4* 5.1.52–4: 'the contrarious
winds that held the King / So long in
his unlucky Irish wars / That all in
England did repute him dead'; also
Daniel, 1.105: Richard returned from
Ireland 'with greatest speed; / But was
by tempests, windes, and seas debarr'd'.
Shakespeare's source is probably
Holinshed (3.499), who reports that
bad weather prevented Richard from
receiving satisfactory dispatches from
England: 'the seas were so troubled by
tempests, and the winds blew so contrarie for anie passage, to come ouer
foorth of England to the king, remaining still in Ireland, that for the space of
six weeks, he receiued no aduertisements from thence'.

1+ SP] *King Q; Rich. F*   1 Barkloughly] Harlechly *Oxf*   they] you *Q2–F*

KING RICHARD

Needs must I like it well. I weep for joy
To stand upon my kingdom once again.   5
Dear earth, I do salute thee with my hand,
Though rebels wound thee with their horses' hoofs.
As a long-parted mother with her child
Plays fondly with her tears and smiles in meeting,
So weeping, smiling, greet I thee, my earth,   10
And do thee favours with my royal hands.
Feed not thy sovereign's foe, my gentle earth,
Nor with thy sweets comfort his ravenous sense,
But let thy spiders that suck up thy venom

---

late recent

4   **Needs** of necessity (Abbott, 25)

4–5 **I weep . . . again.** In his self-conscious, aestheticized manner, Richard is as emotional in his patriotism as Mowbray (cf. 1.3.159–60), Bolingbroke (cf. 1.3.268–70, 306–9) and Gaunt (cf. 2.1.40–66). Love of the land is a pervasive theme in the tragedy (see Introduction, pp. 69–71). 'The contrast with Bolingbroke's business-like' *Bring forth these men* (3.1.1) 'could not be more vivid' (Adams, 150). Tears and weeping form a significant matrix of action and imagery in the tragedy and provide a clue to its dominant tone: see, e.g., 1.3.59, 2.2.27, 3.3.165, 4.1.188, 5.1.48.

6   **Dear earth** Cf. Gaunt's *dear dear land* (2.1.57); also Bolingbroke's *Sweet soil* (1.3.306).
    I pronoun emphatic, contrasted with *rebels* (7)
    salute greet solemnly; Richard stoops down to touch, or even caress, the ground (cf. 11 and 1.3.306n.). See LN.

8   **long-parted mother with** mother long parted from. Among the 'amiable parts' of Richard's character Coleridge remarks on the 'feminine feeling' in 'his intense love of his country' (125); see also 1.3.54n. Ure (94) compares *1H6* 3.3.47, where Joan la Pucelle

likens beholding the ruins of France to 'the mother' looking on 'her lowly babe' as the child dies.

9–10 Richard 'dallies with both tears and smiles – not yielding to the full sway of either. . . . Here is an exquisite mingling of both senses' (Kittredge[2], 149), i.e. deep affection and a sense of folly. Wells (214), following Malone and others, notes Shakespeare's attraction to the combination of tears and smiles or grief and joy; cf. 5.2.32 and *KL* 4.3.17–22, *RJ* 3.2.102–4, *Tem* 3.1.73–4.

9   **fondly** dotingly; foolishly
    smiles noun; cf. 5.2.32.

11 **do . . . hands** bestow royal grace upon thee by caressing (see 6LN)

13 **sweets** good things, rich bounty
    comfort . . . sense satisfy his voracious appetite. In varying forms the word *comfort* echoes throughout the scene like a leitmotif (cf. 36, 65, 75, 206, 208, 144).

14 **spiders . . . venom** Spiders were believed to be mortally dangerous, sucking their poison from the earth; cf. *E3* 2.1.285–6: 'And not a poison-sucking envious spider, / To turn the juice I take to deadly venom'. Richard has earlier associated *venom* (2.1.157) with the Irish rebels; York has applied it to the evil of royal flattery (2.1.19).

---

8 long-parted] *Pope;* long parted *QF*   11 favours] fauour *Q2–F*

And heavy-gaited toads lie in their way,   15
Doing annoyance to the treacherous feet
Which with usurping steps do trample thee.
Yield stinging nettles to mine enemies;
And when they from thy bosom pluck a flower,
Guard it I pray thee with a lurking adder   20
Whose double tongue may with a mortal touch
Throw death upon thy sovereign's enemies.
Mock not my senseless conjuration, lords.
This earth shall have a feeling, and these stones
Prove armed soldiers, ere her native king   25
Shall falter under foul rebellion's arms.

15 **heavy-gaited toads** referring to their lumbering and clumsy movement; like spiders, toads were thought to be venomous.

16 **annoyance** injury, harm (not mere irritation); cf. *2H6* 3.1.67: 'thorns that would annoy our foot'.
   treacherous feet a synecdoche: either the feet of traitorous soldiers or, possibly, the hooves of the horses ridden by them (cf. 7). The latter would enhance the effect of futile fancy and impracticality. *Treacherous* is probably dissyllabic ('treach'rous').

17 **usurping steps** With characteristic intemperance, Richard attributes usurpation not only to Bolingbroke but to his entire army.

18–22 Ure (95) notes that Richard's invocation of natural powers to punish his enemies is similar to Lear's calling upon 'dear goddess' Nature for the same purpose (*KL* 1.4.275).

19–20 common iconography for the idea of danger or evil as apparent good; cf. *2H6* 3.1.228–9, *RJ* 3.2.73, *Mac* 1.5.65–6. Proverbial associations (Dent, S585).

20 **Guard** defend, protect (possibly punning on 'trim' or 'ornament', as with braid)

21 **double** forked; cf. *MND* 2.2.9.
   mortal deadly; the belief that the snake's tongue rather than its fangs contained the poison was current in Shakespeare's time.

22 **Throw** inflict, cast

23 **Mock not** Richard, ever aware of his audience, senses the possible derision to which his emotional rhetoric may have exposed him and attempts to forestall it.
   my senseless conjuration either 'my earnest appeal addressed to something like the earth which possesses no senses', i.e. can neither feel (cf. *feeling*, 24), hear nor understand, or 'my solemn entreaty which makes no sense to you' (because of its fantastic impracticality). Perhaps Richard plays on both meanings. *Conjuration* carries overtones of magical incantation or the mystical invocation of supernatural as well as natural agents.

24–5 **these ... soldiers** perhaps alluding to the fable of Cadmus, who sowed dragon's teeth which then sprang up as soldiers. See LN.

25 **armed** armèd
   native legitimate by right of birth (not native-born); Richard was born in Bordeaux. See List of Roles, ln.

26 rebellion's] rebellious *Q3–F*

CARLISLE

Fear not, my lord. That Power that made you king
Hath power to keep you king in spite of all.
The means that heavens yield must be embraced
And not neglected; else heaven would,   30
And we will not. Heaven's offer we refuse –
The proffered means of succour and redress.

AUMERLE

He means, my lord, that we are too remiss,
Whilst Bolingbroke, through our security,
Grows strong and great in substance and in power.   35

27 *The comma after *lord* in QF is ambiguous. Most editors interpret it as a stop;
but Elizabethans sometimes used the
comma as a substitute for 'that' (i.e.
'doubt not, my lord, "that" that Power').
The difference in meaning is slight.
Fear not do not doubt
29–32 a confusing passage. Pollard (93–4)
suggests that F's omission of these
lines was owing to the obscurity of
'else heaven . . . redress' (30–2); see
Appendix 1, p. 508. Pope's emendation
(see 30t.n.) yields a kind of sense,
although rather tautologically: 'otherwise (*else*), if heaven wishes us to help
ourselves and we obey our own will by
failing to do so, we then spurn the offer
of divine assistance, namely the available means of aid and remedy'. Pope's
reading also smoothes the metre in 30
by adding the wanting tenth syllable.
By repunctuating, however, it is possible to wrest an equally acceptable
meaning from the lines as they stand in
Q: 'otherwise, we run counter to heav-
en's wish. We refuse the offer of heav-
en – the offered (*proffered*) means of
assistance (*succour*; see 32n.) and relief
(*redress*)'. Q's metrically deficient line
30 can be made to scan by introducing

a pause (or beat) after *neglected*. F's
omission of 29–32 provides no solution, for, as Pollard observes, Aumerle
is then left 'without any foundation for
the meaning he attributes to the
Bishop's speech' in 33–5.
29–30 **heavens yield . . . neglected**
heaven affords . . . disregarded
32 **proffered** offered, proposed. RP suggests that the word may be 'preferred'
(= uttered, pronounced, put forth,
adduced; see t.n.); the two words could
be spelled identically and tended to fall
together (see *OED*).
***succour** Pope's emendation has been
almost universally accepted as more
idiomatic. For Q's addition or subtraction of a single letter, see Appendix 1,
p. 537, n. 2. But in this case the compositor may simply have misread a MS
comma as an *s* (cf. 1.4.20n.).
34 **security** overconfidence, negligence
(literally, 'being without care'); cf.
2.1.266n.
35 **substance . . . power** resources, material advantages . . . manpower, troops.
F's substitution of specific 'friends' for
abstract *power* seems distinctly weaker.
For defence of the F reading, see
Jowett & Taylor, 188.

27 lord.] *(Lord,)*, F Power] F; power *Q* 29–32] *om.* F 30 else heaven] else if heaven *Pope*
31 will] would *Q3* not. Heaven's] *Q3 (*not; heauens*)*; not, heauens *Q* offer] *Capell*; offer, *Q*
32 proffered] *(profered)* succour] *Pope*; succors *Q* 33 lord] *(Lo:)*, F 35 power] friends *F*

KING RICHARD

Discomfortable cousin, knowst thou not
That when the searching eye of heaven is hid
Behind the globe and lights the lower world,
Then thieves and robbers range abroad unseen
In murders and in outrage boldly here;   40
But when from under this terrestrial ball
He fires the proud tops of the eastern pines

36 **Discomfortable** disheartening, discouraging. A word used only here in Shakespeare, possibly influenced by Holinshed's report that Richard was 'greatlie discomforted' (see headnote); cf. also 2.2.76n. There may be an echo of Ecclesiasticus, 18.14: 'speake no discomfortable wordes'.

37 **searching . . . heaven** another of the several comparisons of Richard to the sun (cf. 2.4.19–21n.); *heaven* is monosyllabic. Cf. also Gaunt's phrase, *eye of heaven* (1.3.275).

38 ***and** Hanmer's emendation clarifies the syntax and makes the sentence more readily intelligible in the theatre, since, in Q, *globe* (the earth) rather than *searching eye* (37) could be mistakenly understood as the subject of *lights*. In order to make sense of the text as it stands, the phrase 'that lights the lower world' must be heard as standing in apposition to *eye of heaven*, an awkward sense for an actor to convey. Q's 'that' may be a memorial blunder – a substitution influenced by *That* in 37.

lower world 'the other hemisphere, the opposite side of the world from that which I now occupy in Wales'. Richard compares his absence in Ireland to the darkness caused by the sun's departure to illuminate the underside of *the globe* (38) and those who dwell there, *the Antipodes* (49); his return re-illuminates his half of the world, lighting up the horizon at dawn

by coming 'from under this terrestrial ball' (41), and firing the 'tops of the eastern pines' (42). In Ptolemaic astronomy, the sun revolved around the earth (cf. 2.4.9n.), not vice versa.

39–40 For the common notion that robberies are most likely to occur at night, cf. Falstaff's comment in *1H4* 1.2.13–14: 'we that take purses go by the moon and the seven stars'. Some editors cite Job, 24.13–17.

39 **range abroad** prowl about (in search of booty)

40 **murders . . . outrage** From an audience's point of view, these words are loaded with ironic resonance, recalling Richard's own involvement in Gloucester's death (cf. *Murder's bloody axe*, 1.2.21) as well as Bolingbroke's summary execution of Bushy and Green in 3.1 – another political murder-outrage if viewed from the King's perspective.

***boldly** Hudson's emendation (following Collier's conjecture) yields a much more forceful reading than Q2's 'bloudy' (note the antithesis to *trembling*, 46). Q's 'bouldy' is readily explained as mis-setting of 'bouldly' (see 32n. on *succour*).

41 **terrestrial ball** the earth (cf. *globe*, 38)

42 **He fires** He (the sun) sets afire (metaphorically)

proud lofty

eastern pines pines on the eastern horizon

36 knowst] knowest *F*   38 and] *Hanmer;* that *QF*   40 boldly] *Hudson (Collier);* bouldy *Q;* bloudy *Q2–F*   41 this] *QF;* his *Q2*

And darts his light through every guilty hole,
Then murders, treasons and detested sins,
The cloak of night being plucked from off their backs,   45
Stand bare and naked, trembling at themselves?
So, when this thief, this traitor, Bolingbroke,
Who all this while hath revelled in the night
Whilst we were wand'ring with the Antipodes,
Shall see us rising in our throne, the east,   50
His treasons will sit blushing in his face,
Not able to endure the sight of day,
But, self-affrighted, tremble at his sin.
Not all the water in the rough rude sea
Can wash the balm off from an anointed king;   55

43 **guilty hole** hiding place of the guilty
44 **treasons** Q's plural form makes the word parallel to *murders* and *sins* in the same line; but 'treason' could be correct if the compositor mistook a comma after the word for a terminal *s* (cf. 32n.).
   detested detestable (see 2.1.268n.)
46 **trembling at themselves** i.e. fearful because their wickedness has been discovered
47 **thief** Richard perhaps already suspects that Bolingbroke will steal his crown.
49 F's omission of this line is probably a compositorial slip; but it could have been cut in the theatre on account of the syntactical obscurity caused by Q's 'that' in 38 or because the metaphorical identification of the Irish with *the Antipodes* (see n. below) seemed too strained or incomprehensible.
   we were royal plural
   the Antipodes pronounced 'th'Antipodes'; i.e. the people who dwell on the other side of the world (not the geographical region) – metaphorically, the Irish (continuing Richard's conceit from 38). The word means literally

'those whose feet are opposite ours, i.e. who are upside down' (see *OED sb. pl.* 1).
50 **the east** because the sun rises in the east. Richard has travelled from the west (Ireland).
51 **blushing** out of shame (but also reflecting the red of the rising sun)
53 **tremble at** Cf. 46n. Richard applies his earlier generalization specifically to Bolingbroke.
54–7 quoted in *Parnassus* (no. 862) under the heading of 'Kings'; *The Noble Gentleman* (1626?), 5.1.238–9, gives an altered version of these lines: 'Not all the water in the river Sene, / Can wash the blood out of these Princely veines' (Fletcher, 3.194).
54 **rude** stormy, turbulent
55 **balm** consecrated oil (used in anointing monarchs at their coronation); cf. 4.1.207, also *3H6* 3.1.17: 'The balm wash'd off wherewith thou was anointed'. Holinshed (3.416) is very explicit about Richard's anointing: 'The archbishop . . . hauing stripped him, first anointed his hands, then his head,

43 light] Lightning *F*   every] eu'ry *F*   49] *om. F*   53 self-affrighted] *F;* selfe affrighted *Q*   tremble] *QF;* trembled *Q2*   55 off from] from *F*

The breath of worldly men cannot depose
The deputy elected by the Lord.
For every man that Bolingbroke hath pressed
To lift shrewd steel against our golden crown,
God for His Richard hath in heavenly pay   60
A glorious angel. Then, if angels fight,
Weak men must fall, for heaven still guards the right.

Enter SALISBURY.

brest, shoulders, and the ioints of his armes with the sacred oile, saieng certeine praiers, and in the meane time did the quéere [choir] sing the antheme, beginning, *Vnxerunt regem Salomonem, &c.*'

off F's omission of this word smoothes the metre, but the line in Q scans if *an* receives only light stress ('an a-nòint- | ed king') or is elided to 'a'nointed'.

56–7 Holinshed refers several times to Richard's assumption of semi-divine status: in 1397 Bushy addressed the King, not using 'titles of honour, due and accustomed, but inuent[ing] vnused termes and such strange names, as were rather agreeable to the diuine maiestie of God, than to any earthlie potentate' (3.490); Richard 'esteem[ed] himselfe higher in degree than anie prince liuing, and so presumed further than euer his grandfather did, and tooke vpon him to beare the armes of saint Edward, ioining them vnto his owne armes' (3.492). See also 6LN.

56 **breath . . . men** words of earthly men, mere mortals; contrast Bolingbroke's *breath of kings* (1.3.215).

57 **deputy** surrogate, representative. See 1.2.38n., 4.1.127; cf. also *stewardship*, 3.3.78, and Romans, 13.3–4.
   elected chosen, singled out

58 **pressed** impressed, conscripted

59 **shrewd** injurious, keen, biting (with a possible quibble on 'beshrewed' = 'accursed'); some editors gloss *shrewd* as 'sharp, piercing', which, according to *OED* (*a.* 9), is post-Shakespearean.

59–61 **crown . . . angel** probably punning on the coins with these names (cf. *heavenly pay*, 60; also 5.5.67–8n.). Richard imagines angels as wage-earning soldiers in God's army and therefore invincible. Shakespeare could have been thinking of the double row of angels that decorated the roof of Westminster Hall, each bearing a shield emblazoned with the royal arms, placed there when Richard rebuilt that edifice. Cf. 3.3.87n.; also the numerous angels on the panel opposite Richard II in the Wilton Diptych (see 2.1.46LN).

60–1 **God . . . angel** Wilson (184–5) cites Matthew, 26.53: 'Thinkest thou that I can not now pray to my father, and he shall cause to stand by mee more than twelve legions of angels?'

61–2 **if . . . right** The stress falls on *men* (in contrast to *angels*). This passage was anthologized in *Parnassus* (no. 5) under the heading, 'Angels'.

62 **heaven . . . right** heaven always protects those in the right (see 1.1.203n.); *heaven* is monosyllabic.

60 God] Heauen *F*   Richard] *(*Ric:*), F*   62.1 SALISBURY] *(Salish.), F*

Welcome, my lord. How far off lies your power?
SALISBURY
Nor near nor farther off, my gracious lord,
Than this weak arm. Discomfort guides my tongue   65
And bids me speak of nothing but despair.
One day too late, I fear me, noble lord,
Hath clouded all thy happy days on earth.
O, call back yesterday, bid Time return,
And thou shalt have twelve thousand fighting men!   70
Today, today, unhappy day too late,
O'erthrows thy joys, friends, fortune and thy state;
For all the Welshmen, hearing thou wert dead,
Are gone to Bolingbroke, dispersed and fled.
AUMERLE
Comfort, my liege. Why looks your grace so pale?   75

---

63 **power** army
64 **Nor near** neither nearer. In Elizabethan usage, Q's spelling 'neare' is
used also for the comparative (see
OED adv. 1b); cf. 5.1.88 and n. *Near* is
a monosyllable.
65 **Discomfort** discouragement (here
almost equivalent to 'helplessness'); cf.
36.
67 **One . . . late** your arrival from Ireland
one day too late. Shakespeare heightens
Holinshed (3.499); see 2.4 headnote.
I . . . lord Since Q's reflexive construction, 'I fear me', makes good
sense, most editors retain it; Q3's
unauthoritative emendation of *me* to
'my', adopted by F (see t.n.), may be
justified, however, since this is
Salisbury's form of address at 64.
68 **clouded** beclouded (contrasting with
the earlier imagery of sunshine)
happy fortunate; joyful
69 **call back yesterday** proverbial
(Dent, Y31)
70 **twelve thousand** Holinshed (3.499)

reports 'fortie thousand', which does
not fit the metre. But as Wilson (185)
observes, 'historical arithmetic is of no
interest to Shakespeare'; cf. *twenty
thousand* at 76 and 1.3.159n.
71–4 Salisbury's couplets make his dreadful news almost tuneful as well as making the situation seem more irretriev-
able. Cf. Scroop's *care-tuned tongue*
(92) when he delivers even worse news
and Richard's reponse at 121. Créton
(96/323) writes that when Salisbury
met the King, 'instead of joy, there was
very great sorrow. Tears, lamentations,
sighs, groans and mourning quickly
broke forth. Truly it was a piteous
sight to behold their looks and countenance, and woeful meeting.'
72 ***O'erthrows** F's elided form improves
the metre and may reflect theatrical
practice; see Appendix 1, p. 526.
state royal authority, regal power
75–9 See 2.1.118–19n.
75, 82 **Comfort** take courage (probably a
response to *Discomfortable cousin*, 36)

---

63 Welcome] *F; King* Welcome *Q*   63, 64, 67 lord] *(Lo:), F*   67 fear me,] *(feare me); feare, my*
Q3–F   72 O'erthrows] *F; Ouerthrowes Q*

KING RICHARD

But now the blood of twenty thousand men
Did triumph in my face, and they are fled;
And till so much blood thither come again,
Have I not reason to look pale and dead?
All souls that will be safe, fly from my side,   80
For Time hath set a blot upon my pride.

AUMERLE

Comfort, my liege. Remember who you are.

KING RICHARD

I had forgot myself. Am I not king?
Awake, thou coward Majesty, thou sleepest!
Is not the King's name twenty thousand names?   85
Arm, arm, my name! A puny subject strikes
At thy great glory. Look not to the ground,

76–81 Richard's entire speech is a sextain, the same form that often comprises the sestet of a sonnet (cf. Shakespeare's 'sugred sonnets' (Meres)) – a subtle means of dramatizing his 'sweet way . . . to despair' (205); see also 71–4n.

76 **But now** even now, only a moment ago **twenty thousand** See 70n. Again, the requirements of metre may account for the discrepancy. But it is characteristic of Richard in his self-dramatizing mode to exaggerate or even fictionalize his plight.

77 **triumph** shine brightly, glow exultantly

79 **pale and dead** perhaps a stock phrase: cf. *1H6* 4.2.38: 'Shall see thee withered, bloody, pale, and dead'; also *Woodstock*, 4.2.110: 'Strikes her amazèd greatness pale and dead'.

80 **fly** imperative; or 'let them fly' (subjunctive); QF punctuate 'safe, flie'. Some editors, removing the comma, treat *fly* as indicative.

81 **blot** stain (cf. 4.1.236)
pride splendour, glory; arrogance,

haughtiness. Richard's unawareness of the second meaning creates a powerful dramatic irony (cf. 83–4).

84 **coward* cowardly. Q's lack of punctuation in this line creates a syntactical ambiguity, which Q2 attempted to clarify by inserting a comma between *coward* and *Majesty*, thus interpreting *coward* as a noun (addressed by Richard to himself). Treating *coward* as an adjective and placing the comma after *Majesty* (as in F), however, makes *Majesty* rather than *coward* the subject of *Awake*. Either solution makes acceptable sense, but the latter seems slightly stronger. F's 'sluggard' for *coward* weakens the speech.
sleepest probably monosyllabic ('sleep'st')

85 See 70n. and 76n.

87 **Look . . . ground** If Richard is not merely imagining this, embarrassment as much as discouragement might motivate his followers (cf. 23n.).

---

76 twenty thousand] *Q3–F;* 20000. *Q*   81 Time] *F;* time *Q*   84 coward Majesty,] *Pope;* coward Maiesty *Q;* coward, Maiesty *Q2;* sluggard Maiestie, *F;* coward! Majesty, *Cam²*   85 twenty] fortie *F*
86 name!] *F (*Name:*);* name *Q*

Ye favourites of a king. Are we not high?
High be our thoughts! I know my uncle York
Hath power enough to serve our turn.

Enter SCROOP.

But who comes here?   90

SCROOP

More health and happiness betide my liege
Than can my care-tuned tongue deliver him.

KING RICHARD

Mine ear is open and my heart prepared.
The worst is worldly loss thou canst unfold.
Say, is my kingdom lost? Why, 'twas my care;   95
And what loss is it to be rid of care?
Strives Bolingbroke to be as great as we?
Greater he shall not be. If he serve God,
We'll serve Him too, and be his fellow so.

---

88 **we** royal plural
high i.e. in title and position
89 **High** ambitious, optimistic
90 an alexandrine
power troops; perhaps also 'powerful friends'
SD Sir Stephen Scroop has either come from Bristol, since he bears news of the executions there (142), or has learned from some intermediary source the disasters he reports. Wilson (182) thinks that Shakespeare has confused Sir Stephen with his brother, the Earl of Wiltshire, one of Richard's friends beheaded at Bristol. This seems unlikely since Holinshed mentions the younger Scroop as being among Richard's attendants at Conway (3.499).
91 **betide** befall, happen to (optative subjunctive: 'may (they) betide')
92 **care-tuned** 'tuned by sorrow', or perhaps 'tuned to a sorrowful key'

deliver him report to him
93–103 See LN.
94 **worldly loss** loss of worldly possessions
unfold reveal
95 **kingdom lost** Cf. Créton (97–8/ 324–5), where Salisbury reports to Richard that 'All is lost' and where the King, lamenting to God, says, 'for I know right well, that unless thou shouldst speedily deign to regard me, I am lost'. For the psychology revealed here, cf. Bloom's comment on Richard's 'moral masochism' – 'a theatrical tendency in which the ego dramatizes its doom-eagerness in order to achieve a priority in self-destructiveness' (2).
care source of anxiety, burden of responsibility (echoing Scroop's *care* from 92); cf. wordplay at 4.1.194–9.
99 **We'll** royal plural
his fellow his fellow-server of God, his equal in that respect

90] *F lines* turne. / here? / SD] *Oxf; after* here? *QF*   92 care-tuned] *F;* care tunde *Q*   97 we?] *Q3–F;* we, *Q*

324

Revolt our subjects? That we cannot mend.   100
They break their faith to God as well as us.
Cry woe, destruction, ruin and decay.
The worst is death, and Death will have his day.

SCROOP

Glad am I that your highness is so armed
To bear the tidings of calamity.   105
Like an unseasonable stormy day,
Which makes the silver rivers drown their shores
As if the world were all dissolved to tears,
So high above his limits swells the rage
Of Bolingbroke, covering your fearful land   110
With hard bright steel and hearts harder than steel.
Whitebeards have armed their thin and hairless scalps

100 **mend** remedy
101 because the King is the 'deputy elected by the Lord' (57); cf. *Woodstock*,
5.3.59: 'Breaking your holy oaths to
heaven and us'. See also 4.1.235n.
102 *Some editors treat this line as a subjunctive clause dependent on the
following line ('(Although you may)
cry woe . . ., The worst is') rather than
an independent clause in the imperative. QF's comma after *decay* makes
this interpretation possible.
Cry proclaim, announce (directed principally, but not exclusively, to Scroop)
and At least two modern editors accept
F's emendation ('Losse') as a Shakespearean revision; see Jowett & Taylor,
who regard this reading as 'more concrete, forceful and specific' (187–8).
103 **The . . . death** Cf. *E2*, 3.2.59–60: 'The
worst is death, and better die to live, /
Than live in infamy under such a king'.
Death . . . day 'probably proverbial'
(Ard[1], 60); see Dent, D464.
104 **armed** i.e. with fortitude (cf. *my
heart* [is] *prepared*, 93). Gurr (119) suggests 'a possible sarcasm about military

preparedness', but, as Scroop is one of
Richard's most faithful supporters,
this seems unlikely.
107 **silver . . . shores** Shakespeare was
much given to imagery of flooding: cf.
KJ 3.1.23, 5.4.53–7; *MND* 2.1.90–2;
Ham 4.5.100–1.
109–10 **above . . . Bolingbroke** Gurr
(119) points to possible wordplay on
Bolingbroke's name (pronounced
'Bullingbrook') with relation to the
water imagery (see List of Roles, 6n.);
cf. Daniel, 2.8: 'the all-receiuing *Bullingbrooke* . . . What he imagind neuer
could be wrought / Is powrd vpon him'.
109 **his** its (Abbott, 228)
110 **covering** dissyllabic ('cov'ring')
fearful terrified (literally, 'full of fear')
111 **steel** weapons and armour; cf. 59.
112 **Whitebeards** old men (a synecdoche); cf. 119n.
armed with helmets (echoing *armed*
in the metaphorical sense from 104)
thin balding; *thin and hairless* could
simply mean 'thin-haired' or 'almost
hairless' (hendiadys). Scalps perhaps =
skulls.

102 and] Losse, *F*   decay.] *(decay,)*   103 Death] *F;* death *Q*   107 makes] make *Q3–F*   110 cover-
ing] *Q, Fc;* coueting *Fu*   112 Whitebeards] White Beares *F*

Against thy majesty; boys with women's voices
Strive to speak big and clap their female joints
In stiff unwieldy arms against thy crown;   115
Thy very beadsmen learn to bend their bows
Of double-fatal yew against thy state;
Yea, distaff-women manage rusty bills
Against thy seat. Both young and old rebel,
And all goes worse than I have power to tell.   120

KING RICHARD

Too well, too well, thou tell'st a tale so ill.
Where is the Earl of Wiltshire? Where is Bagot?
What is become of Bushy? Where is Green? –
That they have let the dangerous enemy
Measure our confines with such peaceful steps?   125
If we prevail, their heads shall pay for it!

---

113 **majesty** dissyllablic ('maj'sty')
114 **big** with deep voices (imitating men)
114–15 **clap . . . arms** hurriedly thrust
their youthful limbs into rigid, clumsy
armour
116 **beadsmen** almsmen, pensioners,
sometimes spelled 'bedesmen' (usually
old men), who earned their stipends by
saying daily prayers for benefactors;
bead = prayer; the bead of a rosary (as
in 'telling one's beads'). Cf. *H5*
4.1.298–300.
117 **double-fatal** deadly in two ways:
because the yew's berries and foliage
are poisonous, and because its wood
was used for making longbows (death-
dealing weapons)
state Cf. 72n.
118 **distaff-women** women normally
occupied with spinning (*distaff* = staff
which holds the unspun flax or wool,
symbolic of the domestic role of women)
manage rusty bills wield pikes (or
halberds) rusty from disuse; cf. 2.3.80.
The bill was a long-handled weapon,

with a hooked blade or axe blade, often
surmounted by a spike; cf. Holinshed
in 5.5.98–118n.
119 **seat** throne
young and old Créton writes that
while Richard was still in Ireland a messenger reported Bolingbroke's successes
to him: 'Then might you have beheld
young and old, the feeble and the strong,
. . . stir themselves up with one accord
. . . [and begin] to flee towards the duke';
and a little later: 'Taking towns and cas-
tles for his own, he brings young and old
under subjection' (53–5/311).
122 **Where is Bagot?** See LN.
125 **Measure our confines** travel
through (literally, 'around the boundaries of') my territory
peaceful steps unresisted advances
126 **heads shall pay** Cf. *Woodstock*,
5.3.90–1, where Richard threatens his
uncles in similar terms: 'And by my
crown, if still you thus persist / Your
heads and hearts ere long shall answer
it.'

---

113 boys] and boies *Q2–F*   116 bows] *QF;* browes *Q3*   117 double-fatal] *Warburton;* double fatall
QF   yew] *(ewe), F (*Eugh*);* wo *Q3*   118 distaff-women] *F;* distaffe women *Q*   122 Bagot] he got
Theobald   125 steps?] *F;* steps, *Q;* steps. *Q3*

I warrant they have made peace with Bolingbroke.

SCROOP

Peace have they made with him indeed, my lord.

KING RICHARD

O, villains, vipers damned without redemption!

Dogs easily won to fawn on any man!   130

Snakes, in my heart-blood warmed, that sting my heart!

Three Judases, each one thrice worse than Judas!

Would they make peace? Terrible hell

Make war upon their spotted souls for this!

SCROOP

Sweet love, I see, changing his property,   135

Turns to the sourest and most deadly hate.

Again uncurse their souls. Their peace is made

127 **warrant they have** The metre requires either that: *warrant* be elided to a monosyllable ('warr'nt'); or *they have* be shortened to 'they've'. The first option seems preferable.

127–8 **peace . . . Peace** For a comparably grim *double entendre* on 'peace', see *Mac* 4.3.178–9: '*Macduff.* The tyrant has not batter'd at their peace? *Ross.* No, they were well at peace when I did leave 'em'; see Introduction, pp. 89–90.

129 probably an allusion to Matthew, 23.33: 'Ye serpentes, ye generation of vipers, how wyl ye escape the dampnation of hell?'

without beyond hope of

130 The metre of the first two feet of this line – a spondee followed by an elided 'eas'ly' ('Dògs èas- | 'ly wòn') – effectively conveys Richard's anger (ironically unjustified).

Dogs . . . fawn See 5.5.83–9LN.

131 See LN and cf. 19–20n.

132 **Three Judases** See 122LN. Richard

again compares his betrayers to the betrayer of Jesus at 4.1.171–2 (see n.). Judas, however, was a common synonym for traitor; Ure (101) cites *3H6* 5.7.33; *True Tragedy*, l. 600; *Edward I*, l. 891 (Peele, 2.102); *Ironside*, l. 1625. Cf. also *LLL* 5.2.596.

133–4 For discussion of F's changed lineation and addition of 'Offence' in 134, see Appendix 1, pp. 528–9.

133 **Would they** were they willing to (Abbott, 331)

make peace Pollard (85) suggests that these words 'are a cry of rage which can only be adequately rendered by giving to each the time of a whole foot'.

134 **spotted** stained (with treason), sinful; cf. *blot* (81). There may be additional wordplay on the pale-spotted skin of some species of vipers.

135–6 a common proverb (Dent, L513)

135 **his property** its essence or distinctive quality; for *his*, cf. 109n.

137 **uncurse** See 2.1.16n.

127 Bolingbroke] *(Bulling), F (Bullingbrooke)*   130 won] *(woon)*   131 heart-blood] *F3;* hart bloud *QF*   133–4] *F lines* warre / this Offence. /   134 this] this Offence *F*   135 love] *QF;* loue's *Q3;* Ioue's *Q5*   136–7 hate. / Again] *Q3–F;* hate, / Againe, *Q;* hate, / Againe *Q2*

With heads, and not with hands. Those whom you
   curse
Have felt the worst of death's destroying wound
And lie full low, graved in the hollow ground.   140

AUMERLE

Is Bushy, Green and the Earl of Wiltshire dead?

SCROOP

Ay, all of them at Bristol lost their heads.

AUMERLE

Where is the Duke my father with his power?

KING RICHARD

No matter where. Of comfort no man speak!
Let's talk of graves, of worms and epitaphs,   145
Make dust our paper and with rainy eyes
Write sorrow on the bosom of the earth.
Let's choose executors and talk of wills.
And yet not so, for what can we bequeath
Save our deposed bodies to the ground?   150
Our lands, our lives and all are Bolingbroke's,
And nothing can we call our own but death
And that small model of the barren earth

138 **With . . . hands** by dying on the
block rather than by signing documents of submission, shaking hands in
agreement or with raised hands swearing oaths of allegiance; see 127–8n.

139 **wound** F's 'hand' probably represents a compositorial slip of memory
influenced by *hands* in 138; it violates
the rhyme with *ground* (140), an indication, incidentally, of how Elizabethans pronounced 'wound'. A similar rhyme on 'found/wound' appears
in *RJ* 2.1.42–2.2.1.

140 **graved** entombed, laid in the grave
(cf. *Tim* 4.3.166)

141–3 See 122LN. 'Richard's failure – or

inability – to speak here may give a cue
to the actor. As often in Shakespeare,
affliction does not find immediate
expression' (Wells, 219).

141 **Is** are (Abbott, 333)

143 **power** army

150 **deposed** deposèd. Characteristically,
Richard anticipates and, in a sense,
invites the worst before it actually happens; cf. Gaunt's statement that his
nephew is 'possessed now to depose'
himself (2.1.108). See also 95n.

153 **model . . . earth** The human body
was commonly conceived of as a
microcosm of the earth, a small-scale
copy or *model*; but there may be the

138 heads] *QF;* head *Q2*   139 wound] hand *F*   142 Ay] *(1);* Ye *Q2;* Yea *Q3–F*   152 death] *Q2, F*
*(*Death,*);* death: *Q*

Which serves as paste and cover to our bones.
For God's sake let us sit upon the ground   155
And tell sad stories of the death of kings –
How some have been deposed, some slain in war,
Some haunted by the ghosts they have deposed,
Some poisoned by their wives, some sleeping killed –
All murdered. For within the hollow crown   160

additional idea of *model* as that 'mold', shape or raised mound of earth that finally encloses or envelops a body in burial (however unlikely such a humble grave would be for royalty). If the latter meaning is operative, Richard would be saying that this close-fitting envelope of earth is all, apart from *death* (152), that a man can finally possess. Ure (102) thinks that Shakespeare may have envisioned the *model* of a pie (see 154n.), 'the grave and its contents' being likened to meat baked in a crust.

154 **paste** pastry, crust (the covering of a pie, also called a 'coffin'; cf. *Tit* 5.2.187–8, 5.3.60–1). Johnson (1.441) thought the metaphor indecorous – 'not of the most sublime kind'. Cf. also *Duchess of Malfi*, 4.2.125–6: 'what's this flesh? a little crudded milk, fantastical puff-paste'.

155 **sit . . . ground** In view of Richard's earlier postures (occupying a throne or standing), this position marks an important contrast. Sitting on the ground, the site 'of graves, of worms and epitaphs' (145), is an obvious emblem of mortality – a stage action that physicalizes the theme of death on which Richard is about to expatiate; such sitting was also a sign of mourning (cf. 178). It is not entirely clear whether Richard sits alone or is joined by his courtiers; but the latter action is improbable since it would violate traditional decorum (note that the others remain uncovered in the King's presence; see 171–3n. and 1.1.15n.). Richard's sitting alone (as on his throne) would appropriately

emphasize his isolation both as king and man. There may, however, be some memory of *E2*, 4.7.14–18, in which Edward, hiding from his enemies at Neath Abbey, meditates on the transience of 'rule and empery' and invites his companions, Spencer and Baldock, to 'come sit down by me' and 'Make trial' of 'that philosophy' which they have learned 'in our famous nurseries of arts'. Cf. also Job, 2.13, in which Job's comforters sit with him on the ground.

156 See LN.
    sad solemn, serious (as at funerals); sorrowful

158 **ghosts** ghosts of kings. Shakespeare could hardly have failed to recall his own *R3* 5.3, in which the ghosts of the tyrant's victims return to plague his sleep.
    deposed deprived (of life; see *OED v.* 4b). A slightly different sense from *deposed* (dethroned) in 157 (cf. 4.1.192).

159 **some sleeping killed** Cf. Hamlet's father (*Ham* 1.5.59–64) and Duncan (*Mac* 1.7.61–70).

160–3 **For . . . pomp** See LN.
160 **All murdered** another of Richard's 'doom-eager' anticipations, since he seems self-consciously to include himself among the 'sad stories of the death of kings'; cf. 95n., 150n.
    hollow crown echoing *hollow ground* (140) and so linking the two ideas. Symbolically, *hollow* also plays on the sense of 'meaningless, empty (because transitory)'; cf. also 160–3LN and 2.1.100n.

That rounds the mortal temples of a king
Keeps Death his court; and there the antic sits,
Scoffing his state and grinning at his pomp,
Allowing him a breath, a little scene,
To monarchize, be feared and kill with looks,   165
Infusing him with self and vain conceit,
As if this flesh which walls about our life
Were brass impregnable; and humoured thus,
Comes at the last and with a little pin

161 **rounds** encircles, surrounds
  mortal human; marked for death,
  doomed (cf. 160n.)
162 **antic** jester, grotesque buffoon. Cf.
  1H6 4.7.18: 'Thou antic Death, which
  laugh'st us here to scorn'; and *KJ*
  5.2.176–7: 'and in his forehead sits / A
  bare-ribb'd death'. See 160–3LN.
163 **Scoffing his state** deriding (scoffing
  at) his regal status (cf. 72n., 117). *State*
  probably has the secondary meaning of
  'chair of state' (see 1.3.190n.), playing
  on the folly of a royal throne in
  Death's *court* (162).
164 **breath** moment, breathing space
  little scene implying the brevity as
  well as the ultimate triviality of a
  king's life as compared with eternity;
  cf. *Mac* 5.5.24–6: 'Life's but a walking
  shadow, a poor player, / That struts
  and frets his hour upon the stage, /
  And then is heard no more.' Life as a
  play was a common trope. The word
  scene connects imagistically with *antic*
  (162).
165 **monarchize** play the part of a king;
  cf. *Christ's Tears Over Jerusalem*
  (1593): 'the spyrite of monarchizing
  in pryuate men is the spyrite of
  Lucifer' (Nashe, 2.91). *Caesar's
  Revenge* (1592–6?), l. 538, perhaps
  borrows the word from *R2*: 'And
  in proud *Africa* to monarchize';
  see 1.1.109n. For the conception
  of Richard as an actor-king, see

Introduction, pp. 17, 34–6, 45–6.
  kill with looks be able to doom subjects with a mere glance (perhaps suggesting also the theatricality of
  'monarchizing' or role-playing in
  which royal power is a matter of mere
  stage pretence or simulation). Ure
  (102) points out that the king threatened by Death in the woodcut adduced
  in 160–3LN is depicted as frowning,
  with a poor subject who supplicates for
  justice on his knees before him.
166 **self . . . conceit** an empty (or foolish) concept of himself (as though he
  were immortal); *conceit* = fancy, idea
  (not 'unwarranted self-regard'); *self* is
  adjectival (syntactically parallel to
  vain).
168 **brass impregnable** Cf. Job, 6.12: 'Is
  my strength the strength of stones? or
  is my flesh of brasse?' See also 170n.
168–9 **and . . . Comes** either 'and Death,
  being so inclined (or having thus
  amused himself by making the king his
  sport), comes', or 'and Death, having
  thus indulged the king, comes'. A few
  editors take 'the king' (understood
  from 161) as the subject of *humoured*,
  in which case the meaning would be:
  'and while the king is in this humour
  (mood, whim), Death comes' (cf. *MV*
  4.1.43). The first two interpretations
  give a more macabre and therefore
  more forceful sense than the third.

162 Death] *F*; death *Q*   antic] *(antique)*, *Pope (Antick)*

Bores through his castle wall, and farewell, king!   170
Cover your heads, and mock not flesh and blood
With solemn reverence. Throw away respect,
Tradition, form and ceremonious duty,
For you have but mistook me all this while.
I live with bread like you, feel want,   175
Taste grief, need friends. Subjected thus,
How can you say to me I am a king?

170 *through Q2's re-spelling (cf. Q's 'thorough'), carried over into F, may have been introduced to smooth the metre; cf. 5.5.20n.
his castle wall the wall of his mortal body (cf. 167, also *KJ* 3.3.20). The body is suddenly conceived of as a castle under siege, Death's *little pin* (169) serving as the tiny weapon or petard (a small bell-shaped bomb), to pierce its defences, but there is also a backward reference to penetrating the *brass impregnable* of 168.
farewell, king According to some editors, Richard should remove his crown at this point – a prolepsis of his abdication in 4.1. Such a gesture would give additional force to 171–3 where it becomes clear that the other characters onstage continue to be uncovered; see 171–3n.
171–3 Richard's followers, who may remain standing while he sits (see 155n.), have deferentially removed their headgear in the sovereign's presence. Richard invites them to discard the usual protocol and wear their hats (*Cover your heads*), thus symbolically erasing the distinction between king and subject. To persist with the traditional formality, he claims, would be to *mock* his *flesh and blood* as though his body were more exalted than theirs. In the depth of his depression Richard temporarily abjures the doctrine of the king's two bodies, here

emotionally distancing himself from the semi-divine Body Politic (which demands ceremonial or *solemn reverence*, 172) and identifying himself rather with the natural Body Personal, the mortal body, that unites him with the generality of men; see Kantorowicz, 24–41. At the core of his meditation is the concept of Death the leveller.
173 **Tradition,   form** traditional homage, formal observances
175–6 The metrical anomaly of these tetrameter lines is obviously deliberate, requiring the actor to slow down his delivery and employ pauses for emotional effect.
175 **bread** Richard, who so easily compelled Bolingbroke to eat 'the bitter bread of banishment' (3.1.21; see n.), now in his own isolation acknowledges his reliance on the common food that sustains all men.
feel want experience needs and deficiencies
176 **Taste . . . friends** Although Richard is generalizing, he may be thinking of the loss of Wiltshire, Bushy and Green about whom he has just been informed (141–2).
Subjected thus 'since I am liable thus to grief (and to ordinary human necessities)', quibbling on the sense of 'since I am reduced thus to the condition of a subject'

170 through] *Q2–F;* thorough *Q*   wall] walls *Q2–F*

CARLISLE

My lord, wise men ne'er sit and wail their woes,
But presently prevent the ways to wail.
To fear the foe, since fear oppresseth strength,   180
Gives in your weakness strength unto your foe,
And so your follies fight against yourself.
Fear and be slain – no worse can come to fight;
And fight and die is death destroying Death,
While fearing dying pays Death servile breath.   185

AUMERLE

My father hath a power. Enquire of him,

178 **sit . . . woes** possibly proverbial; see
Dent, M999a, who cites Arthur Brooke,
Romeus and Juliet (1562; arguably the
source for Shakespeare's use of the
phrase): 'A wise man in the midst of
troubles and distress, / Still standes not
wayling present harme, but seeks his
harmes redres' (ll. 1359–60; Bullough,
1.321). Cf. *3H6* 5.4.1–2: 'Great lords,
wise men ne'er sit and wail their loss /
But cheerly seek how to redress their
harms.' *TxC* (311) argues that F's 'waile
their present woes' represents a
Shakespearean revision undertaken 'to
avoid the close similarity between his
original line' and that in *3H6*. F's 'present' does, however, allow a further pun
on *presently* (179) in line with other repetitions and puns on *wail* (178–9), *fear*
(180–5), *foe* (180–1), *strength* (180–1),
fight (182–4), *death* (184–5) and *die*
(184–5). Nevertheless, given the importance of Richard's emblematic posture
(see 155n.), the retention of Q's *sit*
seems justified.

179 **presently** promptly
prevent . . . wail probably 'avoid, or
forestall (*prevent* by anticipating), the
courses (*ways*) that lead one to lament
(*wail*)'; the wording is curious but it reinforces the speech's general alliterative
nature. Verity (149) glosses *ways* as 'occasion', which finds no support in *OED*.

180 **oppresseth** weighs down, over-
whelms
181 **Gives . . . strength** Cf. *TC* 1.3.137:
'Troy in our weakness stands, not in
her strength.'
182 probably an accidental omission in F;
but it is striking that an earlier F omission (29–32) also involves Carlisle's lines.
183 **no . . . fight** Nothing worse (than
being *slain*) can come by fighting.
184–5 a somewhat cryptic couplet in which
the Bishop condenses and sums up his
gnomic wisdom: 'and to die fighting is
to destroy the power of Death by dying,
whereas to live in the fear of death is to
pay Death obsequious flattery (*breath*)';
syntactically, the phrase *fight and die*
(184) is treated like a compound gerund
('fighting and dying' or 'dying in the
course of fighting') parallel to *fearing*
(185). Wilson (188) compares *JC*
2.2.32–3: 'Cowards die many times
before their deaths, / The valiant never
taste of death but once.' The elaborate
patterning throughout Carlisle's speech
(see 178n.) conveys episcopal gravity,
not gratuitous ingenuity.
184 Cf. *1H6* 4.7.28: 'Had Death been
French, then Death had died to-day.'
186, 192 **power** army
186 **of** 'from', or possibly 'about' (cf. 192
where Richard asks after York's whereabouts)

178 sit . . . woes] waile their present woes *F*   181 foe,] Foe; *F*   182] *om. F*   184, 185 Death] *this*
edn; death *QF*

And learn to make a body of a limb.

KING RICHARD

Thou chid'st me well. Proud Bolingbroke, I come
To change blows with thee for our day of doom.
This ague fit of fear is overblown.   190
An easy task it is to win our own.
Say, Scroop, where lies our uncle with his power?
Speak sweetly, man, although thy looks be sour.

SCROOP

Men judge by the complexion of the sky
The state and inclination of the day;   195
So may you by my dull and heavy eye.
My tongue hath but a heavier tale to say.
I play the torturer by small and small
To lengthen out the worst that must be spoken:
Your uncle York is joined with Bolingbroke,   200

187 **make . . . limb** make a small band of
loyalists serve effectively as a whole
army. Mustering additional men may
be implied.
189 **change** exchange
for . . . doom to determine which of
us shall be doomed to defeat and death
190–3 Richard's jaunty couplets magnify
the effect of shallow and unjustified
optimism.
190 **ague** chill-causing fever (dissyllabic:
'à-gue')
is overblown has blown over, has dis-
sipated (not 'is exaggerated'). Richard
mixes his metaphors, combining disease with weather imagery.
191 **our own** my own realm (or perhaps
'my own subjects')
193 **sweetly** encouragingly
194–7 a quatrain (rhyming abab); see
198n. Cf. *AW* 5.3.32–4: 'I am not a day
of season, / For thou mayst see a sunshine and a hail / In me at once.'
194 **complexion** external appearance

(not limited to colour)
195 **inclination** tendency (of the weather)
196 **heavy** sad, gloomy
196–7 *This edn interprets QF's colon
after *eye* as a stop; some editors (like
Theobald) allow the sentence to run
on, interpreting the syntax as: 'so may
you (judge) by my dull and heavy eye
(that) my tongue has'. Ure (104)
prefers the latter alternative, reading
Q's colon, however, not as a stop but as
the equivalent of 'that'.
197 **heavier** gloomier, more sorrowful
(than the message that the sad *eye* of
196 betokened)
198 **by . . . small** little by little (like the
torturer who prolongs a prisoner's
agony on the rack). Scroop recognizes
that by holding back his bad news he is
ironically only intensifying Richard's
pain. The quatrain at 194–7 enhances
the effect of indirection.
200 **uncle York** Cf. 89.
is joined has joined (Abbott, 295)

188 well.] *Q4 (*well;*), *F (*well:*); well, *Q*   193 sour] *(sower), *F*   196–7 eye. / My] *(eie: / My);*
eye, / My *Theobald*

> And all your northern castles yielded up,
> And all your southern gentlemen in arms
> Upon his party.
>
> KING RICHARD   Thou hast said enough.
>
> [*to Aumerle*]
>
> Beshrew thee, cousin, which didst lead me forth
> Of that sweet way I was in to despair.   205
> What say you now? What comfort have we now?
> By heaven, I'll hate him everlastingly
> That bids me be of comfort any more.
> Go to Flint Castle. There I'll pine away.

202 **gentlemen in arms** The sense is ambiguous: the primary meaning seems to be 'men of rank who are armed'; but the phrase could also refer to 'gentlemen who have coats of arms' or 'gentlemen who are up in arms'.

203 **Upon his party** on his side. Although it presumably comes from the promptbook (see Appendix 1, pp. 513–14), F's substitution of 'Faction' for Q's 'partie' seems more specific and perhaps more limiting (as at 2.2.57). However, the same change from 'partie' to the more pejorative 'faction' occurs also with reference to the King's opponents in F's reprint of Q *R3* 5.3.13: 'the King's name is a tower of strength, / Which they upon the adverse faction [Q party] want'. RP notes that F's change in both *R2* and *R3* is congruent with the politics of James I's reign, i.e. with monarchist absolutism, and may therefore reflect a 'shift of emphasis' between 1597 and 1623.

204 **Beshrew** confound (literally, 'curse', but always used mildly)
which who (Abbott, 265)

204–5 **forth / Of** away from, out of

205 **sweet . . . despair** *Way* seems to mean both 'path' and 'habit' (as in 'getting into the way of despondency'). 'This admirable stroke goes to the

core of Richard's artist nature. Keenly alive to the effectiveness of the parts he plays, he prefers the heroic rôle of the magnificent and absolute king; failing this, he will have the pathetic rôle of the ruined and hapless king. Aumerle's futile suggestion has disturbed his growing acquiescence in this secondary but still effective part' (Herford, 181).

207–8 Johnson's comment on these lines is famous: 'This sentiment is drawn from nature. Nothing is more offensive to a mind convinced that his distress is without a remedy, and preparing to submit quietly to irresistible calamity, than these petty and conjectured comforts which unskilful officiousness thinks it virtue to administer' (1.441–2).

209–14 The rhymed couplets effectively express Richard's *sweet way* with *despair* (205).

209 **Flint Castle** a Welsh fortress near Chester on the estuary of the River Dee. Holinshed momentarily confuses Conway with Flint (3.499), misnaming the castle as Flint in a marginal note to a passage which reports that the King 'got him to the castell of Conwaie'. For Shakespeare's omission of the ambushing of Richard between Conway and Flint, see headnote. Froissart (6.364–5), whom Shakespeare may

203 party] Faction *F*   204 SD] *Theobald*

A king, woe's slave, shall kingly woe obey.   210
That power I have, discharge, and let them go
To ear the land that hath some hope to grow,
For I have none. Let no man speak again
To alter this, for counsel is but vain.

AUMERLE

My liege, one word.

KING RICHARD   He does me double wrong   215
That wounds me with the flatteries of his tongue.
Discharge my followers. Let them hence away,
From Richard's night to Bolingbroke's fair day.   ᶠ*Exeunt.*ᶠ

have consulted at this point, has
Richard proceeding directly to Flint
on the advice of his nobles, once he has
received news of Bolingbroke's successes and after he is told that his
'puyssaunce is nat sufficient' and that
'it cannat aveyle [him] to make batayle
agaynst' his enemies: 'The nexte day
the kynge, with suche as were of his
householde, rode to the castell of
Flynte, and entred into the castell
without makynge any semblaunt to
make any warre, but to abide there and
to defende the castell if they were
assayled.'

210 **kingly woe** See 5.6.45n.

211 **power** army, military force

212 **ear** plough (and sow), cultivate
hope to grow 'prospect of producing
a harvest'. Richard contrasts his own
barren future to the more fruitful
promise of Bolingbroke's burgeoning
career. Cf. 5.6.46n.

215–16 **He . . . tongue.** The injury is
double because it both *wounds* (i.e.
increases grief) and afflicts with the lies
of flattery (i.e. raises false hopes). See
207–8n. Wells (222) suggests that the
'notion of the *double* or forked *tongue* of
a snake may be present' (cf. 20–1).

218 Richard reverses the sun image which
he had invoked at 37, transferring it
histrionically to his rival; cf. Daniel,

2.1, where Richard's former subjects
'All turn'd their faces to the rising
sunne [Bolingbroke] / And leaues his
setting-fortune[,] night begun'. See
also 2.4.19–21n. Holinshed's comment
at this point on Richard's declining
fortunes could have influenced
Shakespeare's notable increase in the
sympathy evoked for his title character: 'This suerlie is a verie notable
example, and not vnworthie of all
princes to be well weied, and dili-
gentlie marked, that this Henrie duke
of Lancaster should be thus called to
the kingdome, and haue the helpe and
assistance (almost) of all the whole
realme, which perchance neuer thereof
thought or yet dreamed; and that king
Richard should thus be left desolate,
void, and in despaire of all hope and
comfort, in whom if there were anie
offense, it ought rather to be imputed
to the frailtie of wanton youth, than to
the malice of his hart: but such is the
deceiuable iudgement of man, which
not regarding things present with due
consideration, thinketh euer that
things to come shall haue good suc-
cesse, with a pleasant & delitefull end.
But in this deiecting of the one, & aduancing of the other, the prouidence of
God is to be respected, & his secret
will to be woondered at' (3.499).

211 them] 'em *F*

335

[3.3]   Enter ^{F}with [Trumpet,] Drum and Colours^F
BOLINGBROKE, YORK, NORTHUMBERLAND, ^{F}Attendants^F
[and Soldiers].

3.3 This scene, which stages the first meeting between Richard and Bolingbroke
after the latter's banishment, represents
the major turning point of the play,
dramatically reversing the dynamics of
power between the antagonists with
striking visual symbolism. It is founded
mainly on Holinshed, although with
omissions (as explained in 3.2 headnote
and 3.2.209n.). The omission of
Northumberland's use of guile and
force places 'the whole onus on
[Richard's] despair' and emphasizes his
rival's greater 'military power' (Cam^2,
124). In Holinshed, Bolingbroke, having mustered his army near Flint
Castle, arrives with his men and
arranges to confront the King in person
in the courtyard, but only after Richard
has been safely confined there; he continues, during these manoeuvres, to
employ Northumberland as an emis-
sary and one of his negotiators. At this
point Shakespeare picks up the story.
Froissart (6.364) also omits the intervening events and has Richard moving
directly to Flint Castle after his landing
on the Welsh coast. As Ure (106) points
out, it is unnecessary to suppose that
the dramatist suddenly shifted from
relying on Holinshed (his primary
source so far) to the French chronicler,
although Froissart's less intricate narrative could well have prompted him to
streamline the plotting in the interests
of greater dramatic forcefulness.
Froissart excludes Northumberland
altogether from the account of
Richard's capture. Shakespeare, like
Holinshed, makes important use of
him, nevertheless omitting his betrayal
of the King – perhaps, as Wilson (189)
suggests, by way of preparation for his
treatment of the Percys in *1H4* where,
as rebels against Bolingbroke, they

speak with nostalgic reverence about
Richard. Aumerle's involvement in the
scene is largely imagined.
   The shifting locations (see 2.3 headnote) again illustrate the flexibility of
the Elizabethan stage. In the opening
episode, Bolingbroke and his men are
just approaching Flint where they
shortly receive news of Richard's presence 'Within the limits of yon lime and
stone' (26). Bolingbroke then commissions Northumberland as envoy to go to
the *rude ribs* of the castle (32), its walls
represented by the tiring-house wall, to
parley with the King while he and his
forces 'march / Upon the grassy carpet
of this plain' (49–50). This military
action, however executed, must be brief
because the focus shifts immediately to
the King above. At 61.1–3 Richard with
his small group of loyalists appears *on
the walls* of Flint Castle (represented by
the upper level), at which point
Bolingbroke comments below on the
ceremonial entry while the King
remains impressively mute above.
Northumberland then conducts the
negotiations between Richard and
Bolingbroke by moving back and forth
between the two groups on the lower
level. At 183 Richard leaves the upper
level, probably descending behind the
tiring-house facade, and reappears
below at 185, where for the first time in
the scene he meets Bolingbroke face to
face ('in the base court', 176, 180, 182).
The main stage now becomes the castle
courtyard. In addition to a plastic conception of space, it is clear that the
scene calls for considerable formality in
the staging.
0.1 **Trumpet* trumpeter
   **Drum* drummer
   **Colours* probably a standard-bearer
   with a banner (cf. 3.2.0.1n.)

3.3] F (Scaena Tertia.)   0.1–3] Enter Bull. Yorke, North. Q; Enter with Drum and Colours, Bullingbrooke,
Yorke, Northumberland, Attendants. F   0.1 Trumpet] this edn   0.3 and Soldiers] Capell (subst.)

BOLINGBROKE

So that by this intelligence we learn
The Welshmen are dispersed, and Salisbury
Is gone to meet the King, who lately landed
With some few private friends upon this coast.

NORTHUMBERLAND

The news is very fair and good, my lord: 5
Richard not far from hence hath hid his head.

YORK

It would beseem the Lord Northumberland
To say 'King Richard'. Alack the heavy day
When such a sacred king should hide his head.

NORTHUMBERLAND

Your grace mistakes; only to be brief   10
Left I his title out.

YORK   The time hath been,

---

1 **So that** The scene begins in mid-
conversation (cf. 1.4.1n.). Bolingbroke
may hold in his hand a dispatch containing the matter to which he refers;
or perhaps he has simply received an
oral briefing from Northumberland on
events already dramatized in 2.4 and
3.2. The dramatic point is that the
audience is given to understand that
Bolingbroke shares their awareness of
recent events. See 3.2 headnote.
intelligence military information
4 **private friends** Aumerle, Salisbury,
Scroop and Carlisle (cf. 27–30 and n.);
but at this point Bolingbroke appears
not to know their identities.
6 **hid his head** taken shelter. Northumberland conceives of Richard as
hiding, implying cowardice or fear, or
perhaps alluding to the setting sun; an
ironic contrast to Richard's image of
himself as the sun rising majestically at
3.2.39–43.

7–9 York's tart rebuke of his new political
ally effectively conveys the old Duke's
residual respect for the *sacred king* he
has recently deserted – or at least for
the semi-divine office which Richard
still occupies.
7 **beseem** befit
8 **heavy** sad
9 **should** must
   hide See 6n.
10 a metrically deficient line, requiring a
pause (or beat) after the semi-colon.
Rowe's emendation (see t.n.) regularizes the metre but is difficult to defend
bibliographically. The pause, which is
dramatically effective, is probably
intentional.
11–13 ***The . . . shorten you** F's emendation rhetorically balancing *with him*
(12) and *with you* (13), while at the
same time correcting the metre, apparently derives from the theatre promptbook; see Appendix 1, pp. 526–7.

1+ SP]*(Bul[l].)*   10 mistakes] mistakes me *Rowe*   11–13 The . . . shorten you] *as F; Q lines*
him, / shorten you, /

337

Would you have been so brief with him, he would
Have been so brief ^{F}with you^F to shorten you,
For taking so the head, your whole head's length.

BOLINGBROKE

Mistake not, uncle, further than you should.   15

YORK

Take not, good cousin, further than you should,
Lest you mis-take: the heavens are o'er our heads.

BOLINGBROKE

I know it, uncle, and oppose not myself
Against their will.

Enter [HARRY] PERCY.

But who comes here?

12–14 The elaborate quibbling of these lines, far from trivializing York's reproach, lends it sarcastic edge. York uses *brief* in the double sense of 'brief in language' (and therefore disrespectful) and 'hasty' (in pronouncing a sentence of death); *shorten* glances backward at *brief* in the verbal sense while punning on the meaning of 'behead'; *taking so the head* ('thus depriving (the King) of his title') and *taking . . . your whole head's length* ('decapitating you') play on two senses of *head. Taking so the head* may also suggest wordplay on 'being headstrong (and presumptuous), acting without restraint' and 'referring without proper deference to the head of state'. Hall (fol. xiiii), reporting the execution of the Duke of Exeter, Richard's half-brother, says that he was 'made shorter by the hed'. For Baron's imitation, see 3.2.156LN.

13 **to shorten** as to shorten (Abbott, 281)

15 **Mistake** misconstrue, misunderstand

16 **Take not** do not interpret (your right); do not seize (your political advantage)
   cousin nephew

17 **mis-take* transgress, take that to

which you have no proper claim (playing on the senses of *Take* in 16); take amiss, commit an error (playing on Bolingbroke's *Mistake* in 15). GWW suggests a parallel instance of 'hyphenated wordplay' in *Mac* 5.3.40: 'a mind diseased [dis-eased]'. Rowe's punctuation after *mis-take* seems to be justified; Q and F both run the sentence on, creating an idiomatic awkwardness and requiring us to understand *mis-take* in the sense of 'fail to recognize that'. Wilson (190) notes that Rowe's punctuation yields 'better rhythm and greatly superior sense', adding that Q's 'punctuation is often scanty elsewhere'.
   the . . . heads 'We must not forget that we are under the judgement of God'; *heavens* is monosyllabic.

18 a hypermetrical line, scannable by hurrying over *not* or by making the final foot anapaestic ('not mysèlf'). RP suggests that *uncle* has a hanging syllable at the caesura, and that *and oppòse* is also anapaestic.

19 a tetrameter line, or perhaps a pentameter with a long pause after the full

17 mis-take:] *Capell;* mistake; *Rowe;* mistake *QF*   o'er] *F;* ouer *Q*   our heads] your heads *Q3;* your head *F*   19 will] *QF;* willes *Q4*   SD] *Oxf; after* here? *QF*   HARRY] *Wells*

Welcome, Harry. What, will not this castle yield?　　　20

HARRY PERCY

　The castle royally is manned, my lord,

　Against thy entrance.

BOLINGBROKE

　　　　　　Royally?

　Why? It contains no king.

HARRY PERCY　　　　　　　　Yes, my good lord,

　It doth contain a king. King Richard lies　　　25

　Within the limits of yon lime and stone,

　And with him are the Lord Aumerle, Lord Salisbury,

　Sir Stephen Scroop, besides a clergyman

　Of holy reverence – who, I cannot learn.

NORTHUMBERLAND

　O, belike it is the Bishop of Carlisle.　　　30

---

stop. GWW suggests two short lines.
SD Presumably Percy enters through
the door opposite to that through
which Bolingbroke and his party had
entered; apparently he has been sent
ahead to reconnoitre the defensibility
of the castle.

20 probably a regular pentameter with
　extra-metrical *What*
　What a casual, half-humorous inter-
　jection ('Well') used (as often in
　Shakespeare) to introduce a question
　or express impatience (Abbott, 73a)
　this castle Flint (see headnote)

21–6 That Richard commands Flint
Castle and appears prepared to offer
resistance is unhistorical. The departure from Holinshed is clearly due to
Shakespeare's elimination of the capture of Richard between Conway and
Flint; see 3.2 and 3.3 headnotes, also
3.2.209n.

25 **King Richard** Harry Percy's use of

this title may register ironically with
the audience, given the exchange
between Northumberland and York at
6–9.

lies lodges, dwells

26 **limits** walls

27–30 For Richard's companions at Flint,
Shakespeare drew on a passage in
Holinshed (3.501) later than that on
which the earlier part of the scene is
based: 'The king accompanied with
the bishop of Carleill, the earle of
Salisburie, and sir Stephan Scroope
knight, who bare the sword before
him, and a few other, came foorth into
the vtter ward [of Flint Castle], and
sate downe in a place prepared for
him'; see also 190n.

30 possibly an alexandrine, but more likely a regular pentameter introduced by
extra-metrical *O*
　belike doubtless, very likely

21+ SP] *Oxf; H. Per. Q; Per. F*　21 royally is] *QF;* is royally *Q2*　23–4 Royally . . . king] *as
Steevens; one line QF*　23 Royally?] *F;* Royally, *Q*　24 Why? It] *this edn;* why it *Q;* Why, it *F*
26 yon] yond *F*　27 are the] the *Q2–F*

339

BOLINGBROKE [*to Northumberland*]
    Noble lord,
    Go to the rude ribs of that ancient castle;
    Through brazen trumpet send the breath of parley
    Into his ruined ears, and thus deliver:
    Henry Bolingbroke   35
    On both his knees doth kiss King Richard's hand
    And sends allegiance and true faith of heart
    To his most royal person, hither come
    Even at his feet to lay my arms and power
    Provided that my banishment repealed   40
    And lands restored again be freely granted.
    If not, I'll use the advantage of my power

31 **lord** F's singularization of Q's 'Lords'
probably derives from the promptbook
(see Appendix 1, pp. 526–7); since
Northumberland is clearly the person
addressed, the plural makes no dramatic sense. Again Q's compositor may have
confused a comma with terminal *s* in the
MS (cf. 1.4.20n.).

32 **rude ribs** rough walls (cf. 5.5.20; also
KJ 2.1.384: 'The flinty ribs of this contemptuous city'). Bolingbroke's imagery
is anthropomorphic: the fortress is like a
ribcage protecting the vital organs within (the King and his followers). Cf.
Spenser's House of Alma (*FQ*, 2.9.22),
which allegorically in its architecture
represents soul, mind and body.

33 **brazen** made of brass; shrill-sounding
(cf. *AC* 4.8.35–6: 'Trumpeters / With
brazen din')
    breath of parley call (of a trumpet)
    summoning opponents to a conference

34 **his ruined ears** literally, 'the battered
slits or loopholes of the castle's walls'
(cf. *tattered battlements*, 52). For *his* see
3.2.109n.; but *his* may also, as
Coleridge (122) believed, refer to the
King's own ears, *ruined ears* being a

synecdoche for 'ruined man'. Cf. also
KJ 2.1.215: 'your city's eyes, your
winking gates'.
    deliver announce, proclaim

35–8 **Malone's relining restores the metre,
dislocated in Q perhaps by crowding of
35–6 into a single line of print or, more
likely, by crowding in the MS from
which Q was set (see Appendix 1,
pp. 517–18). F's attempt to repair the
problem only worsened matters.

38 **hither come** 'I, Henry Bolingbroke,
being hither come'; the syntax shifts
from third person to first person to
avoid confusion (cf. *my arms*, 39), but
the change also enhances the aggres-
siveness of Bolingbroke's ultimatum.

39 **Even** probably monosyllabic ('E'en')
    my . . . power my weapons and the
    power to command their use

40–1 **my . . . again** 'the revocation of my
banishment and the restoration of my
lands to me'; grammatically, the participles *repealed* and *restored* do duty
for abstract nouns.

42 **the . . . power** my superiority in military force; *the advantage* is probably
elided ('th'advantage').

31 SD] *Rowe*   lord] *F;* Lords *Q*   33 parley] *(parlee);* Parle *F*   35–8] *as Malone; Q lines* hand, /
heart / come /; *F lines* kisse / allegeance / come /   35 Henry Bolingbroke] *(H. Bull.), F (Henry
Bullingbrooke)*   36 On both] vpon *F*   38 most royal] Royall *F*

And lay the summer's dust with showers of blood
Rained from the wounds of slaughtered Englishmen –
The which how far off from the mind of Bolingbroke   45
It is such crimson tempest should bedrench
The fresh green lap of fair King Richard's land
My stooping duty tenderly shall show.
Go signify as much, while here we march
Upon the grassy carpet of this plain.   50
[*Northumberland with Trumpet goes to the walls.*]
Let's march without the noise of threat'ning drum,

43–4 Cf. Daniel, 1.121 (see 97n.); also 46–7n.

43 **summer's dust** Bolingbroke met Richard in August 1399. Cf. 3.2.146.
  showers monosyllabic ('show'rs)

45–8 Coleridge (122–3) thought that Bolingbroke's sudden shift at this point from a threatening to a humbler mode of speech betokens a warning gesture on the part of the actor who plays York, the young speaker being 'checked by the eye' of the older and more reluctant rebel. Coleridge also believed that the same warning glance occurs again after 57. But, as Wells (224) observes, Bolingbroke's change of tone could just as well be motivated by hypocrisy as humility. Cf. Henry V's threats of violence to the citizens of Harfleur, followed by a much gentler tone after the town yields (*H5* 3.3).

45 **The which** as to which; cf. 1.1.172n. The antecedent of *which* is the entirety of Bolingbroke's threat.

46–7 **crimson . . . lap** Cf. 50 and 5.6.46: 'That blood should sprinkle me to make me grow'; also 4.1.138: 'The blood of English shall manure the ground'. For the play's collocation of blood and nature imagery, see Introduction, pp. 70–1.

46 **It is** it is that

47 **lap** Cf. 5.2.47: 'the green lap of the new-come spring'.
  fair handsome (a touch of flattery by Bolingbroke; cf. *stooping duty*, 48); or *fair* may qualify *land*.
  King Richard's Cf. 36, 54, 61 and 62. Herford (182) notes that, unlike Northumberland, Bolingbroke 'never . . . omits Richard's title'. Shakespeare keeps his motive hidden: perhaps Bolingbroke bows outwardly to York's feelings, or deliberately conceals his true intentions, or both. Or is he genuinely respectful of Richard at this point? Adams (168) notes that 'the whole of [this] speech gives the impression of careful preparation; even the richness of its imagery (untypical of Bolingbroke's usual manner of speaking) seems calculated for his cousin's benefit'; cf. 62–7n.

48 **stooping duty** kneeling in submission, dutiful humility
  tenderly gently, solicitously; affectionately, with kindness

50 SD* *Trumpet* See 0.1n.

51 **Let's march** Bolingbroke obviously wishes to impress Richard with the strength and discipline of his army.
  without . . . drum The absence of the drum signifies peaceful intention.

43 showers] *(showres),* F   45 Bolingbroke] *(Bulling.),* F *(Bullingbrooke)*   47 land] *Q2,* F *(* land,*);* land: *Q*   50 SD] *Oxf (subst.)*

That from this castle's tattered battlements
Our fair appointments may be well perused.
Methinks King Richard and myself should meet
With no less terror than the elements   55

52 **tattered** either 'ragged, delapidated'
(in contrast to *Our fair appointments*,
53) or 'crennelated, jagged, denticulat-
ed, having pointed projections' (see
OED a. 1, 5); Q's 'tottered' is a variant
spelling of 'tattered' (Q3, F). The
word is not used contemptuously, nor
does it necessarily imply that the castle can be easily overwhelmed, since
ruined ears probably applies as much to
Richard himself as to the building (see
34n.).

53–61.3 Holinshed (3.500–1) writes:
'King Richard being thus come vnto
the castell of Flint . . . and the duke of
Hereford being still aduertised from
houre to houre by posts, how the earle
of Northumberland sped, the morow
following . . . he came thither & mustered his armie before the kings presence, which vndoubtedlie made a
passing faire shew, being verie well
ordered by the lord Henrie Persie, that
was appointed generall, or rather (as
we maie call him) master of the
campe, vnder the duke, of the whole
armie. . . . The king that was walking
aloft on the braies [ramparts] of the
wals, to behold the comming of the
duke a farre off, might see, that the
archbishop [of Canterbury] and the
other [persons] were come, and (as he
tooke it) to talke with him: wherevpon
he foorthwith came downe vnto them,
and beholding that they did their due
reuerence to him on their knees, he
tooke them vp . . . and as it was reported, the archbishop willed him to be of
good comfort, for he should be
assured, not to haue anie hurt, as
touching his person; but he prophe-
sied not as a prelat, but as Pilat. For,

was it no hurt (thinke you) to his person, to be spoiled of his roialtie, to be
deposed from his crowne, to be translated from principalitie to prison, & to
fall from honor into horror. All which
befell him to his extreame hart greef
(no doubte:) which to increase,
meanes alas there were manie; but to
diminish, helps (God wot) but a few.'
Froissart (6.368) reports: 'all the
countrey about the castell [of Flint]
was full of men of warre: they within
the castell myght se them out at the
wyndowes, and the kynge whan he
rose fro the table myght se them hym-
selfe'.

53 **fair appointments** gallant military
showing, handsomely equipped presence (cf. *glittering arms* and *barbed
steeds*, 116–17)
perused observed, surveyed

54, 91 **Methinks** it seems to me

55 **With** causing

55–7 **elements . . . heaven** It was commonly believed that thunder was
caused by a clash of elements (*fire and
water*). Leonard Digges, *A Prog-
nostication Everlasting of Right Good
Effect* (1576), explains: 'Thunder is the
quenching of fyre, in a cloude. Or
thunder is an exhalation, hot and dry,
mixt with moisture caryed vp to the
middle Region, there thicked and
wrapped into a cloud; of his hotte matter coupled in moystnes, closed in the
cloud, groweth a strife, the heate
beatinge, and breaking out the sides of
ye cloude wyth a thundringe noyse:
the fyre then dispersed, is the light-
ninge' (sig. D1ʳ); see also *Atheist's
Tragedy*, 2.4.141–51.

52 tattered] *(tottered)*, *Q3, F*

Of fire and water, when their thund'ring shock
At meeting tears the cloudy cheeks of heaven.
Be he the fire, I'll be the yielding water;
The rage be his, whilst on the earth I rain
My waters – on the earth and not on him.   60
March on, and mark King Richard how he looks.

56 **fire and water** in the form of lightning and rain, or moisture-filled clouds
shock Cf. 1.3.136n. Q2's 'smoke', carried over into F, possesses no authority, exemplifying one of Compositor A's notorious substitutions; see Appendix 1, p. 537 and n. 1.

57 **cloudy . . . heaven** probably glancing at the puff-cheeked cherubs at the corners of old maps, depicting the winds; cf. *Tem* 1.2.4: 'th' welkin's cheek'; cf. also 45–8n.

58–60 difficult and complex lines. Because *fire* precedes *water* in the traditional hierarchy of the natural order (according to the Great Chain of Being), just as kings precede subjects in the political order, water would necessarily be the *yielding* element. Logically, therefore, Bolingbroke identifies the King with fire (wrath) and himself with water (submission). The irony of this utterance is quickly perceptible since Bolingbroke's actual behaviour, apart from his outward show of submission, involves no *yielding* (58) at all (see 3.2.109–10). Pursuing the weather symbolism further, Bolingbroke states that Richard may rage above (like lightning in the heavens), while he himself will 'rain / [his] waters – on the earth' rather than on the King, i.e. dropping tears of sorrow for his adversary, or perhaps even nourishing the earth of

England with the moisture of his more benevolent rule, as opposed to raining down vengeance upon his oppressor. In addition, Bolingbroke in a half-suppressed manner may quibble on 'reign' (59), hinting at the extent of his political ambition. Q's spelling, 'raigne', could mean either 'rain' or 'reign' (see OED). See 59–60n.

59–60 ***rain . . . earth** Most editors accept F's repunctuation, removing Q's full stop and treating Q's contraction 'water's' ('water is') as a plural ('waters'). F's pointing certainly yields better sense and is more idiomatic. Q's anomalous full stop and apostrophe are plausibly explained by *TxC* (311): 'The line-break is also a page-break between formes [F4–F4ᵛ] in Q' – a circumstance that could partly account for compositorial misunderstanding and consequent mispunctuation.

61 **how he looks** Cf. Abbott, 414; also 5.4.1. Bolingbroke's command to his men that they *mark* Richard's appearance helps underline the iconographic importance of the King's entrance *on the walls*. Note that Richard remains silent for ten lines (62–71) while Bolingbroke and York in turn direct elaborate rhetorical attention to the impressive sunburst of his presence.

56 shock] smoke *Q2–F*   59 whilst] while *F*   59–60 rain . . . – on] *Rowe³ (*waters; on*);* raigne. / My water's on *Q;* raigne / My water's on *Q3;* raine / My Waters on *F*

The trumpets sound [a] [F]*parley without and answer within; then a*
flourish. [F] [KING] RICHARD *appeareth [above] on the walls [with*
Bishop of] [F]CARLISLE, AUMERLE, SCROOP [and] SALISBURY[F].

See, see, King Richard doth himself appear,
As doth the blushing discontented sun

61.1–3 *Richard's ceremonial appearance on the upper level (*on the walls*) makes the title figure the new centre of dramatic interest. This is preceded by a trumpet call signalling a request for *parley* from the stage (*without*), which is then answered from offstage (*within*); the royal entry itself is now announced by a more elaborate fanfare (from offstage or possibly with the trumpeters in view above). As Wells (225) points out, probably no words should be spoken until Richard has formally taken up his position for Bolingbroke and York to comment upon (see 61n.), although it is possible, as GWW thinks, that the entrance of the royal party above would be covered by their comments (62–71). Q's SD is '*Richard appeareth on the walls*', but it is obvious that Aumerle enters with him since the two later converse (127–33). F adds Carlisle, Scroop and Salisbury as mute supporters of the King, almost certainly following the theatre promptbook. Mowat & Werstine (lv), doubting theatrical authority for the additional figures, object that there would be insufficient room 'in the gallery above the stage' of the Elizabethan theatre to accommodate five actors; but Hodges's drawing of a possible staging at the Swan shows the five actors occupying the space without difficulty (see Cam[2], 39). The Swan drawing itself shows many people occupying the 'above' (Cam[2], 36). Also the reconstructed Globe in modern London has enough space for at least five players, in addition to which in other Shakespearean scenes comparable numbers occupy the 'above': see, for instance, *TS* Induction 2, 0.1–2; *Tit* 1.1.0.1–2, 295.1–2.

61.1 *parley* See 1.1.192n.

62–7 Bolingbroke's rhetoric is unusually florid for the matter-of-fact politician who tends to speak more plainly, perhaps thereby suggesting a note of disingenuousness in the character; but, just as likely, Shakespeare may wish to dramatize the true awe which the grandeur of Richard's presence inspires, or, less probably (as F.E. Schelling thought), to suggest a Bolingbroke who momentarily mocks Richard's style (see Black, 215). See LN. There is no authority for reassigning the lines to York or Percy, as many editors have done (see Black, 214–15). Q's unnecessary repetition of the SP at 62 probably reflects only the interruption caused by the preceding SD.

63 **blushing discontented sun** an ominous note: a red sun in the morning was traditionally supposed to be the sign of a stormy day; cf. *1H4* 5.1.1–6 and the old jingle 'Red sky in the morning, / Sailors take warning; / Red sky at night, / Sailors' delight'. (A variant refers to shepherds rather than sailors.) Richard's flushed face is also meant to symbolize his anger (his 'discontent'): as the sun, because of the *envious clouds*; as the king, because of his political vulnerability. For Richard's changing facial colouration, see 2.1.118–19n.

61.1–3] *Parle without, and answere within: then a Flourish. Enter on the Walls, Richard, Carlile, Aumerle, Scroop, Salisbury. F* 61.2 *above*] *this edn* 62 See] *F; Bull. See Q*

From out the fiery portal of the east,
When he perceives the envious clouds are bent   65
To dim his glory and to stain the track
Of his bright passage to the Occident.

YORK

Yet looks he like a king. Behold, his eye,
As bright as is the eagle's, lightens forth
Controlling majesty. Alack, alack for woe   70
That any harm should stain so fair a show!

KING RICHARD [*to Northumberland*]

We are amazed, and thus long have we stood
To watch the fearful bending of thy knee
Because we thought ourself thy lawful king.

---

64 **fiery portal** blazing gateway; cf. 3.2.42n.

65 **he** the sun
envious hostile, spiteful (not merely 'jealous')
are bent are determined, intend

66 **stain** darken, obscure the lustre of (cf. *Son* 33.14: 'Suns of the world may stain, when heaven's sun staineth')

67 **Occident** west (where the sun sets; from Latin *occido* = fall down)

68 **Yet . . . king.** York echoes Bolingbroke's *looks* (61), stressing yet again the impressiveness of Richard's appearance ('so fair a show', 71). Richard's uncle seems to allude to the sad discrepancy between the outward display of royal authority and the actual weakness that underlies it. Probably *Yet* means 'still, as before' (showing that York remains a reluctant convert to Bolingbroke's cause); or, despite the absence of a comma, it may mean simply 'nevertheless'.

69 **bright . . . eagle's** 'The eagle, king of birds, was believed to be able to look into the sun, chief of the heavenly bodies, without coming to harm' (Wells, 226). Tillyard points out that 'in short space' during this scene 'we have four of the traditional primacies [of the Great Chain of Being]: fire

among the elements [55–8], the sun among the planets [62–7], the king among men [72–4], the eagle among the birds [69]' (*Picture*, 28).

69–70 **lightens . . . majesty** flashes with the appearance of majestic authority (like lightning). Jupiter hurled bolts of lightning as divine punishment.

70 an alexandrine

71 **stain** spoil (echoing Bolingbroke's *stain* at 66 with a slight difference)
so . . . show so beautiful a spectacle (see 68n.)

72–3 Richard puts maximal distance between himself and Northumberland through his use of pronouns – by using the royal *we* (instead of the more informal 'I') and the contemptuous *thy* (in lieu of the more formal 'your'). The hierarchical distance, supported by the mentioned postures (standing and kneeling), is reinforced visually by the staging – the King above, the subject below. Richard continues to use the royal plural until 85.

72 **amazed** astounded, stunned, at a loss to comprehend (much stronger than in modern usage; literally, 'in a maze')

73 **To watch** in the expectation of seeing, to wait for
fearful reverential

66 track] tract *F*   72+ SP] *King Q; Rich. F*   72 SD] *Rowe (subst.)*

And if we be, how dare thy joints forget   75
To pay their awful duty to our presence?
If we be not, show us the hand of God
That hath dismissed us from our stewardship;
For well we know no hand of blood and bone
Can gripe the sacred handle of our sceptre,   80
Unless he do profane, steal or usurp.
And though you think that all, as you have done,
Have torn their souls by turning them from us,
And we are barren and bereft of friends,
Yet know: my Master, God omnipotent,   85
Is mustering in His clouds on our behalf
Armies of pestilence, and they shall strike

75 **And if** Some editors interpret the phrase as 'An if' (= if), which is possible (cf. 77) See 4.1.50n.

75–6 **how . . . presence** Northumberland's failure to kneel is significant and in character; cf. his earlier omission of Richard's title (6). Stirling (30–1) says that Shakespeare here uses a technique of 'dramatic suggestion' by which the character, through ' "unconscious" disclosure', reveals his master's hidden intention to claim the crown. In Holinshed, however, Northumberland and the other lords do kneel: 'they did their due reuerence to him on their knees' (see 53–61.3n.).

76 **awful duty** reverential homage, respect full of awe; cf. 1.1.118n.
presence Cf. 1.1.15n.

77 **hand of God** written hand, signature (or possibly used figuratively to mean simply 'manual sign of God', i.e. 'divine revelation'. Doubtless Richard's stress on divine right and the important antithesis to 'hand of blood and bone' (79) prevented F from altering *God* to 'Heaven' (cf. 1.3.11n., 2.1.200n., 251n.)

78 **stewardship** Cf. 4.1.127; see also 3.2.57n.

79 **hand . . . bone** human hand (as contrasted with *hand of God*)

80 **gripe** seize, grasp. 'Grip' may be a variant of the same word (see *OED*).

81 **profane** commit sacrilege, blaspheme (another of Richard's references to divine right)

83 **torn . . . us** 'damned themselves by forsaking their allegiance'. 'Torn' sometimes meant 'lacerated'. The wordplay on *torn* and *turning* is deliberate. The image may imply the tearing up of a legal document, a bond of fealty.

84 **And we are** and that we are (continuing the relative clause from 82)

85 **my Master** Cf. 2 Kings, 6.15. Richard's lapse into the singular pronoun here and later in the speech marks a shift from his initial conception of himself as king to that of an individual.

86 **mustering** probably dissyllabic ('must'ring')

87 **Armies of pestilence** Cf. 3.2.59–61n., 5.3.3n.
strike blast, visit disease upon (used metaphorically). Cf. 2 Kings, 19.35: 'And the selfe same night the angel of the Lord went out, & smote in the host of the Assyrians and hundred fourescore & fiue thousand: and when the remnant were vp earely in the morning, behold they were all dead coarses.'

75 And] An *Oxf (Delius)*

Your children, yet unborn and unbegot,
That lift your vassal hands against my head
And threat the glory of my precious crown.   90
Tell Bolingbroke – for yon methinks he stands –
That every stride he makes upon my land
Is dangerous treason. He is come to open
The purple testament of bleeding war;
But ere the crown he looks for live in peace,   95
Ten thousand bloody crowns of mothers' sons
Shall ill become the flower of England's face,

88–9 **Your ... your** 'the children of you ... who lift your'. Cf. *Daniel*, 1.90: 'The babes vnborne, shall ô be borne to bleed / In this thy quarrell if thou doe proceede'; also *Homily* (2.303): '[rebels] vndoe all men where they come, that the childe yet vnborne may rue it, and shall many yeeres hereafter curse them'. Cf. also Carlisle's prophecy at 4.1.137–50 and 150n. For Baron's imitation, see 3.2.156LN.

89 Cf. *Woodstock*, 5.3.57: 'That draw your swords against our sacred person'. The image of the hand rebelling against the head may derive from the familiar concept of the body politic, which in turn is analogous to the body of Christ, i.e. the Church with its Head and obedient members (1 Corinthians, 12.12–28).
vassal subject

90 **threat** threaten

91 **yon ... stands** *Yon* = yonder, over there. Bolingbroke and York are separated onstage from Northumberland and his men (see 61.1–3n.).

92–3 **every ... treason** Cf. *Daniel*, 1.90: 'Stay here thy foote, thy yet vnguilty foote.' Cf. 2.3.90–1, 3.2.16n., 125.

93 **dangerous** both to Richard and to posterity; perhaps dissyllabic ('dang'rous')
open perhaps monosyllabic ('op'n'; cf. F's 'ope'). Wills and legacies must

be formally opened before their provisions can be legally executed (see 94n.).

94 **purple testament** blood-stained will or legacy (by which war will be bequeathed to the nation); cf. *Jeronimo*, 2.2.87: 'Then I vnclaspe the purple leaues of war' (Kyd, 311). See also *Daniel*, 2.122: 'Her fieldes engrain'd with bloud, her riuers dide / With purple streaming wounds of her owne rage'.

95–7 Richard's bitter wordplay on the many heads (*crowns*) that will have to be sacrificed (by warfare or execution) to pay for Bolingbroke's seizure of the royal *crown* suggests that his enemy has nothing but the force of arms to back his claim.

95 **crown ... for** the crown he seeks. Again Richard assumes the worst before it occurs (cf. 3.2.95n., 160n.); the actions of Bolingbroke may make him a likely suspect for usurpation, but he has carefully avoided making any such claim.

97 **flower ... face** A combination of senses is implied: England (especially its blooming surface) is like a flower that will be defaced by war; the human face is flower-like in its beauty; the young manhood of England constitutes the flower of the nation. As in

91 yon] yond *F*   stands] is *F*   93 open] ope *F*

Change the complexion of her maid-pale peace
To scarlet indignation, and bedew
Her pastor's grass with faithful English blood.   100
NORTHUMBERLAND
The King of Heaven forbid our lord the King
Should so with civil and uncivil arms
Be rushed upon! Thy thrice-noble cousin,

his caressing of the ground at 3.2.6–26, Richard tends to image England anthropomorphically (cf. *maid-pale peace*, 98). There may be a debt to Daniel, 1.121: 'Th' vngodly bloudshed that did so defile / The beauty of thy fields, and euen did marre / The flowre of thy chiefe pride ô fairest Ile'. Cf. also *1H4* 1.1.5–9.

98 **complexion** colour
  maid-pale virgin-white. Cf. *1H6* 2.4.47: 'this pale and maiden blossom'.

99 **scarlet indignation** red-faced anger; bloody wrath

99–100 **bedew . . . blood** Cf. Carlisle's prophecy of civil war at 4.1.138: 'The blood of English shall manure the ground'.

100 **pastor's** shepherd's (i.e. Richard's). The image of the king as shepherd was common, deriving ultimately, for Elizabethans, from the idea of Christ as *bonus pastor*; cf. *E3* 1.1.41 where the sovereign is referred to as 'the true shepherd of our commonwealth'; also Hall (fol. lxxxi), who speaks of Henry V as 'a shepherde whom his flocke loued and louyngly obeyed'. Theobald's emendation ('Pasture's'), or Capell's ('pastures''), which many editors accept, is less effectively personal; but the difference would be hard to hear in performance (Cam[1], 192).

101 **Heaven** monosyllabic
  ***forbid** Grammatically, Q's colon,

like Q4's comma, substitutes for the relative 'that' and so does not represent a heavy stop. F's removal of punctuation simply clarifies the syntax.

102 **civil . . . arms** 'arms used in civil war which are also uncivil because violent and barbarous' – a quibbling oxymoron. Cf. *RJ* Prologue, 4: 'civil blood makes civil hands unclean'.

103 The metre is irregular, the final two feet being trochaic: 'Thy thrice- | nòble | còusin'. Q's lower-case 'be' at the start of the line (see t.n.) conceivably implies an unintended omission.
  thrice-noble because descended from Edward III (his grandfather) and from John of Gaunt (his father), both of whom were royal, as well as having titles of nobility in his own right (see List of Roles, 6n.). Northumberland justifies the triple claim at 105–10, though, confusingly, he cites four (overlapping) grounds for it. Gurr (128) sees a possible 'hint of a threat' to Richard, since such expressions are commonly reserved for kings and queens; cf. *thrice-gracious Queen* (2.2.24) where *thrice* seems to be little more than rhetorical intensification. With less plausibility, Chambers (128) and Petersson (142) take the word to refer to the three titles of Bolingbroke, i.e. Earl of Derby, Duke of Hereford and Duke of Lancaster.

100 pastor's] *QF;* Pasture's *Theobald;* pastures' *Capell*   101 forbid] *F;* forbid: *Q;* forbid, *Q4*   lord]
(Lo:), F   103 Be rushed] *(be rusht), F (*Be rush'd*)*   thrice-noble] *F;* thrise noble *Q*

Harry Bolingbroke, doth humbly kiss thy hand;
And by the honourable tomb he swears   105
That stands upon your royal grandsire's bones,
And by the royalties of both your bloods –
Currents that spring from one most gracious head –
And by the buried hand of warlike Gaunt,
And by the worth and honour of himself,   110
Comprising all that may be sworn or said,
His coming hither hath no further scope
Than for his lineal royalties, and to beg

104 a somewhat irregular line; the first two feet should probably be scanned as a trochee followed by a dactyl ('Hàrry | Bòlingbroke').

105–20 Herford (184) notes that Northumberland fails to repeat his master's message 'in literal terms': 'Bolingbroke has in fact given no pledge and taken no oath. Northumberland seeks merely to get possession of Richard, without committing his chief.' GWW observes that 'Northumberland repeats pretty closely his master's message (35–41) without repeating the threat (42–8)', noting in addition that in *1H4* Hotspur says that his father heard Bolingbroke 'swear and vow to God / He came but to be Duke of Lancaster' (4.3.60–1). The oath appears in Holinshed (see 2.3.114n.).

105 **honourable tomb** of Edward III (in Westminster Abbey); cf. *royal grandsire's bones* (106). In *Woodstock*, 2.1.142–3, York also swears by Edward III's tomb: 'by my birth I swear, / My father's tomb, and faith to heaven I owe'.

107 **royalties . . . bloods** royal status through the lineage of both of you (a meaning slightly different from that in 113)

108 **Currents** streams; the separate bloodlines are conceived of as rivers issuing from a single source (*head*), i.e. Edward III. Cf. 1.2.12–13n.

gracious noble

109 **buried . . . Gaunt** an ellipsis for 'the hand of Gaunt, now buried, that once wielded the sword of chivalric honour'; an allusion to Gaunt's hand in the swearing of oaths (cf. *sworn*, 111) may also be intended. Gaunt was buried in St Paul's Cathedral (Holinshed, 3.496).

110 **worth and honour** here almost synonymous terms

112–14 a paraphrase of Holinshed (3.501), where Bolingbroke himself rather than Northumberland speaks: 'My souereigne lord and king, the cause of my comming at this present, is (your honor saued) to haue againe restitution of my person, my lands and heritage, through your fauourable licence.' For the fuller context, see 190n.

112 **scope** intention, aim

113 **lineal royalties** hereditary rights as a member of the royal family (cf. *KJ* 2.1.85; also 1.1.58n., 2.1.190n.). Gurr (128) suggests that *lineal* 'might imply not only inheritance through Gaunt but from Richard, a hint not in Bullingbrook's instructions to Northumberland at 35–48'. Historically, though not in the sources Shakespeare appears to have known, Bolingbroke's claim to the throne, should Richard die without children, was debated seriously: the young Earl of March

Enfranchisement immediate on his knees;
Which on thy royal party granted once,   115
His glittering arms he will commend to rust,
His barbed steeds to stables and his heart
To faithful service of your majesty.
This swears he, as he is a prince and just;
And, as I am a gentleman, I credit him.   120

KING RICHARD
Northumberland, say thus the King returns:

had been designated heir presumptive, but since his claim was through the female line and there existed strong feeling at the time that titles and great estates should descend through the male line only, Gaunt in Parliament (according to at least two medieval writers) petitioned the crown that his son Henry be acknowledged the rightful heir. March objected, and Richard forthwith silenced the debate (see Saul, 396–7).

114 **Enfranchisement** release (from banishment); restitution of Bolingbroke's property rights and titles is also implied.
on his knees In Holinshed (3.500) Northumberland negotiates with the King before the ambush when he is still at Conway; Northumberland proposes that if Richard would 'pardon the duke of Hereford of all things wherin he had offended him, the duke would be readie to come to him on his knees, to craue of him forgiuenesse, and as an humble subiect, to obeie him in all dutifull seruices'.

115 **thy royal party** your majesty's part (or perhaps 'your side of the dispute, as king'; cf. 3.2.203n.)

116 **glittering** dissyllabic ('glitt'ring')
commend commit, hand over (not 'recommend')

117 **barbed** barbèd; caparisoned and armoured with 'barbs', a corrupted form of 'bards' (metal protectors covering the chest and flanks); cf. *R3* 1.1.10: 'mounting barbed steeds'.

119 *a . . . just** Sisson[2] (2.24) argues plausibly that Q's compositor found an ampersand in his copy after *prince*, which he misread as *es* (a similar form in secretary hand), thus spelling the combined word 'princesse'. Q3 attempted an unsatisfactory alteration, which F further emended to 'a Prince, is iust' – a reading that Sisson rightly pronounces 'awkward and artificial'. Sisson's explanation does not account for Q's omission of *a*, but such an omission would be characteristic of the compositor's known habits (see Appendix 1, p. 537 and n. 2). RP suggests that F's reading could be correct and that Q's 'princesse' possibly stems from misreading of a MS comma as a terminal *s* (see 1.4.20n.).
just true

120 **credit** believe

121 *thus . . . returns** Q's punctuation is ambiguous, making it possible to place the stop after either *thus* (Q3, F) or *returns* (Q2). Both alternatives provide acceptable sense.
returns replies (cf. 1.3.122n., where the meaning is slightly different)

119 a prince and just] *(Sisson[2])*; princesse iust *Q*; a Prince iust *Q3*; a Prince, is iust *F*   121 thus . . . returns:] *Q2* *(thus . . . returnes,)*; thus, . . . returnes, *Q*; thus: . . . returnes, *Q3–4, F*; thus: . . . returnes *Q5*

His noble cousin is right welcome hither,
And all the number of his fair demands
Shall be accomplished without contradiction.
With all the gracious utterance thou hast,   125
Speak to his gentle hearing kind commends.
    [*Northumberland with Trumpet returns to Bolingbroke.*]
[*to Aumerle*] We do debase ourselves, cousin, do we not,
To look so poorly and to speak so fair?
Shall we call back Northumberland and send
Defiance to the traitor, and so die?   130

AUMERLE

No, good my lord. Let's fight with gentle words
Till time lend friends, and friends their helpful swords.

KING RICHARD

O God, O God, that e'er this tongue of mine
That laid the sentence of dread banishment
On yon proud man should take it off again   135

---

123 **fair demands** reasonable requests
124 **accomplished** fulfilled, carried out
125 **gracious** courteous
126–7 Northumberland's failure to reply to the King is characteristically unceremonious (see 75–6n.). See also 127n.
126 **gentle** noble
  commends greetings, regards
  SD* *Trumpet* See 0.1n.
127–30 Cf. *E2*, 4.5.4–7: 'What, was I born to fly and run away, / And leave the Mortimers conquerors behind? / Give me my horse, and let's r'enforce our troops, / And in this bed of honour die with fame.'
127 *a rough line metrically, the final two feet possibly scanned 'còusin, | do we nòt'. Q repeats the SP at this line; Q4 and F remove it. Muir (104) speculates that 'a line of Northumberland' may have 'dropped out' –

a possibility made likelier, perhaps, by Q's indentation of the redundant SP. Maybe an intervening speech of one or more lines was cancelled in Q's copy.
  debase prepares for the bitter wordplay on *base* at 176–82 and 190–1
128 **poorly** abject, pitifully lacking in spirit and courage; 'look poorly' was a stock phrase (*OED*)
  fair politely
131–2 a common sentiment; cf. Barnabe Googe, translator of Palingenius' *Zodiac of Life* (1576): 'The wyseman will refraine, / And spie hys time, and eke geue place his foe with wordes to traine / That pleasant seme' (59).
133–41 Reyher (64) notes that Daniel (2.13–21) develops Richard's plaints at length.

126 SD] *Oxf (subst.)*   127 SD] *Rowe*   We] *Q4–F; King* We *Q*   ourselves] our selfe *F*   131 No, good] *F;* No good *Q*   lord] *(Lo:), F*   135 yon] yond *F*

With words of sooth! O, that I were as great
As is my grief, or lesser than my name!
Or that I could forget what I have been,
Or not remember what I must be now!
Swell'st thou, proud heart? I'll give thee scope to beat,   140
Since foes have scope to beat both thee and me.
[*Northumberland returns to the walls.*]

AUMERLE
Northumberland comes back from Bolingbroke.

KING RICHARD
What must the King do now? Must he submit?
The King shall do it. Must he be deposed?

---

136 **words of sooth** soothing words,
words of appeasement, blandishments;
sooth does not mean 'truth', as often in
Shakespeare (cf. *1H4* 4.1.6–7: 'I do
defy / The tongues of soothers').

137 **my name** One of Richard's several
mentions of his name, i.e. title (cf.
146), as distinct from the substance of
his kingship; see Introduction,
pp. 67–8.

138–9 Cf. *E2*, 5.1.110–11: 'Come, death,
and with thy fingers close my eyes, /
Or, if I live, let me forget myself.'

139 **must** another significant word to
which Richard recurs, underscoring
his frustration; see 143–6n.

140 *****Swell'st . . . heart?** F's interrogative
punctuation seems dramatically superi-
or, although Q's implied meaning is also
possible: 'if you swell, proud heart, I'll
give'. Wells (228) notes, 'Presumably the
King's excited state of mind has a physical effect; the actor would naturally put
his hand to his heart.'
scope space, room; permission, liberty
(a more modern use than in 112, but
perhaps ironically echoing Northumberland since Richard twice repeats
the word; cf. 141)

141 **beat** quibbling on *beat* in 140; cf. the
similarly bitter wordplay at 95–6.

thee my heart

143–59 Wilson (193) suggests that the
'germ of this famous speech' is a sentence in Hall (fol. ix) describing
Richard's abdication: 'And then with a
lamentable voyce and a sorowfull
countenance, [he] deliuered his scepter
and croune to the duke of Lancastre,
requiryng euery persone seuerally by
their names, to graunt and assente that
he might liue a priuate and a solitarie
life, with the swetnesse whereof, he
would be so well pleased, that it should
be a paine and punishement to hym to
go abrode.'

143–6 Cf.   3.2.95n., 150n., 160n.;
'Richard, in his agitation, now loses
his head and throws himself into his
enemy's hand. By holding Bolingbroke to his word, he could have
placed him in the dilemma of having
either to disband his forces or to seize
the king by violence. Instead, he
offers the resignation which Bolingbroke desires to receive but not to
demand' (Herford, 184–5). Richard
begins his speech in the third person,
suggesting that he is 'conscious of the
division between the man and the
office' (Wells, 228). Forker (*E2*, 36)
observes, 'Shakespeare makes much

---

140 thou, proud heart?] *F* *(*thou prowd heart?*)*; thou (prowd heart) *Q*   141 SD] *Oxf (subst.)*

The King shall be contented. Must he lose   145
The name of King? I'God's name, let it go.
I'll give my jewels for a set of beads,
My gorgeous palace for a hermitage,
My gay apparel for an almsman's gown,
My figured goblets for a dish of wood,   150
My sceptre for a palmer's walking staff,
My subjects for a pair of carved saints
And my large kingdom for a little grave,
A little, little grave, an obscure grave;
Or I'll be buried in the King's highway,   155
Some way of common trade, where subjects' feet
May hourly trample on their sovereign's head;

of the paradox of a monarch who is theoretically absolute, yet constrained by lesser mortals – a king who "must". . . . Suggestions for such frustration may have come from Marlowe's Edward, who expresses similar sentiments' (see, e.g., 'Am I a king and must be overruled?' (1.1.134); 'I see I must, and therefore am content' (1.4.85); 'Must! 'Tis somewhat hard when kings must go' (4.7.83); cf. also *E2*, 5.1.36, 56–7, 70). When Elizabeth I was mortally ill in 1602–3, her secretary Robert Cecil, implored her: 'Madame, to content the people you must go to bed', to which her withering reply was, 'Little man, little man, the word *must* is not to be used to princes' (see Jenkins, 323). Cf. also 4.1.228.

145 **contented** willing, content to agree
146 **name of King** i.e. royal title (cf. 137n.)
   God's name Richard plays on the earlier sense of *name* in the line.
147 **set of beads** rosary
148 **hermitage** dwelling place of a religious recluse, monastery
149 **gay apparel** splendid clothing, showy and costly garments (see

1.4.44n., 2.1.21n., 21–3n.)
   almsman's gown the mean garb of a beggar who lives on charity; *gown* suggests the habit or dress of a particular charitable order or institution.
150 **figured** ornamented, embossed
   dish of wood begging bowl, such as almsmen might use (perhaps used also for eating)
151 **palmer's** pilgrim's. Palmers took vows to wander from one religious shrine to another; originally they were named for the palm branch from the Holy Sepulchre at Jerusalem which they carried as proof of their visit.
152 **carved saints** carvèd; probably of wood, like those used by monks for devotional purposes
154 **obscure** òbscure
155 **in . . . highway** in the most public and common of places rather than a sacred or consecrated space such as Westminster Abbey. Note the irony of the road's being designated as the King's (since it belongs to the crown). Cf. Aumerle's flippant wordplay on *high* and *highway* at 1.4.3–4.
156 **trade** traffic, passage to and fro

146 of King] *QF*; of a King *Q2*   I'God's] *Mowat & Werstine;* a Gods *Q;* o'Gods *F*

For on my heart they tread now whilst I live,
And, buried once, why not upon my head?
Aumerle, thou weep'st, my tender-hearted cousin!   160
We'll make foul weather with despised tears;
Our sighs and they shall lodge the summer corn
And make a dearth in this revolting land.
Or shall we play the wantons with our woes
And make some pretty match with shedding tears,   165
As thus, to drop them still upon one place
Till they have fretted us a pair of graves
Within the earth; and, therein laid, there lies
Two kinsmen digged their graves with weeping eyes?
Would not this ill do well? Well, well, I see   170
I talk but idly, and you laugh at me.
[*to Northumberland*]
Most mighty prince, my Lord Northumberland,
What says King Bolingbroke? Will his majesty

158 **heart** Cf. 140n.
　　tread quibbling on *trade* in 156 (see Cercignani, 78)
159 **buried once** 'once I am buried' or 'I being once buried' (Abbott, 378)
161 **despised** despisèd; unimportant, not worth noticing (or perhaps 'despicable')
162 **Our . . . they** our sighs and tears (like wind and rain)
　　lodge beat down, flatten; cf. *2H6* 3.2.176: 'Like to the summer's corn by tempest lodged'.
　　corn wheat
163 **dearth** famine
　　revolting rebellious
164 **play the wantons** behave sportively, frolic; cf. 5.1.101n., 5.3.10n.
165 **make** devise
　　pretty match clever game, pleasing contest
166 **still** continually, incessantly
167 **fretted us** eroded for us, hollowed out on our behalf (by washing away the soil); 'fret' means, literally, to 'eat away'.

There may also be wordplay on *fretted* = complained. Cf. *KL* 1.4.285: 'with cadent tears fret channels in her cheeks'.
168–9 **therein . . . eyes** 'we being laid therein, (a passer-by might say that) there lies . . .'; possibly Richard imagines an epitaph over the two graves: 'There lies . . . weeping eyes'. The rhymed couplet helps convey this impression.
169 **digged** who dug (Abbott, 244)
170–1 For Richard's self-conscious awareness of his onstage audience, cf. 3.2.23n.
170 **this ill do well** 'this unhappiness (*ill*) make a pleasing impression (*do well*)'
171 **idly** foolishly
172–3 **Most . . . Bolingbroke?** mock titles spoken with bitter sarcasm
173–4 **Will . . . die?** on the surface a piece of theatrical sarcasm, meaning 'Will the all-powerful Bolingbroke grant Richard leave to exist?' But, deeply distrustful of his enemy's true plans for him if captured, Richard also tries to

166 As thus] *QF*; And thus *Q2*   171 laugh] mock *F*   172 SD] *Irving (subst.)*

Give Richard leave to live till Richard die?
You make a leg, and Bolingbroke says 'ay'.   175

NORTHUMBERLAND

My lord, in the base court he doth attend
To speak with you. May it please you to come down?

KING RICHARD

Down, down I come, like glist'ring Phaëton,

manoeuvre Northumberland into revealing his chief's strategy; whatever answer Northumberland makes will constitute an acknowledgement that Bolingbroke intends to have Richard under his thumb.

175 **make a leg** bow the knee, make an obeisance. Either Richard interprets a gesture by Northumberland as signifying Bolingbroke's intention to show clemency, or, as Wells (229) implies, Richard makes an ironic slur on Northumberland's skill in manipulating his master, insinuating that Bolingbroke will grant Richard his life (or perhaps any favour) if Northumberland will show sufficient outward deference in asking for it. According to Ure (114), 'Richard describes in his ironical fantasy the anticipated answer to the sinister trick-question of [173–4] . . . – a question that demands the answer "ay", whatever Bolingbroke's intentions really are in regard to Richard's life. Richard sees Bolingbroke and Northumberland as carrying out the set lines of a policy which has been determined elsewhere'.

176 **base court** lower or outer court of the castle, surrounded by stables and the dwellings of servants (from French *basse cour*). Cf. *Traïson* (59/209): 'When the King had dined, and grace had been said, the King went down from the Donjon into the lower court'; also Froissart (6.368): 'downe into the courte'. Holinshed (3.489) repeatedly uses the same phrase, though in a different context: when Gloucester was

abducted from Pleshy in 1397, Richard rode 'into the base court, his trumpets sounding before him. The duke herewith came downe into the base court, where the king was, hauing none other apparell vpon him, but his shirt.' The phrase *base court* then appears twice again in the same passage.

attend wait

177 **May it** probably elided ('May't')

178 **glist'ring** glittering, glistening

178–9 **Phaëton . . . jades** a favourite image of the emblem-writers. *Phaëton*, or Phaëthon (pronounced trisyllabically; the second *h* is silent), was the son of Apollo, the sun-god of classical mythology; cf. Ovid, *Met.*, 1.747–78, 2.1–339. He borrowed his father's chariot, which drew the sun across the sky, and, losing control of the horses, was carried perilously close to the earth, thus almost burning it up. Zeus prevented disaster by felling him with a thunderbolt. Ironically, as the prototype of rash and youthful incompetence, Phaëton suits Richard perfectly. The sun was one of Richard's own chosen symbols; see 62–7 and 2.4.19–21n. In Greek the name means 'glistering one' or 'shining one'. Talbert (169–71), citing *TGV* 3.1.153–6 and *3H6* 1.4.33–4, where the emphasis is on Phaëton's ambition, and *3H6* 2.6.11–17, where the myth is used to illustrate the failure of a king to rule wisely, suggests that Shakespeare intends the image to reflect proleptically upon Bolingbroke as well as Richard, thus allowing 'antithetical meanings to exist concurrently'.

175 ay] *(I)*

Wanting the manage of unruly jades.
In the base court? Base court where kings grow base   180
To come at traitors' calls and do them grace.
In the base court? Come down? Down court, down
     king!
For night-owls shriek where mounting larks should
     sing.   [*Exeunt King Richard and his Followers from above.*]
[*Northumberland returns to Bolingbroke.*]

179 **Wanting** lacking
manage control (a technical term
from French *manège* = the art of
horsemanship); cf. 1.4.39, 3.2.118n.
Daniel (1.43) also uses the word in a
political context: 'And yet I doe not
seeme herein to excuse / The Iustices,
and Minions of the king / Which
might their office and their grace
abuse, / But onely blame the course of
managing.'
jades nags, horses (a contemptuous
term; cf. 5.5.85n.). The *unruly jades*,
Apollo's horses, are of course, metaphorically, Richard's rebellious nobles.
180–1 **where . . . calls** See 127n. on
debase. Richard puns acerbically on the
symbolic 'debasement' of having to
descend to obey the summons of inferiors (Northumberland and Bolingbroke), who, as subjects, are not only
inferior in rank but also in morality,
since they are traitors.
181 **do them grace** be courteously submissive to them; grant them favour
182 **Down . . . king!** Picking up *court*
(courtyard) from the earlier part of
the line, Richard twists it to mean 'royal
court', the symbol of his exalted status, whose ruin necessarily accompanies the King's personal fall from
grandeur.
183 A shrieking owl was considered an
omen of death and disaster; cf. *Mac*

2.2.3–4: 'It was the owl that shriek'd,
the fatal bellman, / Which gives the
stern'st good-night.' 'It is nightfall
when it should be daybreak, because
Richard's sun is setting' (Cam², 131).
GWW notes the rich assemblage of
connotations and images concisely
embedded in the contrast which
Richard's line evokes and related visually to the stage action: dark vs. light,
since the owl is the bird of night and
the lark of morning; ill omen vs. hope,
since the owl is associated with death
and the lark with the hopefulness of
dawn; shrieking vs. singing (ugly
sounds vs. beautiful ones); upward vs.
downward movement since owls fly low
and larks mount highest of all. Richard
contrives to associate his enemy with all
the negative connotations and himself
with the positive ones.
SD1 *Richard's descent with his followers from the upper level to the
main stage (see headnote) focuses the
de casibus theme of the tragedy powerfully in a visually realized action:
Richard's political ruin, reinforced by
the allusion to *Phaëton* and joined to
the broader concept of tragic fall in
the tradition of *Mirror*, becomes a
kind of stage emblem. Modern productions often make the staircase itself
visible so as to reinforce the symbolism even more pointedly, but, as

180 court?] *F*; court, *Q*   182 court?] *Keightley;* court *QF*   down?] *Pope;* downe: *QF*   183 night-
owls] *F*; nightowles *Q*   SD1 *Exeunt . . . above*] *Capell*   SD2 *Northumberland . . . Bolingbroke*]
Johnson¹ (*subst.*) *after* 179

BOLINGBROKE

What says his majesty?

NORTHUMBERLAND   Sorrow and grief of heart

Makes him speak fondly like a frantic man.   185

[Flourish. Enter below KING RICHARD and his Followers.]

Yet he is come.

BOLINGBROKE

Stand all apart,

And show fair duty to his majesty.   *He kneels down.*

My gracious lord.

Shewring (14–15) notes, Richard's brief absence from view 'allows the audience a prophetic glimpse' of the political eclipse that is to follow. For a few symbolic moments onstage there is no visible king. Shakespeare's text does not allow much time (two lines only) between the exit of the King's party from the upper level and their reappearance below. However, Northumberland's onstage move to rejoin Bolingbroke and the editorial *Flourish* at 185.1 would suffice to cover any awkwardness. The main stage, which had earlier represented the grounds outside Flint Castle, now becomes the castle courtyard.

184 probably a pentameter with redundant unstressed syllables (or syllable if *majesty* is elided) at the caesura and trochaic third foot: 'What sàys | his màjesty? | Sòrrow | and grìef | at hèart'

185 **Makes** make (Abbott, 333)
  fondly foolishly (cf. *idly*, 171)
  frantic raving mad

185.1 *Flourish See 1.3.122 SDn. It seems appropriate to add a fanfare here as F specifies one at the King's exit

(209). Cf. 2.1.68.1n.

187 **Stand all apart** i.e. ordering his own men to clear a space for his meeting with Richard. Créton (167/373) gives an elaborate account of the formal courtesy: 'Then they made the king ... come down to meet Duke Henry, who, as soon as he perceived him at a distance, bowed very low to the ground; and as they approached each other he bowed a second time, with his cap in his hand; and then the king took off his bonnet, and spake first'.

188 **fair duty** proper reverence (i.e. kneeling and perhaps also removing hats or bonnets). See 187n.
  SD based on Holinshed, who reports that Bolingbroke knelt thrice (see 190–206n.); but cf. also Daniel, 2.63: 'He kneeles him downe euen at his [Richard's] entering, / Rose, kneeles againe (for craft will still exceed) / Whenas the king approcht, put off his hood / And welcomd him, though wishd him little good.' Although F omits Q's SD (one of the few such in Q), it is nevertheless clear that Bolingbroke kneels (see 190).

185.1 *Flourish*] *this edn   Enter . . . Followers*] *Capell (subst.)*   188 SD] *om.* F

357

KING RICHARD

Fair cousin, you debase your princely knee   190
To make the base earth proud with kissing it.
Me rather had my heart might feel your love
Than my unpleased eye see your courtesy.
Up cousin, up. Your heart is up, I know,
[*Raises Bolingbroke.*]

190–206 Holinshed (3.501) is obviously the principal source for this part of the scene: 'then the earle of Northumberland passing foorth of the castell to the duke, talked with him a while in sight of the king, being againe got vp to the walles, to take better view of the armie, being now aduanced within two bowe shootes of the castell, to the small reioising (ye may be sure) of the sorowfull king. The earle of Northumberland returning to the castell, appointed the king to be set to dinner (for he was fasting till then) and after he had dined, the duke came downe to the castell himselfe, and entred the same all armed, his bassenet [helmet] onelie excepted, and being within the first gate, he staied there, till the king came foorth of the inner part of the castell vnto him. The king [with Carlisle, Salisbury, Scroop and others; see 27–30n.] . . . came foorth into the vtter ward. . . . Foorthwith as the duke got sight of the king, he shewed a reuerend dutie as became him, in bowing his knee, and comming forward, did so likewise the second and third time, till the king tooke him by the hand, and lift him vp, saieng; Deere cousine, ye are welcome. The duke humblie thanking him said; My souereigne lord and king, the cause of my comming at this present, is (your honor saued) to haue againe restitution of my person, my lands and heritage, through your fauourable licence. The king hervnto answered; Deere cousine, I am readie to accomplish your will, so that ye may inioy all that is yours, without exception.'

190 **Fair cousin** picking up Bolingbroke's *fair* from 188; cf. Créton (167/373): 'Fair cousin of Lancaster, you be right welcome'; also *Traïson* (59/209): 'Fair cousin of Lancaster, ye are right welcome'. Stow, undoubtedly following either Créton or *Traïson*, also has 'faire cousin of Lancaster' (511). In Froissart's account of the deposition (6.378) Bolingbroke is referred to by the King as 'Fayre cosyn'; see 4.1.304–5n. Richard repeatedly addresses his enemy as *cousin* (cf. 194, 204), perhaps, though not necessarily, an ironic means of underscoring his disdain.
debase See 127n., 180–1n.
192 **Me rather had** I had rather (Abbott, 230)
193 **courtesy** politeness, civility; curtsy, obeisance. Originally, 'courtesy' and 'curtsy' were the same word; cf. 1.4.33n.
194–5 imitated in *Wonder of a Kingdom* (1636), 5.2.121–2: 'nay, nay, pray rise, / I know your heart is up, tho your knees downe' (Dekker, 3.638); also Heywood, *1 If You Know Not Me* (1605), l. 1266: 'My heart it bends, farre lower than my knee' (see 1.1.160n.). Ure (116) cites *Mirror* (497) where Wolsey describes his ambitious dissimulation with Henry VIII: 'Than downe I lookt, with sober countnaunce sad, / But heart was vp, as high as hope could go, / That suttel fox, might win some fauour so' ('Cardinal Wolsey', ll. 47–9).
194 SD *based on Holinshed (see 190–206n.)

190] *F lines* Cousin, / Knee, /   194 SD] *Capell (subst.)*

Thus high at least,   [*Indicates crown.*]
                          although your knee be low.   195
BOLINGBROKE
My gracious lord, I come but for mine own.
KING RICHARD
Your own is yours, and I am yours and all.
BOLINGBROKE
So far be mine, my most redoubted lord,
As my true service shall deserve your love.
KING RICHARD
Well you deserve. They well deserve to have   200
That know the strong'st and surest way to get!
[*to York*]
Uncle, give me your hands. Nay, dry your eyes.
Tears show their love, but want their remedies.
[*to Bolingbroke*]
Cousin, I am too young to be your father,

---

196 **but . . . own** also from Holinshed (see
190–206n.); see also 113n. and
2.3.148–9n.

197 Cf. Holinshed: 'all that is yours'
(190–206n.). Richard means: 'What
you claim is already yours (since you
have taken possession of it), just as you
have taken possession of me and everything else.'

198–9 'Be my friend so far . . . as my loyal
service to you deserves your friend-
ship'; Bolingbroke wrenches Richard's
I am yours (197) into a new sense.

198 **redoubted** dreaded, held in awe; cf.
the common phrase, 'my dread lord'.

200 **you deserve** spoken ironically, as the
following sentence makes clear

202 **hands** F's 'Hand' may represent a
genuine correction as 3.3.149–205 is
one of the areas of text that, according
to Jowett & Taylor (174), show evidence of the heaviest collation of Q3
against the MS promptbook (see
Appendix 1, pp. 524–7). Richard's

taking both York's *hands*, however,
seems dramatically more appropriate
for consoling an old man in distress.

203 'Tears show love for the person for
whom they are shed but lack power to
remedy the misfortunes that caused
them to flow.' Gurr notes, 'York is the
only character outside the king's own
party to weep for his fall' (132). Cf.
Heywood, *1 If You Know Not Me*, ll.
513–15: 'wishes and teares / Haue both
one property, they shew their loue that
/ want the remedy' (see 1.1.160n.).

204 **too young** Historically, Richard and
Bolingbroke were the same age (thirty-
three); see List of Roles, 1n. and 6n.,
and 2.1.69n. It has been suggested,
however, that Richard is meant to
impress us as being more youthful;
unlike Marlowe's Edward II, who was
forty-three at the time of his murder
(cf. *E2*, 5.2.119, 'agèd Edward', and
Forker's note), grief seems not to age
him (see 4.1.277–9).

---

195 SD] *Hudson (subst.); touching his own head. / Malone*   200] *F lines* you deseru'd: / haue, /   you
deserve] you deseru'd *F*   202 SD] *Hanmer*   hands] Hand *F*   204 SD] *Hanmer*

Though you are old enough to be my heir.   205
What you will have, I'll give, and willing too;
For do we must what force will have us do.
Set on towards London, cousin, is it so?

BOLINGBROKE
Yea, my good lord.

KING RICHARD   Then I must not say no.   ^F*Flourish. Exeunt.*^F

[3.4]   *Enter the* QUEEN *with two* Ladies.

205 **be my heir** inherit my crown. Richard speaks sardonically; see 113n.
206–9 Apart from the conventional use of couplets as a means of signalling the end of a scene, Richard's rhymes enhance the effect of total capitulation.
206 **will have** wish to have
   willing willingly, gladly
207, 209 **must** See 139n., 143–6n.
207 **will have** will compel (playing on *will have* and *willing* from 206); note that 'force will have us do' actually negates *willing*.
208 **Set on** lead on, set forward
   towards London the traditional location of coronations and parliaments. Cf. Holinshed's marginal note (3.501): 'The king and the duke iournie together towards London'; the passage to which this note refers specifies the route, naming, among other towns, Chester, Newcastle, Lichfield, Coventry and St Albans. Holinshed's geography is somewhat confused since Richard and Bolingbroke meet at Flint, yet the chronicler says that after the two had drunk some wine, 'they mounted on horssebacke, and rode that night to Flint, and the next daie vnto Chester'. Holinshed suggests in addition the privation to which Richard, who was normally 'exceeding

sumptuous in apparell', was subjected: 'neither was the king permitted all this while to change his apparell, but rode still through all these townes simplie clothed in one sute of raiment'. In Froissart the route to London is entirely different.
   is it so 'Is it ordered so?' or 'Is this your command?'
3.4 This scene is choric in function (like 2.4), allowing for reflection and commentary on Richard's misrule by means of its sustained allegory, and drawing additional sympathy to Richard in defeat through its portrayal of the Queen's anguish (see Introduction, pp. 33, 69–70, 76, 135). It fills the time gap between Richard's capture at Flint Castle and his reappearance in London and is entirely unhistorical. H.N. Coleridge, attributing the phrase to his uncle S.T. Coleridge in *Literary Remains*, referred to it as a beautiful 'islet of repose – a melancholy repose' (Forker, 133). The speeches of the gardeners on the maintenance of political and horticultural order may be indebted to Henry IV's words to the bishops as reported in *Traison* (92–3/247); see 50–2 and 2.3.167n. But the concept of England as a garden is already implicit in

QUEEN

What sport shall we devise here in this garden
To drive away the heavy thought of care?

1 LADY

Madam, we'll play at bowls.

QUEEN

'Twill make me think the world is full of rubs,

Gaunt's metaphor of an *other Eden, demi-paradise* (see 2.1.42n.). For possible indebtedness to Lodge, see 38LN. Froissart (6.370–1) writes of the Queen's desolation after Richard's fall: 'the state of the quene was so tourned and broken, for there was lefte nouther man, woman, nor chylde of the nacion of France, nor yet of Englande, suche as were in any favour with the kyng: her house was newly furnisshed with ladyes and damoselles, and other offycers and servauntes: they were charged all, that in no wyse they shuld nat speke of the kynge, nat one to another'. From the Gardener's words at 69–70 we may infer that the action takes place at one of York's homes – possibly Langley (see 3.1.36n.). Holinshed (3.515) locates the Queen only later at Sunning (a manor near Reading) at the time of the Abbot of Westminster's abortive plot against Henry IV in 1400; Froissart (6.388) and *Traïson* (33/178) place her respectively at Havering and Wallingford. The gardeners, among the few commoners in the play, are not distinguished by their speech as belonging to the working class; their characterization is emblematic rather than naturalistic (see List of Roles, 35n.). Heywood seems to have imitated this scene in his own garden episode of *2 If You Know Not Me*; see especially ll. 2325–30 and Forker, 'Heywood', 170–1 (also 1.1.160n.).

0.1 *F's specification of 'two Ladies' for Q's 'attendants' probably comes

from the promptbook. Although the division of speeches between them in this edn is arbitrary, giving both ladies a voice seems more natural than allowing one to remain mute; see Introduction, p. 169. Some editors have suggested that Shakespeare may have originally conceived of more than two ladies – one for each of the diversions suggested at 3, 6, 10 and 19; if so, economies of casting must have intervened. In number the three ladies balance the three gardeners. The Queen's ladies reappear in 5.1.

1–23 Cf. the similar situation in *AC* (1.5.1–10, 2.5.1–18) where Cleopatra's ladies (Charmian and Iras) attempt to entertain their mistress.

1 **here . . . garden** important information on a stage without scenery; see 25n.

2 **heavy** sad

3, 6, 10, 11, 19, 21 **Madam** The spelling 'Madame' is used by Q only in the ladies' speeches in this scene (elsewhere 'Madam'). Muir (107) suggests that the French spelling may be intended to suggest that the ladies came with the Queen from her own country; but see Froissart in headnote.

3 **bowls** a common Elizabethan pastime; bowling greens were often located in gardens.

4 **rubs** obstacles or impediments which diverted a bowl from its proper course (a technical term). Metaphorically, the word often meant simply 'difficulty' or 'hindrance'; cf. *Ham* 3.1.64: 'ay, there's the rub'.

3, 10, 11 SP] *Capell; Lady Q; La. F*

And that my fortune runs against the bias.   5

2 LADY

Madam, we'll dance.

QUEEN

My legs can keep no measure in delight
When my poor heart no measure keeps in grief.
Therefore, no dancing, girl; some other sport.

1 LADY

Madam, we'll tell tales.   10

QUEEN

Of sorrow or of joy?

1 LADY   Of either, madam.

QUEEN

Of neither, girl.
For if of joy, being altogether wanting,
It doth remember me the more of sorrow.
Or if of grief, being altogether had,   15
It adds more sorrow to my want of joy.
For what I have I need not to repeat,
And what I want it boots not to complain.

---

5   **against the bias** Bowls contain a
weight (*bias*) in one side, causing them,
when rolled, to swerve or run in a pre-
dictable arc. The Queen will reflect
that her fortune, unlike a weighted
bowl, runs contrary to its usual bent.
The phrase is proverbial (Dent, B339).

7–8   **measure . . . measure** stately dance
step (cf. 1.3.291) . . . moderation (or
proper limit)

10   **tell tales** amuse ourselves by telling
stories. The narrative impulse becomes a motif of the drama: cf.
3.2.156LN, 5.1.40–5 and 44n. See also
Introduction, pp. 39, 56, 138–9, 142.

11   ***joy** Rowe's emendation is obviously
correct (as proved by *joy* in 13). QF's
'griefe' could represent compositorial

error (an end-of-line repetition from
'griefe' at 8, although the words are
three lines apart).

13   **being altogether wanting** 'since it is
entirely absent'; *being* is probably
monosyllabic ('be'ng').

14   **remember** remind

15   **being altogether had** 'since I am
entirely possessed by it' or 'since it
occupies my whole mind'; *had* is used
in antithesis to *wanting* in 13. As in 13,
being is probably monosyllabic.

16   **want** lack

18   **want** The Queen turns her noun of 16
into a verb; see 2.3.87n.
      it boots not it is useless
      complain lament, bewail, complain
      about

6, 19, 21   SP] *Wells; Lady Q; La. F*   11   joy] *Rowe³;* griefe *QF*

362

2 LADY

Madam, I'll sing.

QUEEN   'Tis well that thou hast cause;

But thou shouldst please me better, wouldst thou weep.   20

2 LADY

I could weep, madam, would it do you good.

QUEEN

And I could sing, would weeping do me good,

And never borrow any tear of thee.

Enter GARDENER ᶠ*and [his] two* Menᶠ.

But stay, here come the gardeners.

Let's step into the shadow of these trees.   25

My wretchedness unto a row of pins

---

19 **I'll sing** Wroughton, in his 1815 adaptation of *R2* at Drury Lane (in which Edmund Kean played the King), introduced a pastiche Elizabethan song; see Wroughton, 49–50.

'Tis . . . cause It is fortunate that you are happy enough to sing.

20 **shouldst . . . wouldst** would certainly . . . should; modern English transposes the force of the two words.

21 a slightly irregular line the second foot of which is probably to be scanned as a spondee: 'I còuld | wèep, mà- | dam, wòuld'. But if the line is spoken by 1 Lady, the stress would have to fall on *I*.

22–3 The syntax is obscurely condensed. The Queen seems to mean: 'I would sing for joy if weeping could make me feel better, and would have no need for you to weep for me.'

23 **of** from

23.1 *It is clear from the Gardener's first speech 'that there are two undergardeners' and that their superior, the head gardener, although he also engages in physical work (37–9), 'is a man of

authority'. The formally laid out gardens 'of great Elizabethan estates were internationally famous', and those in charge of their upkeep bore 'heavy responsibility' (Wells, 232). Despite a tendency of modern directors, there is nothing 'rustic' or comic in the speech of the gardeners; see List of Roles, 35n.

24 a tetrameter line, made natural by the entrance of the gardeners

25 **shadow . . . trees** During or at the end of this speech (see 28 SD) the Queen and her ladies probably retire behind one of the stage pillars. For the staging, cf. the similar overhearing actions in *MA* 2.3.36, 3.1.23 and *TN* 2.5.20.

26 'I'll wager my wretchedness against something as worthless as a row of pins'; pins were proverbial examples of insignificance (Dent, P333, P334; cf. *Ham* 1.4.65).

*pins Q's 'pines' makes little sense. F's alteration probably derives from the theatre promptbook even though *OED* (pin *sb.* 1) lists 'pine' as a rare spelling; see Appendix 1, pp. 526–7.

---

19 weep, . . . good.] *F; weepe; . . . good? Q; weepe . . . good. Q2*   23.1] *Enter Gardeners Q; Enter a Gardiner, and two Seruants. F   his] Wells   Men] Wells; Seruants F*   24 come] *commeth Q2; comes F*   26 pins] *F (Pinnes); pines Q*

They will talk of state, for everyone doth so
Against a change; woe is forerun with woe.
[*Queen and Ladies stand apart.*]

GARDENER [*to one Man*]

Go bind thou up young dangling apricocks,
Which, like unruly children, make their sire   30
Stoop with oppression of their prodigal weight.

27 **They will** that they will. Almost certainly elided to a monosyllable ('They'll'; see t.n.).
state politics, affairs of state

28 **Against a change** 'on the eve of a change' (in the political situation), 'when change is imminent' (Abbott, 142). The Queen obviously anticipates a change for the worse; cf. her presentiments at 2.2.9–13, 28–32, 34–40.
***change; woe** F's punctuation is vital to the sense.
woe . . . woe 'Gloomy happenings (in politics) are heralded by gloomy predictions' (cf. 2.4.15; contrast *2H4* 4.2.81–2). The Queen, not yet informed of her husband's captivity, nevertheless senses that disaster is in the offing.

29 **young** Q's reading ('yong') has authority (see t.n.), being well justified by Pollard (56): 'surely the picture of the new shoots, as yet only twigs, borne down by the weight of the young green fruit, is vivid enough to stand, and it is the word "yong" that suggested the comparison of the fruit to "vnruly children" in the next line'; cf. also *too fast-growing sprays* (34). No precise season is indicated in this scene (Holinshed, 3.501–2, places Richard's imprisonment in the Tower in late summer, i.e. September 1399); this 'would be the right time for "young" apricots, and would come between the *disordered spring* and *the fall of leaf* (48–9). The pruning of which the Gardener speaks at 34 and 57–8

belongs to spring, and Richard's *fall* (49, 76) to the autumn' (Cam², 134). Wilson (196–7) regards Q2's 'yon' (F's 'yond') as a legitimate correction necessitated by the speaker's pointing to a particular tree: 'I conjecture that Shakespeare wrote "yond," that the "d," accidentally set up "p," was corrected to "g" on the press.'
dangling Cf. 31n., 32n. The trees are clearly standards; training fruit trees to grow against orchard walls (where additional *supportance* (32) would be unnecessary) was still a novelty in Shakespeare's age (see *Shakespeare's England*, 1.371).
apricocks apricots; Shakespeare's habitual older spelling relates to the Portuguese rather than the French form of the word; cf. *MND* 3.1.166, *TNK* 2.2.236. Chambers (131) notes the anachronism: 'Apricots had not been brought into England in the fourteenth century.'

30 **sire** tree (from which the fruit grows); father

31 **Stoop** bend (as with heavy-laden boughs); become stooped in body (as with the back of an old man); see 59n.
prodigal excessive, extravagant (perhaps glancing at the parable of the prodigal son, Luke, 15.11–32; cf. *unruly children*, 30); probably elided to a dissyllable ('prod'gal')
weight physical and emotional (applying to both the fruit and the parental suffering)

27 They will] They'le *F*   28 change;] *F;* change *Q1–5*   SD] *Pope (subst.)*   29+ SP] *(Gard.)* 29 SD] *Cam¹ (subst.)*   young] yon *Q2;* yond *F*   apricocks] *Q3* (Apricockes*), F;* Aphricokes *Q;* Aphricocks *Q2*

Give some supportance to the bending twigs.
[*to the other Man*]
Go thou, and, like an executioner,
Cut off the heads of too fast-growing sprays
That look too lofty in our commonwealth.   35
All must be even in our government.
You thus employed, I will go root away
The noisome weeds, which without profit suck
The soil's fertility from wholesome flowers.

1 MAN
Why should we in the compass of a pale   40

---

32 **supportance** support (cf. *TN* 3.4.300, the only other instance in Shakespeare); cf. *dangling* (29n.).
bending with the weight of fruit, since it is late summer

33 **like an executioner** At this point the likening of a garden to a kingdom, suggested earlier by Gaunt at 2.1.42 (see n.; also 3.4 headnote) and by Bolingbroke's reference to the favourites as *caterpillars* (see 2.3.166n., 167n.), becomes explicit. The parallel had numerous classical and other precedents (including Livy, Ovid and Herodotus), which Ure discusses in detail (li–lvii, 119); cf. also *Catiline* (1611), 3.1.644–6, which alludes to the familiar story of Tarquin cutting off the tallest poppies as a lesson to his son on how to suppress ambitious nobles (Jonson, 5.490).

34 *****too** F's alteration of Q's 'two' yields better sense and probably represents a change introduced from the theatre promptbook by the annotator of Q3. The spellings 'two' and 'too' could both be used for the numeral (see *OED* two *sb.* A1) but not 'two' for the adverb; see Appendix 1, pp. 526–7. Wilson (197) believes that Q's compositor merely normalized 'to' (a

Shakespearean spelling) incorrectly.
sprays new branches; conceivably there is a subliminal link here with 'bushy' and 'green' (the ironic names of the favourites whose heads have just been *Cut off*).

35 **look** appear
lofty tall; overweening, presumptuous

36 **even** uniform, level, neat (implying impartiality)

37 **You thus employed** elliptical ('while you are thus employed')

38 **noisome** harmful, noxious

38, 44 **weeds** Cf. Bolingbroke's threat at 2.3.167 (see n.) to 'weed and pluck away' Bushy, Bagot and their accomplices. See LN.

38 **without profit** devoid of beneficial effect, doing no good (yielding no fruit)

40, 67 SP *See 23.1n.; also Introduction, p. 169.

40 **in . . . pale** within the limits of an enclosure (a walled garden) – i.e. contrasting the limited space with the kingdom at large (*our sea-walled garden*, 43); *pale* = fenced-in area, paling. Cf. also the 'English pale', the area surrounding Dublin controlled by England (see 1.4.42n.).

---

33 SD] *Cam*¹ (*subst.*)   34 too] *F;* two *Q*   fast-growing] *Collier;* fast growing *QF*   35 commonwealth] *Rowe;* common-wealth *QF*   38 which] that *Q2–F*   40, 67 SP] *Capell; Man. Q; Ser. F*

Keep law and form and due proportion,
Showing, as in a model, our firm estate,
When our sea-walled garden, the whole land,
Is full of weeds, her fairest flowers choked up,
Her fruit trees all unpruned, her hedges ruined,   45
Her knots disordered and her wholesome herbs
Swarming with caterpillars?

GARDENER   Hold thy peace.
He that hath suffered this disordered spring
Hath now himself met with the fall of leaf.
The weeds which his broad-spreading leaves did shelter,   50
That seemed in eating him to hold him up,

---

41 **proportion** four syllables
42 **model** pattern; copy in miniature (cf. 3.2.153n.)
   firm estate stable condition; well-established state
43 **sea-walled garden** sea-wallèd. A pointed repetition of Gaunt's imagery; cf. 2.1.42n., 43–4n., 48n., 61–3.
44 **flowers** probably monosyllabic ('flow'rs')
45 **unpruned** Cf. *1 Troublesome Reign*, ll. 1481–2, where King John alludes to actions taken against the Pope: 'Sith we have proynd the more than needfull braunch / That did oppresse the true wel-growing stock'.
46 **knots** flower beds arranged in intricately geometrical designs. An example in Thomas Hill, *Gardener's Labyrinth* (1577), is reproduced in *Shakespeare's England*, 1.389.
   disordered obscured by the growth of weeds
47 **caterpillars** This use of Bolingbroke's term (see 2.3.166n.) invokes an awareness of Richard's favourites.
48–66 Mahood (78) comments on the emblematic nature of the Gardener's two speeches (48–53 and 55–66): in the first Richard is 'a young tree choked by upstart weeds . . . while in the second

he is a neglectful gardener . . . whose trees bear no fruit because he has failed to prune them. These are conflicting images, but their contradiction is obscured by the way they are made to intertwine: in the first, Richard is also the owner of a blessed plot who has allowed ("suffered") it to become rank, and in the second he is seen as on the point of being felled and deprived of his arboreal "crown" [65]. . . . The wordplay and the shifting metaphors it accompanies thus carry us over an emotional watershed. Distressing and awesome as is the thought of deposition, the kingdom calls for good government, and Bolingbroke, by his readiness to pluck weeds up root and all, has shown himself well able to tend and order the realm.'
48 **suffered** permitted (perhaps with a play on 'undergone')
49 **fall of leaf** autumn (see 29n.). Cf. *Mac* 5.3.22–3: 'my way of life / Is fall'n into the sear, the yellow leaf'.
50–2 See 2.3.167n.
51 **eating him** feeding on him, devouring him (metaphorically); there may be a suggestion of parasitical or creeping vines such as ivy.

---

42 as in] *QF;* in *Q2*   50 which] that *Q2–F*   broad-spreading] *F;* broad spreading *Q*

Are plucked up, root and all, by Bolingbroke –
I mean the Earl of Wiltshire, Bushy, Green.

2 MAN

What, are they dead?

GARDENER   They are. And Bolingbroke
Hath seized the wasteful King. O, what pity is it   55
That he had not so trimmed and dressed his land
As we this garden! We at time of year
Do wound the bark, the skin of our fruit trees,
Lest, being over-proud in sap and blood,
With too much riches it confound itself.   60
Had he done so to great and growing men,
They might have lived to bear and he to taste

54 SP1 *See 23.1n.; also Introduction, p. 169.
54–7 ***They . . . year** Capell's relineation and repunctuation, as well as his emendation (see 57n.), improve both sense and metre. The mislining in Q may derive from copy rather than the compositor as it saves no space on Q's page. It seems likely that the MS squeezed a line and a half onto one line, inducing Q's further misdivision, uncorrected by F. For other examples, see Appendix 1, pp. 517–18.
55 probably best scanned by treating *O* after the caesura as an extra-metrical interjection
56 **dressed** put in order, taken care of, kept in a proper state
57 *****garden! We** Capell's emendation (inserting a second *We* in the line) seems essential to the meaning. 'The *We* in Capell's emendation is balanced by the *he* of 61, and the same antithesis recurs in lines 64 and 65'

(Ard², 121). RP suggests that what was intended to read 'garden, that at' in the MS could have been shortened to 'garden at' through haplography.
at . . . year in season, at the proper time of year
58 **Do** 'F's emendation of "Do" to "And" looks like an attempt to make sense of Q' (Cam², 135); see 54–7n. and 57n.
skin heightens the human–horticultural parallel
59 **over-proud in** excessively burgeoning with, too luxuriant in
sap and blood *Sap* is the *blood* of trees: Shakespeare maintains the double level of reference (arboreal and human); cf. *bark* and *skin* in 58, also 30n., 31n. The Duchess of Gloucester sets up a similar parallel at 1.2.11–21.
60 **confound** destroy, ruin; cf. 5.3.85. The Gardener means that without pruning the tree will produce only unprofitable woody extremities rather than fruit.

52 plucked] puld *Q3–F*   54 SP1] *Wells; Man. Q; Ser. F*   54–7 They . . . year] *as Capell; QF line* are. / king, / trimde, / yeare /   55 seized] *(ceasde), Q3–F*   is it] *QF;* it is *Q2*   57 garden! We at] *Capell;* garden at *Q;* Garden, at *Q3–F*   58 Do] And *F*   59 over-proud] *F;* ouer prowd *Q*   in] with *Q2–F*

Their fruits of duty. Superfluous branches
We lop away that bearing boughs may live.
Had he done so, himself had borne the crown,   65
Which waste of idle hours hath quite thrown down.

1 MAN

What, think you then the King shall be deposed?

GARDENER

Depressed he is already, and deposed
'Tis doubt he will be. Letters came last night
To a dear friend of the good Duke of York's   70
That tell black tidings.

QUEEN   O, I am pressed to death

---

63 a rough pentameter with metrical pause after the caesura: 'Their frùits | of dù- | ty. ^ | Supèr- | fluous brànches'
64 **bearing** fruit-bearing
65–6 The Gardener's couplet provides a fitting conclusion to his sustained comparison; cf. 90–1 where the same technique is used. His last speech (102–7), which concludes the scene, is made up of couplets.
65 **himself had borne** he would have continued to wear (playing on *bearing* from 64)
   crown royal diadem; crown of a tree. See 48–66n.
66 **waste** Cf. *wasteful King* (55).
   idle unproductive; foolish
   thrown down anticipating Richard's later reference at 5.1.24–5 to winning 'a new world's crown, / Which our profane hours here have thrown down'. The line also recalls 1.3.118: 'The King hath thrown his warder down.'
67 ***then** Pope's emendation restores the needed extra syllable to an irregular line. Ure (121) speculates that Shakespeare may have abbreviated *then* as

'the' with a tilde over the *e* and that the compositor mistakenly read the following word (*the*) as a redundant repetition. Craven agrees; see Appendix 1, pp. 537–8, 538, ns 1 and 2.
68 **Depressed** subjugated, humbled, brought low in fortune
69 **'Tis doubt** it is feared that
69–70 **Letters . . . York's** These lines place the scene in one of York's houses (possibly Langley; see headnote and 3.1.36n.). *Letters* = a letter? (cf. 3.1.40–1n.).
71 **black tidings** 'Although the Gardener regrets the way in which Richard has allowed the country to run to ruin, these words suggest that he feels a basic sympathy for the King's predicament' (Adams, 188).
71–2 **I . . . speaking** I must speak or die. Alludes to the Elizabethan punishment of *la peine forte et dure* (the piling of weights upon the chests of accused felons, designed to force them to plead guilty or not guilty; most died under the torture). There may also be word-play on the meaning of 'oppressed to the point of death'. For possible indebtedness to Nashe, see Introduction, p. 114, n. 2.

---

66 of] and *F*   67 you then] *Pope;* you *QF*   68 SP] *(Gard.), F (Gar.)*   69 doubt] doubted *F*
70 good Duke] Duke *Q3–F*   71–4 O . . . news] *as Malone; QF line* speaking / garden, / news? /

Through want of speaking!
[*Queen and Ladies come forward.*]
                 Thou, old Adam's likeness,
Set to dress this garden, how dares
Thy harsh rude tongue sound this unpleasing news?
What Eve, what serpent hath suggested thee   75
To make a second fall of cursed man?
Why dost thou say King Richard is deposed?
Dar'st thou, thou little better thing than earth,
Divine his downfall? Say where, when and how
Cam'st thou by this ill tidings? Speak, thou wretch!   80

GARDENER

Pardon me, madam. Little joy have I
To breathe this news; yet what I say is true.
King Richard he is in the mighty hold

---

72 **want of speaking** failure to speak

72, 77, 78, 80 **Thou** The Queen uses the familiar form of the pronoun contemptuously to an inferior.

72 **old Adam's likeness** Adam was the prototype of gardeners, being the first; see LN.

73 **Set** appointed
dress Cf. 56n.

74 Cf. *KJ* 4.2.150: 'rude harsh-sounding rhymes'.

75 **suggested** tempted, prompted (to evil); cf. 1.1.101n. The Queen conflates the two temptations implicit in the story of the Fall (Genesis, 3.1–7, 17–19): Satan in the form of a serpent tempted Eve, and Eve, having succumbed, then made Adam her accessory in disobedience.

76 **make . . . fall** because the deposition of the King would be as calamitous as the fall of mankind. The Queen represents her husband not as Christ (in contrast to Richard himself; cf.

3.2.132, 4.1.171, 239–42) but as Adam expelled from the garden. In her anguished distraction, she blames the messenger for the message.
cursed cursèd; under a curse (like Adam after his fall from grace; cf. Genesis, 3.17–19)

78 **thou, thou** The repetition is intended to demean. See 72n.; also *Tem* 1.2.314, 3.2.26–7.

79 **Divine** prophesy, foretell by supernatural means (more solemnly portentous than 'predict'); perhaps the Queen plays ironically on *earth* in 78.

80 **this ill tidings** Cf. 2.1.272n.

82 **breathe** utter, tell

83 **he** For the inserted pronoun, see Abbott, 243.
hold grasp, possession, custody, with a possible pun on 'fastness, castle' since, according to Holinshed (3.501), Richard was confined in the Tower of London

---

72 SD] *Capell (subst.)*   80 Cam'st] *Q2–F; Canst Q*   tidings?] *Q2–F; tidings Q*   82 this] these *Q2–F*

Of Bolingbroke. Their fortunes both are weighed:
In your lord's scale is nothing but himself   85
And some few vanities that make him light;
But in the balance of great Bolingbroke,
Besides himself, are all the English peers,
And with that odds he weighs King Richard down.
Post you to London and you will find it so.   90
I speak no more than everyone doth know.

QUEEN

Nimble Mischance, that art so light of foot,
Doth not thy embassage belong to me,

84–9 **Their . . . down.** The Gardener's
scale conceit subtly anticipates
Richard's bucket-and-well speech; see
4.1.184–9n.; Gurr (136), following
Ure (122), cites Psalms, 62.9, especially in relation to 86: 'As for the children
of men, they are but vaine: the children of men are deceitfull vpon the
weights, they are altogether lighter
then vanitie it selfe.' But, unlike the
Psalmist, the Gardener is more concerned with political than with moral
lightness (cf. 86n.).
84 **weighed** against each other in a pair of
balances
85 **scale** pan, one side of the balances
86 **vanities** follies, worthless things (or
perhaps more specifically Richard's
flatterers, balancing *English peers* of
88)
    light light in weight; frivolous, wan-
ton, irresponsible; of little value
87 **balance** pan, the other side of the balances
    great powerful
89 **odds** advantage
    weighs . . . down i.e. outweighs
Richard. The Gardener speaks paradoxically: Bolingbroke's greater weight
in one pan of the balances makes him
physically lower but politically

stronger than Richard since all the
peers (88) increase his heft, whereas
Richard's corresponding position in
the other pan is higher and politically
weaker because his 'vanities . . . make
him light' (86) and because he has lost
his supporters; but the lighter weight
of Richard nevertheless *weighs* him
down politically since his fortunes are
falling whereas Bolingbroke's career is
on the rise. Richard will reverse the
contrast at 4.1.184–9, making Bolingbroke light and himself heavy.
90 **Post you** hasten, ride quickly
    you will probably monosyllabic
('you'll'; see t.n.). But the line could be
spoken with a hanging extra syllable
just before the caesura ('Pòst you | to
Lòn- | don and yòu | will find | it
sò').
92 **light of foot** speedy (*Mischance* is
personified and conceived of as a run-
ner); the Queen may also be playing on
the Gardener's word *light* at 86.
93 **embassage** errand, mission (the
report you bring)
    belong to me pertain to me. The
Queen asks why she is the last to know
news that concerns her more nearly
than others.

84 weighed:] *Q3 (weyde.), F;* weyde *Q*   85 lord's] *(Lo.), F*   90 you will] you'l *F*

And am I last that knows it? O, thou think'st
To serve me last that I may longest keep   95
Thy sorrow in my breast. Come, ladies, go
To meet at London London's king in woe.
What, was I born to this, that my sad look
Should grace the triumph of great Bolingbroke?
Gard'ner, for telling me these news of woe,   100
Pray God the plants thou graft'st may never grow!

                                        Exit [with Ladies].

GARDENER

Poor Queen, so that thy state might be no worse,
I would my skill were subject to thy curse.
Here did she fall a tear. Here in this place
I'll set a bank of rue, sour herb of grace.   105

94 **last . . . it** Shakespeare may have been influenced here by Froissart's report that after Richard's capture the Queen was isolated – surrounded by servants who were forbidden to 'speke of the kynge' even to each other (see quotation in headnote).

95 **serve me last** do your service as a messenger to me last of all (perhaps implying also the legal sense of 'to serve a writ')

96–101 The Queen concludes her final speech with three couplets – a formalizing, quasi-incantatory effect reflecting heightened emotion. The rhymes 'set the seal on Isabel's grief and the inevitability of the events which have aroused it' (Adams, 190).

96 **Thy sorrow** the sorrow that you report
   go let us go (hortatory subjunctive)

97 **in woe** qualifying *meet* or *king*

98 **What** probably an exclamation, or *What* could mean 'Why' (see Abbott, 253); without Q's comma (see t.n.), the line would mean 'Why was I born to this . . . ?'
   look appearance; facial expression. Cf. Daniel, 2.74–7, where the poet dwells at length upon the Queen's facial

reaction to Bolingbroke's triumphal procession.

99 **triumph** triumphal procession, victory parade; cf. *AC* 5.1.66, 5.2.109.
   Bolingbroke rhymes with *look* (98); see List of Roles, 6n.

100 **these news** 'News' (new things) was originally plural. See 2.1.272n.

102–7 See 65–6n., 96–101n.

102 **so that** provided that, on condition that, if (not 'in order that')
    state condition; royal status

103 **subject** liable to

104 **fall** drop, let fall

105 **sour** sad, sorrow-making
    herb of grace Cf. *Ham* 4.5.181–3: 'There's rue for you . . . we may call it herb of grace a' Sundays'. Perhaps also an echo of Nashe (see Introduction, p. 114, n. 2.). The plant 'rue' was also called 'herb of grace' because, coincidentally, to 'rue' meant to repent, and one can repent only through God's grace. It was therefore sometimes mingled with holy water. Here, however, the herb is associated chiefly with pity (see 106n.).

94 think'st] *F*; thinkest *Q*   98 What,] What *F*   100 Gard'ner] Gardiner *Capell*   these] this *F*   101 Pray God] I would *F*   SD *with Ladies*] *Pope (subst.)*   102 SP] *(Gard.), F (G)*   104 fall] drop *Q2–F*

> Rue e'en for ruth here shortly shall be seen
> In the remembrance of a weeping queen.   *Exeunt.*

[**4.1**]   *Enter* BOLINGBROKE *with the lords,* ^FAUMERLE,
NORTHUMBERLAND, [HARRY] PERCY, FITZWATER,
SURREY, [Bishop of] CARLISLE, ABBOT of Westminster,
[another Lord,] *Herald*^F *[and Attendants] to Parliament.*

106 **e'en for ruth** for sheer compassion; as an appropriate emblem or symbol of pity (punning on *rue* in 105). *Ruth* refers to the Queen's compassion as well as the Gardener's.

4.1 For this climactic and emotionally crucial scene, located in Westminster Hall (which Richard himself had caused to be impressively rebuilt in the two years before his deposition), Shakespeare again relied principally on Holinshed, at the same time radically condensing and rearranging the sequence of events that took place in the final months of 1399 into the vicissitudes of a single day. On 29 September in the presence of his successor Richard formally abdicated in the Tower of London, Parliament being notified of his action on the following day by the commissioners who had witnessed the act. That body immediately accepted the resignation, and Bolingbroke claimed the throne with the approval of the lords and commons; he was crowned Henry IV on 13 October, following which (on 16 and 18 October respectively) Bagot and Fitzwater accused Aumerle of involvement in Gloucester's murder. On 22 October the Bishop of Carlisle spoke in opposition to the proposal of the commons that Richard be tried and judged guilty of various crimes so that the realm could effectively be rid of him as a political force. Henry's directive

that Mowbray be recalled from exile was made on 27 October, and the Abbot of Westminster's plot against Henry was hatched at the cleric's house after Parliament had disbanded – either in mid-December or early January. Shakespeare reconfigures these actions into the four movements of a single extended scene; see LN. His most striking and effective innovation, however, consists not merely in the reordering of events but in an entirely changed emphasis: this he achieves by concentrating on Richard's extravagantly volatile personality and on the effective irony of a defeated king's verbal and emotional domination of the action, while the political victor is reduced dramatically to the role of *silent King* (290).

0.1–4 Bolingbroke obviously presides over the ensuing quarrel (as Richard presided in the similar circumstances of 1.1), but although the raised throne is again present onstage, Bolingbroke must either stand in front of it or sit elsewhere, as becomes clear at 114 when he is about to 'ascend the regal throne', thus provoking Carlisle's objection. 'Parliament was formally *rex in parliamento*, the king, lords and commons together' (Cam², 137). However, the commons as a body are not represented onstage, presumably because of personnel limitations (cf. 155n., 156n.). Rackin suggests that the staging decisions in this play implicate the

106 e'en] *F (*eu'n*);* euen *Q*   107 the remembrance] *QF;* remembrance *Q2*   SD] *Exit. F*
4.1] *F (Actus Quartus. Scoena Prima.)*   0.1–5] *Enter Bullingbrooke with the Lords to parliament. Q; om.*
Q3; Enter Bullingbrooke, Aumerle, and others. Q4; Enter as to the Parliament, Bullingbrooke, Aumerle,
Northumberland, Percie, Fitz-Water, Surrey, Carlile, Abbot of Westminster. Herauld, Officers, and Bagot.
F   0.2 HARRY] *Oxf*   0.4 *another* Lord] *Capell   and Attendants] Capell (subst.)*

BOLINGBROKE
Call forth Bagot.

Enter ᶠ*Officers with*ᶠ BAGOT.

Now, Bagot, freely speak thy mind,

audience as commoners, providing them with 'two temporal perspectives' – on the one hand 'a long, historical view of the action' seen as 'already completed and reduced to the stasis of formal tableaux', on the other an 'insistent, present reality', 'a disturbing . . . process that reaches out to involve and implicate the audience' (*History*, 119).

0.4 **another* **Lord** Capell's addition here is clearly necessary since Q gives this anonymous character a single speech and a specific action at 53–7 (omitted, however, in F).

*Herald The herald's function apart from enhancing the obvious pageantry of the occasion is not entirely clear. Perhaps he sounds a trumpet to announce Bolingbroke's entrance (and exit?) or to accompany the latter's ascent (or attempted ascent) of the throne at 114 (see 0.1–4n. and 114n.). If the regalia is brought in at this point (see n. following), the herald might carry it. See LN.

to Parliament As Wells (235) observes, Q's wording and also F's '*as to the Parliament*' suggest a processional entry. Gurr thinks 'the royal regalia' would be 'carried at the head of the procession, before the new judge Bullingbrook' (137); but see notes on 107.1, 162.2, 181 and 183.

1 This peremptory two-foot line quickly establishes Bolingbroke's authority; cf. his similar opening line in 3.1 (see 3.1.1n.).

Bagot apart from Aumerle, the lone survivor among Richard's special favourites (see 3.2.122LN; also 2.2.134–40n., 2.3.165n.). The arraignment of Bagot, his accusation of Aumerle and the quarrels that ensue are based closely upon

Holinshed (3.511–12) although somewhat altered and simplified. See LN. The episode 'leaves a strong presumption of Aumerle's guilt; but it is not definitely brought home to him, still less is he punished for it' (Herford, 192). Later, of course, Aumerle is reduced in rank (see 5.2.41–3n.) but only 'for being Richard's friend'. Bolingbroke entertains no suspicion of him until the moment when he kneels to be pardoned for treason (5.3.29).

1.1 **Halliwell's* transposition of F's '*Officers*' (included for typographical economy in F's general entry direction) to Q's separate SD one line later makes obvious dramatic sense.

2–5 Cf. Holinshed (3.511): 'Thus much adoo there was in this parlement, speciallie about them that were thought to be guiltie of the duke of Glocesters death, and of the condemning of the other lords that were adiudged traitors [the earls of Arundel and Warwick; see 1.1.88–103n.] in the forsaid late parlement holden in the said one and twentith yeare of king Richards reigne. Sir Iohn Bagot knight then prisoner in the Tower, disclosed manie secrets, vnto the which he was priuie; and being brought on a daie to the barre, a bill was read in English which he had made, conteining certeine euill practises of king Richard; and further what great affection the same king bare to the duke of Aumerle, insomuch that he heard him say, that if he should renounce the gouernement of the kingdome, he wished to leaue it to the said duke, as to the most able man (for wisdome and manhood) of all other.'

2 a tetrameter line whose brevity again helps convey Bolingbroke's dominance

1 SP] *(Bull.), F (Bullingbrooke.)*   1.1 *Officers with*] *Halliwell; in opening SD F*

What thou dost know of noble Gloucester's death,
Who wrought it with the King, and who performed
The bloody office of his timeless end.   5

BAGOT
Then set before my face the Lord Aumerle.

BOLINGBROKE
Cousin, stand forth, and look upon that man.
    [*Aumerle comes forward.*]

BAGOT
My Lord Aumerle, I know your daring tongue
Scorns to unsay what once it hath delivered.
In that dead time when Gloucester's death was plotted,   10
I heard you say, 'Is not my arm of length,

---

as judge (cf. 1n.)

freely speak a repetition of Richard's
words at 1.1.17

4 **wrought** This word, meaning literally 'worked', is ambiguous, probably
deliberately so. As Ure (125) observes, it can mean either 'worked
upon the King so that the murder was
effected', or 'joined with the King in
effecting the murder'. Holinshed's
report (3.512) leaves either or both of
these meanings possible: 'there was
no man in the realme to whom king
Richard was so much beholden, as to
the duke of Aumarle: for he was
the man that to fulfill his mind, had
set him in hand with all that was
doone against the said duke [of
Gloucester]'.

5 **office** service, duty, task

timeless untimely (or possibly, 'everlasting')

7 **Cousin** Bolingbroke uses the same
familiar address to Aumerle that
Richard used to him (cf. 1.1.28, 84,
186) in the corresponding challenge
scene with which the play opens. The

term again raises suspenseful uncertainty in the audience's mind as to the
nature of the relationship between
monarch and subject.

8–13 No source for the claim attributed to
Aumerle has been discovered. It may
be Shakespeare's invention, and perhaps Bagot is fabricating to save his
skin; cf. 17n.

9 **unsay** deny, retract (cf. 2.1.16n.)

delivered reported, uttered

10 **dead** fatal, deadly (cf. *MND* 3.2.57,
WT 4.4.434); ominous, dismal, grim
(cf. *Ham* 1.1.65). The word has also
occasionally been glossed as 'past, long
ago' (cf. *TGV* 2.6.28).

11 **of length** long; cf. Lyly, *Euphues*:
'Knowest thou not . . . that kinges
haue long armes & rulers large rech-
es?' (1.221); also *2H6* 4.7.81: 'Great
men have reaching hands'. See also
Dent, K87, and Ovid, *Heroides*,
17.166. The words attributed to
Aumerle could be taken to imply once
more that Richard was guilty of
Gloucester's murder (cf. 1.1.100n.,
1.2.39n.); but see 17n.

7+ SP] *(Bul[l].)*   7 SD] *Bevington*   9 once it hath] it hath once *F*

That reacheth from the restful English court
As far as Calais to mine uncle's head?'
Amongst much other talk, that very time,
I heard you say that you had rather refuse   15
The offer of an hundred thousand crowns
Than Bolingbroke's return to England –
Adding withal how blest this land would be
In this your cousin's death.

AUMERLE

Princes and noble lords,   20
What answer shall I make to this base man?

---

12 **restful** quiet (untroubled by Gloucester's political scheming and turbulence; see 1.1.88–103n.)
13 **Calais** the place of Gloucester's death (see 1n.); for pronunciation, see 1.1.126n. Cf. also 83.
mine uncle's head i.e. Gloucester's life
15 probably scanned with an anapaestic final foot: 'Rà- | ther refùse'
16 **an . . . crowns** According to Holinshed (3.512): a bill was read to the Parliament in which Bagot claimed that he 'had heard the duke of Aumerle say, that he had rather than twentie thousand pounds that the duke of Hereford were dead, not for anie feare he had of him, but for the trouble and mischeefe that he was like to procure within the realme'. Since a crown was worth a quarter of a pound, 100,000 crowns = £25,000.
17–19 *Q's mislining (the compression of three lines into two) resulted from the need to save space in setting cast-off copy.
17 **Than** than have (elliptical; see Abbott, 390)
Bolingbroke's return The chronology in Bagot's charge is seriously

wrong: Gloucester's death (cf. 10) occurred in September 1397, a full year before Bolingbroke was exiled (September 1398), so that the two remarks attributed to Aumerle could not possibly have been made at the same time (*that very time* (14)). It is tempting to interpret Bagot's words as recognizably untruthful rather than as an historical slip on Shakespeare's part. See 8–13n.
England probably pronounced trisyllabically ('Eng-e-land'); otherwise the line is short by a syllable. This pronunciation 'is frequent in the pre-Shakespearian drama, especially in Peele' (Herford, 190).
18 **withal** at the same time, besides (Abbott, 196)
19–20 These two short lines (both trimeters) make rhetorical sense: Bagot ends his speech of accusation with deliberate curtness, while Aumerle begins his answer by addressing the entire assemblage, after which there is a natural pause.
19 **this . . . death** the death of this, your cousin
21 **base** villainous; low in rank (since Bagot is not of noble birth)

13+ Calais] (Callice), *F* (Callis)   13 mine] my *F*   17–19] *as Capell; QF line* withall, / death. /

Shall I so much dishonour my fair stars
On equal terms to give him chastisement?
Either I must, or have mine honour soiled
With the attainder of his sland'rous lips.   25
   [*Throws down his gage.*]
There is my gage, the manual seal of death
That marks thee out for hell. I say thou liest,
And will maintain what thou hast said is false
In thy heart-blood, though being all too base
To stain the temper of my knightly sword.   30

---

22 **my fair stars** my high rank, or destiny (determined by the stars that influenced the circumstances of my birth); Johnson (1.444–5) remarks that 'our authour with his usual licence takes "stars" for "birth" '. Cf. *Ham* 2.2.141: 'a prince out of thy star'.

23 **On equal terms** in formal combat as though we were equals. Aumerle, being a duke, could theoretically refuse to fight a mere knight; cf. 29–30.
   to as to. Cf. 3.3.13n.
   chastisement chàstisement; punishment (in a duel or tournament)

25 **attainder** dishonouring accusation, stigma, disgrace (originally a legal term meaning that those convicted of treason or felony would forfeit their honours and estates but which became confused with 'taint')

26 **gage** See 1.1.69n. Gloves rather than hoods are probably used as 'gages' in this scene as in 1.1, since to do otherwise would detract from the parallel with the action of the play's opening (see following n.). Holinshed (3.512) does not specify the nature of the gage: 'After that the bill had beene read and heard, the duke of Aumarle rose vp

and said, that as touching the points conteined in the bill concerning him, they were vtterlie false and vntrue, which he would proue with his bodie, in what manner soeuer it should be thought requisit.' But later in the same passage, he reports that Fitzwater, twenty other lords, Aumerle himself and the Duke of Surrey all used hoods as gages (see 34–41n., 53–7n. and 61–71n.).
   manual . . . death This phrase seems to mean both 'gauntlet' and 'death warrant signed and sealed by my hand'. Or else, if *death* is taken as a personification (cf. 2.1.270n., 3.2.162), the warrant bears the signature and seal (*the manual seal*) of Death himself. 'Aumerle is being grimly witty' (Ard[2], 126). For *manual seal*, cf. *Ironside*, l. 439: 'Then for a manuell seale receaue this kisse'; also *VA* 516: 'Set thy seal manual on my wax-red lips'.

27, 39, 45, 66 **liest** monosyllabic

29 **though being** although it (the blood) is. See Abbott, 378.
   base Cf. 21n.

30 **temper** quality (i.e. well-tempered steel); cf. *1H4* 5.2.93–4: 'A sword, whose temper I intend to stain / With the best blood that I can meet withal'.

---

23 him] *Q3–F*; them *Q*; my *Q2*   25 sland'rous] *F*; slaundernous *Q*   SD] *Irving (subst.)*   27 I say thou] thou *Q2–F*   29 heart-blood] *Theobald*; heart bloud *QF*

BOLINGBROKE

Bagot, forbear. Thou shalt not take it up.

AUMERLE

Excepting one, I would he were the best
In all this presence that hath moved me so.

FITZWATER [*to Aumerle*]

If that thy valour stand on sympathy,
There is my gage, Aumerle, in gage to thine.   35
   [*Throws down his gage.*]
By that fair sun which shows me where thou stand'st,
I heard thee say – and vauntingly thou spak'st it –
That thou wert cause of noble Gloucester's death.
If thou deniest it twenty times, thou liest!
And I will turn thy falsehood to thy heart,   40

---

31 Aumerle's challenge to Bagot remains unaccepted and the gage is not picked up; cf. 78 SDn.

32–3 'I wish that the person (Bagot) who has so aroused my anger (*moved me so*) were the highest in rank (*the best*) in this entire assembly with the exception of *one* (Bolingbroke).' Presumably Aumerle also detests Bolingbroke (cf. his attitude at 1.4.3–19) but must conceal his hostility out of political prudence.

34–41 Cf. Holinshed (3.512): 'The lord Fitzwater herewith rose vp, and said to the king [Bolingbroke], that where the duke of Aumarle excuseth himselfe of the duke of Glocesters death, I say (quoth he) that he was the verie cause of his death, and so he appealed him of treason, offering by throwing downe his hood as a gage to proue it with his bodie.'

34 **thy valour** your courageous self (probably meant ironically)

   stand on sympathy 'require a knight as good as yourself'; *stand on* = insist on (cf. 'stand on ceremony'). Some

editors gloss this phrase as 'demand equality in rank'; but although Fitzwater, unlike Bagot, was a peer, he was only a baron, not a duke (see List of Roles, 26n.). *Sympathy* = correspondence (in fortune, condition or rank). Shakespeare never uses 'sympathy' to mean 'compassion, fellow-feeling'.

35 **in gage** as a pledge of defiance; engaged

36 **fair sun** another instance of the pervasive sun imagery, now applied to Bolingbroke; cf. 56n. 'They all show an uneasy consciousness of Bullingbrook's ambiguous "presence" before the throne' (Cam², 139).

37 **vauntingly** boastfully

39 **deniest** dissyllabic ('deni'st')
   it ... thou F's placing of the comma after *it* (rather than after *times* as in Q), although possible, seems mistaken. Cf. Holinshed's mention of the twenty other lords who also challenged Aumerle (53–7n.).

40 **turn** fling back, return; cf. *1H6* 2.4.79: 'I'll turn my part thereof [of the slanders] into thy throat'.

---

34 SD] *this edn* sympathy] sympathize *F*   35 SD] *Irving (subst.)*   36 which] that *Q2–F*
39 it] it, *F*

Where it was forged, with my rapier's point.

AUMERLE

Thou dar'st not, coward, live to see that day.

[*Takes up gage.*]

FITZWATER

Now, by my soul, I would it were this hour!

AUMERLE

Fitzwater, thou art damned to hell for this.

HARRY PERCY

Aumerle, thou liest. His honour is as true   45
In this appeal as thou art all unjust.
And that thou art so, there I throw my gage
To prove it on thee to the extremest point
Of mortal breathing.   [*Throws down his gage.*]
                        Seize it if thou dar'st.

AUMERLE

And if I do not, may my hands rot off   50

---

41 **forged** forgèd; conceived, engendered
rapier's point an obvious anachronism, since rapiers (long slender two-
edged swords with a sharp point) came
into use only in the later sixteenth century; see LN.
43 **it** the combat
44 *****Fitzwater** historically, Fitzwalter;
for the spelling, see List of Roles, 26n.
F altered Q's 'Fitzwaters', probably by
reference to the theatre promptbook
(see Appendix 1, pp. 526–8). But see
5.6.12.1, where QF retain 'Fitzwaters'.
45–9 **Harry Percy** (often known as Lord
Percy; see List of Roles, 16n.) is
Shakespeare's invention in this
episode, not being mentioned by
Holinshed nor any other source in
connection with the accusation of

Aumerle. Perhaps his action, like that
of the anonymous Lord at 53–7, was
suggested by Holinshed's 'twentie
other lords' (see 53–7n.).
46 **appeal** charge, accusation (see 1.1.4n.)
all unjust entirely false, altogether
untrue
47 **that** in token that, to symbolize
48 **the extremest** elided to three syllables ('th'extremest')
48–9 **point . . . breathing** point of death
50 **And if** possibly 'An if' (= if); 'and', as
well as being a conjunction, could be a
variant spelling of 'an' (used on its
own meaning 'if' or combined with the
conditional as an intensifier). Both
interpretations yield sense. See also
notes on 264, 2.3.133–4, 3.3.75, 5.3.67
and 112.

41 forged,] *Q4;* forged *QF*   42 to see that] I to see the *Q2;* to see the *F*   SD] *Bevington (subst.)*
44 Fitzwater] *(Fitzwaters),* F   45 SP] *Oxf; L. Per. Q; Per. F*   49 SD] *Irving (subst.) after 47*
Seize] *(ceaze), Q3–F*   50 And if] An if *Delius (Capell)*

And never brandish more revengeful steel
Over the glittering helmet of my foe!
[*Takes up gage.*]

ANOTHER LORD

I task the earth to the like, forsworn Aumerle,
And spur thee on with full as many lies
As may be holloaed in thy treacherous ear   55
From sun to sun.   [*Throws down his gage.*]
There is my honour's pawn.

51 **never brandish more** never again brandish
    revengeful avenging
52 **glittering** dissyllabic ('glitt'ring'; cf. 3.3.116n.)
53–60 F's omission of these lines probably represents little more than a cut in length: 'the scene is a long one and it was thought [probably] that three challenges were enough – as indeed they are' (Pollard, 95). Pollard, however, ignores the further challenges after F's cut. Wilson (202) adds: 'The cut also saved a small speaking part, always a nuisance to a producer.' Mahood (*Parts*, 72), however, argues for the importance of this character, who never speaks again: 'the unnamed Lord . . . vividly recalls the opening scene's presentation of speech as action ("with a foul traitor's name stuff I thy throat" [see 1.1.44n.]) by his tactile verb "spur" and his startling pun upon "hollowed/holloaed". The parallelism of the two gage scenes and the contrast between their two presiding figures are bound to be a little diminished when, as happened even before the compilation of the Folio, the anonymous figure is cut out.'
53–7 The dramatist apparently introduces this anonymous Lord in lieu of the group of noblemen in Holinshed

(3.512) who supported Fitzwater in his challenge to Aumerle: 'There were twentie other lords also that threw downe their hoods, as pledges to proue the like matter against the duke of Aumerle.' See 53–60n.; also 45–9n.
53 **task . . . like** 'burden the earth in a similar manner (by throwing down my gage)'. The language is 'high-flown' but 'in keeping with the conventional tone of the challenge' (Herford, 191). The metre requires *to the like* to be elided to two syllables ('to'th' like').
54 **spur** incite (see Mahood's comment in 53–60n.)
    lies assertions that you lie
55 ***As may** Capell's emendation mends the metre. Compositorial interpolation of small words is not uncommon; see Craven[2], 189–90, 196.
    holloaed in shouted loudly into (cf. the slang word 'hollered', which is close to Q's 'hollowed') with a pun on 'hollowed' ('reverberated in the emptiness of, sounded hollowly'); cf. *1H4* 1.3.222: 'in his ear I'll hollow "Mortimer"'; and also *E2*, 2.2.127–8: 'I'll thunder such a peal into his ears / As never subject did unto his king.'
56 ***sun to sun** sunrise to sunset; cf. Saviolo: 'The time appointed for Duello hath alwaies bene twixt the rising and setting of the Sunne' (sig. Bb4); also

52 SD] *Bevington (subst.)*   53–60] *om. F*   53 task] take *Q2;* tax *(Sisson²)*   55 As may] *Capell;* As it may *Q*   holloaed] *Cam;* hollowed *Q*   56 sun to sun] *Capell;* sinne to sinne *Q*   SD] *Irving (subst.) after 53*   pawn.] *Q3* (pawne,*);* pawne *Q*

Engage it to the trial if thou dar'st.

AUMERLE

Who sets me else? By heaven, I'll throw at all.

[*Takes up gage.*]

I have a thousand spirits in one breast

To answer twenty thousand such as you.   60

SURREY

My Lord Fitzwater, I do remember well

Cym 3.2.68. Wilson (203) cites *Traïson* (15/147), '*entre deux soleilz*' ('between sunrise and sunset'), but the phrase had already become current in English. Q's 'sinne to sinne' probably derives from misreading of minims (short downward strokes) in the MS. Although Wells (238) states that Q's reading 'could conceivably be defended', he, like all other editors, accepts Capell's emendation. Mahood (*Parts*, 72) points to the pervasiveness of sun imagery throughout, linking it here especially to Fitzwater's swearing by the *fair sun* in 36.

honour's pawn pledge of honour; cf. 71 and 1.1.74n.

57 **Engage . . . trial** 'Accept it by pledging your agreement (by taking up the gage) to meet me in combat (*trial*)'; see 72n. Note the wordplay on *engage* and *gage*. **trial** dissyllabic

58 **Who . . . else?** 'Who else challenges me (puts up a stake against me)?' *Sets* and *throw* are both figures from dicing. **throw at all** 'wager against everything that has been staked' (see previous n.). There is wordplay on throwing down gages as well as dice. Possibly, in addition to accepting the anonymous Lord's challenge (by picking up his gage), Aumerle also flings down a second glove of his own, which may explain his need to borrow an additional glove at 84 (but see 86 SDn.).

59 **spirits** of courage; cf. *R3* 5.3.347: 'A thousand hearts are great within my

bosom'.

60 **twenty thousand** possibly suggested by an earlier passage in Holinshed (3.512) in which Aumerle was alleged by Bagot to have said that he would prefer Bolingbroke's death to 'twentie thousand pounds' (see 16n.). See also 1.3.159n.

61–71 Surrey's involvement comes directly from Holinshed (3.512): 'The duke of Surrie stood vp also against the lord Fitzwater, auouching that where he had said that the appellants were causers of the duke of Glocesters death, it was false, for they were constrained to sue the same appeale, in like manner as the said lord Fitzwater was compelled to giue iudgement against the duke of Glocester, and the earle of Arundell [see 2–5n.]; so that the suing of the appeale was doone by constraint, and if he said contrarie he lied: and therewith he threw downe his hood. The lord Fitzwater answered herevnto, that he was not present in the parlement house, when iudgement was giuen against them, and all the lords bare witnesse thereof.' Like Aumerle, Surrey was of Richard's faction, being a nephew of the King; see List of Roles, 24n.

61–3 F's relining together with the interpolation of 'My Lord' at 63 (in F a separate line) is undoubtedly the result of deliberate space-wasting on the part of the compositor (see Appendix 1, p. 540).

---

57 dar'st] *Q2;* darest *Q*   58 SD] *Bevington (subst.)*   61–3] *F lines Fitz-water*: / time / talke. / My Lord, / then, /

The very time Aumerle and you did talk.

FITZWATER

'Tis very true. You were in presence then,

And you can witness with me this is true.

SURREY

As false, by heaven, as heaven itself is true!   65

FITZWATER

Surrey, thou liest.

SURREY   Dishonourable boy!

That lie shall lie so heavy on my sword

That it shall render vengeance and revenge

Till thou the lie-giver and that lie do lie

In earth as quiet as thy father's skull,   70

In proof whereof there is my honour's pawn.

[*Throws down his gage.*]

Engage it to the trial if thou dar'st.

FITZWATER

How fondly dost thou spur a forward horse!

---

63 **in presence** Possibly this phrase means 'in the King's presence-chamber', i.e. present at court (cf. 1.1.15n., 2.3.63n., 3.3.76); but it could mean merely 'present'.

65 **heaven . . . heaven** monosyllabic in both instances

66 **boy** a wounding insult, since the word was used chiefly for servants and inferiors (cf. *Cor* 5.6.100); Fitzwater was thirty-one, Surrey's senior by some six years.

67 Cf. 1.2.47.
That lie both the content of Fitzwater's accusation (that Surrey lies) and the lie that the act of accusing him constitutes. Surrey's ingenious quibbling on *lie* in 69 intensifies his scorn.
heavy heavily (Abbott, 23)

68 **render** return, give back

vengeance and revenge synonyms; the redundancy implies something like 'vengeance redoubled'; cf. *TNK* 1.1.58: 'vengeance and revenge'. Wilson's phrase (203) is 'ceremonious tautology'. See Introduction, pp. 86–7.

70 **thy father's skull** Walter Fitzwalter, fourth Baron, had died thirteen years earlier (1386) in Galicia, Spain, serving with John of Gaunt in the latter's unsuccessful campaign to obtain the crown of Castile.

71 **honour's pawn** See 56n.

72 an exact repetition of 57

73 **fondly** foolishly
spur proverbial: 'Do not spur a willing horse' (Dent, H638); perhaps echoing the anonymous Lord's verb at 54 (see n.). Cf. *LLL* 2.1.118–20, *2H6* 1.3.150–1.
forward eager, zealous

---

62 Aumerle] *Q2–F*; (Aumerle) *Q*   63 'Tis] My Lord, / 'Tis *F*   true.] *Q2* (true,), *F* (true:); true *Q*   65] *F lines* heauen, / true. /   66–7 Dishonourable . . . sword] *as F; one line Q*   71 my] mine *Q2, F*   SD] *Irving (subst.)*

[*Takes up gage.*]
If I dare eat, or drink, or breathe, or live,
I dare meet Surrey in a wilderness   75
And spit upon him, whilst I say he lies,
And lies, and lies. There is ᶠmyᶠ bond of faith
To tie thee to my strong correction.
[*Throws down his second gage.*]
As I intend to thrive in this new world,
Aumerle is guilty of my true appeal.   80
Besides, I heard the banished Norfolk say

75 **in a wilderness** where no help is
available; see 1.1.64–6n.

76–7 **he . . . and lies** The triple repetition is meant to intensify; cf. *vengeance
and revenge* (68).

77 ***my** Q3's emendation for Q's omitted
word seems necessary (the other challengers in the scene have thus far
referred to 'my' gage). Pollard (60)
believes it 'somewhat less than self-
evidently right' because Q2's 'the' or
'a' 'would be as good or better'. The
defective metre obviously requires the
addition of a syllable. Ure (128–9)
accepts Q3 (which F simply took
over), but cites the conjecture of H.F.
Brooks that the missing word could be
'this': the compositor's eye might have
skipped 'this' because of the preceding
is; Fitzwater, having already thrown
down one gage at 35, 'might well
emphasize now: "here's this – yet
another gage!"'. Q3's reading, though
it lacks authority, seems the simplest
solution and has been universally
accepted by editors.

bond of faith gage; cf. *honour's pawn*
(56, 71).

78 **tie** bind. Cf. *Son* 117.4: 'Whereto all
bonds do tie me'.

strong correction severe punishment
(of you); *correction* = four syllables
(cor-rèct-i-on).

SD *Fitzwater has already thrown
down his glove at 35 in challenging
Aumerle; now apparently he throws
down a second glove to challenge
Surrey. Wells (238) suggests that perhaps Fitzwater merely 'points to the
one he threw' earlier, but this seems
unlikely; the same gage can scarcely do
duty for two separate challenges.
Aumerle, who may also have thrown
down more than one glove, has to borrow an additional one at 84; see 58n.,
82–91n. and 84–5n. The text is unclear
as to whether Fitzwater's second gage
and Aumerle's borrowed one, thrown
down at 78 and 86 respectively, are
picked up. Perhaps, like the gage with
which Aumerle challenged Bagot (see
31n.), they remain on the floor until
Bolingbroke announces at 87 that all
the challenges must remain unsettled
until Mowbray has been recalled. At
this point the unclaimed gloves would
be gathered up.

79 **this new world** the world of Henry
IV (who will restore order to the
realm). Cf. 5.2.50: 'this new spring of
time'; also 5.5.58–9: 'my time / Runs
posting on in Bolingbroke's proud
joy'.

80 **true appeal** just accusation; cf. 46 and
1.1.4n.

81 **Norfolk** Mowbray

73 SD] *Bevington (subst.)*   77 my] *Q3–F; the Q2*   78 SD] *Bevington (subst.)*

That thou, Aumerle, didst send two of thy men
To execute the noble Duke at Calais.

AUMERLE

Some honest Christian trust me with a gage –
That Norfolk lies, here do I throw down this,   85
If he may be repealed to try his honour.

[*Borrowing a gage, throws it down.*]

BOLINGBROKE

These differences shall all rest under gage
Till Norfolk be repealed. Repealed he shall be,
And, though mine enemy, restored again

82–91 Cf. Holinshed (3.512): 'Moreouer, where it was alledged that the duke of Aumarle should send two of his seruants to Calis, to murther the duke of Glocester, the said duke of Aumarle said, that if the duke of Norfolke affirme it, he lied falselie, and that he would proue with his bodie, throwing downe an other hood which he had borowed. The same was likewise deliuered to the constable and marshall of England, and the king [Henry] licenced the duke of Norfolke to returne, that he might arraigne his appeale.'

84–5 *gage . . . lies QF have a comma after *gage*, making it uncertain whether the succeeding phrase (*That Norfolk lies*) belongs syntactically with *gage* or forms the start of a new sentence. Collier's more natural punctuation is adopted here.

85 That to assert that

86 repealed recalled home (from banishment); cf. 2.2.49.
try test in combat
SD* If Aumerle has already thrown down both gloves (see 25 and 58n.), his need to borrow a third is explained. However, if he has thrown only one gage, Shakespeare may be recalling Holinshed (see 82–91n.) and

inadvertently imagining Aumerle's gages not as gloves (as he would still have an unused one) but as hoods at this point, which would again explain his need to borrow a gage.

87–8 Holinshed mentions the decision to recall Mowbray from banishment twice – first at 3.512 (see 82–91n.), then again when Fitzwater petitions Bolingbroke for his day of reckoning (3.513): 'After this came the lord Fitzwater, and praied to haue day and place to arreigne his appeale against the earle of Rutland [Aumerle]. The king [Henry] said he would send for the duke of Norffolke to returne home, and then vpon his returne he said he would proceed in that matter.'

87, 106 differences disputes, quarrels; trisyllabic ('diff'rences')
rest under gage remain as standing challenges; cf. 106n.

88 Repealed . . . be This 'rather self-righteous expression of clemency, immediately followed by the news of Mowbray's death, is probably intended to convey the suggestion . . . that Bolingbroke knows the facts before Carlisle speaks' (Cam[1], 203). But surely a more benign interpretation of Bolingbroke's words is possible (see 90n. and 102n.).

---

83 at] *QF*; of *Q2*   84–5 gage – . . . lies,] *Collier (subst.)*; gage, . . . lies, *Q*; Gage, . . . lyes: *F*
86 repealed] repeal'd, *F*   SD] *Bevington (subst.)*

To all his lands and signories. When he is returned,   90
Against Aumerle we will enforce his trial.

CARLISLE

That honourable day shall ne'er be seen.
Many a time hath banished Norfolk fought
For Jesu Christ in glorious Christian field,
Streaming the ensign of the Christian cross,   95
Against black pagans, Turks and Saracens,
And, toiled with works of war, retired himself
To Italy, and there at Venice gave
His body to that pleasant country's earth

90 **signories** estates (cf. 3.1.22n.). Bolingbroke's promise to restore Mowbray's properties – a detail that may ameliorate our impression of the usurper at this point – is Shakespeare's invention; but later, according to Shakespeare at least, the family's rights and estates were restored to Mowbray's son (see *2H4* 4.1.108–10). Holinshed reports only the fact of Mowbray's death; see 92–101n. Bolingbroke is at pains to appear both authoritative and magnanimous in his handling of the dispute; cf. his pardoning of Aumerle at 5.3.130.

   he is perhaps elided ('he's'; see t.n.), although *he is* would seem to deserve emphasis. The line is an alexandrine, the fifth foot being either a trochee with the elision ('when he's') or an anapaest without it ('when he is'). Var 1773 attempted to regularize the metre by deleting *all*.

91 **we** Note Bolingbroke's premature use of the royal plural here and elsewhere in the scene (see 0.4LN).

   enforce his trial 'see that his trial by combat takes place'; *his* refers either to Aumerle (*his trial* = his making good of his challenge) or to Mowbray (*his trial* = trial by combat with Aumerle).

92–101 Mowbray's crusading adventures in the Holy Land and subsequent

death in Venice as recounted by Carlisle serve as preparation for King Henry's vow of expiation at the end of the play (5.6.49–50). There may be an implication that Mowbray was atoning for his role in the death of Gloucester, as King Henry will later plan to do for his guilt in Richard's murder. Shakespeare's Henry IV, of course, never manages the expiatory voyage to Jerusalem, dying ironically at home in a chamber named 'Jerusalem' (*2H4* 4.5.232–40). For the historical background of Mowbray's death, see LN.

94 **in . . . field** in glorious defence of Christianity (*field* = field of battle)

95 **Streaming** flying in the wind
   ensign See 101n.

96 **black pagans** perhaps Moors, Arabs (cf. *TC* 1.1.77–8: 'blackamoor'); but *black* may be used figuratively (= wicked, evil; cf. 132).

97 **toiled** worn out, exhausted; cf. *MND* 5.1.74.
   retired himself withdrew; cf. French *se retirer.*

99 **pleasant country's earth** Wilson (203–4) cites Hall (fol. i): 'who can reherce what mischefes and what plages the plesant countree of Italy hath tasted . . . ?'; cf. also *TS* 1.1.4: 'The pleasant garden of great Italy'.

90 all] *om. Var 1773*   he is] hee's *F*   92 ne'er] *F;* neuer *Q*   94 field,] field. *Q2;* field *F*   99 that] *QF;* a *Q2*

And his pure soul unto his captain Christ,   100
Under whose colours he had fought so long.

BOLINGBROKE

Why, Bishop, is Norfolk dead?

CARLISLE

As surely as I live, my lord.

BOLINGBROKE

Sweet Peace conduct his sweet soul to the bosom
Of good old Abraham! Lords appellants,   105
Your differences shall all rest under gage
Till we assign you to your days of trial.

Enter YORK.

101 **colours** banner (usually bearing a red cross); see 95.

102 Is Bolingbroke's surprise here feigned (cf. 88n.) or genuine? As Ure (130) points out, there is no warrant in Holinshed for inferring 'statesmanlike hypocrisy' on Henry's part, because the new king's decision to recall Mowbray (3.512, 513) and the report of his death (3.514) are entirely unconnected in the chronicle. By juxtaposing the two details in this scene, Shakespeare may have wished to imply such hypocrisy. But the juxtaposition may represent nothing more sinister than dramatic economy through compression and the desire to communicate information about the death of a character who had figured prominently in earlier scenes.

104–5 **Sweet . . . Abraham!** Cf. Luke, 16.22: 'Abrahams bosome'; also *R3* 4.3.38, *H5* 2.3.9–10 (where 'Arthur's bosom' is a comic blunder for 'Abraham's bosom'). The phrase became proverbial for 'heaven'. *Bosom* may be monosyllabic ('bos'm') although a feminine ending is equally possible. Chambers (135) takes Bolingbroke's words as 'a sneer at the expense

of his dead enemy'; Adams (200) interprets them as perhaps more generous. See also 2.1.154n.

105 a metrically irregular line with a natural beat (or pause) after *Abraham*. Or could the final word of the line be stressed *àppellànts*?

Lords appellants The official term for lords who have made formal accusations or challenges (here Aumerle, Fitzwater, Percy, the anonymous Lord and Surrey).

106 a formulaic expression, virtually a repetition of 87 (see n.)

107 **we** Talbert (179) interprets the royal pronoun as evidence of Bolingbroke's hypocrisy; see 0.4LN.

days of trial individual dates for the various contests of honour (cf. 57n., 91n.)

107.1 Holinshed (3.504) makes no mention of the Duke of York in connection with Richard's abdication: 'all the lords spirituall and temporall, with the commons of the said parlement, assembled at Westminster, where, in the presence of them, the archbishop of Yorke, and the bishop of Hereford, according to the kings request, shewed vnto them the voluntarie renouncing

102 Bishop] *Q3–F*; B. *Q*; Bishop of Carlisle *Oxf*   103 surely] sure *Q2–F*   104–6] *F lines* Soule / *Abraham.* / gage, /   104 Peace] *this edn*; peace *QF*

YORK

Great Duke of Lancaster, I come to thee
From plume-plucked Richard, who with willing soul
Adopts thee heir, and his high sceptre yields   110
To the possession of thy royal hand.
Ascend his throne, descending now from him,
And long live Henry, of that name the fourth!

of the king, with the fauour also which he bare to his cousine of Lancaster to haue him his successour'. See LN. Bevington (782) suggests that the regalia, which most editors take to accompany Richard's entrance at 162.1–2 (see 162.2n.), may be brought in at this point in view of York's words at 110–11, but these lines need not imply the physical presence of the sceptre onstage. See also 0.1–4n.

109 **plume-plucked** humbled, stripped of his glory. The term has proverbial overtones (Dent, P441.1). Ure (131) sees an allusion to the Aesopian fable (Yoder, 11, 79) of the crow that decked itself out in stolen feathers and was shamed when the other birds plucked them away; cf. also *1H6* 3.3.5–7: 'Let frantic Talbot . . . like a peacock sweep along his tail; / We'll pull his plumes and take away his train'. For Richard's extravagant dress, see 1.4.44n.

110–11 Cf. Holinshed (3.504): 'Now foorthwith . . . he [Richard] subscribed the same [the instrument of abdication], and after deliuered it vnto the archbishop of Canturburie, saieng that if it were in his power, or at his assignement, he would that the duke of Lancaster there present should be his successour, and king after him. And in token heereof, he tooke a ring of gold from his finger being his signet, and put it vpon the said dukes finger, desiring and requiring the archbishop of Yorke, & the bishop of Hereford, to shew and make report vnto the lords of

the parlement of his voluntarie resignation, and also of his intent and good mind that he bare towards his cousin the duke of Lancaster, to haue him his successour and their king after him.' See also the passage from Froissart in 204–15LN.

112 **descending . . . him** 'which you now inherit as his heir'. York implies that Richard has already abdicated. Carlisle's protest, which follows, seems to take the position that Richard cannot abdicate. After Richard's entrance at 162.1–2, the remainder of the scene exploits this contradiction dramatically. See 163n.

113 ***of . . . fourth** F's reading, which both improves the metre and lends an appropriately ceremonious tone to the line, probably has promptbook authority; see Appendix 1, pp. 526–7. This may represent an alteration of Shakespeare's original word order introduced by an actor in performance, despite Jowett & Taylor's belief that the change represents 'authorial adjustment' (190). On the other hand, Q's compositor may simply have scrambled the line (see Craven[2], 190, 196). Some editors, not very persuasively, attempt to justify Q by making *Henry* trisyllabic or *fourth* dissyllabic. F's reading is clearly preferable on both aesthetic and bibliographical grounds. Cf. also *Woodstock*, 2.2.115: 'Long live King Richard, of that name the second'.

110 thee] *(the), Q2–F*   113 Henry . . . fourth] *F*; Henry fourth of that name *Q*

BOLINGBROKE

In God's name I'll ascend the regal throne.

CARLISLE

Marry, God forbid!   115

114 The sudden baldness of Bolingbroke's action (without at this point
attempting any legal justification for his
claim) is revealing. Cf. Créton
(201–3/391–3): Bolingbroke 'accepted
of the regal power, since it was (*thus*)
ordained of God'; and when general
assent was given by the bishops and
other lords with 'a marvellously loud
voice', their '"Yea" . . . so quickened
him, (put such a flea in his ear) that
without farther delay he accepted and
took possession of the Crown of
England'. Then, after making a speech
in both Latin and English, 'without any
gainsaying, he sat down upon the royal
seat'. Cf. also *Traïson* (69/220): 'The
Duke [in Parliament] . . . sat himself
down on the throne before he was
crowned, in the place where the King is
accustomed to sit.' We may question
whether Bolingbroke actually does sit in
Richard's throne as York invites him to
do at 112. The action would make a bold
dramatic statement, and Bolingbroke
could scarcely be intimidated by
Carlisle's intervention, since Northumberland (with the Duke's consent or
even by his tacit command) instantly
arrests him. Irving goes so far as to add
a SD specifying that Bolingbroke 'takes
his place on the throne' (see Black, 258).
But Bolingbroke is elsewhere presented
as coolly deliberative, politically cautious and eager to preserve decorum (cf.
156–8 and 271), so that Carlisle's sudden
objection may prompt second thoughts
in him. This was the interpretation of
Giles's production in which Jon Finch
(as Bolingbroke) waited until he had
received the crown and sceptre before he
sat in the royal chair. If Bolingbroke does
occupy the throne during Carlisle's
protest and its immediate aftermath, he

presumably leaves it before Richard
enters at 162.1–2, after which York
explains to the fallen king that he has
been summoned specifically for the purpose of resigning his *state and crown*
(180) to Bolingbroke. It would be politically inept for Bolingbroke to sit in the
state before Richard has formally
renounced it, and in any event
Bolingbroke must stand for the episode
at 182 when both he and Richard have
their hands on the crown. But see 218n.
In God's name another of the several
anomalous instances in which F fails to
alter *God* to 'Heaven'; cf. Créton in
previous n. and 3.3.77n. Undoubtedly
the name of God is used in too serious
a manner at this juncture to be trifled
with by a censor; cf. also 130.

115–50 Shakespeare's alteration of the circumstances in Holinshed (see headnote)
converts this speech into 'a perfect dramatic prelude to the "Deposition" scene
that follows, and one calculated to enlist
the sympathies of an Elizabethan audience on behalf of the fallen monarch'
(Cam[1], 204). To give it greater weight
and significance not only for Richard's
personal tragedy but also for that of the
entire nation, Shakespeare lays heavier
stress on the doctrine of divine right
(virtually ignored in Holinshed) and
introduces the long-range vision of civil
strife in future generations (omitted
altogether by Holinshed). The prophecy, of course, could well also have been
preparation for the later dramas on the
troubles of Henry IV (as yet unwritten)
and a reminder of the already popular
plays about Henry VI and Richard III.
Baxter (184–7) analyses Carlisle's
speech as a *sermo humilis*, cast in the
form of a classical oration with *exordium*
(116–17), *narratio* (118–23), *explicatio*

115 Marry] *(Mary)*   God] Heauen *F*

387

Worst in this royal presence may I speak,
Yet best beseeming me to speak the truth.
Would God that any in this noble presence
Were enough noble to be upright judge
Of noble Richard! Then true noblesse would   120
Learn him forbearance from so foul a wrong.
What subject can give sentence on his king?
And who sits here that is not Richard's subject?
Thieves are not judged but they are by to hear,
Although apparent guilt be seen in them;   125
And shall the figure of God's majesty,

(124–30), *partitio* (130–2), *amplificatio*
(133–6), *refutatio* (137–45) and *peroratio*
(146–50), and exhibiting the 'lowly'
style of Christian humility suitable for
attacking presumption in high places.
See LN.
115 **Marry, God forbid!** For *Marry*, see
1.4.16n. The short line obviously suits
Carlisle's sudden protest.
116–17 'In the presence of royalty I, who
am humbly born, may speak only as a
person of the meanest station and least
competence (the *worst*); yet it befits me,
as a priest (or perhaps, as the only 'lord
spiritual' present), more than anyone
else to speak the truth.' *Royal presence*
may be spoken sarcastically (see 118n.).
118 **any** Verity (163) calls this 'a stroke at
Bolingbroke'.
noble presence Note the change from
royal presence (116). The modification
may reflect Carlisle's intention 'to
deny Bolingbroke's regality' (Wells,
240) in what follows (see 135n.). But
Carlisle toys with the words *noble* and
noblesse in 119–20; and cf. *noble
Richard* (120).
119 **upright** Cf. 1.1.121n.
120 **noblesse** nobility (of both soul and
rank). Used only here in Shakespeare;
but Q2's 'noblenesse' is merely an

alternative and, in this case, metrically
less graceful form.
121 **Learn him forbearance** teach him
to refrain
122 Cf. *Daniel* (2.109): 'Durst subiects
euer here or any where / Thus impi-
ously presume so fowle offence? / To
violate the power commanding all /
And into iudgement maiestie to call';
also *Homily* (2.279): 'what a perilous
thing were it to commit vnto the
Subiects the iudgement which Prince
is wise and godly, and his gouernement
good, and which is otherwise: as
though the foot must iudge of the
head' (see 115–50LN). For additional
parallels, see Ard², 132. Hayward (102)
may have recalled Carlisle's words: 'As
for force, what subiecte can attempt, or
assist, or counsaile, or violence against
hys Prince, and not incurre the high
and heynous crime of treason?'
124 **Thieves** 'even robbers' (emphatic).
Cf. Holinshed's 'so errant a theef' (see
115–50LN).
but . . . by except when they are present
125 **apparent** manifest, evident; cf.
1.1.13.
126–30 See LN.
126 **figure** image, symbolic representation

116 may I] *QF;* I may *Q2*   118 that any] *QF;* any *Q2*   120 noblesse] noblenesse *Q2–F*   123 sits]
QF; sits not *Q2*

His captain, steward, deputy elect,
Anointed, crowned, planted many years,
Be judged by subject and inferior breath,
And he himself not present? O, forfend it, God,   130
That in a Christian climate souls refined
Should show so heinous, black, obscene a deed.
I speak to subjects, and a subject speaks,
Stirred up by God, thus boldly for his king.
My Lord of Hereford here, whom you call king,   135
Is a foul traitor to proud Hereford's king.
And if you crown him, let me prophesy

127 **steward** manager (on God's behalf)
   *****deputy elect** Cf. 1.2.38n., 3.2.57n.;
   elect = chosen. F treats *deputy elect* as
   virtually a compound phrase, whereas
   Q's punctuation makes *elect* the first of
   a series of modifying past participles
   parallel to *Anointed, crowned, planted*
   (128). Both readings are defensible,
   but most editors prefer F.
128 **crowned** crownèd
   planted many years 'firmly established'. Richard had been king for
   twenty-two years (since 1377). The
   image of a *planted monarch* clearly
   relates to the garden scene (3.4); cf.
   5.1.63.
129 **subject** of a subject (adjectival)
   inferior breath the language of inferiors; cf. 1.3.215n., 3.2.56n., 3.4.82n.
130 an alexandrine
   forfend it, God may God forbid (or
   avert) it
131–2 Ure (132) suggests that Hayward
   (115) 'may be remembering this passage' in his description of how the
   people of Bordeaux reacted to
   Richard's deposition: 'Who would
   euer haue thought that Christians, that
   ciuill people, that any men, would thus
   haue violated all religion, all lawes, and
   all honest and orderlie demeanure?'

131 **climate** country, region
   souls refined 'civilized people' or
   'people who have been purified by
   Christianity'
132 **obscene** abominable, odious, foul
135 **My . . . Hereford** Carlisle refers to
   Bolingbroke by his title before banishment, refusing to acknowledge his
   claim to regality, or even his title as
   Duke of Lancaster; cf. 116–17n., 118n.
   whom . . . king probably echoed by
   Hayward (109): 'the Duke whom you
   call king'
137 **let me prophesy** Wilson (205)
   observes that 'Carlisle's prophecy balances Gaunt's' at 2.1.31–9 and that
   both proved to be historically true. For
   the political content of this speech, cf.
   Homily (2.295): 'countreymen to dis-
   turbe the publique peace and quietnesse of their countrey, for defence of
   whose quietnesse they should spend
   their liues: the brother to seeke, and
   often to worke the death of his brother,
   the sonne of the father, the father to
   seeke or procure the death of his sons
   . . . and by their faults to disinherite
   their innocent children and kinsemen
   their heires for euer'; see also
   3.3.88–9n.

127 deputy elect] *F;* deputy, elect *Q*   130 forfend] forbid *F*   132 deed.] *Q2 (*deed,*), F;* deed *Q*
134 God,] *(*God*);* Heauen, *F*

The blood of English shall manure the ground,
And future ages groan for this foul act.
Peace shall go sleep with Turks and infidels,   140
And in this seat of peace tumultuous wars
Shall kin with kin and kind with kind confound.
Disorder, horror, fear and mutiny
Shall here inhabit, and this land be called
The field of Golgotha and dead men's skulls.   145
O, if you raise this house against this house,

138 Cf. *Caesar's Revenge*: 'And Cole-black *Libians* shall manure the grounde . . . with bleeding hearts of men' (ll. 155–6); see 1.1.109n. The ironic association of blood with fertility reappears at 5.6.46: 'That blood should sprinkle me to make me grow'. For Baron's imitation, see 3.2.156LN.

140 **infidels** non-Christians

141 **seat of peace** Contrast with Gaunt's phrase *seat of Mars* (2.1.41).

142 **kin with kin** kindred by means of kindred (*kin* = blood relations)
kind with kind countrymen by means of fellow-countrymen (*kind* = breed, race, natural group)
confound destroy, bring to ruin. Shakespeare in an emblematic scene of *3H6* (2.5.55–122) had already dramatized the bloodshed between fathers and sons predicted here. Father–son warfare became shorthand for the worst evils of civil war (see 137n.). Cf. also Daniel, 1.1: 'Whil'st Kin their Kin, brother the brother foyles, / Like Ensignes all against like Ensignes band'.

143 **mutiny** insurrection, civil strife

145 **field** battlefield; perhaps also 'arable land'
Golgotha Calvary, where Christ was crucified; cf. *Mac* 1.2.40: 'Or memorize another Golgotha'.
dead men's skulls Cf. Matthew, 27.33: 'a place called Golgotha, that is to say, a place of a skull'. Mark, 15.22

(Geneva Bible) is verbally closer ('a place of dead mens skulles'), as is also the Gospel for Good Friday in the *Prayer Book* (John, 19.17): 'the place of dead men's skulls, but in Hebrew, Golgotha'. Carlisle imagines all England as a graveyard, a place of skulls like Golgotha (so called because the remains of executed criminals lay about). The Bishop's placing of this reference prepares the audience for Richard's comparison of his deposition to Christ's Passion; cf. 171–2n., 239–42 and 3.2.132n.

146 **raise** stir up, cause to rise in rebellion. See t.n. and Appendix 1, pp. 513, 529.
this . . . house Cf. Mark, 3.25: 'if a house be diuided against it self, that house cannot continue'; also Matthew, 12.25. Carlisle foresees the Wars of the Roses (already dramatized by Shakespeare in *H6* and *R3*) in which the two branches of a single Plantagenet dynasty, the houses of York and Lancaster, contest bloodily. There may also be a secondary reference in *this house* to the Parliament (cf. *3H6* 1.1.71) – i.e. indicating a prophecy of future strife within the legislative body that represents the nation. Gurr (143) notes a production in Oregon (1980) in which 'Carlisle gestured first at the assembled Parliament and then at heaven, giving point to his invocation of the divinity of kingship'.

139 this] his *Q2–F*   146 raise] reare *F*   against this] *QF;* against his *Q3*

It will the woefullest division prove
That ever fell upon this cursed earth.
Prevent it, resist it, let it not be so,
Lest child, child's children, cry against you, 'Woe!'.   150
NORTHUMBERLAND
Well have you argued, sir; and for your pains,
Of capital treason we arrest you here.
My Lord of Westminster, be it your charge

148 **cursed** cursèd; 'cursed because of the Fall' (cf. Genesis, 3.14) or, proleptically, 'cursed by the conflicts that civil war will unleash'
149–50 As often in Shakespeare, a rhymed couplet provides the ringing conclusion to an important utterance.
149 **Prevent it** forestall it (cf. 5.2.55). 'The irregular metre makes for dramatic effect, but Pope's conjecture may be right' (Ard², 133). Although compositorial interpolation of an extra syllable is possible (see Craven², 189–90), and an intrusive 'it' could plausibly be explained by the presence of *it* twice more in the same line, it is safer here to accept the hypermetricality as an intentional rhetorical device.
150 echoes Richard's own prediction in 3.3 (see 3.3.88–9n.).
child's children Cf. Psalms, 103.17: 'But the Mercifull goodnesse of the Lord endureth for euer . . . and his righteousnesse vpon childrens children'; also Psalms, 128.7.
*****Woe!** Conceivably *woe* (without a preceding comma in Q) could be understood adverbially (in woe, woefully) rather than as an exclamation.
151–5 Only Froissart (6.378) mentions Northumberland's presence in London at the time of Carlisle's speech (see 107.1LN). Shakespeare's use of the character as Bolingbroke's henchman represents a skilful means of preserving a degree of sympathy for the usurper

by shifting the onus of his strong-arm tactics to a subordinate; cf. 222–7, 243, 253–4, 269–71. The negative portrayal of Northumberland may also owe something to the Conway episode in Holinshed, in which the Earl treacherously broke his faith to Richard and captured him; see 3.2 and 3.3 headnotes, also *Traïson* in 171–2LN. Holinshed (3.512) says that Carlisle was arrested by the Earl Marshal, i.e. the Earl of Westmoreland after Richard's deposition; (see 153–4n.); Northumberland held the post of 'high constable of England' (3.510).
152 **Of capital treason** on a charge of treason punishable by death
153–4 The sources are unanimous in reporting that custody of Carlisle was given to the Abbot of St Albans rather than of Westminster; cf. Holinshed (3.512): 'As soone as the bishop had ended this tale, he was attached by the earle marshall [see 151–5n.], and committed to ward in the abbeie of saint Albons.' Wilson (206–7) attributes Shakespeare's change to a mistaken inference drawn from *Traïson* (76/228), but it is more likely due, as Ure (134) observes, to mere 'dramatic convenience . . . since Westminster and Carlisle are to remain on the stage to represent' the hatching of the plot against Bolingbroke, which Holinshed describes at a later point in his narrative and which includes Carlisle (3.514); see 324n.

149 Prevent it] Prevent *Pope*   let] and let *Q2–F*   150 you, 'Woe!'] *F;* you wo *Q*

To keep him safely till his day of trial.

[*Bishop of Carlisle is taken into custody.*]

^FMay it please you, lords, to grant the commons' suit?   155

BOLINGBROKE

Fetch hither Richard, that in common view

He may surrender. So we shall proceed

Without suspicion.

YORK   I will be his conduct.   *Exit* [*with Officers*].

BOLINGBROKE

Lords, you that here are under our arrest,

155–318 *This passage (the so-called
deposition scene), presumably deleted
from the MS from which Q was set, is
necessarily based on F, the most reliable text available. Occasionally, however, readings from Q4 (the first
printing of the lines, probably derived
from an acted version) must be seriously considered. Only departures
from F, however, will have asterisks
within this passage. See Introduction,
p. 10, n. 2, 165, and Appendix 1,
pp. 506–7, 507, n. 1, 515–17, 517, n. 1.

155 the commons' suit i.e. the demand
that the terms of Richard's abdication
(including the charges against him) be
publicly declared in Parliament and
that he be judged unworthy of kingship (see 272; also Holinshed, 3.512,
502 in 115–50LN and 225n.).
Holinshed makes it clear that the commoners in London were particularly
hostile to Richard. The historical reason for Northumberland's request
goes unexplained, but it may be
inferred from Bolingbroke's words at
156–8.

156–8 Fetch . . . suspicion. Q4's continuation of these lines as Northumberland's may reflect a theatrical version
different from F's; or perhaps, since
mislineation is involved (three lines of

type printed as two), the compositor
may have misunderstood his copy or,
despite ample room in his measure for
indentation and a new SP, have econo-
mized on space.

156 Fetch hither Richard Bolingbroke
consents to Northumberland's request
by summoning Richard in person,
thus agreeing by implication with
Carlisle's objection that no judgement
should be pronounced in his absence.
    in common view perhaps playing on
Northumberland's *commons' suit* from
155

157 surrender abdicate, surrender (the
crown)
    we royal plural; see 0.4LN.

158 Without suspicion Cf. headnote
and 114n.
    conduct escort

159 here are Q4's interpolation of a second 'are' (together with the addition of
a comma after *here*; see t.n.) is probably
a sophistication; but since Q4 can be
made to scan and yield a kind of sense,
it may be further evidence of a different acting version; see 156–8n.
    our arrest our restraint (until your
quarrels of honour have been settled;
cf. 87–8n., 106 and 107n.); *our* is royal
plural.

---

154 SD] *Capell (subst.)*   155–318] *Q4–F; not in Q1–3*   155 commons'] *F; common Q4*   156 SP]
F (Bull.); not in Q4   157–8 He . . . suspicion] *as F; one line Q4*   158 SD Exit] *F; not in Q4   with
Officers] Capell (subst.)*   159+ SP] *Q4, F(Bul[l].)*   159 here are] *F; are heere, are Q4*

Procure your sureties for your days of answer. 160
Little are we beholding to your love,
And little looked for at your helping hands.

Enter [KING] RICHARD *and* YORK
[*with Officers bearing the crown and sceptre*].

KING RICHARD
Alack, why am I sent for to a king

160 'Arrange for guarantors (*sureties*) who will vouch for your appearance on your respective days of combat (when you must answer to the enemies who have challenged you).' The same procedure had obtained when Bolingbroke himself was summoned before the King at Coventry; see 1.1.2n.
161–2 These lines are presumably addressed specifically to the challengers, who have created an awkward problem for the new ruler by raking up old quarrels, not the whole body of lords in Parliament.
161 **beholding** indebted, beholden. Shakespeare often uses the present in lieu of the passive participle (see Abbott, 372); cf. *R3* 2.1.130, *MV* 1.3.105, *KJ* 1.1.239. Since he never uses 'beholden', Pope's emendation, though sometimes adopted, can be safely rejected.
162 **And . . . for** 'and (I) little expected (love (= support))'. Q4's 'looke for' (meaning 'I little expect support') may be correct; but F, implying that Bolingbroke has already assessed the potential disloyalty of those who have caused him difficulty, seems richer. Cf. Mowbray's line, 1.3.155: 'all unlooked for at your highness' hands'.
  at from
162.1 *KING RICHARD In SDs and SPs in Acts 1–3 F rarely adds 'King' to

Richard. From this SD onwards it never does so again. See Introduction, pp. 168 and Appendix 1, pp. 510–11.
162.2 *The added SD is necessary to account for the presence of the crown and sceptre, which figure in the action at 181, 199 and 204–5; see 181n. and 183n., but cf. also 0.4n., 107.1n. Cf. also *KL* (Q) 1.1.33.1: ' *Enter one bearing a coronet*'. The chronicles characterize Richard as reluctant to part with the crown, and in Froissart he keeps possession of it even during his imprisonment in the Tower (see 204–15LN); it therefore seems appropriate to have it accompany him at his entrance here as opposed to being brought in at an earlier point. In *2H4* 4.5.21–2 the dying king keeps the crown on a 'pillow' beside him as a 'troublesome . . . bedfellow'.
163–222 See LN.
163 **to a king** ambiguous phrase: either 'as a king' (i.e. 'as though I were (still) a king'; see Abbott, 189); or 'to the presence of a (new) king'. Richard continues to feel like a king while recognizing his loss of command, so that he is both a king and not a king at the same time. Since it is characteristic of him to anticipate events, as in 3.2 and 3.3, he speaks of himself as already deposed (cf. Holinshed's account of his formal abdication in the Tower before the action was reported to

161 beholding] *Q4, F*; beholden *Pope* 162 looked] *F*; looke *Q4* 162.1] *Enter king Richard. Q4;*
Enter Richard and Yorke. F 162.2 *with . . . sceptre*] *White² (subst.); bearing the Regalia. / Capell*
163+ SP] *Cam (subst.); Rich. Q4, F*

Before I have shook off the regal thoughts
Wherewith I reigned? I hardly yet have learned   165
To insinuate, flatter, bow and bend my knee.
Give Sorrow leave awhile to tutor me
To this submission. Yet I well remember
The favours of these men. Were they not mine?
Did they not sometime cry 'All hail' to me?   170
So Judas did to Christ, but He in twelve
Found truth in all but one; I, in twelve thousand,
          none.

Parliament); see 110–11n. and head-note. With typically self-indulgent hyperbole Richard underlines his pow-erlessness. Dramatically, however, the formal abdication has yet to take place, as becomes clear when York explains to Richard at 178–81 that he has been escorted into Parliament to perform the *office* that was earlier only *offered* – the *resignation* of his *state and crown* to Bolingbroke. So Richard may mean that it is too soon for him to accept a summons to another king when he has not got used to thinking of himself as anything but *the* king.

164 **shook** shaken (a common past participle in Elizabethan usage)

166 a difficult line metrically. *To insinuate* is probably elided to three syllables ('T'in-sin-uate') or to four ('T'in-sin-u-ate'); in the latter case the second foot of the line becomes anapaestic.
  insinuate ingratiate myself (literally, 'make my way by sinuous and subtle means'); cf. Milton, *Paradise Lost* (4.347–50): 'the Serpent sly / Insinuating, wove with Gordian twine / His breaded train, and of his fatal guile / Gave proof unheeded'.

168–70 **I . . . me** For Richard's painful nostalgia, see Holinshed (3.507) in 4.1LN.

169 **favours** probably a quibble on three different senses of the word: faces,

countenances; kindnesses, friendly actions; tokens of affection (cf. 5.3.18)

170 **sometime** once
  All hail a probable echo of Matthew, 26.49: 'And foorthwith when he [Judas] came to Jesus, he said Haile master'; cf. also Mark, 14.45. Similar words are spoken by Judas in the York mystery cycle: *Agony in the Garden* (l. 248), 'All hayll maistir' (Beadle, 240). See 171–2n. The phrase has many analogues elsewhere in Shake-speare: e.g. *Mac* 1.3.48–50; *JC* 2.2.58; *1H6* 2.2.34; *Tit* 5.3.141.

171–2 The concept of the martyr-king, especially the analogy of Richard to Christ, is notably absent from Holinshed, Hall, Froissart and Daniel, whereas the anti-Lancastrian French chroniclers emphasize the parallel. See LN and Introduction, pp. 17–19, 30–2, 34–8, 49, 65–6, 77–8, 156–7.

172 an alexandrine, which, by lengthening the measure, has the ingenious effect of enhancing the contrast between *twelve* (171) and *twelve thousand*; cf. 3.2.70n., 76n. Note also the internal rhyme on *one* and *none* – a hint of the more lyrical style that tends to set Richard's speech apart from other characters; cf. his couplets at 173–6, 192–3, 196–9, 201–2, etc. But see also Introduction, pp. 57, 60–1.
  truth fidelity

166 knee] *F;* limbes *Q4*   167–71] *as F; Q4 lines* submission: / men, / hayle / twelue, /   167 tutor] *Q4, F (*tuture*)*   170 sometime] *F;* sometimes *Q4*

God save the King! Will no man say 'Amen'?
Am I both priest and clerk? Well then, Amen.
God save the King, although I be not he,   175
And yet Amen, if heaven do think him me.
To do what service am I sent for hither?

YORK

To do that office of thine own good will
Which tired majesty did make thee offer –
The resignation of thy state and crown   180
To Henry Bolingbroke.

KING RICHARD [*to York*] Give me the crown. [*Takes crown.*]

---

174 **both . . . clerk** alluding to the
   Anglican liturgical practice in which
   the officiant (*priest*) read most of the
   prayers while a server (*clerk*) at the
   reading desk spoke the responses,
   often simply 'Amen'; cf. 1.4.65n. Cf.
   also 1 Kings, 1.34, 36. The idea of
   playing both roles was proverbial
   (Dent, P587.1).
175 **God . . . King** the traditional acclamation used at coronations and other
   royal ceremonies (now enshrined in
   the British national anthem), here spoken paradoxically by a king who is also
   a subject; see 163n.
176 **if . . . me** Richard never fully relinquishes his belief in the sacramental
   authority of his kingship 'except formally', as Chambers (137) puts it, 'and
   in such terms as to reassert the right he
   is pretending to abandon'; cf.
   5.5.109–10.
177 **service** business, duty (with possible
   punning on 'religious service' in reference to the priest–clerk relationship of
   174 and on 'service' as feudal homage)
178 **office** function (probably extending
   Richard's wordplay of 177: *office* =
   church service or rite)
179 **tired** dissyllabic ('tirèd' or perhaps

'ti-erd'). *Tired majesty* = the stress of
being king, the weariness of kingly
responsibility. Hall (fol. viii[v]) says that
Richard 'desyred to be disburdoned of
so great a charge and so heauy a bur-
dein'. Cf. also Holinshed (3.503),
where Richard in the Tower is reminded that at Conway he had promised
'that he for insufficiencie which he
knew himselfe to be of, to occupie so
great a charge, as to gouerne the
realme of England, he would gladlie
leaue of and renounce his right and
title'.
180 **resignation** Cf. 190n.
   state kingly rank; throne (see 114n.)
181 **Give . . . crown.** Q4's lack of this
   sentence (correct in Malone's view)
   has led some editors, including
   Wilson, to believe that F's addition of
   it may betray 'clumsy conflation on the
   part of the scribe preparing copy for
   Jaggard' (Cam[1], 208). But F's repetition of *Here, cousin* (182) and the near-
   repetition of 'Give me the crown'
   (181–2), as Ure (135) points out, give
   us valuable clues about 'dramatic business' and are probably not redundant.
   John (82) suggests, for instance, that at
   182 Bolingbroke 'hesitates to take hold

---

181 Henry] *F; Harry Q4* SD1] *this edn* SD2] *Bevington (subst.)* 181–3 Give . . . thine] *Wells;*
Sease the Crowne. / Here Coosin, on this side my hand, and on that side yours: *Q4;* Giue me the
Crown. Here Cousin, seize y[e] Crown. / Here Cousin, on this side my Hand, on that side thine. *F*

[*to Bolingbroke*]
Here, cousin, seize the crown. Here, cousin,
On this side my hand, and on that side thine.
Now is this golden crown like a deep well

of the crown at Richard's first invitation' and only 'puts his hand on' it
when the King impatiently reiterates,
Here, cousin. The missing phrases in
Q4's version may reflect an alternative
staging (see 183n.) or faulty transmission from the putative MS copy (see
Appendix 1, pp. 506–7 and 506, n. 1).
SD1, 2 *Verity (220) suggests that
Holinshed's account of how Richard
in the Tower placed his signet-ring
on Bolingbroke's finger (see
110–11n.) 'may have suggested the
highly dramatic transfer of the
crown', the latter being more visually
and symbolically effective than a ring.
The crown is probably displayed in
some prominent position onstage,
perhaps on a ceremonial pillow.
Wilson (73), following editors as
early as Capell, imagines that it is
borne in procession by attendants
when Richard, '*stripped of his royal
robes*', enters with York at 162.1.
Some editors substitute '*the regalia*'
for the crown in the entry direction
since Richard also handles the sceptre
at 205. Such an arrangement seems
likely enough and is adopted here,
but other stagings would be possible
(see notes on 0.4, 107.1 and 183).
Richard must receive the crown from
an *officer* or from York (who has taken
it from the *officer*) so that he can then
offer it to Bolingbroke (181–2) as a
symbol of the transfer of power.
York, as the senior member of the
royal family and the noble who
escorts Richard into Parliament,
would appropriately have charge of
the regalia. Adams (204) notes that
Richard's gesture of taking the crown
'is as dramatically eyecatching as any

he made at the height of his power'.
RP points out that Richard's entry
SD in Q4, '*Enter king Richard*', may
imply that, at least in this version of
the scene, Richard may still actually
be wearing the crown; cf. Jowett in
183n.

182 *metrically irregular – appropriately
so in view of the dramatic situation.
The line opens with an attention-
arresting trochee ('Hère, cous- | in,
sèize'), then introduces a beat (or
pause) in the fourth foot between the
full stop and the beginning of the new
sentence. *Seize* carries obvious legal
overtones.

183 *and Q4's *and* is required by the
metre according to the lineation adopted in this edn. F's omission of the
word may represent editorial or compositorial adjustment in conjunction
with the variants mentioned in 181n.
Gurr (145) suggests that there may
have been 'some elaboration in the
playhouse to clarify a difficult piece of
staging, and that the F text reflects the
change'. Jowett (*TxC*, 312) believes
that Q4's 'substantial omission may
reflect an alternative staging whereby
Richard enters bearing the crown and
sceptre himself'.

184–9 Richard's extended conceit of the
two buckets obviously mirrors the chiastic structure of *R2* and relates thematically to the *de casibus* tradition of
political rise and fall; see 3.3.183
SD1n., 3.4.84–9n. and Introduction,
pp. 36, 80, 160. Coghill (94) cites
Chaucer's description of Arcite's
emotional state in *The Knight's Tale* (l.
1533): 'Now up, now doun, as boket in
a welle'. Cf. also *Isle of Gulls* (1606),
3.1.18–21: 'I can compare my lord and

182 SD] *this edn*

That owes two buckets, filling one another,   185
The emptier ever dancing in the air,
The other down, unseen and full of water.
That bucket down and full of tears am I,
Drinking my griefs whilst you mount up on high.

his friend to nothing in the world so fitly as to a couple of water buckets, for whilst hope winds the one up, dispaire plunges the other downe.' Patch (53–4) illustrates the connection with the goddess Fortuna in medieval literature: the rising and descending buckets represent the fabled instability of Fortune. Kiefer (242) calls attention to an emblem in Guillaume de la Perrière's *La Morosophie* (1553) in which the figures of Fortuna on the right and Virtus on the left 'jointly hold a crown above a monarch's head' (see Fig. 4); Kiefer sees Richard as conceiving of himself as Fortune's victim in medieval *de casibus* tradition, whereas Bolingbroke, embodying Machiavellian *virtú*, represents the capacity to rise above Fortune. Actors sometimes misguidedly hold the crown upside down, occasionally raising and lowering it, to make the bucket-and-well imagery visually clearer, although Shakespeare's simile identifies the crown with the well, not with its rising and falling buckets. See also 185n.

185 **owes** has, possesses
  filling one another based on a familiar proverb (Dent, B695); cf. *Malcontent* (3.3.63–6): 'did you e'er see a well with two buckets; whilst one comes up full to be emptied, another goes down empty to be filled? Such is the state of all humanity'; also *White Devil*, 1.1.29–30. George Herbert seems to have recalled Shakespeare's passage in 'Justice (II)': 'Thy scales like buckets, which attend / And interchangeably descend, / Lifting to heaven from this well of tears'

(Herbert, 141, 527); *tears* figures in both contexts and *interchangeably*, an unusual word, appears twice in the play (1.1.146, 5.2.98). For additional parallels, see Ure (136).

186–9 In applying the analogy of the buckets, Richard manages cleverly to imply that Bolingbroke, the higher bucket, is *emptier* (lacking the weight of legitimacy as well as light-hearted, emotionally shallow and insensible of suffering), while he himself, the lower bucket, is tragically heavier (not only because he is 'down and full of tears' but also because he possesses the gravitas of divine right). The ironically inapposite point in the comparison, of course, is that, unlike the lower bucket, *unseen* because it is submerged, Richard is highly visible and indeed contrives to make himself the centre of dramatic attention. Note also that in the Gardener's parallel image of the balances (3.4.84–9), Richard occupies the *light* side of the *scale*, while Bolingbroke 'weighs King Richard down'. Johnson (1.447) thought Richard's comparison 'not easily accommodated to the subject, nor very naturally introduced', although he admired the detail by which Shakespeare 'makes the usurper the *empty* bucket'.

189 **Drinking my griefs** Cf. Isaiah, 30.20: 'the water of aduersitie'; see also Holinshed in 5.2.37n. After he has finished the bucket-and-well speech, during which both men have a hand on the crown (183), Richard may take it again into his own possession, thus provoking Bolingbroke's question at 200. He does not give it

189 griefs] *F;* griefe *Q4*

397

BOLINGBROKE

I thought you had been willing to resign.   190

KING RICHARD

My crown I am, but still my griefs are mine.

You may my glories and my state depose,

But not my griefs; still am I king of those.

BOLINGBROKE

Part of your cares you give me with your crown.

KING RICHARD

Your cares set up do not pluck my cares down.   195

My care is loss of care, by old care done;

Your care is gain of care, by new care won.

The cares I give, I have, though given away;

They 'tend the crown, yet still with me they stay.

---

to Bolingbroke until 204–5 where he also relinquishes the sceptre. 204 ('from off my head') may suggest that during this brief interval Richard again wears the crown; see 204n.

190 Cf. York's earlier report that Richard had agreed to abdicate *with willing soul* (109), also his use of the word *resignation* (180). Wilson (209) remarks on the 'bluntness of Bolingbroke's speeches in this scene'.

192–202 Richard resumes his rhymed couplets (cf. 172n.). Here, curiously, they have the effect of conveying heightened feelings of personal hurt mingled with verbal ingenuity, word-play, paradox, even flippancy; note the nine persistent repetitions of the word *care* in 195–8 (see n.), triggered by Bolingbroke's use of the word in 194.

192 **state** Cf. 180n.

depose take away, deprive me of (cf. 3.2.158n.)

195–8 Richard plays on *care* in a variety of senses including 'responsibility', 'sorrow', 'diligence', 'anxiety' and 'effort':

'The fact that you are taking on new responsibilities as king does not diminish my sorrows in forfeiting the kingship. My grief is the loss of my old responsibilities occasioned by the exhaustion of my efforts and the failure to be sufficiently attentive; your anxiety comes from your fresh responsibility won through your zealous political efforts.'

195 The antithesis between *up* and *down* extends the bucket-and-well imagery from 184–9.

196 **by . . . done** a somewhat obscure phrase: possibly 'caused by my old (and insufficient exercise of) care', or, as Ure glosses it, 'through having finished with old care' (136).

198–9 The idea is proverbial (Dent, C863).

198 **have** still possess (because I grieve for their loss)

199 **'tend** attend, accompany. Q4's missing apostrophe ('tend') does not change the meaning. Shakespeare uses 'tend' and 'attend' more or less interchangeably; cf. *KJ* 5.6.32, *Tem* 1.2.47.

199 'tend] *F;* tend *Q4*

BOLINGBROKE

Are you contented to resign the crown?   200

KING RICHARD

Ay, no. No, ay; for I must nothing be.
Therefore, no 'no', for I resign to thee.
Now mark me how I will undo myself:
I give this heavy weight from off my head,

[*Gives crown to Bolingbroke.*]

---

200 Cf. *E2*, 5.1.49–50: 'My lord, why waste you thus the time away? / They stay your answer; will you yield your crown?' See 189n.

201–2 Richard's chop-logic turns on two elaborate quibbles: a *double entendre* on *I*, meaning both *ay* ('yes') and also the personal pronoun; and a pun on *no* and 'know'. In the first instance F and Q4 use the spelling 'I' for both meanings, as is characteristic of Elizabethan orthography; cf. *RJ* 3.2.45–50 and see 3.2.142n. Shakespeare makes Richard, in his narcissistic distress, toy with ambiguous significances which can only emerge in heard speech. Although the nuances of Richard's wordplay tend to blur into each other, at least two ways of understanding these lines may be suggested which perhaps operate simultaneously: (1) 'Yes, no. No, yes. But "no" is the equivalent of "I"; for, having lost my identity as king, I am now nothing ("no thing"). Therefore saying "no" isn't permissable (*no 'no'*), so I resign to you.' (2) 'I, no. No, I', which in delivery can sound like 'I know no "I"'; in this reading, we may paraphrase: 'Since I am now reduced to a nonentity, I cannot even know who I am, and therefore whatever I say is meaningless: given such erasure of distinctions, "no 'no'" (or "no 'know'") might just as well mean "yes".' Stripped of its quibbling intricacy, Richard's fundamental response to Bolingbroke's straightforward (and probably impatient) question is that he cannot disentangle 'yes' from 'no' in the disoriented psychic state to which the questioner has consigned him. For further discussion of this complicated passage, see Mahood, 87, and Gilman, 88. See also 202n., and Introduction, pp. 61, 88–9.

202 *no 'no'* Q4's punctuation, implying that the second *no* could be understood as a noun (accepted by most editors since Theobald), makes better sense than F's double interjection. F's intrusive comma may represent compositorial misunderstanding of the passage.

203 **mark me how** Cf. 3.3.61 (Abbott, 414).

undo myself annihilate my royal identity, unmake myself; ceremonially divest myself (cf. *undeck*, 250). See also 2.1.16n. Richard ritualizes his self-deposition as a kind of coronation service in reverse, an 'inverted rite' as Pater famously called it (Forker, 298). See LN.

204–15 As Gurr (145) notes, this passage draws significantly upon the wording and content of the instrument of abdication as given in Holinshed (3.504); *hand* (205, 208), *crown* (208), *release* (210), *oaths* (210) and *majesty* (211), for instance, also appear in the legal document. See LN; also Holinshed in 110–11n.

204 Richard may have put on the crown somewhere between 189 and this point. Certainly this line (or 208) could

---

201 Ay, no. No, ay;] *F (*I, no; no, I:*);* I, no no I; *Q4*   202 no 'no'] *Q4 (*no no*);* no, no *F;* no No *Theobald*   204 SD] *Bevington (subst.), combined with 205 SD after 203*

And this unwieldy sceptre from my hand,   205
[*Takes up sceptre and gives it to Bolingbroke.*]
The pride of kingly sway from out my heart;
With mine own tears I wash away my balm,
With mine own hands I give away my crown,
With mine own tongue deny my sacred state,
With mine own breath release all duteous oaths.   210
All pomp and majesty I do forswear;
My manors, rents, revenues I forgo;
My acts, decrees and statutes I deny.
God pardon all oaths that are broke to me;
God keep all vows unbroke are made to thee.   215

be made dramatically more effective if Richard is literally removing the crown from his head (see Froissart in 204–15LN).

heavy weight heavy with grief as well as with responsibility; see 179n. Cf. *2H4* 3.1.31: 'Uneasy lies the head that wears a crown'.

205 **unwieldy** difficult to manage (not physically, but because of the authority it represents); cf. 3.2.115.

207 Richard contradicts the doctrine of sacred kingship to which he elsewhere clings (cf. 3.2.54–5: 'Not all the water in the rough rude sea / Can wash the balm off from an anointed king'); see 3.2.55n. But see also 176n.

208 Cf. Daniel, 2.119: ''Tis said with his owne hands he gaue the crowne / To *Lancaster*, and wisht to God he might / Haue better ioy thereof then he had knowne'; also Froissart (6.378): 'take the crowne fro his heed with bothe his handes' (see 204–15LN). Hayward (88), in turn, may have echoed Shakespeare, though he too could have consulted earlier sources: 'and then he deliuered with his owne hands the Crowne, the Septer, and the Robe to the Duke of Lancaster'.

209 **deny . . . state** 'repudiate my status as a king by divine right'.

210 **release . . . oaths** 'release my subjects from all the oaths of allegiance which they dutifully swore to me' (elliptical); cf. 214; also Bolingbroke's *My stooping duty* (3.3.48) and York's *oath / And duty* (2.2.112–13). Some editors prefer Q4's 'duties rites' as clearer, but both readings mean essentially the same thing. Cf. Daniel, 2.118: 'There he his subiects all in generall / Assoyles and quites of oth and fealty'. In Holinshed (3.504) the instrument of abdication uses similar language: Richard does 'acquit and assoile' all his subjects 'from their oth of fealtie and homage . . . and from all manner bonds of allegiance'.

211 **pomp and majesty** splendour of majestic ceremony (hendiadys); cf. *Oth* 3.3.354: 'pride, pomp, and circumstance'.

212 **revenues** revènues (a common Elizabethan pronunciation; but for 'rèvenues', see 1.4.46, 2.1.161, 226)

213 **deny** annul, repeal

214 Cf. 210n.

215 **are made** that are made (Abbott, 244); Q4's variant 'that sweare' = 'of them that swear fealty'.

205 SD] *Bevington (subst.), combined with 204 SD after 203*   210 duteous oaths] *F;* duties rites *Q4*
212 manors] *Q4 (*Manners*), F*   215 are made] *F;* that sweare *Q4*

Make me, that nothing have, with nothing grieved,
And thou with all pleased that hast all achieved.
Long mayst thou live in Richard's seat to sit,
And soon lie Richard in an earthy pit!
'God save King Henry', unkinged Richard says,   220
'And send him many years of sunshine days!' –
What more remains?

[*Northumberland presents a paper to King Richard.*]

NORTHUMBERLAND   No more, but that you read

216 **Make me** God make me (continuing the subjunctive mood from 215)
with nothing grieved 'There is deliberate paradox here. Richard asks to be grieved by having nothing, but also to be grieved by nothing. The ambiguity is highly expressive of the delicate balance of Richard's state of mind, wishing to be relieved of his care yet reluctant to give up his crown' (Wells, 244).

217 For the sentiment, cf. Daniel in 208n. For Elizabethan use of the nominative ('thou') where we should expect the accusative ('thee'), see Abbott, 216.
with all Q6's spelling ('withall'; see t.n.) may imply a *double entendre*: 'withal' = with everything; also, too. Cf. the similar punning on *mis-take* (3.3.17n.).
achieved won

218 Does this line suggest that Bolingbroke is already sitting *in Richard's seat* or merely that he soon will sit in it? Either staging is possible. See 114n.

219 **earthy pit** perhaps an extension of Richard's imagery at 3.3.153–4. Cf. *E2*, 5.1.110, where Edward also wishes for death at the moment of his abdication: 'Come, death, and with thy fingers close my eyes.'

220 **unkinged** Cf. 5.5.37, the only other use of this word in Shakespeare; see

also 2.1.16n.

221 **sunshine days** In defeat Richard bitterly applies the sun image (traditionally associated with any kingship) to his rival; cf. 3.2.218n. But *sunshine day* is a stock phrase: cf. *3H6* 2.1.187; *E2*, 5.1.27; *Ironside*, l. 1355. For Baron's imitation, see 3.2.156LN.

222–3 **read / These accusations** Holinshed (3.502–3) mentions '33 solemne articles', printing these in an abridged form, but nowhere suggests that Richard was meant to read them out in public. They spell out 'manie heinous points of misgouernance and iniurious dealings in the administration of his kinglie office'. The chronicle does suggest that Richard in the Tower 'read the scroll of resignation' aloud (3.504), but adds that the oral presentation of the specific charges in Parliament 'was deferred' (3.505). Northumberland's role in trying to impose this further humiliation upon the fallen king illustrates Shakespeare's dramatic inventiveness – a way of garnering sympathy for the protagonist by showing his tormentor in an ugly light. As Ure (138) notes, the dramatist probably wanted his audience to be aware of the written accusations and yet avoid the tedium (and opprobrium?) of having their details exposed by making Richard 'evade the task' of public confession.

217 with all] *Q4–F;* withall *Q6*   219 earthy] *Q4, F;* earthly *Q5*   220 Henry] *F; Harry Q4*
221 sunshine] *Q4, F;* Sun-shines *Q5*   222 SD] *Capell (subst.) after* read

These accusations, and these grievous crimes
Committed by your person and your followers
Against the state and profit of this land,   225
That, by confessing them, the souls of men
May deem that you are worthily deposed.

KING RICHARD

Must I do so? And must I ravel out
My weaved-up follies? Gentle Northumberland,
If thy offences were upon record,   230
Would it not shame thee in so fair a troop
To read a lecture of them? If thou wouldst,
There shouldst thou find one heinous article
Containing the deposing of a king

224 **followers** presumably elided to two syllables ('follow'rs')
225 **state and profit** ordered prosperity, profitable state (hendiadys). Holinshed (3.502) says that the articles against Richard were intended to persuade Parliament 'that he was an vnprofitable prince to the common-wealth, and worthie to be deposed'; the writ of abdication, also printed in Holinshed (3.504), echoes the same language: Richard acknowledged and 'deeme[d]' himself to have 'beene insufficient and vnable, and also vnprofitable, and for [his] open deserts not vnworthie to be put downe'. See 227n.
226 **by confessing them** by (your) confessing them (Abbott, 378)
226–7 **the . . . deem** 'men in their deepest convictions may judge'
227 **worthily deposed** deservedly deprived of kingship. Cf. Holinshed's 'worthie to be deposed' (225n.).
228 **Must . . . must** See 3.3.143–6n.
ravel out unravel, expose
229 **Gentle** noble; amiable, tender (with extreme sarcasm)
230 **thy** Richard here begins to use the familiar form of the pronoun

disdainfully to Northumberland.
record recòrd (cf. *Ham* 1.5.99); but cf. also rècord (1.1.30).
231 **so . . . troop** so fine a company, so splendid a gathering. Richard speaks with corrosive irony; cf. 'a sort of traitors here ' (246).
232 **read a lecture** read aloud (as though preaching a sermon or inculcating a moral lesson)
232–3 **wouldst . . . shouldst** Although today standard English would reverse these auxiliaries, there was no consistent distinction between them in Elizabethan usage.
233 **heinous** Cf. Carlisle's 'so heinous, black, obscene a deed' (132); Holinshed (3.502) reports that the thirty-three articles drawn up against Richard were 'heinous to the eares of all men', a phrase lifted from Hall (fol. vi'): 'articles very heynous to the eares of men'. Cf. also Holinshed in 222–3n.
article item, entry (see previous note); Richard glances mordantly at the *accusations* (223) – the paper that Northumberland has thrust upon him; the Earl himself uses the word at 243.

229 follies] *F*; Folly *Q4*

And cracking the strong warrant of an oath,   235
Marked with a blot, damned in the book of heaven.
Nay, all of you that stand and look upon me,
Whilst that my wretchedness doth bait myself,

235 **strong . . . oath** 'binding assurance in your oath of fealty to me'. Cf. *Homily* (2.293): 'rebels by breach of their faith giuen, and the oath made to their Prince, bee guiltie of most damnable periurie' (see 2.2.112n.). An audience might recall Northumberland's detailed oath to Richard on behalf of Bolingbroke at 3.3.105–20 but would probably know little of Northumberland's perjury at Conway, which Shakespeare chose to omit from the play but to which he may allude here. See LN.

236 probably a biblical echo; cf. Exodus, 32.33: 'And the Lord said unto Moses, Whosoever hath sinned against me, him will I blot out of my book' (AV); also Psalms, 69.28: 'Let them be blotted out of the book of the living, and not be written with the righteous' (AV). In these passages, however, neither Bishops' nor Geneva Bible uses the word 'blot'; but see Revelation, 3.5: 'blot . . . out of the book of life' (Bishops' Bible) and 1.3.202n.

Marked . . . damned modifying *article* (233)

damned . . . heaven 'condemned in the celestial record of those living on earth' (biblical: see Isaiah, 4.3, Malachi, 3.16, Psalms, 69.28). The familiar *Sermon Against Swearing and Perjury* (*Homilies*, 1.47) underlines the sacredness of oaths, sworn in God's name and therefore 'part of Gods glory, which we are bound by his commandements to giue vnto him'; cf. also *Homily* (2.296): rebels 'against God, their Prince and Countrie . . . iustly doe fall headlong into hell'.

237 **look upon me** Most recent editors have preferred F's reading with the added word *me* at the end of the line (see t.n.). It is possible that *look upon* stood in the original MS but was altered to *look upon me* in the theatre for purposes of clarity and that Shakespeare assented. The added syllable creates no metrical problem if *upon me* is treated as a weak ending. Q4's 'look vpon', however, might be right; cf. *TC* 5.6.10: 'He is my prize, I will not look upon'; also *3H6* 2.3.26–7: 'whiles the foe doth rage, / And look upon'. *Look upon* without the pronoun, being less personal, would alter the meaning of the clause to 'all of you who stand here as onlookers', characterizing the spectators as already morally detached or even evasive. Such an interpretation might be effective if realizable on-stage. Jowett (*TxC*, 312) pronounces Q4's reading 'distinctive and acceptable' and thinks it 'more plausible that the Folio compositor should have supplied "me", perhaps under the influence of "my" immediately below ["my selfe", 238], than that the last word of the line should have been omitted in Q4.'

238 **Whilst . . . bait** 'while I in my wretchedness torment'. Kittredge[2] (171) suggests that the figure comes 'from bear-baiting'; *bait* = harass, attack. Mowat & Werstine (166) elaborate: 'the bear is tied to a stake and set upon by dogs. Here the spectators watch Richard being attacked by his own *wretchedness*.'

237 all of] *F;* of *Q4*   upon me] *F;* vpon *Q4*   238 bait] *F;* bate *Q4*

Though some of you, with Pilate, wash your hands,
Showing an outward pity, yet you Pilates   240
Have here delivered me to my sour cross,
And water cannot wash away your sin.

NORTHUMBERLAND

My lord, dispatch. Read o'er these articles.

[Presents the paper again.]

KING RICHARD

Mine eyes are full of tears; I cannot see.
And yet salt water blinds them not so much   245
But they can see a sort of traitors here.
Nay, if I turn mine eyes upon myself,
I find myself a traitor with the rest;
For I have given here my soul's consent
T'undeck the pompous body of a king,   250

239–42 Cf. Matthew, 27.24–5. See 171–2n., 239n. and 3.2.132n.

239 **with Pilate** like Pilate. See 3.1.5–6 and n., a passage in which Bolingbroke compares himself (unconsciously?) to Pilate washing his hands, as he does again at 5.6.50 (see n.). Cf. also Holinshed in 3.3.53–61.3n.

241 **delivered** Cf. John, 18.30, 19.16, the Gospel for Good Friday in the *Prayer Book*, where Christ is 'delivered' to Pilate, and by Pilate 'delivered' to the Jews to be crucified.
sour bitter

243 **dispatch** make haste, don't waste time
articles Cf. 222–3n., 225n., 233n.

244 Richard replicates the Queen's imagery at 2.2.16: 'Sorrow's eyes, glazed with blinding tears'.

246 **But they can** that they cannot
sort pack, gang (a term of contempt); cf. *R3* 5.3.316: 'A sort of vagabonds, rascals, runaways'. Wells

(245), somewhat implausibly, suggests a possible 'pun on *salt*' from 245.

247 Thematically, this line anticipates the mirror episode at 276–88.

248–50 Cf. *E2*, 5.1.97–9: 'Here, receive my crown. / Receive it? No, these innocent hands of mine / Shall not be guilty of so foul a crime.'

250 **T'undeck** to divest of its regalia; cf. *undo* (203 and n.). See also 2.1.16n.
pompous splendidly arrayed, ceremonially clad. Shakespeare never uses the word in its modern pejorative sense.
body Note the antithesis to *soul's* in 249 – a repeated theme in the play; cf. 1.1.37–8, 103, 1.3.195–6, 3.1.3, 4.1.99–100, 5.5.111–12. 'Richard asserts his right to the crown while renouncing its attributes' (Wells, 245).

243 SD] *this edn*   245 salt water] *Q4;* salt-Water *F*   250 T'undeck] *F;* To vndecke *Q4*

Made Glory base and Sovereignty a slave,
Proud Majesty a subject, State a peasant.

NORTHUMBERLAND

My lord –

KING RICHARD

No lord of thine, thou haught insulting man,
Nor no man's lord! I have no name, no title –   255
No, not that name was given me at the font –

251 *and Sovereignty Most editors accept Q4's reading as idiomatic and natural, although F's 'a Soueraigntie' was defended by Malone and accepted by a few followers (see Black, 272). Wilson (211) not unreasonably believes the F reading to be 'a misprint'. Ironically, Richard's words recall Gaunt's 'Thy state . . . is bondslave' (2.1.114).

252 State royal stateliness, magnificence

253–4 Cf. *E2*, 5.1.112–13: '*Winchester.* My lord – / *Edward.* Call me not lord! Away, out of my sight!'

254 *haught arrogant, haughty; cf. *R3* 2.3.28, also *E2*, 3.1.28. Q4's *haught insulting* is acceptable; F's compound ('haught-insulting') suggests that in the theatre *haught* may have been regarded as having adverbial force (haughtily insulting). But since a compositorial corruption seems to have invaded 255 (see n.), F could be unreliable at this point.

255 *Nor no F's 'No, nor no' destroys the metre and is probably a compositorial mistake influenced by *No, not* in the next line.
    no name, no title Cf. 3.3.145–6: 'Must he lose / The name of King?' In Holinshed (3.504) Richard gives up 'the name, worship, and regaltie and kinglie highnesse' of his office.

'Richard reasons with the logic of despair and completely "undoes [unmakes] himself" (l. 203). The usurper has stripped him of his royalty, which was his by right of birth, and so has destroyed his identity. If not *King*, how can he be *Richard*? He is a nameless outcast' (Kittredge[2], 171–2). Cf. also *KL* 5.3.121–2: 'my name is lost, / By treason's tooth bare-gnawn and canker-bit'. Richard's total 'undoing' of himself has its logical end in the image of the 'mockery king of snow' (260) and in the shattering of his image as reflected in the mirror (288).

256–7 name . . . usurped Richard's claim that even his baptismal name (Richard) has been stolen may be nothing more than characteristic hyperbole. Or he could mean that since he is now unkinged and 'has no identity', he may himself usurp a name to which he is no longer entitled (Wells, 245). For the libel that Richard was illegitimate, see LN.

256 was given that was given (Abbott, 244)
    at the font possibly an echo of Froissart (6.377), where Bolingbroke mentions that Richard's mother was Edward III's 'gossyp [godparent] of two chyldren at the fonte'

251 and Sovereignty] *Q4*; a Soueraigntie *F*   254 haught insulting] *Q4*; haught-insulting *F*
255 Nor] *Q4*; No, nor *F*

But 'tis usurped. Alack the heavy day,
That I have worn so many winters out
And know not now what name to call myself.
O, that I were a mockery king of snow,   260
Standing before the sun of Bolingbroke,
To melt myself away in water-drops!
Good King; great King – and yet not greatly good –
An if my word be sterling yet in England,
Let it command a mirror hither straight,   265
That it may show me what a face I have,
Since it is bankrupt of his majesty.

BOLINGBROKE
    Go, some of you, and fetch a looking-glass.   [*Exit Attendant.*]
NORTHUMBERLAND [*to King Richard*]
    Read o'er this paper while the glass doth come.
    [*Presents the paper again.*]

---

258 **so many winters** Although Richard
was relatively young at the time of his
deposition (thirty-two), he imagines
that his sufferings have aged him (cf.
277–9); similarly in *E2* Kent speaks of
his brother as 'agèd Edward' (5.2.119)
and the King of himself as 'old
Edward' (5.3.23). *Winters* = 'years'
(with a suggestion of life's tribula-
tions).

260–2 Richard continues his transfer of
the sun imagery to Bolingbroke (cf.
221n.). Wilson (212) suggests that the
snowman image is an extension of *winters* (258) and that it may derive ultimately from *Doctor Faustus* (A-text),
5.2.119–20 : 'O soul, be changed into
little waterdrops, / And fall into the
ocean, ne'er be found!' (see also 270n.,
281–6n.). Cf. the Queen's *dissolve to
dew* (5.1.9); also *Ham* 1.2.129–30: 'O
that this too too sallied flesh would

melt, / Thaw, and resolve itself into a
dew!'
260 **mockery** counterfeit, imitation; dissyllabic ('mock'ry')
262 **water-drops** tears; cf. 'Mine eyes are
full of tears' (244).
264 ***An if** F's 'And' may be an alternative spelling of 'An', intensifying 'if'
(see 50n.).
    sterling valid currency (cf. 1.3.231n.).
The financial imagery continues in
bankrupt (267).
265 **hither straight** 'to be brought here
immediately'
266 **what a face** what kind of face
267 **his** its (Abbott, 228)
268 **some of you** probably singular,
'someone'; cf. *Per* 5.1.9–10: 'there is
some of worth would come aboard; / I
pray greet him fairly'.
269 **while** till (Abbott, 137); cf. 1.3.122n.

---

260 mockery king] *Q4;* Mockerie, King *F*   264 An if] *Theobald;* And if *Q4, F*   word] *F;* name *Q4*
268 SD] *Capell (subst.)*   269 SD1] *this edn*   SD2] *this edn*

KING RICHARD

Fiend, thou torments me ere I come to hell!   270

BOLINGBROKE

Urge it no more, my Lord Northumberland.

NORTHUMBERLAND

The commons will not then be satisfied.

KING RICHARD

They shall be satisfied. I'll read enough

When I do see the very book indeed

Where all my sins are writ, and that's myself.   275

Enter one with a glass.

Give me that glass, and therein will I read.

[*Takes looking-glass.*]

---

270 **Fiend** Richard conceives of Northumberland as a devil. Ure (140) suggests that Shakespeare may be recalling the final speech of the protagonist
in *Doctor Faustus* (A-text), 5.2.121–3,
where the devils drag him off to hell;
cf. 260–2n., 281–6n.
   torments tormentest (an older form
of the second person singular present;
see Abbott, 340); cf. *sets* (5.3.121).
271 **Urge . . . more** *Urge* = insist upon
(cf. 3.1.4n.). Editors are divided about
the tone of Bolingbroke's restraint
upon Northumberland. Herford (195)
detects 'absence of personal rancour
against Richard' while Wilson (212)
sees rather 'contempt'.
272 Cf. *the commons' suit* (155 and n.).
274–5 Cf. Psalms, 139.15: 'Thine eyes did
see my substance, yet being vnperfect:
and in thy booke were all my members
written.'
275.1 The complex symbolic and iconographic significances of the mirror, its
relation to such themes as wisdom,
self-knowledge, vanity, narcissism, his-

torical truth (the 'mirror for princes'
tradition), true and false counsel, and
even death, have been much discussed;
see especially Ure 'Looking-Glass',
219–24; Talbert, 187–90; Dillon,
69–72; Grabes, 111, 202, 214–16;
McMillin, 46. The concept of the *flat-
t'ring glass* (279) was proverbial (Dent,
G132.1). See also Introduction, pp.
36–8, 75, 87, 102–5, 135, 138, 164.
276–86 This passage contains numerous
Q4–F variants in addition to Q4's
irregular division of lines – an indication, perhaps, of different acting versions (note Q4's omissions) as well as
scribal or compositorial difficulties in
Q4; see 155–318n.
276 **that** F's demonstrative pronoun may
be defended as perhaps more characteristic of Richard's fondness for gesture, though many editors prefer Q4's
'the', probably on the grounds of
maintaining consistency with *the glass*
(269). Both readings are acceptable;
see 285n.

275.1] *F; not in Q4*   276–86] *as F; Q4 lines* yet? / this / woundes? / prosperitie! / his / men? / follies, / Bullingbrooke? /   276 that] *F; the Q4*   and . . . read] *F; not in Q4*   SD] *Bevington (subst.)*

No deeper wrinkles yet? Hath Sorrow struck
So many blows upon this face of mine
And made no deeper wounds? O, flatt'ring glass,
Like to my followers in prosperity,   280
Thou dost beguile me. Was this face the face
That every day under his household roof
Did keep ten thousand men? Was this the face
That like the sun did make beholders wink?
Is this the face which faced so many follies,   285

280 **followers in prosperity** 'those who
followed me when I was king', fair-
weather friends
281–6 **Was . . . Bolingbroke?** a clear reminiscence of the famous and memorable speech to the apparition of Helen
of Troy in *Doctor Faustus* (A-text),
5.1.91–2: 'Was this the face that
launched a thousand ships / And burnt
the topless towers of Ilium?'; see
260–2n., 270n. and Introduction,
p. 164. The symbolic link between the
mythical Helen whose beauty burned
Troy and the handsome monarch
whose deposition became the catalyst
for a long period of civil war might well
have occurred to many in
Shakespeare's audience. Shakespeare
echoed the lines again in *TC* 2.2.81–2:
'she is a pearl, / Whose price hath
launch'd above a thousand ships'. Gurr
(148) cites Isaiah, 14.16: 'Is this the
man that brought all landes in feare,
and made the kingdomes afraide?'
281 **beguile** deceive (with overtones of
'charm, enchant')
283 **keep** maintain
ten thousand men Cf. Holinshed
(3.508): '[He [Richard] kept the greatest port, and mainteined the most
plentifull house that euer any king in
England did either before his time or
since. For there resorted dailie to his

court aboue ten thousand persons that
had meat and drinke there allowed
them.' *Woodstock* insists on the detail,
repeating it no fewer than three times:
'The hall at Westminster shall be
enlarged . . . Wherein I'll daily feast
ten thousand men' (2.2.194–6); 'every
day I feast ten thousand men' (3.1.85);
'He daily feasts, they say, ten thousand
men' (3.2.28).
284 Cf. 3.2.37–46; also 2.4.19–21LN.
wink blink, shut their eyes.
285 **Is . . . which** Q4's reading ('Was this
the face that'), which corresponds to
F's phrase from 283–4, is appealing
since it repeats the same rhetorical pattern and tense used in 281–2. It may
well represent what was actually said
in some performances (see 276–86n.;
also Appendix 1, pp. 506–7 and 506, n.
1). On the other hand, Q4's faulty lineation may point to corruption in the
quarto text. **faced** countenanced,
sanctioned; the term comes from tai-
loring where 'facing' means enhancing
the appearance of a garment by covering over one fabric with another.
'Richard covered over many follies by
adorning them with the splendour of
his own state' (Ard², 141); cf. *1H4*
5.1.74–5: 'To face the garment of
rebellion / With some fine color that
may please the eye'.

277 struck] *F;* stroke *Q4*   279 flatt'ring] *F;* flattering *Q4*   281 Thou . . . me] *F; not in Q4*   this
face] *F;* this *Q4*   282 household] *Q4* (Houshould*); *House-hold *F*   283–4 Was . . . wink] *F; not in
Q4*   285 Is . . . which] *F;* Was this the face that *Q4*

That was at last outfaced by Bolingbroke?
A brittle glory shineth in this face –
As brittle as the glory is the face!   [*Shatters glass.*]
For there it is, cracked in an hundred shivers.
Mark, silent King, the moral of this sport,   290
How soon my sorrow hath destroyed my face.

BOLINGBROKE

The shadow of your sorrow hath destroyed

286 **That** Q4's reading ('And') is defensible; see 285n.
outfaced stared down, successfully challenged; supplanted (cf. *KJ* 2.1.97). The word occurs again in *LLL* 5.2.623, with a slightly different shade of meaning (put out of countenance, embarrassed).

287–8 Donne's sentence from *Devotions* (1624) serves as an illuminating gloss on these lines: 'A glasse is not the lesse brittle, because a *Kings* face is represented in it; nor a King the lesse brittle, because *God* is represented in him' ('Eighth Meditation', 41). Cf. also *MM* 2.2.117–20, where 'proud man, / Dress'd in a little brief authority', is conceived of as having a 'glassy essence'.

289 **an** Q4's 'a' is also possible; see 285n.
shivers splinters, small shards; cf. *TC* 2.1.39 (the only other use as a noun in Shakespeare). The superstition that breaking a mirror brought misfortune, or even portended death, is ancient, going back even to the first century AD before breakable or glass mirrors were invented, and apparently deriving from the primitive notion that a person's reflected image was his soul looking back at him. Because, theologically speaking, the soul could not be separated from the body except through death, any injury to an object that reflected the soul was regarded as extremely threatening. By deliberately smashing the mirror Richard not only

invites disaster but might be thought in some sense actually to commit suicide (see Grose, 48).

290 **silent King** Once again with pointed irony (cf. 3.3.172–3n.) Richard refers to Bolingbroke as *King* before he has been crowned. The word *silent* is also telling, underlining Richard's theatrical control of the scene and his rival's passive discomfort, even extreme embarrassment, or, according to Wilson (213), his 'contemptuous taciturnity'; see headnote and Introduction, pp. 38, 68–9.
sport a game of play-acting; with characteristic self-consciousness, Richard acknowledges that the mirror episode is a performance.

291 **face** Here the word connotes both Richard's identity (the face being the signature of human uniqueness) and his physical handsomeness (cf. 2.1.117–19; also 3.3.62–71). York had made the audience especially conscious of Richard's face by suggesting that it bore the lineaments of his heroic father, the Black Prince (2.1.176–7). See LN.

292–3 **shadow . . . shadow** a heavily freighted word in *R2* (see 2.2.14n.), which carries a range of associations including emotional darkness, unsubstantiality and distorted perception. Bolingbroke's literal-minded meaning is 'reflection', by which he implies sharply that the dark *shadow* cast by Richard's fancied sorrow is unreal,

286 That] *F;* And *Q4*   outfaced] *Q4* (outfaast); out-fac'd *F*   288 SD] *Oxf (subst.)*   289 an] *F; a Q4*

The shadow of your face.
KING RICHARD   Say that again!
The shadow of my sorrow? Ha, let's see.
'Tis very true, my grief lies all within;   295
And these external manners of laments
Are merely shadows to the unseen grief
That swells with silence in the tortured soul.

factitious, illusory, theatrically induced
– and that his affected or feigned emotion has caused him to destroy the
mere *shadow* (or image) of his face –
that is, the looking-glass as opposed to
the face itself. Thus one *shadow* (imagined grief) has obliterated another (the
reflected face). The Elizabethan connection of shadows with the theatre
('shadow' sometimes meant 'actor'; see
McMillin, 46, *MND* 5.1.423) reinforces the notion of illusion or falsity.
See 294n.; also LN.
294 shadow . . . sorrow Richard inge-
niously picks up Bolingbroke's deroga-
tory term *shadow*, wrenching it to serve
an entirely new and more self-flattering
significance – namely, the inexpress-
ibility of grief by external means: the
shadows (297) of Richard's grief are
'these external manners of laments'
(296) – a crude appearance only, that
which can be outwardly observed but
comes between the viewer and the real
object of his contemplation – while *the
unseen grief* (297) that lies deeper,
swelling 'with silence in the tortured
soul' (298), is the true *substance* (299).
Richard's shadow–substance dichotomy, derived ultimately from Neoplatonism, links up interestingly with
Bushy's speech on *perspectives* (see
2.2.18LN) and ties into the themes of
identity and perception that inform the
play as a whole. Cf. 'Each substance of
a grief hath twenty shadows, / Which
shows like grief itself, but is not so'

(2.2.14–15); also *Ham* 1.2.85–6: 'But I
have that within which passes show, /
These but the trappings and the suits
of woe.'
296–8 Cf. Bushy's characterization of the
Queen's grief as *naught but shadows*
(2.2.23) and see 292–3n. and 294n.
296 *manners of laments manifestations
of grief, kinds, or forms, of lamentation
(gestures and utterances). Many editors
accept Q4's *manners* because of the
agreement with *these*, but follow Capell
in emending *laments* to 'lament'. Wilson
(213) prefers this latter solution, specu-
lating that a scribe in preparing copy for
F perhaps 'deleted the wrong *s* in his
copy'. Other editors retain F's 'manner',
arguing for 'an archaic construction
comparable with "all manner of"'
(Wells, 246). This interpretation (on the
principle of *lectio difficilior*) has its
attractions and may be correct, in which
case the *s* in Q4's *manners* would be a
sophistication. Q4's unaltered *manners of
laments* sounds awkward to modern ears,
but could represent what was spoken on
Elizabethan stages (see 285n.). F's deletion of the *s* in *manners* could be either a
compositorial omission or a scribal
sophistication in its copy.
297 to compared with
    unseen ùnseen
298 swells Cf. 2.1.228n. Gurr (149)
interprets this word as an 'image of
pregnancy', relating it to the Queen's
conceit of 'unborn sorrow, ripe in
Fortune's womb' (2.2.10).

293–300 Say . . . giv'st] *as F; Q4 lines* sorrow; / griefe / manners / vnseene, / soule: / giuest /
296 manners] *Q4;* manner *F*   laments] *Q4–F;* lament *Capell*

There lies the substance. And I thank thee, King,
For thy great bounty that not only giv'st   300
Me cause to wail, but teachest me the way
How to lament the cause. I'll beg one boon,
And then be gone and trouble you no more.
Shall I obtain it?

BOLINGBROKE   Name it, fair cousin.

KING RICHARD
'Fair cousin'? I am greater than a king;   305
For when I was a king, my flatterers
Were then but subjects. Being now a subject,
I have a king here to my flatterer.
Being so great, I have no need to beg.

BOLINGBROKE
Yet ask.   310

KING RICHARD
And shall I have?

BOLINGBROKE
You shall.

KING RICHARD
Then give me leave to go.

BOLINGBROKE
Whither?

---

299 **There** in my soul
  substance reality (of my sorrow); see
  292–3n. and 294n.
  thank thee, King Cf. 290n. Richard's
  tone is bitterly sarcastic.
300 **thy . . . that** the great munificence of
  you who (see Abbott, 218)
304–5 **fair . . . cousin** Bolingbroke echoes
  Richard's form of address to him at
  3.3.190 (see n.); but his attempt to
  appear conciliatory and diplomatic back–
  fires with Richard's mocking repetition.
305 **cousin** Q4's 'Coose, why?', according

to Wilson (213), 'suggests an actor's
  addition'. See 285n.
307 **now a subject** Cf. 3.2.176n.
308 **to** as, for
311 **have** Q4's 'haue it' may represent
  another actor's change (for the sake of
  clarity?); see 285n.
313 'Richard's request seems anti-climactic.
  It may represent a calculated deflation
  of Bolingbroke, Richard having led
  him to expect a more taxing request'
  (Wells, 247).
  Then For Q4's 'Why then', see 285n.

---

299 There . . . substance] *F; not in Q4*   300 For . . . bounty] *F; not in Q4*   giv'st] *F;* giuest *Q4*
304 Shall . . . it] *F; not in Q4*   305 cousin] *F;* Coose, why? *Q4*   306–9] *as F; Q4 lines* subiects, /
heere / beg. /   311 have] *F;* haue it *Q4*   313 Then] *F;* Why then *Q4*

KING RICHARD
> Whither you will, so I were from your sights.   315

BOLINGBROKE
> Go, some of you, convey him to the Tower.

KING RICHARD
> O, good – 'Convey'! Conveyers are you all
> That rise thus nimbly by a true king's fall.[F]

> [*Exit King Richard under guard.*]

BOLINGBROKE
> On Wednesday next we solemnly set down

---

315 **so** provided that, as long as (Abbott, 133)
from your sights out of the sight of each of you; cf. *KL* 4.6.35.

316 **convey** conduct, escort. Bolingbroke uses a stock phrase: cf. *3H6* 3.2.120; *R3* 1.1.45; also 317n. Shakespeare's choice of the word may derive from Holinshed's 'conueieng of' (see 5.2 headnote).
Tower Shakespeare postdates. In Holinshed (3.501) Richard's incarceration in the Tower occurs almost immediately after he has arrived in London as Bolingbroke's prisoner (2 September 1399 or thereabouts): 'The next day after his comming to London, the king from Westminster was had to the Tower, and there committed to safe custodie.'

317–18 The couplet gives Richard's angry exit an appropriate tone of unanswerable finality.

317 **'Convey'! Conveyers** Cf. 2.1.137n. Richard picks up Bolingbroke's word in the euphemistically pejorative sense of 'steal'. Bolingbroke has stolen his crown while those who support him become thieves by being accessories to the crime. Cf. *E2*, 1.1.199, where the same pun is implied: '*Edward.* Convey this priest to the Tower. *Coventry.* True, true!' Later in *1H4* 3.2.50 Bolingbroke admits that in pursuing his ambitious career, he 'stole

all courtesy from heaven'.

318 **rise . . . fall** continues the pervasive *de casibus* imagery; cf. the descent from the walls of Flint Castle (3.3.178–83) and the bucket-and-well analogy (see 184–9n.).
nimbly a word often applied to thieves; cf. *WT* 4.4.671–2: 'a nimble hand is necessary for a cutpurse'.

319–20 *This is the point where Q1's text resumes after omitting the deposition (see 155–318n.). Perhaps originally the copy for Q read: 'On Wednesday next, we solemnly proclaime / Our coronation, Lords be ready all.' Q's mislining would then have resulted simply from the addition of 'let it be so, and loe', which almost certainly represents an adjustment made to help bridge the gap created by the excision of the abdication episode. Editors, however, almost universally accept Q4–F's version of these lines, since they seem to have promptbook authority and the final word of Q's 'be ready all' rhymes somewhat awkwardly with Richard's exit couplet at 317–18 (all/fall). See Appendix 1, pp. 515–17, 516, n. 1.

319 **Wednesday next** Holinshed (3.507) states that 'the feast day of saint Edward the king and confessor' (13 October) was proclaimed as the date when 'the coronation should be

---

317 good –] *F (good:); good Q4*   318 SD] *Collier (subst.)*   319–20] *as Q4–F; Q lines* next, / Coronation, / all.   319 On] *Q4–F; Let it be so, and loe on Q*   set down] *Q4–F; proclaime Q*

Our coronation. Lords, prepare yourselves.   320

Exeunt all but [Abbot of] Westminster,
[Bishop of] Carlisle [and] Aumerle.

ABBOT

A woeful pageant have we here beheld.

CARLISLE

The woe's to come. The children yet unborn
Shall feel this day as sharp to them as thorn.

AUMERLE

You holy clergymen, is there no plot

---

solemnized'. In 1399 (see headnote) this was a Monday, not a Wednesday. Shakespeare probably misread Holinshed (3.511): 'The solemnitie of the coronation being ended, the morow after being tuesdaie'; or did he take over Créton's error (206/396) in claiming that St Edward's day fell on 'Wednesday'? Ure (143) attributes Shakespeare's mistake, not implausibly, to hasty misappropriation of the day from a paragraph on the following page of Holinshed (3.512), which begins with the phrase, 'on Wednesdaie following', but which actually refers to Carlisle's speech and arrest.

we royal plural; see 0.4LN

***set down** decree

321 **woeful pageant** grief-inducing dramatic spectacle; theatrical display of sorrow. Cf. *AYL* 2.7.137–9: 'This wide and universal theatre / Presents more woeful pageants than the scene / Wherein we play in'; also Carlisle's earlier use of the word *Woe* (150). The phrase may reflect Richard's self-dramatization. Without Richard's ritualized 'performing' of the abdication (see 155–318n.), the term *pageant* makes little sense. See Appendix 1, p. 516, n. 1.

322–3 *Carlisle summarizes his earlier prediction at 137–50 (see 150n., also 3.3.88–9n.). The syntax of these lines is

ambiguous: since both Q and F print commas after *come* and *unborn* (322), it is possible to understand 'the children yet unborn, / (who) Shall feel' as being in apposition to *woe*; but most editors treat the comma after *come* as a stop (as in Q4), delete the comma after *unborn*, and interpret 'The children . . . Shall feel' as independent. Meaning is little affected either way. The rhymed couplet gives the prelate's words a fittingly gnomic quality.

323 **sharp . . . thorn** Carlisle may allude to Genesis, 3.18, which says that the first fruits of the Fall were the thorns; cf. also Milton, *Paradise Lost*, 4.256, 10.203. In *1H4* 1.3.176 Hotspur speaks scornfully of 'plant[ing] this thorn, this canker, Bullingbrook'.

324–5 Aumerle's couplet seems flat in comparison to Carlisle's arresting couplet that precedes it. The contrast may imply a corresponding contrast in character – strength as opposed to weakness.

324 **plot** 'plan that can be devised' (not necessarily implying evil intent). The conspiracy against Bolingbroke, mentioned first here and again in 5.2 and 5.3, is based mainly on Holinshed (3.514): 'shortlie after [the coronation of Henry IV] he [King Henry] was put in danger to haue beene set besides the seat, by a conspiracie

---

320 prepare yourselves] *Q4–F;* be ready all *Q*   SD] *Exeunt. / Manent West. Caleil, Aumerle. Q; Exeunt.*
F   all but] this edn; Manent Q   322 woe's] Woes *F*   come.] *Q4 (come;); come, QF;* come – *Cam¹*

To rid the realm of this pernicious blot?   325
ABBOT
My lord,
Before I freely speak my mind herein,
You shall not only take the sacrament
To bury mine intents, but also to effect
Whatever I shall happen to devise.   330
I see your brows are full of discontent,
Your hearts of sorrow and your eyes of tears.
Come home with me to supper. I'll lay
A plot shall show us all a merry day.   *Exeunt.*

begun in the abbat of Westminsters house, which, had it not beene hindered, it is doubtfull whether the new king should haue inioied his roialtie, or the old king (now a prisoner) restored to his principalitie'. Holinshed lists among the plotters 'Edward earle of Rutland late duke of Aumarle sonne to the duke of Yorke' and 'Iohn the bishop of Carleill'. Daniel's extended account (3.26–54) may also have been influential. Interestingly, Shakespeare suppresses the Abbot's personal motive for the plot as given in Holinshed, namely his belief that the new king would be hostile to the Church: 'this abbat . . . vpon a time heard king Henrie saie, when he was but earle of Derbie, and yoong of yeares, that princes had too little, and religious men too much' (cf. also Daniel (3.27) and 1LN).

325 **blot** referring to the deposition itself rather than to those responsible for it. Aumerle echoes Richard's word (cf. 236 and n.).

328 **take the sacrament** receive the Eucharist (to solemnize an oath). Daniel alone among the sources mentions this detail: 'The Sacrament the pledge of faith they take, / And euery man vppon his sword doth sweere / By

knighthood, honor, or what els should binde, / To assecure the more each others minde' (3.34). Holinshed (3.514) reports that the conspirators 'sware on the holie euangelists to be true and secret each to other, euen to the houre and point of death'.

329 **bury mine intents** conceal my plans

333 ***supper. I'll** QF print a comma after *supper*, which may mean that 'Come home with me to supper' should be taken as a conditional subjunctive, '(If you) come home . . ., I'll', rather than a simple imperative. Either reading makes good sense. According to Pope's relineation, which brings out the rhyme on *lay* and *day* and makes the scene end conventionally with a couplet (cf. 149–50 and n.), the line is deficient by a syllable. Possibly *I'll* should not be elided despite its spelling ('Ile') in QF (cf. Malone's emendation, 'I will'); but more likely, a pause or beat should follow *supper*. RP suggests 'where I'll' as 'another possible emendation'. Holinshed (3.514) reports that 'The abbat highlie feasted these lords, his speciall freends'.

334 **plot shall** plan that will (Abbott, 244). See Holinshed in 5.2.41–117n.
    merry happy; fortunate

326 My lord] *Q1–2 (*My Lo.*); om. Q3–F*   326–7] *as Cam; one line Q1–2*   332 hearts] *heart Q2–F*
333–4] *as Pope; QF line* plot, / daie. /   333 supper.] *Kittredge; supper, Q*   I'll] *and I'll Pope; I will Malone*

[5.1]   *Enter the* QUEEN *with* Ladies.

QUEEN

This way the King will come. This is the way
To Julius Caesar's ill-erected tower,
To whose flint bosom my condemned lord
Is doomed a prisoner by proud Bolingbroke.
Here let us rest, if this rebellious earth   5

5.1 The scene of Richard's parting from the Queen, set in a public street near the Tower of London, has no counterpart in Holinshed and is largely Shakespeare's invention. It follows from the Queen's proposal at 3.4.96–7 that she and her ladies 'go / To meet at London London's king in woe' and from Bolingbroke's order at 4.1.316 that Richard be conveyed *to the Tower*. The episode seems, however, to have been significantly influenced by a long passage in Daniel (2.71–98) – the single source that describes the last meeting of the married pair before her sailing for France. See LN. After the great public *pageant* of Richard's deposition, this quieter, more personal episode shows the fallen king in a more reflectively sensitive and wiser vein, though his style of speech, which extends also to the Queen, retains much of its theatrical self-consciousness and artificiality. Thus it prepares us for 5.5 – his final isolation in the cell at Pomfret. A single factual detail from Holinshed concerning Richard's transfer from the Tower to Pomfret appears in 51–2.

0.1 *Q's 'attendants'* are the *Ladies* of 3.4 (F substitutes '*Ladies*' for '*attendants*' in both scenes); see 3.4 headnote and 0.1n.

2 The late medieval tradition that Julius Caesar built the Tower of London persisted into Shakespeare's age, being mentioned, sometimes sceptically, by such historians as Polydore Vergil, Stow, Lambarde and Grafton, and by poets such as Lydgate and Peele. Cf. *Edward I*, l. 971: 'Julius Caesars towre' (Peele, 2.105); also *STM* (ll. 1580–3); *R3* 3.1.69–71. The Tower was actually built by William the Conqueror to hold London in check.

ill-erected 'built for evil purposes or to evil effect' (since many crimes had occurred there and especially since it is about to become Richard's prison), or perhaps 'ill-omened'; not 'badly constructed'. See LN.

3 **flint bosom** pitiless breast (as hard as flint); cf. 5.5.20–1: 'flinty ribs / Of this hard world'.

condemned condemnèd

4 **doomed** sentenced

5 **rest** pause. The Queen and her ladies probably remain standing. Trewin (*Neville*, 57) reports that in Benthall's Old Vic production John Neville as Richard and Virginia McKenna as the Queen sat 'on the ground' during this scene and that this staging proved mistakenly hampering to the players.

rebellious earth Hyperbolically, the Queen thinks of the very ground on which she stands as *rebellious* since it has permitted a usurper to tread upon it; cf. Richard's petition to his *Dear earth* (3.2.6), asking that it resist 'the treacherous feet / Which with usurping steps do trample thee' (3.2.16–17).

5.1] F *(Actus Quintus. Scena Prima.)*   0.1] *Enter the Queene with her attendants. Q; Enter Queene, and Ladies. F*   2 ill-erected] *F;* ill erected *Q*

Have any resting for her true king's queen.

Enter [KING] RICHARD ^{F} *and Guard* ^{F}.

But soft, but see, or rather do not see
My fair rose wither. Yet look up, behold,
That you in pity may dissolve to dew
And wash him fresh again with true-love tears.   10
Ah, thou, the model where old Troy did stand,
Thou map of honour, thou King Richard's tomb,

6   **resting** resting place
6.1 *F's '*Guard*'* may imply more than
one person; see 50.1 n.
7   **soft** hush, wait a moment, hold (literally, 'go slowly')
     but . . . see The Queen probably
addresses herself rather than her ladies.
Cf. Daniel, 2.83: 'Thus as shee stoode
assur'd and yet in doubt, / Wishing to
see, what seene she grieud to see'.
8   **fair rose** echoed by Hotspur in *1H4*
1.3.175: 'To put down Richard, that
sweet lovely rose'. Roses, being at the
top of the floral hierarchy in the Great
Chain of Being, were naturally associated with kings (see Tillyard, *Picture*,
28); cf. the red and white roses which
became respectively the badges of the
Lancastrian and Yorkist factions in the
Wars of the Roses.
9   Cf. 4.1.260–2; also *Ham* 1.2.130: 'resolve
itself into a dew', and *TS* 2.1.173:
'morning roses newly washed with dew'.
     you The Queen addresses herself.
11 **thou** The Queen turns to address
Richard, who is aware of her presence;
it is not clear, however, at what point
he hears her words, since much of the
speech has the effect of an apostrophe.
     model . . . stand 'the ruins of Troy'.
The Queen compares her husband in
defeat to the mere outline of the walls
where a magnificent city once stood. In
legend London was founded by Brut, a
great grandson of Aeneas (who, according to Virgil, founded Rome and led

survivors of the Trojan war to Britain);
the new city was named Troynovant (or
Troia-Nova = New Troy). This association may be induced by the mention of
the Tower with its supposed link to
Julius Caesar (2) and therefore to classical civilization. For other uses of
model, see 1.2.28, 3.2.153 and 3.4.42;
here the word 'gains force through its
previous associations with earth and
death' (Ard², 146). Cf. also Proverbs,
25.27: 'He that can not rule himselfe, is
like a citie which is broken downe, and
hath no walles.'
12 **map of honour** mere image (or outline) of former grandeur; cf. *2H6*
3.1.203, where Duke Humphrey's face
is called the 'map of honor, truth, and
loyalty'; also *Tit* 3.2.12: 'Thou map of
woe'. Shakespeare ordinarily uses
'map' (in its figurative sense) to mean
'image' or 'embodiment' with 'emphasis on the *resemblances* between a map
and that which it represents', whereas
here 'the stress seems to be on the way
a map *differs* from the thing it represents' (Ard², 146). Like a 'model', a
'map' is a small-scale representation.
12–13 **Richard's . . . Richard** hyperbolic
way of suggesting that the lively,
splendid figure she remembers now
seems dead; ordinarily, when monarchs cease to be kings they are
entombed. Bolingbroke refers to the
body as 'this frail sepulchre of our
flesh' (1.3.196). See also 26–8n.

6.1] *Enter Ric. Q; Enter Richard, and Guard. F*   KING] *Rowe*   10 true-love] *F*; true loue *Q*

416

And not King Richard! Thou most beauteous inn,
Why should hard-favoured Grief be lodged in thee,
When Triumph is become an alehouse guest?   15

KING RICHARD

Join not with grief, fair woman, do not so,
To make my end too sudden. Learn, good soul,
To think our former state a happy dream,
From which awaked, the truth of what we are
Shows us but this. I am sworn brother, sweet,   20
To grim Necessity, and he and I
Will keep a league till death. Hie thee to France,

13–15 Thou . . . guest? another fanciful conceit stressing Richard's physical attractiveness (see, e.g., 3.3.68–70, 4.1.277–9, 291n.): Richard is the beautiful and dignified *inn* (town residence, mansion, noble abode; see *OED sb.* 1) which houses *Grief*, while Bolingbroke is the vulgar *alehouse* where victory is celebrated. Richard's grief, which is *hard-favoured* (ugly, harsh-featured), should properly be embodied in his ignoble rival rather than in a body that is handsomely royal. Wilson (216) suggests that the imagery 'is founded upon an unexpressed quibble on "entertain," which = (*a*) receive a guest, (*b*) harbour a feeling or thought'; cf. 2.2.7: 'welcome such a guest as Grief'. See LN.

15 Triumph exultation (perhaps with overtones of 'conquest')

16–17 Join . . . sudden. Johnson glosses: 'Do not thou unite with grief against me; do not, by thy additional sorrows, enable grief to strike me down at once' (1.449).

18 state condition of splendour, stateliness

20 but only

this either 'this wretched condition in

general' (possibly with a gesture to indicate his unroyal dress), or introducing the sentence which follows. Q's colon after *this* makes either interpretation possible.

sworn brother bosom friend (member of a knightly brotherhood or, possibly, a religious order); cf. *H5* 2.1.12–13: 'we'll be all three sworn brothers to France'; also *MA* 1.1.73–4. In chivalric tradition knights sometimes vowed to share each other's fortunes as *fratres iurati* (sworn brothers).

21 Necessity Richard personifies this word in its philosophical sense, signifying not only 'that which cannot be avoided' or 'the power of unalterable circumstances', but also a force close to 'tragic destiny' (cf. Chaucer, *Troilus and Criseyde*, 4.1048–50: 'men may wel yse / That thilke thynges that in erthe falle, / That by necessite they comen alle'; also *FQ*, 1.5.25: 'But who can turne the streame of destinee, / Or breake the chayne of strong necessitee . . . ?'

22 league dedicated companionship, covenant (alluding to his being a *sworn brother*)

Hie thee hasten

---

14 hard-favoured] *F;* hard fauourd *Q*   Grief] *F;* greife *Q*   15 Triumph] *F;* triumph *Q*   16 SP] *Cam (subst.); Rich. QF*   21 Necessity] *F;* necessitie *Q*

And cloister thee in some religious house.
Our holy lives must win a new world's crown,
Which our profane hours here have thrown down.   25

QUEEN

What, is my Richard both in shape and mind
Transformed and weakened? Hath Bolingbroke
Deposed thine intellect? Hath he been in thy heart?
The lion, dying, thrusteth forth his paw
And wounds the earth, if nothing else, with rage   30
To be o'erpowered; and wilt thou, pupil-like,

23 **cloister . . . house** sequester yourself
in some convent; i.e. withdraw from
the political to the contemplative
world. Cf. 3.3.147–8.
24 **win . . . crown** i.e. in heaven; cf. 2
Timothy, 4.8: 'Henceforth there is laid
vp for me a crowne of righteousnesse,
which the Lord the righteous iudge
shall giue mee at that day'. Cf. also *E2*,
5.1.107–9: 'Now, sweet God of heaven,
/ Make me despise this transitory
pomp, / And sit for aye enthronizèd in
heaven.'
25 'which our carelessly secular lives on
earth have endangered'. Cf. 3.4.66:
'Which waste of idle hours hath quite
thrown down' (and n.).
thrown probably dissyllabic ('throw-
en', a common spelling; see 5.2.30t.n.);
F's substitution ('stricken') shows the
need of an extra syllable. Dissyllabic
hours ('howers'; cf. 1.2.7n., 5.5.58n.)
has been suggested, which would make
the third foot trochaic.
26–8 Cf. Daniel, 2.82: 'Let me not see
him, but himselfe, a king; / For so he
left me, so he did remoue: / This is not
he, this feeles some other thing.'
26 **shape and mind** *shape* = appearance,
body (cf. 12–13n.); the emphasis falls
on *mind*.
27 **weakened** The scansion might seem
to require *weakenèd* (three syllables);
but Q's 'weakned' and F's 'weaken'd'

argue against this pronunciation.
There is probably a beat (or pause)
after the question mark and before
Hath.
28 probably an alexandrine; or five stresses
could fall on *Depòsed*, *intellect*, *Hath*, *in*
and *heart*.
Hath . . . heart? 'Has he also quelled
your courage?' The heart was supposed to be the prompter of will and
the seat of spirited self-assertion; cf.
TC 3.2.113: 'Boldness comes to me
now, and brings me heart.'
29 **lion** The lion was *king of beasts* (34),
analogous to the sun among planets
and the rose among flowers (Tillyard,
Picture, 28); see 8n. The reference here
ironically recalls Richard's 'Lions
make leopards tame' (1.1.174; see n.).
Daniel, 1.58, compares Richard as an
'vnbridled king' to 'a Lion that escapes
his bounds'.
thrusteth . . . paw Cf. *E2*, 2.2.202–3:
'shall the crowing of these cockerels /
Affright a lion? Edward, unfold thy
paws'; also 5.1.11–14: 'But when the
imperial lion's flesh is gored, / He
rends and tears it with his wrathful
paw, / And highly scorning that the
lowly earth / Should drink his blood,
mounts up into the air.'
31 **To be** at being
31–2 **wilt . . . rod** Cf. *1H6* 1.1.35–6: 'an
effeminate prince, / Whom like a

25 thrown] stricken *F*   27 weakened] *(weakned), F (weaken'd)*

418

Take the correction mildly, kiss the rod
And fawn on rage with base humility,
Which art a lion and the king of beasts?

KING RICHARD

A king of beasts, indeed! If aught but beasts,   35
I had been still a happy king of men.
Good sometimes queen, prepare thee hence for France.
Think I am dead, and that even here thou tak'st,
As from my death-bed, thy last living leave.

---

schoolboy you may overawe'; also *E2*,
3.1.28–31: 'This haught resolve
becomes your majesty, / Not to be tied
to their affection / As though your
highness were a schoolboy still, / And
must be awed and governed like a
child.' See 32n.

32 *Q's punctuation, placing the comma
after *correction* (punishment), makes
equally good sense, and Pollard (56–7)
argues that it should be retained. But, as
Ure (148) points out, 'Take the correction mildly' seems to have been something like a stock phrase in the sixteenth
century, and *kiss the rod* (without a modifying adverb) was proverbial (Dent,
R156); cf. Tyndale: 'Yf [the child]
knowleadge his faute and take the cor-
reccion mekely and even kysse the
rodde and amende him selfe . . . then is
the rodde take[n] awaye and brunte
[burnt]' (fol. xlvi); also *TGV* 1.2.58–9:
'scratch the nurse / And presently, all
humbled, kiss the rod'.
   Take the Q2's 'Take thy', uncorrected
by F, represents either a memorial slip
or an unauthorized 'improvement'.

33 **fawn on rage** behave obsequiously
towards enmity or violence
   base humility the humility proper to
underlings; *base* recalls Richard's bitter
punning on the word (see 3.3.127n.,
180–1n.). The Queen's demand for

kingly rage contrasts with the patient
endurance York clearly admires in
Richard at 5.2.30–3; her attitude is
somewhat parallel to that of the
Duchess of Gloucester at 1.2.33–4.
See 1.2.37–41n.

34 **Which** you who (referring to *thou* in 31)
   the . . . beasts See 29n. Some editors
accept Q2's unauthoritative emendation ('a' for *the*) on the grounds that
the phrase should agree with Richard's
rejoinder in the following line; but 'the
difference between the Queen's *the* and
Richard's *a*' marks 'the distinction
between her spirited exhortation and
his resignation'; she 'accents *king* and
he *beasts*' (Cam[1], 217).

35 **aught but beasts** anything other than
beasts (beastly subjects). Verity (169)
notes Richard's habit of 'catching up
words' and compares 4.1.305. For another example see 4.1.317. Richard almost
certainly means Bolingbroke and the
rebels; Chambers (142), however, thinks
he means 'his idle court of flatterers'.

37 **sometimes** former. Cf. 1.2.54n.
   hence 'to go hence' or, possibly,
'henceforward'

38 **even** probably elided to 'e'en' or 'er'n'
(see t.n.)

39 **last living leave** last farewell before
death. Richard's alliteration conveys his
sense of their dissolving companionship.

32 Take] Take thy *Q2–F* correction mildly,] *F;* correction, mildly *Q* 34 the king] a King
Q2–F 35+ SP] *Cam (subst.); King. Q; Rich. F* 35 indeed!] *F (*indeed:*);* indeed, *Q* 37 some-
times] sometime *Q3–F* 38 even] ev'n *Pope* tak'st] *F;* takest *Q* 39 death-bed] *F;* death bed *Q*
thy last] my last *Q2–F*

419

In winter's tedious nights sit by the fire   40
With good old folks, and let them tell thee tales
Of woeful ages long ago betid.
And ere thou bid good night, to quite their griefs,
Tell thou the lamentable tale of me
And send the hearers weeping to their beds.   45
For why the senseless brands will sympathize
The heavy accent of thy moving tongue
And in compassion weep the fire out;
And some will mourn in ashes, some coal-black,

40–50 perhaps influenced by Daniel, 3.65, where Richard in his prison at Pomfret muses upon the difference between the peasant's situation and his own: 'Thou sit'st at home safe by thy quiet fire / And hear'st of others harmes, but feelest none; / And there thou telst of kinges and who aspire, / Who fall, who rise, who triumphs, who doe mone: / Perhappes thou talkst of mee, and dost inquire / Of my restraint, why here I liue alone, / O know tis others sin not my desart, / And I could wish I were but as thou art.' Cf. also *WT* 2.1.25: 'A sad tale's best for winter' (which may have suggested the title, *The Winter's Tale*).

41 *thee Q2's apparent emendation, which nearly all editors accept, may be nothing more than an alternative spelling; see 1.3.58n.

42 woeful See 4.1.321n.
long ago betid 'which happened long ago'; *betid* is governed by either *tales* or *ages*. See Abbott, 342.

43 quite their griefs 'repay them in full for their tales of woe'; 'match their mournful stories' (*quite* = requite). F's 'quit' is merely an alternative spelling.

44 lamentable làmentable
tale of me F's 'fall' is unnecessary as *tale* has already been used at 41, and it also recalls Richard's memorable 'tell

sad stories of the death of kings' (see 3.2.156LN); cf. also *Astrophil and Stella* (1591), 45.12–14: 'Then thinke my deare, that you in me do reed / Of Lover's ruine some sad Tragedie: / I am not I, pitie the tale of me' (Sidney, 187). See LN.

45 send by doing so you will send
46 For why 'and with good reason' (literally, 'for which reason, because', i.e. weeping because); cf. *TGV* 3.1.99. See Abbott, 75.
46–7 the . . . tongue 'Even the firebrands, which are inanimate (*senseless*), will respond to, or match (*sympathize*), the doleful tone (*heavy accent*) of your affecting narration (*moving tongue*).'
48 Richard may refer to the resin that green wood often 'weeps' as it burns. Cf. *KJ* 4.1.105: 'the fire is dead with grief'; also *Tem* 3.1.18–19, where burning 'logs' will 'weep' (i.e. exude sap).
fire probably two syllables (cf. 1.3.294n., 2.1.34n.); or perhaps *compassion* should be pronounced with four syllables.
49 some some of the *brands*
mourn in ashes Scattering ashes on the head and wearing sack-cloth begrimed with ashes was an ancient form of expressing grief (biblical: see Joshua, 7.6; Job, 2.12, 42.6; 2 Samuel,

41 thee] *Q2–F;* the *Q*   42 betid] *(betidde);* betide *Q2–F*   43 quite] *(quit) F*   griefs] griefe *Q2–F*
44 tale] fall *F*   46 why] *Dyce;* why, *Q.;* why? *F*   sympathize] *QF;* simpathie *Q2*   49 coal-black] *F;*
cole blacke *Q*

For the deposing of a rightful king.   50

Enter NORTHUMBERLAND [*with Attendants*].

NORTHUMBERLAND
My lord, the mind of Bolingbroke is changed.
You must to Pomfret, not unto the Tower.
And, madam, there is order ta'en for you:

13.19); cf. *KJ* 4.1.110: 'strew'd repen-
tent ashes on his head'.
some coal-black i.e. some of the
brands, once charred, will simulate the
black of mourning dress
50.1 Shakespeare extends Northumberland's role as the unsympathetic agent
of Bolingbroke's policies; see
4.1.151–5n.
*with Attendants Editors are divided
as to whether Northumberland should
appear in this scene with 'Others' (as
Capell and his many followers have
supposed) or '*solus*' (since the presence
of the '*Guard*' – one or more – for
Richard, as specified in F at 6.1, makes
the presence of additional figures
functionally unnecessary). See, however, 102 SDn. on the Queen's exit.
GWW argues that Shakespeare may
wish to preserve a visual balance
between three women (the Queen and
her ladies) and three men (Richard,
and two Guards), as in 3.4. Such a
symmetry is possible and may extend
to Northumberland here, who, as
spokesman for royal authority, should
be attended.
51–2 based on Holinshed, 3.507: 'For
shortlie after his resignation, he
[Richard] was conueied to the castell of
Leeds in Kent, & from thence to
Pomfret, where he departed out of this
miserable life (as after you shall
heare)'. The transfer to Pomfret
occurred in late autumn, 1399.
51 **Bolingbroke** Northumberland brus-
quely omits to refer to his leader as a

monarch or even by a lesser style. Cf.
his failure to use Richard's proper title
and York's rebuke at 3.3.6–9; also
Bagot's use of the name at 4.1.17.
52 **Pomfret** Pontefract Castle in Yorkshire, originally a Norman stronghold,
some twenty-two miles from the city of
York. *Pomfret* is the common pronunciation and spelling in Shakespeare: cf.
R3 3.3.9–12: 'O Pomfret, Pomfret! O
thou bloody prison! / Fatal and ominous to noble peers! / Within the
guilty closure of thy walls / Richard
the Second here was hacked to death';
also *KJ* 4.2.148.
53 **there . . . ta'en** 'arrangements have
been made' (cf. *R3* 4.2.52, *2H4*
3.2.185–6); *ta'en* is pronounced 'tane'.
Shakespeare's dramatic economy is to
have Bolingbroke dispose of Richard
and the Queen at the same time. In
history, the new king detained Isabel
in England until June or July 1401,
when he finally sent her back to her
own country (Cam¹, 218). Holinshed
(3.519) reports that, after negotiations
with the French about a second
English marriage and a possible repay-
ment of her dowry, 'she was shortlie
after sent home, vnder the conduct of
the earle of Worcester . . . hauing with
hir all the iewels, ornaments, and plate
which she brought into England, with
a great surplusage besides giuen to hir
by the king [Henry IV]'. Froissart
(6.370) says that soon after his accession Henry sent Isabel's French attendants home: 'So all Frenche men and

50.1 *with Attendants*] Capell (*subst.*)

With all swift speed you must away to France.

KING RICHARD

Northumberland, thou ladder wherewithal   55
The mounting Bolingbroke ascends my throne,
The time shall not be many hours of age
More than it is ere foul sin, gathering head,
Shall break into corruption. Thou shalt think
Though he divide the realm and give thee half   60
It is too little, helping him to all.
He shall think that thou, which knowst the way

women departed, and they were conveyed to Dover, and . . . toke shippyng . . . and so arryved at Boloyne' (cf. also 3.4 headnote). Shakespeare may have derived the idea for the Queen's sudden forced departure from this detail.

54 **away** go away, be sent away (Abbott, 32)

55–9 **Northumberland . . . corruption.** Despite Bolingbroke's absence from this scene, these lines are recalled by a sick and depressed King Henry in *2H4* 3.1.65–79: 'But which of you was by . . . When Richard, with his eye brimful of tears, / Then check'd and rated by Northumberland, / Did speak these words, now prov'd a prophecy? / "Northumberland, thou ladder by the which / My cousin Bullingbrook ascends my throne" / (Though then, God knows, I had no such intent, / But that necessity so bow'd the state / That I and greatness were compell'd to kiss), / "The time shall come," thus did he follow it, / "The time will come, that foul sin, gathering head, / Shall break into corruption": so went on, / Foretelling this same time's condition / And the division of our amity.' In *R2* the lines are already replete with irony, for Elizabethan audiences knew that Richard's prediction had proved only too true.

55–6 **ladder . . . throne** Shakespeare used the image again with a different twist in *JC* 2.1.22–3: 'lowliness is

young ambition's ladder, / Whereto the climber-upward turns his face'; for non-Shakespearean examples, see LN.

55 **wherewithal** by means of which

58–9 **foul . . . corruption** The image is that of a carbuncle or abscess that culminates by discharging pus; *gathering head* = 'coming to a head', 'festering more'. There may, however, be a submerged pun on *head* (insurrection, armed force); see *1H4* 1.3.284, where Worcester, Northumberland's brother, speaks of the 'raising of a head [army]'.

58 **gathering** dissyllabic ('gath'ring')

60–8 Cf. Daniel, 2.3, where the same idea is elaborated in regard to Northumberland's brother, Worcester: 'And kings loue not to be beholding ought, / Which makes their chiefest friends oft speed the worst: / For those by whom their fortunes haue bin wrought / Put them in mind of what they were at first: / Whose doubtfull faith if once in question brought / Tis thought they will offend because they durst, / And taken in a fault are neuer spar'd, / Being easier to reuenge, then to reward.' Cf. also *1H4* 5.2.4–11, *JC* 2.1.21–7.

61 **helping . . . all** 'inasmuch as you have helped him get all of it' (see Abbott, 378)

62 **He** Rowe's emendation ('And he'), which Pollard (57) pronounced 'necessary', smoothes the metre; but

62 He] And he *Rowe*   knowst] *Q2–F;* knowest *Q*

422

To plant unrightful kings, wilt know again,
Being ne'er so little urged, another way
To pluck him headlong from the usurped throne.   65
The love of wicked men converts to fear,
That fear to hate, and hate turns one or both
To worthy danger and deserved death.

NORTHUMBERLAND
My guilt be on my head, and there an end.
Take leave and part, for you must part forthwith.   70

KING RICHARD
Doubly divorced! Bad men, you violate
A twofold marriage, 'twixt my crown and me

syncopating the line with a beat (or pause) at the start accomplishes the same effect. GWW conjectures that the MS may have had 'He then shall think'; the rapid succession of words beginning in *th* might perhaps account for Q's omission of 'then'.
which who
63 **plant** establish. The garden imagery persists; cf. 4.1.128n. Gurr (153) detects a 'submerged metaphor . . . of the Plantagenet line and the Tree of Jesse' (see 1.2.12–13n.); cf. *3H6* 1.1.48: 'I'll plant Plantagenet, root him up who dares'.
64 **Being** monosyllabic
ne'er . . . urged hardly urged at all
65 **the usurped** probably elided to 'th'usurpèd'; or perhaps 'the ùsurped'
66 **love . . . men** for each other. F's substitution ('friends' for *men*), if it comes from the promptbook, may represent an actor's attempt to clarify the idea that the 'love of wicked men' is for each other rather than for someone else. Although both readings can be defended, nearly all editors follow Q.
converts changes (intransitive)
67–8 **hate turns . . . danger** 'Hatred brings one or both parties (either the

usurper or his sponsor, or both of them) into deserved peril (*worthy danger*).' See 60–8n.
68 **deserved** deservèd
69 **My . . . head** Cf. Matthew, 27.25, where the Jews answer Pilate regarding the Crucifixion: 'His blood be on us, and on our children'. With unwitting irony, Northumberland casts himself in an unenviable position in relation to Richard as Christ.
and . . . end a common phrase for dismissing a topic: 'and let that be the end of it'; cf. *TGV* 1.3.65, *1H4* 5.3.61.
70 **part . . . part** part from each other . . . depart. Northumberland's wordplay helps dramatize his heartlessness. There may be a perverse echo of the marriage rite in the *Prayer Book*: 'till death us depart'.
71–3 See LN.
72 **marriage . . . me** Shortly after her crowning in 1559, when a parliamentary deputation implored her to marry, Elizabeth I withdrew her coronation ring (an element of the regalia) and, showing it to them, said: 'I am already bound unto a husband, which is the Kingdom of England' (Jenkins, 76).

64 urged,] *F2;* vrgde *QF* way] *Pope;* way, *QF*   66 men] friends *F*   71 divorced!] *Q2 (*diuorst,*),* *Q3–F (*diuorc'd?*);* diuorst *Q*   you] ye *F*   72 'twixt] *QF;* betwixt *Q2*

And then betwixt me and my married wife.
[*to Queen*]
Let me unkiss the oath 'twixt thee and me –
And yet not so, for with a kiss 'twas made.   75
[*to Northumberland*]
Part us, Northumberland: I towards the north,
Where shivering cold and sickness pines the clime;
My wife to France, from whence, set forth in pomp,
She came adorned hither like sweet May,
Sent back like Hallowmas or short'st of day.   80

QUEEN
And must we be divided? Must we part?

74 **unkiss** annul with a kiss; see 2.1.16n.
   oath wedding vow
75 A kiss to seal the vows was sometimes
   used as part of the marriage rite,
   although the *Prayer Book* specifies only
   the joining of hands; cf. *TS* 3.2.122–3:
   'bid good morrow to my bride, / And
   seal the title with a lovely kiss!', also
   Insatiate Countess, 5.1.195: 'The kiss
   thou gavest me in the church, here
   take'. Richard seems to mean, 'yet let
   us not kiss, since our vow, ratified with
   a kiss, cannot so easily be kissed away'.
   For similar quibbling logic about kissing, see *RJ* 1.5.107–10. Cf. also notes
   on 96, 97, 98, 99–100.
76 **the north** Yorkshire (see 52n.)
77 **pines the clime** afflicts the climate;
   causes the region to suffer (one of only
   two transitive uses of 'pine' in
   Shakespeare; cf. *VA* 602 and see *OED*
   v. 1). See 2.2.16–17n.
78–9 Richard's sad reminiscence of his
   queen recalls Edward II's even more
   pathetic memory of his own courting
   days in *E2*, 5.5.67–9: 'Tell Isabel, the
   queen, I looked not thus / When for
   her sake I ran at tilt in France / And
   there unhorsed the Duke of
   Cleremont.' That both queens were
   named Isabel could have strengthened

the parallel in Shakespeare's mind.
78 **wife** F's 'Queene' – a more formal,
   less intimate word – could be an actor's
   substitution influenced by *pomp* in the
   same line; see Appendix 1, pp. 513,
   529.
   set . . . pomp 'splendidly arrayed' or
   'having set out with great pageantry';
   Holinshed (3.487) details the extravagant ostentation of the wedding festivities.
79–80 The seasons mentioned here are
   poetic rather than historical. See LN.
   Rhymed couplets from here to 102
   contribute to the stylized gravity of
   the actual parting.
79 **adorned** adornèd. Richard seems to
   imply that at her departure, in contrast to
   her arrival, the Queen will be *un*adorned.
   But this is unhistorical; see 53n.
80 **short'st of day** i.e. the winter solstice
   – 10 not 22 December in Shakespeare's
   time because of the uncorrected calen-
   dar, and therefore closer to Hallowmas
   (All Saints Day, 1 November), then
   than now: the line, however, does not
   equate *Hallowmas* with *short'st of day*,
   though the sad occasion unites them
   symbolically.
81 **must . . . Must** Cf. 3.3.143–6n.,
   4.1.228.

74 SD] *Rowe (subst.)*   'twixt] *QF;* betwixt *Q2*   76 SD] *this edn*   78 wife] Queene *F*

KING RICHARD

Ay, hand from hand, my love, and heart from heart.

QUEEN [*to Northumberland*]

Banish us both, and send the King with me.

NORTHUMBERLAND

That were some love, but little policy.

QUEEN

Then whither he goes, thither let me go.   85

KING RICHARD [*to Queen*]

So two together, weeping, make one woe.

Weep thou for me in France, I for thee here;

Better far off than, near, be ne'er the near.

Go count thy way with sighs, I mine with groans.

---

84 SP *Q's assignment of this line to Richard has been preferred by some on the grounds that it better preserves the pattern of formal stichomythic alternation between the lovers. But the intrusion of Northumberland's political realism in the phrase *little policy* (unastute politics, poor statesmanship) is dramatically effective and suits the ambitious nobleman better than Richard. It is clear that the Queen addresses Northumberland in 85, and her *Then* implies that she is replying to him. As GWW suggests, Q's error could be explained as compositorial carelessness induced by the repetition of SPs up to and beyond this point. F's change of speaker probably has promptbook authority; see Appendix 1, pp. 526–7.

85 possibly an echo of Ruth's words to Naomi, Ruth, 1.16: 'Entreate me not to leaue thee, and to returne from thee: for whyther thou goest, I will go also.'

86–96 These lines 'bring together many

of the words in the play's vocabulary of grief – *weeping, woe, sighs, groans, moans, sorrow,* and *grief*' (Wells, 251). See also Wells, 'Tale'.

86 perhaps indebted to Daniel, 2.91–2, where the Queen says, 'Nor my teares without thine are fullie teares, / For thus vnioyn'd, sorrow but halfe appeares. / Ioine then our plaints & make our griefe ful griefe, / Our state being one, ô lets not part our care'. So in that case

88 *'It is better to be distant from each other than, being near, yet be no closer to meeting'; or, more literally, 'Better far off than near, be the nearness never so much the nearer'. The second *near* is a contracted form of the comparative (nearer); cf. 3.2.64n. *Ne'er the near* is proverbial (Dent, N135.2); Johnson (1.450) glosses the phrase as 'never the nigher' and reports that in the eighteenth century it was still current in the Midlands.

89 **count thy way** measure your distance

---

82 Ay] *(I)*   83 SD] *Wells*   84 SP] *F; King Q*   86 SD] *this edn*   87 Weep thou] *QF;* Weepe *Q2*
88 off than, near,] *Ard²;* off than neere *Q;* off, then neere, *F*

QUEEN
So longest way shall have the longest moans.   90
KING RICHARD
Twice for one step I'll groan, the way being short,
And piece the way out with a heavy heart.
Come, come, in wooing Sorrow let's be brief,
Since, wedding it, there is such length in grief.
One kiss shall stop our mouths, and dumbly part;   95
Thus give I mine, and thus take I thy heart.
    [*They kiss.*]
QUEEN
Give me mine own again; 'twere no good part
To take on me to keep and kill thy heart.
    [*They kiss again.*]
So now I have mine own again, be gone,

90 'If I count my way with sighs, as you suggest, then (*So*) I shall have the *longest moans* (on account of the greater distance).'
longest way to France (as opposed to Pomfret)
92 **piece . . . out** lengthen the journey (with a possible quibble on 'pace'). Richard counters his wife's logic by saying that he will double the number of his groans to compensate for his shorter journey.
93–4 Richard suggests that because being married to grief involves a life-long commitment, the courting of it ought to be mercifully brief. Ironically, wedding grief means the divorce of Richard from his queen.
95 **stop our mouths** silence us. The phrase was often associated with kissing; cf. *MA* 2.1.310–11, 5.4.98, *2H6* 3.2.396, *TC* 3.2.133.
dumbly part make us part silently. Cf. *E2*, 1.4.134: 'Therefore, with dumb embracement, let us part –'.
96 Figuratively, Richard and the Queen exchange their hearts in kissing – thus

paradoxically enacting a second marriage in parting (continuing the nuptial imagery of 93–4). The conceit of lovers giving their hearts to each other through kissing was a staple of Elizabethan love poetry (cf. *RJ* 1.5.107–10); the hearts were conceived of as passing through the open lips. Cf. also Sidney's lyric (75): 'My true love hath my hart, and I have his, / By just exchange, one for the other giv'ne'.
97 **part** action, behaviour (on your part); probably punning on the sense of 'parting' (see 95), reinforced by rhyme
98 **to . . . heart** 'to keep your heart as a part of myself and thereby kill it (when I die from the grief that I shall experience by your absence)'; cf. the death of Falstaff in *H5* 2.1.88: 'The King has kill'd his heart'. *Keep* combines the senses of 'keep with me' and 'guard'. A second kiss makes possible the repossession of their own hearts.
99–100 'Now that I possess my own heart once more, leave, so that I can try to kill it with the groan that your departure will elicit from me.'

91 groan, . . . short,] *Q2–F;* grone . . . short *Q*   93 Sorrow] *F;* sorrow *Q*   95 dumbly] *QF;* doubly *Q2*   96 SD] *Rowe*   98 SD] *Rowe (subst.)*

That I may strive to kill it with a groan.   100
KING RICHARD
We make woe wanton with this fond delay.
Once more, adieu. The rest let Sorrow say.   *Exeunt.*

[5.2]   *Enter* Duke of YORK *and the*
                             DUCHESS [OF YORK].

101–2 Dillon (69) observes that
'Richard's last words' are 'reminiscent
of Bolingbroke's refusal to be *prodigal*
of tongue' (cf. 1.3.256).
101 We are trifling with sorrow in foolishly
extending our loving farewell; *fond* =
both 'affectionate' and 'useless, foolish'; *wanton* = playful, frivolous; self-
indulgent, promiscuously unrestrained. Cf. 3.3.164: 'play the wantons
with our woes' (see n.). As Wells (252)
observes, the highly self-conscious
wordplay of Richard and the Queen in
this exchange recalls the similar dialogue between Richard and Gaunt at
2.1.84–94. Richard's awareness of
rhetorical self-indulgence may be compared to 'I talk but idly, and you laugh
at me' (3.3.171).
102 **Once more, adieu** possibly with yet
another kiss, although this would damage the elaborately worked out system
of conceits explained above
Sorrow silent sorrow
SD Clearly Richard and the Queen
exit 'severally', i.e. by separate doors.
Since Northumberland has informed
her that she must be conducted to
France 'With all swift speed' (54), one
or more of his attendants may accompany her through one door, while
Northumberland himself may exit
with Richard and the Guard through
the other.
5.2 This scene is located either at Langley
or at one of York's other houses in, or

near, London (see List of Roles, 4n.);
Langley is nearer Windsor, where
King Henry is, than London (see
Black, 294). It falls into two sections:
York's evocative description of
Bolingbroke's triumphal entry into
London with Richard as his prisoner
(1–40); and his discovery of Aumerle's
involvement in the Abbot of
Westminster's plot against Henry IV
(41–117). The first magnifies yet further the pathos of Richard's abjection
by contrasting it with Bolingbroke's
popularity; the second dramatizes the
divided loyalties that attend the new
king's accession and that create instability not only in the realm but also
within a single family.
Historically, the festive and hostile
receptions of Bolingbroke and Richard
occurred on separate days. Holinshed
(3.501) generally avoids specific detail:
Bolingbroke 'was receiued with all the
ioy and pompe that might be of the
Londoners . . . It was a woonder to see
what great concursse of people, & what
number of horsses came to him
. . . till his comming to London, where
(vpon his approch to the citie) the
maior rode foorth to receiue him, and a
great number of other citizens. Also
the cleargie met him with procession,
and such ioy appeared in the countenances of the people, vttering the same
also with words, as the like [has] not
lightlie [= readily] beene seene. For in

102 Sorrow] *F;* sorrow *Q*
5.2] *F (Scoena Secunda.)*   0.1–2] *Enter Yorke, and his Duchesse. F*

DUCHESS OF YORK

My lord, you told me you would tell the rest,
When weeping made you break the story off
Of our two cousins' coming into London.

euerie towne and village where he passed, children reioised, women clapped their hands, and men cried out for ioy. But to speake of the great numbers of people that flocked togither in the fields and streets of London at his comming, I here omit; neither will I speake of the presents, welcommings, lauds, and gratifications made to him by the citizens and communaltie.' The next day, when Richard was transferred from Westminster to the Tower, Holinshed continues, 'Manie euill disposed persons, assembling themselues togither in great numbers, intended to haue met with him, and to haue taken him from such as had the conueieng of him, that they might haue slaine him. But the maior and aldermen gathered to them the worshipfull commoners and graue citizens, by whose policie, and not without much adoo, the other were reuoked from their euill purpose.' Holinshed's 'juxtaposition of these two very different receptions might have suggested the sharp contrasts' in York's description (Ard², 152). Shakespeare was also probably influenced by Daniel, 2.66–77, twelve stanzas that immediately precede those on which he had based the previous scene – a passage that describes Bolingbroke riding in procession in front of the newly humbled Richard. For possible influence of the French chroniclers, see LN.

For the story of York's discovery of Aumerle's intended treason, Shakespeare followed Holinshed, possibly also consulting Hall, Holinshed's source (who in turn drew on *Traïson*), and probably deriving a few touches from Daniel. Invented wholly by Shakespeare is the role of the Duchess

of York, a figure intended to balance the Duchess of Gloucester in 1.2. York's first wife, Aumerle's mother, Isabella of Castile, died in 1394, five years before the action dramatized here; his second wife, the one presented in this scene, was historically Aumerle's stepmother, Joan Holland (the sister of the Duke of Surrey and also Richard's niece), a young woman of only thirty-three and thus about seven years older than Aumerle; see List of Roles (5n.), Appendix 3 and 109n. Shakespeare's concern was simply to provide for Aumerle a doting mother whose entirely private concern for her child could be made to contrast emblematically with her husband's public (and harshly political) condemnation of him.

1–3 As the two cousins' coming to London must have taken place between 3.3 and 4.1 (3.3.208), the timing of York's resumption of his tale may seem chronologically and psychologically unrealistic, but Shakespeare's more important aim is to evoke pathos for the fallen king. Charles Kean in 1857 turned York's description into a lavishly mounted spectacle with costumes and scenery based upon current antiquarian research (see Forker, 17–18, and Introduction, pp. 93–5).

2   **weeping** Despite York's conversion to Bolingbroke's cause, his sympathy for Richard continues; see notes on 3.3.7–9, 12–14, 45–8, 68, 203.
    story This reference to a story so sad that the tears of the narrator (and possibly of the listener) caused it to be interrupted reminds us of Richard's prediction at 5.1.44–5.

3   ***cousins'** nephews' (Richard and Bolingbroke). See LN.

2 off] *(of)*, F; *om.* Q2–5   3 cousins'] *Keightley;* cousins *QF*

YORK

   Where did I leave?

DUCHESS OF YORK   At that sad stop, my lord,

   Where rude misgoverned hands from windows' tops   5
   Threw dust and rubbish on King Richard's head.

YORK

   Then, as I said, the Duke, great Bolingbroke,
   Mounted upon a hot and fiery steed,
   Which his aspiring rider seemed to know,
   With slow but stately pace kept on his course,   10

4   **leave** leave off. Herford (200) suggests
    that this expression may be 'a mark of
    York's age, which is elsewhere insisted
    on' (cf. 2.2.74: *his aged neck*); cf. also
    Ham 2.1.50–1, where Polonius, losing
    the thread of his discourse, says, 'By
    the mass, I was about to say something.
    / Where did I leave?' There is, however,
    no necessary implication of bumbling;
    in Warner's production Michael
    Bryant played York with great dignity.
    stop pause, point

5   **rude** brutal (not merely 'ill-man-
    nered')
    misgoverned unruly, ill-behaved
    windows' tops upper windows, those
    at the tops of houses. Elizabethan case-
    ment or lattice windows had no 'tops'
    such as modern sash windows possess.
    Possibly Shakespeare derived the gen-
    eral idea from 'the window' out of
    which the Queen observes the street
    procession in Daniel (2.78).

6   **Threw . . . rubbish** This desecration
    of the royal person is Shakespeare's
    invention and contrasts significantly
    with the mob savagery described in
    Holinshed (see headnote) and with the
    attempt of Londoners to have Richard
    beheaded even before he reached the
    capital, as reported in Créton
    (176–7/376) and *Traïson* (62/212).
    The besmirching reappears at 30 and
    is recalled by the Archbishop of York
    in *2H4* 1.3.103–7: 'Thou, that threw'st

dust upon his goodly head / When
through proud London he came sighing on / After th' admired heels of
Bullingbrook, / Cri'st now, "O earth,
yield us that king again, / And take
thou this!" '

King The Duchess gives Richard his
royal title even after his capture and
degradation.

8   **hot . . . steed** Cf. 'his proud steed's
    neck' (19). Some editors interpret this
    as *roan Barbary*, the horse mentioned
    by Richard's groom at 5.5.78 and by
    Richard himself at 5.5.81; but the
    Groom describes a horse used for the
    coronation, not one already ridden by
    Bolingbroke in Richard's presence.
    The *steed* is fictional, but the idea may
    have come from Daniel's 'white cours-
    er' (2.74), in turn derived from
    Froissart (6.380). See 5.2LN and
    9–10n.

9–10 The subject of *know* is *Which* (=
    steed) and *his aspiring rider* its object.
    Bolingbroke rides the horse as though
    the animal were already accustomed to
    (*seemed to know*) him; Herford (201)
    adds, 'The spirited horse instinctively
    felt that it bore a spirited rider'. Cf. the
    Groom's description at 5.5.83 of
    Barbary with his new rider, advancing
    'So proudly as if he disdained the
    ground'; but see 8n.

9   **aspiring** gallant, high-spirited; ambi-
    tious

Whilst all tongues cried, 'God save thee, Bolingbroke!'.
You would have thought the very windows spake,
So many greedy looks of young and old
Through casements darted their desiring eyes
Upon his visage, and that all the walls   15
With painted imagery had said at once,
'Jesu preserve thee! Welcome, Bolingbroke!',
Whilst he, from the one side to the other turning,

12–13 *spake, / So F's comma (unlike Q's colon) clarifies the syntax, showing that the following clause (*So many . . . visage*) belongs with 'You would have thought' and is not grammatically separate.

13 **young and old** Cf. 3.2.119 and n.

16 **painted imagery** York suggests that the faces at the windows with their clamorous mouths resemble the speaking figures in painted wall-coverings. Cloths, often depicting biblical or classical themes and incidents, on which were painted human figures, from whose mouths issued lettered sayings or mottoes as in a modern cartoon strip, often decorated the interior walls of Elizabethan houses and could be hung from windows on the outside on celebratory occasions. Cf. *Luc* 244–5: 'who fears a sentence or an old man's saw / Shall by a painted cloth be kept in awe'; also *FQ*, 7.7.10: 'tapestry, / That princes bowres adorne with painted imagery'. Shakespeare's mother, Mary Arden, possessed eleven such cloths (see Honan, 22). Froissart mentions such decorations (see 5.2LN), and Daniel (2.68) may imply them in his line, 'Houses impou'r-isht were t'inrich the streetes'.
at once in chorus, all together

17 *thee! Welcome F's emendation, accepted by all editors, is not only more idiomatic but is likely to have promptbook authority; see 1.3.58n. and Appendix 1, pp. 526–7.

18–20 York's description of Bolingbroke's demeanour recalls Richard's words at 1.4.23–36. The bowing to the crowds

may derive from Daniel (2.74), where the Queen, at first mistaking the mounted Bolingbroke for Richard, is impressed by 'the thronging troupes of people' whom he greets: 'I know him by his seate, he sits s'vpright: / Lo now he bows: deare Lord with what sweet grace.' Froissart (6.361), Daniel's possible source, credits Bolingbroke with the same trait, although on the occasion of his reception by Londoners when he had just returned from exile: 'and alwayes as he rode he enclyned his heed to the people on every syde'. Shakespeare could have remembered one or both of these passages or simply have invented the bowing, which would doubtless be customary (Ard², 154). Hayward (71) may perhaps imitate Shakespeare in reporting that upon arriving from France Bolingbroke was 'not negligent to vncouer the head, to bowe the body, to stretch forth the hand to euery meane person, and to vse all other complements of popular behauiour'.

18 **the one** probably elided ('th'one'); F's omission of the article (see t.n.), if done for metrical reasons, is not strictly necessary, although Craven³ (56–7) and Gurr (155), not implausibly, suggest that Q could have inserted *the* in trying to balance *the one side* with *the other*. GWW thinks that F's deletion of Q's *the* occurred because F's compositor recognized that Q had mistakenly anticipated *the* from the later occurrence of the word in the same line. See Appendix 1, pp. 537–8 and 537, n. 2.

11 Whilst] While *Q2–F*   thee] *(the), F*   12 spake,] *F;* spake: *Q*   17 thee! Welcome, Bolingbroke!] *F (*thee, welcom *Bullingbroke.); the welcome Bullingbrooke, *Q*   18 from the] from *F*

430

Bare-headed, lower than his proud steed's neck,
Bespake them thus: 'I thank you, countrymen';   20
And thus still doing, thus he passed along.

DUCHESS OF YORK
Alack, poor Richard! Where rode he the whilst?

YORK
As in a theatre the eyes of men,
After a well-graced actor leaves the stage,
Are idly bent on him that enters next,   25
Thinking his prattle to be tedious,
Even so, or with much more contempt, men's eyes
Did scowl on gentle Richard. No man cried God save
    him!
No joyful tongue gave him his welcome home,

19 **Bare-headed** with his hat removed (a sign of deference)
lower bending lower (in deference to the crowd)
20 **Bespake them** addressed the crowd
21 **still** continually, all the time
22 **Alack** F's 'Alas' is an indifferent variant (see Appendix 1, pp. 513–14).
the whilst during that time
23–36 Dryden, in the earliest critical statement on *R2*, singled out this passage of 'passionate description' for special praise (Preface to *Troilus and Cressida*, 1679): 'the painting of it is so lively, and the words so moving, that I have scarce read any thing comparable to it, in any other language. Suppose you have seen already the fortunate Usurper passing through the croud, and follow'd by the shouts and acclamations of the people; and now behold King *Richard* entring upon the Scene: consider the wretchedness of his condition, and his carriage in it; and refrain from pitty if you can' (Vickers, 1.265). Next to Gaunt's speech on England (especially 2.1.40–50), this description probably remains the most popular passage of the play; Saintsbury called it 'the most famous . . . of many

famous ones' in the drama (Forker, 441).
23–8 Cf. Daniel, 2.70: 'Behind him all aloofe came pensiue on / The vnregarded king, that drooping went / Alone, and but for spight scarce lookt vpon'.
23 **theatre** an obvious anachronism since public theatres did not exist in 1399 and only came into being in London about 1575. For other anachronisms, see 3.4.29n. on *apricocks* and 4.1.41n. on *rapier's point*.
24 **well-graced** attractive, graceful, accomplished (and therefore 'well-liked, favoured, popular')
25 **idly** listlessly, inattentively, without much interest
27 **Even** probably monosyllabic ('E'en')
28 an alexandrine in Q. F's omission of *gentle* (cf. 31) may be correct (see Craven³, 58), but the 'correction', if it is one, originates in Q2 (a mere reprinting of Q1), not the theatre prompt-book, and can therefore possess no authority. See Appendix 1, pp. 537–8.
gentle noble and magnanimous; 'a word with a much stronger and wider connotation then than now' (Ard², 154). Cf. 1.3.95n., 2.3.45n., 4.1.229n.
29 **home** i.e. from Ireland and Wales

22 Alack] Alas *F*   rode] rides *Q2–F*   28 gentle Richard] *(Ric.);* Richard *Q2, F*

But dust was thrown upon his sacred head,   30
Which with such gentle sorrow he shook off,
His face still combating with tears and smiles,
The badges of his grief and patience,
That had not God for some strong purpose steeled
The hearts of men, they must perforce have melted   35
And barbarism itself have pitied him.
But heaven hath a hand in these events,
To whose high will we bound our calm contents.
To Bolingbroke are we sworn subjects now,

30 **thrown** See t.n. and 5.1.25n.
   sacred York instinctively clings to the
   notion of Richard's sacramental status
   even though he has acknowledged
   Bolingbroke as sovereign; cf. 2n., 45n.
32 The combination of *tears* and *smiles* is a
   favourite motif in Shakespeare; cf. *KL*
   4.3.17–19, *Mac* 1.4.33–5, *Cor* 1.9.3,
   Tem 3.1.73–4. The same detail, perhaps
   coincidentally, appears also in Créton
   (237/421) in a passage describing the
   Queen's return to France, where 'her
   coming caused many a tear and smile'.
   The theme was already popular in the
   continental literature of the fifteenth
   century (see Huizinga, 283–4).
   combating with struggling between;
   còmbating. Cf. 3.2.9.
33 **badges** tokens, outward signs; *tears*
   are the emblems of *grief*, *smiles* of
   patience.
   patience three syllables. For the association of *smiles* (32) with *patience*, see
   TN 2.4.114–15: 'like Patience on a
   monument, / Smiling at grief'.
34 **some strong purpose** i.e. a divine,
   not a human, purpose
35–6 Wilson (221) cites *MV* 4.1.30–3; also
   Créton (116/340): 'There lives not a
   man so hard-hearted or so firm, who
   would not have wept at sight of the disgrace that was brought upon him.'
   Later in Créton (157/370) the same
   sentiment is applied to Richard and his
   friends, as they weep: 'no creature in

this mortal world . . . could have beheld
[them] . . . without being heartily sorry
for them'.
35 **perforce** of necessity, inevitably
36 **barbarism itself** i.e. even savages
37–8 The rhymed couplet suits York's
   conventional piety, which Herford
   (201) interprets as a means of 'dis-
   guis[ing] his timidity'; see 37n. and
   Introduction, pp. 40–1.
37 Cf. 1.2.6. Possibly Shakespeare recalled Holinshed's moralistic comment
   on Richard's reign (3.508): 'the wrath
   of God was dailie prouoked to
   vengeance for the sins of the prince
   and his people. How then could it continue prosperouslie with this king?
   against whom for the fowle enormities
   wherewith his life was defamed, the
   wrath of God was whetted and tooke
   so sharpe an edge, that the same did
   shred him off from the scepter of his
   kingdome, and gaue him a full cup of
   affliction to drinke.'
38 **bound . . . contents** 'confine our
   peaceful contentment'; *calm contents* is
   proleptic. Some editors read *bound* as
   the past tense of 'bind' and interpret
   the phrase as a reference to York's oath
   of allegiance.
39–40 York has acknowledged Bolingbroke's claim to the throne and already
   confirmed it by swearing allegiance,
   but he still finds it hard to use Henry's
   new title.

30 thrown] *(*throwen*)*, *Q2–F*   39 subjects] *QF;* subiect *Q4*

Whose state and honour I for aye allow.   40

^F*Enter* AUMERLE.^F

DUCHESS OF YORK
Here comes my son, Aumerle.
YORK   Aumerle that was,

---

40 **state** royal status, kingship; throne
I . . . allow 'I totally accept and
approve' (literally, 'I acknowledge forever'); note the wordplay on *I* and *aye*
(cf. 4.1.201–2n.).

41–117 based mainly on Holinshed
(3.514–15), who reports that the
Abbot of Westminster assembled at
his house the chief conspirators, 'his
speciall freends', the earls of
Huntingdon and Kent, Aumerle,
Salisbury, Lord Hugh Spenser,
Carlisle, Sir Thomas Blunt and
Richard Maudelyn, a priest of King
Richard's chapel. After dinner they
retired to 'a secret chamber' to devise
a stratagem for assassinating King
Henry. The plan was to lure him to
Oxford on the pretext of his presiding
at a festal jousting contest between
twenty knights sponsored by
Huntingdon and twenty others sponsored by Salisbury: when the King
'should be most busilie marking the
martiall pastime, he suddenlie should
be slaine and destroied, and so by that
means king Richard, who as yet liued,
might be restored to libertie, and haue
his former estate & dignitie. . . .
Hervpon was an indenture sextipartite
made, sealed with their seales, and
signed with their hands, in the which
each stood bound to other, to do their
whole indeuour for the accomplishing
of their purposed exploit. Moreouer,
they sware on the holie euangelists to
be true and secret each to other, euen
to the houre and point of death.' After
Huntingdon had informed the King at
Windsor of the proposed tournament

and secured his agreement to attend,
the conspirators dispersed to make
preparations, coming together again at
Oxford – 'except the earle of Rutland,
by whose follie their practised conspiracie was brought to light and disclosed to king Henrie. For this earle of
Rutland departing before from
Westminster to see his father the duke
of Yorke, as he sat at dinner, had his
counterpane [copy] of the indenture
of the confederacie in his bosome.
The father espieng it, would needs see
what it was: and though the sonne
humblie denied to shew it, the father
being more earnest to see it, by force
tooke it out of his bosome; and perceiuing the contents therof, in a great
rage caused his horsses to be sadled
out of hand, and spitefullie
reprouing his sonne of treason, for
whome he was become suertie and
mainpernour [guarantor] for his good
abearing in open parlement, he incontinentlie mounted on horssebacke to
ride towards Windsore to the king, to
declare vnto him the malicious intent
of his complices. The earle of Rutland
seeing in what danger he stood, tooke
his horsse, and rode another waie to
Windsore in post, so that he got thither before his father.'

Since Hall's more colourful and
detailed account (fols xii^v–xiii) of
York's anger contains Shakespeare's
word *pledge* (44), which is not in
Holinshed, the dramatist may also
have consulted this version: 'thou
knowest wel inough that I am thy
pledge borowe and mayneperner' (for

40.1] *Q4 (after* son, Aumerle. *41), F*   41 my] our *(Craven¹)*

But that is lost for being Richard's friend;
And, madam, you must call him Rutland now.
I am in Parliament pledge for his truth
And lasting fealty to the new-made king.   45

the full context, see LN). Hall's source was *Traïson*, which also uses the phrase 'pledge-borrow' (81/233), although the French chronicler differs from Hall (as well as Holinshed) in reporting that instead of Aumerle's hiding the incriminating document in his 'bosom', he 'placed' it 'upon the table' in his father's presence (80/233). But as Ure (155) notes, Shakespeare's word *pledge* may represent nothing more than a translation of Holinshed's more technical term, 'mainpernour'; and he also points out that in general 'the particular features in which Hall really is more vivid than Holinshed . . . are not reflected in Shakespeare's text' (152). Daniel (3.48) treats Aumerle's betrayal of the conspiracy in general terms only: '*Aumarle* became the man that all did marre / Whether through indiscretion, chance or worse, / He makes his peace with offring others bloud / And shewes the king how all the matter stood.'

This episode contains a large number of metrically irregular lines – a technique used to convey the agitation or emotional stress of the speakers. Black (301) remarks that Shakespeare 'appears to be experimenting with lines of irregular lengths' to suggest 'distraction'; see 57n. The anomalies sometimes border on prose, but most can be explained in terms of normal metrical licence within the somewhat elastic limits of the play's verse structure. For a stimulating analysis of the comic elements and function of this scene and its companion (5.3), see Zitner, also Introduction, pp. 41–3.

41–3 After Henry IV's accession, Aumerle was punished with the loss of his ducal title but retained his earlier title of Earl of Rutland; cf. Holinshed (3.513): 'Finallie, to auoid further inconuenience, and to qualifie the minds of the enuious, it was finallie enacted, that such as were appellants in the last parlement against the duke of Glocester and other, should in this wise following be ordred. The dukes of Aumarle, Surrie, and Excester there present, were iudged to loose their names of dukes, togither with the honors, titles and dignities thereunto belonging.' Daniel (3.15) has a similar passage: 'And to abase the too high state of those / That were accusd, and lessen their degrees, / *Aumarle*, *Surry*, *Exceter*, must lose / The names of Dukes, their titles, dignities, / And whatsoeuer honour with it goes'. See also 4.1.1n. This reference to Aumerle's demotion is the only consequence of the nobles' parliamentary quarrels of 4.1 mentioned in the play.

41 **my son** Historically, Aumerle was her stepson; see headnote. Craven[1] (59–60) believes that Q substituted *my* for 'our', anticipating the Duchess's *my son* in 46; see Appendix 1, p. 538. Although this is possible, Q's *my* makes acceptable sense.

42 **that** that title

43 **And** and therefore

44 **pledge . . . truth** guarantor of his loyalty (see 41–117n.); *truth* = troth (cf. 78n.).

45 **fealty** allegiance, fidelity
new-made This term calls attention to the fact that Henry 'has been "made" a king, and has not attained the crown by birth or succession' (Cam[2], 156).

45 new-made] *F;* new made *Q*

DUCHESS OF YORK

Welcome, my son. Who are the violets now
That strew the green lap of the new-come spring?

AUMERLE

Madam, I know not, nor I greatly care not.
God knows I had as lief be none as one.

YORK

Well, bear you well in this new spring of time,   50
Lest you be cropped before you come to prime.
What news from Oxford? Do these jousts and
    triumphs hold?

AUMERLE

For aught I know, my lord, they do.

46–7 Who ... spring? 'Who are the new favourites at the freshly formed court of Henry IV?'; cf. *Son* 98.6–8. The metaphor of *violets*, the most ephemeral and short-lived of flowers, is obviously charged with irony – an irony made explicit by York's warning at 50–1. See 4.1.79n.

48 nor ... not double negative used for emphasis (Abbott, 406); cf. 4.1.255.

49 I ... one 'I had just as soon not be a favourite as be one'; *had as lief* = 'would find it as pleasant'. Aumerle's protest of indifference to Henry's favour may be taken as a clue to his guilty intentions. No wonder his father is suspicious.

50–1 York's rhymed couplet reinforces the sententious nature of his advice.

50 bear you well conduct yourself prudently (perhaps with a pun on *bear* = bring forth leaves or fruit)
this ... time Cf. 4.1.79n.

51 cropped plucked, harvested; beheaded. Cf. 2.1.134; also *R3* 1.2.247.
prime maturity, full bloom

52 an alexandrine in Q. F reduces the line to an ordinary pentameter (see t.n.), and Jowett & Taylor (190) regard this as an instance of 'authorial adjustment' or revision. But an extra-metrical line just before two irregularly short ones

makes good dramatic sense; see 41–117n. For an implied defence of Q, see Pollard, 86–7.

What ... Oxford? The question probably startles Aumerle or causes him to react nervously; cf. 49n. Holinshed is mistaken about the location of the proposed tournament, which was in fact Kingston (near Windsor), not Oxford (see following n.).

Do ... hold? elliptical: 'Do (the plans for) these jousts and triumphs hold firm?' or 'Will these jousts and triumphs be held?' *Triumphs* = processional festivities (usually chivalric or allegorical), here intended as part of the tournament pageantry, but the word could mean simply 'festive activities, spectacles' (see *OED sb.* 4) including the jousts themselves (cf. 66, also 5.3.14); the name derives from Roman triumphs. Cf. Holinshed (3.514): 'it was deuised, that they [the conspirators] should take vpon them a solemne iusts to be enterprised betweene him [the Earl of Huntingdon] and 20 on his part, & the earle of Salisburie and 20 with him at Oxford, to the which triumph K. Henrie should be desired [invited]'; see also 41–117n.

53 For aught as far as

---

46 are] *QF*; art *Q4*   47 new-come] *F*; new come *Q*   52 Do ... hold] Hold those Iusts & Triumphs? *F*

YORK

You will be there, I know.

AUMERLE

If God prevent it not, I purpose so.   55

YORK

What seal is that that hangs without thy bosom?

Yea, look'st thou pale? Let me see the writing.

AUMERLE

My lord, 'tis nothing.

YORK   No matter, then, who see it.

I will be satisfied. Let me see the writing.

AUMERLE

I do beseech your grace to pardon me.   60

It is a matter of small consequence,

Which for some reasons I would not have seen.

---

55 *****prevent it** Capell's insertion of *it*, accepted by most editors, mends the halting metre. Compositorial omission (see Craven[2], 189, 191–5) is especially likely in the present case since the hypothetically omitted word (*it*) ends with the same letter as the preceding word (*prevent*). Cf. 4.1.149n. QF's 'preuent not' is, however, idiomatically possible. The entire line carries sinister implications (cf. 49n.).

56 **seal** a wax seal carrying the impression of a person's device, emblem or signet, attached to the bottom of a document by a narrow strip of parchment; see Holinshed in 41–117n. 'The "bond" was in Aumerle's doublet, and the seal, red and therefore likely to catch the eye, dangled outside [*without*] – a good point for the theatre' (Cam[1], 222). The visible seal, which arouses York's suspicion, is Shakespeare's invention.

bosom Aumerle's partially unbuttoned tunic or doublet (the equivalent of a pocket (*OED sb*. 2b)). Figuratively,

bosom also meant 'receptacle of secrets' (see *OED sb*. 6a) because it enclosed the heart.

57–63 **Let . . . see**. Cf. *KL* 1.2.30–5 where Gloucester plucks a letter from his son's pocket: '*Gloucester*. What paper were you reading? *Edmund*. Nothing, my lord. *Gloucester*. No? What needed then that terrible dispatch of it unto your pocket? . . . Let's see. Come, if it be nothing, I shall not need spectacles.'

57 A pause (or beat) may be introduced before *Let*. Johnson (1.450) thought that 'Such harsh and defective lines as this, are probably corrupt', but see end of 41–117n.

58 **see** subjunctive (Abbott, 368)

59 Metrically irregular; see end of 41–117n.

   satisfied fully enlightened

60 **pardon me** excuse me (from showing it); cf. 70. See also 5.3.118n.

62–3 **seen . . . see** Cf. Holinshed ('espieng', 'see', 'shew') and Hall ('espied', 'bee sene', 'see') in 41–117n.

---

55 prevent it] *Capell;* preuent *QF;* prevent me *Rowe*   58 see] sees *F*

YORK

Which for some reasons, sir, I mean to see.
I fear, I fear –

DUCHESS OF YORK   What should you fear?
'Tis nothing but some bond that he is entered into   65
For gay apparel 'gainst the triumph day.

YORK

Bound to himself? What doth he with a bond
That he is bound to? Wife, thou art a fool.
Boy, let me see the writing.

AUMERLE

I do beseech you, pardon me. I may not show it.   70

YORK

I will be satisfied. Let me see it, I say.
He plucks it out of his bosom and reads it.
Treason, foul treason! Villain, traitor, slave!

---

65 another alexandrine, made rougher than usual by the weak ending (*into*); see end of 41–117n. and Craven³, 60 (see t.n.).
*bond agreement. For consistency with Q's *bond* at 67, I follow F's rather than Q's spelling ('band'); but the two forms were interchangeable, as is demonstrated by Q's use of both spellings within three lines. Shakespeare himself perhaps had no preference, and Q's compositor probably followed copy in setting 'band' at 65 and 'bond' at 67; the occurrence of *Bound* (67), which intervenes, may have influenced the shift. See also 1.1.2n.
is entered into has committed himself to
66 **gay apparel** splendid clothing
'gainst in preparation for, in expectation of
triumph day Cf. 52n.
67–8 **Bound . . . to?** York makes the cogent point that if Aumerle had borrowed money to purchase clothing (as the Duchess supposes), the document

binding his debt would be in the possession of his creditor, not of his son.
67 **bond** See 65n.
69 **Boy** The word illustrates York's anger as well as dramatizing the high value set upon filial obedience.
the writing Holinshed and Shakespeare treat this paper as though it were the actual 'indenture' binding Aumerle to his fellow conspirators; see 41–117n. Historically, the incriminating document was a letter to Aumerle from his confederates urging him to join them without further delay.
70 an alexandrine
71 another irregular line
SD F's substitution ('*Snatches it*') conveys the suddenness of York's action onstage. 'Q, which hitherto has been scanty of SDs, is from now onwards fuller than is usual in dramatic texts' (Cam¹, 222). See Appendix 1, pp. 509–10, 517.
72 For metrical roughness here, clearly dramatic, see end of 41–117n.

---

65 bond] *(*band*), F*   that he is] he's *Pope*; he is *(Craven³)*   66 'gainst] against *Q2–F*   day] *om. Q2–F*   70 I do beseech] Beseech *Capell*   71 SD] *Snatches it F*

DUCHESS OF YORK

What is the matter, my lord?

YORK [*Calls offstage.*]

Ho! Who's within there?

[*Enter* Servingman.]

Saddle my horse.

God for His mercy, what treachery is here!   75

DUCHESS OF YORK

Why, what is't, my lord?

YORK

Give me my boots, I say. Saddle my horse.

[*Exit Servingman.*]

Now, by mine honour, by my life, by my troth,

73–110 See LN.

74 SD2* The Servingman is presumably the character who enters with information about Aumerle and news of the Duchess of Gloucester's death at 2.2.85.1. His 'comic business' as he halts between York's repeated call for his boots at 84 and 87 and his wife's attempt to prevent the order from being obeyed at 85–6 'is very welcome to the audience at this point, and the more of it that can be sustained by the servant without his rendering his master ludicrous, the more useful he is to the actor of York, whose part disintegrates if its occasional absurdity is over-exploited. One wonders whether the original actor in this role achieved such a good comic effect that Shakespeare gave him the chance to repeat it in the first part of *Henry the Fourth* when the drawer, Francis, "stands amazed, not knowing which way to go" (2.4.79)' (Mahood, *Parts*, 4–5). Many editors add no entrance

and exit for the servant at 74 and 77, apparently interpreting the comedy as deriving in part from York's frustrated and impatient calls offstage to an unresponsive servant who delays his appearance until 84. Either staging is possible.

75 **God . . . mercy** See 2.2.98n.

77 **boots** These would be long leather boots to protect the calves and thighs in riding – onstage often typifying a traveller. They usually required assistance to put on.

78–9 **Now . . . villain!** See LN.

78 **by my . . . troth** Q's double repetition of *by* (omitted by Q2–F; see t.n.) is probably correct, although one of them adds an extra-metrical syllable, which Pope characteristically removed. Q's compositor may have mistakenly interpolated the third *by*, but, as noted in 41–117n., metrical irregularities are characteristic of this context.

troth faith to God and man

---

73 What is] What's *F*   74 SD1] *Mowat & Werstine (subst.)*   Who's] *F*; who is *Q*   SD2] *Capell (subst.)*   75 God] Heauen *F*   76 is't] *F*; is it *Q*   77 SD] *Capell (subst.)*   78 mine] my *F*   by my . . . troth] my life, my troth *Q2–F*; by my life, my troth *Pope*

I will appeach the villain!

DUCHESS OF YORK   What is the matter?

YORK

Peace, foolish woman!   80

DUCHESS OF YORK

I will not peace. What is the matter, Aumerle?

AUMERLE

Good mother, be content. It is no more

Than my poor life must answer.

DUCHESS OF YORK   Thy life answer?

YORK [*to Servingman offstage*]

Bring me my boots! I will unto the King.

His Servingman *enters with his boots.*

DUCHESS OF YORK

Strike him, Aumerle! Poor boy, thou art amazed.   85

[*to Servingman*]

Hence, villain! Never more come in my sight!

---

79 **appeach** denounce, inform against (an alternative form of 'peach'); cf. 102. 'York's vehemence against his son may be explained partly by the fact that he has entered into surety for Aumerle's loyalty (lines 44–5). Aumerle has thus let him down personally, as well as endangered him' (Wells, 255).
  What is perhaps elided ('What's')
80 **Peace** either an exclamation ('Silence'; see *OED sb.* 6a) or a verb in the imperative (*OED v.* 2); the distinction is purely technical since neither choice could be heard in oral delivery.
81 **peace** 'hold my peace'. If York's *Peace* is a noun (see 80n.), the Duchess turns it into a verb; otherwise she merely repeats his use. Cf. *KL* 4.6.102. Cf. also York's similar trick with *Grace* at 2.3.87 (see n.).
  Aumerle F's 'Sonne' may be a metrical adjustment, but otherwise seems to carry no particular authority (see

Appendix 1, pp. 513–14, 529), even though it agrees with the Duchess's earlier address at 46 (*Welcome, my son*); clinging to his old status (see 41–3n.), she calls him *Aumerle* again at 85 and 111 (cf. her similar attitude to Richard; see 6n.).
82 **be content** calm down
83 **answer** pay the price for, answer for
85 **him** the Servingman. In her desperation, the Duchess instructs Aumerle to strike the servant so as to prevent him from helping York put on his boots or otherwise prepare to leave for Windsor. Aumerle, however, is too dazed or stunned (*amazed*) to act.
86–7 The Servingman obviously obeys York rather than his wife, not leaving the stage until he has assisted his master with the boots (see 77). A brief hesitation after 86, however, would enhance the comic effect of this moment. Zitner

81 Aumerle] Sonne *F*   84 SD] *this edn*   84.1] *His man enters with his bootes. Q; Enter Seruant with Boots. F, after 83*   Servingman] *this edn; man Q; Seruant F*   86 SD] *Pope (subst.)*

YORK

Give me my boots, I say.

[*Servingman helps York put on his boots, then exit.*]

DUCHESS OF YORK

Why, York, what wilt thou do?

Wilt thou not hide the trespass of thine own?

Have we more sons? Or are we like to have?   90

Is not my teeming date drunk up with time?

And wilt thou pluck my fair son from mine age

And rob me of a happy mother's name?

Is he not like thee? Is he not thine own?

YORK

Thou fond madwoman,   95

Wilt thou conceal this dark conspiracy?

A dozen of them here have ta'en the sacrament

(247) thinks that York puts his boots on somewhere 'between lines 85 and 110', perhaps 'without the servant's aid'. *Away, fond woman!* (101) could be a response to the Duchess blocking York's attempted exit (implying that by then he has his boots on); but it could equally well relate to her continuing attempt to prevent him putting on the boots.

87 SD *exit* The Servingman could exit at any convenient point before York's own exit at 110 or possibly with him to help him to his horse. Since QF provide no exit for the Servingman, some editors suppose that he should indeed remain onstage until 110 'as a bewildered, perhaps amused, observer of the quarrel between his master and mistress' (Wells, 255). This edition follows Kittredge (in having him exit whenever York has his boots on) and also Wilson (in having him help York get into them). Capell first added the early exit, but made it coincide with the Duchess's *Hence, villain!* at 86, thus leaving York still bootless in the following line; see 86–7n.

90 **Have . . . sons?** Shakespeare omits to mention York's younger son Richard, who was created Earl of Cambridge in 1414. In *H5* Cambridge appears among the Yorkist traitors beheaded for treason, while Aumerle has become the staunchly Lancastrian Duke of York, but Shakespeare never mentions their kinship. See 5.3.144n.
like likely
91 **teeming date** time for bearing children (*date* = period, season)
drunk up exhausted, used up
92 **mine age** me in my old age; cf. 5.3.89, *old dugs*.
95 **fond** foolish
97 **A dozen** an apparent exaggeration; Holinshed (3.514) mentions only nine conspirators (see 41–117n.). *Traïson* (77/229) says that eleven persons were present when the plot was hatched.
here indicating the document. Irving added a SD directing the actor to strike the paper with his hand (see Black, 305).
ta'en the sacrament See 4.1.328n.; *ta'en* is pronounced 'tane'.

87 SD *Servingman . . . boots*] *Cam¹ (subst.)*   *then exit*] *Kittredge (subst.)*   89 thou not] *QF*; not thou *Q2*   94 thee] *(the), Q2–F*

And interchangeably set down their hands
To kill the King at Oxford.

DUCHESS OF YORK   He shall be none;
We'll keep him here. Then what is that to him?   100

YORK

Away, fond woman! Were he twenty times my son,
I would appeach him.

DUCHESS OF YORK   Hadst thou groaned for him
As I have done, thou wouldest be more pitiful.
But now I know thy mind. Thou dost suspect
That I have been disloyal to thy bed,   105
And that he is a bastard, not thy son.
Sweet York, sweet husband, be not of that mind.
He is as like thee as a man may be,
Not like to me, or any of my kin,   109
And yet I love him.

98 **interchangeably . . . hands** i.e. the conspirators signed the *bond* reciprocally (cf. 1.1.146), each having a record of the oath sworn by the others; Holinshed speaks of 'an indenture sextipartite' (see 41–117n., 97n.). Cf. also *1H4* 3.1.79–80: 'And our indentures tripartite are drawn, / Which being sealed interchangeably'.

99 **Oxford** See 52n.
  shall be none shall not be one of them

100 **what . . . him** 'How does what they do concern him?' Verity (192) takes *that* to refer simply to the *bond*, which is also possible and which Black (306) believes to be 'more actable'.

101 another alexandrine, unless we consider *Away* an extra-metrical interjection; cf. the analogous *Away* in 117, and see Abbott, 512. Ure (158), pointing to 'similar phrases' (*Thou fond madwoman*, 95; *Make way, unruly woman*, 110) suspects 'memorial corruption', but metrical irregularities seem to be part of the style at this point; see 41–117n.

fond Cf. 95n.

102 **appeach** Cf. 79n.
  groaned for him experienced the pangs of giving birth to him; cf. *AW* 1.3.147, 4.5.11.

103 *a pentameter with trochaic third foot and weak double ending. An alternative and perhaps preferable pentameter may be achieved by contracting Q's 'thou wouldst' to a monosyllable ('thou'dst'), which is Ure's solution (158). Webster and Dekker may have travestied the line in *Westward Ho* (1604), 3.3.64–5: 'I, I, I, if you had groand fort as I haue done you wold haue bin more natural' (Dekker, 2.355).
  pitiful compassionate, full of pity

109 This comment may suggest Shakespeare's underlying awareness that the Duchess was in fact Aumerle's much younger stepmother; see headnote and List of Roles, 5n. But it is clear that he chose for dramatic reasons to portray her as past child-bearing (see 90–3, 5.3.89). See LN.

98 their] *(there)*, *Q2–F* 99–100 He . . . him?] *as F*; *Q lines* heere, / him? / 101–2 Away . . . him] *prose F* 102–3 Hadst . . . pitiful *as Rowe³*; *QF line* done, / pittifull. / 103 wouldest] *F*; wouldst *Q* 108 a man] *Qc, F*; any man *Qu* 109 to me] *QF*; me *Q2* or any] *Qc*; or a *Qu*; nor any *F*

YORK   Make way, unruly woman.   *Exit.*
DUCHESS OF YORK
After, Aumerle! Mount thee upon his horse!
Spur, post, and get before him to the King
And beg thy pardon ere he do accuse thee.
I'll not be long behind. Though I be old,
I doubt not but to ride as fast as York.   115
And never will I rise up from the ground
Till Bolingbroke have pardoned thee. Away, be gone!
                                                        ᶠ*Exeunt.*ᶠ

[5.3]   *Enter* ᶠBolingbroke,ᶠ [*as*] KING [HENRY,] *with*
         [HARRY] ᶠPERCY *and other Lords*ᶠ.

111 **After** go after him
  Mount . . . horse! York has left by this
  point. Apparently the Duchess tells
  Aumerle to overtake his father and
  mount the already saddled horse (Ard²,
  159). Holinshed (3.515) and Hall (fol.
  xiii) refer to Aumerle's own steed (see
  41–117n.).
112 **Spur, post** 'Urge forward (your
  horse), make haste.' 'The Duchess's
  vigor of speech, as well as the Q1
  pointing, suggests that we should take
  post as a verb rather than as an adverb'
  (Black, 307). Many editors, however,
  prefer F's removal of the comma:
  'Spurre post' ('Spur post haste, ride as
  fast as possible'), which may be correct. 'Post' was common as both verb
  and adverb, but Shakespeare conceivably recalled Holinshed's phrase, 'in
  post', or Hall's 'riding in post', meaning that Aumerle arrived at Windsor
  before his father by galloping with
  relays of post-horses, 'whiche his
  father being an olde man could not do'
  (Hall; see 41–117LN).
113 **thy pardon** pardon for yourself

114–15 Shakespeare invents the
  Duchess's prediction that she can ride
  as rapidly as her husband, but a hint for
  it could have come from Hall's contrast
  between Aumerle's youthfully fast riding and his father's slower pace owing
  to old age; see 112n., also 2.2.74n.
116–17 *****And . . . thee**. In 5.3 the
  Duchess proves as good as her word.
117 **Bolingbroke** Like her husband, the
  Duchess seems to avoid the new king's
  title; cf. 6n., 39–40n.
5.3 This scene presents Bolingbroke for the
  first time in the play as a crowned
  monarch; his SP therefore now changes
  to 'King Henry'. (For further discussion
  of SPs, see Introduction, pp. 168, and
  Appendix 1, pp. 510–12.) The opening
  conversation concerning Prince Hal's
  youthful high jinks and dissolute behaviour (1–22), which balances Aumerle's
  unfilial offence, is based on tradition
  going back almost to the Prince's own
  time. Shakespeare's sources could have
  included Elyot, fols 122–3ᵛ, Stow, 547,
  and *Famous Victories*, as well as Hall,
  Fabyan and Holinshed. Humphreys

112 Spur, post] Spurre post *F*   114 behind.] *F (* behind:*)*; behind, *Q*   116 And] *Q2–F*; An *Q*
117 SD] *F (Exit), Rowe*
5.3] *F (Scoena Tertia.)   0.1–2] Enter the King with his nobles. Q; Enter Bullingbrooke, Percie, and
other Lords. F   0.1 HENRY] Kittredge   0.2 HARRY] Oxf*

KING HENRY

Can no man tell me of my unthrifty son?
'Tis full three months since I did see him last.
If any plague hang over us, 'tis he.
I would to God, my lords, he might be found.

(xxvi–xxxvi) discusses the background of the Prince's wildness. Holinshed (3.543) contains enough of the tradition to have suggested the entire passage in *R2*: 'But this king [the newly crowned Henry V] . . . determined to put on him the shape of a new man. For whereas aforetime he had made himselfe a companion vnto misrulie mates of dissolute order and life, he now banished them all from his presence . . . calling to mind how once to hie offense of the king his father, he had with his fist striken the cheefe iustice for sending one of his minions (vpon desert) to prison, when the iustice stoutlie commanded himselfe also streict to ward, & he (then prince) obeied.' Prince Hal's offstage presence together with his father's disappointment and worry about him suggests that Shakespeare was already thinking ahead to *1H4* and perhaps beyond.

The main body of the scene (23–145) continues and concludes the story of Aumerle's involvement in the Abbot of Westminster's conspiracy (begun in the previous scene) and is based chiefly on Holinshed, although, as in 5.2, there is a remote possibility that Hall might also have been consulted. Again the part played by the Duchess of York is wholly fictional. The location is Windsor Castle (see 5.2.41–117n.).

0.1–2 Again the throne is doubtless present (as in 4.1), but now Bolingbroke is unambiguously king and can take his place in the royal chair, probably wearing his crown, although Q is silent about his posture. No fanfare is specified in either Q or F although such would be appropriate and could have been used in the theatre; cf. F's '*Flourish*' for the analogous

entrance at 5.6.0.1. In Woodman's production, Paul Shenar, playing Henry, sat in the royal chair without a crown, wearing it for the first time only in the final scene after Richard's death (5.6).

1 Q has eleven syllables; F, probably trying to smooth the metre, deleted *me* (see t.n.).
   unthrifty prodigal, dissolute, profligate (cf. 2.3.122n.); may allude to the biblical parable of the prodigal son, in which case Shakespeare's first reference to Hal adumbrates the story of the wayward youth who ultimately returns to his father's good graces (as dramatized in *1* and *2H4*). According to Holinshed (3.511), Prince Hal was only twelve years old at the time of his father's coronation in 1399, when he was created Prince of Wales. Shakespeare clearly conceives of him as some years older; but cf. 'young wanton and effeminate boy' (10). Preparing for *1H4*, the dramatist already begins unhistorically to equalize the ages of Hotspur (in fact three years older than Bolingbroke; cf. 2.3.21n., 36) and Hal.

2 **full** fully
   three months Literally, this would imply a lapse of three months since the coronation, at which Hal had to be present since he participated in the ceremony; the dramatic point here is only to stress Hal's prolonged absence from court and therefore the emotional strain between father and son.

3 **plague** Cf. Richard's prediction of *pestilence* (3.3.87) and Carlisle's prophecy of more general disaster, which Henry undoubtedly recalls (4.1.137–50).
   hang over See 1.3.284n.
   us royal plural

1 SP] *King H. Q; Bul. F*   tell me] tell *F*   4 God] heauen *F*

Enquire at London, 'mongst the taverns there,   5
For there, they say, he daily doth frequent,
With unrestrained loose companions,
Even such, they say, as stand in narrow lanes
And beat our watch and rob our passengers,
While he, young wanton and effeminate boy,   10
Takes on the point of honour to support
So dissolute a crew.

HARRY PERCY

My lord, some two days since I saw the Prince,
And told him of those triumphs held at Oxford.

---

6 **frequent** resort, visit
7 **unrestrained** unrestrainèd; undisci-
plined, licentious, lawless
loose immoral, unprincipled
companions four syllables; the term
is probably used pejoratively (cf. *2H4*
2.4.94, 123: 'swaggering companions',
'scurvy companion').
8 **Even** probably monosyllabic ('E'en')
9 **watch** night-watchmen, civic police
passengers wayfarers, travellers,
passers-by. Shakespeare develops this
part of the legend in the Gadshill rob-
bery episode of *1H4* (2.2). Reminiscences by the fourth Earl of Ormonde,
a contemporary of the Prince (Humphreys, xxx), supply the basis of this
story, but the dramatist could have
found versions of it in Stow and
Famous Victories (see headnote).
10 *****While** Many editors retain QF's
'Which' as a vulgar use of the relative
without antecedent (cf. *OED pron.*
24b), or else as meaning 'whom' or 'as
to which' (Abbott, 272); but the clum-
siness of the construction makes 'so
dissolute a crew' almost unintelligible
in performance. Pope's emendation is
justifiable if Q's compositor misread or
misremembered his copy; the

'assumed misprint is one of a common
type' (Cam[1], 225). Capell's 'Whilst' is
also possible.
young wanton spoiled child, prodigal
youth (*wanton* is probably a noun); cf.
3.3.164.
effeminate self-indulgent, volup-
tuous; frivolous, capricious (probably
trisyllabic: 'effem'nate'). Cf. Daniel,
1.70, where Richard II is referred to as
'this wanton young effeminate'; also
the description of Richard with whom
Henry IV compares his son in *1H4*:
'The skipping King, he ambled up and
down, / With shallow jesters, and rash
bavin wits, / Soon kindled and soon
burnt' (3.2.60–2).
11–12 possibly an allusion to the story of
Prince Hal's confrontation with the
Chief Justice for imprisoning 'one of
his minions' (see Holinshed in headnote). Shakespeare alludes to the incident again in *1H4* 3.2.32–3, and dramatizes its aftermath in *2H4* 5.2.
11 **Takes on the** undertakes as a
14 **those** F's 'these' is another indifferent
variant; see Appendix 1, pp. 513–14,
529.
triumphs See 5.2.52n.
held appointed to be held, planned

---

9 beat . . . rob] rob . . . beate *F*   10 While] *Pope*; Which *QF*; Whilst *Capell*   wanton] wanton, *F*
11–12] *as F; one line Q*   13 SP] *Oxf; H. Percie Q; Per. F*   14 those] these *F*

KING HENRY

And what said the gallant?   15

HARRY PERCY

His answer was he would unto the stews,
And from the common'st creature pluck a glove
And wear it as a favour, and with that
He would unhorse the lustiest challenger.

KING HENRY

As dissolute as desp'rate! Yet through both   20
I see some sparks of better hope, which elder years
May happily bring forth.

Enter AUMERLE, *amazed.*

But who comes here?

15 **gallant** gallànt; fashionable young gentleman (with heavy irony)
16 **would** would go (Abbott, 405)
  stews either 'brothels' or 'the quarter of the city notorious for houses of prostitution'
17 **common'st** most promiscuous (referring to prostitutes)
18 **favour** mark of favour, love-pledge (here a lady's token worn by knights in jousts). Cf. *E2*, 2.2.185–6. Harry Percy, the Hotspur of *1H4* and a future model of chivalry, reports that Prince Hal is mocking aristocratic tradition. 'This is unlike the Prince of *Henry IV*, who possesses a sense of decency and always keeps the life of Eastcheap distinct from that of the Court' (Cam¹, 225).
  that the glove (as a talisman)
19 **lustiest** most stalwart and vigorous
20 **desp'rate** reckless
  both both traits (dissoluteness and recklessness)
20–2 **Yet . . . forth.** Cf. Holinshed's

report of the maturer Henry's becoming 'a new man' and rejecting his 'misrulie mates' (see headnote).
21 an alexandrine. Shakespeare dramatizes King Henry's agitation here and immediately after Aumerle's entrance (24) by giving him two irregularly long lines.
  sparks bright particles. Cf. also 5.6.29: *sparks of honour.*
  better hope hope of better things
  years F's 'dayes' is probably another indifferent variant; see Appendix 1, pp. 513–14, 529. Jowett (*TxC*, 312), however, speculates that 'the Q1 compositor introduced a substitution contaminated by "heere" at the end of the following line' or that Shakespeare later altered 'yeeres' to 'dayes', emending 'the prompt-book to avoid the jingle with "heere"'.
22 **happily** perhaps, by good luck, perchance ('haply'); to a happy issue, with a happy result
  SD *amazed* distraught (cf. 24 and 5.2.85)

15 SP] *King. Q; Bul. F* 16 SP] *Oxf; Per. QF* unto] *QF;* to *Q2* 20, 24 SP] *King H. Q; Bul. F*
20–4] *F lines* both, / dayes / heere? / King? / stares / wildely? / ; *Capell lines* both, / hope, / forth. / means / wildly? / ; *Ard² lines* yet / hope, / forth. / means / wildly? / ; *Cam² lines* both / hope in him / forth. / means / wildly? / 20 desp'rate] *F;* desperat *Q* Yet] But yet *Ard²* 21 sparks] *QF;* sparkles *Q2* hope] hope in him *Cam²* years] dayes *F* 22 SD] *Oxf; after* here? *QF* SD] Enter Aumerle. *F*

AUMERLE

    Where is the King?

KING HENRY

    What means our cousin that he stares and looks so
      wildly?

AUMERLE

    God save your grace! I do beseech your majesty   25
    To have some conference with your grace alone.

KING HENRY [*to Lords*]

    Withdraw yourselves, and leave us here alone.

               [*Exeunt all but King Henry and Aumerle.*]
    What is the matter with our cousin now?

AUMERLE

    For ever may my knees grow to the earth,   [*Kneels.*]

23–145 based chiefly on Holinshed (3.515), continuing the account cited in 5.2.41–117n.: 'when he [Aumerle] was alighted at the castell gate, he caused the gates to be shut, saieng that he must needs deliuer the keies to the king. When he came before the kings presence, he kneeled downe on his knees, beseeching him of mercie and forgiuenesse, and declaring the whole matter vnto him in order as euerie thing had passed, obtained pardon. Therewith came his father, and being let in, deliuered the indenture which he had taken from his sonne, vnto the king, who thereby perceiuing his sonnes words to be true, changed his purpose for his going to Oxenford, and dispatched messengers foorth to signifie vnto the earle of Northumberland his high constable, and to the earle of Westmerland his high marshall, and to other his assured freends, of all the doubtfull danger and perilous ieopardie.' Hall (fol. xxxi), although somewhat fuller than Holinshed, adds

nothing that Shakespeare could have used except the detail of York's knocking at the gate (see 37n.); but for this Shakespeare would need no source (cf. the knocking in such plays as *RJ*, *1H4*, *MM*, *Oth* and *Mac*). After the plot to assassinate Henry IV had failed, the conspirators rebelled openly; the earls of Huntingdon and Kent were trapped at Cirencester, and most of the others were also hunted down and beheaded.

24 another alexandrine (cf. 21n.); or possibly an irregular pentameter in which the stresses of the first three feet fall on *means*, *còusin* and *stares*

24, 28 **cousin** used precisely, since Aumerle and Henry IV were first cousins

25 **majesty** probably dissyllablic ('maj'sty')

26 **conference** conversation; dissyllabic ('conf'rence')

29 Cf. 92, 105 and 5.2.116; also *King Leir* (1594), where Cordella kneels to her father (sc. 24.228): 'But I will never rise from off my knee'. Aumerle probably continues to kneel until 37.
grow be fixed

27+ SP] *King. Q; Bul. F*   27 SD1] *Oxf*   SD2] *Capell (subst.)*   29 SD] *Rowe*

My tongue cleave to the roof within my mouth,　　　30
Unless a pardon ere I rise or speak.

KING HENRY

Intended or committed was this fault?
If on the first, how heinous e'er it be,
To win thy after-love I pardon thee.

AUMERLE

Then give me leave that I may turn the key,　　　35
That no man enter till my tale be done.

KING HENRY

Have thy desire.　　*[Aumerle locks the door.]*
　　The Duke of York knocks at the door and crieth.

YORK ᶠ(*within*)ᶠ

My liege, beware! Look to thyself!
Thou hast a traitor in thy presence there.

KING HENRY *[to Aumerle]*

Villain, I'll make thee safe.　　*[Draws his sword.]*　　40

AUMERLE

Stay thy revengeful hand. Thou hast no cause to fear.

---

30 Cf. Psalms, 137.6: 'If I doe not remember thee, let my tongue cleaue to the
roofe of my mouth'.
　*the roof QF's 'my rooffe' undoubted-
ly resulted from a mis-setting by Q's
compositor, influenced by *my* later in
the line (see Craven³, 48–9). Apart from
the idiomatic awkwardness, the biblical
echo (see previous n.) is too familiar to
make an intentional 'my rooffe' credible. See Appendix 1, p. 538.
31 **Unless a pardon** elliptical: either
'unless you grant, or I have, a pardon'
or 'unless a pardon be granted'. The
compressed idiom suits Aumerle's
'breathlessness' (Cam², 161).
33 **If . . . first** if the former (the *intended*
as opposed to the *committed* act)
　how heinous e'er however heinous

34 **after-love** future loyalty
35 **turn the key** Cf. Holinshed: 'he
caused the gates to be shut' (see
23–145n.).
37–8 These irregularly short lines (a
dimeter followed by a tetrameter) fit
the excited nature of the speeches at
this point. See also the tetrameter at 45.
37 SD2 *knocks . . . door* perhaps suggested by Hall (fol. xiii): 'While the kyng
and the duke talked together, the duke
of Yorke knocked at the castel gate';
see 23–145n.
40–1 two more irregular lines (a trimeter
followed by an alexandrine); see 37–8n.
40 **safe** harmless (by running him
through with his sword); cf. *Mac*
3.4.24: 'But Banquo's safe?'
41 **revengeful** avenging

---

30 the roof] *Dyce² (Lettsom)*; my rooffe *QF*　34 after-love] *F2*; after loue *QF*　35 I may] *Q2–F*;
May *Q*　37 SD1 *Aumerle . . . door.*] *Capell (subst.)*　SD2 *The Duke . . . crieth.*] *om. F*　38 SD] *F*
(Yorke within.), opp. 37　40 SD1] *Oxf*　SD2] *Johnson¹ (subst.)*

447

YORK [*within*]

Open the door, secure, foolhardy King!
Shall I for love speak treason to thy face?
Open the door, or I will break it open.
[*King Henry unlocks the door.*]

^F*Enter* YORK.^F

KING HENRY

What is the matter, uncle? Speak!   45
Recover breath. Tell us how near is danger,
That we may arm us to encounter it.

YORK

Peruse this writing here, and thou shalt know
The treason that my haste forbids me show.
[*Presents the paper.*]

AUMERLE [*to King Henry*]

Remember, as thou read'st, thy promise passed.   50

---

42 **secure** unsuspecting, overconfident, heedless; cf. 2.1.266n.
*foolhardy Q's 'foole, hardie' shows the not uncommon use of a comma substituting for a hyphen.

43 **Shall . . . treason** 'Must I out of love and loyalty speak treasonably (use such disrespectful language)?'

44.1 Departing from Holinshed (see 23–145n.), Shakespeare heightens the dramatic excitement and suspense by having York enter to expose his son's intended treason before Aumerle has had an opportunity to reveal the plot himself.

46–7 **us . . . us** royal plural

48 **this writing** the indenture seized from Aumerle's *bosom* (5.2.71 SD); see 5.2.69n.

49 **treason** Setting from Q3, F's compositor may have omitted the *t* (a broken

letter in some copies of Q3), mistakenly believing that he was correcting 'rrea-son' and thus producing 'reason'; but 'reason' makes some sense and could possibly be a deliberate F substitution (cf. 14n., 21n.).
haste forbids me because he is out of breath from riding so fast (*forbids* = prevents)
show showing (Abbott, 349)

50 ***passed** just given (at 34). Dyce's apparent emendation is probably only a normalization of QF's spelling ('past') for the past participle of 'pass' (see *OED v.* 48a, *a.* 2). Although a few editors retain the original spelling, taking 'past' as an adjective ('made in the past'), Dyce's interpretation of the grammar seems more natural and idiomatic.

---

42 SD] *Capell*   foolhardy] *Hudson;* foole-hardy *F;* foole, hardie *Q*   44 SD] *Malone (subst.)*   45–6]
as Johnson¹; QF line breath, / daunger, /   49 treason] reason *F*   SD] *Oxf (subst.)*   50 SD] *Mowat & Werstine (subst.)*   passed] *Dyce;* past *QF*

I do repent me. Read not my name there;
My heart is not confederate with my hand.

YORK [*to Aumerle*]

It was, villain, ere thy hand did set it down.
I tore it from the traitor's bosom, King.
Fear, and not love, begets his penitence.   55
Forget to pity him, lest pity prove
A serpent that will sting thee to the heart.

KING HENRY

O heinous, strong and bold conspiracy!
O loyal father of a treacherous son!

---

51 **repent me** For the common use of the reflexive, see Abbott, 296.
52 proverbial overtones; possibly a variation on (and reversal of) 'What the heart thinks the tongue speaks' (Dent, H333). Cf. also 'With heart and hand' (Dent, H339).
confederate a fellow conspirator; three syllables ('confed'rate')
hand signature, handwriting
53 rough pentameter, with anapaestic second foot ('villain, ère')
it Aumerle's signature on his part of the indenture
54 Cf. 5.2.56n., 71 SD.
56 **Forget to pity** 'forget your promise to forgive'; cf. *3H6* 2.6.74: 'Thou pitiedst Rutland, I will pity thee.'
*lest pity Craven's conjecture for QF's 'lest thy pittie' improves both the metre and the force of York's line. As Craven points out, 'the word *thy* occurs eleven times' on the quarto page (sig. I2), e.g. at 37, 39, 50, 64, so that the pronoun 'thy' 'may have intruded' into the compositor's memory on 'the mistaken assumption that a phrase parallel to *his penitence* [55] was required' (Craven³, 56). Jowett (*TxC*, 312) suggests that the interpolation could have resulted from contamination by 'thee' (directly below 'thy') in 57.
57 **serpent . . . heart** Cf. 3.2.131LN; the

repetition of 'Richard's image about traitors' gives 'point to the Aumerle plot as a parody of the question of loyalty' (Cam², 162). The issue of Aumerle's loyalty is complex; in attempting to be loyal to Richard he becomes a traitor to Henry IV, and, when exposed in treachery, then allows his duty to his father to take precedence over his sworn loyalty to his fellow conspirators whose lives now become forfeit.
58–65 Henry's emotional outburst at this point has seemed out of character to some critics and actors since he is usually so self-possessed and tightly controlled in stressful situations. It has been suggested that he may feign greater excitement than he feels so as to draw York out and thereby test the sincerity of his motive in condemning his own son; cf. the Duchess's comment at 87 and n.
58 **strong** flagrant (an obsolete sense applied to crimes; see *OED a.* 11e); dangerous; determined
59 For a similar juxtaposition, see Mowbray's words about the relationship between Gaunt and Bolingbroke at 1.1.136: 'The honourable father to my foe'.
treacherous probably dissyllabic ('treach'rous')

---

53 SD] *this edn*   56 lest] *this edn (Craven³); lest thy QF*

Thou sheer, immaculate and silver fountain   60
From whence this stream through muddy passages
Hath held his current and defiled himself!
Thy overflow of good converts to bad,
And thy abundant goodness shall excuse
This deadly blot in thy digressing son.   65

YORK

So shall my virtue be his vice's bawd,
And he shall spend mine honour with his shame,
As thriftless sons their scraping fathers' gold.
Mine honour lives when his dishonour dies,
Or my shamed life in his dishonour lies.   70

60–2 The metaphor is that of a pure source (York) from which *this stream* (Aumerle) is later contaminated; cf. *TS* 5.2.142–3: 'like a fountain troubled, / Muddy'. Cf. also Lyly, *Euphues*: 'as the water that springeth from the fountaines head and floweth into the filthye channell is not to be called cleere bicause it came of the same streame: so neyther is he that discendeth of noble parentage, if he desist from noble deedes, to be esteemed a gentleman in that he issued from the loynes of a noble sire, for that he obscureth the parentes he came off, and discrediteth his owne estate' (1.317).
60 **sheer** pure, clear; cf. *FQ*, 3.2.44: 'a fountaine shere'.
fountain spring
62 **held his current** taken its course
himself itself (but including also the personal reference to Aumerle)
63 **overflow** excess; continuing the *fountain* imagery from 60
converts changes (i.e. in Aumerle)
64 **excuse** be warrant for excusing, compensate for
65 **deadly blot** 'damnable and death-dealing sin', possibly quibbling on *blot*

('ink signature') on the indenture. The phrase contributes to the succession of stain images in the play; see 2.1.63–4n.
digressing wayward, transgressing, deviating from virtue (as the *stream* wanders from the purity of its source)
66–72 Lothian remarks, 'York is clearly prompted by self-interest in this unnatural degree of loyalty to his new master' (173); but York's reaction can also be interpreted simply as devotion to good order and obedience to the crowned king.
66 **be . . . bawd** serve as pander to his wickedness
67 ***And** The meaning is ambiguous since *And* could represent either the conjunction or 'an' (= if). Nearly all editors accept *And* here as a conjunction. However, *And* (= if) also makes sense. See 4.1.50n.
68 'in the same way that prodigal (*thriftless*) sons (spend) the gold of their saving (*scraping*) fathers'; cf. 1 (*unthrifty son*) and n.
69–72 See LN.
69 **lives** revives, comes to life
dishonour dies i.e. on the block
70 **in . . . lies** depends on his dishonour

62 held] hald *Q3;* had *F*   67 And] *Q2–F;* An *Q*

Thou kill'st me in his life: giving him breath,
The traitor lives, the true man's put to death.

DUCHESS OF YORK ^F(*within*)^F

What ho, my liege! For God's sake, let me in!

KING HENRY

What shrill-voiced suppliant makes this eager cry?

DUCHESS OF YORK [*within*]

A woman, and thy aunt. Great King, 'tis I.   75
Speak with me, pity me, open the door!
A beggar begs that never begged before.

KING HENRY

Our scene is altered from a serious thing,
And now changed to 'The Beggar and the King'. –

---

71 **in his life** by allowing him to live
giving him breath in (your) sparing
him (Abbott, 372). York repeats himself
– possibly a way of characterizing his age.
74 ***shrill-voiced** Q3's unauthoritative
correction is clearly right. Probably
Q's compositor misread 'voicd' for
'voice' – a common confusion of terminal *d* and *e* in secretary hand.
eager sharp; impetuous, vehement
76 The Duchess's cry, although decasyllabic, is radically irregular – appropriately so in view of her extreme pertur-
bation. The line may be scanned as a
rough tetrameter, the stresses falling
on *Speak*, *pity*, *òpen* and *door*.
77 The effect of the contrived repetitions
(*beggar*, *begs*, *begged*) is comic.
78–81 King Henry's amused response to
the quasi-farcical situation of having to
admit three competing visitors
(Aumerle, York and his Duchess) in
rapid succession occasions his rhymes.
Then the rhyming continues until 135,
which, together with the kneeling of
each of the suppliants at various points,
produces an undeniable shift towards

comedy – a continuation of the vein
that began with the business of York's
boots in the preceding scene. 5.2 and
5.3 are often cut in productions, but, as
RP points out, King Henry's balance
and ability to be amused contrast
favourably with Richard's treatment of
similar issues in Act 1. See LN; also
Introduction, pp. 41–3.
78 **Our scene** 'our little drama here'
79 **The . . . King** probably a reference to
the popular ballad of King Cophetua
and the Beggar Maid, referred to also in
2H4 5.3.102, *RJ* 2.1.14 and *LLL*
1.2.109–14, 4.1.64–6. As John (99)
points out, it is merely the title, not the
content, of the ballad that brings the
allusion to Henry's mind. Richard
Johnson included such a ballad ('A Song
of a Beggar and a King') in his *Crown
Garland of Golden Roses* (1612), reprinted in Percy's *Reliques* (series 1, book II,
6). Samuel Johnson (1.451) suggested,
not unreasonably, that 'an interlude well
known in the time of our authour' may
also have existed, though he could find
no copy of it. See David, 66–7.

---

71 life: giving] *F (*life, giuing)*; life giuing *Q*   73 SD] *F (Dutchesse within.), after* 72   God's]
heauens *F*   74 SP] *King H. Q; Bul. F*   shrill-voiced] *Q3 (*shrill voic'd*), F (*shrill-voic'd*); shril voice
Q   75 SD] *Capell*   thy] thine *F*   aunt. Great] *this edn;* aunt (great *QF*   King,] *(*king*))*   I.] *F;* I, *Q*
78 SP] *King Q; Bul. F*

451

My dangerous cousin, let your mother in.   80
I know she's come to pray for your foul sin.
[*Aumerle opens the door.*]

^F*Enter* DUCHESS [OF YORK].^F

YORK [*to King Henry*]
If thou do pardon whosoever pray,
More sins for this forgiveness prosper may.
This festered joint cut off, the rest rest sound;
This let alone will all the rest confound.   85

DUCHESS OF YORK
O King, believe not this hard-hearted man.
Love loving not itself none other can.

YORK
Thou frantic woman, what dost thou make here?
Shall thy old dugs once more a traitor rear?

80 **dangerous** probably dissyllabic ('dang'rous')

82–7 Both York and his wife seem to be mouthing familiar *sententiae* or drawing upon proverbial wisdom. For a similar opposition between the claims of strict justice and pity, see *MM* 2.2.99–104.

82 **whosoever pray** anyone who begs for pardon (subjunctive); F's insertion of a comma after *pardon* changes the syntax, making *whosoever pray* a subordinate clause ('no matter who prays') rather than the direct object of *pardon*. Either interpretation makes sense.

83 **More sins** i.e. future attempts upon the King's life ('which might succeed' (*prosper*))
   for because of

84 perhaps an echo of Matthew, 18.8, applied to the body politic: 'If then thy hande or thy foote offende thee, cut them off, and cast them from thee: it is better for thee to enter into life halt or maimed, rather then thou shouldest, hauing two hands or two feete, be cast into the euerlasting fire'; see also Matthew, 5.30, and Mark, 9.43.
   festered joint infected limb
   cut off being cut off
   rest rest rest (of the body politic) remain. Cf. 77n. and 119n.; see also 2.3.87n.

85 **let alone** left untreated
   confound destroy (or perhaps 'infect, corrupt')

87 i.e. if York cannot love his own child, he cannot love anyone else (including his sovereign); cf. 43 where he makes *love* of Henry his motive for speaking bluntly.

88 **frantic** deranged, hysterical
   make do

89 'Shall your old breasts (*dugs*) once more suckle a traitor?' York suggests scornfully that his wife's intercession on behalf of Aumerle is equivalent to her nourishing the treason of her grown son as she once fed him when he was still an infant; he puns on *rear* in the double sense of 'raise a child' and 'raise a traitor to life'. See also 5.2.92n.

81 she's] *F;* she is *Q* SD] *Collier* 81.1] *Wells (subst.); after* 85 *F* 82 SD] *this edn* pardon whosoever] pardon, whosoeuer *F* 84 rest rest] rest rests *F*

DUCHESS OF YORK
Sweet York, be patient.   [*Kneels.*]
                                Hear me, gentle liege.   90
KING HENRY
Rise up, good aunt!
DUCHESS OF YORK   Not yet, I thee beseech.
For ever will I walk upon my knees
And never see day that the happy sees
Till thou give joy, until thou bid me joy,
By pardoning Rutland, my transgressing boy.   95
AUMERLE
Unto my mother's prayers I bend my knee.   [*Kneels.*]
YORK
Against them both my true joints bended be.   [*Kneels.*]
Ill mayst thou thrive if thou grant any grace.
DUCHESS OF YORK
Pleads he in earnest? Look upon his face.
His eyes do drop no tears; his prayers are in jest;   100
His words come from his mouth, ours from our breast.

90 **patient** calm, quiet
92 **walk . . . knees** a traditional act of penance, possibly alluding to the famous Scala Sancta near the papal church of St John Lateran in Rome which penitents ascended on their knees; see LN. Wilson (227) compares Shakespeare's contribution to *Sir Thomas More* (Addition II, sc. vi, ll. 233–4), where More urges the rebels: 'and your vnreuerent knees / make them your feet to kneele to be forgyven' (*STM* 77).
93 **happy** happy person
94 **joy** first used as noun (give me joy), then verb (rejoice); see also 2.3.87n.
95 **pardoning** dissyllabic ('pard'ning')
96 **Unto** in support of (Abbott, 190) **prayers** usually, as here, monosyllabic; but metre of 100 and 109 suggests dissyllabic pronunciation (see also 100n.).

97 **true** loyal
98 F's omission of this line, necessary to the rhyme scheme, is probably accidental; see Pollard, 95. Or could 'Ill mayst thou thrive', addressed to a newly crowned usurper, have been considered so politically inept as to cause an actor (or censor) to cut the line deliberately? **grace** mercy
99 **he** York
100 yet another alexandrine if *prayers* is pronounced dissyllabically (see 96n.); but Capell's omission of *in* (see t.n.) yields smoother rhythm, although at the cost of strained sense. Possibly Q's compositor mistakenly set 'in iest', affected by *in earnest*, 99. **drop** shed
101 **breast** heart

90 SD] *Rowe*   91, 128 SP] *King H Q; Bul. F*   92 walk] kneele *F*   96 SD] *Rowe*   97 SD] *Rowe*
98] *om. F*   100 are in] are *Capell*   101 words come] *QF;* words do come *Q2*

He prays but faintly and would be denied;
We pray with heart and soul and all beside.
His weary joints would gladly rise, I know;
Our knees still kneel till to the ground they grow.   105
His prayers are full of false hypocrisy;
Ours of true zeal and deep integrity.
Our prayers do outpray his; then let them have
That mercy which true prayer ought to have.

KING HENRY
Good aunt, stand up.

DUCHESS OF YORK   Nay, do not say 'Stand up'.   110
Say 'Pardon' first, and afterwards 'Stand up'.
An if I were thy nurse, thy tongue to teach,
'Pardon' should be the first word of thy speech.
I never longed to hear a word till now.
Say 'Pardon', King; let pity teach thee how.   115
The word is short, but not so short as sweet;
No word like 'Pardon' for kings' mouths so meet.

---

102 **faintly** feebly
would be would like to be
103 **with . . . soul** Cf. Deuteronomy, 4.29: 'seeke [God] with all thy heart, and with all thy soule'.
105 **still** perpetually. F's emendation ('shall') may be correct; Jowett (*TxC*, 313) suggests that Q's *still* was 'perhaps contaminated' by *till* in the same line.
109 **true** sincere, heartfelt
have This second *have*, rhyming with the same word in the line above, could be a mistake on the part of Q's compositor. Wilson (227) thinks that he set the second *have* 'in place of a word, such as "crave" [W.S. Walker's conjecture], that rhymes with it'. But Shakespeare deliberately rhymes on the same word ('ring') in *MV* 5.1.193–7, 199–202; cf. also the repetition of *Stand up* in the following couplet (110–11).
110 SP1 *Q2's correction is obviously

necessary. York could hardly address his own wife as *aunt*, but the King does so at 91 and 128.
112 *An if Considering the context here, Theobald's interpretation seems to make the likelier sense, but 'And' as conjunction is also possible; see 4.1.50n.
nurse . . . teach Cf. 1.3.170n.
114 **longed** perhaps referring to a woman's longings during pregnancy (Cam[1], 227); cf. *TC* 3.3.237. But the Duchess is long past child-bearing (cf. 89, also 5.2.90–2).
a word such a word
116 **short as sweet** proverbial (Dent, S396: 'short and sweet')
117 a proverbial idea (Dent, M898); cf. *E3* 5.1.41–2, *MV* 4.1.188–95, *MM* 2.2.59–63. Chambers (149) notes that the 'delicate flattery of the new king is very clever'.
meet proper, fitting, appropriate

---

105 still] shall *F*   109 prayer] prayers *F*   have] crave *(Walker)*   110 SP1] *Q2 (King); Bul. F; yorke Q*   111 Say] But *F*   112 An if] *Theobald;* And if *QF*

YORK

Speak it in French, King; say '*Pardonne-moi*'.

DUCHESS OF YORK [*to York*]

Dost thou teach Pardon pardon to destroy?

Ah, my sour husband, my hard-hearted lord,   120

That sets the word itself against the word!

[*to King Henry*]

Speak 'Pardon' as 'tis current in our land;

The chopping French we do not understand.

Thine eye begins to speak, set thy tongue there;

Or in thy piteous heart plant thou thine ear,   125

That, hearing how our plaints and prayers do pierce,

---

118 *Pardonne-moi* 'Forgive me for refusing you' (*pardonnez-moi*), a courteous way of saying no to a request (cf. *MM* 4.2.181; also *Jew of Malta*, 4.4.45); York quippingly reverses his wife's meaning. The pronunciation of *Pardonne*, as in France, is trisyllabic, while *moi*, in anglicized pronunciation (see Q's 'moy'), rhymes with *destroy*. On the Elizabethan stage English vowel qualities would probably have been used (see Cercignani, 247–8); an actor today confronts an unhappy choice between (a) preserving the rhyme at the risk of losing the sense and (b) jettisoning the rhyme in the interest of saying what a modern audience is likely to understand (i.e. standard French pronunciation). See also LN.

119 **Pardon pardon** In addition to rhyme, repetition (e.g. 69–70) and inverted word order (e.g. 83) are distinctive features of the epigrammatic style of this section of the scene.

120 **sour** bitter

121 i.e. that makes the word *pardon* contradict itself (referring to the pun in 118; see n.)
   sets Cf. 4.1.270n.
   word . . . word perhaps punning on *word* (scripture); cf. 5.5.13–14. Those

who compared one verse from the Bible against another to spread misinterpretation or doubt were often criticized. The habit was sometimes ascribed to Puritans.

123 **chopping** probably including a mixture of senses: shifting the sense of words as in 'chop-logic' and 'chop and change' (see *OED v.* 8b); mincing, affected (Schmidt); jerky (Lothian). 'The home of Ramist rhetoric, which could be parodied as chop-logic, was in Paris' (Cam[2], 164). Cf. also Mercutio's jibe in *RJ* 2.4.31–4: 'is not this a lamentable thing . . . that we should be thus afflicted with these strange flies, these fashion-mongers, these pardon-me's, who stand so much on the new form'.

124 **speak** express tender emotion or pity
   set . . . there 'Let your tongue imitate your eye (in expressing pity).'

125 'or listen to your pitiful heart'

126 **hearing** you hearing (see Abbott, 378)
   plaints lamentations, expressions of grief
   pierce penetrate ears and heart (pronounced to rhyme with *rehearse*; see Cercignani, 79, 169). Cf. *LLL* 4.2.83–4: 'Master Person [Parson], *quasi* pers-one [Pierce-one]. And if one should be pierc'd, which is the one?'

---

118 *Pardonne-moi] Cam (*pardonne moi*); Pardonne moy *Q, F (Pardon'ne moy); Pardonnez moy *Rowe[3]*; Pardonnez-moi *Oxf* 119 SD] *Irving* Pardon] *this edn;* pardon *QF* 120 sour] *(sower), F* 122 SD] *Irving (subst.)* 125 thy piteous] *Qc, F;* this piteous *Qu*

Pity may move thee 'Pardon' to rehearse.

KING HENRY

Good aunt, stand up.

DUCHESS OF YORK   I do not sue to stand.

Pardon is all the suit I have in hand.

KING HENRY

I pardon him, as God shall pardon me.   130

DUCHESS OF YORK

O, happy vantage of a kneeling knee!

Yet am I sick for fear. Speak it again,

Twice saying 'Pardon' doth not pardon twain,

But makes one pardon strong.

KING HENRY   With all my heart

I pardon him.

DUCHESS OF YORK   A god on earth thou art!   135

[*York, Duchess of York and Aumerle rise.*]

127 **rehearse** say aloud, pronounce
128 **sue** beg for permission, petition
129 **suit** petition, request (perhaps with a pun on 'suit of cards'; cf. *hand*)
130 **as . . . me** 'as I hope God will forgive me for my sins at the day of judgement'; cf. the 'Our Father' in the *Prayer Book*: 'forgive us our trespasses, as we forgive them that trespass against us'. The phrase is conventional, but King Henry may hint at the guilt he feels for usurping the throne; cf. 5.6.45–52.
131 Since 'vantage' was originally a military term applied to the superiority of a combatant's position, the Duchess plays on the paradox of her submissive posture as an element in her victory. **happy** fortunate; joyous
132 **Yet** still, even now (probably not 'nevertheless')
133 **twain** two persons (i.e. Aumerle and someone else). Ure (166) takes *twain* as a verb (divide in two, 'a rare usage not found elsewhere in Shakespeare'; see *OED v.* 1), in which case the Duchess

means that saying 'Pardon' twice (as the Duchess herself has done at 119) does not weaken or nullify its effect (as double negatives logically cancel each other out) but rather strengthens pardon by reaffirming it. A quibble on both meanings may be intended.
134–5 **With . . . him.* Pope's rearrangement of the word order and relining preserve the couplet (see 78–81n.) and avoid an awkward mid-line rhyme. The few editors who prefer the unemended text presumably believe that Henry's 'I pardon him with all my heart' is theatrically stronger than Pope's inverted word order.
135 **god on earth** a commonplace of Tudor doctrine (see Dent, G275.1); see LN. The somewhat risible context of *god on earth* may undermine the concept of divine right on which Richard has insisted; or does it ironically call attention to the distance between Richard's divinely ordained legitimacy and Henry IV's shaky claim to royal authority?

130 SP] *King Q; Bul. F*   God] heauen *F*   134, 136 SP] *King H. Q; Bul. F*   134–5 With . . . him]
Pope; I pardon him with al my heart *QF*   135 SD] *Wells (subst.)*

KING HENRY

But for our trusty brother-in-law and the Abbot,
With all the rest of that consorted crew,
Destruction straight shall dog them at the heels.
Good uncle, help to order several powers
To Oxford, or where'er these traitors are;   140
They shall not live within this world, I swear,
But I will have them if I once know where.
Uncle, farewell, and so, cousin, adieu.
Your mother well hath prayed, and prove you true.   144

136 a metrically rough line that signals
the shift from jingling rhymes to blank
verse, i.e. to a more serious tone and a
more dangerous concern – the threat
posed by Aumerle's confederates. The
final foot of the pentameter may be
elided ('and th'Abbot') while *brother-in*
becomes 'broth'r-in'. F omits *and*, thus
improving the metre at the cost of
implying that the Abbot of
Westminster and the brother-in-law
are one and the same.
    for as for
    trusty brother-in-law John Holland,
Earl of Huntingdon; cf. 2.1.281n.
Trusty is obviously meant sarcastically
(cf. *dangerous*, 80). The plot to lure
Henry IV to a joust was 'by the aduise
of . . . Huntington' (Holinshed, 3.514).
137 **consorted crew** conspiring gang;
crew is obviously scornful (cf. 12); *consorted* = allied, confederated.
138 a repetition from *R3* 4.1.39: 'Death
and destruction dogs thee at thy heels'.
See 5.6.7–8, 13–16.
    straight immediately
139 **order several powers** 'marshal separate bodies of troops (or military
units) to be sent'
141–5 The rhyming resumes with a couplet and a rare triplet – here not for

reasons of levity but conventionally to
mark the scene's conclusion.
143 *so, cousin Since the line in QF is
awkwardly unmetrical in a place
where regularity might reasonably be
expected, most editors since
Theobald have accepted Q6's conjectural emendation ('Cosin too'),
although Wilson (228) and Ure (167)
are both unhappy with it. Craven[3]
(55–6) argues plausibly that Q's compositor may have dropped *so* from the
line (cf. *R3* 3.5.97; 'and so, my lord,
adieu'). Since this solution makes bibliographical sense, improves the
metre and is idiomatically acceptable,
it is adopted here. Jowett's refinement
of Craven, reversing the two words
(Oxf, 442), has slightly smoother
rhythm to recommend it but seems
less natural idiomatically.
144 **prove you true** either 'may you
prove loyal' (optative subjunctive) or
'be sure you prove loyal' (imperative). The first seems likelier.
Aumerle, the inheritor of his father's
dukedom, did ultimately vindicate
himself at Agincourt (cf. *H5*
4.6.3–32, where his heroic death
as Duke of York is elaborately
described).

136 brother-in-law] *F;* brother in law *Q* and the] the *F* 140 are;] *F* (are:); are, *Q* 143 so,
cousin] *this edn (Craven[3]);* cousin *QF;* Cosin too *Q6;* cousin, so *Oxf*

DUCHESS OF YORK
Come, my old son. I pray God make thee new.   *Exeunt.*

[5.4]   *Enter* Sir Piers [of] EXTON *and* [*two*] Servants.

145 **old** unreformed, unregenerate (in the biblical sense)
  make thee new Cf. 2 Corinthians, 5.17: 'Therefore if any man be in Christ, he is a newe creature: Olde things are passed away, behold, all things are become newe'; also the baptismal rite in the *Prayer Book*: 'grant that the old Adam in this child may be so buried, that the new man may be raised up in him'. The phrase 'new man' became proverbial (Dent, M170). Cf. also *MM* 2.2.78–9: 'And mercy then will breathe within your lips, / Like man new made.'

5.4 This brief scene lays the groundwork for Richard's murder in 5.5, without which the action there would seem too sensationally unexpected and only marginally intelligible. After the lowered tension of the previous scene, it also reinvolves the audience in tragic expectations and suggests Henry's responsibility for the protagonist's death. Herford (204) compares the episode with *KJ* 3.3.64–7, where John hintingly commissions Hubert to rid him of Prince Arthur; Chambers (151) thinks the scene exposes Henry's 'cold-blooded ingenuity'. As in the previous scene, the place apparently is Windsor Castle. The main source is Holinshed (3.517): 'One writer, which seemeth to haue great knowledge of king Richards dooings, saith, that king Henrie, sitting on a daie at his table, sore sighing, said; Haue I no faithfull freend which will deliuer me of him, whose life will be my death, and whose death will be the preseruation of my life? This saieng was much noted of them which were present, and especiallie of one called sir Piers of Exton. This knight incontinentlie departed from the

court, with eight strong persons in his companie, and came to Pomfret.' Shakespeare's indebtedness to this account continues at 5.5.98–118 (see n.). A single stanza of Daniel's may have contributed to the scene in a minor way (see 2n. and 7n.). It has often been noted that Henry II is supposed to have got rid of Thomas à Becket by similar means (cf. Holinshed, 3.78).
  *Unlike F, Q contains no act or scene designations; but F marks no separate scene at this point, even though the exit just before Exton's entrance has obviously cleared the stage of all characters from the previous episode. F designates the prison scene (5.5 of modern texts) '*Scaena Quarta*'. Q's bewildering SD directing Exton and his assistants to remain onstage ('*Manet sir Pierce Exton, &c.*') makes nonsense of the action since he has not entered. Exton could be one of the courtiers who enter with Henry at the beginning of 5.3, but, if so, he would depart when the King commands them to *withdraw* and *leave* him onstage *alone* with Aumerle (5.3.27). Probably, as Gurr (165) suggests, something has been deleted – either a bit of action and dialogue at the end of 5.3 or even a brief scene that would explain Exton's presence: 'The evidence of F's incomplete adjustment strengthens the assumption that Q1 shows a deletion incompletely recorded'; see also Appendix 1, pp. 510, 512. RP goes further, postulating that 5.4 could have resulted from the deliberate cutting of a longer scene 'in which Henry spoke the quoted words', a scene 'drafted and then truncated as too dangerously explicit for staging'; such an explanation might 'account for the anomalous SD and F's lack of scene

145 God] heauen *F*
5.4] *Steevens; continuous with previous scene in QF*   0.1] *Manet sir Pierce Exton, &c. Q (after 5.3.145 SD); Enter Exton and Seruants. F*   of] *Collier*   two] *this edn*   and . . . Servants] *F; &c. Q*

EXTON

Didst thou not mark the King, what words he spake:
'Have I no friend will rid me of this living fear?'
Was it not so?

1 SERVANT   These were his very words.

EXTON

'Have I no friend?' quoth he. He spake it twice,
And urged it twice together, did he not?   5

2 SERVANT

He did.

EXTON

And speaking it, he wishtly looked on me,

number' but would also be consistent with 'the dramaturgy of this play' which 'frequently ends scenes with a small group of conspirators staying onstage when most other characters have left (a favourite structure of Shakespeare from *2H6* to *KL* and beyond)'.

0.1 EXTON See List of Roles, 30n.

1 For the grammatical construction, see 3.3.61n.

mark hear, pay attention to

2 an alexandrine

will who will (Abbott, 244)

rid . . . fear *Fear* = cause of fear. Cf. Daniel (3.56), where King Henry, musing on the peril of Richard's continued existence, 'wisht that some would so his life esteeme / As rid him of these feares wherein he stood: / And therewith eies a knight [Exton], that then was by, / Who soone could learne his lesson by his eie'. Shakespeare may be echoing Daniel's 'rid him of these feares'; Holinshed's equivalent phrases are 'to rid himselfe of anie such like danger' (3.516) and 'deliuer me of him, whose life will be my death' (3.517). Cf. also *Gorboduc* (1562), 2.2.36–7: 'Send to your father eke; he shall appease / Your kindled minds and rid you of this fear.' Hayward (131) elaborates on Holinshed,

but Shakespeare's line could have suggested the further question he attributes to King Henry: 'for how can I bee free from feare, so long as the cause of my daunger dooth continue?'

3, 6 SP *Cf. F's '*Seruants*' (0.1); the SPs (Q's '*Man*', F's ' *Ser.*') make it unclear whether one or both men speak. Following Oxf, this edition shares out the two lines rather than making one of the actors remain mute.

5 urged . . . together insisted on it by repetition

7 wishtly fixedly, intently, desirously, perhaps also 'with secret meaning'; the form is recorded as an obsolete spelling of 'wishly' (*OED adv.*). Q3–F's 'wistly' (see t.n.) is found at *VA* 343, *Luc* 1355, *PP* 6.12, where it also means 'intently' and is associated with looking. Exton is reporting that King Henry singled him out by giving him a significant or scrutinizing look, as in Daniel (see 2n.) but not Holinshed. Wilson (229) sees Q's form as an echo of Daniel's 'wisht'. Ure (168) cites *The Life of Sir Thomas More* by 'Ro: Ba:' in which Henry VIII, on hearing that More's execution had just taken place, 'turned hym to Queene Ann, who then stood by, wistlie looking vpon her, [and] said, "Thou, thou, art the cause of this

1 King] *(K.)*, *F*   3 SP] *Oxf (subst.)*; *Man Q*; *Ser. F*   These] Those *F*   4 friend] *QF*; friends *Q2 (TCC copy)*   twice,] *Q3–F*; twice. *Q*   6 SP] *Oxf (subst.)*; *Man Q*; *Ser. F*   7 wishtly] wistly *Q3–F*

> As who should say, 'I would thou wert the man
> That would divorce this terror from my heart',
> Meaning the King at Pomfret. Come, let's go. 10
> I am the King's friend, and will rid his foe. [F]*Exeunt.*[F]

[5.5] *Enter* [KING] RICHARD *alone.*

KING RICHARD
I have been studying how I may compare

---

mans death"' (263–4); one extant MS
of *The Life* reads 'wishly' for 'wistlie'.
8 **As . . . say** as if to say (Abbott, 257)
9 **divorce this terror** separate this fear;
cf. 2n.
10 **Pomfret** See 5.1.52n.
11 **rid** rid him of (possibly echoing
Holinshed or Daniel or both; see 2n.);
cf. also *3H6* 5.5.67: 'As deathsmen, you
have rid this sweet young prince!'
5.5 Richard's murder is based on Holinshed
(3.516–17), with the remote possibility
that Hall was consulted (see 114–16n.).
The long meditative soliloquy which
opens the episode has no precise source
but could have been influenced by a passage in Daniel (3.63–71), where the
account of Richard's death is also preceded by such a speech. Although its
substance is very different, Daniel's passage develops the contrast between the
lot of kings and commoners (cf.
5.1.40–50n.), a theme which Shakespeare's character touches upon; and,
like Shakespeare, Daniel follows his
monologue with the hasty entrance of a
minor figure to announce the presence of
Exton, who has just arrived from court –
this in turn succeeded by the sudden
breaking in of the assassins. Holinshed
may also contain the germ of the faithful
groom in his account of Jenico d'Artois,
a Gascon loyalist (Ard[2], 169; see 66.1n.).
For the possible influence of Froissart on
the disloyalty of *roan Barbary*, see 83–9

LN. Most of what occurs and is said
prior to the actual murder is freely
invented by the dramatist to increase
sympathy for the protagonist and to
show his power to inspire affection, even
in defeat. The place is Pomfret Castle
(see 5.1.51–2n., 52n.); the historical time
some unspecified date in February 1400
(Saul, 425). Shakespeare eschews the
psychological terror and physical horrors of the death scene in *E2*, choosing
instead an emphasis on royal dignity and
unalloyed pity; Holinshed's alternative
accounts of Richard's death by starvation (3.516), which the dramatist rejected, would have allowed an approach
closer to Marlowe's (cf. 19–21n.).
1–66 Richard's only soliloquy; there are
but two in the play, the other being
Salisbury's speech of forboding
(2.4.18–24). Now that Richard's realm
has shrunk to a mere cell, and since
there is no onstage audience, the self-
dramatizing speaker (cf. 31) must create an imaginary kingdom of hearers
out of his *still-breeding thoughts* (8). For
the putative relation to Daniel, see
headnote and Introduction, pp. 141.
1–9 In trying to sustain an analogy
between the world at large and his
dungeon, Richard copes with the logical difficulty of there being no people
except himself in the prison, whereas
the great world *is populous* (3). He
determines therefore to people the cell

---

11 SD] *Q4, F (Exit.)*
5.5] *Steevens; Scaena Quarta. F* 0.1] *Enter Richard. F* KING] *Rowe* 1+ SP] *Cam (subst.); Rich.
QF* 1 I may] to *Q2–F*

This prison where I live unto the world;
And, for because the world is populous
And here is not a creature but myself,
I cannot do it. Yet I'll hammer't out. 5
My brain I'll prove the female to my soul,
My soul the father, and these two beget
A generation of still-breeding thoughts;
And these same thoughts people this little world,
In humours like the people of this world, 10
For no thought is contented. The better sort,
As thoughts of things divine, are intermixed
With scruples and do set the word itself
Against the word, as thus: 'Come, little ones';

with his own *thoughts*, engendered by his *soul* (the male) in conjunction with his *brain* (the female); and these thoughts, which are continually producing offspring of their own (new thoughts), multiply to fill the void. The conceit is further complicated as the head in which Richard's thoughts are confined is itself a kind of prison.

1 **studying** dwelling on, intently meditating upon; dissyllabic ('stud-ying'). The term well suggests the element of self-conscious fancy and verbal ingenuity in Richard's make-up.
2 **unto** with, to
3 **for because** because, for the reason that (Abbott, 151)
5 *hammer't out puzzle it out, beat it into shape, work hard at it (a metaphor from the forge)
6 **prove** consider to be, establish as
7 The syntax is elliptical: 'my soul (I'll establish as) the father, and these two (shall) beget'.
8 **generation** progeny, family
   still-breeding always reproducing, ever-breeding
10 **humours** varied temperaments, psychological moods, dispositions.

'Richard says that he will fill the world of his prison with thoughts as diverse as the temperaments of the people who inhabit the real world: *thoughts of things divine* [12], *Thoughts tending to ambition* [18], *Thoughts tending to content* [23], thoughts of kingship and poverty [32–8]' (Adams, 250).

11 **sort** category, class (of thought)
12–17 Richard's thoughts of heaven are mixed with doubt (*scruples*) as he does not know whether to rely on the offer of salvation to the innocent (*little ones*) or to fear its denial to the rich, both applicable (in his own mind) to himself but seemingly contradictory. The two biblical texts cited at 14 and 16–17 are close together in the same chapter in each of the three relevant gospels (Matthew, Mark and Luke).
12 **As** such as, for example
13–14 **set . . . word**: Cf. 5.3.121n.; *word* here = scripture. The repetition of this phrase is curious in what Chambers (151) calls 'such a carefully written play'. See LN.
14–15 *For the lineation see Appendix 1, pp. 517–18.
14 **Come, little ones** biblical: cf. Luke,

5 hammer't] *F*; hammer it *Q* 13 word] Faith *F* 14–15] *as Wells; one line QF* 14 the] *QF*; thy *Q2*
word] Faith *F*

And then again: 15
'It is as hard to come as for a camel
To thread the postern of a small needle's eye.'
Thoughts tending to ambition, they do plot
Unlikely wonders – how these vain weak nails
May tear a passage through the flinty ribs   20
Of this hard world, my ragged prison walls,

18.16: 'Jesus . . . sayd, Suffer litle children to come vnto me, and forbid them not: for vnto such belongeth the kingdome of God'; also Matthew, 19.14, Mark, 10.14.

16–17 Cf. Luke, 18.25: 'For it is easier for a Camel to goe thorow a needles eye, then for a rich man to enter into the kingdome of God'; also Matthew, 19.24, Mark, 10.25. Scholars have questioned whether Shakespeare was familiar with the famous cruces contained in *camel* and *needle*, *camel* in some interpretations meaning 'cable-rope' and *needle* perhaps 'small pedestrian entrance in a city-gate'. Shakespeare's phrase, *thread the postern* (17), could reflect a cognizance of *needle* meaning 'gate' (cf. *postern*) while at the same time hinting that *needle* may also have retained its everyday significance (cf. *thread*). Ure (170) shows that the dramatist could have found the less obvious understanding of the problematic words in sources such as Erasmus's *Paraphrases*, a marginal annotation in the Geneva Bible (which prints 'camel' at Matthew, 19.24 but gives 'cable rope' as a possible alternative) and Thomas Lupset's *A Treatise of Dying Well* (1534). As for the meaning of *needle* in the play, Ure suggests that Shakespeare perhaps 'compromised' between the two interpretations 'in his choice of words'.

17 **postern** narrow back gate
needle's monosyllabic ('neele's' or 'needl's'); cf. *KJ* 5.2.157, also Cercignani, 317.

18 **they** For the redundant pronoun, see Abbott, 243.

19–21 **how . . . walls** Ure (170) believes that Shakespeare may have recalled the proverb, 'Hunger breaks stone walls' (Dent, H811), reinforced perhaps by a passage describing Famine in Sackville's Induction to 'Buckingham' in *Mirror* (310): 'Great was her force whom stonewall could not stay, / Her tearyng nayles snatching at all she saw' (ll. 358–9). Richard's lines contain no reference to hunger, but, as Ure suggests, the association might have been triggered in Shakespeare's mind by one of the versions of Richard's death provided by Holinshed – death by starvation; see headnote.

19 **vain** ineffectual, useless

20 *****through** F's spelling, which nearly all editors accept, regularizes the metre; cf. 3.2.170n. Ard² and *Riv* prefer Q's metrically irregular 'thorow' ('thorough'); RP believes that the irregularity 'would generate more energy than the smooth line'.
flinty ribs Cf. 3.3.32n., 5.1.3n.; RP suggests that Shakespeare's use of *flint bosom* and *flinty ribs* as architectural metaphors may imply some subliminal connection with Flint Castle and his decision to make Richard's capture occur there rather than at the historically correct Conway Castle.

21 **hard** difficult, painful; stone-walled
ragged rough, rugged

17 thread] *(threed)*, *Q5–F*   postern] *QF;* small posterne *Q3*   small needle's] Needles *F*   18 plot] *Q2–F;* plot, *Q*   20 through] *F;* thorow *Q*

And, for they cannot, die in their own pride.
Thoughts tending to content flatter themselves
That they are not the first of Fortune's slaves,
Nor shall not be the last, like silly beggars   25
Who sitting in the stocks refuge their shame
That many have and others must sit there;
And in this thought they find a kind of ease,
Bearing their own misfortunes on the back
Of such as have before endured the like.   30
Thus play I in one person many people,
And none contented. Sometimes am I king;

22 *for . . . pride The syntax is compressed: ' because *they* (the *nails*) cannot penetrate the wall, the "Thoughts
tending to ambition" *die* in their full
vigour (*pride*)'; cf. *1H6* 4.6.57: 'let's die
in pride' and 4.7.15–16: 'died . . . in his
pride'. Or perhaps Richard means that
his ambitious thoughts die in the pride
of their own 'thwarted ambition'
(Cam², 167).
23 **content** contentment
24 **of Fortune's slaves** to become slaves
to Fortune
25 **Nor** and (Abbott, 408)
   silly simple-minded
26 **stocks** an instrument of public punishment: a heavy timber frame with
holes to confine the ankles of a seated
offender; cf. *KL* 2.2–2.4, where Kent
is so punished.
   refuge their shame 'solace (seek
refuge from) their disgrace by thinking'; *refuge* as a verb appears only here
in Shakespeare.
27 **have** have sat
   *sit Q3's spelling, which F takes over,
is probably an alternative form of Q's
'set'; see 1.2.47n. and Pollard, 61. Cf.
MV 1.3.112, 126, 131 where 'spet' is a
variant form of 'spit'.
31 Cf. *AYL* 2.7.142, 'And one man in his
time plays many parts', where the various

parts are played in chronological succession rather than, as here, randomly.
person The word carries overtones of
'dramatic role, guise, semblance' (*OED
sb.* 1) as well as meaning 'individual
human being' or 'actor'; the complex
implication is that of a speaker whose
identity is already a kind of role taking
on various additional roles. For a subtle
exploration of the entire speech in relation to Richard's role-playing and its
link with the deliberately difficult
effort of sustaining the similitude
between prison and world, see
Nowottny, 88–91. Nowottny observes:
'At the climax of the speech it is impossible to separate Richard's one meaning
– that as soon as he has an impulse to
pretend, the pretence takes possession
of him – from his other meaning, that
his tragic predicament makes every rôle
short-lived; nor can we separate, from
these, his meaning that there are
enough mutually contradictory facts in
his situation to make every rôle equally
possible and impossible' (90).
32–3 **Sometimes . . . beggar** an ironic
echo of King Henry's lines at 5.3.78–9:
'Our scene is altered . . . to "The Beggar
and the King".' H. Craig (138) compares these lines to Edward's speech in
prison to Leicester (*E2*, 5.1.5–37).

22] *F (*And . . . cannot, . . . pride.*);* And . . . cannot . . . pride, *Q*   24 Fortune's] *F;* fortunes *Q*
25 silly] *(*seely*), F*   27 many have] *QF;* haue many *Q2*   sit] *Q3–F;* set *Q*   29 misfortunes] misfortune *F*   31 person] prison *Q2–F*   32 am I] *QF;* am I a *Q2*

Then treasons make me wish myself a beggar,
And so I am. Then crushing penury
Persuades me I was better when a king;   35
Then am I kinged again, and by and by
Think that I am unkinged by Bolingbroke,
And straight am nothing. But whate'er I be,
Nor I nor any man that but man is
With nothing shall be pleased till he be eased   40
With being nothing.   *The music plays.*
                Music do I hear?

33 **treasons make** the thought of treasons makes
36 **kinged** For a different sense, cf. *H5*
2.4.26.
  by and by shortly, in a moment
37 **unkinged** deposed; cf. 4.1.220.
38 **straight** immediately
39–41 **Nor . . . nothing.** a tangled utterance, which seems to mean, 'Neither I
nor any man, who is merely mortal
(*that but man is*), shall be fully satisfied
with anything (in this life) until he be
released by death (*being nothing*).' The
first *nothing*, apparently, is part of a
double negative. According to an alternative interpretation – rather more
strained and harder to take in aurally –
Richard's sentence would mean,
'Neither I nor anyone . . . shall be
pleased with having nothing (i.e. with
losing everything) until he is relieved
of his pain by death.' The internal
rhyme (*pleased/eased*) may point to a
familiar saying or epitaph. Richard
dwells on conflicting senses of his own
identity, which tend to cancel each
other out and reduce him to nonentity
or nothingness; cf. notes on 31,
4.1.201–2, 216, 260–2, 291, 292–3.
Here, of course, his words ironically
anticipate his actual death at the close
of the scene. See also Introduction,
pp. 17, 43, 45–6, 61, 67–8.

39 **Nor . . . nor** neither . . . nor
41 SD F's printing of this direction three
lines earlier (see t.n.) possibly reflects
an advance warning cue in the promptbook, but Richard's failure to react to
the music until 41 suggests that Q's
placement is correct.
41 ***Music do I hear?** This edition follows F's punctuation, but Q's
comma is ambiguous; possibly a
declarative statement rather than a
question is intended. The offstage
music probably comes from a single
stringed instrument, perhaps a lute
(see 46, 64n.). Woodman used an
unseen lute in his production. For a
penetrating analysis of the symbolic
importance of music in this scene –
its complex relation to memory,
tragedy, myth, time and madness,
see Iselin, 180–3, 185–6. Mahood
suggests the possibility that the
Groom, who enters at 66.1, may also
be the musician; in Kyle's RSC production Roger Moss, playing the
Groom, appeared with 'the lute
slung across his back' (Mahood,
Parts, 86). The question arises, however, whether a lowly groom would
possess or could play a lute, normally
an instrument of the aristocracy (see
also 47–8n.).

33 treasons make] Treason makes *F*   36 kinged] *QF;* king *Q2;* a King *Q3*   38 be] am *F*   41 SD]
opp. 41, Q; Musick (opp. 38) F   hear?] *F;* heare, *Q;* heare; *Q4*

Ha, ha, keep time! How sour sweet music is
When time is broke and no proportion kept!
So is it in the music of men's lives.
And here have I the daintiness of ear   45
To check time broke in a disordered string,
But for the concord of my state and time
Had not an ear to hear my true time broke.
I wasted time, and now doth Time waste me;

42 **Ha, ha** an exclamation of surprise or annoyance, not a laugh
   keep time This phrase initiates a chain of complex wordplay on *time* in a variety of senses: musical time (42, 43, 46), lifetime or season (47, 48, 58), the times (47), the duration of hours, days and years (49, 58), Father Time (49, 50), a specific time of day (58), and the time Richard keeps, like a clock, as he contemplates Bolingbroke (58).
   How . . . is Richard responds to the inadequate performance of music that would otherwise be *sweet*.
43 **time is broke** the rhythm is faulty, the playing is out of time.
   proportion musical time, metrical beat, orderly rhythm
44 **in** in the case of (Abbott, 162)
45 **daintiness of ear** aural acuteness or discernment, musical refinement; cf. Gaveston's comment on Edward II (*E2*, 1.1.50–3): 'I must have . . . Musicians that, with touching a string, / May draw the pliant king which way I please. / Music and poetry is his delight'.
46 **check** find fault with, reprove
   string Many commentators gloss this as a synecdoche (stringed intrument), but one faulty string can cause as much disorder or dissonance in music as a whole instrument which is out of tune. Cf. *TS* 3.1.24–5, 38–40.
47–8 Naylor (33) relates the *disordered*

string (46) to Richard himself, 'who has been playing his part "out of time" (*disordered* simply means "out of its place" – i.e., as we now say, "a bar wrong"), and this has resulted in breaking the *concord* – i.e., the harmony of the various parts which compose the state'. The image, in other words, involves both rhythmic and harmonic disorder: incorrect rhythm, the failure to give notes their proper time value, causes disharmony in relation to the other voices of a polyphonic composition. Richard contrasts his critical sensitivity to music with his lack of political, and perhaps ethical, perception.
47 **for** with respect to
   my . . . time my realm and my life. Some editors gloss *time* as 'the times' or 'the age'; *my* is emphatic.
48 **my . . . broke** the disharmony of my own life and reign
49 **I wasted time** Cf. 'waste of idle hours' (3.4.66); also *E2*, 5.1.121–2, where Edward also regrets his self-indulgent reign: 'Commend me to my son, and bid him rule / Better than I'.
   waste me cause me to waste away; lay me waste. Elizabethan psychology held that sighing (cf. 51–4n.) depleted the blood supply and so caused emaciation and loss of physical energy. Cf. 2.2.3n.

45 ear] *QF;* care *Q5*   46 check] heare *F*   in a] *QF;* in *Q2*   49 Time] *F;* time *Q*

For now hath Time made me his numb'ring clock.   50
My thoughts are minutes, and with sighs they jar
Their watches on unto mine eyes, the outward watch,
Whereto my finger, like a dial's point,
Is pointing still, in cleansing them from tears.
Now, sir, the sound that tells what hour it is   55

50 **numb'ring clock** one whose face has
the hours marked upon it, not an hour-
glass or sundial
51–4 an intricate and somewhat strained
conceit, which Adams (252) explains
as follows: 'The disturbed state of
Richard's mind is reflected in the
complexity of the metaphor: his
thoughts are minutes and the frequent and regular sighs to which they
give rise are the groaning of the pen-
dulum which ticks them out (*jar(s)
Their watches*). While it does so, the
passage of time is also being traced on
the face of the clock (*the outward
watch* – represented by Richard's
eyes) by its hand (*dial's point* – the finger with which he wipes away his
tears). Thus, the sad thoughts passing
through Richard's mind are revealed
both by his sighs and also by the
expression in his eyes.' Chambers
(153) remarks, 'The point of the comparison [between *thoughts* and *minutes*] lies in the monotonous recurrence of the same thoughts'; cf. also
AYL 3.2.303–5: 'sighing every minute
and groaning every hour would detect
the lazy foot of Time as well as a
clock'.
52 an alexandrine; the length and regularity may be onomatopoeic
watches numbers on a clock; periods
of insomnia. The imagery is partly
based on the imagined similarity
between a clock-face and the human
eye, since the hand of a clock points to
the hour and then passes over it
as the finger wipes away tears (53–4),
and also since the eye keeps watch

physically as the clock does metaphorically. It should be remembered that in
the sixteenth century watches and
clocks could be synonymous terms
(see *OED* watch *sb.* 20a, where the
present instance is cited); this passage, however, complicates understanding by using the word *watch* in
several overlapping senses, i.e. the
interval of time marked by the tick-
ing of the clock, the clockface or dial
with its numerals, and the length of
the watch (a division of the day),
with special reference to night watches or wakefulness, which a clock measures.
54 **still** continually (possibly with a pun
on 'motionless' since hour and minute
hands on a clock-face can move almost
imperceptibly). Cf. *Oth* 4.2.53–5: 'to
make me / The fixed figure for the
time of scorn / To point his slow
unmoving finger at!'
them Richard's eyes
55 **Now, sir** For a moment it suits
Richard's rhetorical stance to address
an imaginary interlocutor – perhaps a
projection of himself. Or perhaps he
addresses the audience directly as
Launce does in a soliloquy in *TGV*
2.3.19–20: 'Now, sir, this staff is my
sister'.
55–6 **sound . . . Are** The disagreement
in number can be explained in two
plausible ways: *sound that tells* is a simple transposition of 'sounds that tell'
(Abbott, 337; see Pope's emendation in
t.n.); the verb *Are* 'is attracted to the
predicate *groans*' (Verity, 177).

50 Time] *F;* time *Q*   made me] *QF;* made *Q2*   52 eyes,] *F;* eyes *Q*   55 sound that tells] sounds that tell *Pope*

Are clamorous groans which strike upon my heart,
Which is the bell. So sighs, and tears, and groans
Show minutes, times, and hours. But my time
Runs posting on in Bolingbroke's proud joy,
While I stand fooling here, his jack o'the clock.   60
This music mads me! Let it sound no more;   [*Music ceases.*]
For though it have holp madmen to their wits,
In me it seems it will make wise men mad.
Yet blessing on his heart that gives it me,
For 'tis a sign of love; and love to Richard   65
Is a strange brooch in this all-hating world.

58 **times** Possibly this means quarter- and half-hours (as struck by the clock or marked on the clock-face), in which case Q's sequence is a logical progression from smaller to larger units of time. But *times* could also mean 'seasons' or 'whole ages', as is perhaps suggested by F's changed order (see t.n.).
hours dissyllabic (cf. the common Elizabethan spelling, 'howers'); see 1.3.261t.n.
my time my life on earth (probably punning on 'the time I keep as though I were a clock')
59 **posting** hurrying, speeding
60 *****jack o'the clock** the small mechanical figure on certain old clocks of a man who struck the bell with his mallet to mark the hours or quarter-hours. Richard complains that for the politically triumphant Henry time passes rapidly and joyfully, whereas he himself must eke out his poor existence hour by hour in prison. The term conveys a certain self-contempt; cf. *R3* 4.2.114–15.
61 **mads me** maddens me, drives me insane
SD *If the Groom has provided the music (see 41n.), he obviously stops playing before his entrance; but in any case the music probably stops or has

died away by 66, beyond which it would be distracting.
62 **have holp** may have helped (subjunctive; see Abbott, 366); *holp* is an archaic form of 'helped'.
madmen ... wits Elizabethans shared the ancient belief that music could be therapeutic for the insane; mentioned by Galen, the idea derives in part from the biblical story of David curing Saul's evil possession by playing the harp (1 Samuel, 16.14–23); cf. *KL* 4.7.23.2 (in Q only), where 'soft music' helps to restore the mad king to sanity. Burton calls music 'a soveraigne remedy against Despaire and Melancholy' (2.114).
63 **wise** sane, having their wits (an antithesis to *madmen*); Richard claims no unusual sagacity.
64 **his** may imply a single musician
gives it me gives it to me
65 **to** for; Gurr (168) notices the irony of *love to Richard* 'in view of what is to follow'.
66 **strange brooch** rare jewel (often worn prominently on hats). Expanding upon her notion that the Groom may derive from Holinshed (see 66.1n.), Mahood (*Parts*, 87) suggests that the character, in addition to providing the music, may have worn the *brooch* in his cap 'in the form of Richard's emblem' – a white

56 which] that *F*   58 times, and hours] Houres, and Times *F*   60 o'the] *F* (o'th'); of the *Q*
61 SD] *Oxf (subst.), after 63*   62 have] *QF;* hath *Q5*   65 a sign] (asigne), *Q2–F*

Enter a Groom *of the Stable.*

GROOM
Hail, royal Prince!
KING RICHARD   Thanks, noble peer.
The cheapest of us is ten groats too dear.
What art thou, and how comest thou hither

hart (see Fig. 16); cf. *sign of love* (65), and see also headnote.
all-hating world Johnson's gloss (1.451), 'world in which I am universally hated', is probably correct. For *all* used intensively, see Abbott, 28.
66.1 For the significant role of the loyal servant, in large part Shakespeare's invention, cf. Holinshed (3.500), where the chronicler describes Richard's relative isolation after being ambushed and captured near Conway: 'The king had verie few about him of his freends, except onelie the earle of Salisburie, the bishop of Carleill, the lord Stephan Scroope, . . . and Jenico Dartois a Gascoigne that still ware the cognisance or deuise of his maister king Richard, that is to saie, a white hart, and would not put it from him, neither for persuasions nor threats; by reason whereof, when the duke of Hereford vnderstood it, he caused him to be committed to prison within the castell of Chester. This man was the last (as saieth mine author) which ware that deuise, and shewed well thereby his constant hart toward his maister, for the which it was thought he should haue lost his life, but yet he was pardoned, and at length reconciled to the dukes fauour, after he was king.' Daniel (2.28) also refers admiringly to Jenico d'Artois, but without mentioning the details of his loyalty. See also 66n., 75–6n.
67–8 **royal . . . noble . . . groats** Further wordplay, to which the rhyming of *peer* with *dear* helps call attention, is

obviously intended on these three coins: royals were worth ten shillings (120 pence), nobles six shillings and eightpence (80 pence), *groats* only fourpence. Being a mere prisoner, Richard says he is the *cheapest* (the cheaper of the two men present onstage) and therefore worth no more than a *noble*, which is also the adjective Richard has just applied to the Groom; to call Richard *royal*, as the Groom has just done, is therefore to price him *ten groats* (40 pence) *too dear* (too high), since the difference between a royal and a noble is ten groats. Cf. *1H4* 2.4.287–91, where Mistress Quickly announces 'a nobleman' at the door, and Prince Hal responds in jest, 'Give him as much as will make him a royal man'; cf. also the jocular exchange between Parolles and Helena in *AW* 1.1.106–9: '*Parolles*. Save you, fair queen! *Helena*. And you, monarch! *Parolles*. No. *Helena*. And no.' See also LN.
67 The line may be scanned as a tetrameter, each of the two speeches commencing with a spondee: 'Hàil, ròy- | al Prince ! | Thànks, nò- | ble pèer'.
peer Richard puns on the two senses of 'nobleman' and 'equal'.
69 an irregularly short line, the main stresses of which fall on *What, thou, how, còmest* and *hither*. Ure (173) thinks that a pause occurs after the comma 'while Richard scrutinizes the groom'; Craik suggests that 'fellow', 'the obvious word to complete the metre', may somehow have dropped

66.1] *Enter Groome. F*   69 comest] com'st *F*

Where no man never comes but that sad dog 70
That brings me food to make misfortune live?

GROOM

I was a poor groom of thy stable, King,
When thou wert king, who, travelling towards York,
With much ado, at length have gotten leave
To look upon my sometimes royal master's face. 75
O, how it erned my heart when I beheld
In London streets, that coronation day,

out before the caesura or been added in
performance; cf. *H5* 4.8.58. 'Fellow',
however, tends to be used derogatively
(see 95n.) and Richard elsewhere treats
the Groom with respect (see 81n. on
gentle).
What who (Abbott, 254)
how . . . hither Richard asks how the
Groom has managed to gain access to
his presence.
70 **never** ever; Q5 and F both eliminate
the double negative (see t.n. and
Appendix 1, p. 507, n. 3).
  sad dog gloomy fellow, dismal lackey
  (*sad* = grave, solemn, unsmiling).
71 **make misfortune live** 'allow me,
the embodiment of misfortune, to
survive', 'perpetuate my unfortunate
life'
73 **travelling towards** four syllables
required: either *travelling* may be given
three syllables and *towards* one
('t'wards'); or *travelling* may be elided
to two syllables ('trav'ling') and
towards expanded to two ('tò-wards').
74 **ado** difficulty
75–6 Shakespeare's use of both *master's*
and *heart* might count as verbal evidence (despite the commonness of
both words) of the influence of
Holinshed's phrase describing
d'Artois: 'his constant hart toward his
maister' (see 66.1n.).
75 an alexandrine. See LN.
  sometimes royal master's either

'once royal master's' (*sometimes* = formerly); or 'royal former master's'; cf.
1.2.54n. Kittredge[2] (188), taking *sometimes* in the first sense, remarks that the
Groom thus 'unconsciously emphasizes the King's bitter jest' (see
67–8n.).
76 **erned** grieved, moved to compassion;
cf. *MW* 3.5.44: 'yearn your heart'.
77–83 The Groom describes a different
procession from the one York evokes
at 5.2.7–36, i.e. Bolingbroke's entry
into London from Wales with Richard
as his captive, the victor riding 'a hot
and fiery steed' (5.2.8). Henry IV's
coronation took place on 13 October
1399. Holinshed (3.511) says only
that 'from the Tower the king rode
through the citie to Westminster,
where he was consecrated, annointed,
and crowned king by the archbishop
of Canturburie with all ceremonies
and roiall solemnitie as was due and
requisit'. Froissart's more detailed
account (6.380–2), which mentions
Henry's 'whyte courser' (see 5.2LN),
may have influenced the conception
of *roan Barbary*. Neither Holinshed
nor Froissart suggests that King
Henry's horse had originally been
Richard's, so that the pathos and
irony of the Groom's account (like
the character himself) are presumably
the product of Shakespeare's imagination. See LN and 83–9LN.

70 never] euer *Q5–F*   73 travelling] (trauailling*), Q3–F*   76 erned] *(*ernd*)*; yern'd *F*

When Bolingbroke rode on roan Barbary,
That horse that thou so often hast bestrid,
That horse that I so carefully have dressed!   80

KING RICHARD
Rode he on Barbary? Tell me, gentle friend,
How went he under him?

GROOM
So proudly as if he disdained the ground.

KING RICHARD
So proud that Bolingbroke was on his back?
That jade hath eat bread from my royal hand;   85
This hand hath made him proud with clapping him.
Would he not stumble? Would he not fall down,
Since pride must have a fall, and break the neck
Of that proud man that did usurp his back?
Forgiveness, horse. Why do I rail on thee,   90
Since thou, created to be awed by man,

---

78 **roan** darkly dappled or mottled bay colour, variegated reddish-brown
Barbary The horse's name is derived from its Arabian breed, a highly prized strain associated with the Barbary Coast of North Africa.
79 **bestrid** bestrode (an older form)
80 **dressed** groomed, combed, tended
81 a slightly irregular line; the stresses probably fall on *Rode*, *Bàrbary*, *Tell*, *gèntle* and *friend*.
gentle Richard uses a polite form of address, showing that he continues to regard the Groom as a gentleman; cf. *noble peer* (67).
friend a significant epithet since Richard's friends are now so few; cf. 96 and 3.2.176n.
82 a trimeter; 'How did the horse behave with Bolingbroke as his rider?'
83–9 See LN.
85 **jade** old nag, worthless horse (cf. 3.3.179n.)

eat eaten (pronounced 'et'); an obsolete form of the past participle (Abbott, 343)
86 **proud** Richard attributes human feelings to the horse, i.e. pride in being petted by a king.
clapping patting, stroking
87–9 Cf. *TNK* 5.4.48–82 where Pirithous gives an elaborate account of how Arcite's horse, rearing up and falling backwards, crushed its rider beneath its weight. The sudden reversal of fortune which befalls the rivals in love (Palamon's delivery from execution and Arcite's death from the riding accident) suggests a structural similarity to the rise of Bolingbroke and the fall of Richard.
88 **pride . . . fall** proverbial (Dent, P581); the origin is biblical: Proverbs, 16.18.
89 **usurp** a loaded word, glancing at Bolingbroke's usurpation of the crown as well as of the horse's back
90 **on** against

79 bestrid] *F;* bestride *Q*   83 he] he had *F*   84 SP] *Cam (subst.); Ric. Q; Rich. F*   85 eat] *(eate)*

Wast born to bear? I was not made a horse,
And yet I bear a burden like an ass,
Spurred, galled and tired by jauncing Bolingbroke.

Enter Keeper *to* [*King*] *Richard with* ᶠ*a dish*ᶠ [*of*] *meat.*

KEEPER [*to Groom*]

    Fellow, give place. Here is no longer stay.   95

KING RICHARD [*to Groom*]

    If thou love me, 'tis time thou wert away.

GROOM

    What my tongue dares not, that my heart shall say.   *Exit.*

---

94 **Spurred, galled** F's emendation ('Spur-gall'd') improves neither the sense nor the metre, although it is apparently the more usual form (see *OED v.*; *ppl. a.*). Nashe (1.199, 3.126) uses 'spur-gall' in *Piers Penniless* (1592) and *Have With You to Saffron Walden* (1596). Cf. also *The Mad Lover* (1617), 5.3.16: 'your spurgall'd conscience' (Fletcher, 5.81).
galled made sore
jauncing probably either 'prancing' or 'moving up and down with the motion of the horse, rough-riding' (cf. *RJ* 2.5.52: 'catch my death with jauncing up and down'). Some editors gloss: 'making the horse prance'; originally 'jaunce' meant 'to fatigue a horse by riding him hard' (see *OED v.*).

94.1 **meat** food (cf. 2.1.76); but Shakespeare presumably thought of the meal as including meat since a 'keruing knife' figures importantly in Holinshed's account (see 98–118n.).

95–9 a triplet followed by a couplet, unusual in Shakespeare; cf. 100–1n. and 5.3.141–5n. Wells (264) observes that the change to rhyme 'heightens the tension'.

95 **Fellow** Unlike Richard, the Keeper addresses the Groom as an inferior.
give place yield your place to me
Here . . . stay. 'You must stay here no longer'; cf. *TGV* 1.3.75: 'No more of stay'.

96 Richard's recognition and appreciation of the Groom's devoted loyalty are notable. This 'discovery helps him to find . . . a last reserve of strength' so that he can die 'proclaiming the royalty he disaverred on the Groom's first appearance' (Mahood, *Parts*, 88).

97 Conceivably there is implied wordplay on *heart* with reference to the white hart which Richard's loyal servants wore, although Shakespeare never mentions the emblem itself (see 66n.); cf. Holinshed's account of Jenico d'Artois, which uses the same spelling ('hart') for both meanings (see 66.1n. and 75–6n.). Cf. also *Ham* 1.2.159: 'But break my heart, for I must hold my tongue.' The 'Groom's humanity is deepened for us by the brutality of the Keeper who turns him out' (Mahood, *Parts*, 90).

---

94 Spurred, galled] Spur-gall'd *F*   94.1] *Enter Keeper with a Dish. F*   Keeper] *F; one Q*   King] *this edn*   95 SD] *Rowe (subst.)*   96+ SP] *Cam (subst.); Rich. QF*   96 SD] *Wells (subst.)*   97 SD] *Q (Exit Groome.), F*

KEEPER

My lord, will't please you to fall to?

KING RICHARD

Taste of it first, as thou art wont to do.

KEEPER

My lord, I dare not. Sir Piers of Exton, who lately   100

98–118 Shakespeare's indebtedness to Holinshed (3.517) resumes at this point: Sir Piers of Exton, having arrived at Pomfret, commanded 'the esquier that was accustomed to sew [serve] and take the assaie [taste the food] before king Richard, to doo so no more, saieng; Let him eat now, for he shall not long eat. King Richard sat downe to dinner, and was serued without courtesie or assaie, wherevpon much maruelling at the sudden change, he demanded of the esquier whie he did not his dutie; Sir (said he) I am otherwise commanded by sir Piers of Exton, which is newlie come from K. Henrie. When king Richard heard that word, he tooke the keruing knife in his hand, and strake the esquier on the head, saieng The diuell take Henrie of Lancaster and thee togither. And with that word, sir Piers entred the chamber, well armed, with eight tall men likewise armed, euerie of them hauing a bill [long-handled weapon] in his hand. King Richard perceiuing this, put the table from him, & steping to the formost man, wrung the bill out of his hands, & so valiantlie defended himselfe, that he slue foure of those that thus came to assaile him. Sir Piers being halfe dismaied herewith, lept into the chaire where king Richard was woont to sit, while the other foure persons fought with him, and chased him about the chamber. And in conclusion, as king Richard trauersed his ground, from one side of the chamber to an other, & comming by the chaire, where sir Piers

stood, he was felled with a stroke of a pollax which sir Piers gaue him vpon the head, and therewith rid him out of life, without giuing him respit once to call to God for mercie of his passed offenses. It is said, that sir Piers of Exton, after he had thus slaine him, wept right bitterlie, as one striken with the pricke of a giltie conscience, for murthering him, whome he had so long time obeied as king.' In a marginal note, Holinshed calls the reader's attention to 'The desperat manhood of king Richard'.

98 a short line (tetrameter) appropriate to the abruptness of the Keeper's request and the general nervousness of the situation. From this point until 106 the dramatist introduces various metrical irregularities, doubtless in preparation for, and in tandem with, the suddenness, violence and excitement of the stage action. See 100–1n.
  fall to commence eating
99 **Taste . . . first** It was the duty of an appointed servant regularly to taste ('assay') a king's food before it was consumed – originally as a precaution against poison (cf. *KJ* 5.6.23), later as a royal formality; see Holinshed in 98–118n. Chambers (154) thinks the Keeper's refusal to taste the food signifies, as in Holinshed, 'not poison, but only discourtesy'; see, however, 105n.
  wont accustomed
100–1 *No relineation can entirely remove the metrical roughness of these lines. The solution proposed here makes 100 an irregular pentameter, the stresses falling on *lord, dare,*

Came from the King, commands the contrary.
KING RICHARD
The devil take Henry of Lancaster and thee!
Patience is stale, and I am weary of it.   [*Attacks Keeper.*]
KEEPER
Help, help, help!

*The murderers, *^F*EXTON and [four of his] Servants,*^F *rush in.*

KING RICHARD
How, now! What means Death in this rude assault?   105

Piers, *Èxton* and *làtely*; 101 then falls into place as a normal decasyllabic line with an initial trochaic foot. Malone's relineation assumes that *who* rhymes with *to* and *do* (98–9), thus completing the second of two triplets; but the verse remains rough, and a rhyme on *who* seems most uncharacteristic. Wilson (233) thinks these lines, which were 'clearly once verse', can now 'only be printed as prose', the 'text as it stands' being 'probably the result of adaptation'; but prose appears nowhere else in the play, and the Keeper's earlier lines are obviously verse. Verses containing proper names are sometimes irregular; cf. 2.1.279n.

102 a verbatim quotation from Holinshed; see 98–118n.
    devil probably monosyllabic ('de'il'); cf. *Ham* (Q2) 2.2.599: 'deale'; also Scots 'deil'.

103–4 Richard's violent resistance conforms to the Queen's idea of how a king should die: 'The lion dying, thrusteth forth his paw . . . with rage / To be o'erpowered' (5.1.29–31). Cf. also Holinshed (98–118n.).

103 **stale** worn out, futile; a stronger word in Shakespeare's age than ours, possibly because of its association with the urine (*stale*) of horses (see *OED a.* 3)

104.1 **four . . . Servants* Although Holinshed mentions eight servants (see 98–118n.), the action requires no more than four. Richard kills two of these (106–7) before being struck down himself (107), leaving two others – the minimum needed to assist Exton in carrying off the three dead bodies (118); see 117–18n.

105 an ambiguous and problematic line. Richard seems to personify death as he has done earlier at 3.2.103, 162 (see also 2.1.270n.), in which case he probably intends, 'What does Death mean by assaulting me so violently?' He had earlier expected to *pine away* in grief (3.2.209), and the Keeper's refusal to taste his food (100–1) may have aroused suspicion of death by poison, hence his surprise at the patently violent form death will take. If the line is repunctuated, *Death* de-personified and *means* interpreted as a second person singular present (mean'st; Abbott, 340), Richard could be saying, 'What? Do you (i.e. the servant from whom he seizes the weapon in 106) mean my death by your rough assault?' A third way of reading Richard's question is: 'What, Death, do you mean to attack me so violently?' The first of these interpretations seems likeliest.

---

103 SD] *Rowe (subst.)*   104.1] *Enter Exton and Seruants.* F   *four of his*] *this edn*   105 SP] *Cam (subst.)*; *Rich.* Q; *Ri.* F

Villain, thy own hand yields thy death's instrument.
[Seizes a Servant's weapon and kills him with it.]
Go thou, and fill another room in hell!
[Kills another Servant.] Here Exton strikes him down.
That hand shall burn in never-quenching fire
That staggers thus my person. Exton, thy fierce hand
Hath with the King's blood stained the King's own land.   110
Mount, mount, my soul! Thy seat is up on high,

106 metrically irregular; as the line is heavily emphatic it could be scanned in a wide variety of ways. The most regular of these would be as a pentameter with trochaic first foot and anapaestic second foot: 'Villain, | thy own hànd | yields thỳ | death's ìn- | strumènt'.

107 **room** empty space, place (not 'chamber'); see *OED sb.* 1.
SD *Exton . . . down* Cf. *R3* 3.3.9–12, where Rivers, on the eve of execution, recalls his historical predecessor: 'O Pomfret, Pomfret! . . . Within the guilty closure of thy walls / Richard the Second here was hack'd to death'. The account of Richard's assassination derives ultimately from *Traïson*, possibly Hall's source, though it also appears in Fabyan; modern historians, however, dismiss it 'as an invention', considering it more probable that Richard 'was starved to death by his gaolers' (Saul, 425) – one of the possibilities mentioned by Holinshed (see headnote and 19–21n.).

108–12 Neither Holinshed (98–118n.) nor Daniel (3.74–85) gives Richard any dying speech.

108 **never-quenching** unquenchable

109–18 The scene concludes with a series of rhymed couplets – here not only for the conventional reason of signalling the action's closure but also for the purpose of restoring calm and establishing a tone of stateliness. The couplets clearly assist the required dramatic shift to emotional elevation, formal dignity and moral

weight. Verity (179) sees the rhymes as appropriate to 'the close of [Richard's] life's tragedy, as of the scene'.

109 an alexandrine, unless *Exton* is regarded as extra-metrical (see t.n. and 100–1n.)
staggers causes to stagger
my person my royal person. 'Richard reasserts his royalty at the last, notwithstanding his enforced renunciation of it' (Chambers, 155); *person* includes the idea of the king's sacred body. Cf. also 31n.

111–12 Cf. Heywood, *1 If You Know Not Me*, l. 1340: 'My bones to earth I giue, to heauen my soule lift'; see also 1.1.160n. 'The idea that the soul, like air or fire, rises while the body (earth) falls is related to the elemental imagery, the concept of the king's two bodies and the implication of Christian martyrdom' (Cam[2], 171). In 1899, C.E. Montague described Benson's delivery of these lines: he spoke the final words 'much as any other man might utter them under the first shock of the imminence of death', then, half rising 'from the ground with a brightened face', he repeated 'the two last words with a sudden return of animation and interest, the eager spirit leaping up, with a last flicker before it goes quite out, to seize on this new "idea of" the death of the body' (Forker, 368–9).

111 **seat** place in heaven (probably quibbling on 'royal throne')

106 thy own] thine own *Q5–F* SD] *Hanmer (subst.)*   107 SD *Kills . . . Servant*] *Pope (subst.)* *Here*] *om. F*   108 That] *F; Rich.* That *Q* never-quenching] *F;* neuer quenching *Q* 109 Exton] *om. Pope*

Whilst my gross flesh sinks downward here to die.
[*Dies.*]

EXTON

As full of valour as of royal blood!
Both have I spilled. O, would the deed were good!
For now the devil that told me I did well   115
Says that this deed is chronicled in hell.
This dead King to the living King I'll bear.
[*to Keeper and remaining Servants*]
Take hence the rest, and give them burial here.

^F*Exeunt* [*with the bodies*].^F

114–16 **O . . . hell.** Holinshed's account of Richard's death (3.516–17) is taken almost verbatim from Hall (fol. xiiii'), but the latter stresses Exton's tortured conscience much more heavily than his redactor: 'When this knight [Exton] perceiued that he [Richard] was deade, he sobbed, wept, and rent his heare criyng, Oh Lord, what haue we done, we haue murthered hym whom by the space of xxii. yeres we haue obeied as king, and honored as our soueraigne lord, now all noble men will abhorre vs, all honest persons will disdaine vs, and all pore people will rayle and crie out vpon vs, so that duryng our naturall liues, we shal be poincted with the finger, and our posterite shal be reproued as children of Homecides, ye of Regicides & prince quellers.' Shakespeare may well have ignored Hall for the story of Richard's murder, but the latter's emphasis on Exton's fear of ostracism could have partly suggested King Henry's negative reaction to Exton's deed and his command: 'never show

thy head by day nor light' (5.6.44; see also 5.6 headnote and 5.6.34–44LN). Daniel (3.80–1) also comes down heavily on Exton's 'blacke infamie', 'disgrace' and 'hatefull skorne to all posterity', calling him the 'out-cast of the world', but declines to speculate upon his remorse; see 5.6.43n. Ure (176) notes that Matrevis in *E2* (5.6.2) and Lapoole in *Woodstock* (5.1.32–44), both murderers of royal figures, also suffer pangs of conscience; cf. also Shakespeare's earlier guilt-haunted characters, the second murderers in *2H6* 3.2.3–4, and *R3* 1.4.271–3, 276–8.

114 **spilled** destroyed; poured out. Exton has both extinguished Richard's *valour* and *spilled* his *blood*.

115 **devil** probably monosyllabic; see 102n.

117–18 Presumably Exton carries Richard's body himself (*I'll bear*), perhaps with the Keeper's help, while the other two corpses are removed by the two surviving Servants (cf. 104.1n.).

118 **rest** others

---

112 SD] *Rowe*   113 valour] *(valure), F*   118 SD1] *this edn*   SD2 Exeunt] *Q4–F (Exit.), Rowe*
with the bodies] *Capell (subst.)*

[5.6]   ^F*Flourish.*^F *Enter* Bolingbroke [*as* KING HENRY]
with the Duke of YORK, ^F*other Lords, and Attendants*^F.

KING HENRY
Kind uncle York, the latest news we hear

5.6 For the final scene Shakespeare took most of what he could use directly from Holinshed, including the names of the executed conspirators, the Abbot of Westminster's death, the pardoning of Carlisle and the ceremonious conveying of Richard's corpse from Pomfret to London, compressing and to some extent rearranging the historical sequence as he did so. In fact, the crushing of the insurrection against Henry predated Richard's murder (the direct consequence of the earls' rising), and the final conspiratorial head to be sent for public display on London Bridge arrived there on 29 January 1400, more than a month before Richard's corpse actually departed from Pomfret (see Chambers, 156; Saul, 424–6). As in 5.3, the location is probably Windsor, although King Henry learned at Oxford rather than at his southern residence that the rebellion against him had been suppressed. Shakespeare seems to have invented Exton's presentation of Richard's body to Henry IV and the latter's repudiation of the murderer (but see 34–44LN and 5.5.114–16n.). Daniel, however, having omitted the repudiation from the first version of his *Civil Wars*, added it to his 1609 revision (see 34–44n.), having undoubtedly picked up the detail from the play. The dramatic technique of the scene replicates that of 3.2 in its use of successive messengers entering to announce new political developments – in this case favourable news (from the point of view of King Henry) in contrast to the earlier crescendo of disasters reported to Richard near Barkloughly Castle. The assignment of

the various duties performed by Northumberland, Fitzwater and Harry Percy is fictional (but see 7–12n.). Chambers (156), who seems oddly to ignore Carlisle's fate, regards the concluding episode as 'a counterpart' to 4.1: 'Those who there took Richard's part are now either won over to Bolingbroke, or have "made peace" with him by death.' Richard's career has ended and his successor's reign is now underway; but despite Henry's political victory, Richard's murder casts a shadow over the future, hinting at the ineluctable truth of Carlisle's prophecy (4.1.137–50) and preparing perhaps for the several revisionary allusions to Richard that will crop up in the later dramas of the tetralogy. Richard's tragedy seems already to have contaminated Henry's best hopes.

0.1–2 As in 5.3, King Henry enters processionally with his nobles and presides, probably, from the throne; see 5.3.0.1–2n.

0.1 **Flourish* Cf. 5.3.0.1–2n.

1–4 Holinshed (3.515) reports that when the rebels 'were aduertised of the kings puissance', they 'departed from thence [Colbroke] . . . to Berkhamsteed, and so to Circester, & there the lords tooke their lodging. The earle of Kent, and the earle of Salisburie in one Inne, and the earle of Huntington and lord Spenser in an other . . . wherevpon in the night season, the bailiffe of the towne with fourescore archers set on the house, where the erle of Kent and the other laie, which house was manfullie assaulted and stronglie defended a great space. The earle of Huntington being in an other Inne with the lord

5.6] *Steevens; Scoena Quinta. F*   0.1–2] *Flourish. Enter Bullingbrooke, Yorke, with other Lords &*
attendants. F   0.1 *as* KING HENRY] *Dyce (subst.)*   1+ SP] *Capell (subst.); King Q; Bul. F*

Is that the rebels have consumed with fire
Our town of Ci'cester in Gloucestershire,
But whether they be ta'en or slain we hear not.

Enter NORTHUMBERLAND.

Welcome, my lord. What is the news?   5
NORTHUMBERLAND
First, to thy sacred state wish I all happiness.
The next news is, I have to London sent

Spenser, set fire on diuerse houses in the towne, thinking that the assailants would leaue the assault and rescue their goods, which thing they nothing regarded. The host lieng without, hearing noise, and seeing this fire in the towne, thought verelie that king Henrie had beene come thither with his puissance, and therevpon fled without measure, euerie man making shift to saue himselfe, and so that which the lords deuised for their helpe, wrought their destruction.' According to an alternative version, also in Holinshed (3.516), 'a preest that was chapleine to one of [the rebel lords] . . . set fire vpon certeine houses in the towne'. Significantly, Henry uses the royal plural as at 5.3.9 (but see 18n.).

2   **consumed** destroyed
3   **Ci'cester** trisyllabic; Cirencester, spelled 'Cicester' in QF. Holinshed's spellings are 'Circester' (see 1–4n.) and 'Circiter'.
4   **ta'en** captured; pronounced 'tane'
6   probably an irregular pentameter, the stresses falling on *First*, *sàcred*, *state*, *wish* and *hàppiness*
    sacred state royalty by divine authority (cf. 4.1.209). Given Bolingbroke's usurpation, Northumberland's adjective seems both ironic and slightly oily; cf. 2.3.6–7n.
    happiness good fortune
7–16 Cf. Holinshed (3.515): 'The earle of Huntington . . . seeing no hope of com-

fort, fled into Essex. The other lords which were left fighting in the towne of Circester, were wounded to death and taken, and their heads stricken off and sent to London.' In another account redacted by Holinshed (3.516), the townspeople, 'to reuenge themselves of' the lords who had set fire to their houses, 'brought them foorth of the abbeie where they had them in their hands, and in the twilight of the euening, stroke off their heads. The earle of Salisburie . . . a scorner of the sacraments, ended his daies . . . without the sacrament of confession . . . The lord Hugh Spenser, otherwise called earle of Glocester, as he would haue fled into Wales, was taken and carried to Bristow, where (according to the earnest desires of the commons) he was beheaded. . . . Manie other that were priuie to this conspiracie, were taken, and put to death, some at Oxford, as sir Thomas Blunt, sir Benet Cilie knight, . . . but sir Leonard Brokas, and [others] . . . were drawne, hanged, and beheaded at London. There were nineteene in all executed in one place and other, and the heads of the cheefe conspirators were set on polles ouer London bridge, to the terror of others.'
7–12 The succession of jingling couplets introduced at this point and continuing intermittently throughout the scene produces, some of the time at least, a certain perfunctory if not almost comic effect.

3 of] *QF; om. Q5*   Ci'cester] *Oxf;* Ciceter *QF;* Cicester *Rowe*   4.1] *QF; after 5 Q4*

The heads of Salisbury, Spencer, Blunt and Kent.
The manner of their taking may appear
At large discoursed in this paper here.   10

[*Presents a paper.*]

KING HENRY

We thank thee, gentle Percy, for thy pains,
And to thy worth will add right worthy gains.

Enter Lord FITZWATER.

FITZWATER

My lord, I have from Oxford sent to London

The dramatist's intention, apparently, was to communicate information rapidly in a formal and deliberately stylized manner. For Northumberland's mission, see Holinshed (3.515): having been informed of the conspiracy, King Henry 'dispatched messengers foorth to signifie vnto the earle of Northumberland his high constable, and to the earle of Westmerland his high marshall, and to other his assured freends, of all the doubtfull danger and perilous iopardie'.

7   **next** most pressing (*OED a*. 4a)

8   *****Spencer** F corrects Q's historical mistake (the introduction of 'Oxford' as an executed rebel), making the names conform to Holinshed's account; see Appendix 1, pp. 514–15, 526–7. Shakespeare, writing in haste, may have blundered inasmuch as the city of Oxford (as distinct from the earldom) is mentioned frequently in Holinshed's account of the conspiracy, or perhaps Q's compositor made a faulty substitution, infected by *Oxford* in 13. Q2 made matters worse by omitting 'Blunt' (apparently for metrical reasons), and F eventually repaired the factual error, probably by reference to the theatre promptbook. *Spencer* is Thomas le Despenser (1373–1400), created Earl of

Gloucester by Richard II but degraded by Henry IV (cf. 5.2.41–3n.), called 'Hugh Spenser' by Holinshed. The brother-in-law of Aumerle, he was among the insurrectionists at Cirencester but beheaded at Bristol (see Holinshed in 1–4n. and 7–16n.).

Blunt Sir Thomas Blunt (or Blount), not to be confused with the Sir Walter Blunt of *1H4*. He attended the Abbot of Westminster's supper at which the conspiracy was planned (see 5.2.41–117n.); captured at Oxford, he was decapitated only after being hanged, eviscerated and quartered (see 7–16n. and *DNB*).

Kent Thomas Holland, Earl of Kent – Surrey's title after he had forfeited his dukedom (see List of Roles, 24n. and 5.2.41–3n.)

9   **taking** capture; cf. 4n.

10   **At large discoursed** discoursèd; fully recounted

11   **Percy** Northumberland (Henry Percy)

12   **worth** deserving, demonstrable merit; present assets

     right worthy gains well-deserved and substantial rewards

12.1 *****FITZWATER** For the normalization of the name (here by Q6), see List of Roles, 26n., 4.1.44n. and Appendix 1, pp. 526–8.

8 Salisbury, Spencer, Blunt] *F;* Oxford, Salisbury, Blunt *Q;* Oxford, Salisbury *Q2–5*   10 SD] *Rowe (subst.)*   11–12] *Q, Fc; not in Fu*   12.1 Lord] *om. F*   FITZWATER] *(Fitzwaters), F (Fitz-waters), Q6*

The heads of Brocas and Sir Bennet Seely,
Two of the dangerous consorted traitors   15
That sought at Oxford thy dire overthrow.

KING HENRY

Thy pains, Fitzwater, shall not be forgot.
Right noble is thy merit, well I wot.

Enter HARRY PERCY ^F^*with* [Bishop of] CARLISLE^F^[, *as prisoner*].

HARRY PERCY

The grand conspirator, Abbot of Westminster,

14 See Holinshed (7–16n.).

Brocas Sir Bernard Brocas, son of
another Sir Bernard who was chamberlain to Anne of Bohemia, Richard's
first queen; the younger Sir Bernard
was Master of the Buck-hounds (an
office inherited from his father) as well
as carver to Richard II. Holinshed calls
him 'sir Leonard Brokas' (see French,
51–2).

Sir Bennet Seely spelled 'Cilie' by
Holinshed; his surname is variously
given as Scheveley, Sely and Shelley by
historians, some of whom assert that
his Christian name was John rather
than Bennet or Benedict. He seems to
have been a retainer of Richard's half-
brother, the Earl of Huntingdon.
Apart from his involvement in the conspiracy, little is known about him. He
was probably an ancestor of the
Romantic poet (see Black, 347). Wylie
distinguishes between 'Sir Benedict
Sely', who had 'a manor near
Winchelsea' and was associated in the
conspiracy with Sir Thomas Blunt
(1.91), and 'Sir Thomas Shelley of
Aylesbury', who accompanied Huntingdon in his attempted escape
(1.102).

15 **consorted** conspiring; cf. 5.3.137n.
16 **Oxford** See 5.2.41–117n.

dire disastrous

18 **merit** deserving

I wot I know. From this point forward
Henry abandons the royal plural (cf.
1–4n.) – perhaps Shakespeare's way
of suggesting the uneasy tension
between his official role and his private feelings, especially as regards
Carlisle and the murdered Richard,
both of whom remind him of the conflicting imperatives of conscience and
political necessity.

19–29 Cf. Holinshed (3.516): 'Shortlie
after, the abbat of Westminster, in
whose house the conspiracie was
begun (as is said) gooing betweene
his monasterie & mansion, for
thought [on account of depression]
fell into a sudden palsie, and shortlie
after, without speech, ended his life.
The bishop of Carleill was
impeached, and condemned of the
same conspiracie; but the king of his
mercifull clemencie, pardoned him
of that offense, although he died
shortlie after, more through feare
than force of sicknesse, as some haue
written.' Actually, Carlisle did not
die until about 1409; see List of
Roles, 21n.

19 **grand** chief, principal

17 Fitzwater] *(Fitz.)*, F *(Fitzwaters)*, *Q6* not] *Q2–F*; nor *Q* 18.1] *Enter Percy and Carlile.* F
HARRY] *Oxf*; H *Q*; Henry *Q3*; om. F *as prisoner*] *Cam^1 (subst.)* 19 SP] *Oxf*; Percie *Q*; Per. *Q4–F*

With clog of conscience and sour melancholy,   20
Hath yielded up his body to the grave.
But here is Carlisle living, to abide
Thy kingly doom and sentence of his pride.

KING HENRY

Carlisle, this is your doom:
Choose out some secret place, some reverend room,   25
More than thou hast, and with it joy thy life.
So as thou liv'st in peace, die free from strife;
For though mine enemy thou hast ever been,
High sparks of honour in thee have I seen.

Enter EXTON [*and Servants bearing*] *the coffin.*

20 **clog of conscience** the burden of a
(guilty) conscience; cf. 1.3.200: 'The
clogging burden of a guilty soul' (see
n.), also *Oth* 1.3.198.
sour bitter; cf. 4.1.241.
melancholy Here conceived of as a
bodily fluid (black bile), the excess of
which caused illness according to the
theory of humours. Cf. also 2.2.3n.
22 **abide** await submissively; undergo,
submit to
23 **doom** punishment, judgement
of for
25 **secret** private, discreet
***reverend room** venerable place (cf.
5.5.107n.), dignified abode or perhaps
'some place of religious retirement'
(such as a monastery); see List of
Roles, 21n. Q's 'reuerent' suggests the
modern sense 'respectful' rather than
the required 'worthy of respect',
rverend (Q3). In the period the two
spellings were interchangeable for
both senses. Cf. *1H6* 3.1.49–50
('reuerent', F; 'Reuerend', F3).
26 **More . . . hast** 'more ample than your
prison cell' or perhaps 'more suitable
for your dignity as a clergyman'
joy enjoy, possess, have the benefit of

(*OED v.* 4). Since Carlisle has been
deprived of his episcopal title and all
courtly influence, Henry may use the
verb with mild irony.
27 **So as** provided that; cf. 4.1.315n.
28 **enemy** perhaps two syllables ('en'my')
29 **High** noble
sparks bright particles (metaphorical); cf. 5.3.21n., also *King Leir*
(1594), sc. 7.140: 'I see such sparks of
honor in your face'. King Henry's
leniency to Carlisle matches that
shown earlier to Aumerle. Henry
wishes to show that he can be merci-
ful as well as stern in administering
justice.
29.1 *coffin* Perhaps open so that
Richard's face can be recognized by
the audience (cf. Holinshed in
30–52n.). Shewring (19) suggests that
a bier may have been used, since the
'final stage picture depends, as in so
many key scenes in the play, on the
presence of both Richard and
Bolingbroke on stage'. On the other
hand, Exton's identification of the
contents of the coffin suggests that it is
closed.

25 reverend] *Q3–F;* reuerent *Q*   29.1 *and Servants bearing*] Capell *(subst.)   the*] *with the Q; with
a F*

EXTON

Great King, within this coffin I present   30
Thy buried fear. Herein all breathless lies
The mightiest of thy greatest enemies,
Richard of Bordeaux, by me hither brought.

KING HENRY

Exton, I thank thee not, for thou hast wrought

30–52 Cf. Holinshed (3.517): 'After he [Richard] was thus dead, his bodie was imbalmed, and seered, and couered with lead, all saue the face, to the intent that all men might see him, and perceiue that he was departed this life: for as the corps was conueied from Pomfret to London, in all the townes and places where those that had the conueiance of it did staie with it all night, they caused dirige to be soong in the euening, and masse of *Requiem* in the morning; and as well after the one seruice as the other, his face discouered, was shewed to all that coueted to behold it. Thus was the corps first brought to the Tower, and after through the citie, to the cathedrall church of saint Paule bare faced, where it laie three daies togither, that all men might behold it. There was a solemne obsequie doone for him, both at Paules, and after at Westminster, at which time, both at dirige ouernight and in the morning at the masse of *Requiem*, the king and the citizens of London were present. When the same was ended, the corps was commanded to be had vnto Langlie, there to be buried in the church of the friers preachers. The bishop of Chester, the abbats of saint Albons and Waltham, celebrated the exequies for the buriall, none of the nobles nor anie of the commons (to accompt of) being present . . . He was after by king Henrie the fift remooued to Westminster, and there honorablie intoomed with queene Anne his wife.' Cf. Henry V's soliloquy before Agincourt (*H5* 4.1.295–305), where, still labouring under the inherited guilt of his father's crime, he begins: 'I Richard's body have interred new, / And on it have bestowed more contrite tears, / Than from it issued forced drops of blood.'

30 **present** The presentation of the corpse to the King is dramatic licence; but Henry IV did attend a requiem mass for Richard at St Paul's and, later, at Westminster Abbey (see 30–52n.).

31 **buried fear** buried object of fear; an echo of *this living fear* at 5.4.2 (see n.) **all** totally (an intensive use); cf. 5.5.66n.

33 **of Bordeaux** so called because of his birthplace; see List of Roles, 1n. and 3.2.24–5n. Exton pointedly avoids Richard's royal title.
   by me Exton 'emphasises his own services. In spite of his momentary qualms [5.5.113–16] . . . he still hopes to pose as *the King's friend* [5.4.11]' (Chambers, 157).

34–44 Since none of the established or possible sources says anything about Henry's disavowal of Exton, scholars reasonably assume that Shakespeare's imagination is the sole authority, but see LN. Daniel, undoubtedly influenced by Shakespeare's tragedy, revised his *Civil Wars*, 3.78–9 (1609), to read in part: 'What great aduancement hast thou [Exton] hereby wonne, / By being the instrument to perpetrate / So foul a deed? where is thy grace in Corte, / For such a seruice, acted in this sort? / First, he for whom thou dost this villanie / (Though pleas'd therewith) will not auouch thy fact, / But let the weight of thine owne infamie / Fall on thee, vnsupported and vnbackt.' The repudiation of a murderer by the ruler for whom the crime had been undertaken has many literary and historical precedents; Ure (179) discusses some of these. Elizabeth I punished Secretary

A deed of slander with thy fatal hand 35
Upon my head and all this famous land.

EXTON

From your own mouth, my lord, did I this deed.

KING HENRY

They love not poison that do poison need,
Nor do I thee. Though I did wish him dead,
I hate the murderer, love him murdered. 40
The guilt of conscience take thou for thy labour,
But neither my good word nor princely favour.
With Cain go wander thorough shades of night,

Davison for going forward with the execution of Mary Queen of Scots even though he had done so with her knowledge and permission (see Jenkins, 279). Cf. also *JC* 2.1.175–7: 'And let our hearts, as subtle masters do, / Stir up their servants to an act of rage, / And after seem to chide 'em.'

34 **wrought** committed

35 **of slander** 'that will bring disgrace by making slanderous tongues wag'; cf. 1.1.113n.

37 **From . . . mouth** 'in accordance with your own words'; see 5.4.2 and *KJ* 4.2.182–248, where King John confronts Hubert after the supposed death of Prince Arthur. See also 34–44n.

38–40 a version of the proverb, 'A King loves the treason but hates the traitor' (Dent, K64), which was popular in the theatre; cf. *R3* 1.4.254–5: 'O, sirs, consider, they that set you on / To do this deed will hate you for the deed'; also *1 Honest Whore*, 4.4.48–50: 'I banish thee for euer from my court. / This principle is olde but true as fate, / Kings may loue treason, but the traitor hate' (Dekker, 2.87). Hayward (133–4) also underlines the irony of Exton's murder: 'Sir *Pierce* expecting great fauour and rewards for his vngracious seruice, was frustrated of both, and not only missed that countenance for

which he hoped, but lost that which before he had: so odious are vices euen when they are profitable.'

40 In order to preserve the rhyme with *dead* in 39, *murdered* must be given three syllables ('murderèd'); *murderer* could then be elided to a dissyllable ('murd'rer').

love him murdered Abbott (246) would gloss as 'love him (who is) murdered', a reading that seems to accord with 'Though I did wish him dead' (39); but the phrase could also mean 'am happy about the fact that he is dead (without approving of the means by which his death was accomplished)'. Lothian (140) suggests that the ambiguity may be deliberate.

41 **guilt** Henry may be punning cynically on 'gilt' since Exton undoubtedly expected a monetary reward; cf. Hayward (38–40n.).

43–4 For the possible influence of Hall and Daniel on Exton's exile, see 5.5.114–16n. Cf. also Joan la Pucelle's curse in *1H6* 5.4.86–91.

43 **Cain** The biblical allusion to the first murderer (who killed his brother Abel) recalls Bolingbroke's words in the first scene, reinforcing a significant motif of the tragedy; see 1.1.104n. and Introduction, pp. 75–7. Cf. Genesis, 4.11–12:

35 slander] slaughter *Q2–F*   37 lord] *(Lo.), Q2, F*   43 thorough shades] *Cam;* through shades *Q;* through the shade *Q2–F*

And never show thy head by day nor light.   [*Exit Exton.*]

Lords, I protest, my soul is full of woe   45

That blood should sprinkle me to make me grow.

Come, mourn with me for what I do lament

And put on sullen black incontinent.

I'll make a voyage to the Holy Land

'And nowe art thou cursed from the earth . . . A fugitiue and a vagabond shalt thou be'; also Daniel (3.81), where Exton is described as 'The out-cast of the world, last of thy race, / Of whose curst seed, nature did then deny / To bring forth more her faire workes to deface'; see also 5.5.114–16n.

*thorough Cam's emendation (an alternative spelling of Q's 'through') supplies the needed extra syllable by simpler means than Q2's addition of 'the'; cf. *MND* 2.1.3: 'Thorough bush, thorough brier'.

shades of night an echo of Mowbray's description of his own exile at 1.3.177: 'shades of endless night' (with the same rhyme on *light*)

44 **day nor light** Adams (262) explains: 'Exton is condemned to be a man of shadows, skulking away from the brightness of the sun or that of artificially lit rooms.' Black, citing *OED* (*sb.* 4b), glosses *light* as 'an ignited candle, lamp, or the like'. It has been noted by several commentators that, but for the rhyme on *night*, *light* could easily be taken for a misprinting of 'night'. 'Night' could indeed be correct; cf. the use of identical rhyme at 5.3.108–9, 110–11 (see 5.3.109n.).

nor sometimes substitutes for 'or' in Elizabethan usage (see Abbott, 406)

45 **protest** solemnly declare

full of woe echoes Richard's *kingly woe* (3.2.210)

46 Cf. *True Tragedy*, l. 51: 'Blood sprinkled, springs: blood spilt, craues due reuenge'; Wilson, '*R3*', argues persuasively that this was a source for

Shakespeare's *R3*. According to Mc-Millin & MacLean (164–6), Shakespeare had probably been a member of the Queen's Men, to whom the anonymous play belonged. The image of blood watering the growth of the new king is portentous and charged with irony (cf. 3.2.211–13 and 212n.); it ties in significantly with the garden scene (3.4) and the play's pervasive evocation of the green world. Cf., for instance, Richard's phrase at 5.1.63: 'To plant unrightful kings'. See also Introduction, pp. 33, 69–71, 135.

48 **sullen** mournful, gloomy; cf. 1.3.227n.

incontinent immediately

49 Numerous references to Henry IV's unfulfilled intention to atone for his guilt by undertaking a crusade reappear in the next two plays of the tetralogy; cf. *1H4* 1.1.19–29, 48, 102; *2H4* 3.1.108, 4.4.3–4, 4.5.209–10, 238. At this point the vow may signify merely a plan to make a pilgrimage of expiation to Jerusalem, which Bolingbroke had already visited in 1392–3 (see Bevan, 31–3). Ure (180) notes Henry's 'religious gravity' in the later plays, seeing his behaviour here as a prolepsis of it. Shakespeare invents Henry's remorse as a motive for the proposed crusade, which the chronicles associate with the end rather than the beginning of his reign without mention of Richard's murder; Holinshed (3.540) writes only that in Henry's final year (1413) 'order was taken for ships and gallies to be builded and made readie, and all other things necessarie to be prouided for a voiage which he meant

44 SD] *Wells*   47 what] that *F*

To wash this blood off from my guilty hand.   50
March sadly after; grace my mournings here
In weeping after this untimely bier.   ^F*Exeunt.*^F

FINIS.

to make into the holie land, there to recouer the citie of Ierusalem from the Infidels'. Holinshed (3.508), however, moralizes heavily and at length on Henry's responsibility for the murder: 'What vnnaturalnesse, or rather what tigerlike crueltie was this, not to be content with his [Richard's] principalitie? not to be content with his treasure? not to be content with his depriuation? not to be content with his imprisonment? but being so neerelie knit in consanguinitie, which ought to haue moued them like lambs to haue loued each other, wooluishlie to lie in wait for the distressed creatures life, and rauenouslie to thirst after his bloud, the spilling whereof should haue touched his conscience so, as that death ought rather to haue beene aduentured for his safetie, than so sauagelie to haue sought his life after the losse of his roialtie.' Perhaps Holinshed's phrase, 'should have touched his conscience', influenced the characterization at this point. GWW suggests that King Henry's ultimate failure to make the journey to Jerusalem, of which audiences could well have been aware, might be

interpreted as the result of divine Providence – God's frustrating a regicide from washing the blood from his guilty hands. Henry's final speech could also be taken as containing an element of politic hypocrisy, as a public expression of guilt and sorrow calculated to soften or disarm future opposition.

50 a pointed and ironic reminder of Richard's phrase at 3.2.55: 'wash the balm off from an anointed king'. By alluding to Pilate, Henry ironically echoes both himself and Richard; see 3.1.5–6n., 4.1.171–2LN, 239n.

51 **sadly after** solemnly behind the coffin
    grace my mournings 'dignify with your presence the obsequies that I shall arrange'; the plural form *mournings* suggests actual rites (cf. Holinshed in 30–52n.).

52 **after** in procession after the corpse. The processional exit following a coffin, sometimes accompanied by muffled drums, became a traditionally sombre way of ending Elizabethan tragedies; cf. *E2*, which concludes with Edward III leaving the stage in 'funeral robes' behind his 'father's hearse' (5.6.93–4).

51 mournings] mourning *F*

LONGER NOTES

1.1.100 plot . . . death Later in the play Gaunt asserts that Richard has *caused* Gloucester's *death* (1.2.39), and York seems to refer to the event as an execution by mentioning his brother's beheading (2.2.102). Later still, when Bolingbroke (functioning already as Henry IV) inquires about *Gloucester's death*, 'Who wrought it with the King, and who performed / The bloody office' (4.1.4–5), he is answered by Bagot, who implicates Aumerle (see Holinshed in 4.1.2–5n.); Aumerle then vehemently denies the accusation (4.1.27). Fitzwater also alleges that Aumerle sent two of his men 'To execute the noble Duke at Calais' (4.1.83).

1.1.139 But a press correction in Q. The corrected state of the inner forme of sheet A (preserved in BL) mends the bungled metre of the line on sig. A4; the other surviving copies (uncorrected in this forme) print 'Ah but', a mistake by Compositor S, who was setting seriatim at this point. Pollard (35) suggests that the mistake could have crept in through the compositor's interjecting an extra syllable while dictating the line to himself as a mnemonic device. See Appendix 1, pp. 533, 537.

1.1.171 Slander's In Q many of these personifications are capitalized, which may reflect authorial intention; numerous others appear in F. This edn tends to retain them: cf. also *Shame* (1.1.195), *Envy* (1.2.21), *Murder* (1.2.21, 32), *Grief* (1.2.55, 1.3.274, 2.1.75, 2.2.7, 5.1.14), *Fortune* (1.3.85, 2.2.10, 5.5.24), *Virtue* (1.3.98), *Valour* (1.3.98), *Ignorance* (1.3.168), *Death* (1.3.224, 2.1.270, 2.2.70, 3.2.103, 162, 184, 185), *Sorrow* (1.3.292, 302, 2.2.16, 26, 4.1.167, 277, 5.1.93, 102), *Age* (2.1.133), *Counsel* (2.1.27), *Will* (2.1.28), *Wit* (2.1.28), *Nature* (2.1.43), *Justice* (2.1.227), *Majesty* (3.2.84, 4.1.252), *Hope* (2.2.69, 72), *Time* (1.3.229, 2.1.195, 3.2.69, 81, 5.5.49, 50), *Mischance* (3.4.92), *Glory* (4.1.251), *Sovereignty* (4.1.251), *State* (4.1.252), *Triumph* (5.1.15), *Necessity* (5.1.21), *Pardon* (5.3.119).

1.1.195 SD* A number of twentieth-century productions retained the early exit. In the 1971 promptbook for Barton's production Gaunt's departure is marked to occur after 199, apparently owing to sickness – a clear visual preparation for 2.1; see also 1.3.258n. Bradley (46–7) suggests that F's SD 'for Gaunt's exit may have been prompted in part by a Stage-reviser's inspiration to change the sense of *place* [in 1.2] from London to Plashy, . . . which is given some prominence in the dialogue, and where the Duchess is later reported to have died'. Some modern directors avoid the awkwardness by having Gaunt remain onstage for the beginning of 1.2, even though this solution obscures the change of location and the implied lapse of time between scenes. Such was the staging in the productions of Kent and Pimlott.

1.1.199 Saint Lambert's Day Lampe (79) calls attention to the irony implicit in Shakespeare's date – the day on which both the combatants will be exiled: Saint Lambert, a popular seventh-century bishop of Utrecht, was banished unjustly and later restored in triumph (like Bolingbroke). Ultimately he was martyred in a family feud. Gail McMurray Gibson, as reported by GWW, points out that Richard chooses an ironically inauspicious date for a contest of *swords and lances* (200) since Saint Lambert was honoured for his pacifism and, like Richard, was slain by 'armed men'. The Bishop's supporters had killed a kinsman of the assassins as Richard's adherents had murdered Gloucester; then relatives of the murdered man sought vengeance against the prelate as Bolingbroke sought vengeance against Richard for his murdered uncle. See *The Golden Legend* as translated by Caxton (5.147–9).

1.3   Richard's intervention in the combat was to be viewed as a fatal decision by later generations: in *2H4* 4.1.123–7, for instance, Mowbray's son recalls the event as the source of all the tragedy to follow: 'O when the King did throw his warder down / (His own life hung upon the staff he threw), / Then threw he down himself and all their lives / That by indictment and by dint of sword / Have since miscarried under Bullingbrook'. Hayward in 1599 compared Richard's action in arranging for the combat and then stopping it to that of Caligula in France: the Roman emperor 'with a great armie nere the sea shoare, gaue the signe of battell, set his men in aray, marched foorth as if it had bene to some great piece of seruice, & suddenly commanded them all to gather cockles' (48).

1.3.250   SD* A few editors include Aumerle in the general exit of Richard and his train at 248, making him deliver his final couplet, awkwardly, as he follows after the court. Bevington directs Aumerle to 'retire' with the Lord Marshal but remain in view – another unlikely (because unmotivated) solution. Most others keep Aumerle silent onstage, apparently unseparated from the speakers, until the end of the scene, supposing that an earlier exit would contradict his statement at the beginning of 1.4 that he accompanied Bolingbroke on the first leg of his journey into exile (see 250n.). Unless Aumerle stands apart with the Marshal (as in Bevington), his presence during the emotional leave-taking of Gaunt and his son would be dramatically awkward, even intrusive (see 252n.); moreover, spectators can easily conceive of Aumerle rejoining Bolingbroke in the imaginary interval between the two scenes, especially as they are not informed of the action until it has already taken place. GWW suggests that (a) Shakespeare forgot when he came to write 1.4 that it was Aumerle in 1.3 who had left the stage (as he had to in order to be available in the following episode) and that it was the Marshal who travelled with Bolingbroke; and (b) since it was Aumerle's character that he wished to develop in 1.4 rather than the Marshal's, the dramatist finally made Aumerle Bolingbroke's companion on the road.

1.4.23   *Q's metrically clumsy half-line leaves Bagot and Green awkwardly unidentified in the first scene in which they function as more than supernumeraries and just before the latter is to speak for the first time in the play. Q6's emendation, or something similar, would appear to be dramaturgically essential, particularly as Shakespeare in *R2* is scrupulous about identifying speakers. Several explanations of the textual anomaly have been attempted (see especially Pollard, 85; Cam¹, 150; Ard², 41; *TxC*, 308–9). Q's short line 'Our selfe and Bushie' may be explained by the hypothesis that the line was altered, in conjunction with the decision to make Bushy the messenger at 52, by removal of 'here' (if we take F's correction as a restoration of the original line). This hypothesis involves the assumption that more was inadvertently deleted from Q's copy than was necessary, or that Q's compositor misunderstood the deletion of 'here' as extending to the rest of the line. F's compositor or the annotator who prepared Q3 as copy for F (see Appendix 1, pp. 509–10, 510n.) hit on the expedient of separating 'Bushie' from 'heere' with a colon. Q6 proposed the alternative, adopted in this edn, of transposing *here* and *Bagot*.

1.4.24–36   Wilson (148–9) believes that Froissart's 'more vivid' description was determinative: 'there were in the stretes mo thanne fourtie thousande men, wepyng and cryeng after hym, that it was pytie to here; and some said: O gentyll erle of Derby, . . . This realme shall never be in joye tyll ye retourne agayne. . . . The mayre of London and a great nombre of the chiefe burgesses accompanyed therle . . . out of the cytie. Some rode to Dartforde and some to Dover, and saw hym take shippyng, and than they retourned'; the same passage implies also that Richard reduced the sentence of banishment specifically on account of Bolingbroke's popularity – 'to appease therby the people' (6.319–20). Cf. also Froissart's account of Bolingbroke's return from exile: 'and alwayes as he rode he enclyned his heed to the people on every syde' (6.361), which Wilson thought influenced the phrase 'his courtship to the common people' (24); see also 5.2.18–20 and n. Daniel, describing the events at Coventry, also mentions Bolingbroke's popularity, but specifically as Richard's motive for banishing him: since Bolingbroke was 'Belov'd of all', his victory over Mowbray 'might advance his pride' and he therefore 'become more popular by this, / Which he [Richard] feares, too much he already is' (1.64).

1.4.31 This line seems to have been echoed at least twice by Elizabethan writers. Brereton ('Notes', 102) cites an anonymous poem attacking Raleigh after his fall in 1603, which contrasts the subject's characteristic disdain with Essex's praiseworthy self-abasement: 'Renowned Essex, as he past the streets, / Would vail his bonnett to an oyster wife, / And with a kind of humble congie greet / The vulgar sort that did admire his life'; J.O. Halliwell printed the poem in his *Poetical Miscellanies* (1845), *Early English Poetry*, xv, Percy Society publications, p. 17. In contrast Everard Guilpin in *Skialetheia* (1598) attacks Essex as 'great *Foelix*', who 'passing through the street / Vayleth his cap to each one he doth meet, / And when no broome-man that will pray for him, / Shall have less truage then his bonnets brim, / Who would not thinke him perfect curtesie? / Or the honny-suckle of humilitie?' (Satire I, sig. C3ᵛ; cited by Harrison, *TLS*, 1931). The opposed attitudes to Essex which these passages illustrate suggest the similar dividedness with which *R2* portrays Bolingbroke.

1.4.45 **farm . . . realm** *Woodstock*, 4.1.180–93, is more specific in its dramatization of what Holinshed records as merely a rumour: 'These gentlemen [Green, Bagot, Bushy and Scroop] . . . all jointly here stand bound to pay your majesty, or your deputy, wherever you remain, seven thousand pounds a month for this your kingdom; for which your grace, by these writings, surrenders to their hands: all your crown lands, lordships: manors, rents: taxes, subsidies, fifteens, imposts; foreign customs, staples for wool, tin, lead and cloth: all forfeitures of goods or lands confiscate; and all other duties that do, shall, or may appertain to the king or crown's revenues; and for non-payment of the sum or sums aforesaid, your majesty to seize the lands and goods of the said gentlemen above named, and their bodies to be imprisoned at your grace's pleasure'. Cf. 2.1.57–60, 113.

1.4.52.1–53 *Wilson hypothesizes: 'if "Enter Bushie" was written in the margin against "wᵗ newes", after "Enter a Messenger" or some such words had been deleted, the compositor would be faced with "Enter Bushie wᵗ newes" which he would naturally take as a SD'. Wilson, followed by Sisson² (18), takes the second 'Bushie' to be an editorial addition to F, whereas Ure, citing H.F. Brooks, believes that it was already part of the original correction in the MS and that the name was erroneously dropped. The promptbook, which the annotator of Q3 consulted in preparing copy for F, must have contained the corrected reading in its complete and clearer form.

2.1.40–64 Gaunt's patriotic speech on England, which has no counterpart in Holinshed and which quickly became popular (it is the longest passage quoted in *Parnassus* (no. 1927), though its editor ascribed it mistakenly to Michael Drayton), appears to have been based on a diversity of sources that coalesced in Shakespeare's imagination; these include Daniel; Froissart; *Woodstock*; John Eliot's *Ortho-Epia Gallica* (1593) – a conversation book containing a translation of part of a passage by Du Bartas in praise of France; possibly an early printing of Sylvester's translation of the same Du Bartas passage (adapted as an encomium of England, 1592–5?); and Lodge's 'Truth's Complaint over England' (1584). Cf. also a similar passage in *KJ* (2.1.23–8), which may be likewise indebted to Daniel. Muir (*Sources*, 58–65) gives a detailed analysis of the indebtedness. See also the discussion of sources in the Introduction, pp. 134, 142, 149, 164–5, 165 n. 1. Mahood (79–82) comments provocatively on the speech as well as on the context in which it is embedded. McAvoy shows that the form accords with the strategies of Renaissance handbooks on the rhetoric of praise, particularly with the *Progymnasmata* of Aphthonius and the *scholia* of Reinhardus Lorichius.

2.1.46 **precious . . . sea** Gordon (*Diptych*, 38, 57–8) suggests the remote possibility that this line may contain an allusion to the famous Wilton Diptych (*c.* 1395), the left interior panel of which depicts the youthful Richard II kneeling in front of three standing saints (Edmund, Edward the Confessor and John the Baptist), while the opposite panel shows the object of Richard's devotion – the Virgin and child with angels. In the upper left-hand corner of the right panel we see a white banner with a red cross (probably evoking both Saint George, the patron saint of England, and the Resurrection), the pole (which is carried by an angel) being surmounted by an orb within which appears a minute map-like image of a green island with trees and blue sky surrounded by a sea, originally of silver leaf, on which a ship in full sail can be observed. At the centre of the island is a white castle with turrets. This tiny detail, a mere centimetre wide, only became visible in 1992 after the painting had been cleaned. The island is probably intended to symbolize England, a 'little world . . . set in the silver sea', offered like a jewel by Richard as a dowry to Our Lady, which his open hands are about to receive back with her blessing into his royal protection (see Saul, 305–7). That Shakespeare could have seen and remembered this specific image, depicted so minutely on a treasured portable royal altarpiece, seems most unlikely; as Gordon points out in an earlier article, the 'symbolism' incorporated inside the orb, being so difficult to see, is 'extremely personal' (Gordon, 'Discovery', 667). Our earliest record of the diptych is a catalogue of 1639 which lists it as among Charles I's pictures; it was supposedly given to King Charles by Sir James Palmer. It did not become part of the Pembroke estate at Wilton House until the early eighteenth century. It is now in the National Gallery, London. Shakespeare, like the anonymous painter of the diptych, may have been drawing upon an iconographic tradition of England, a precious jewel set in the sea, as the *Dos Mariae* (Mary's Dowry), a realm under the special protection of Our Lady. Gordon argues that 'by the time of Henry IV . . . the concept of England as the dowry of the Virgin was common parlance' (Gordon, 'Discovery', 667), and Richard's devotion to Mary was well known and certainly available to the dramatist: Froissart (3.239) says that he prayed before her image in Westminster Abbey before riding out to meet the peasants in Smithfield in 1381; and in 1383 he made a pilgrimage to the Shrine of Our Lady of Walsingham (see Saul, 307–8). But as Gordon also suggests, the similarity of Shakespeare's line to the island image in the painting may be nothing more than 'a coincidence' (Gordon, *Diptych*, 58).

2.1.48 ***a moat defensive** Cf. *3H6* 4.1.43–5: 'Let us be back'd with God, and with the seas, / Which he hath giv'n for fence impregnable, / And with their helps only defend ourselves'; also *KJ* 2.1.23–8: 'that pale, that white-fac'd shore, / Whose foot spurns back the ocean's roaring tides / And coops from other lands her islanders, / Even till that England, hedg'd in with the main, / That water-walled bulwark, still secure / And confident from foreign purposes'. The passage from *KJ* may be indebted to Daniel (2.49). Sylvester's adaptation of Du Bartas praises England as 'Fenc'd from the World . . . *With triple Wall (of Water, Wood, and Brasse)* / *Which neuer Stranger yet had power to passe* / *(Saue when the Heau'ns haue for thy haynous Sinne,* / *By some of Thine, with* false *Keyes let them in*' (463); Sylvester's 'false Keyes' apparently refers to the secret plots of English traitors (especially Jesuits), who assisted Catholic proselytization from abroad. See also 40n., 43–4n.

2.1.167–8 **prevention . . . marriage** Richard, charging Bolingbroke with disloyal behaviour, blocked his projected alliance with Marie, Charles VI's cousin and daughter of the Duc de Berri, contracted while Bolingbroke was in exile in Paris.

Holinshed gives a full account: 'At his comming into France, king Charles hearing the cause of his banishment (which he esteemed to be verie light) receiued him gentlie, and him honorablie interteined, in so much that he had by fauour obteined in mariage the onelie daughter of the duke of Berrie . . . if king Richard had not beene a let in that matter, who being thereof certified, sent the earle of Salisburie with all speed into France, both to surmize by vntrue suggestion, heinous offenses against him, and also to require the French king that in no wise he would suffer his cousine to be matched in mariage with him that was so manifest an offendor. This was a pestilent kind of proceeding against that nobleman then being in a forren countrie, hauing beene so honorablie receiued as he was at his entrance into France, and vpon view and good liking of his behauiour there, so forward in mariage with a ladie of noble linage' (3.495). Froissart provides even greater detail, emphasizing Bolingbroke's fury at being labelled a traitor (6.341–7). This allusion to a matter nowhere else mentioned in the play is puzzling since there is little reason to suppose that Shakespeare could assume audience knowledge of the incident from some remoter source. Wilson's argument that this 'loose thread' is evidence for Shakespeare's use or revision of a lost play is unconvincing (lxv–lxvi). The dramatist's memory of Holinshed (and perhaps Froissart) is explanation enough for the dramatic oversight. Since Bolingbroke has barely left England (see 1.4.1–37), there has been no interval during which Richard could have intervened; but, as Adams (106) suggests, the detail may be intended to create the illusion that time has elapsed since the Coventry lists; for the telescoping of time in this scene, see 289–90n. Bolingbroke's first wife, Mary de Bohun, had died in 1394.

2.1.250 **benevolences** Cf. *Jack Straw*, in which the Archbishop of Canterbury speaks of 'this last beneuolence to the King, / Giuen at high Court of Parliament' but resented by the people as 'more requirde for priuate good, / Than helpe or benefite of common weale' (ll. 190–3). The term is anachronistic, being first used in connection with Edward IV's extortions in 1473 for an anticipated invasion of France: King Edward, according to Holinshed, 'deuised this shift, to call afore him a great number of the wealthiest sort of people in his realme', demanding 'of euerie of them some portion of monie, which they sticked not to giue. And therefore the king, willing to shew that this their liberalitie was verie acceptable to him, he called this grant of monie, A beneuolence: notwithstanding that manie with grudge gaue great sums toward that new found aid, which of them might be called, A maleuolence' (3.694). The term 'plesance' is Holinshed's equivalent of *benevolence* as applied to the *new exactions* referred to in 249; a marginal note explains: 'The paiment of these fines was called a plesance as it were to please the K. withall, but yᵉ same displeased manie that were thus constreined to paie against their willes' (3.496). Some scholars, dating back as far as Richard Simpson in 1874 (see Forker, 242), have argued that Shakespeare deliberately introduced the anachronism in order to suggest a covert parallel to the hated policies of Lord Burghley, Elizabeth's Lord Treasurer. In *A Declaration of the True Causes of the Great Troubles, Presupposed to be Intended against the Realm of England* (1592), for instance, Richard Rowlands (?) fulminates against Burghley's tyrannical means of extorting funds: 'it is a woonder to consider, what great & grieueous exactions, haue from tyme to tyme bene generally emposed vpon the people, as all the *Lones* [loans], the *Lottery*, *gathering* for the steeple of Paules, newe *impostes* and *customes* of wynes, clothes, and other marchandize, *forfaictures* [forfeitures] and *confiscations* of the goodes of Catholikes, *forced beneuolences* for the sucouring of rebellious bretheren, huge masses of mony raised by *priuy seales*, and last of all, the great number of *subsidies*, which haue bene more in the tyme of this Queene, then those that haue beene leyued by diuers of her predecessors, and do amount to many *millions* of *poundes*' (60).

2.2.18 **perspectives** Perspectives are trick paintings or drawings which, viewed directly (*rightly gazed upon*), appear confused or distorted, but when looked at from an
oblique angle (*awry* (19)) resolve into a clear image. For instance, a grotesquely
elongated portrait of Edward VI, by an unknown artist, in the National Portrait
Gallery, London, must be viewed from the right-hand edge before the face comes
into proper focus (see Fig. 5). The most famous example is Holbein's *The
Ambassadors*, housed in the National Gallery, London. Although painted conventionally for the most part, this picture features a mysterious anamorphic object in
the foreground which, when observed *awry*, is seen to be a skull – a *memento mori*
concealed, as it were, at the feet of men who symbolize transitory prowess and are
visually associated with such emblems of human knowledge and achievement as a
globe, compasses, a clock, a volume on arithmetic and a lute. Holbein is thought to
have produced the distorted image by copying the reflection of a death's-head in a
curved mirror. In 16–17 Bushy alludes to a different kind of perspective, namely a
glass cut to produce the optical deception of multiplied images (cf. *TN*
5.1.216–17). The Queen's teardrops form tiny mirrors which, like shards of a shattered glass, convert a single object into many, thus distorting her vision (cf.
Richard's 'Mine eyes are full of tears; I cannot see' at 4.1.244). Invoking two different kinds of perspective in the same speech creates a puzzling ambiguity: trying
to comfort the Queen, Bushy suggests that her tears falsify her perception of imminent disaster through multiplication – that is, her feelings exaggerate the reality of
her true situation; but then, contradictorily, he refers to the experience of viewing
a perspective painting like that of Edward VI which necessitates oblique viewing in
order to *Distinguish form* (20). According to Bushy, then, looking awry yields both
false and true images. Ironically, when Green enters at 40.1 with the chilling news
of Bolingbroke's threatening actions, the Queen's intuitive sense of approaching
catastrophe is shown to be more reliable than Bushy's highly-wrought but sophis-
tical attempt to allay her fears, based on analogies to painting and optics. Gilman
relates the double perspective of Bushy's speech to the larger dualities of the play,
especially to the paradox of the king's two bodies. The perspective simile also
relates to the play's complex symbolism of mirrors – mirrors that paradoxically
reflect both truth and falsity by evoking the traditions of self-knowledge and the
'mirror of princes' genre as well as those of susceptibility to flattery, self-deception,
vanity and death (see 4.1.292–3n., 294n.). McMillin interprets Bushy's speech as a
key to the play's themes of perception, identity and loss.

2.2.122 **at . . . seven** The term derives from a dicing game called 'hazard' in which the
original expression was 'to set on cinque and sice' (from the French for 'five' and
'six', the most risky numbers to 'set on' or shoot for; see *OED* six *sb*. 5). Later the
connection with the rules of the game seems to have been lost and the numbers
shifted to six and seven, signifying confusion or impossibility, since the numerical
combination cannot be produced on a single throw, six being the highest number
on a single die. There may also be some suggestion of unluckiness implied by the
number thirteen (the combination of six and seven).

2.2.134–40 Rossiter (238) finds some reconciliation of this discrepancy in *Woodstock*,
5.6.6–7, where it is implied that Bagot flies to Bristol 'to make strong the castle' en
route to Ireland, but is then prevented at the port when he attempts to 'fly the land',
thus never managing to escape from England. Ure (78), however, rejects Rossiter's
explanation, attributing the discrepancy to 'sheer carelessness' on the dramatist's part.

2.3.99–102 Some editors adduce *Woodstock*, 5.1.67–72, where the ghost of the Black
Prince incites the sleeping Gloucester: 'Had I the vigour of my former strength /
When thou beheldst me fight at Crecy field / Where, hand-to-hand, I took King
John of France / And his bold sons my captive prisoners, / I'd shake these stiff
supporters of thy bed / And drag thee from this dull security.' The parallel,

however, is inexact and the verbal similarity slight. Nestor's speech chiding Greek cowardice and recalling his own youthful prowess (Homer, *Iliad*, 7.157–62), at which Shakespeare glances in *TC* 1.3.291–301, has also been suggested as a possible inspiration for York's lines (see Arthur Hall's translation, *Ten Books of Homer's Iliads* (1581), 125); but again, the parallels are too general to be convincing.

2.3.166 **caterpillars** In *Woodstock* Bagot and Green are referred to as 'caterpillars' – 'cankers' who 'eat the fruit / That planting and good husbandry hath nourished' (1.3.155–8) and commoners are demeaned as 'caterpillars' (3.3.138); cf. *Duchess of Malfi*, 1.1.51. The word was incorrectly taken to be cognate with 'pillage' (see *OED*, caterpillar, and 2.1.246n.). As Gurr (111) observes, the metaphor has biblical precedents (Isaiah, 33.4; Jeremiah, 15.14, 27) and was applied to usurers, to greedy friars and (by the puritan Stephen Gosson) even to poets, musicians and actors (see *OED sb*. 2) as well as to corrupt officials. Chambers (117) cites William Harrison's *Description of England* (1577), a part of Holinshed, where beggars are referred to as 'thieves and caterpillars in the commonwealth'; as Muir (*Sources*, 65) points out, Lodge uses the phrase, 'the Caterpillers of a Common weale', in *An Alarum against Usurers* (1584). Bolingbroke's use of it here ties in with the symbolism of England as a garden (see 2.1.42n. and 3.4 headnote).

2.4.9–15 Daniel, for instance, mentions 'Warnings of wrath, foregoing miseries; / In lines of fire and caracters of blood, / There fearefull formes in dreadfull flames arise, / Amazing Comets, threatning Monarches might / And new-seene stares, vnknowne vnto the night' (1.114); also 'burning Meteors, poynted-streaming lights, / Bright starres in midst of day appeare in skie' (1.115).

2.4.19–21 The sun imagery (associated symbolically with the monarch because of the sun's analogical position in the Great Chain of Being) is clearly thematic and pervasive in the play (cf. especially 3.3.178: 'Down, down I come, like glist'ring Phaëton', which the lines in the present scene subtly anticipate; see n.). The historical Richard used two different sun badges – the 'sunburst' (with clouds) and the 'sun-in-splendour' (the full orb surrounded by rays); see Scott-Giles, 65–6. The first is engraved on the cloak Richard wears in his tomb effigy; the second is illustrated in one of the illuminations from the Créton manuscript (Harleian MS 1319, fol. 18b), which shows a sail of Richard's ship on his return from Ireland so emblazoned.

3.1.11–15 Holinshed speaks of Richard's 'lasciuious liuing' (3.502) and mentions the sexuality of his court: 'there reigned abundantlie the filthie sinne of leacherie and fornication, with abhominable adulterie, speciallie in the king, but more cheefelie in the prelacie' (3.508); but he says nothing specifically about homoeroticism. The detail probably comes from *E2*, in which the sexual liaison between Edward and Gaveston is not only patent but also produces grief and jealousy in the Isabella of that play. Shakespeare might well have recalled her hostile words to Gaveston: 'thou corrupts my lord, / And art a bawd to his affections. . . . Villain, 'tis thou that rob-b'st me of my lord' (*E2*, 1.4.150–60). *Woodstock* depicts Richard as especially intimate with Green (see, for instance, 2.1.8–10, 2.2.202–4, 218–19, 3.1.76–80, 4.1.216–18, 5.4.3, 25–35) and the Queen (Anne of Bohemia) as hostile to his minions (2.3.10–37). Like Holinshed, however, the anonymous play is unspecific about homosexuality, though it is possible to detect hints of it in the Duchess of Ireland's comment that Richard 'was the cause' that her dead husband 'left [her] bed' (2.3.12), and in Richard's lament over Green: 'Hard-hearted uncles . . . That here have murdered all my earthly joys!' (5.4.29–30). The same is true of *Mirror* (113), which merely refers to Richard's 'lecherous minde' and predilection to 'Venus pleasures'. Shakespeare appears to present Bolingbroke as seeking further to besmirch the characters of Bushy and Green for his own political advantage while chivalrously holding up the Queen as a symbol of virtue from which they have led Richard astray. That the accused do not deny the charges except to protest

Bolingbroke's *injustice* in general terms (31–4) means only that they know their fates are sealed whatever defence they should attempt. The dramatic effect is to make Bolingbroke reveal himself as more expediently propagandist and Machiavellian than before and thus subtly to initiate a certain alienation of our sympathies from the usurper at a moment in the action when the dramatist needed to prepare his audience for a somewhat warmer response to Richard. Wilson (181) says that a deliberately 'false charge . . . would ill suit with the character of Bolingbroke'; however, ambiguous, unproved and perhaps unprovable accusations are a recurring feature of the play (see 1.1.88–103n. and 4.1LN).

3.1.43 **Glendower** Glendower was indeed in the general vicinity and, according to Holinshed, 'serued king Richard at Flint castell, when he was taken by Henrie duke of Lancaster' (3.518), which may explain Shakespeare's mention of him at this point in the action. After Richard's capture, Glendower escaped into Wales. Ure (93) suggests that the dramatist was merely adding a 'bit of historical colour', while Adams (148) thinks the detail helps to establish Bolingbroke's 'capacity for organisation and the thoroughness and efficiency with which he copes with problems as they arise' (in contrast to Richard). That the Welsh tended to be hostile to Bolingbroke and friendly to Richard is borne out by Créton (104/327); see also 2.4.6n. The fiery Welsh chieftain is never mentioned again in *R2*, but since he figures prominently in *1H4*, Shakespeare may have been planning ahead. For the possible identification of Glendower with the Welsh Captain of 2.4, see List of Roles, 31n. Gurr (114), following Theobald and other eighteenth–century editors, believes that 43 'may be a late insertion' since it interrupts a concluding couplet, and that possibly it reflects an attempt at 'belated preparation' for *1H4*. However, a continuity of sorts is preserved in *R2*, as we learn, in 3.3, that Bolingbroke has reached Wales when he immediately refers to the dispersal of the Welsh troops.

3.2 Wilson (182) believes that Shakespeare also consulted *Traïson* (42/190) and Créton (97/324), both of whom make Salisbury the bearer of evil tidings; however, the playwright could himself have invented such a strategy in the interests of effective dramaturgy. As Ure (97) argues, Salisbury is 'the obvious person to bring the bad news of the Welsh defection' since in Holinshed he had been sent from Ireland to gather troops in Wales and has already been shown in 2.4 with the Welsh Captain. The present scene is symmetrically structured to convey both Richard's unfounded overconfidence and his 'vtter despaire' (Holinshed's phrase in a side-note on the description quoted in 3.2 headnote) by dramatizing the rapid oscillation between these extremes as the tidings of disaster accumulate. The technique, as Herford (176) remarks, is a little like that of 2.2, involving a succession of entrances; see also 5.6 headnote. This arrangement gives dramatic immediacy to the situation described by Créton (113/337): 'for on all sides, one after another, came pouring in upon him mischief and trouble'. Johnson believed that 2.4 and 3.1 were 'accidentally transposed' and that 2.4 should more logically appear as 'the second scene' of Act 3 (1.438).

3.2.6 **salute** There are overtones here of the 'royal touch' – the ancient belief in England and France that the King, having been anointed with a special chrism, had the power to cure 'the King's evil' or scrofula (a term used over time for a variety of ailments); cf. *Mac* 4.3.141–56, where Malcolm describes the 'most miraculous work' of Edward the Confessor, to whose hand heaven has lent 'Such sanctity' that the diseased 'presently amend'. The ancient practice of royal touching (famously used by Edward the Confessor, whose arms Richard adopted; see 56–7n.) was newly formalized by Edward III, Richard's grandfather, used regularly by the Tudors and Stuarts, and continued intermittently until the reign of Queen Anne. Elizabeth I practised the traditional ceremony, the liturgy for which was published in 1597 by William Tooker, an Anglican priest (see Bloch, 190, 386–7); certain editions of the *Prayer Book* contained the rite. The word *wound* (7) reinforces the curative implications of Richard's action as does his maternalist conception of kingship and his anthropomorphic imaging of the earth (cf. 8–11, 19, 24–5).

3.2.24–5 **these . . . soldiers** Wilson (183) sees a possible echo of Luke, 3.8 ('God is able of these stones to raise up children unto Abraham') or 19.40 ('I tell you that if these would hold their peace then shall the stones cry immediately'). Michel (20–1) suggests a debt to Daniel (2.30) where Salisbury tries to persuade Richard to remain in his place of protection and thus avoid possible capture by Bolingbroke: 'Here haue you craggy rockes to take your part / That neuer will betray their faith to you; . . . If men will not, these very cliffes will fight / And be sufficient to defend your right.' RP proposes a conceivable allusion to the use of stones as weapons at Poitiers when the soldiers ran out of arrows (represented in *E3* 4.6.13–16); GWW suggests the possibility of an allusion to the myth of Deucalion, who renewed the world's population after a devastating flood by throwing stones, the metaphorical bones of mother earth, over his shoulder and thus turning them into men (cf. Ovid, *Met.*, 1.348–415).

3.2.93–103 Johnson comments on this speech: 'It seems to be the design of the poet to raise Richard to esteem in his fall, and consequently to interest the reader in his favour. He gives him only passive fortitude, the virtue of a confessor rather than of a king. In his prosperity we saw him imperious and oppressive, but in his distress he is wise, patient, and pious' (1.440).

3.2.122 **Where is Bagot?** Of the quartet of favourites mentioned here, Bagot is the only one to survive; he reappears in 4.1 where he accuses Aumerle. See 2.2.134–40n. Having raised the question of Bagot's whereabouts here, however, neither Richard nor the other characters onstage engage with it: Richard later exclaims against only *Three Judases* (132), Aumerle omits Bagot from his question 'Is Bushy, Green and the Earl of Wiltshire dead?' (141), and Scroop, replying to Aumerle, confirms only that Bushy, Green and Wiltshire were the three who *lost their heads* (142) at Bristol. Theobald, however, assuming that an error in transmission had occurred, proposed to emend *Bagot* to 'he got', thus making Richard's question apply to Wiltshire; but as Chambers (124), noting the absence of parallels, observes, 'the phrase sounds hardly Shakespearian'. Wells (217–18) suspects that the confusion at this point 'may be the result of imperfect revision on Shakespeare's part', while Gurr (120) adds that an 'explanation' of Bagot's separate destiny may have somehow been omitted 'between 122 and 132', the putative omission being connected also with 'incomplete adjustments to the movements of the minor figures evident in 2.2'. The fogginess is further worsened by the decision to exclude Wiltshire (apparently one of the *Three Judases*) as a dramatic character, for the audience have already been encouraged to regard Bushy, Bagot and Green as a trio (cf. 2.2.123–48). Wilson (186) believed that Shakespeare 'identified "Bagot" with "the Earl of Wiltshire"' in 122, the two names being meant to be understood 'in apposition'; but this seems most unlikely, given their obvious separateness at 2.2.135 and in Holinshed. In performance, where the whole point is the rapid agglomeration of evil tidings, the puzzle about Bagot tends to pass by unnoticed. The narrative effect of the unanswered question about Bagot may be to remind the audience that he was not executed in 3.1 with the other favourites, thus preparing for his reappearance in 4.1.

3.2.131 *Vipers* (129) were fabled for their treachery, and, as Ure (100) notes, the comparison of traitors to snakes in the bosom – 'in my heart-blood warmed' – was commonplace, even proverbial; cf. 5.3.57 and *2H6* 3.1.343–4: 'you but warm the starved snake, / Who, cherish'd in your breasts, will sting your hearts'; also Dent, V68. The idea may have arisen from a familiar fable of Aesop illustrating ingratitude – concerning a peasant who warmed a nearly frozen serpent in his breast out of pity and was fatally bitten (Yoder, 18, 117–18). See also Daniel, 2.60: 'These vipers spoile the wombe wherein they lie'; *Woodstock*, 5.3.30–1: 'Never such vipers were endured so long / To grip, and eat the heart of all the kingdom.' RP adds 'Vipers are also, as their etymology reveals, ovo-viviparous (hatching eggs inside the mother's body and so giving birth to living offspring), and could be imagined as gnawing their way out of the mother (cf. *1H6* 3.1.72–3, *Per* 1.1.64–5), which is Daniel's image.'

3.2.156 Richard invokes the literary tradition of *de casibus* tragedy such as Lydgate's *Fall of Princes* (an adaptation of Boccaccio's *De Casibus Virorum Illustrium*), Chaucer's *Monk's Tale* and, most popular of all, *The Mirror for Magistrates* (1559–78), a tradition on which *R2* is itself founded. Cf. also the *death of kings* in Shakespeare's earlier plays (especially *3H6*, *R3* and, perhaps, *KJ*) and Marlowe's *E2*. Wolsey's speech on 'the state of man' (*H8* 3.2.351–72) develops the idea of tragic fall in a political context. For the tradition of Fortune's wheel as vital to *R2*, see Farnham, 415–18. See also 3.4.10n. Robert Baron's pervasive indebtedness to *R2*, found substantially in his two works, *Cyprian Academy* (1647) and *Mirza* (1655), begins here. This line is imitated in *Mirza*, 95, 'Come my good Lord . . . you and I / Will sit, and tell sad stories'. Baron further echoes *R2* 3.2.160–3 ('Here Death keepeth his Court', *Academy*, 3.43); 3.3.12–14 ('to lop him shorter by the head', *Mirza*, 44); 3.3.88 ('Children unborn, and Priests not yet begotten', *Mirza*, 82); 4.1.138 ('what land, what fields / Has not his sword manur'd with hostile blood!', *Mirza*, 76); 4.1.221 ('many yeares of Sun-shine dayes', *Academy*, 3.58–9); and 5.1.55–6 ('Staves in the ladder we ascend a Throne by', *Mirza*, 21). See also 5.1.44n. and Forker, 'Baron', 184–5, 193–4.

3.2.160–3 **For . . . pomp** Douce in 1807 (see Forker, 92–3) was the first to suggest that this image may derive from a woodcut in the famous series *Imagines Mortis* (*Dance of Death* by Hans Holbein the Younger), which shows a grinning skeleton rising from behind an enthroned king and about to remove the crown from his head. As Collier pointed out, Death in this print does not actually sit *within* the crown or keep *his court* there, so that the influence on Shakespeare, if any, would be rather general. The *memento mori* tradition, as in Holbein's *Dance of Death*, commonly depicted a skull or skeleton mocking the pretensions and false security of the great (see Fig. 8). Johnson (1.441) noted here 'an allusion to the "antick" or "fool" of old farces, whose chief part is to deride and disturb the graver and more splendid personages'; cf. *little scene* (164). Reyher (63) cites *1 Tamburlaine*, 5.1.111–12, where on the point of Tamburlaine's sword 'sits imperious death, / Keeping his circuit by the slicing edge'. As Wilson (187) observes, 'circuit' is Shakespeare's synonym for *crown* in *2H6* 3.1.352: 'the golden circuit on my head'. For Baron's imitation, see 156LN.

3.3.62–7 The imagery describing Richard as the crimson sun emerging at dawn to overwhelm the opposing clouds comes as a confirmatory, if ironic, recrudescence of the King's own comparison of himself to the 'searching eye of heaven' hidden at first 'Behind the globe' (3.2.37–8) but soon 'rising in our throne, the east' (3.2.50); see also 2.4.19–21LN. Some commentators, beginning with Oscar Wilde (see Forker, 280), have believed that Shakespeare was influenced by seeing Richard's effigy in Westminster Abbey (the sunburst obscured by or emerging from clouds on the King's mantle is reproduced in Senior, 91).

3.4.38 **weeds** The upstart-weed metaphor was not uncommon: cf. *Woodstock*, 5.6.3–5, where Lancaster (Gaunt) says that Richard's uncles 'Have toiled to purge fair England's pleasant field / Of all those rancorous weeds that choked the grounds / And left her pleasant meads like barren hills'. Rossiter (237) cites *1 Troublesome Reign*, ll. 1543–7, where King John recalls his first investiture as monarch: 'Once since that time ambicious weedes have sprung / To staine the beautie of our garden plot: / But heavens in our conduct rooting thence / The false intruders, breakers of worlds peace, / Have to our joy, made Sunshine chase the storme'; also *2H6*

494

3.1.31–3, where Queen Margaret warns her husband about upstarts: 'Now 'tis the spring, and weeds are shallow-rooted; / Suffer them now, and they'll o'ergrow the garden, / And choke the herbs for want of husbandry.' Cf. also *3H6* 2.6.21. Since Lodge's 'Truth's Complaint' seems to have been otherwise influential in the play (cf. 2.1.43–4n., 70n.), it is possible that a stanza comparing weeds to 'wicked men' may have prompted Shakespeare in this passage, especially at 37–9 and 43–5; see Muir, *Sources*, 64. The general idea of weeds as destructive is proverbial (Dent, W241–2): cf. Hamlet's comparison of the world to 'an unweeded garden / That grows to seed' – a garden which 'things rank and gross in nature / Possess . . . merely' (*Ham* 1.2.135–7). Since his context is also political, Heywood may have had Shakespeare in mind for *2 If You Know Not Me*, ll. 2329–30: 'Weedes must bee weeded out, yet weeded so, / Till they doe hurt, let them a Gods name grow' (see 1.1.160n.).

3.4.72 **old Adam's likeness** Cf. *2H6* 4.2.134: 'Adam was a gardener'; also *Ham* 5.1.36–7 and Genesis, 2.15: 'Then the Lorde God tooke the man, and put him into the garden of Eden, that he might dresse it and keepe it' (Geneva Bible). He was often portrayed in pictures as an old man, partly, no doubt, because medieval Christian typology conceived of Christ as the 'new Adam' (saviour of the world) in contrast to the 'old Adam' (agent of the Fall; cf. 75–6); cf. also his namesakes in *CE* ('old Adam . . . that keeps the prison', 4.3.13–18) and *AYL* ('*Adam*. Is "old dog" my reward?', 1.1.82). See also 5.3.145n.

4.1 The first movement (1–107) presents the acrimonious quarrelling of the nobles – the challenges to Aumerle by Bagot, Fitzwater and others, the impassioned denials of the accused, and the reopening of the matter of Gloucester's death, responsibility for which remains still unclear from the early scenes of the play but which the present wrangling only serves further to confuse and obfuscate. The furious throwing down and taking up of gages in the presence of Bolingbroke replicates the situation of the play's opening scene at which Richard had presided – but now with more cynical, indeed almost parodic, effect. When Bolingbroke proposes to recall Mowbray as a means of importing fresh evidence into the dispute, Carlisle quashes all hope of certainty by reporting his death abroad. We see immediately that the usurper must begin his reign in a climate of rancour and instability among his courtiers. The second movement (108–62) commences with the entrance of York (who does duty for all the commissioners in Holinshed's account) to announce that Richard has willingly renounced the throne. Bolingbroke instantly responds by proclaiming his accession, which in turn prompts Carlisle's eloquent speech of protest with its appeal to divine-right legitimacy and its prophecy of civil war. The Bishop's summary arrest and Bolingbroke's decision to have Richard surrender *in common view* (156), so that the transfer of power may be clothed in the garment of legality, bring the second section to an end. Richard's operatic spectacle of self-humiliation and royal martyrdom constitutes the dominant third movement (163–320). This is almost wholly the product of the dramatist's imagination, including Richard's ritualized discrowning (but see 181n.) and the episode with the mirror. A few generalities in Holinshed, however, were doubtless influential: he reports, for instance, that at the prospect of losing his crown Richard was 'with sorrow almost consumed, and in manner halfe dead . . . vtterlie despairing of all comfort' (3.503); and that when his former subjects retracted their allegiance, the moment 'was a redoubling of his greefe, in so much as thereby it came to his mind, how in former times he was acknowledged & taken for their liege lorde and souereigne, who now (whether in contempt or in malice, God knoweth) to his face forsware him to be their king' (3.507). The third movement closes with the symbolic contrast of Richard's being returned to prison, now as a private person, and Bolingbroke's announcement of his imminent coronation. After this *woeful pageant*

(321), at which point all but Aumerle, Carlisle and the Abbot of Westminster leave the stage, the scene concludes with the brief fourth movement (321–34) – a *coda* which introduces plans for a counterplot to restore Richard to the throne, an obvious preparation for 5.2 and 5.3. The roles of Harry Percy, York and Northumberland are largely invented although Hall and Froissart (see 107.1LN and 151–5n.) may have slightly influenced the latter two.

4.1.0.4 ***Herald*** Although Bolingbroke only becomes king *de jure* when Richard yields him the crown at 204 (or perhaps even later at his coronation; cf. 319–20), he behaves like a king from the beginning of the scene (1n. and also his use of the royal plural at 91, 107, 157, 159–61 and 319–20); the herald may therefore be intended simply as a symbol of Bolingbroke's royalty or at least of his new political status. It seems unlikely that the herald would announce Richard's entrance at 162.1 since at this point the King is already *plume-plucked* (109) and arrives in Parliament as a virtual prisoner – stripped of his authority and in the custody of York. Jowett & Taylor (198) argue that in neither Q nor F 'is a herald required' and speculate that the survival of the figure in F's SD represents the vestige of an earlier version of the scene in which the herald had a speaking part: 'Shakespeare's first draft may have been censored, and the text as it stands in F may be a rewritten version which actually avoids political controversy.' Just how the presence of a herald would contribute to a hypothetically more controversial episode, however, is far from obvious. The safest solution is to retain the herald as a mute attendant in Bolingbroke's train.

4.1.1 **Bagot** Shakespeare omits the following complications in Holinshed: Bagot's disclosure that Richard's dislike of Bolingbroke was owing partly to the latter's enmity to the Church; Bagot's report that Mowbray had tried to save Gloucester's life at Calais and that he had finally complied with Richard's orders only out of fear for his own life (see 1.1.133–4n.); Bagot's claim that he had tried to warn Bolingbroke in exile of Richard's secret malice towards him; the Duke of Exeter's challenge to Bagot that he had secretly plotted to have Bolingbroke killed on the pretext of resisting arrest; Bagot's implicating of one John Hall, a yeoman, in the death of Gloucester as a result of which Hall was condemned and executed; Surrey's explanation, in denouncing Fitzwater for mendacity, that those accused of causing Gloucester's death were acting under constraint when they voted in Parliament to condemn him.

4.1.41 **rapier's point** Johnson (1.445) thought that this desertion of 'the manners of the age' was 'without necessity': 'The edge of a sword had served [Shakespeare's] purpose' just as well, 'and he had then escaped the impropriety of giving the English nobles a weapon which was not seen in England til two centuries afterwards.'

4.1.92–101 Holinshed mentions Mowbray's death twice, first at the time of his exile (3.496): 'Norfolke departed sorowfullie out of the relme into Almanie [Germany], and at the last came to Venice, where he for thought [depression] and melancholie deceassed: for he was in hope (as writers record) that he haue beene borne out in the matter [of Gloucester's death] by the king [Richard], which when it fell out otherwise, it greeued him not a little'; and again shortly after Bolingbroke proposes to recall him (3.514): 'This yeare [1399] Thomas Mowbraie duke of Norffolke died in exile at Venice, whose death might haue beene worthilie bewailed of all the realme, if he had not beene consenting to the death of the duke of Glocester.' The association of Mowbray with the Crusades probably derives from Stow (515), who reports that the Duke 'dyed at Venice, in his returne from Jerusalem'; Stow, however, does not specify whether he had been in the Holy Land as a soldier or as a pilgrim. Wilson (203) cites *Traïson* (22/158) at the point where Mowbray is sentenced to banishment: 'That Thomas of Mowbray, Duke of Norfolk, shall quit the realm for the rest of his life, and shall choose whether he would dwell in Prussia, in Bohemia, or in Hungary, or would go right beyond sea to the land of the Saracens and unbelievers; that he shall never return to set foot again on Christian land'. Ure (129) argues persuasively that the French account 'is not very close to Shakespeare, and implies in its last sentence a contradiction of Shakespeare and Holinshed, whom Shakespeare follows in respect of the death at Venice'. Conceivably the reference to the Crusades owes something to Froissart (6.317), who writes that, after Bolingbroke's banishment, people speculated on that lord's possible travels to the Holy Land: 'thoughe he have been sore traveyled in his dayes in farre countreis, as into Pruce, and to the Holy Sepulchre, to Cayre, and to saynt Katheryns mount, so he may do yet, goo some other voyages to passe the tyme if he lyste . . . Whan he cometh into Spaygne he maye move theym [the Queens of Spain and Portugal] to make warre upon the Sarazyns.' Theoretically, Shakespeare could have enriched Holinshed with the new detail from Stow (which seems probable); or used Holinshed in conjunction with *Traïson* or Froissart's association of Bolingbroke with crusading; or have employed any combination of these sources. But it may be just as credible that he invented the colourful description of Mowbray's crusading adventures as an effective bit of historical and dramatic heightening. In historical fact, however, as Newbolt (122) points out, 'there was no Crusade between 1396 and 1439, nor did any Crusader reach Jerusalem after the twelfth century'.

4.1.107.1 If Shakespeare relied exclusively on Holinshed at this point, the mention of the Archbishop of York could have supplied his cue. Hall (fol. vii^v), however, reports that Bolingbroke relied on the Duke of York's assistance at the time of Richard's abdication: 'The Duke of Lancastre [Bolingbroke] the nexte daye [after Richard had agreed to resign the crown] declared all kyng Richardes hole mind to the councel, but especially to his vncle Edmunde duke of Yorke (whose helpe he much vsed) whiche hearyng al thynges to be in a broyle, a fewe daies before was come to London.' Froissart (6.378) also records that York was in London: 'the next day [after Bolingbroke had consulted with Richard in the Tower concerning his handing over the crown] he sent forthe mo commaundementes into all parties of the realme, to cause noble men and other to come to London. His uncle the duke of Yorke came to London, and the earl of Rutlande his sonne, the earle of Northumberlande, and the lorde Thomas Percy his brother.' Ure (131) argues cogently, however, that Shakespeare need not have relied on either Hall or Froissart for York's function in this scene: 'York provides continuity with the earlier part of the play', and some character was obviously needed to serve as an intermediary between the new king and the old. The appearance of York at this point is also significant in view of his developing role and the events to follow in Act 5.

4.1.115–50 Holinshed (3.512) writes: 'request was made by the commons [on 22 October 1399], that sith king Richard had resigned, and was lawfullie deposed from his roiall dignitie, he might haue iudgement decreed against him, so as the realme were not troubled by him, and that the causes of his deposing might be published through the realme for satisfieng of the people: which demand was granted. Wherevpon the bishop of Carleill, a man both learned, wise, and stout of stomach, boldlie shewed foorth his opinion concerning that demand; affirming that there was none amongst them woorthie or meet to giue iudgement vpon so noble a prince as king Richard was, whom they had taken for their souereigne and liege lord, by the space of two & twentie yeares and more; "And I assure you (said he) there is not so ranke a traitor, nor so errant a theef, nor yet so cruell a murtherer apprehended or deteined in prison for his offense, but he shall be brought before the iustice to heare his iudgement; and will ye proceed to the iudgement of an anointed king, hearing neither his answer nor excuse? I say, that the duke of Lancaster whom ye call king, hath more trespassed to K. Richard & his realme, than king Richard hath doone either to him, or vs: for it is manifest & well knowne, that the duke was

497

banished the realme by K. Richard and his councell, and by the iudgement of his owne father, for the space of ten yeares, for what cause ye know, and yet without licence of king Richard, he is returned againe into the realme, and (that is woorse) hath taken vpon him the name, title, & preheminence of king. And therfore I say, that you haue doone manifest wrong, to proceed in anie thing against king Richard, without calling him openlie to his answer and defense." As soone as the bishop had ended this tale, he was attached by the earle marshall, and committed to ward in the abbeie of saint Albons.'

Daniel (3.22) also seems to have influenced Shakespeare's wording: 'Neuer shall this poore breath of mine consent / That he that two and twenty yeeres hath raignd / As lawfull Lord, and king by iust discent, / Should here be iudgd vnheard, and vnraignd / By subiects two [too]: Iudges incompetent / To iudge their king vnlawfully detaind, / And vn-brought forth to plead his guiltles cause, / Barring th'annointed libertie of lawes.' Wilson (199), while acknowledging that Holinshed is verbally closer to Shakespeare in this scene, argues that *Traïson* (70–1/221–2) was also consulted for Carlisle's words of protest, because the French chronicle 'places the speech almost immediately after Bolingbroke's assumption of the throne'. Although this is possible, Shakespeare does so much rearranging of incidents in the fourth act (see headnote) that there is no need to attribute this particular proximity to *Traïson*. Ure (132) cites other sources, especially the homilies on obedience and against rebellion, that Shakespeare may have drawn upon in a general way for the received idea that subjects must not presume to judge a king (see *Homily*, 2.279).

4.1.126–30 Johnson (1.446) notes that the doctrine of divine right clearly preceded the Stuarts: 'Here is another proof that our authour did not learn in King James's court his elevated notions of the right of kings. I know not any flatterer of the Stuarts who has expressed this doctrine in much stronger terms. It must be observed that the poet intends from the beginning to the end to exhibit this bishop as brave, pious, and venerable.'

4.1.163–222 Talbert (184–5) argues that the dialogue in this passage, a section he calls 'the transfer of regalia', is so written as to reflect an alternating sequence of 'Lancastrian' (pro-Bolingbroke) and 'Yorkist' (pro-Richard) attitudes toward deposition: Lancastrian (163–8); Yorkist (168–77); Lancastrian (178–81); Yorkist (182–90); Lancastrian (191–222). In my opinion the dichotomy is less schematic than this. See Introduction, pp. 34–8.

4.1.171–2 Wilson (207–8) cites *Traïson* (49/198, 52/201): 'the said Earl [of Northumberland] . . . can only be likened to Judas or to Guenelon. . . . Then turning to his companions, who were weeping, he [Richard] said with a sigh, "Ah! my good and faithful friends, we are all betrayed, and given without cause into the hands of our enemies; for God's sake have patience, and call to mind our Saviour, who was undeservedly sold and given into the hands of his enemies."' A third passage from *Traïson* (56/206) has Carlisle saying to Richard, 'if we must die, let us accept death willingly, and call to mind the passion of our Saviour and of the holy martyrs in Paradise'. Créton (179/377–8) contains a passage comparing Richard to Christ before Pilate: 'Then spake Duke Henry quite aloud to the commons of the said city [London], "Fair Sirs, behold your king! consider what you will do with him!" And they made answer with a loud voice, "We will have him taken to Westminster." And so he delivered him unto them. At this hour did he remind me of Pilate, who caused our Lord Jesus Christ to be scourged at the stake, and afterwards had him brought before the multitude of the Jews, saying, "Fair Sirs, behold your king!" who replied, "let him be crucified!" Then Pilate washed his hands of it, saying, "I am innocent of the just blood." And so he delivered our Lord unto them. Much in the like manner did Duke Henry, when he gave up his rightful lord to the rabble of London, in order that, if they should put him to death, he might say, "I am innocent of this deed."' Ure (xlvi–xlix) doubts the influence of either *Traïson* or Créton on Shakespeare.

4.1.203 **undo myself** Ranald shows how this aspect of the play draws upon traditions of ceremonial degradation in chivalric, military and ecclesiastical contexts. Particularly relevant to Shakespeare's invented ritual of discrowning could have been the solemn public stripping of vestments and episcopal appurtenances from Archbishop Cranmer, Primate of all England, in the cathedral at Oxford in 1556 prior to his execution. As elaborately celebrated by Foxe in *Acts and Monuments* (1583), Cranmer became the archetypal martyr of the English Church, parallel historically to Richard II as the royal martyr. Cranmer was ceremonially degraded by bishops inferior to him in rank, a technical violation of authority, whereas Richard, to prevent such violence to tradition, discrowns himself as Celestine V had done at his abdication of the papacy in 1294; see Ranald, 183–8. In Woodman's television film, David Birney as Richard knelt while giving up the sceptre and crown. See Introduction, pp. 35–6.

4.1.204–15 Cf. also Froissart (6.378): 'kynge Rycharde was brought into the hall [of the Tower], aparelled lyke a kynge in his robes of estate, his septer in his hande, and his crowne on his heed. Than he stode up alone, nat holden nor stayed by no man, and sayde aloude: I have been kynge of Englande, duke of Acquytany, and lorde of Irelande, about xxii. yeres, which sygnory, royalte, cepter, crowne, and herytage, I clerely resygne here to my cosyn Henry of Lancastre: and I desyre hym here in this open presence, in entrynge of the same possessyon, to take this septour: and so delyvered it to the duke, who toke it. Than kynge Rycharde toke the crowne fro his heed with bothe his handes, and set it before hym, and sayd: Fayre cosyn, Henry duke of Lancastre, I gyve and delyver you this crowne, wherwith I was crowned kyng of Englande, and therwith all the right therto dependyng. The duke of Lancastre tooke it, and the archebysshop of Caunterbury toke it out of the dukes handes'. The note of personal suffering in Hall (fol. ix) could also have been influential: 'I of my owne mere mocion and frewill, do putte and depose my self out of all royall dignite, preheminence and sofferaignitee, and resigne the possession, title and vse of this realme, with all rightes there vnto apperteigyng, into his handes and possession. And then with a lamentable voyce and a sorowfull countenance, delivered his scepter and croune to the duke of Lancastre, requiryng euery persone seuerally by their names, to graunt and assente that he might liue a priuate and a solitarie life, with the swetnesse whereof, he would be so well pleased, that it should be a pain and punishement to hym to go abrode.'

4.1.235 **strong . . . oath** Northumberland lured Richard from the safety of Conway Castle on the pretext of arranging a meeting with Bolingbroke to discuss their grievances and come to peaceful agreement; Richard, 'vpon the earles oth, for assurance that the same should be performed in ech condition, agreed to go with the earle to meete the duke', and so was trapped by Northumberland's prearranged ambush (Holinshed, 3.500; see 3.2 and 3.3 headnotes). *Traïson* (49/199) gives Northumberland's betrayal heavy emphasis, the Earl being required to 'assure us [Richard] by your loyal oath, and swear upon the sacred body of our Lord, that what you have told us from our cousin of Lancaster is true'. Créton (146/363) also underlines Northumberland's guile: here Richard laments, 'it is the earl who hath drawn us forth upon his oath'. In Daniel (2.24), Northumberland falsely 'laies his soule to pledge, and takes his oth / The [h]ost of Christ an [h]ostage for his troth'.

4.1.256–7 **name . . . usurped** Some historians, excluding Hall and Holinshed, mention a rumour, circulated among Lancastrian partisans, that Richard was the illegitimate son of a priest of Bordeaux and that his true name was 'Jehan' (John). Froissart (6.377) has Bolingbroke telling Richard in the Tower 'that the common renome rynneth through Englande, and in other places, that ye were never sonne to the prince of Wales, but rather sonne to a preest or to a chanon; for I have herde of certayne knightes that were in the princes howse, myne uncle, howe that he knew well that his wyfe had nat truely kepte her maryage'. *Traïson* (64/215, 72/223, 94/248) refers to the story thrice: first, making the London populace curse Richard as 'this wicked bastard'; second, having Bolingbroke arrange for the sentencing and imprisonment of 'John of Bordeaux, who has been called Richard King of England'; and, finally, in the command that Exton 'deliver straightway from this world John of London, called Richard'. Rossiter (216) thinks that the same rumour may be alluded to in *Woodstock*, 2.2.100, where the King, referring to the disputed date of his own birth, says, 'thereby hangs a secret mystery'. Elizabethan audiences were unlikely to be familiar with the story.

4.1.291 **face** Richard was 'seemelie of shape and fauor' (Holinshed, 3.507); Nigel Saul, Richard's biographer, writes that he 'showed an almost obsessive interest in projecting and manipulating his own image', flaunting 'an idealized royal image before his subjects' in 'every artistic medium – in sculpture, writing and in painting' (238); and again that he 'was highly conscious of his image, . . . more likenesses surviv[ing] of him than of any English ruler before Henry VIII' (450). The tradition of Richard's handsomeness is summed up by Richard Baker in *A Chronicle of the Kings of England From the Time of the Romans' Government unto the Reign of our Sovereign Lord King Charles* (1643), 2.27: 'He was of such a comly and graceful Personage, that he is said to be the most Beautiful Prince, that ever wore the *English* Diadem.'

4.1.292–3 **shadow . . . shadow** The concept of the shadow-king also connects this passage to *E2*, one of Shakespeare's obvious models: cf. 'But what are kings when regiment is gone / But perfect shadows in a sunshine day?' (*E2*, 5.1.26–7). Forker (*E2*, 29–30, 40–1) discusses the possible development of the shadow-king idea from Shakespeare's original use of it in *3H6* 4.3.49–50 through Marlowe to *R2*. Daniel (2.113) also introduces the idea when he makes Richard ask his enemies to allow him to retain the 'name' and 'title' of king while he cedes the power to others: 'Leaue me that shew and I will be content, / And let them rule and gouerne without feare: / O can they not my shadowe now indure / When they of all the rest do stand secure?'

5.1 Daniel's treatment is much less dramatic than Shakespeare's. In the poem, to be sure, the Queen waits for her husband to appear in a London street, but she looks out of a window, and the occasion is Bolingbroke's processional entry into London with Richard as his prisoner. Observing the riders from a distance, she at first mistakes the triumphant Bolingbroke for her husband, swoons when she recognizes Richard in humble attire, then swears to love him steadfastly for himself despite his degradation; finally she contrives to be alone with him at night in a chamber whither she has come by 'a close concealed way' (Daniel, 2.93). After he has briefly welcomed her, both lovers become speechless with grief; only at the end of the passage does Richard attempt to assuage his wife's sorrow, though Daniel at this point gives him no words to speak. The greater part of Daniel's episode is devoted to a long meditative soliloquy by the Queen in which she tries, with only partial success, to master her desolation. Shakespeare, transforming lyrical complaint and the stasis of protracted lamentation into drama, equalizes the speeches of the lovers, and introduces Northumberland as the harsh instrument of their separation. Pathos is increased by the sense of *Realpolitik* intruding upon personal devotion and intimacy – emotions which challenge Bolingbroke's earlier assertion that Bushy and Green had sinfully 'made a divorce betwixt' them (see 3.1.11–15n.). *Traïson* (27/167–8) also stresses Richard's devotion to his queen at the point when he departs for Ireland: 'I never saw so great a lord make so much of, nor shew such great affection to, a lady, as did King Richard to his Queen. Great pity was it that they separated, for never saw they each other more.' But there is nothing in the French source that Shakespeare could not more easily have derived from Daniel.

5.1.2 **ill-erected** Elizabethan theatre-goers might have recalled the various malignant events connected with the Tower in Shakespeare's earlier histories, e.g. the sordid quarrelling of Lord Protector Gloucester and the Bishop of Winchester at the Tower gates and, later, the death of embittered Mortimer who, recalling Richard II's deposition by Bolingbroke, provides the stimulus for Richard Plantagenet's attempt to reclaim the crown for the Yorkists in the bloody civil wars that follow (*1H6* 1.3, 2.5); the imprisonment and murder of Henry VI by Plantagenet's evil son, 'misshapen Dick' *(3H6* 5.6); the slaughter of Clarence and the smothering of the young princes as described by Tyrrel (*R3* 1.4, 4.3).

5.1.13–15 **Thou . . . guest?** Cf. Thomas Walkington, *The Optic Glass of Humours* (1607), which may imitate Shakespeare: 'His comely body is a beautious Inne, / Built fairely to the owners princely minde, / Where wandring vertues lodge oft lodg'd with sinne, / Such pilgrims kindest entertainment finde. / An Inne, said I, O no that names vnfit, / Sith there stay not a night, but dwell in it' (fols 84–84ᵛ). Fletcher and Massinger probably echo Shakespeare's lines in *The Lovers' Progress* (1623?), 5.3.63–6: ''tis my wonder, / If such mishapen ghests, as lust and murther, / At any price should ever finde a lodging / In such a beauteous Inne!' (Fletcher, 10.518); see also 3.1.21n.

5.1.44 **tale of me** F's 'fall' is probably an indifferent variant. It has been suggested that *tale* may be a memorial slip on the part of Q's compositor, triggered by *tales* in 41, but this is unlikely as, according to Craven, a different compositor took over at 43 (see Appendix 1, p. 537).

5.1.55–6 **ladder . . . throne** In *Ironside*, ll. 76–8, Edricus refers to himself as 'tho'nely ladder vppon wᶜʰ' King Canute 'Clymed' to the 'kindome'; cf. also Daniel, 1.74: 'Who will throw downe himselfe for other men / That make a ladder by his fall to clime?' Heywood in *1 If You Know Not Me*, ll. 38–9, borrowed the idea for Queen Mary's accession: 'The suffolke men . . . was to the Queene / The very stayres, by which she did ascend' (see also 1.1.160n.). For Baron's imitation of this image, see 3.2.156LN.

5.1.71–3 conceivably influenced by Créton (117/340), who lays heavy stress on Richard's pain in being separated from his wife, although the King expresses his grief at Conway, where the Queen is not present, rather than in London: 'My mistress and my consort! accursed be the man, little doth he love us, who thus shamefully separateth us two. I am dying of grief because of it.'

5.1.79–80 Queen Isabel is associated with *May* because of her youth and the traditions of 'Maying', i.e. gathering flowers and courting (cf. *H5* 1.2.120; *TNK* 2.3.36), whereas *Hallowmas* (All Saints Day, November 1) is symbolic of autumn and the onset of winter (cf. *1H4* 1.2.158–9). The historical seasons were nearly opposite to those invoked here: Richard and Isabel were married at Calais on 4 November 1396; she was returned to France in June or July 1401, or thereabouts.

5.2 For Richard's reception in London, some scholars have suggested that *Traïson* lies behind both Shakespeare and Daniel. The most suggestive passage from the French account (63–4/215) reads: 'And, as he [Richard] rode through London on a little horse on his way to prison, they kept an open space round him, that every one might see him; and there was a boy behind him, who pointed him out with his finger, saying, "Behold King Richard, who has done so much good to the kingdom of England!" It is true that some pitied him much, and others were exceedingly glad, cursing him loudly in their language, and saying, "Now are we well revenged of this wicked bastard who has governed us so ill." And in this manner was he taken to the Tower of London.' Créton's mention (172–3/375) of 'two little horses that were not worth forty franks', one of which 'the king mounted' when he was conducted humiliatingly from Flint to Chester, could conceivably have been relevant; as could Froissart's description of Henry IV's coronation procession (6.380), which speaks of the new king as 'mounted on a whyte courser' (a touch taken by Daniel and imported into his description of the entry of Bolingbroke and Richard into London; see 8n.). Froissart's unique detail that 'the streates [were] hanged as he passed by', could also have prompted Shakespeare's allusion to street decorations ('all the walls / With painted imagery', 15–16). If Shakespeare drew upon Froissart, however, he clearly disregarded his statement that Richard was not made to ride in public through the streets (6.370); and, in fact, none of the French chroniclers can be considered a proven or even very likely source for York's distinctive account, however suggestive the parallels that have been adduced.

5.2.3 *cousins'* Some editors interpret the word as a noun in the accusative followed by a present participle (*coming*) rather than (as here) a plural possessive with a gerund (see Abbott, 93, 164, 178). In terms of oral delivery, the grammatical distinction is purely technical, could not be registered by audiences and therefore affects meaning not at all.

5.2.41–117 Hall writes: 'This duke of Aumerle went before from Westminster to se his father the duke of Yorke, and sittyng at diner had his counterpaine of the endenture of the confederacie whereof I spake before in his bosome. The father espied it and demaunded what it was, his sonne lowely and beningly [benignly] answered that it myght not bee sene, and that it touched not him. By saint George quod the father I will see it, and so by force toke it out of his bosome, when he perceaued the contente and the sixe signes and seales sette and fixed to the same, whereof the seale of his sonne was one, he sodainlie rose from the table, commaundying his horses to be sadeled, and in a greate furie saied to his sonne, thou trayter thefe, thou hast bene a traitour to kyng Richard, and wilt thou nowe be falce to thy cosen kyng Henry? thou knowest wel inough that I am thy pledge borowe and mayneperner, body for body, and land for goodes in open parliament, and goest thou about to seke my death and destruction? by the holy rode I had leauer see the strangeled on a gibbet. And so the duke of Yorke mounted on horsbacke to ride toward Windsor to the kyng and to declare the hole effecte of his sonne and his adherentes & partakers. The duke of Aumerle seyng in what case he stode toke his horse and rode another way to Windsor, riding in post thither (whiche his father being an olde man could not do)' (fols xii^v–xiii).

5.2.73–110 George Pierce Baker, the famous American teacher of playwriting, particularly admired the 'theatrical' expertise of this episode, its way of looking at the action 'through the eyes and feelings of each participator', its 'swift contrasting of the doting mother and the outraged, sternly loyal father', and especially its 'climax gained by having York so long hold back the exact nature of what he has read in the indenture, and in the frenzied cry of the Duchess to Aumerle as the servant enters [at 84] to receive the orders of the infuriated Duke: "Strike him, Aumerle!"' (see Forker, 430).

5.2.78–9 Now . . . villain! Swinburne's extreme distaste for this episode has become famous: 'Style and metre are rough, loose, and weak: the dotage of York becomes lunacy. *Sa folie en furie est tournée*' (see Forker, 398).

5.2.109 Herford (200) considers that the 'change was perhaps deliberately made with a view to the part [the Duchess] is made to play in this and the following scene'; though he adds that 'It is unlikely . . . that Shakespeare knew' she 'was in reality young and the niece of Richard'. Zitner (248), however, believes that the playwright 'could have deduced from Holinshed' that the second duchess 'was probably much younger than her husband'. Chambers (147) thinks that Shakespeare conflates 'the two duchesses, as he does the two queens' (Anne of Bohemia and Isabel); see List of Roles, 2n.

5.3.69–72 The stiffly contrived style of York's advice falls into rhymed couplets – a symptom, perhaps, of his unnaturally severe moralism. York protests that the intolerable contradiction between his honour and his son's shame can only be resolved by the death of one of them: either his reputation for loyalty will continue unblemished because his son will have been justly executed, or he will die of shame because his son's dishonour goes unpunished. RP adduces *A Knack to Know a Knave* (1594), sc. 3, as an analogue to 'the bloodthirstily legalistic father'.

5.3.78–81 The comedy from this point to the end of the scene has elicited various responses. Wilson (226) says that this 'farcical upshot is quite in the manner of *The Troublesome Reign*', citing *Part 1*, 1.1.412–15. Swinburne famously objected to the 'relapse into rhyme and rhyming epigram, into the "jigging vein" dried up (we might have hoped) long since by the very glance of Marlowe's Apollonian scorn' (Forker, 256); Saintsbury regarded the 'squabble' of the Duke and Duchess over their son as 'one of the few' scenes in Shakespeare that unintentionally 'approach the ridiculous' – a 'sign of immaturity' (Forker, 442). Zitner analyses what he takes to be intentionally parodic and burlesque elements in this and the previous scene. Gurr (162) suggests that 'The rhymes . . . together with the stage actions of hammering at the door and kneeling . . . bring the scene very close to the few surviving examples of the jig or knockabout act which commonly followed the performance of a public-theatre play on the Elizabethan stage'. Apart from the rhyming and occasional knocking, however, the examples in Baskervill's classic study of jigs (371–605) provide no really comparable parallels.

5.3.92 **walk . . . knees** The stairway was believed to have been that which Christ ascended in Jerusalem to receive judgement from Pontius Pilate, which was later brought to Rome to serve as the ceremonial entrance to the Lateran palace. In 1589, just a few years before *R2* was written, Pope Sixtus V ordered the stairs to be transferred to their present site leading up to the Sancta Sanctorum. The stairway was much celebrated by religious pilgrims from all over Christendom.

5.3.118 *Pardonne-moi* Johnson's distaste for the wordplay (on *Pardon* from the previous line) is famous (1.451): 'This whole passage is such as I could well wish away'. Later commentators have been more vehemently negative: Henry Hallam in 1837 spoke of 'this stupid quibble' in a line 'both atrocious and contemptible' (Forker, 136), while A.W. Verity in 1886 pronounced the *double entendre*, including its context, 'intolerable' (Forker, 285); Dowden's adjective is 'execrable' (see Herford, 203).

5.3.135 **god on earth** Cf. the Shakespearean part of *Sir Thomas More* (Addition II, sc. vi, ll. 225–7): '[God] hath not only lent the king his figure / his throne, [his] sword, but gyven him his owne name, / calls him a god on earth' (*STM* 77); also *Homily*, 2.278: 'as the name of the king is very often attributed and giuen vnto God in the holy Scriptures, so doeth God himselfe in the same Scriptures sometime vouchsafe to communicate his Name with earthly Princes, terming them gods'. Bacon's 'Essay of a King' (1642) opens with the statement: 'A King is a mortal God on Earth, unto whom the living God hath lent his own name as a great honour' (*Works*, 12.387); and William Baldwin in his dedication of *The Mirror for Magistrates* (1559) writes that, as justice is of such importance in a state, so 'hath God established it with the chiefest name, honoring & calling Kinges . . . by his owne name, Gods' (*Mirror*, 65). See also Holinshed in 3.2.56–7n. For the god-like role of mercy in administering justice, cf. *MV* 4.1.193–5: 'But mercy is above the sceptred sway, / It is enthroned in the hearts of kings, / It is an attribute to God himself.' Classical rulers were called gods on earth. For other parallels and the scriptural and theological provenance of the phrase, tortuously derived from Psalms, 82, John, 10.34–5 and other texts; see Ure (166).

5.5.13–14 **set . . . word** F's alteration ('Faith' for *word*) was probably made in the theatre to avoid echoing a phrase already used earlier; but, as Ure (169) correctly observes, F's new wording 'certainly weakens the precision of what Richard says'. GWW suggests that F's change may reflect religious censorship since 'the word . . . Against the word' might be considered to 'strike at the integrity of the Scriptures' whereas setting 'the Faith . . . Against the Faith' would have been 'a daily occurrence'. That F saw no need to alter the phrase at 5.3.121 could mean that no religious implications were detected in the earlier context.

5.5.67–8 **royal . . . noble . . . groats** 'The cheapest of us is ten groats too dear' could also contain the notion of depreciation, as though Richard were saying, 'I exaggerate the value of both of us'; Chambers (154) suggests that the jest may contain 'an allusion to some rise in the value of the coins'. 'A Letter Containing an Account of Some Antiquities between Windsor and Oxford' (Hearne, 5.153) contains a version of the same witticism. The story concerns John Blower, an Anglican priest, who 'preach'd but one *Sermon* in his Life, which was before Queen *Elizabeth*': 'as he was going about to caress the *Queen*, he first said *my Royal Queen*, and a little after *my Noble Queen*. Upon which says the *Queen, what am I ten Groats worse than I was?* At which *Words* being baulked (for he was a Man of *Modesty*) he could not be prevail'd with to preach any more, but he said he would always read the *Homilies* for the future.'

5.5.75 'The man's distress as he studies Richard's features can be felt in the hesitant parenthesis [of 73] and the extra syllables of the last line [75]' (Mahood, *Parts*, 87). Craik, unhappy with the additional syllables, proposes that *sometimes* and *royal* could originally have been 'alternatives' in Shakespeare's MS. Craik thinks that on the one hand the Groom might be hesitant to use *royal* again after 67–8 but that on the other he might deliberately wish to show 'his heartfelt loyalty' by stressing the word through repetition. What would not please Richard, however, would be the gauche double attribute, *sometimes royal*. Craik accordingly concludes that Shakespeare may have tinkered uncertainly while composing the line, leaving 'less-than-clear copy' for the compositor.

5.5.77–83 Since Richard's lavish tastes were well known, perhaps Shakespeare was aware of, or took for granted, Richard's love of fine horses, for which John Webb in an editorial note (Créton, 99–101) gives the historical evidence. Hayward (85), perhaps taking a hint from Shakespeare, reports that 'All the Kings treasure & Iewels, with his horses, and al his fardage came to the Dukes [Bolingbroke's] hands'.

5.5.83–9 Froissart's story of Richard's favourite greyhound (6.369) has often been suggested as a possible source for Barbary's fickleness: 'kynge Rycharde had a grayhounde called Mathe, who alwayes wayted upon the kynge, and wolde knowe no man els: for whansoever the kynge dyde ryde, he that kept the grayhounde dyde lette hym lose, and he wolde streight rynne to the kynge and fawne upon hym, and leape with his fore fete upon the kynges shulders. And as the kyng and the erle of Derby [Bolingbroke] talked togyder in the courte [the courtyard of Flint Castle], the grayhounde, who was wont to lepe upon the kyng, left the kynge and came to the erle of Derby, duke of Lancastre, and made to hym the same frendly countinaunce and chere as he was wonte to do to the kyng. The duke, who knewe nat the grayhounde, demaunded of the kyng what the grayhounde wolde do. Cosyn, quod the kyng, it is a gret good token to you, and an yvell signe to me. Sir, howe know you that? quod the duke. I knowe it well, quod the kyng: the grayhounde maketh you chere this day as kynge of Englande, as ye shal be, and I shal be deposed: the grayhounde hath this knowledge naturally; therfore take hym to you, he wyll folowe you and forsake me. The duke understode well those wordes, and cherisshed the grayhounde, who wolde never after folowe kyng Rycharde, but folowed the duke of Lancastre.' Wilson (229) speculates that 'this is just the tale Shakespeare himself would have been likely to seize upon and elaborate', while Ure (174), who tends to discount Froissart's influence altogether, regards the putative connection as 'not

. . . very plausible'. Bullough, who believes that Froissart contributed to Shakespeare's 'treatment of Gaunt' and the Queen, and who thinks that he likewise influenced the playwright's 'unusually sympathetic attitude to Richard in his fall' (3.369), nevertheless omits the passage quoted here from his collection of significant source materials. If Shakespeare read Froissart at all, it would be strange if he were not attracted by the story of the suddenly disloyal greyhound, which could also have prompted Richard's disgust with 'Dogs easily won to fawn on any man' (3.2.130). But of course the thematic parallel between the behaviour of the favourite dog and the favourite horse could be fortuitous.

5.6.34–44 Holinshed (3.515) reports that in the course of the Abbot of Westminster's conspiracy Richard Maudelyn, a cleric, impersonated Richard II as part of the conspirators' strategy for rescuing the latter from prison. Later (at 3.516) Holinshed has the following ambiguous sentence: King Henry 'caused king Richard to die of a violent death, that no man should afterward faine himselfe to represent his person, though some haue said, he was not priuie to that wicked offense'. It is unclear whether 'he was not priuie to that wicked offense' relates to Henry's complicity in the murder of Richard or (perhaps less likely) to Richard's assent to the impersonation. However, as Ure (179) points out, Henry's disavowal of Exton in *R2* could have been influenced by this sentence in Holinshed if Shakespeare interpreted the phrase as relating to Henry. Elsewhere, Holinshed seems simply to assume that Henry ordered the murder of Richard (see 49n.).

APPENDIX 1

TEXTUAL ANALYSIS

The text of *Richard II* exists in eight early editions: five quartos, each
printed from its immediate predecessor – Q or Q1 (1597), Q2 (1598),
Q3 (1598), Q4 (1608) and Q5 (1615); the First Folio (F or F1, 1623);
and a final quarto, Q6 (1634), its text derived from the Second Folio
(F2, 1632). Scholars agree universally that Q1 is the text closest to
Shakespeare's holograph and must therefore serve as the basic text
for modern editions. The obvious exception is the large part of
Act 4 (4.1.155–318), the so-called deposition episode, which Q1
omits and which was supplied in a good text for the first time by F.
An inferior version of the missing lines appeared in Q4 and was
reprinted in Q5. This version, set from a manuscript of dubious ori-
gin,[1] contains numerous mislineations and verbal errors which the
Folio usually sets right, although in a few instances Q4 supplies the

---

1   Editors have differed on the nature of the copy used for the Q4 additions. Wilson
    (112–13) suggests that they derive 'from copy acquired by underhand means' – perhaps
    from some subordinate employee of the theatre or, following Pollard, from a shorthand
    reconstruction. Ure, pronouncing Pollard's shorthand theory untenable on account of
    the 'comparatively "good"' text that resulted, proposes that the new lines represent 'a
    memorial reconstruction' (xv); Evans also speaks of 'a memorially contaminated text'
    (*Riv*, 837) and Jowett of 'a reported text' (*TxC*, 307). Mowat and Werstine, however,
    point out that differences between the Q4 and F versions of the deposition scene 'hardly
    resemble the kinds of differences attributed to memorial reconstruction in other texts to
    which this theory has been affixed' (liv); Maguire (298, 325) concurs. Gurr, noting the
    'instances of mislineation and mishearing', thinks that the Q4 additions 'suggest . . . a
    hasty transcript probably made from dictation' (176). P.A. Daniel (xi) speculates that
    Matthew Law, the publisher of Q4, inherited from the previous holder of the copyright
    (Andrew Wise) a quarto copy which contained the additions in manuscript. Greer
    argues that Q4's version of the deposition episode, since it contains no actual 'corrup-
    tions of meaning', derives from 'Shakespeare's original' (perhaps a theatre manuscript)
    and that its small omissions and unmetrical characteristics are the result of a copyist
    'working hurriedly' under time pressure ('Deposition', 50). Talbert speculates merely
    'that the quarto version was derived from a theatrical performance' (194).

better reading[1] and cannot therefore be wholly disregarded; Q4's deposition scene, however, also lacks several lines and part-lines to be found in F. The later pre-Folio quartos, which occasionally correct obvious misprints in Q1 but which also introduce and multiply many fresh errors, can possess no independent authority. Apart from Q1 and Q4 (for the deposition scene alone), the only text which deserves careful consideration is that of the 1623 Folio.

The Folio text was probably printed in the main either from a complete exemplar of Q3[2] or from a defective copy of Q3 whose missing final leaves were supplied from a copy of Q5.[3] But it is fairly clear that the Folio editor in preparing his copy for the printer also consulted a manuscript that seems to have had a close connection with theatrical

1   E.g. 'and Soueraigntie' for 'a Soueraigntie' (4.1.251), 'Nor' for 'No, nor' (4.1.255), 'mockerie King' for 'Mockerie, King' (4.1.260) and 'manners' for 'manner' (4.1.296). RP suggests that a few variant spellings, e.g. 'tutor' for 'tuture' (4.1.167) and 'haught insulting' for 'haught-insulting' (4.1.254), may point to F's having been 'set from MS copy, rather than annotated Q4/Q5, for this passage'.

2   Although Pollard noticed the possibility that Q3 might have lain behind the Folio text, he nevertheless accepted the traditional finding that a copy of Q5 was the source. There is now, however, substantial agreement that an annotated copy of Q3 rather than of Q5 was that used by the Folio printer (at least for most of the play), although a few editors (such as Muir, Mowat and Werstine) have clung to the older view. F retains a substantial number of the putative errors in Q1 plus most of the additional errors introduced by Q2 and Q3, while only one of the eighteen new variants of Q4 and four of the thirty-eight new ones in Q5 appear in the Folio text; see Pollard, 49–51. For a summary of the argument that Q5 rather than Q3 was the source of F, see Black, 378–82.

3   Such is the contention of Hasker, who follows up a suggestion tentatively made by Pollard (51–3; see p. 507, n. 2). Walton points out that since Hasker's case for the part-use of Q5 'rests on' only 'four readings where F agrees with Q5 against Q3', most of which are 'indifferent', 'we do not have to suppose that any quarto other than Q3' lies behind the Folio text (116–17). The four Q5–F readings are 'euer' for 'neuer' (5.5.70), 'wert' (F 'wer't') for 'art' (5.5.99), 'thine own' for 'thy own' (5.5.106) and the spelling 'tels' for 'tells' (5.5.55). The first of these merely replaces a double with a single negative, the second simply changes the tense of the verb, the third alters the form of a pronominal adjective before a vowel (ostensibly for reasons of euphony) and the fourth involves only a variant spelling which can be accounted for by the habits of Folio Compositor B. None involves any significant change of meaning or affects metre. A fifth variant, 'formerly' (a Q5–F mistake for 'formally' at 1.3.29), is a fairly common error and, since it occurs in a part of the text where F seems otherwise to have relied on Q3, was probably made independently by the compositors of Q5 and F. The concentration of the four Q5–F variants in the same scene – indeed within fifty-one lines of each other – is indeed suggestive, and Jowett and Taylor point to a few additional Q5–F agreements in the positioning and wording of SDs within the same area of text; but on the principle of Ockham's razor, it is easier to suppose that the Folio editors used an ordinary copy of Q3 in addition to a manuscript source, which may already have contained the variants.

production – perhaps the promptbook[1] itself – and that he compared the printed copy, somewhat desultorily to be sure, with the manuscript for purposes of correction and annotation.[2] The most significant differences between the early quartos and F fall into several categories.

First, as mentioned above, F gives a fuller and more satisfactory version of the deposition episode in Act 4 than had appeared in Q4–5, presumably restoring the original lines excised from the printer's copy of Q1 by reason of censorship but set from the transcript of these lines from the promptbook.[3] Second, in addition to smoothing out the metre in numerous places, F restores many readings from Q1 that had been corrupted in subsequent quartos (e.g. 'and I' for 'and' (1.1.60), 'beggar-feare' for 'begger-face' (1.1.189), 'liues' for 'life' (1.1.198), 'at' for 'a' (1.3.72), 'vpon' for 'with' (1.3.233), 'our' for 'your' (1.4.10)) while at the same time leaving uncorrected a large number of mistakes that had crept into these same reprints (e.g. 'a King' for 'the King' (1.1.70), 'said' for 'speake' (1.1.87), the omission of 'duely' (1.1.127), 'mine' for 'my' (1.1.133), 'you shall' for 'we shall' (1.1.202), 'my' for 'thy' (1.2.62)). Third, the Folio omits some nine passages (amounting to fifty lines), at least six of which appear to be deliberate theatrical cuts (1.3.129–33, 239–42, 268–93, 2.2.77, 3.2.29–32, 4.1.53–60), but three of which (3.2.49, 182, 5.3.98) may be accidental instances of a dropped line.[4]

1 Long (93) objects to the term 'promptbook' on the grounds that it distorts or even falsifies what limited evidence the extant playhouse manuscripts actually provide, suggesting rather that we substitute the term 'playbook'. Although in substance I agree, the older term has been so commonly used by scholars that it is difficult to avoid it. Recognizing that the playhouse copy of *Richard II* undoubtedly contained markings more diverse than those attributable to a hypothetical 'prompter', I nevertheless use the term 'promptbook' throughout.

2 It is also theoretically possible that the copy compared with Q3 was a printed text that had been emended and added to by reference to the theatre promptbook. Gurr (176) mentions this possibility. Pollard believed that an annotated copy of Q1 had itself served as prompt copy and that whoever prepared the text for Jaggard's shop compared this with the later quarto (probably Q5) that he was using as his primary copy-text. Direct collation of Q3 against a playhouse manuscript would seem, however, to be the simpler and likelier means of accounting for most features of the Folio text. See, however, p. 522, n. 1.

3 Most scholars now believe that the copy for Q1 originally contained the deposition scene. For the view that it was added later, see p. 516, n. 1.

4 F's omission of York's line, 'Ill maist thou thriue if thou graunt any grace' (5.3.98), looks especially inadvertent, since it destroys the rhymed couplet formed by his wife's rejoinder, 'Pleades he in earnest: looke vpon his face' (5.3.99); but see also 5.3.98n. A tenth omission from the Folio text may also be mentioned – the words 'My Lord' at 4.1.326 – which in modern editions is usually printed as a separate line.

Fourth, F supplements the SDs of the quartos, adding many necessary entrances and exits such as we might expect to be marked in the theatre book-keeper's script, sometimes elaborating the descriptions for group entries (i.e. at 2.3.0.1, 3.2.0.1, 3.3.0.1–2, 4.1.0.1–4, 5.3.0.1–2 and 5.6.0.1–2), and specifying more systematically than the quartos such effects of production as drums, trumpets, banners and the use of a specific prop for Richard's food in the prison scene (e.g. '*A charge sounded*' (1.3.117 SD), '*A long flourish*' (1.3.122 SD), '*Flourish*' (2.1.223 SD), '*Drums: Flourish, and Colours*' (3.2.0.1), '*Enter with Drum and Colours*' (3.3.0.1), '*Parle without, and answere within: then a Flourish*' (3.3.61.1–2) and '*Enter Keeper with a Dish*' (5.5.94.1)). Although in general the Folio makes the quarto SDs tidier and more consistent, it falls short in a few places: it omits Q's '*Exeunt*' at 1.3.309; it fails to supply Q's missing exits at 2.2.107, 3.1.35, 4.1.268 (in the passage added to Q4–5) and 5.3.27; and it occasionally supplies a singular exit where a plural one is needed (2.2.148, 5.2.117, 5.4.11 and 5.5.118) or fails to make plural a singular exit already present (3.4.101).

In several instances F clarifies staging which is ambiguous or problematic in the quartos. At the end of the first scene, for instance, Q makes Gaunt exit with the other characters, leaving no interval for his immediate re-entrance with Gloucester's widow in scene 2; F supplies the necessary exit ten lines earlier (1.1.195) before Richard's concluding speech.[1] When Bushy enters to Richard and his favourites at 1.4.52.1, F alters Q's somewhat awkward '*Enter Bushie with newes*' to the simpler '*Enter Bushy*', then adds a dramatically natural line ('*Bushy, what newes?*') to the King's speech, thus identifying the messenger and making the situation more comprehensible. In the same scene, F also removes Bushy from Q's opening SD ('*Enter the King with Bushie, &c*'), which obviously contradicts the later entrance, at the same time clarifying the presence of '*Greene*' and '*Bagot*',

---

The Folio, however, took over this lacuna from Q3, which reads 'Before I freely speeake my minde heerein', omitting the hypermetrical words of the line as it appears in Q1–2 ('My Lo. before I freely speake my mind heerein').

1 GWW once suggested that perhaps Shakespeare, forgetting that he needed Gaunt back onstage immediately for 1.2, belatedly added the exit in 1.1 at a not very convincing place, after he became aware of the staging problem. Possibly the actors pointed it out to him. Since then GWW has been persuaded by Foster's computerized evidence for the roles taken by Shakespeare (based on the chronological clustering of 'rare-words' in his entire corpus), evidence suggesting that the playwright himself played Gaunt and would therefore have needed no prompting for the change. See Foster, 32, and 1.1.195 SDn.

the latter of whom remains mute except for the concluding 'Amen!' which he speaks in unison with everyone else.[1] In 3.4, F specifies the Queen's '*two Ladies*' and the Gardener's '*two Seruants*' whereas the quarto directions refer only to the Queen's '*attendants*' and to undifferentiated '*Gardeners*'. Unlike Q, F supplies two necessary SDs for the Duchess in 5.3, making it clear that she first speaks offstage, '*Dutchesse within*' (73), before her subsequent entry. At the end of 5.3 where Q prints the confused direction, '*Exeunt. Manet sir Pierce Exton, &c.*', when Exton is not onstage, F corrects the mistake to a simple '*Exeunt.*'. On the other hand, when Bolingbroke confronts Richard at Flint Castle, F omits one of Q's few descriptive directions ('*he kneeles downe*', 3.3.188). Since the quartos and Folio are sparing of gestural directions contained in or implied by the dialogue, editors have indicated specific actions for the guidance of readers: for instance, when gages are hurled down and taken up, when the King's baton is thrown down, when Bolingbroke and Mowbray lay their hands on Richard's sword, when various characters kneel and rise, when Northumberland moves back and forth between the battlements of Flint Castle and Bolingbroke's party, when the Queen and her ladies stand apart to overhear the gardeners, when Richard shatters the looking-glass, when Richard and his queen kiss in parting, when York puts on his boots, when King Henry draws his sword upon Aumerle and unlocks the door to admit York, and when Richard attacks his gaoler and kills two of Exton's servants.

Fifth, F tends in a progressive fashion to regularize the somewhat erratic naming of the two central characters in both SDs and SPs. Q refers to the protagonist in the opening SD and first SP as '*King Richard*', but immediately shortens this to '*King*' or '*the King*' in the remaining prefixes and directions until 3.3.61.2 where '*Richard*' appears on the walls. Omitting the deposition episode, Q then reverts to the use of '*King*' until 5.1.6.1 when '*Enter Ric.*' marks his entrance in the scene of parting from the Queen, during which both '*Rich.*' and '*King*' show

---

1   As Wilson (149–50) points out, Q's SD at 1.4.0.1–2 probably represents Shakespeare's original intention to have Richard enter with all three of his favourites, '*Bushie, &c*' standing for Bushy, Bagot and Green. When it was decided, apparently at a later point, to make Bushy serve as the messenger who brings news of Gaunt's illness at 1.4.52.1, the copy for Q at line 23 ('Our selfe and Bushie here, Bagot and Green') was clumsily and unmetrically emended to read simply 'Ourself and Bushy' since, after the adaptation, Bushy would still be offstage. But whoever made the alteration failed to notice that the unchanged SD at the beginning of the scene left a contradiction in the action still unresolved. See 1.4.0.1n., 23LN and 52.1–53n.

up as SPs. At the character's final appearance in prison, the SDs refer to
him as '*Richard*', varying between '*Rich.*' and '*Ric.*' in SPs. F follows the
quarto designations for the first scene (except for one SP abbreviated to
'*Kin.*') and then marks Richard's entrance in 1.3 as '*King*', while for the
rest of the scene designating his speeches either '*Rich.*' or '*Ric.*'. F again
marks his entrance in 1.4 as '*King*' but reverts to '*Ric.*' or '*Rich.*' for the
SPs. Thereafter, except for the entry SD in 2.1.68.1 ('*Enter King . . .*'), F
invariably refers to the King in SDs as '*Richard*' and in SPs as '*Rich.*' or
'*Ric.*' except for two instances of '*Ri.*' (2.1.72 SP, 5.5.105 SP). In the
naming of Bolingbroke, Q is even more inconsistent. In 1.1 the character enters as '*Bullingbrooke*' with SPs varying among '*Bulling.*', '*Bull.*'
and '*Bul.*'.[1] He becomes '*Duke of Hereford*' at his entrance in 1.3 but
retains the SPs '*Bul.*' and '*Bull.*', the same forms being repeated in 2.3
and 3.1, except in the opening SD of 2.3 where his title is abbreviated to
'*Hereford*'. Both 3.3 and 4.1 commence with '*Enter Bull.*' and '*Enter
Bullingbrooke*' respectively, the SPs of both scenes remaining '*Bull.*'
(except for '*Bul.*', 3.3.209). In 5.3, however (again we skip over the absent
pageant of abdication), Bolingbroke enters as '*King*' and is given SPs
that vary between '*King H.*' and '*King*'. Yet in the closing scene he loses
his royal designation in the SD ('*Enter Bullingbrooke*') but retains it for
the SPs ('*King*'). F in contrast calls the character '*Bullingbrooke*' in all
SDs except for his entrances in 1.3 and 2.3 where he is designated
'*Hereford*' and '*Duke of Hereford*' respectively. In SPs he is referred to
throughout as '*Bul.*', '*Bull.*' or '*Bullingbrooke*' (the last only once, in the
opening speech of 4.1). The same tendency of F to normalize holds true
with Mowbray and the Abbot of Westminster. In the SDs of the two
scenes in which the first of these characters appears, Q refers to him initially as '*Mowbray*' (1.1) and later as '*Duke of Norfolke*' (1.3), while the
SPs in these scenes vary between '*Mowb.*' and '*Mow.*'. F regularizes
throughout to '*Mowbray*' in SDs and to '*Mow.*' (except for a single '*Mo.*')
in the SPs. Whereas Q designates the Abbot as '*West.*' in the only SD
that applies to him and then goes on to mark his speeches '*Abbot.*'
(4.1), F clarifies by normalizing to '*Abbot of Westminster*' and '*Abbot.*'

1 Although Q, F and Holinshed spell the name 'Bullingbrooke', this edition adopts the
preferred traditional form 'Bolingbroke', which is consistent with the principles of
modernization generally used in the Arden Shakespeare. The form, Bolingbroke,
however, is of medieval, not modern, origin (see *Register*, nos. 109, 265, 1036;
Traïson, 124; Capgrave, 98).

respectively. These differences in naming practice between Q and F are at least potentially of more than bibliographical interest, for, as McLeod has suggested, Q's unstable habits, taken in conjunction with the speeches and dramatic action of the tragedy, are interpretively suggestive; the changing SPs, for instance, may offer clues to Shakespeare's intuitive and developing notions of how certain characters, under pressure of circumstance, shift their conceptions and self-conceptions of personal and political identity.[1]

Sixth, whereas the quartos specify no act or scene divisions, the Folio marks both in Latin – '*Actus Primus, Scaena Prima*', '*Scaena Secunda*', etc. These are the divisions which have become canonical in modern editions as far into the text as 5.4 (the brief scene in which Exton and his servants first appear), which, despite the clearing of the stage at this point, is continuous in the Folio with the preceding action (the pardoning of Aumerle). In consequence, '*Scaena Quarta*' and '*Scoena Quinta*' of Folio Act 5 become respectively 5.5 and 5.6 in modern texts. Whether the Folio divisions – particularly the numbering of scenes – represent Shakespeare's original conception or simply reflect Jacobean editorial or theatrical convention is a nice question. It is possible, of course, that the Folio's separation into five acts evinces little more than the increasing respect for classical tradition that fully established itself, in the popular theatres at least, only in the seventeenth century; although it may hint in addition at a shift towards structural breaks in post-Elizabethan theatrical practice. On the evidence of other quartos as close to holograph origin as *Richard II*, it seems unlikely that the formal marking of acts and scenes ever appeared in Shakespeare's drafts; but such a conclusion, of course, by no means rules out a conscious five-movement principle of structure on the dramatist's part.[2]

---

1   See McLeod, 137–67. For an interesting discussion of related problems, see also Williams, *Headings*.
2   Baldwin, who believed that most dramatists of the period including Shakespeare conceived their plays in terms of acts and scenes, argued that the marking of such divisions in play manuscripts is evidence of their authorial derivation. It is also worth noticing that the manuscript of *Woodstock*, a play that almost certainly preceded Shakespeare's *Richard II*, contains act divisions (added in the hand, apparently, of a seventeenth-century playhouse scribe) as well as 'vestigial' scene designations at the beginning – these latter ostensibly of authorial origin; see Long, 97. Jewkes presents evidence to show that even if Shakespeare thought in terms of a five-movement structure (as, for instance, in *Henry V*), he 'did not originally mark act divisions in his plays' (39), and that these were increasingly added to promptbooks and printed

Seventh, the Folio routinely, though not invariably, expurgates the quartos by replacing references to 'God' with the word 'heaven'. This practice constitutes further evidence that theatrical copy influenced F since the Act to Restrain Abuses (1606), enacted to curb profanity in the theatre, did not apply to printed texts. Not surprisingly, therefore, the quartos of 1608 and 1615, printed after the statute went into effect, retain the older form of such oaths. Perhaps the most notable passage that curiously escapes the usual sanitizing in F comprises two very formal speeches by the Lord Marshal and Mowbray in the tournament episode (1.3.11–25) which contain no fewer than five references to 'God' and may have been thought permissible on account of their ritualistic, even formulaic, character.[1] In any case, the general avoidance of profanity in the Folio probably reflects stage necessity during the period between 1606 and 1623 and can have little authorial warrant.

Finally, the Folio emends the quarto text in two additional respects. (1) It substitutes a large number of words for readings in Q that can hardly be classified as simple blunders or printers' errors. Most of these seem to be alternatives of an indifferent kind (e.g. 'time' for 'month' (1.1.157), 'iust' for 'right' (1.3.55), 'verie' for 'grieuous' (1.4.54), 'Kinsman' for 'cousin' (2.3.125), 'sluggard' for 'coward' (3.2.84), 'Faction' for 'party' (3.2.203), 'mock' for 'laugh' (3.3.171), 'reare' for 'raise' (4.1.146), 'Queene' for 'wife' (5.1.78), 'that' for 'which' (5.5.56)).

---

texts after his death in 1616 (as was the case with most plays in the Folio) by playhouse adapters, scribes or even literary editors. Hunter argues that pauses between acts were a regular feature of Elizabethan theatrical production, and therefore of Shakespearean dramaturgy from the beginning, and further that the absence of act divisions in the quartos and their presence in the Folio merely reflects a change of fashion among printers. On Hunter's principle it is possible to discern such pauses at the ends of Acts 1, 2, 3 and 4 in Folio *Richard II*: the first after Richard's shocking irreverence at the news of Gaunt's impending death and his show-stopping curtain line, 'Pray God we may make haste and come too late!' (1.4.52); the second after Salisbury's ominous couplets predicting Richard's defeat in cosmic imagery (2.4.21–4); the third after the Gardener's rhymed chorus on the 'weeping queen' and his symbolic intention to plant 'a bank of rue' in remembrance of her (3.4.102–7); and the fourth after the 'pageant' of Richard's abdication and the Abbot's concluding speech inviting Carlisle and Aumerle to join him in a counter-revolutionary plot (4.1.326–34). But whether these four moments are more emphatic than those at the ends of other scenes (e.g. Bolingbroke's departure to begin his exile in 1.3 or Richard's parting from the Queen in 5.1) is debatable.

1   Knight noted in 1839 that the Folio's characteristic change from 'God' to 'heaven' is not indiscriminate and that the editors of F retain the sacred name 'when it is used in a peculiarly emphatic, or reverential manner' (1.142). In F 'God' occurs 37 times, 'heaven' 50; in Q 'God' appears 64 times, 'heaven' 30.

A few of these may be defended as genuine improvements, and some scholars have believed them to represent authorial revisions or 'second thoughts';[1] but they have more commonly been attributed to a combination of sources including compositorial preferences or lapses of memory, substitutions made by players and recorded in the book-keeper's copy, and possibly even alterations made by an editor annotating copy for the printer. (2) At least two Folio variants, however, seem to possess somewhat greater authority and are therefore sometimes adopted by modern editors. These clarify and correct historical facts in a way that would probably be desirable, if not absolutely necessary, in performance. They seem therefore to lie beyond the purview of a mere printing-house corrector. When Gaunt refuses his sister-in-law's demand early in the play that he personally avenge Gloucester's death, he refers in Q to 'the part I had in Woodstockes bloud' (1.2.1). The Folio emends this to 'Glousters blood', which conforms with all other references to the murdered Duke in Q and obviates the problem of a name that audiences might not recognize – unless of course they were already familiar with *Woodstock*, the anonymous play on the same reign which some scholars believe was one of Shakespeare's sources,[2] or unless the name was already more generally familiar than most scholars have supposed. The second instance involves a seemingly necessary emendation at 5.6.8 where Northumberland announces the execution of rebels against Henry IV and mentions the severed heads of 'Oxford, Salisbury, Blunt and Kent'. As most editors have pointed out, the Earl of Oxford (Aubrey de Vere) was certainly not involved in the Abbot of Westminster's conspiracy, and the Folio's alteration to '*Salsbury*, *Spencer*, *Blunt*, and *Kent*' renders a genuine service to audiences by making an important historical correction; for, according to Holinshed (3.516), Hugh (or Thomas) Spencer was indeed beheaded at Bristol. One cannot be sure whether Shakespeare, perhaps writing in haste, here misremembered Holinshed, or whether the eye of Q1's compositor

---

1 P.A. Daniel (xvii–xviii) so regarded them in 1890. Evans wrote in 1974 that 'substantive readings which appear for the first time in F1 deserve some consideration as possible Shakespearean second thoughts' (*Riv*, 838). Jones speaks of 'isolated touches of revision' (42). Jowett defends the acceptance of 'over forty Folio readings' (*TxC*, 306) on the grounds that these occur in parts of the text where the annotator of Q3 was carefully collating the printed copy against the prompt copy. For the most detailed defence of this latter position, see Jowett & Taylor.

2 See Chambers, *WS*, 1.352–3, and Introduction, pp. 144–52.

skipped to the 'Oxford' (5.6.13) five lines later in his copy.[1] The correction in F, however, almost certainly resulted from comparing Q3 with the promptbook, which had possibly been corrected by the book-keeper or someone in the theatre familiar enough with the chronicle source to make the change, or even by Shakespeare himself if the promptbook, as has been suggested, was an authorial transcript of the dramatist's own first draft.

Despite general agreement on the primary authority of Q1 for all but the deposition scene of *Richard II* and on the value of the Folio as probably containing 'sprinklings of authority',[2] scholars have vigorously debated both the nature of the manuscript from which Q1 was set and that of the copy against which Q3 was collated in preparing a text for the compositors of the Folio in Jaggard's printing house. Let us first consider Q1.

That the first quarto derives from a generally clean and unproblematic manuscript purchased by Andrew Wise from the Lord Chamberlain's Servants only a brief time before the play was set in type at Valentine Simmes's shop is not in dispute.[3] Although the title-page omits the dramatist's name, an omission that was remedied in the subsequent quartos, it mentions the company by which the play '*hath beene publikely acted*' (see Fig. 17). Compared to many early texts of Shakespeare used as the basis of modern editions, *Richard II* requires relatively little emendation. Although it has been proposed that the missing deposition episode was a late addition to the play, inserted at some point between 1601 (when *Richard II* was probably the play revived on behalf of the Essex conspirators) and a later restaging by the King's Men as advertised on the title-page of Q4 (1608), it was almost certainly present in the original copy but

1 Ure (xvi–xvii) argues that the mistake cannot have occurred in the printing house because the intrusive 'Oxford' is too far in advance of what a compositor in the process of setting type would be able to hold in memory. He thinks that the error might more naturally arise in the transcribing of the author's holograph by a copyist. It is questionable, however, despite Ure's attempt to contrast their habits, whether there would be much difference between a compositor's and a scribe's memorial capacity. Authorial error seems the likeliest explanation.
2 See Jowett & Taylor, 151.
3 Certain features of the press correction gleaned from the surviving copies of Q1 establish that the text was set from manuscript rather than from a previously printed book. As Gurr (175) points out, Wise may have had 'a steady . . . and legitimate arrangement with Shakespeare's company for printing popular plays', for he 'also produced an edition of *Richard III* in 1597 sometime after the *Richard II*' and also *1 Henry IV* (in 1598) and *Much Ado About Nothing* and *2 Henry IV* (both in 1600).

marked for deletion from the printed version for reasons of censorship.[1] In 1597 the issue of who would succeed Elizabeth on her throne was as politically delicate as it was potentially threatening, and, as has been noted in the Introduction (p. 5), identification of the ageing monarch with Richard II had become common. No one can be sure whether an official censor (perhaps the Bishop of London or even the Archbishop of Canterbury) enjoined the publisher to exclude the scene, or whether Wise, or even Simmes, omitted it voluntarily out of prudence or fear. We know, however,

---

1 P.A. Daniel (x) observed in 1890 that Bolingbroke's order that Richard be conveyed 'to the Tower' (4.1.316) near the end of the passage missing from Q agrees totally with the opening of the following scene (included in Q) in which we see the deposed King conducted under guard to 'Iulius Caesars ill erected Tower' (5.1.2). Furthermore, most scholars have believed that the Abbot of Westminster's line, 'A woeful pageant have we here beheld' (4.1.321), must refer to Richard's self-dramatizing resignation in the extended episode that almost immediately precedes his remark, and that therefore the missing passage must have belonged to the tragedy as originally composed. Bergeron, however, challenges the interpretation, arguing that the deposition scene would ill suit the propagandistic motives of Essex and his faction and that it must therefore have been composed after 1601 when the danger of dramatizing such controversial issues had passed. The 'woeful pageant', Bergeron (37) believes, could refer simply to 'the arrest of Carlisle, the announcement of Richard's abdication, Bolingbroke's ascent to the throne, and his plans for coronation'. Professor Bergeron is a recognized authority on pageantry; but the word 'pageant', which had explicit connotations of public spectacle, theatricality and allegorical meaning in the sixteenth century (see *OED*), would probably not have been used in the loose sense he implies.

   The poetic style of the deposition scene accords perfectly with the drama as a whole and seems to date from the period of its original composition. Foster's conclusions, based on as yet unpublished computer data on *Richard II* (in his 'Shaxicon' database; see Foster, 25), seem to confirm the assumption that the deposition scene formed part of Shakespeare's original text and that from its inception it was performed in the theatre, although deleted from the Elizabethan quartos. It is true that the replacement title-page of Q4 (dated, like the original title-page which it replaced, 1608) refers to 'new additions of the Parliament Sceane, and the deposing of King Richard' (see Fig. 18), but this notice almost certainly means only that the added material was being printed for the first time. There are indications in the Q text itself that the copy for Q1 was altered in an attempt to bridge the hiatus caused by the excision of the deposition scene by the addition, after Carlisle's arrest (4.1.154) and before Bolingbroke's 'on Wednesday next, / We solemnly proclaime our Coronation, / Lords be ready all' (4.1.319–20), of the phrase 'Let it be so, and loe'. Q4–F, restoring the deposition scene, then removed this inserted phrase, which served no further purpose. They also introduced variants in lines 319–20, replacing Q's 'proclaime' and 'be ready all' with 'set downe' and 'prepare your selues'. Although it seems likely that Q's lines represent Shakespeare's original version, mislined to accommodate the added bridging phrase (Q's 'proclaime', for example, is certainly closer to Holinshed's 'proclamations' of Henry's accession (3.507) than Q4–F's 'set downe'), the later variants are regarded by Jowett and Taylor as instances of authorial revision, and are accordingly adopted in this edition (see 4.1.319–20n.).

that Simmes had got into difficulty with the authorities in 1595, having had his press confiscated and his types destroyed, and that later when he was engaged in printing Q1 *2 Henry IV* (1600), an entire scene of the play (3.1) was omitted in some copies and subsequently replaced in others by the insertion of a cancel sheet – circumstances that led McManaway to conclude that the publishers (Andrew Wise and William Aspley) had instructed Simmes to delete it 'through timidity' rather than because it had been officially forbidden.[1] Whether the episode in 4.1 was also disallowed in the theatre is likewise uncertain – if so, a different authority, the Master of the Revels, would have prohibited it – but there is some reason, given the slightly clumsy transition in Q from the point where the deposition begins in F and where it ends, to believe that it had been played all along as originally conceived.

It is obvious, too, that the manuscript from which the deposition scene was cut, although undoubtedly a property of Shakespeare's company until Wise bought it, was 'authorial' rather than 'theatrical' in type, the traditional distinction being admittedly problematic in the case of a professional actor-dramatist such as the author of *Richard II*. As pointed out above, Q's SDs are shorter, less explicit and less complete than would presumably be needed in the book-keeper's working copy (Q sometimes resorts to '*&c.*', as in the case of Green and Bagot at 1.4.0.1, rather than specifying minor characters or numbering attendants and supernumeraries); and the directions occasionally contain descriptive or literary features ('*Enter Duke of Hereford appellant in armour*', '*Enter Bushie with newes*', '*he kneeles downe*', '*He pluckes it out of his bosome and reades it*', '*His man enters with his bootes*', '*Enter Aumerle amazed*', '*The Duke of Yorke knokes at the doore and crieth*', '*Enter Richard alone*', '*the musike plaies*', '*The murderers rush in*', etc.) that have been regarded as uncharacteristic of prompt copy. As also noted earlier, Q is less consistent in the naming of characters than we might expect in a copy actually associated with theatrical production. Since the manuscript from which Q was printed was apparently very close to Shakespeare's original, the question that remains is whether it was actually the dramatist's holograph or a scribal copy thereof. On this point the evidence proves inconclusive.

There are instances in Q of mislineation created, apparently, by the running together of a full line with a part-line that precedes or follows it

1   See McManaway, 69–73, 80.

– a habit of crowding that Wilson believed to be characteristic of Shakespeare when he was running out of space at the foot of his manuscript pages,[1] and that seems unlikely, some of the time, to be compositorial in origin. At least nine examples may be noted: (1) 'Farewel, & for my hart disdained that my tongue' (1.4.11–12); (2) 'And al the houshold seruants fled with him to Bullingbrook' (2.2.60–1); (3) 'Ile dispose of you: Gentlemen, go muster vp your men' (2.2.116–18); (4) 'Tut tut, grace me no grace, nor vnckle me no vnckle' (2.3.86–7); (5) 'H.Bull. on both his knees doth kisse king Richards hand' (3.3.35–6); (6) 'Dishonorable boy, that lie shall lie so heauie on my sword' (4.1.66–7); (7) 'My Lo. before I freely speake my mind heerein' (4.1.326–7); (8) 'Takes on the point of honour to support so dissolute a crew' (5.3.11–12); (9) 'Against the word, as thus: Come little ones, & then againe' (5.5.14–15). Of course, the first, fourth and seventh examples can be interpreted as alexandrines, and a copyist of Shakespeare's manuscript might conceivably have followed his original in the matter of line arrangement or else have introduced such crowding on his own initiative. Nevertheless, it is just as logical to infer that the distinctive pattern of merged lines points to a Shakespearean holograph – and this despite disturbances of metre in other places that may well be laid to a compositor.[2]

Pollard found corroborative evidence in the punctuation of some of the longer speeches, particularly those which introduce the colon in places where a dramatic pause shorter than a full stop is called for, even though to modern eyes such pointing violates grammatical logic. To Pollard (64–70) this punctuation, being a hallmark of the dramatist's sensitivity to oral delivery and the subtleties of a specific dramatic situation, was fundamentally authorial. But he went on to observe that apart from certain set speeches the punctuation of Q is inadequately light and 'obviously careless', giving the impression, assuming it was printed from the author's manuscript, that Shakespeare in the heat of rapid composition 'paid little attention' to pointing in any systematic way.[3] In addition, we find numerous

---

1   See Wilson, *Manuscript*, 221.
2   Some of the mislineation, as Hinman shows in his introduction to the Q1 facsimile (Greg, xi–xiii), is probably compositorial crowding – the result of mis-estimation of space needed in casting-off copy. Among the nine examples listed, 2.2.60–1 may be a case in point, since it occurs on D4 in a sheet where other evidence of compositorial crowding is demonstrable.
3   Graham-White also analyses the punctuation of Q1 and, like Pollard, discovers in it dramatic subtleties – indeed, even signs of significant change in the title character.

abbreviations that seem too cryptic for a compositor and have the earmarks of authorial rather than scribal copy – e.g. '*Exeunt Duke, Qu man.* [for *manent*] *Bush. Green*', meaning that York and the Queen exit while Bushy and Green remain onstage (2.2.122), but confusing because '*man.*' could easily be misread as a reference to the '*Seruingman*' whose earlier exit at 2.2.107 is unmarked; 'Lo. scale' for 'lord's scale' (3.4.85); 'Why B.' for 'Why, Bishop' (4.1.102); 'the K.' for 'the King' (5.4.1); and 'Thy paines Fitz.' for 'Thy pains, Fitzwater' (5.6.17).[1]

Although most scholars have preferred to believe that Shakespeare's own draft served as copy for Q,[2] some have detected signs of an intervening transcription. Ure (xviii) argues, for instance, that in certain respects Q reflects 'memorial contamination', citing the substitution of 'Oxford' for 'Spencer' (5.6.8) mentioned earlier (pp. 514–15 and 515, n. 1), as well as metrical irregularities that might be traceable to the faulty memory of a scribe or actor.[3] Almost every critic, after all, has noted the habitual smoothness of Shakespeare's iambic pentameter in *Richard II*. Traits of punctuation and orthography in Q have also been adduced as evidence for a transcriber. Feuillerat (187) points unconvincingly to the substitution of parentheses for commas, a characteristic to be found in later manuscripts prepared by Ralph Crane, a scrivener of Shakespeare's company.[4] The 1597 quarto regularly spells the exclamation 'Oh', instead of 'O' (twenty-eight times as opposed to eight), which latter is the preferred form of the so-called good quartos (usually thought to derive from

---

Although he argues that the pointing 'aids the actor in conveying the different emotions through which Richard passes' (94), he cautiously refrains from claiming that it is authorial. Partridge is sceptical of Pollard's argument. Noting Shakespeare's supposed neglect of careful pointing in a set speech from Hand D's section of *Sir Thomas More* as well as other conflicting evidence, he concludes that with few exceptions 'the last refinements of punctuation in published plays were . . . added by [a] playhouse editor, scribe, or printer' (59–60). Generally, I agree with Partridge.

1 Although he admits that abbreviated names and titles are rare in the texts or parts of text set by Simmes's Compositor A, Craven nevertheless attributes this characteristic to the same compositor in Q1 *Richard II* 'even when there is no need to save space'; that Compositor S also abbreviates twice in the same way in Q1 *Richard II*, however, seems to weaken the case further (see Craven[1], 46).

2 See Greg, xv; Jowett & Taylor, 199.

3 Hinman and Craven, however, have cast doubt on Ure's theory of scribal intervention between Shakespeare's draft and Q1 (see Greg, xv–xvi, and Craven[1], 57–8).

4 Howard-Hill points out that, apart from the fact that the earliest known transcript by Crane is more than twenty years later than the 1597 quarto of *Richard II*, Feuillerat fails to take into account other kinds of evidence (hyphenation, characteristic spellings, act and scene headings, the proportion of parentheses to commas and the like) that necessarily complicate reliable ascriptions to Crane.

autograph copy). On the basis of this variance (which is shared with *Titus Andronicus* only), Jackson (215) concludes that the copy was probably a transcript.[1] This last point, though a small one, is telling. Also, the relative clearness of Q's text might be taken to support Jackson's conclusion, the only 'indecipherable passage', according to Feuillerat (187), being 'This sweares he, as he is princesse iust' (3.3.119), which all editors emend. The arguments for holograph copy, however, cannot be wholly dismissed. Jowett and Taylor believe that the compositors had before them Shakespeare's 'foul papers', but a script that was nevertheless 'much fairer' than many others belonging to this elastically defined category; and Alexander, using punctuation as evidence, classes Q1 *Richard II* with Q2 *Hamlet* and the putatively Shakespearean part of the manuscript of *Sir Thomas More*.[2]

The nature of the copy against which Q3 was compared in preparing a text for the Folio printer is even more problematic. And the issue is important, not only because this copy must have been the source for the good version of the deposition episode but also because it contained some variants that are clearly superior to readings of the quartos (see pp. 509, 514–15). Expanded and occasionally corrected SDs seem to lend F additional authority. Several theories have been proposed, none of which can safely be regarded as self-evidently reliable.

P.A. Daniel, who believed that Q5 was the basis of F, thought that this quarto had been corrected throughout 'on the authority of *an* acting copy' (xiii) that might have been part-print and part-manuscript (the latter for the deposition scene at least) but that was most likely wholly manuscript – a manuscript that embodied important substantive revisions including the numerous substituted synonyms. Although Daniel did not believe this hypothetical acting manuscript to be 'the author's autograph' (xviii), he nevertheless considered its authority so high as to make F the necessary basis for a modern edited text. Pollard, who contributed a classic textual analysis of the play, hypothesized that the

1   The most exhaustive demonstration of Shakespeare's preference for 'O' over 'Oh' appears in Taylor & Jowett, 248–56; these authors suggest that the anomaly of Q1 *Richard II*'s preference for 'Oh' might possibly 'be due to early composition', i.e. to the period before *c*. 1593 when Shakespeare's 'habitual spelling of this word changed' (251). The shift from 'O' to 'Oh' in Folio *King John*, as Taylor and Jowett show, is probably due to two different scribes, so that 'no one will want to attribute the disparity . . . to Shakespeare' (253).
2   See Jowett & Taylor, 199; Alexander, *Hamlet*, 390–4.

original manuscript promptbook was destroyed and then replaced by a copy of Q1 because of its greater legibility and handiness, and that this in turn was kept up to date to reflect current habits of performance by more or less continuous annotation. These annotations, he believed, comprised theatrical cuts, altered SDs, removal of profanity, new words introduced by actors, and a manuscript insertion of the deposition scene reconstructed from players' individual parts. According to Pollard (98–9), it was this heavily annotated copy of Q1 that the Folio editors consulted in their imperfect correction of Q5, but that remained in the theatre library and was not available to Jaggard's compositors. Rejecting Pollard's hypothesis of an annotated quarto as prompt copy, Wilson proposed the simpler notion that the promptbook collated with Q5 was wholly manuscript – an independent transcript of Shakespeare's autograph, which would be precious to the company because of its inscription by the Revels-office censor authorizing performance as an 'allowed book' and therefore never destroyed, and which would also be more convenient in the theatre because of its larger format, displaying 'before the eye twice the quantity of dialogue that an open quarto could show' (Cam[1], 110). The manuscript promptbook, however, in Wilson's view, would also reflect non-authorial changes (cuts, emended SDs, expurgations and the like) adopted for practical purposes in the course of production.

Although Pollard had entertained but rejected the possibility that Q3 rather than Q5 was the chief basis for F (see p. 507, ns 2 and 3), Hasker was the first to argue seriously for this position. Hasker followed Pollard, however, in supposing that a printed text had replaced the original manuscript promptbook after having been collated with its worn-out counterpart. According to Hasker's hypothesis, this printed text, an annotated exemplar of Q3, later suffered damage to its final three leaves and was repaired by the addition of the corresponding text (two leaves) from a copy of Q5. By such a hypothetical sequence of events Hasker attempted to account for a Folio text that showed an 'overwhelming preponderance' of evidence 'in favor of Q3' as copy-text (60) but that nevertheless shared uniquely with Q5 a cluster of substantive variants at the end of the play (5.5.55–106).[1] The made-up promptbook consisting

---

1   See, however, p. 507, n. 3. Distinctive spellings have also been adduced as evidence against F's use of Q3 as copy-text. Among the points that Pollard (53) lists is 'the curious misspelling "percullist" for "portcullist" [i.e. portcullised]' at 1.3.167 – a

of parts of two mutilated quartos, and probably also containing the man-uscript insertion of the good version of the deposition scene, then served, according to Hasker's theory, as copy for Jaggard's compositors.[1] Ure (xx–xxv) accepted much of Hasker's case but modified it to postulate the survival of the original manuscript promptbook – a promptbook derived from Shakespeare's draft and containing the censor's allowance, as well as the superior version of the deposition episode and various alterations introduced by the theatre book-keeper. In Ure's opinion, then, it was this manuscript promptbook against which the Folio editors collated a copy of Q3 – probably a defective copy of Q3 supplemented by two leaves from Q5 because of some accident to the earlier quarto, or because its missing pages went unnoticed until after the collation had begun.

Gurr, reconsidering the arguments of his predecessors and adding fresh observations of his own, concurs in general with Ure's conclusion: the printers of the Folio used as their 'basic text' 'a copy of Q3' collated with another text of 'some authority – evidently one that had been used in the playhouse'. Although this second text 'may have been a manuscript, possibly even a promptbook' or 'a printed text emended by reference to the promptbook' (Cam[2], 176), and although many of the Q3/F variants probably reflect preferences of a Folio editor or of the compositors, Gurr believes it most likely that 'F is the result of a collation between a raw copy of Q3 and a playhouse manuscript'. Pointing out, however, that F corrects only about half of Q3's errors, and that even some of these appear to have been made conjecturally, or at least without reference to a source like Q1 (which a manuscript promptbook would presumably resemble), he concludes that the Folio editor allowed himself consider-able liberty 'in his conflation of printed text and manuscript' (Cam[2], 180).

---

mistake apparently taken over from Q4–5 – whereas Q3 correctly prints 'portcullist'. Observing, however, that the noun 'percullis' is a recognized spelling recorded by *OED*, Hasker writes that the Q5–F agreement on 'percullist' is 'not the obstacle [to Q3] Pollard felt it to be' (61). Conversely, the spelling 'vnpruin'd' for 'vnprunde' (i.e. unpruned) at 3.4.45 is shared by Q3 and F. Pollard and Hasker cite this as an error, but as *OED* lists 'pruin(e)' as a seventeenth-century spelling of 'prune' (*v*. 2), there are no grounds for treating it as erroneous.

1   Although Hasker finally accepted that a transcript of the deposition episode (origi-nally missing in Q3) was added to the made-up printed promptbook when it was compared with the disused manuscript promptbook, Evans and Black both chose to believe that leaves from Q5 (which contains an imperfect version of Richard's depo-sition) were added to the theatre copy of Q3 and that these added leaves were then emended to produce the good text of the episode found in F. See *Riv*, 838, and Black[2], 636; also p. 524, n. 1.

Jowett and Taylor in their complex examination of the interrelation-ship of the play's several texts revert (though on the basis of more exhaustive and sophisticated research) to Daniel's theory of F as incorporating authorial revisions or second thoughts. According to their hypothesis, Shakespeare's original draft served two purposes: first it was copied and the transcript prepared for use as a promptbook when the play was originally staged; later it served as printer's copy for Q1. This transcript, possibly scribal but more likely an 'autograph fair copy', embodied a certain amount of 'authorial tinkering' (199) including, presumably, some of the substituted synonyms – what Ure (xxi) called 'words of nearly equivalent meaning' that distinguish F's text from that of the quartos – and also perhaps a revised version of the deposition episode, an earlier version of which had been scored out in the draft from which Q1 was set. At some point after the publication of Q5 (1615), so Jowett and Taylor argue, it was noticed that the manuscript promptbook had lost one of its pages. Someone (perhaps the theatre book-keeper?) then repaired the gap by transcribing the corresponding text from a copy of the most recent printed edition (Q5), so that one manuscript leaf now contained a few localized readings unique to this quarto that would eventually show up in the Folio text. Some time after the repair, when copy for Jaggard's printing shop was being readied, a Folio editor (probably someone closely associated with Jaggard's business) annotated a clean copy of Q3 with reference to the patched manuscript promptbook, inserting a transcript of the superior version of the deposition episode, supplying on his own initiative scene (and perhaps act) divisions, transferring new readings and expurgations, bringing SDs and SPs into accord with those of the promptbook, and marking for omission cuts adopted in previous performances. This extensively emended copy of Q3 then became the source from which Jaggard's compositors set the Folio text. The difficulty with Jowett and Taylor's elaborate hypothesis, of course, is their assumption that the annotator of Q3 would trouble to introduce a cluster of such unimportant readings from Q5, even if these had somehow got into the promptbook (see p. 507, n. 3).

It is scarcely necessary, however, to accept all of Jowett and Taylor's conclusions to acknowledge the signal advance on previous work that their investigation of the text of *Richard II* has made possible. A primary effect of their scholarship, for instance, is to confirm the belief of Hasker, Ure and Gurr in Q3 as the printed text from which F was set, and further to establish an overwhelming probability that the prompt-book against which Q3 was collated was a manuscript rather than a marked-up quarto.[1] Additionally, among their most valuable achievements is clarification of the specific areas of the play in which the heaviest collation of Q3 against the promptbook appears to have occurred. Many of the most significant variants, for instance, are concentrated in a single scene (3.2); and the evidence seems to point to more extensive annotation of the quarto up to about 2.2.50–1 than later, as well as to more salient intervention in the printed text in scenes when Richard himself is onstage. Jowett and Taylor usefully distinguish between the annotator's more or less uniform or systematic alteration of the quarto SDs and SPs, and his much more intermittent emendation of the dialogue – a procedure doubtless facilitated by the three-column layout of the typical manuscript promptbook, which placed SPs in the left column, dialogue in the centre and exits and other SDs (apart from centred entrances) to the right.

For the modern editor of *Richard II* the two most challenging problems are to decide, first, which of the apparently numerous annotations of Q3 derive from the manuscript promptbook (as opposed to those that might originate from the annotator or printing-house editor) and, second, which of such theatre-derived variants may be thought to carry authorial weight. As Long makes clear in his analysis of the *Woodstock* manuscript, numerous agents over a substantial period of time were likely to be involved in the copying and marking-up of a theatre promptbook, including authors, scribes, book-keepers and actors, with the probability of considerable overlapping of these functions. Even if it were possible to distinguish such hypothetically multiple hands in a lost manuscript (which obviously it is not), the difficulty of assigning clear levels of authority to individual readings in it would remain – if for no

---

1   As Sisson has shown, marked-up quartos were occasionally used as promptbooks in the theatre, and a copy of *A Looking Glass for London and England* (1594) annotated for stage use by a London company in the early 1600s survives (Sisson[1], 133–4). The practice, however, seems to have been anomalous and is most unlikely in the case of *Richard II*. Jowett and Taylor (167–8) point to a number of errors in F's text which can best be explained as misreadings of manuscript copy: 'doubly' for 'doubled' (1.1.57), 'complaint' for 'complaine' (1.2.42), 'placed' for 'plated' (1.3.28), 'rigor' for 'vigour' (1.3.71), 'soules' for 'smiles' (1.4.28), 'White Beares' for 'White beards' (3.2.112) and 'sympathize' for 'sympathie' (4.1.34). One may ask, of course, why an annotator would introduce such errors from MS to replace correct readings in Q3.

other reason than that there is still no scholarly consensus as to what constitutes 'authority' in a performance-oriented and culturally contingent document altered in various ways over time and supplemented by many persons. Although it is impossible under these circumstances to eliminate a large element of guesswork and subjectivity (much of it aesthetic) in making individual decisions, we can at least isolate F's substantive departures from Q3 which (1) do not represent restorations of Q1 readings and (2) have garnered the approval of a significant number of modern editors. Accordingly, I list here the major instances apart from the deposition scene (4.1.155–318) in which this edition adopts new Folio readings (i.e. those absent from Q1–3) that may be plausibly credited to the Q3 annotator's consultation of the manuscript promptbook and that have also found favour among modern textual scholars.

		F	Q1–3
(1)	1.1.118	by my	by
(2)	1.1.152	Gentlemen	gentleman
(3)	1.1.192	parle[1]	parlee
*(4)	1.2.47	sit[2]	set
(5)	1.3.172	then, but	but
(6)	1.3.180	you owe	y'owe
(7)	1.3.222	night[3]	nightes
(8)	1.4.20	Cosin (Cosin)	Coosens Coosin
(9)	1.4.52.1–53	*Enter Bushy. / Bushy,* what newes?	*Enter Bushie with newes.*
(10)	2.1.48	as a Moate[4]	as moat
(11)	2.1.102	incaged	inraged
(12)	2.1.177	the number	a number
*(13)	2.1.254	Ancestors	noble auncestors
(14)	2.1.284	*Quoint*	Coines
*(15)	2.2.119	Barkley Castle	Barkly

1 Possibly a variant spelling rather than a different word (see *OED*), but 'parle' (for 'parlee') appears to be rare.

2 Although 'set' might conceivably be interpreted as a variant spelling of 'sit' (according to *OED* the two words were sometimes confounded), this variant would appear to embody two distinct meanings.

3 F's emendation restores the rhyme with 'light' in the previous line. The correction is probably independent of Q4–5, where it had already appeared.

4 The correction appears also in Q4–5. Presumably, F emended independently.

		F	Q1–3
*(16)	2.2.128	that's	that is
*(17)	2.3.65	thankes,	thanke's
(18)	2.3.99	now the	now
*(19)	3.2.72	Orethrowes	Ouerthrowes
(20)	3.3.13	briefe with you	briefe
(21)	3.3.31	Lord	Lords
*(22)	3.4.26	Pinnes[1]	pines
(23)	3.4.34	too[2]	two
*(24)	4.1.44	*Fitzwater*	Fitzwaters
*(25)	4.1.113	of that Name the Fourth	fourth of that name
*(26)	5.1.84	[SP] *North.*	*King*
*(27)	5.2.17	thee, welcom	the welcome
		Bullingbrooke	Bullingbrooke
(28)	5.6.8	*Salsbury*, *Spencer*,	Oxford, Salisbury,
		Blunt	Blunt *Q*; Oxford,
			Salisbury *Q2–3*

* = Items not included in Jowett and Taylor's list of F corrections

Several observations may be drawn from this list. Most striking perhaps is the fact that eighteen of these twenty-eight supposed corrections of Q3 (roughly two thirds of them) fall within the first two acts (or 46 per cent) of the play, while the others are scattered much more sparsely over the remainder. This datum tends to chime with Jowett and Taylor's finding that the annotator's correction was consistently heaviest in the early scenes, actually the first seven. Seventeen of the twenty-eight are validated by Jowett and Taylor's identification of heavily annotated areas in their Table 2 (175–6). Nos. 13 and 26 (not listed by Jowett and Taylor) fall inside their designated areas of annotation and nos. 4 and 24 are on the borders of these areas. Of the remaining seven, six are of a nature to make it unclear whether they are compositorial rather than a result of annotation.

1 Although 'pines' is possibly a variant spelling of 'pinnes' (see *OED*), it appears to be extremely rare.
2 Although *OED* fails to list 'two' as a variant spelling of the adverb 'too', the substitution seems to have occurred occasionally because 'too' was a possible spelling of the numeral. A compositor might therefore easily confuse the words. In Daniel's *Civil Wars* (3.22), for instance, 'two' appears as an error for 'too' in the 1595 edn; it was then corrected in the 1609 edn. See 4.1.115–50LN; also Michel, 314.

Only one substantial correction (no. 15) falls outside their proposed areas. On balance, then, the probability that most of the commonly adopted 'corrections' of Q3 resulted from the annotator's collation of the quarto against the manuscript promptbook seems strong, although certainty is clearly unachievable.

The three categories into which these F emendations of Q3 fall are also revealing. Ten of them (nos. 1, 3, 5, 6, 10, 13, 15, 16, 18 and 19) involve the simple addition or subtraction of syllables to regularize metre and do not alter meaning in any significant way. No. 25 is a similar case, although in addition to syllabic addition, a transposition of words is involved. No. 20 also improves the metrical pattern in which it is embedded (3.3.11–13), but the main effect of the emendation is presumably to restore Shakespeare's effective rhetorical balance through the echoing of 'so briefe with him' (3.3.12) in the previous line. Although one can imagine an annotator or even a compositor introducing such changes on his own initiative, the likelihood that their source was the theatre promptbook is considerable, since, as has already been noted, the verse of *Richard II* is characteristically regular and would ordinarily appear correctly – or at least as the actors spoke it – in the prompt copy. Such a conclusion gains additional force when we note that in five further places (2.2.50–1, 2.3.28–9, 4.1.66–7, 5.2.99–100 and 5.3.11–12), the Folio text corrects the confused lineation of the quartos, probably because the annotator of Q3 followed his manuscript source.

In the second category, a group of thirteen, the F corrections affect sense by clarifying or altering syntax (nos. 8, 17 and 27), by correcting vocabulary (nos. 4, 11, 22 and 23), by making phrases more idiomatic (nos. 7 and 12), by changing singular to plural or vice versa (nos. 2 and 21), by restoring rhyme to a couplet (no. 7), and by making the dramatic action more comprehensible (nos. 9 and 26). In the final pair the action is clarified (a) by restoring to Richard a line of dialogue confounded in Q3 with Bushy's entrance in 1.4 and (b) by reassigning to Northumberland a sardonic remark contextually inappropriate to Richard in 5.1 but given to him (probably mistakenly) in the quartos. The third and final category (nos. 14, 24 and 28) involves the correction of proper names. The substitution of Spencer for Oxford (no. 28) in Northumberland's list of executed rebels has already been mentioned; the correction is a matter of historical fact and may have been made in the theatre when it was realized perhaps that Shakespeare had made a slip in dramatizing Holinshed. The

Folio's correction of Q3's 'Coines' to '*Quoint*' (no. 14), where Holinshed has 'Coint', appears to reflect the usual pronunciation of the name. The change from 'Fitzwaters' to '*Fitzwater*' (no. 24) again follows Holinshed's spelling for a name usually given as 'Fitzwalter' but apparently spoken without sounding the *l* (Fitzwater); in *2 Henry VI* (4.1.31–5), for instance, the dramatist makes much of the pun on 'Walter' and 'water'. Shakespeare may initially have written the name with an idiosyncratic terminal *s*, which was then dropped by the actors in performance. For all of these name changes, however, it is hard to imagine the dramatist withholding his assent, and, consequently, they have been almost universally accepted by recent editors. Their source, like that of the others, was undoubtedly the manuscript promptbook since they appear to reflect habits of performance.

The 'corrections' of Q3 discussed in the preceding paragraphs (including modification of the SDs and the introduction of dubiously authorial act and scene divisions) represent something like a consensus of twentieth-century editorial judgement on which F readings should be admitted into a modern critical edition of *Richard II*. Beyond these boundaries the question of F's 'authority' becomes much more debatable. If one accepts F's improvement of metre in the instances mentioned above, why not also, it will be asked, accept F's relining and metrical regularization of 3.2.133–4?

> Would they make peace? terrible hell
> Make warre vpon their spotted soules for this.
>
> (Q3)

> Would they make peace? terrible Hell make warre
> Vpon their spotted Soules for this Offence.
>
> (F)

Pollard, finding F's 'this Offence' 'pitifully weak', defended the quarto on aesthetic grounds, arguing that 'make peace' in the tetrameter line is 'a cry of rage' (85–6) and must be spoken slowly by giving each of the two monosyllables the value of a separate foot. Jowett and Taylor (with the prior concurrence of a few others) reject Pollard and accept the Folio on the grounds that no editor or printer would be likely to introduce such a change without consulting the promptbook, and that if the reading 'stood in the promptbook', it is 'perverse' to attribute the variant to an actor or some other agent 'when it could originate with the author himself' (170–1). Jowett and Taylor may indeed be correct to assume that the changed lineation and added word were taken from the play-house manuscript, but, even so, it is rash to assume that everything in this document was authorial or possessed authorial warrant, particularly in a case in which, as most editors agree, the quarto gives the dramatically more forceful and poetically superior reading. It is perhaps more difficult to defend the retention of Q3's 'Woodstocks bloud' against F's regularization, 'Glousters blood', at 1.2.1, although virtually all editors, while noting the inconsistency with respect to other references to the murdered Duke, nevertheless follow the quarto. Again this change (as with the other altered names discussed above) probably originates in the theatre promptbook, perhaps because an actor, a book-keeper or even the dramatist himself decided in the course of repeated performances that the regularized name would make clearer the identity of a figure who importantly (and ominously) dominates the political background of the action. For cultural contextualists this might seem authority enough; but since Q1's line makes perfectly good sense as it stands, involves no historical falsification and may contain an intended backward glance at *Woodstock*, the anonymous drama on the earlier events of the reign, conservative editors are content to let the anomaly stand.[1] A similar rationale governs my rejection of most of the other synonyms introduced by F and regarded by Jowett and Taylor as authorial revisions. Some of these may indeed be Shakespeare's 'second thoughts', but even though in most cases their source is probably the promptbook, we cannot know who put them there or when, and must rely ultimately on interpretive subjectivity. At all events, most editors have been content to relegate these variants to collation notes and to regard them, either explicitly or by implication, as poetically and dramatically weaker.

We must now enquire whether the printing history of the play and especially what is known of the habits of the compositors who set Q1 and F throw additional light on the transmission of the text or provide any basis for modifying the editorial policies set out above. The story of how

---

1 An additional reason for retaining Q's mention of Woodstock is the Duchess's extended metaphor involving the trunk of a tree (a wood stock) a few lines later in the scene; the family impresa or badge represented a tree trunk uprooted and cut short (see Fig. 7), and it is possible that the actor who played the Duchess would have worn the symbol on his costume (see 1.2.15n.).

THE
Tragedie of King Richard the second.

As it hath beene publikely acted by the right Honourable the Lorde Chamberlaine his Seruants.

LONDON

Printed by Valentine Simmes for Androw Wise, and are to be sold at his shop in Paules church yard at the signe of the Angel.

1597.

17 Q1 title–page (1597), Huntington Library copy

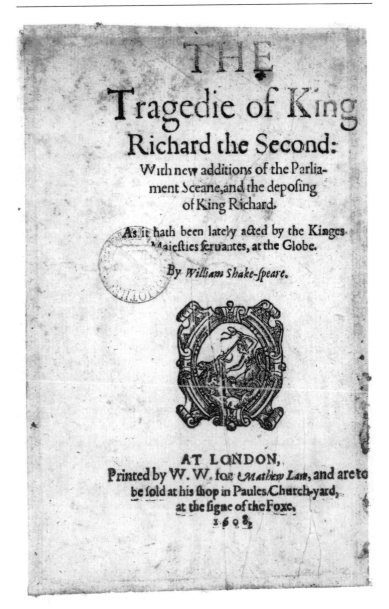

THE
Tragedie of King
Richard the Second:

With new additions of the Parliament Sceane, and the depofing
of King Richard.

As it hath been lately acted by the Kinges
Maiesties feruantes, at the Globe.

By *William Shake-fpeare*.

AT LONDON,
Printed by W. W. for *Mathew Law*, and are to
be fold at his fhop in Paules Church-yard,
at the figne of the Foxe.
1608

18 Q4 title-page (1608), second state, Bodleian Library copy

the successive quartos got into print is straightforward enough. Andrew Wise, to whom Shakespeare's company had sold a manuscript of *Richard II*, paid his fee of sixpence to the Company of Stationers and obtained his authorization to print on 29 August 1597. As was to be expected, the first edition appeared shortly afterwards with a title-page advertising the 'Tragedie' as having '*beene publikely acted by . . . the Lorde Chamberlaine his Seruants*' and printed 'by Valentine Simmes' (Fig. 17). That the book sold uncommonly well is proved by Wise's decision to issue two further editions (Q2 and Q3) the following year, each set from its immediate predecessor and printed by Simmes, but adding the name of '*William Shakes-speare*' (lacking in Q1) to the respective title-pages. As noted above, the first three quartos omit the deposition episode (4.1.155–318), which appeared for the first time in Q4 (1608). By this time copyright had been transferred from Wise to Matthew Law, who had acquired possession on 25 June 1603.[1] Law's printer was William White, the title-page of whose fourth quarto survives in two states: the first of these merely repeats the old name of the acting troupe as 'the Lord Chamberlaine his seruantes' (a name already altered to the King's Men at the accession of James I), whereas the second gives more up-to-date information: 'The Tragedie of King Richard the Second: With new additions of the Parliament Sceane, and the deposing of King Richard, As it hath been lately acted by the Kinges Maiesties seruantes, at the Globe. *By William Shake-speare*' (Fig. 18). The 'new additions' consist of an imperfect version of the deposition episode not included previously in Q1–3 but printed from a source inferior to the Folio text and of doubtful origin (see p. 506, n. 1). Obviously White cancelled his original title leaf, replacing it with one that advertised a Jacobean revival of the play as 'lately acted' by Shakespeare's fellows. No resetting of the text was involved, so that the earlier and later issues of Q4 both contain the deposition episode. Apart from the added lines, Q4 simply reprints Q3 – rather carelessly, however, since it introduces numerous fresh errors. In 1615 Law brought out a fifth edition (Q5) based on Q4 and printed by Thomas Purfoot, but correcting a number of its most obvious misprints. This reprint may also have been prompted by a stage revival although its title-page simply repeats from Q4 the phrase 'lately acted . . . at the Globe'.

1   See Greg, *Bibliography*, 1.18, 227; Black, 368.

Q1 survives in four copies: the Huth copy (in the British Library), the Capell copy (in the library of Trinity College, Cambridge), the Petworth copy (in the library of Petworth House) and the Kemble–Devonshire copy (in the Huntington Library, California) – designated respectively in this edition BL, TCC, P and HN. Collation of these copies discloses no fewer than thirty-three variants due to press correction (see textual notes for details of those affecting the text). As Greg and Hinman have pointed out (Greg, v–vi, ix–xi), two of these are especially interesting, for the Petworth copy shows that Simmes's Compositor A[1] deliberately omitted a line in two places (at 2.1.185–7 and 2.2.32–4 on sigs D1^v and D3^v respectively) in order to save space: (1) '*King* Why Vnckle whats the matter?' and (2) '*Bush.* Tis nothing but conceit my gratious Lady'. Not only are two lines excised, however; in both cases the abridgements constitute entire speeches – responses by Richard (to York) and by Bushy (to the Queen) that intervene between longer utterances by their respective interlocutors, so that the suppressions give the false appearance that York and the Queen speak in these places without interruption. In the corrected state of inner D the omitted lines have been restored, presumably at the insistence of a proofreader, and the normal length of the affected pages consequently extended from thirty-seven to thirty-eight lines to accommodate the stop-press addition (see Fig. 19).

Some of the metrical irregularities in Q1 can perhaps also be traced to the same cause, namely compositorial crowding, as is likely, for instance, at 2.2.50–1 and 2.2.60–1 on D4, where part-lines following a full pentameter are squeezed hypermetrically into a single line of type: (1) 'And with vplifted armes is safe ariude at Rauenspurgh' and (2) 'And al the houshold seruants fled with him to Bullingbrook'. In the first of these instances the evidence for compositorial tampering with authorial lineation is especially strong, for, as we have seen already, F (probably because the annotator of Q3 consulted the theatre promptbook) restored the proper lining of 2.2.50–1 as it very likely stood in the copy for Q1. The missing SD for Green's entrance at 2.2.40.1 where we might expect a separate line of type can also be attributed perhaps to the compositor's shortage of space, since the omission occurs on D3^v, the same page on which Bushy's speech was deleted, and immediately before the

1   Both Hinman and Craven agree on this designation (Greg, xiv; Craven, 'Printing', 36–8).

The Tragedie of

The plate, coine, reuenewes, and moueables
Whereof our Vnckle Gaunt did stand possest.
Yorke. How long shall I be patient? ah how long
Shall tender dutie make me suffer wrong?
Not Glocesters death, nor Herefords banishment,
Nor Gaunts rebukes, nor Englands priuate wrongs,
Nor the preuention of poore Bullingbrooke,
About his mariadge, nor my owne disgrace,
Haue euer made me sower my patient cheeke.
Or bende one wrinckle on my soueraignes face:
I am the last of noble Edwards sonnes,
Of whom thy father Prince of Wales was first,
In warre was neuer Lyon ragde more fierce,
In peace was neuer gentle lambe more milde,
Then was that young and princely Gentleman
His face thou hast, for euen so lookt he,
Accomplisht with a number of thy howers,
But when he frownd, it was against the french,
And not againsl his friends, his noble hand
Did win what he did spende, and spent not that
Which his triumphant fathers hand had wonne:
His hands were guilty of no kinred bloud,
But bloudie with the enemies of his kinne:
Oh Richard, Yorke is too far gone with griefe,
Or elshe he neuer would compare betweene.
King. Why Vncklewhats the matter?
Yorke. Oh my liege, pardone me if you please,
If not I pleasd not to be pardoned, am content with all,
Seeke you to ceaze and gripe into your hands
The roialties and rights of banisht Herefords:
Is not Gaunt dead? and doth not Hereford liue?
Was not Gaunt iust? and is not Harrie true?
Did not the one deserue to haue an heire?
Is not his heire a well deseruing sonne?
Take Herefords rightes away, and take from time
His charters, and his customarie rights;
Let not to morrow when ensue to daie:
Be not thy selfe. For how art thou a King   But

The Tragedie of

The plate, coine, reuenewes, and moueables
Whereof our Vnckle Gaunt did stand possest.
Yorke. How long shall I be patient? ah how long
Shall tender dutie make me suffer wrong?
Not Glocesters death, nor Herefords banishment,
Nor Gaunts rebukes, nor Englands priuate wrongs,
Nor the preuention of poore Bullingbrooke,
About his mariadge, nor my owne disgrace,
Haue euer made me sower my patient cheeke.
Or bende one wrinckle on my soueraignes face:
I am the last of noble Edwards sonnes,
Of whom thy father Prince of Wales was first,
In warre was neuer Lyon ragde more fierce,
In peace was neuer gentle lambe more milde,
Then was that young and princely Gentleman
His face thou hast, for euen so lookt he,
Accomplisht with a number of thy howers,
But when he frownd, it was against the french,
And not againsl his friends, his noble hand
Did win what he did spende, and spent not that
Which his triumphant fathers hand had wonne:
His hands were guilty of no kinred bloud,
But bloudie with the enemies of his kinne:
Oh Richard, Yorke is too far gone with griefe,
Or elshe he neuer would compare betweene.
My liege, pardone me if you please,
If not I pleasd not to be pardoned, am content with all,
Seeke you to ceaze and gripe into your hands
The roialties and rights of banisht Herefords:
Is not Gaunt dead? and doth not Hereford liue?
Was not Gaunt iust? and is not Harrie true?
Did not the one deserue to haue an heire?
Is not his heire a well deseruing sonne?
Take Herefords rightes away, and take from time
His charters, and his customarie rights;
Let not to morrow when ensue to daie:
Be not thy selfe. For how art thou a King   But

19 Uncorrected and Corrected pages from Q (D1ᵛ and D3ᵛ) – uncorrected P (Petworth, on left) and corrected TCC (Trinity College, Cambridge, on right) – showing how the compositor dropped a line in the uncorrected state and then restored it in the corrected one

inner-forme page (D4) on which the metrical anomalies mentioned above show up. Because Q1's proofreader either overlooked or ignored the missing entrance, the omission was carried over into all the quarto reprints before F; F restores the needed entry direction, no doubt because the Q3 annotator found it in the theatre promptbook. Necessity to compress text in these cases arose because Q1 was set by formes, not seriatim, in sheets B to K (though probably not in A),[1] and the copy was cast off (with mis-estimation of the needed space in some places) to allow the setting, locking up and delivery to the press of the outer formes before the corresponding inner formes were set in type. We can verify this procedure because of the pattern of recurring distinctive types and running titles, first identified by Hinman and analysed in greater detail by Craven.[2] Although the evidence is drawn from a very small number of surviving copies, Hinman was probably right to conclude that when the copy manuscript was inaccurately cast off (especially for grouped inner-forme pages) the compositor was prepared to misrepresent it in order to fit it into the quarto page.

On the basis of individual type-recurrences as well as the appearance of numerous unabbreviated SPs lacking a full stop, Hinman tentatively divided Q1 between two compositors, S and A, the first having set 'the equivalent of approximately nineteen full pages of text' and the second 'all the rest – approximately 53 1/2 pages – with the possible exception of certain pages and parts of pages . . . in which the evidence is either wanting or is scanty and inconclusive'.[3] He also concluded that neither of these men was 'grossly incompetent', although both made errors that require correction in modern texts, that the proof-correction 'at least

---

1   Sheet A contains the title-page, the verso of which is blank, and six pages of the opening scene (1.1.1–204); sheet K is a half-sheet containing the three pages that bring the play to a close (5.5.91–5.6.52), K2[v] being blank. Hinman was unsure whether the pattern of setting by formes continued into K. Craven, however, showed by reference to type and headline recurrences that sheet K was composed after outer I and before inner I, and printed by half-sheet imposition (Craven, 'Printing', 43–4).
2   See Greg, x–xvi; Craven, 'Printing', Chapter 3 (27–47); Craven[1] and Craven[2].
3   According to Hinman, '*Compositor S* set A2–4[v], B4[v], most of quire C (all save the lower part of C2 and pages C3[v]–4), G2, H2[v], I1 (probably), I2, I4[v], and part-page K2', whereas '*Compositor A* set' everything else except perhaps 'G2[v] and G3, H1, and at least the lower half of H2'. Davison (109) points out that 'if one adds up the pages he [Hinman] lists it will be seen that these figures should be 18 and 54 1/2' rather than nineteen and fifty-three and a half. Compositor A was first designated and his habits described by Ferguson, who in 1960 studied his work in *2 Henry IV*, *Much Ado About Nothing*, *The First Part of the Contention* and Dekker's *The Shoemakers' Holiday*.

some of the time' was 'remarkably careful', that the proofreader often consulted copy (probably 'in quire A, inner B, and outer C' but certainly in inner D), and that by Elizabethan standards 'Q1 must be regarded as a reasonably well-printed book' (Greg, xiv–xv).

Craven not only carried Hinman's analysis further but arrived at more radical conclusions. Considerably altering the balance of work between Compositors S and A in favour of the latter, he assigned only fifteen pages to S (the equivalent of 1.1.1–204, 1.3.175–305, 1.4.10–47, 2.1.90–125, 3.3.169–204, 5.1.5–42, 5.5.56–90 and 5.6.35–52 in this edition) and fifty-seven and a half pages to A (1.1.205–1.3.174, 1.3.306–1.4.9, 1.4.48–2.1.89, 2.1.126–3.3.168, 3.3.205–4.1.154, 4.1.319–5.1.4, 5.1.43–5.5.55 and 5.5.91–5.6.34). He confirmed also that every sheet (with the probable exception of A) was set by formes.[1] Since, according to Craven's painstaking reinvestigation, Compositor A set roughly four-fifths of the entire quarto, it was obviously desirable so far as possible to isolate his particular habits, to assess his accuracy in following copy and to estimate the degree, if any, to which such information might give warrant for emending the text. Surprisingly (and contrary to the assumption of most earlier scholars), evidence from *Richard II* and other plays in which A is believed to have had a major hand seems to show that this compositor was much given to making substantive alterations of his copy-text in ways that, because they involve few obvious misprints and present superficially plausible readings, are far from self-evident to the casual reader. In resetting the entirety of the first reprint of *Richard II* (Q2, 1598), for instance, Compositor A introduced 155 substantive changes (most of them memorial in nature), including sixty-three substitutions, thirty omissions, fourteen interpolations, twenty-five significant additions or subtractions of single letters ('literals'), eight transpositions, nine alterations of the form of a word ('sophistications') and six purported corrections, whether or not they are actually correct.[2] Substitutions, omissions and literals obviously make up the largest

1 Craven's most detailed analysis of the printing of Q1 appears in his doctoral dissertation (Craven, 'Printing'); see especially Chapter 3; also p. 536, ns 1 and 2.
2 The following lists illustrate the kinds of substantive change characteristic of Compositor A and constitute a sample only of the 155 changes made in resetting Q2 *Richard II*. They are taken from Craven's complete list (Craven[1], 51–4). *Substitutions*: 'of a King' for 'of the King' (1.1.70); 'my brother' for 'thy brother' (1.2.62); 'banist with good' for 'banist vpon good' (1.3.233); 'all in pieces' for 'all to pieces' (2.2.138); 'knowne to you' for 'knowen vnto you' (2.3.158); 'smoke' for 'shocke' (3.3.56);

group, while interpolations compose a somewhat smaller number; trans-positions, sophistications and corrections are still less frequent. The alarming extent of A's general unreliability inferable from his many alter-ations in setting Q2 – an unreliability often ignored, it would appear, by Simmes's somewhat desultory proofreader[1] – seemed to Craven to sup-ply justification for emending thirteen supposedly 'unsatisfactory' readings in Q1. The great majority of these suggested emendations (eleven out of thirteen) repair broken metre, the original problems hav-ing been caused, so Craven theorized, by A's tin-eared tendency to omit or interpolate words, or even to substitute words of different syllabic value, in Shakespeare's consistently regular verse. Two additional emen-dations, in Craven's view, make the sense more idiomatic and, although they involve no metrical change, are justified, he believed, on the grounds of A's known habit of substituting a pronoun for an article ('my' for 'the') or one pronoun for another ('my' for 'our').[2] Although Craven acknowledged that Compositor A would probably have had to work more slowly in setting from manuscript than from printed copy (where it would be easier to take a larger amount of text into memory at a single

'weedes that without' for 'weedes which without' (3.4.38); 'As sure as' for 'As surely as' (4.1.102); 'how to compare' for 'how I may compare' (5.5.1). *Omissions*: 'and spit at him' for 'and I spit at him' (1.1.60); 'flatter those' for 'flatter with those' (2.1.88); 'straunger in' for 'stranger here in' (2.3.3); 'the death of Kings' for 'the death or fall of Kings' (2.4.15); 'In remembrance' for 'In the remembrance' (3.4.107); 'like mee' for 'like to me' (5.2.109); 'Salisbury, and' for 'Salisbury, Blunt and' (5.6.8). *Interpolations*: 'of the noble' for 'of noble' (2.1.171); 'the rest of the reuolted' for 'al the rest reuolted' (2.2.57); 'sits not here' for 'sits here' (4.1.123); 'words do come' for 'words come' (5.3.101); 'through the shade' for 'through shades' (5.6.43). *Literals*: 'Esteeme a foyle' for 'Esteeme as foyle' (1.3.266); 'said your cousin' for 'said our cousin' (1.4.10); 'sorrowes eyes' for 'Sorrowes eye' (2.2.26); 'thee fauour with' for 'thee fauours with' (3.2.11); 'vnder his terrestriall' for 'vnder this terrestriall' (3.2.41); 'some sparkles of' for 'some sparkes of' (5.3.21). *Transpositions*: 'his yong sonne H. Percie' for 'his son yong H. Percie' (2.2.53); 'countrey all are witherd' for 'country are al witherd' (2.4.8); 'Castle is royally' for 'Castle royally is' (3.3.21); 'pres-ence I may speake' for 'presence may I speake' (4.1.116). *Sophistications*: 'to mine owne' for 'to my owne' (1.1.133); 'hate against any' for 'hate gainst any' (2.1.243), 'Hath broke' for 'Hath broken' (2.2.59); 'oath betwixt thee' for 'oathe twixt thee' (5.1.74). *Corrections*: 'outrage bloudy here' for 'outrage bouldy here' (3.2.40); 'Camst thou' for 'Canst thou' (3.4.80); '*King* Good' for '*yorke* Good' (5.3.110). In a subse-quent article, Craven confirmed Compositor A's unreliability by studying his work in two later reprints, Q2 *The First Part of the Contention* (1600) and Q3 *1 Henry IV* (1604), in which similar kinds of change are observable; see Craven[2], 188–93.

1 See Craven[2], 193–6.
2 For details, see the textual notes and accompanying commentary at 1.3.83, 2.1.254, 2.2.109–10, 2.3.158, 3.4.67, 5.2.18, 28, 41, 55, 65, 5.3.30, 56 and 143. See also Craven[3], 47–50, 54–61.

glance), he nevertheless argued that the compositor would be inclined to make the same kinds of memorial error in Q1 as in Q2, though perhaps less frequently.

Davison, reviewing Hinman's revised introduction to Greg's facsimile edition of Q1 and the earliest of Craven's articles (Craven[1]), warns us to be sceptical of their evidence on the grounds of its selectivity; and he goes on to suggest with some force that the demarcation between the habits of Compositors S and A is less clear and definite than Hinman and especially Craven implied. Proof-correction variants in the surviving copies of Q1 make it clear, he reminds us, 'that S is capable of adding a word and omitting an exit and he is as good as A at producing variants that make a kind of sense – such as "A partiall slaunder ought I to auoide" for "A partial slaunder sought I to auoide" [1.3.241]' on C1 (Davison, 128). He particularly questions whether the unstopped SPs, supposedly the fingerprint of A, can be wholly relied upon since the pattern fails to hold up consistently in Q2, which A set in its entirety. And Davison raises the further complicating possibility that A may have corrected pages originally set by S so as to produce a mixture of styles and therefore a clouding of the evidence. Dissenting from both Hinman and Craven in the allocation of pages, Davison (127) would assign forty-eight to A and eighteen to S (including two pages on which Craven saw the need to emend because of A's supposed inaccuracy), leaving seven pages unallocated for lack of evidence (apparently counting sig. K2 as a full page since his page count totals seventy-three). Davison also doubts that A was as radically inaccurate compared to S as Craven believed, for he suggests that at least some of A's supposed errors in setting Q2 may have originated from his following a copy of Q1 whose sheets had not been corrected. He also believes that a few of Compositor A's 'errors' in Q2, often rejected by editors, represent legitimate 'corrections' which can reasonably be defended in modern editions.

Davison's healthy scepticism towards the work of his predecessors in compositor analysis must give us pause, but his caveat need not wholly undermine Craven's general conclusions, for even if some of the errors attributed to A should turn out to be S's, the likely pattern of widespread interpolation, omission and substitution in Q1, extrapolated from the mis-settings in Q2, would seem to be undeniable. One must obviously consider each case in context, individually and on its own merits. I have nevertheless admitted six of Craven's suggested readings into this edition (at 2.1.254, 3.4.67, 5.2.55, 5.3.30, 56 and 143) not only because they improve the metre or the sense but also because, in my view, a convincing case can be made for them bibliographically. In the first of these instances (2.1.254) the argument for acceptance becomes slightly stronger because the emendation, although absent from Q2–5, does appear in F – possibly an indication that it stood in the theatre prompt-book and therefore also, perhaps, in the copy for Q1.

As for the setting of the Folio text (again by formes rather than seri-atim), Hinman showed in his classic study that the two Jaggard compositors involved in *Richard II* were probably those now designated A and B. Compositor A, by much the more accurate of the two (his most characteristic errors involved only individual letters such as those shown in the variants on p. 507, n. 1), was responsible for pages 39–40 in the Histories section (sigs d2–d2^v) on which the deposition episode (4.1.155–318) occurs. According to Hinman, A also set pages 32–7 (c4^v–d1) and page 41 (d3), his total stints being the equivalent in this edition of 2.3.7–3.4.53 and 4.1.73–5.2.6. The more liberty-taking Compositor B, who is usually credited with setting half the entire Folio, probably set the rest of the play, pages 23–31 (b6–c4), page 38 (d1^v) and pages 42–5 (d3^v–d5) – the equivalent of 1.1.1–2.3.6, 3.4.54–4.1.72 and 5.2.7–5.6.52 – although Hinman raised the possibility that d1^v (3.4.54–4.1.72) might have been set by a third man (Compositor C).[1] Problems with spacing as a result of imperfectly cast-off copy similar to those that beset Q1's Compositor A also caused F's Compositor B trouble. At 4.1.61–7 on d1^v, for instance, he reset Q3 to make the dialogue between Surrey and Fitzwater (seven lines of type in the quarto) spread to eleven in the Folio, not only dislocating the metre but also inserting a superfluous 'My Lord' at the beginning of line 63 so as to fill out his column. In order to obvi-ate crowding on d5 he also deleted a two-line speech by Bolingbroke ('*Bul.* We thank thee gentle *Percy* for thy paines, / And to thy worth will adde right worthy gaines' (5.6.11–12)), which was later replaced, appar-ently at the injunction of a proofreader, causing a shift of type from the top of column 2 to the bottom of column 1 in the corrected state of page 45.[2] A's setting of the deposition scene involves no serious textual

---

1 See Hinman, 2.77. Blayney's apportionment of pages agrees with Hinman's except for the elimination of Compositor C as the possible setter of d1^v, which Blayney assigns to 'B?' (Norton, Facsimile, xxvi).

2 See Blayney, 14.

difficulties apart from the need to correct a few minor aberrations by reference to Q4 (see p. 507, n. 1). The Jaggard–Blount syndicate apparently ran into copyright difficulties while *Richard II* was being worked on, for an interruption in the usual composing and printing sequence occurred after the setting of page 36 (c6ᵛ) – well into 3.3. Matthew Law (who had issued Q5 in 1615) still held title to this play as well as to *1* and *2 Henry IV* and *Richard III*, and the publishers seem to have delayed negotiating with him until the setting of *Richard II* was already underway. In any event, work in Jaggard's shop shifted at this point to completion of the printing of the Comedies, after which the compositors were instructed to continue printing the Histories from *Henry V* onwards, leaving on one side the unset section of *Richard II* and the whole of *1* and *2 Henry IV* (plays owned by Law). Since they did not resume the setting of *Richard II* until they were well into *3 Henry VI*, we can infer that Law held out for a high price for dramas that (except for *2 Henry IV*) had been bestsellers.[1]

---

1   See Hinman, 2.522–3; Blayney, 17.

APPENDIX 2
DOUBLING CHART

Actor	1.1	1.2	1.3	1.4	2.1	2.2	2.3	2.4	3.1	3.2
1	King R		-King R-	King R	-King R-					King R
2	-Bol		-Bol				Bol		Bol	
3	[*York]		-[*York]-		York-	-York-	-York		York	
4	Gaunt-	Gaunt	-Gaunt		Gaunt-					Carlisle
5					-North		North		*North-	
6	-Mowb		-Mowb-				-Harry P		*Harry P	
7	[*Aumerle]		Aumerle-	Aumerle	-*Aumerle-		-*Attend (York)			Aumerle
8	[*Bushy]		-*Bushy-	-Bushy	-*Bushy-	Bushy			Bushy-	
9	*Marshal		Marshal				*Sold(North)			-Scroop
10	[*Green]		-*Green-	Green	-*Green-	-Green			Green-	
†11					-Queen	Queen-				
†12	[*Lord]		-[*Lord]-							
†13		Duch G								
14	[*Bagot]		-*Bagot-	Bagot	-*Bagot-	Bagot		Captain-		
15	*Attend(Bol)		-1 Herald-		-Ross		-Ross		*Ross	
16	*Attend(Mowb)		-2 Herald-		-*Attend(Rich)-	-Serv(York)-	-*Attend(York)			*Colours
17					*Serv(Gaunt)-			Salisbury		-Salisbury
18	*Attend(Rich)		-*Attend(Rich)-		-Willoughby		-Willoughby		*Willoughby	
19	*Attend(Rich)		-*Attend(Rich)-		-*Attend(Rich)-		-Berkeley		*Sold(Bol)-	*Sold(Rich)
20					*Serv(Gaunt)-		*Sold(North)		*Sold(Bol)-	*Sold(Rich)
†21	[*Lord]		-[*Lord]-							

Actor	3.3	3.4	4.1	5.1	5.2	5.3	5.4	5.5	5.6	Total Lines
1	-King R		-King R-	-King R				King R		755
2	Bol		Bol-			King H			King H	413
3	York		-York-		York-	-York			*York	288
4	-*Carlisle		Carlisle						-*Carlisle	255
5	North		North-	-North		[*North]-			-North	143
6	-Harry P		Harry P-			Harry P-			-Harry P	180
7	-Aumerle	-Gardener	Aumerle		-Aumerle	-Aumerle			[*Aumerle]	85
8							Exton	-Exton	-Exton-	112
9	-*Scroop		Lord-	-*Attend(North)		[*Lord]-			[*Lord]	67
10	*Trumpet		Fitz-						-Fitz	59
†11		Queen-		Queen						115
†12	*Attend(North)		*Attend(Bol)-		Duch York	-Duch York			*Attend(Bol)	93
†13		1 Lady-	*1 Herald-	*1 Lady					[*Lord]	61
14	*Drum		-Bagot-	-*Attend(North)	-*Serv(York)-			-Groom-	*Attend(Bol)	49
15	*Sold(Bol)		Abbot					-Keeper	-[*Guard(Car)]	33
16	*Colours		Surrey-					-*Serv(Exton)	*Serv(Exton)	22
17	-*Salisbury						1 Serv(Exton)	-*Serv(Exton)		31
18	*Attend(North)		*Attend(Bol)-	-*Guard(Rich)			2 Serv(Exton)	-*Serv(Exton)		13
19	*Sold(Bol)	-1 Man(Gard)	-*Officer-	-[*Guard(Rich)]		*Lord]-		-*Serv(Exton)	-*Serv(Exton)	13
20	*Sold(Bol)	-2 Man(Gard)	-*Officer-			*Lord]-			[*Lord]	17
†21		2 Lady-		*2 Lady					[*Lord]	1

† boy actor
* mute
- enters after beginning or exits before end of scene
[ ] characters whose presence, though possible, is not certain

APPENDIX 3
GENEALOGICAL TABLES

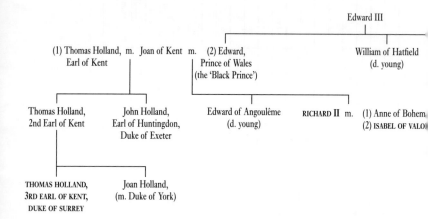

Edward III

(1) Thomas Holland, m. Joan of Kent m. (2) Edward,   William of Hatfield
Earl of Kent   Prince of Wales   (d. young)
(the 'Black Prince')

Thomas Holland,   John Holland,   Edward of Angoulême   RICHARD II m. (1) Anne of Bohem
2nd Earl of Kent   Earl of Huntingdon,   (d. young)   (2) ISABEL OF VALOI
Duke of Exeter

THOMAS HOLLAND,   Joan Holland,
3RD EARL OF KENT,   (m. Duke of York)
DUKE OF SURREY

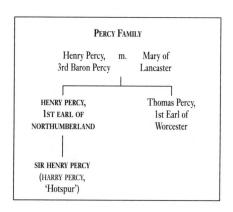

PERCY FAMILY

Henry Percy,   m.   Mary of
3rd Baron Percy   Lancaster

HENRY PERCY,   Thomas Percy,
1ST EARL OF   1st Earl of
NORTHUMBERLAND   Worcester

SIR HENRY PERCY
(HARRY PERCY,
'Hotspur')

Persons who appear as characters in *Richard II* are in bold capitals

544

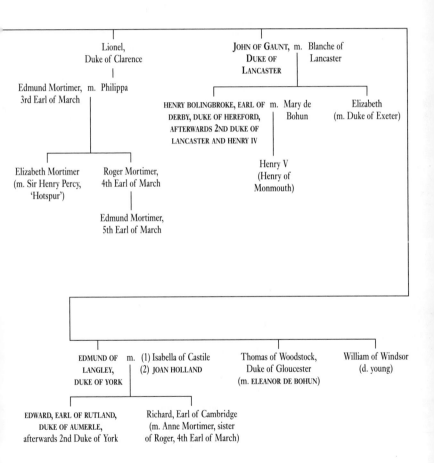

Lionel,
Duke of Clarence

JOHN OF GAUNT, m. Blanche of
DUKE OF Lancaster
LANCASTER

Edmund Mortimer, m. Philippa
3rd Earl of March

HENRY BOLINGBROKE, EARL OF m. Mary de
DERBY, DUKE OF HEREFORD, Bohun
AFTERWARDS 2ND DUKE OF
LANCASTER AND HENRY IV

Elizabeth
(m. Duke of Exeter)

Elizabeth Mortimer
(m. Sir Henry Percy,
'Hotspur')

Roger Mortimer,
4th Earl of March

Henry V
(Henry of
Monmouth)

Edmund Mortimer,
5th Earl of March

EDMUND OF m. (1) Isabella of Castile
LANGLEY, (2) JOAN HOLLAND
DUKE OF YORK

Thomas of Woodstock,
Duke of Gloucester
(m. ELEANOR DE BOHUN)

William of Windsor
(d. young)

EDWARD, EARL OF RUTLAND,
DUKE OF AUMERLE,
afterwards 2nd Duke of York

Richard, Earl of Cambridge
(m. Anne Mortimer, sister
of Roger, 4th Earl of March)

ABBREVIATIONS AND REFERENCES

Unless otherwise stated the place of publication in all references is London. Quotations and references relating to *Richard II* are keyed to this edition. Those relating to other works by Shakespeare are keyed to the *Riverside Shakespeare*, ed. G. Blakemore Evans (Boston, Mass., 1974), unless otherwise specified. The Bishops' Bible (1568 etc.) is the usual source for biblical quotations and citations, although the Geneva (1560) and the Authorized (1611) versions are occasionally used. For titles of collected editions of Shakespeare except the Folios, I simplify to the forms *Works* or *Plays*, depending on whether the non-dramatic pieces are included. For titles of other independent editions of the play including the quartos, I invariably use the short form *Richard II*. I normalize the spelling of the dramatist's name to Shakespeare throughout. Abbreviations of parts of speech are those used in *OED* (2nd edn).

ABBREVIATIONS

ABBREVIATIONS USED IN NOTES

ed., eds	editor, editors
edn	edition
fol., fols	folio, folios
LN	Longer Notes
n.	note
n.s.	new series
om.	omitted
opp.	opposite
SD	stage direction
sig., sigs	signature, signatures
SP	speech prefix
subst.	substantially
this edn	a reading adopted for the first time in this edition
t.n.	textual note (at the foot of each page of the text)
( )	enclosing a reading in the textual notes indicates original spelling; enclosing an editor's or scholar's name indicates a conjectural reading
*	precedes commentary notes when they involve readings in this edn substantively altered from the original editions

WORKS BY AND PARTLY BY SHAKESPEARE

AC	*Antony and Cleopatra*
AW	*All's Well That Ends Well*
AYL	*As You Like It*
Car	*The History of Cardenio*
CE	*The Comedy of Errors*
Cor	*Coriolanus*
Cym	*Cymbeline*
DF	Lewis Theobald, *Double Falsehood*
E3	*The Reign of King Edward III*
Ham	*Hamlet*
1H4	*King Henry IV, Part 1*
2H4	*King Henry IV, Part 2*
H5	*King Henry V*
1H6	*King Henry VI, Part 1*
2H6	*King Henry VI, Part 2*
3H6	*King Henry VI, Part 3*
H8	*King Henry VIII*
JC	*Julius Caesar*
KJ	*King John*
KL	*King Lear*
LC	*A Lover's Complaint*
LLL	*Love's Labour's Lost*
Luc	*The Rape of Lucrece*
MA	*Much Ado About Nothing*
Mac	*Macbeth*
MM	*Measure for Measure*
MND	*A Midsummer Night's Dream*
MV	*The Merchant of Venice*
MW	*The Merry Wives of Windsor*
Oth	*Othello*
Per	*Pericles*
PP	*The Passionate Pilgrim*
R2	*King Richard II*
R3	*King Richard III*
RJ	*Romeo and Juliet*
Son	*Sonnets*
STM	*The Book of Sir Thomas More*
TC	*Troilus and Cressida*
Tem	*The Tempest*
TGV	*The Two Gentlemen of Verona*
Tim	*Timon of Athens*
Tit	*Titus Andronicus*
TN	*Twelfth Night*
TNK	*The Two Noble Kinsmen*

TS	*The Taming of the Shrew*
VA	*Venus and Adonis*
WT	*The Winter's Tale*

REFERENCES

EDITIONS OF SHAKESPEARE
COLLATED OR REFERRED TO

Adams	*Richard II*, ed. Richard Adams, Macmillan Shakespeare (1975)
Alexander	*Works*, ed. Peter Alexander (London and Glasgow, 1951)
Ard[1]	*Richard II*, ed. Ivor B. John, Arden Shakespeare (1912)
Ard[2]	*Richard II*, ed. Peter Ure, Arden Shakespeare (1956)
Bevington	*Works*, ed. David Bevington (Glenview, Ill., 1980)
Bevington[2]	*Richard II*, ed. David Bevington, Bantam Shakespeare (New York, 1988)
BL	Copy of Q1 in the British Library
Black	*Richard II*, ed. Matthew W. Black, New Variorum Shakespeare (Philadelphia, Penn., 1955)
Black[2]	*Richard II*, ed. Matthew W. Black, in Alfred Harbage (gen. ed.), *Works*, Pelican Shakespeare (Baltimore, Md., 1969), 633–67
Cam	*Works*, ed. William George Clark, John Glover and William Aldis Wright, 9 vols (Cambridge and London, 1863–6), vol. 4
Cam[1]	*Richard II*, ed. John Dover Wilson (Cambridge, 1939; repr. with additions, 1951)
Cam[2]	*Richard II*, ed. Andrew Gurr (Cambridge, 1984)
Campbell, O.J.	*Selected Works*, ed. O.J. Campbell (New York, 1949)
Capell	*Plays*, ed. Edward Capell, 10 vols (1767–8), vol. 5
Chambers	*Richard II*, ed. E.K. Chambers, Falcon Shakespeare (London and New York, 1891)
Clark & Wright	*Richard II*, ed. W.G. Clark and W.A. Wright, Clarendon Press Series: Shakespeare Select Plays (Oxford, 1876)
Collier	*Works*, ed. John Payne Collier, 8 vols (1842–4), vol. 4
Craig, H.	*Richard II*, ed. Hardin Craig, Tudor Shakespeare (New York, 1912)
Craig, H.[2]	*Works*, ed. Hardin Craig (Chicago, Ill. 1951)
Daniel, P.A.	*Richard II, The First Quarto, 1597, A Facsimile in Photo-Lithography*, ed. Peter Augustin Daniel (1890)
Delius	*Works (Werke)*, ed. Nicolaus Delius, 7 vols (Elberfeld, 1854–61), vol. 3

Dyce   *Works*, ed. Alexander Dyce, 6 vols (1857), vol. 3
Dyce²   *Works*, ed. Alexander Dyce, 9 vols (1864–7), vol. 4
Edwards   Thomas Edwards, *A Supplement to Mr. Warburton's Edition of Shakespear . . .*, 7th edn (1765)
Evans   See *Riv*
F, F1   *Comedies, Histories, and Tragedies*, The First Folio (1623)
Fc   corrected state in F
Fu   uncorrected state in F
F2   *Comedies, Histories, and Tragedies*, The Second Folio (1632)
F3   *Comedies, Histories, and Tragedies*, The Third Folio (1663)
F4   *Comedies, Histories, and Tragedies*, The Fourth Folio (1685)
Greg   *Richard II: The Quarto of 1597*, Shakespeare Quarto Facsimiles No. 13, ed. W.W. Greg and Charlton Hinman (Oxford, 1966)
Gurr   See *Cam²*
Halliwell   *Works*, ed. James O. Halliwell, 16 vols (1853–65), vol. 9
Hanmer   *Plays*, ed. Sir Thomas Hanmer, 6 vols (Oxford, 1743–4), vol. 3
Harrison   *Works*, ed. G.B. Harrison (New York, 1968)
Herford   *Richard II*, ed. C.H. Herford, Warwick Shakespeare (1893)
HN   Copy of Q1 at the Henry E. Huntington Library, San Marino, Calif.
Hudson   *Works*, ed. Henry N. Hudson, 11 vols (Boston, Mass., 1851–9), vol. 5
Irving   *Works*, ed. Henry Irving and Frank A. Marshall, 8 vols (New York, 1888–90), vol. 2
John   See *Ard¹*
Johnson   *Plays*, ed. Samuel Johnson, 8 vols (1765), vol. 4
Keightley   *Plays*, ed. Thomas Keightley, 6 vols (1864), vol. 3
Kittredge   *Works*, ed. G.L. Kittredge (Boston, Mass., 1936)
Kittredge²   *Richard II*, ed. G.L. Kittredge (Boston, Mass., 1941)
Knight   *Works*, ed. Charles Knight, *Pictorial Edition*, 8 vols (1839–43), vol. 1
Lothian   *Richard II*, ed. John M. Lothian (Oxford, 1938; repr. with corrections, 1939)
Malone   *Works*, ed. Edmond Malone, 10 vols (1790), vol. 5
Mowat & Werstine   *Richard II*, ed. Barbara A. Mowat and Paul Werstine, New Folger Library Shakespeare (New York, 1996)
Muir   *Richard II*, ed. Kenneth Muir, Signet Shakespeare (London and New York, 1963)
Neilson   *Works*, ed. William Allan Neilson (Boston, Mass., 1906)
Newbolt   *Richard II*, ed. Henry Newbolt (1925)
Norton Facsimile   *The Norton Facsimile: The First Folio of Shakespeare*, ed. Charlton Hinman with a new introduction by Peter W.M. Blayney (New York, 1996)

Oxf	*Works*, ed. Stanley Wells, Gary Taylor, John Jowett and William Montgomery (Oxford, 1986)
P	Copy of Q1 at Petworth House, England
Petersson	*Richard II*, ed. Robert T. Petersson, Yale Shakespeare, rev. edn (New Haven, Conn., 1957)
Pollard	*A New Shakespeare Quarto: 'The Tragedy of King Richard II' Printed for the third time by Valentine Simmes in 1598*, ed. A.W. Pollard (1916; facsimile of Q3)
Pope	*Works*, ed. Alexander Pope, 6 vols (1723–5), vol. 3
Q, Q1	*Richard II*, The First Quarto (1597)
Qc	corrected state in Q
Qu	uncorrected state in Q
Qq	Q1–5
Q2	*Richard II*, The Second Quarto (1598)
Q3	*Richard II*, The Third Quarto (1598)
Q4	*Richard II*, The Fourth Quarto (1608)
Q5	*Richard II*, The Fifth Quarto (1615)
Q6	*Richard II*, The Sixth Quarto (1634)
Rann	*Plays*, ed. Joseph Rann, 6 vols (1786–94), vol. 3
Ritson	Joseph Ritson, contributor to Steevens
Riv	*Works*, ed. G. Blakemore Evans *et al.*, *Riverside Shakespeare* (Boston, Mass., 1974)
Roderick	Richard Roderick, see Edwards
Rolfe	*Richard II*, ed. William J. Rolfe (New York, 1876)
Rowe	*Works*, ed. Nicholas Rowe, 6 vols (1709), vol. 3
Rowe[3]	*Works*, ed. Nicholas Rowe, 8 vols (1714), vol. 3
Singer	*Plays*, ed. Samuel W. Singer, 2nd edn, 10 vols (1855–6), vol. 4
Staunton	*Plays*, ed. Howard Staunton, 3 vols (1858–60), vol. 1
Steevens	*Plays*, ed. George Steevens and Isaac Reed, 15 vols (1793), vol. 8
TCC	Copy of Q1 at Trinity College, Cambridge
Theobald	*Works*, ed. Lewis Theobald, 7 vols (1733), vol. 3
Ure	See Ard[2]
Var 1773	*Plays*, ed. Samuel Johnson and George Steevens, 10 vols (1773), vol. 5
Var 1785	*Plays*, ed. Samuel Johnson, George Steevens and Isaac Reed, 10 vols (1785), vol. 5
Verity	*Richard II*, ed. A.W. Verity (Cambridge, 1899)
Warburton	*Works*, ed. William Warburton, 8 vols (1747), vol. 4
Watt	*Richard II*, ed. A.F. Watt, Tutorial Shakespeare (1907)
Wells	*Richard II*, ed. Stanley Wells, New Penguin Shakespeare (Harmondsworth, England, 1969)
White	*Works*, ed. Richard Grant White, 12 vols (Boston, Mass., 1857–66), vol. 6

White[2]	*Works*, ed. Richard Grant White, *Riverside Shakespeare*, 3 vols (Boston, Mass., 1883), vol. 2
Wilson	See Cam[1]
Wright	*Works*, ed. William Aldis Wright, 9 vols (Cambridge, 1891–3), vol. 4

OTHER WORKS

Abbott	E.A. Abbott, *A Shakespearian Grammar*, 3rd edn (1879; references are to section numbers, not to pages)
Advertisement	*An Advertisement Written to a Secretary of My Lord Treasurer's of England*, trans. John Philopatris [i.e. Richard Rowlands?] (Antwerp, 1592)
AEB	*Analytical & Enumerative Bibliography*, The Bibliographical Society of Northern Illinois
Albright	Evelyn M. Albright, 'Shakespeare's *Richard II* and the Essex Conspiracy', *PMLA*, 42 (1927), 686–720
Alexander, 'Hamlet'	Peter Alexander, 'The Text of *Hamlet*', *RES*, 12 (1936), 385–400
Altick	Richard D. Altick, 'Symphonic Imagery in *Richard II*', *PMLA*, 62 (1947), 339–65
AN&Q	*American Notes and Queries*
Ascham	Roger Ascham, *English Works*, ed. William Aldis Wright (Cambridge, 1904)
Aston	Margaret Aston, 'Richard II and the Wars of the Roses', in F.H.R. Du Boulay and Caroline M. Barron (eds), *The Reign of Richard II: Essays in Honour of May McKisack* (1971), 280–317
Atheist's Tragedy	Cyril Tourner, *The Atheist's Tragedy*, ed. Irving Ribner, Revels Plays (1964)
AV	Authorized Version of the Bible ('King James Bible', 1611)
Axton	Marie Axton, *The Queen's Two Bodies: Drama and the Elizabethan Succession* (1977)
Bacon, *Letters*	*The Letters and the Life of Francis Bacon*, ed. James Spedding, 7 vols (1861–72)
Bacon, *Works*	*The Works of Francis Bacon*, ed. James Spedding, R.L. Ellis and D.D. Heath, 15 vols (New York, 1863–4)
Baldwin	T.W. Baldwin, *On Act and Scene Division in the Shakespeare First Folio* (Carbondale, Ill., 1965)
Barber	C.L. Barber, 'From Ritual to Comedy: An Examination of *Henry IV*', in W.K. Wimsatt, Jr (ed.), *English Stage Comedy: English Institute Essays, 1954* (New York, 1955), 22–51
Barkan	Leonard Barkan, 'The Theatrical Consistency of *Richard II*', *SQ*, 29 (1978), 5–19

Baron, *Academy*   Robert Baron, *The Cyprian Academy* (1647)

Baron, *Mirza*   Robert Baron, *Mirza, A Tragedy* (1655)

Barroll   Leeds Barroll, 'A New History for Shakespeare and His Time', *SQ*, 39 (1988), 441–64

Baskervill   Charles Read Baskervill, *The Elizabethan Jig* (Chicago, Ill., 1929)

Baxter   John Baxter, *Shakespeare's Poetic Styles: Verse Into Drama* (1980)

Beadle   Richard Beadle (ed.), *The York Plays* (1982)

Beaumont   See Fletcher

Berger, 'Perspective'   Harry Berger, Jr, '*Richard II*: A Modern Perspective', in Mowat & Werstine, 237–72

Bergeron   David M. Bergeron, 'The Deposition Scene in *Richard II*', Dennis G. Donovan and A. Leigh DeNeef (eds), *Renaissance Papers 1974* (Durham, N.C., 1975), 31–7

Bergeron, 'Hoby Letter'   David M. Bergeron, 'The Hoby Letter and *Richard II*: A Parable of Criticism', *SQ*, 26 (1975), 477–80

Bevan   Bryan Bevan, *Henry IV* (New York, 1994)

Billington   Michael Billington, *The Modern Actor* (1973)

Black, 'Interlude'   James Black, 'The Interlude of the Beggar and the King in *Richard II*', in David M. Bergeron (ed.), *Pageantry in the Shakespearean Theater* (Athens, Ga., 1985), 104–13

Black, 'Sources'   Matthew W. Black, 'The Sources of *Richard II*', in J.G. McManaway, G.E. Dawson and E.E. Willoughby (eds), *Joseph Quincy Adams Memorial Studies* (Washington, D.C., 1948), 199–216

Blayney   Peter W.M. Blayney, *The First Folio of Shakespeare*, Folger Library Publications (Washington, D.C., 1991)

Bloch   Marc Bloch, *The Royal Touch: Sacred Monarchy and Scrofula in England and France*, trans. J.E. Anderson (1973)

Bloom   Harold Bloom (ed.), *William Shakespeare's 'Richard II'*, Modern Critical Interpretations (New York and New Haven, Conn., 1988)

Boas   F.S. Boas, '*Thomas of Woodstock*; A Non-Shakespearean *Richard II*', in *Shakespeare and the Universities* (New York, 1903), 143–66

Bornstein   Diane Bornstein, 'Trial by Combat and Official Irresponsibility in *Richard II*', *SSt*, 8 (1975), 131–41

Bradley   David Bradley, *From Text to Performance in the Elizabethan Theatre* (Cambridge, 1992)

Brereton, 'Notes'   J. Le Gay Brereton, 'Some Notes on *Richard II*', in R.G. Howarth (ed.), *Writings on Elizabethan Drama* (Melbourne, 1948), 98–109

Brooke   Nicholas Brooke, '*Richard II*', in *Shakespeare's Early Tragedies* (1968), 107–37

Bryant	J.A. Bryant, Jr, 'The Linked Analogies of *Richard II*', *Sewanee Review*, 65 (1957), 420–33
Buchon	J.A. Buchon (ed.), *Chronique de Richard II*, in *Collection des Chroniques Nationales Françaises*, 25 (Froissart, vol. 15) (Paris, 1826), Deuxième Supplément, 1–79 (Jean Le Beau's version of *Traïson*)
Bullough	Geoffrey Bullough (ed.), *Narrative and Dramatic Sources of Shakespeare*, 8 vols (London and New York, 1957–75)
Burton	Robert Burton, *The Anatomy of Melancholy*, ed. Thomas C. Faulkner, Nicolas K. Kiessling and Rhonda L. Blair, 5 vols (Oxford, 1989–)
Caesar's Revenge	*The Tragedy of Caesar and Pompey, or Caesar's Revenge*, ed. F.S. Boas, MSR (Oxford, 1911)
Campbell	Lily B. Campbell, *Shakespeare's Histories: Mirrors of Elizabethan Policy* (San Marino, Calif., 1947)
Capgrave	John Capgrave, *Liber de Illustribus Henricis*, ed. Francis Charles Hingeston (1858)
Caxton	*The Golden Legend, or Lives of the Saints, as Englished by William Caxton*, 6 vols (1900)
Cercignani	Fausto Cercignani, *Shakespeare's Works and Elizabethan Pronunciation* (Oxford, 1981)
Chamberlain	A.B. Chamberlain, *Hans Holbein the Younger*, 2 vols (New York, 1913)
Chamberlain, *Letters*	*The Letters of John Chamberlain*, ed. Norman Egbert McClure, 2 vols (Philadelphia, Penn., 1939)
Chambers, 'Gleanings'	E.K. Chambers, 'The Date of *Richard II*', in 'Elizabethan Stage Gleanings', *RES*, 1 (1925), 75–6
Chambers, *ES*	E.K. Chambers, *The Elizabethan Stage*, 4 vols (Oxford, 1923; corrected edn, 1951)
Chambers, *Survey*	E.K. Chambers, *Shakespeare: A Survey* (New York, 1926)
Chambers, *WS*	E.K. Chambers, *William Shakespeare: A Study of Facts and Problems*, 2 vols (Oxford, 1930)
Champion	Larry S. Champion, 'The Function of Mowbray: Shakespeare's Maturing Artistry in *Richard II*', *SQ*, 26 (1975), 3–7
Charles I	*The Works of King Charles the Martyr*, 2 vols (1662)
Charlton & Waller	H.B. Charlton and R.D. Waller (eds), *Christopher Marlowe, Edward II* (1933; rev. F.N. Lees, 1955)
Chaucer	*The Works of Geoffrey Chaucer*, ed. F.N. Robinson, 2nd edn (Boston, Mass., 1957)
Cibber	Colley Cibber, *The Tragical History of Richard the Third* (1718)
Cicero	See *Tusculan Disputations*
Clegg	Cyndia Susan Clegg, '"By the choise and inuitation of al the realme": *Richard II* and Elizabethan Press Censorship', *SQ*, 48 (1997), 432–48

Coghill	Nevill Coghill, 'Shakespeare's Reading in Chaucer', in Herbert Davis and Helen Gardner (eds), *Elizabethan and Jacobean Studies Presented to Frank Percy Wilson* (Oxford, 1959), 86–99
Coit	Charles Wheeler Coit, *The Royal Martyr* (1924)
Coleridge	Samuel Taylor Coleridge, *Coleridge's Criticism of Shakespeare*, ed. R.A. Foakes (Detroit, Mich., 1989)
Collins	Arthur Collins (ed.), *Letters and Memorials of State, in the Reigns of Queen Mary, Queen Elizabeth, King James, King Charles the First . . .*, 2 vols (1746)
Conference	R. Doleman [i.e. Robert Parsons and Others], *A Conference about the Next Succession to the Crown of England* (1594); arranged as two parts separately paginated
Contention	*The First Part of the Contention* (Q1, 1594; Q2, 1600)
Copy of a Letter	[Thomas Morgan?], *The Copy of a Letter Written by a Master of Art of Cambridge . . . about the present state and some proceedings of the Earl of Leicester* (Paris, 1584; repr. as *Leicester's Commonwealth*, 1641 – see Peck)
Cox	Frank Cox, 'Old Vic *Richard II*', *Plays and Players*, vol. 19, no. 8 (1972), 44–6
Craig, *Interpretation*	Hardin Craig, *An Interpretation of Shakespeare* (New York, 1948)
Craik	T.W. Craik, private communication
Craven[1]	Alan E. Craven, 'Simmes' Compositor A and Five Shakespeare Quartos', *SB*, 26 (1973), 37–60
Craven[2]	Alan E. Craven, 'The Reliability of Simmes's Compositor A', *SB*, 32 (1979), 186–97
Craven[3]	Alan E. Craven, 'Compositor Analysis to Edited Text: Some Suggested Readings in *Richard II* and *Much Ado about Nothing*', *Papers of the Bibliographical Society of America*, 76 (1982), 43–62
Craven, 'Printing'	Alan E. Craven, 'The Printing of Shakespeare's *Richard II*, 1597', unpublished dissertation, University of Kansas, Lawrence, Kans., 1965
Créton	Jean Créton, *Histoire du Roy d'Angleterre Richard*, ed. and trans. J. Webb, *Archaeologia*, 20 (1824). The double pagination of the references is to the French text and English translation both contained in the edn. Single pagination indicates reference to editorial matter.
CSPD	*Calendar of State Papers, Domestic Series, Elizabeth, 1598–1601*, Public Record Office, ed. Mary Anne Everett Green (1869; repr. Nendeln, Liechtenstein, 1967), vol. 5 of 12 vol. series covering the reigns of Edward VI, Mary, Elizabeth I and James I

Daniel	Samuel Daniel, *The First Four Books of the Civil Wars Between the Two Houses of Lancaster and York* (1595)
David	Richard David (ed.), *Love's Labour's Lost*, Arden Shakespeare (1956)
David, *Theatre*	Richard David, *Shakespeare in the Theatre* (Cambridge, 1978)
Davison	Peter Davison, 'The Selection and Presentation of Bibliographic Evidence', *AEB*, vol. 1, no. 2 (1977), 101–36
Declaration	[Richard Rowlands?], *A Declaration of the True Causes of the Great Troubles, Presupposed to be Intended Against the Realm of England* (Antwerp, 1592)
Dekker	*Dramatic Works*, ed. Fredson Bowers, 4 vols (Cambridge, 1953–61)
Dent	R.W. Dent, *Shakespeare's Proverbial Language: An Index* (Berkeley, Calif., 1981)
Dillon	Janette Dillon, *Shakespeare and the Solitary Man* (London and Totowa, N.J., 1981)
DNB	*The Dictionary of National Biography*, ed. Sir Leslie Stephen and Sir Sidney Lee, 66 vols (Oxford, 1885–1901)
Doctor Faustus	Christopher Marlowe, *Doctor Faustus, A- and B-texts (1604, 1616)*, ed. David Bevington and Eric Rasmussen, Revels Plays (Manchester, 1993)
Donne, *Devotions*	John Donne, *Devotions Upon Emergent Occasions*, ed. Anthony Raspa (Oxford and New York, 1987)
Dowling	Margaret Dowling, 'Sir John Hayward's Troubles over His *Life of Henry IV*', *The Library*, 4th series, 11 (1931), 212–24
Duchess of Malfi	John Webster, *The Duchess of Malfi*, ed. John Russell Brown, Revels Plays (1964)
Duls	Louisa D. Duls, *Richard II in the Early Chronicles* (The Hague and Paris, 1975)
E2	Christopher Marlowe, *Edward the Second*, ed. Charles R. Forker, Revels Plays (Manchester, 1994)
E3	[William Shakespeare?], *King Edward III*, ed. Giorgio Melchiori (Cambridge, 1998)
Edwards, P.	Philip Edwards, 'Person and Office in Shakespeare's Plays', *Proceedings of the British Academy*, 56 (1970), 93–109
ELH	*English Literary History*
Eliot	John Eliot, *Ortho-Epia Gallica* (1593)
ELR	*English Literary Renaissance*
Elson	John James Elson, 'The Non-Shakespearian *Richard II* and Shakespeare's *Henry IV, Part I*', *SP*, 32 (1935), 177–88
Elyot	Sir Thomas Elyot, *The Book Named the Governor* (1531)
Erasmus	Desiderius Erasmus of Rotterdam, *On Copia of Words and Ideas*, trans. Donald B. King and H. David Rix (Milwaukee, Wis., 1963)

Fabyan	Robert Fabyan, *The Chronicle of Fabyan*, 2 vols (1559)
Famous Victories	*The Famous Victories of Henry The Fifth*, in Bullough, 4.299–343
Farnham	Willard Farnham, *The Medieval Heritage of Elizabethan Tragedy* (Berkeley, Calif., 1936)
Ferguson	W. Craig Ferguson, 'The Compositors of *Henry IV, Part 2, Much Ado About Nothing, The Shoemakers' Holiday*, and *The First Part of the Contention*', *SB*, 13 (1960), 19–29
Feuillerat	Albert Feuillerat, *The Composition of Shakespeare's Plays: Authorship, Chronology* (New Haven, Conn., 1953), 185–230
Fletcher	*The Dramatic Works in the Beaumont and Fletcher Canon*, gen. ed. Fredson Bowers, 10 vols (Cambridge, 1966–96)
Forker	Charles R. Forker (ed.), *Shakespeare: The Critical Tradition: 'Richard II'* (1998)
Forker, 'Baron'	Charles R. Forker, 'Robert Baron's Use of Webster, Shakespeare, and Other Elizabethans', *Anglia*, 83 (1965), 176–98
Forker, 'Heywood'	Charles R. Forker, 'Shakespeare's Histories and Heywood's *If You Know Not Me, You Know Nobody*', *Neuphilologische Mitteilungen*, 66 (1965), 166–78
Foster	Donald Foster, 'Shaxicon 1995', *SN*, 45 (1995), 25, 30, 32
FQ	Edmund Spenser, *The Faerie Queene*, see Spenser
French	G.R. French, *Shakespeareana Genealogica* (1869)
Friar Bacon	Robert Greene, *Friar Bacon and Friar Bungay*, ed. Daniel Seltzer (Lincoln, Nebr., 1963)
Friedman	Donald M. Friedman, 'John of Gaunt and the Rhetoric of Frustration', *ELH*, 43 (1976), 279–99
Frijlinck	Wilhelmina P. Frijlinck (ed.), *The First Part of the Reign of King Richard the Second, or Thomas of Woodstock*, MSR (Oxford, 1929)
Froissart	*The Chronicle of Froissart Translated out of French by Sir John Bourchier Lord Berners (Annis 1523–25)*, (ed.) W.P. Ker, 6 vols (1901–3)
Gielgud	John Gielgud, *Stage Directions* (1963)
Gilbert	Miriam Gilbert, '*Richard II* at Stratford: Role-Playing as Metaphor', in Philip C. McGuire and David A. Samuelson (eds), *Shakespeare: The Theatrical Dimension* (New York, 1979), 85–101
Gilman	Ernest B. Gilman, '*Richard II* and the Perspectives of History', *RenD*, 7 (1976), 85–115
Golding	*Shakespeare's Ovid Being Arthur Golding's Translation of the Metamorphoses*, ed. W.H.D. Rouse (1961)
Gorboduc	Thomas Sackville and Thomas Norton, *Gorboduc, or Ferrex and Porrex*, ed. Irby B. Cauthen (Lincoln, Nebr., 1970)

Gordon, *Diptych*	Dillian Gordon, *The Making and Meaning of The Wilton Diptych* (1993)
Gordon, 'Discovery'	Dillian Gordon, 'A New Discovery in the Wilton Diptych', *Burlington Magazine*, 134 (1992), 662–7
Grabes	Herbert Grabes, *The Mutable Glass: Mirror-imagery in the Titles and Texts of the Middle Ages and English Renaissance*, trans. Gordon Collier (Cambridge, 1982)
Graham-White	Anthony Graham-White, 'The Interpretation of Internal Evidence: Rhetoric and Character in *Richard II*', in *Punctuation and Its Dramatic Value in Shakespearean Drama* (Newark, Del., and London, 1995), 94–104, 163–4
Greer	C.A. Greer, 'The Date of *Richard II*', *N&Q*, 195 (1950), 402–4
Greer, 'Daniel'	C.A. Greer, 'Did Shakespeare Use Daniel's *Civile Warres?*', *N&Q*, 196 (1951), 53–4
Greer, 'Deposition'	C.A. Greer, 'More About the Deposition Scene of *Richard II*', *N&Q*, 198 (1953), 49–50
Greg, *Bibliography*	W.W. Greg, *A Bibliography of the English Printed Drama to the Restoration*, 4 vols (Oxford, 1939–59) vol. 1
Grose	Francis Grose, *A Provincial Glossary with a Collection of Local Proverbs, and Popular Superstitions* (1787)
GWW	George Walton Williams, private communication
Hall	Edward Hall, *The Union of the Two Noble and Illustrate Families of Lancaster & York* (1548)
Harbage	Alfred Harbage, *As They Liked It: An Essay on Shakespeare and Morality* (New York, 1947)
Harris	Kathryn Montgomery Harris, 'Sun and Water Imagery in *Richard II*: Its Dramatic Function', *SQ*, 21 (1970), 157–65
Harrison, *TLS*	G.B. Harrison, *Times Literary Supplement*, 20 November 1930, p. 974, and 15 October 1931, p. 802
Hasker	Richard E. Hasker, 'The Copy for the First Folio *Richard II*', *SB*, 5 (1952–3), 53–72
Hayward	Sir John Hayward, *The First Part of the Life and Reign of King Henry the IV* (1599)
Hearne	Thomas Hearne, *The Itinerary of John Leland, the Antiquary*, 3rd edn, 9 vols (Oxford, 1770)
Heffner	Ray Heffner, 'Shakespeare, Hayward, and Essex', *PMLA*, 45 (1930), 754–80
Heninger	S.K. Heninger, Jr, 'The Sun-King Analogy in *Richard II*', *SQ*, 11 (1960), 319–27
Herbert	*The Works of George Herbert*, ed. F.E. Hutchinson (Oxford, 1941)
Heywood, *If You Know Not Me*	Thomas Heywood, *If You Know Not Me, You Know Nobody*, Parts *1* and *2*, ed. Madeleine Doran, MSR, 2 vols (Oxford, 1935)

Hibbard	G.R. Hibbard, *The Making of Shakespeare's Dramatic Poetry* (Toronto, Ont., 1981)
Hinman	Charlton Hinman, *The Printing and Proof-Reading of the First Folio of Shakespeare*, 2 vols (Oxford, 1963)
Hobson	Harold Hobson, *Theatre* (1948)
Hockey	Dorothy C. Hockey, 'A World of Rhetoric in *Richard II*', *SQ*, 15 (1964), 179–91
Hodges	C. Walter Hodges, *Enter the Whole Army: A Pictorial Study of Shakespearean Staging 1576–1616* (Cambridge, 1999)
Holbein	Hans Holbein the Younger, *The Dance of Death: A Complete Facsimile of the Original 1538 Edition of 'Les simulachres & historiees faces de la mort'; With a New Introduction by Werner L. Gundersheimer* (New York, 1971)
Holinshed	Raphael Holinshed, *The Chronicles of England, Scotland, and Ireland*, 2nd edn, 3 vols in 2 (1587)
Homilies	*Certain Sermons or Homilies Appointed to be Read in Churches In the Time of Queen Elizabeth I (1547–1571)* (1623; facsimile edn by M.E. Rickey and T.B. Stroup, 2 vols in 1, Gainesville, Fla., 1968)
Homily	*A Homily against Disobedience and Wilful Rebellion*, see *Homilies*
Honan	Park Honan, *Shakespeare: A Life* (Oxford, 1998)
Howard-Hill	T.H. Howard-Hill, 'Ralph Crane's Parentheses', *N&Q*, n.s. 12 (1965), 334–40
Huizinga	J. Huizinga, *The Waning of the Middle Ages: A Study of the Forms of Life, Thought and Art in France and the Netherlands in the XIVth and XVth Centuries* (1924)
Humphreys	A.R. Humphreys (ed.), *Henry IV, Part I*, Arden Shakespeare (1961)
Hunter	G.K. Hunter, 'Were There Act-Pauses on Shakespeare's Stage?', in Standish Henning, Robert Kimbrough and Richard Knowles (eds), *English Renaissance Drama: Essays in Honor of Madeleine Doran & Mark Eccles* (Carbondale, Ill., 1976), 15–35
Hunter, *History*	G.K. Hunter, *English Drama 1586–1642: The Age of Shakespeare*, The Oxford History of English Literature (Oxford, 1997)
Ingram	William Ingram, *A London Life in the Brazen Age: Francis Langley, 1548–1602* (Cambridge, Mass., 1978)
Insatiate Countess	John Marston (and Others), *The Insatiate Countess*, ed. Giorgio Melchiori, Revels Plays (Manchester, 1984)
Ironside	*Edmond Ironside; or, War Hath Made All Friends*, ed. Eleanore Boswell, MSR (Oxford, 1928)
Iselin	Pierre Iselin, 'Myth, Memory and Music in *Richard II*, *Hamlet* and *Othello*', in A.J. Hoenselaars (ed.), *Reclamations*

	of Shakespeare (Amsterdam and Atlanta, Ga., 1994), 173–86
Isle of Gulls	John Day, *The Isle of Gulls: A Critical Edition*, ed. Raymond S. Burns (New York and London, 1980)
Jack Straw	*The Life and Death of Jack Straw*, ed. Kenneth Muir, MSR (Oxford, 1957)
Jackson	MacDonald P. Jackson, *Studies in Attribution: Middleton and Shakespeare* (Salzburg, 1979)
JEGP	*Journal of English and Germanic Philology*
Jenkins	Elizabeth Jenkins, *Elizabeth the Great* (New York, 1959)
Jewkes	Wilfred T. Jewkes, *Act Division in Elizabethan and Jacobean Plays, 1583–1616* (Hamden, Conn., 1958)
Jew of Malta	Christopher Marlowe, *The Jew of Malta*, ed. N.W. Bawcutt, Revels Plays (Manchester, 1978)
Johnson	*Johnson on Shakespeare*, ed. Arthur Sherbo, 2 vols (New Haven, Conn., 1968). Vol. 1 contains Johnson's commentary on *Richard II*.
Jones	John Jones, *Shakespeare at Work* (Oxford, 1995)
Jonson	*Ben Jonson*, ed. C.H. Herford and Percy and Evelyn Simpson, 11 vols (Oxford, 1925–63)
Joseph	Sister Miriam Joseph, *Shakespeare's Use of the Arts of Language* (New York, 1947)
Jowett	See *TxC*
Jowett & Taylor	John Jowett and Gary Taylor, 'Sprinklings of Authority: The Folio Text of *Richard II*', *SB*, 38 (1985), 151–200
Kantorowicz	E.H. Kantorowicz, *The King's Two Bodies: A Study in Mediaeval Political Theology* (Princeton, N.J., 1957)
Kelly	H.A. Kelly, *Divine Providence in the England of Shakespeare's Histories* (Cambridge, Mass., 1970)
Kiefer	Frederick Kiefer, *Fortune and Elizabethan Tragedy* (San Marino, Calif., 1983)
Kincaid	A.N. Kincaid, 'Sir Edward Hoby and "K. Richard": Shakespeare Play or Morton Tract?', *N&Q*, n.s. 28 (1981), 124–6
King	T.J. King, *Casting Shakespeare's Plays: London Actors and their Roles 1590–1642* (Cambridge, 1992)
King Leir	*A Critical Edition of the True Chronicle History of King Leir and His Three Daughters, Gonorill, Ragan and Cordella*, ed. Donald M. Michie (New York and London, 1991)
Kipling	Gordon Kipling, 'Richard II's "Sumptuous Pageants" and the Idea of the Civic Triumph', in David M. Bergeron (ed.), *Pageantry in the Shakespearean Theater* (Athens, Ga., 1985), 83–103
Kirby	J.L. Kirby, *Henry IV of England* (1970)

Klinck	Dennis R. Klinck, 'Shakespeare's Richard II as Landlord and Wasting Tenant', *College Literature*, vol. 25, no. 1 (1998), 21–34
Kyd	*The Works of Thomas Kyd*, ed. F.S. Boas, rev. edn (Oxford, 1955)
Lambrechts	G. Lambrechts, 'Sur Deux Prétendues Sources de *Richard II*', *Etudes Anglaises*, 20 (1967), 118–39
Lampe	David E. Lampe, 'Ironic Saint's Lore in *Richard II*, I.i', in John L. Cutler and Lawrence S. Thompson (eds), *American Notes and Queries Supplement, Vol. 1: Studies in English and American Literature* (Troy, N.Y., 1978), 79–80
Lanham	Richard A. Lanham, *A Handlist of Rhetorical Terms*, 2nd edn (Berkeley, Calif., 1991)
Leiter	Samuel L. Leiter (ed.) *Shakespeare Around the Globe: A Guide to Notable Postwar Revivals*, (New York and London, 1986)
Lettsom	[W.N. Lettsom], 'New Readings in Shakespeare – No. II', *Blackwood's Edinburgh Magazine*, 74 (1853), 306–7
Lodge, 'Truth's Complaint'	Thomas Lodge, 'Truth's Complaint Over England', in *An Alarum Against Usurers* (1584)
Logan	George M. Logan, 'Lucan – Daniel – Shakespeare: New Light on the Relation Between *The Civil Wars* and *Richard II*', *SSt*, 9 (1976), 121–140
Long	William B. Long, ' "A bed / for woodstock": A Warning for the Unwary', *Medieval and Renaissance Drama in England*, 2 (1985), 91–118
Lucan, *Pharsalia*	Lucan, *The Civil War*, trans. J.D. Duff, Loeb Classical Library (1928)
Lyly	*The Complete Works of John Lyly*, ed. R. Warwick Bond, 3 vols (Oxford, 1902)
McAvoy	William C. McAvoy, 'Form in *Richard II*, II.i.40–66', *JEGP*, 54 (1955), 355–61
McDonald	Russ McDonald, *Shakespeare and the Arts of Language* (Oxford, 2001)
McGuire	Philip C. McGuire, 'Choreography and Language in *Richard II*', in Philip C. McGuire and David A. Samuelson (eds), *Shakespeare: The Theatrical Dimension* (New York, 1979), 61–84
McLeod	Random Cloud [i.e. R.R. McLeod], 'The Psychopathology of Everyday Art', in G.R. Hibbard (ed.), *The Elizabethan Theatre IX* (Waterloo, Ont., 1986), 100–68
McManaway	James G. McManaway, 'The Cancel in the Quarto of *2 Henry IV*', in Charles T. Prouty (ed.), *Studies in Honor of A.H.R. Fairchild*, University of Missouri Studies, 21 (Columbia, Mo., 1946), 67–80

McManaway, '*R2*'	James G. McManaway, '*Richard II* at Covent Garden', *SQ*, 15 (1964), 161–75
McMillin	Scott McMillin, 'Shakespeare's *Richard II*: Eyes of Sorrow, Eyes of Desire', *SQ*, 35 (1984), 40–52
McMillin & MacLean	Scott McMillin and Sally-Beth MacLean, *The Queen's Men and Their Plays* (Cambridge, 1998)
Maguire	Laurie E. Maguire, *Shakespearean suspect texts* (Cambridge, 1996)
Mahood	M.M. Mahood, *Shakespeare's Wordplay* (1957)
Mahood, *Parts*	M.M. Mahood, *Playing Bit Parts in Shakespeare* (London and New York, 1998)
Malcontent	John Marston, *The Malcontent*, ed. G.K. Hunter, Revels Plays (1975)
Massinger	See Fletcher
Maveety	Stanley R. Maveety, 'A Second Fall of Cursed Man: The Bold Metaphor in *Richard II*', *JEGP*, 72 (1973), 175–93
Michel	Laurence Michel (ed.), *The Civil Wars by Samuel Daniel*, (New Haven, Conn., 1958)
Milton	*The Complete Poetry of John Milton*, ed. John T. Shawcross (New York, 1963)
Mirror	William Baldwin et al., *The Mirror for Magistrates*, ed. Lily B. Campbell (Cambridge, 1938)
Monsarrat	Gilles Monsarrat, 'Shakespeare's Ravenspur(gh)', *N&Q*, n.s. 45 (1998), 316–17
Morse	Ruth Morse, 'Telling the Truth with Authority: From Richard II to *Richard II*', *Common Knowledge*, vol. 4, no. 1 (1995), 111–28
MSR	Malone Society Reprints
Muir, *Sources*	Kenneth Muir, *The Sources of Shakespeare's Plays* (1977)
N&Q	*Notes and Queries*
Nashe	*The Works of Thomas Nashe*, ed. Ronald B. McKerrow, rev. F.P. Wilson, 5 vols (Oxford, 1958)
Naylor	E.W. Naylor, *Shakespeare and Music*, rev. edn (London and Toronto, Ont., 1931; repr. New York, 1965)
Neale	J.E. Neale, *Elizabeth I and her Parliaments, 1559–1601*, 2 vols (New York, 1958)
Nevo	Ruth Nevo, *Tragic Form in Shakespeare* (Princeton, N.J., 1972)
Nichols	John Nichols, *The Progresses and Public Processions of Queen Elizabeth*, new edn, 3 vols (1823)
Nicoll	Allardyce Nicoll, *Shakespeare* (1952)
Nowottny	Winifred Nowottny, *The Language Poets Use* (1962)
O'Brien	Timothy O'Brien, 'Designing a Shakespeare Play: *Richard II*', *SJW* (1976), 23–42

References

OED   *Oxford English Dictionary*, ed. J.A. Simpson and E.S.C. Weiner, 2nd edn, 20 vols (Oxford, 1989)

Ornstein   Robert Ornstein, *A Kingdom for a Stage: The Achievement of Shakespeare's History Plays* (Cambridge, Mass., 1972)

Ovid, *Fasti*   Ovid, *Fasti*, trans. Sir James G. Frazer, Loeb Classical Library (1931)

Ovid, *Heroides*   Ovid, *Heroides and Amores*, trans. Grant Showerman, 2nd edn rev. G.P. Goold, Loeb Classical Library (1977)

Ovid, *Met.*   Ovid, *Metamorphoses*, trans. Frank Justus Miller, 2nd edn, Loeb Classical Library, 2 vols (1921)

Page   Malcolm Page, *'Richard II': Text and Performance* (Atlantic Highlands, N.J., 1987)

Palmer   John Palmer, *Political Characters of Shakespeare* (1945)

Parnassus   *England's Parnassus, Compiled by Robert Allot, 1600*, ed. Charles Crawford (Oxford, 1913)

Partridge   A.C. Partridge, *Orthography in Shakespeare and Elizabethan Drama: A Study of Colloquial Contractions, Elision, Prosody and Punctuation* (1964)

Patch   Howard R. Patch, *The Goddess Fortuna in Mediaeval Literature* (Cambridge, Mass., 1927; repr. New York, 1967)

Peck   *Leicester's Commonwealth*, ed. D.C. Peck (Athens, Ohio, 1985)

Peele   George Peele, *Works*, gen. ed. C.T. Prouty, 3 vols (New Haven, Conn., 1952–70)

Perkin Warbeck   John Ford, *The Chronicle History of Perkin Warbeck, A Strange Truth*, ed. Peter Ure, Revels Plays (1968)

Plutarch, *Lives*   Plutarch, *Lives*, trans. Bernadotte Perrin, Loeb Classical Library, 11 vols (1920)

PMLA   *Publications of the Modern Language Association of America*

PQ   *Philological Quarterly*

Prayer Book   *The Book of Common Prayer 1559: The Elizabethan Prayer Book*, ed. John E. Booty (Charlottesville, Va., 1976)

Rabkin   Norman Rabkin, *Shakespeare and the Common Understanding* (New York, 1967)

Rackin   Phyllis Rackin, 'The Role of the Audience in Richard II', *SQ*, 36 (1985), 262–81

Rackin, *History*   Phyllis Rackin, *Stages of History: Shakespeare's English Chronicles* (Ithaca, N.Y., 1990)

Ranald   Margaret Loftus Ranald, 'The Degradation of Richard II: An Inquiry into the Ritual Backgrounds', *ELR*, 7 (1977), 170–96

Rebhorn   Wayne A. Rebhorn, *The Emperor of Men's Minds: Literature and the Renaissance Discourse of Rhetoric* (Ithaca, N.Y., 1995)

Register   *John of Gaunt's Register, 1379–1383*, ed. E.C. Lodge and R. Somerville, Camden Society, 3rd series, 2 vols (1937)

RenD   *Renaissance Drama*

562

RES	*Review of English Studies*
Reyher	Paul Reyher, 'Notes sur les sources de *Richard II*', *Revue de l'Enseignement des Langues Vivantes*, 41 (1924), 1–13, 54–64, 106–14, 158–68
Ro: Ba:	'Ro: Ba:', *The Life of Sir Thomas More*, ed. E.V. Hitchcock and P.E. Hallett (Oxford, 1950)
Roberts	Josephine A. Roberts, *'Richard II': An Annotated Bibliography*, 2 vols (New York, 1988)
Rossiter	See *Woodstock*
Rossiter, *Angel*	A.P. Rossiter, *Angel with Horns, and Other Shakespeare Lectures*, ed. Graham Storey (1961).
RP	Richard Proudfoot, private communication
RSC	Royal Shakespeare Company
Rutter	Carol Chillington Rutter, 'Fiona Shaw's *Richard II*: The Girl as Player-King as Comic', *SQ*, 48 (1997), 314–24
Saul	Nigel Saul, *Richard II* (New Haven, Conn., and London, 1997)
Saviolo	Vincentio Saviolo, *Of Honour and Honourable Quarrels* (1594)
SB	*Studies in Bibliography*
Schell	Edgar Schell, *Strangers and Pilgrims: From 'The Castle of Perseverance' to 'King Lear'* (Chicago, Ill., 1983)
Schmidt	Alexander Schmidt, *Shakespeare-Lexicon*, 2 vols (Berlin and London, 1874)
Scott-Giles	C.W. Scott-Giles, *Shakespeare's Heraldry* (1950)
Senior	Michael Senior, *The Life and Times of Richard II* (1981)
Shakespeare's England	*Shakespeare's England: An Account of the Life and Manners of his Age*, ed. Sir Walter Raleigh, Sir Sidney Lee *et al.*, 2 vols (Oxford, 1916)
Shapiro	I.A. Shapiro, '*Richard II* or *Richard III* . . . ?', *SQ*, 9 (1958), 204–6
Shewring	Margaret Shewring, *Shakespeare in Performance: King Richard II* (Manchester, 1996)
Shirley	*The Dramatic Works and Poems of James Shirley*, ed. William Gifford and Alexander Dyce, 6 vols (1833)
Sidney	*The Poems of Sir Philip Sidney*, ed. William A. Ringler, Jr (Oxford, 1962)
Sidney, *Apology*	Sir Philip Sidney, *An Apology for Poetry*, ed. Geoffrey Shepherd (Manchester, 1973)
Sisson[1]	Charles J. Sisson, 'Shakespeare Quartos as Prompt-Copies', *RES*, 18 (1942), 129–43
Sisson[2]	Charles J. Sisson, *New Readings in Shakespeare*, 2 vols (Cambridge, 1956)
SJW	*Shakespeare Jahrbuch West*
Smidt	Kristian Smidt, *Unconformities in Shakespeare's History Plays* (1982)

Smith	Robert Metcalf Smith, *Froissart and the English Chronicle Play* (New York, 1915)
SN	*Shakespeare Newsletter*
SP	*Studies in Philology*
Spanish Tragedy	Thomas Kyd, *The Spanish Tragedy*, ed. Philip Edwards, Revels Plays (1959)
Spenser	*The Works of Edmund Spenser*, Variorum Edition, ed. Edwin Greenlaw, C.G. Osgood, F.M. Paddleford, Ray Heffner *et al.*, 10 vols (Baltimore, Md., 1932–49), *FQ* in vols 1–6
Spevack	Marvin Spevack (ed.), *A Complete and Systematic Concordance to the Works of Shakespeare*, 9 vols (Hildesheim, 1968–80), 2.149–213
Sprague	Arthur Colby Sprague, *Shakespeare's Histories: Plays for the Stage*, Society for Theatre Research (1964)
SQ	*Shakespeare Quarterly*
SSt	*Shakespeare Studies*
Statutes	*The Statutes of the Realm: printed from original records and authentic manuscripts . . .*, 11 vols in 12 (1963)
Stavropoulos	Janet C. Stavropoulos, ' "A masque is treason's license": The Design of *Woodstock*', *South Central Review*, vol. 5, no. 2 (1988), 1–14
Stirling	Brents Stirling, 'Bolingbroke's "Decision" ', *SQ*, 2 (1951), 27–34
STM	*The Book of Sir Thomas More*, ed. W.W. Greg, MSR (Oxford, 1911)
Stow	John Stow, *The Annals of England* (1592)
Stredder	James Stredder, 'John Barton's Production of *Richard II* at Stratford-on-Avon, 1973', *SJW* (1976), 23–42
Stubbs	William Stubbs, *The Constitutional History of England*, 3 vols (Oxford, 1875–8)
Sylvester	Joshua Sylvester (trans.), Du Bartas, *Divine Weeks and Works* (1605)
Talbert	Ernest William Talbert, *The Problem of Order: Elizabethan Political Commonplaces and an Example of Shakespeare's Art* (Chapel Hill, N.C., 1962)
Tamburlaine	Christopher Marlowe, *Tamburlaine the Great*, ed. J.S. Cunningham, Revels Plays (Manchester, 1981)
Tate	Nahum Tate, *The History of King Richard the Second* (1681)
Taylor & Jowett	Gary Taylor and John Jowett, *Shakespeare Reshaped, 1606–1623* (Oxford, 1993)
Theobald, *Tragedy*	Lewis Theobald, *The Tragedy of King Richard the II* (1720)
Tilley	Morris P. Tilley, *A Dictionary of the Proverbs in England in the Sixteenth and Seventeenth Centuries* (Ann Arbor, Mich., 1950)
Tillyard	E.M.W. Tillyard, *Shakespeare's History Plays* (London and New York, 1944)

Tillyard, *Picture*	E.M.W. Tillyard, *The Elizabethan World Picture* (1943)
Timberlake	Philip W. Timberlake, *The Feminine Ending in English Blank Verse: A Study of its Use by Early Writers in the Measure and its Development in the Drama up to the Year 1595* (Menasha, Wis., 1931)
Tobin	J.J.M. Tobin, 'Nashe and *Richard II*', *AN&Q*, vol. 24, nos. 1–2 (1985), 5–7
Tomlinson	Michael Tomlinson, 'Shakespeare and the Chronicles Reassessed', *Literature and History*, vol. 10, no. 1 (1984), 46–58
Traïson	*Chronicque de la Traïson et Mort de Richart Deux Roy Dengleterre*, ed. Benjamin Williams (1846). The double pagination of the references is to the French text and English translation both contained in the edn. Single pagination indicates reference to editorial matter.
Trewin	J.C. Trewin, *Shakespeare on the English Stage, 1900–1964* (1964)
Trewin, *Neville*	J.C. Trewin, *John Neville: An Illustrated Study of His Work* (1961)
Troublesome Reign	*The Troublesome Reign of King John*, in Bullough, 4.72–151
Trousdale	Marion Trousdale, *Shakespeare and the Rhetoricians* (1982)
True Tragedy	*The True Tragedy of Richard the Third (1594)*, ed. W.W. Greg, MSR (Oxford, 1929)
Tusculan Disputations	*Those five questions which Mark Tully Cicero disputed in his manor of Tusculanum*, trans. John Dolman (1561; Loeb Classical Library edn, trans. J.E. King, 1945)
TxC	Stanley Wells and Gary Taylor, with John Jowett and William Montgomery, *William Shakespeare: A Textual Companion* (Oxford, 1987)
Tyndale	William Tyndale, *The Obedience of a Christian Man* (Antwerp, 1528)
Ure, 'Du Bartas'	Peter Ure, 'Two Passages in Sylvester's Du Bartas and their Bearing on Shakespeare's *Richard II*', *N&Q*, 198 (1953), 374–7
Ure, 'Looking-Glass'	Peter Ure, 'The Looking-Glass of *Richard II*', *PQ*, 34 (1955), 219–24
Ure, 'Sources'	Peter Ure, 'Shakespeare's Play and the French Sources of Holinshed's and Stow's Account of Richard II', *N&Q*, 53 (1953), 426–9
Vaughan	Henry H. Vaughan, *New Readings & New Renderings of Shakespeare's Tragedies*, 3 vols (1881–6), vol. 1
Vickers	Brian Vickers (ed.), *Shakespeare: The Critical Heritage*, 6 vols (London and Boston, Mass., 1974–81)
Vickers, 'Rhetoric'	Brian Vickers, 'Shakespeare's Use of Rhetoric', in Kenneth Muir and S. Schoenbaum (eds), *A New Companion to Shakespeare Studies* (Cambridge, 1971), 83–98

Walker	W.S. Walker, *A Critical Examination of the Text of Shakespeare*, ed. W.N. Lettsom, 3 vols (1860)
Walton	J.K. Walton, *The Quarto Copy for the First Folio of Shakespeare* (Dublin, 1971)
Wells, *Productions*	Stanley Wells, *Royal Shakespeare: Four Major Productions at Stratford-upon-Avon*, Furman University Lectures (Manchester, 1977)
Wells, 'Tale'	Stanley Wells, 'The Lamentable Tale of *Richard II*', *Shakespeare Studies* (Tokyo), 17 (1978–9), 1–23
Werstine, '*Lear*'	Paul Werstine, 'Folio Editors, Folio Compositors, and the Folio Text of *King Lear*', in Gary Taylor and Michael Warren (eds), *The Division of the Kingdoms: Shakespeare's Two Versions of 'King Lear'* (Oxford, 1983), 247–312
Werstine, 'Verse'	Paul Werstine, 'Line Division in Shakespeare's Dramatic Verse: An Editorial Problem', *AEB*, vol. 8, no. 2 (1984), 73–125
White Devil	John Webster, *The White Devil*, ed. John Russell Brown, Revels Plays (1960)
Williams	George Walton Williams, 'Shakespeare's Metaphors of Health: Food, Sport, and Life-preserving Rest', *Journal of Medieval and Renaissance Studies*, 14 (1984), 187–202
Williams, *Headings*	George Walton Williams (ed.), *Shakespeare's Speech-Headings: Speaking the Speech in Shakespeare's Plays* (Newark, Del., 1997)
Williams, 'Notes'	George Walton Williams, 'Some Notes on Shakespeare's *Henry IV*', *Renaissance Papers 1968* (Durham, N.C., 1969), 49–53
Wilson, M.	Mona Wilson, *Sir Philip Sidney* (1931)
Wilson, *Manuscript*	John Dover Wilson, *The Manuscript of Shakespeare's 'Hamlet'* (Cambridge, 1934)
Wilson, '*R3*'	John Dover Wilson, 'Shakespeare's *Richard III* and *The True Tragedy of Richard the Third*, 1594', *SQ*, 3 (1952), 299–306
Wilson & Worsley	John Dover Wilson and Thomas C. Worsley, *Shakespeare's Histories at Stratford, 1951* (1952; repr. Freeport, N.Y., 1970)
Woodstock	*Woodstock, A Moral History*, ed. A.P. Rossiter (1946)
Wroughton	Richard Wroughton, *Shakespeare's King Richard the Second: An Historical Play Adapted to the Stage with Alterations and Additions* (1815; facsimile reprint with introduction by Leah Scragg, 1970)
Wylie	J.H. Wylie, *History of England under Henry the Fourth*, 4 vols (1884–98)
Yoder	Audrey Yoder, *Animal Analogy in Shakespeare's Character Portrayal* (New York, 1947)
Zitner	Sheldon P. Zitner, 'Aumerle's Conspiracy', *Studies in English Literature*, 14 (1974), 239–57

MODERN STAGE AND TELEVISION
PRODUCTIONS CITED

Barton	RSC, Royal Shakespeare Theatre, Stratford-upon-Avon, and Aldwych Theatre, London, directed by John Barton, 1973–4 (Richard Pasco and Ian Richardson alternating as Richard and Bolingbroke)
Benthall	Old Vic Theatre, London, directed by Michael Benthall, 1955 (John Neville as Richard)
Caldwell	Stratford Festival Theatre, Stratford, Ontario, directed by Zoe Caldwell, 1979 (Stephen Russell, Nicholas Pennell or Frank Maradan as Richard)
Cass	Old Vic Theatre, London, directed by Henry Cass, 1934 (Maurice Evans as Richard)
Cottrell 1968	Prospect Theatre Company (on tour and London), directed by Richard Cottrell, 1968–9 (Ian McKellen as Richard)
Cottrell 1983	Stratford Festival Theatre, Stratford, Ontario, directed by Richard Cottrell, 1983 (Brian Bedford as Richard)
Gielgud 1937	Queen's Theatre, London, directed by John Gielgud, 1937 (Gielgud as Richard)
Gielgud 1953	Lyric Theatre, Hammersmith, London, directed by John Gielgud, 1953 (Paul Scofield as Richard)
Giles	BBC television production company (Cedric Messina), directed by David Giles, 1978 (Derek Jacobi as Richard)
Hall	RSC, Royal Shakespeare Theatre, directed by Peter Hall, John Barton, Clifford Williams, 1964 (David Warner as Richard)
Hands	RSC, Royal Shakespeare Theatre, Stratford-upon-Avon, directed by Terry Hands, 1980 (Alan Howard as Richard)
Jensen	Oregon Shakespeare Festival Theatre, Ashland, Oregon, directed by Howard Jensen, 1995 (Richard Howard as Richard)
Kent	Almeida Theatre Company, Gainsborough Studios Theatre, London, directed by Jonathan Kent, 2000 (Ralph Fiennes as Richard)
Kyle	RSC, Royal Shakespeare Theatre, Stratford-upon-Avon, directed by Barry Kyle, 1986 (Jeremy Irons as Richard); transferred to London, 1987
Littlewood	Theatre Workshop, Theatre Royal, Stratford, East London, directed by Joan Littlewood, 1954 (Harry Corbett as Richard)
Mnouchkine	Théâtre du Soleil, Cartoucherie de Vincennes, near Paris, and Palais des Papes, Avignon (1981), Olympic Arts Festival, Los Angeles (1984), directed by Ariane Mnouchkine (Georges Bigot as Richard)

Pimlott	RSC, The Other Place Theatre, Stratford-upon-Avon, directed by Steven Pimlott, 2000 (Samuel West as Richard)
Quayle	Shakespeare Memorial Theatre, directed by Anthony Quayle, 1951 (Michael Redgrave as Richard)
Richardson	Old Vic Theatre, London, directed by Sir Ralph Richardson, 1947 (Alec Guinness as Richard)
Schaefer	Hallmark Theatre (NBC Hallmark Hall of Fame television series), in conjunction with Maurice Evans Productions, directed by George Schaefer, 1954 (Maurice Evans as Richard)
Tree	His Majesty's Theatre, London, directed by Sir Herbert Beerbohm Tree, 1903 (Tree as Richard)
Warner	Royal National Theatre Company, Cottesloe Theatre, London, directed by Deborah Warner, 1995 (Fiona Shaw as Richard)
Webster	St James Theatre, New York, directed by Margaret Webster, 1937 (Maurice Evans as Richard)
Williams, D.	Royal National Theatre Company, Old Vic Theatre, London, directed by David Williams, 1972 (Ronald Pickup as Richard)
Williams, H.	Old Vic Theatre, London, directed by Harcourt Williams, 1929 (John Gielgud as Richard)
Woodman	Bard Productions Ltd. television production, directed by William Woodman, 1981 (Crest Video, 1982) (David Birney as Richard)

INDEX

This index covers the Preface (except acknowledgements), the Introduction, the Commentary and Appendix 1. It includes the historical personages upon which stage characters are based; *dramatis personae* are indexed only selectively.

Abbott, E.A. 182n., 191n., 195n., 198n., 199n., 202n., 204n., 207n., 211n., 221n., 224n., 226n., 228n., 234n., 235n., 246n., 254n., 260n., 266n., 268n., 269n., 274n., 276n., 277n., 279n., 288n., 292n., 296n., 316n., 325n., 327n., 328n., 333n., 334n., 338n., 339n., 343n., 354n., 357n., 358n., 364n., 369n., 371n., 375n., 376n., 381n., 393n., 399n., 400n., 401n., 402n., 405n., 406n., 407n., 411n., 412n., 414n., 420n., 422n., 435n., 436n., 441n., 444n., 445n., 448n., 449n., 451n., 453n., 455n., 459n., 460n., 461n., 462n., 463n., 465n., 466n., 467n., 468n., 469n., 470n., 473n., 482n., 483n., 502n.

Abel (Genesis) 76–7, 137, 188n., 482n.

Abraham (Bible) 385n., 493n.

Act to Restrain Abuses 197n., 208n., 262n., 268n., 346n., 387n., 513n.

Adam (Genesis) 75–6, 369n., 458n., 495n.

Adams, Richard 212n., 290n., 316n., 341n., 368n., 371n., 385n., 396n., 461n., 466n., 483n., 489n., 492n.

Aeneas (classical legend) 416n.

Aesop 386n., 493n.

Agony in the Garden, The (York mystery cycle) 394n.

Albright, Evelyn 16

Alexander, Peter 520

Allot, Robert 91, 196n., 231n., 232n., 242n., 320n., 321n., 487n.

Altick, Richard D. 65, 69

Amer, Nicholas 101

Amhurst, Nicholas 53–4

Anglican Church 8, 424n., 499n. See also *Book of Common Prayer; Homilies*

Anne of Bohemia (1st queen of Richard II) 145, 146, 147, 150, 174n., 307n., 479n., 491n., 502n.

Anne, Queen of England 492n.

Apollo (classical mythology) 355n., 356n., 503n.

Apthonius 488n.

Arden, Mary 430n.

Arthur, Prince (*King John*) 458n., 482n.

Arundel, 13th Earl of. See Howard, Philip

Arundel, 14th Earl of. See Howard, Thomas

Arundel, Richard Fitzalan, 4th Earl of 186n., 188n., 267n., 271n., 272n., 373n., 380n.

Arundel, Thomas, Archbishop of Canterbury 25, 47n., 133, 156, 269n., 270n., 271n., 272n., 320n., 342n., 386n., 469n., 499n.

Arundel, Thomas, the Younger (nephew of Archbishop Arundel) 270n., 271n.

Arundell, Charles 266n.

Ascham, Roger 243n.

Ashcroft, Peggy 99

Aspley, William 517

Aston, Margaret 47n., 249n.

Atheist's Tragedy, The. See Tourneur, Cyril

Atropos. See Destinies

Aumerle, Edward of York, Earl of Rutland, 2nd Duke of 125, 130, 175–6n., 180n., 185n., 191n., 192n., 207n., 263n., 283n., 289n., 306n., 314n., 315n., 336n., 337n., 344n., 372n., 373n., 374n., 375n., 376n., 377n., 378n., 379n., 380n., 383n., 414n., 427n., 428n., 433n., 434n., 440n., 443n., 446n., 457n., 458n., 478n., 493n., 497n., 502n., 503n.

Axton, Marie 150, 151

Bacon, Sir Francis 213n., 503n.

Bacon, Sir Nicholas 7

Bagot, Sir William 117, 127n., 144, 146, 151, 176n., 192n., 238n., 283n., 288n., 289n., 301n., 372n., 373n., 374n., 375n., 380n., 487n., 490n., 491n., 493n., 496n.

Baker, George Pierce 98, 106, 502n.

Baker, Herschel (*Riverside* editor) 115n., 242n.
Baker, Richard 500n.
Baldwin, T.W. 122, 512n.
Baldwin, William 24n., 138, 139, 503n.
Barbary (Richard II's horse) 429n., 460n., 469n., 470n., 504n.
Barber, C.L. 66
Barentyn, Sir Drew (Mayor of London) 486n.
Barkan, Leonard 60
Baron, Robert 91, 338n., 347n., 390n., 401n., 494n., 501n.
Barroll, J. Leeds 11n.
Barron, Karl 106
Barton, Anne 112n.
Barton, John 44n. 70, 73, 75, 80, 83, 98, 102–5, 111, 168n., 178n., 485n.
Baskervill, Charles Read 503n.
Baxter, John 33n., 57, 63–4, 251n., 387–8n.
Beadle, Richard 394n.
Beattie, Rod 105n.
Beauchamp, Lord Edward (son of Lady Catherine Grey) 9
Beauchamp, Thomas, 12th Earl of Warwick 186n., 267n., 373n.
Beaufort, Henry, Bishop of Winchester 501n.
Beaumont, Henry, 5th Baron 279n.
Becket, Thomas à, Archbishop of Canterbury 458n.
Bedford, Brian 98
benevolences 489n.
Benson, Sir Frank 96–7, 474n.
Benthall, Michael 39n., 98, 101, 415n.
Berger, Harry 33n., 43n.
Bergeron, David M. 115n., 516n.
Berkeley, Thomas, 5th Baron 178n., 295n., 296n., 297n., 299n.
Berners, Lord. See Bourchier, Sir John
Berri, Jean, Duc de (uncle of Charles VI) 488n.
Bevan, Bryan 483n.
Bevington, David 115n., 386n., 486n.
Bible, The 4, 33, 34, 36, 66, 70, 75–8, 80, 83, 137, 156, 157, 201n., 308n., 443n., 455n., 458n., 503n.
    Corinthians (1) 47n., 347n.
    Corinthians (2) 458n.
    Deuteronomy 454n.
    Ecclesiasticus 204n., 275n., 319n.
    Exodus 403n.

    Genesis 70, 75–8, 80, 135, 136, 137, 158, 188–9n., 196n., 201n., 245n., 310n., 360n., 369n., 391n., 413n., 482n., 495n.
    Hebrews 188n.
    Isaiah 311n., 397n., 403n., 408n., 491n.
    James 38
    Jeremiah 196n., 491n.
    Job 319n., 329n.
    John 66, 201n., 390n., 404n., 503n.
    Joshua 420n.
    Kings (1) 311n., 395n.
    Kings (2) 346n.
    Luke 201n., 364n., 385n., 461n., 462n., 493n.
    Malachai 403n.
    Mark 390n., 394n., 452n., 461n., 462n.
    Matthew 157, 247n., 310n., 321n., 327n., 390n., 394n., 404n., 425n., 452n., 461n., 462n.
    Proverbs 416n., 470n.
    Psalms 201n., 204n., 216n., 370n., 391n., 403n., 407n., 447n., 503n.
    Revelations 223n., 226n., 403n.
    Romans 321n.
    Ruth 425n.
    Samuel (1) 204n., 467n.
    Samuel (2) 420n.
    Timothy (1) 247n., 258n.,
    Timothy (2) 418n.
    Zachariah 282n.
Bigot, Georges 109
Billington, Michael 101
Birney, David 499n.
Black, James 42n.
Black, Matthew W. xv, 5n., 89, 110n., 121n., 122n., 158n., 176n., 295n., 300n., 344n., 387n., 405n., 427n., 434n., 440n., 441n., 442n., 479n., 483n., 507n., 522n.
Black Prince, the. See Edward, Prince of Wales
Blanche of Lancaster (1st wife of John of Gaunt) 175n.
blank charters, 22, 116, 148, 238–9n., 267n., 268n.
Blayney, Peter W.M. 540n., 541n.
Bloch, Marc 492n.
Bloom, Harold 26n., 159, 324n.
Blount, Edward 541
Blower, John 504n.
Blunt (or Blount), Sir Thomas 433n., 477n., 478n., 514, 526, 538n.

Blunt, Sir Walter 478n.

Boas, F.S. 95, 117n., 145n.

Boccaccio, Giovanni 494n.

Bodenham, John 91

Bohun, Eleanor de, Duchess of
Gloucester 116, 126, 176n., 200n.,
204n., 275n., 284n., 419n., 428n.,
438n., 485n., 529n.

Bohun, Humphrey de (son of Thomas of
Woodstock) 176n., 284n.

Bohun, Humphrey de, 7th Earl of
Hereford (father of Eleanor and Mary
de Bohun) 175n.

Bohun, Mary de (1st wife of Henry
Bolingbroke) 175n., 176n., 301n.,
489n.

Boleyn, Ann (2nd queen of Henry VIII)
459n.

Bolingbroke, Elizabeth (sister of Henry
Bolingbroke) 272n.

Bolingbroke, Henry, Earl of Derby,
Duke of Hereford, Duke of Lancaster,
afterwards Henry IV 8, 12, 24, 25, 47n.,
128, 129, 130, 131, 135, 137, 138n., 141,
142–3, 146, 149, 154, 155n., 157, 175n.,
176n., 177n., 178n., 179n., 180n., 186n.,
189n., 190n., 191n., 197n., 204n., 207n.,
208n., 213n., 214n., 215n., 217n., 224n.,
226n., 235n., 237n., 239n., 241n., 249n.,
250n., 259n., 261n., 262n., 263n., 265n.,
269n., 272n., 273n., 280n., 283n., 285n.,
286n., 288n., 289n., 291n., 293n., 296n.,
297n., 298n., 301n., 302n., 303n., 304n.,
305n., 306n., 309n., 312n., 313n., 314n.,
315n., 326n., 335n., 341n., 342n., 348n.,
350n., 357n., 358n., 359n., 360n., 371n.,
372n., 375n., 377n., 380n., 382n., 383n.,
384n., 385n., 386n., 387n., 396n., 400n.,
405n., 413n., 414n., 419n., 422n.,
427–8n., 429n., 430n., 431n., 432n.,
433n., 434n., 435n., 442n., 443n., 444n.,
446n., 449n., 457n., 458n., 459n., 467n.,
468n., 469n., 472n., 476n., 477n., 478n.,
481n., 483n., 484n., 485n., 486n., 487n.,
488n., 489n., 491n., 492n., 493n., 495n.,
496n., 497n., 498n., 499n., 500n., 501n.,
502n., 504n., 505n., 540

Bonner, G.W., 94

Book of Common Prayer, The 240n.,
282n., 390n., 395n., 404n., 423n.,
424n., 456n., 458n., 493n., 504n.
See also Anglican Church

Booth, Edwin 95

Booth, Junius Brutus 95

Bornstein, Diane 199n.

Bourchier, Sir John, Lord Berners 124,
152

Bracton, Henry de 19

Bradley, David 174n., 273n., 485n.

Brandes, Georg M.C. 159

Brereton, J. Le Gay 285n., 286n., 487n.

Bridges-Adams, William 95

Brittany, Duke of. See John IV

Brocas, Sir Bernard ('Leonard'), the
Younger 477n., 479n.

Brocas, Sir Bernard, the Elder 479n.

Brooke, Arthur 230n., 332n.

Brooke, C.F. Tucker 159

Brooke, Nicholas 74

Brooks, H.F. 194n., 254n., 382n., 487n.

Brut (classical legend) 416n.

Bryant, J.A. 75

Bryant, Michael 429n.

Buchon, J.A. 124, 188n.

Bukton, Peter (or Piers) 178n.

Bullough, Geoffrey 116–17, 139n.,
146n., 153, 156, 158, 230n., 332n.,
504n.

Burbage, James 120

Burbage, Richard 120, 122, 312n.

Burghill, John, Bishop of Lichfield (i.e.
Chester) 481n.

Burghley, Lord. See Cecil, William

Burton, Robert 467n.

Bushy, Sir John 17, 117, 125, 144,
146, 151, 176n., 177n., 207n., 217n.,
238n., 283n., 288n., 289n., 301n.,
309n., 331n., 487n., 491n., 493n.,
500n.

Cade, Jack 187n.

Cadmus (classical mythology) 317n.

Caesar's Revenge 91, 189n., 198n.,
289n., 330n., 390n.

Cain (Genesis) 76–7, 135, 137, 188–9n.,
482n.

Caldwell, Zoe 106

Caligula (Roman emperor) 486n.

Camden, William 10n.

Campbell, Lily B. 49n., 136, 139n.

Campbell, O.J. 115n.

Canterbury, Archbishop of. See
Arundel, Thomas; Becket, Thomas à;
Cranmer, Thomas; Sudbury, Simon;
Whitgift, John

Canute, King 501n.

Capell, Edward 166, 199n., 214n., 254n., 271n., 348n., 367n., 379n., 380n., 396n., 410n., 421n., 436n., 440n., 444n., 453n., 533
Capgrave, John 511n.
Carey, Henry, 1st Baron Hunsdon 5n., 120n.
Carlisle, Bishop of. See Merke, Thomas
Cass, Henry 98
Catherine of Lancaster, Queen of Spain (Castile) 497n.
Catholics, 5–7, 10, 21, 51, 246n., 266n., 271n., 488n., 489n.
Cavendish, William Spencer, 6th Duke of Devonshire 533
Caxton, William 486n.
Cecil, Sir Robert 5n., 9, 10, 14, 15, 114–15, 122, 353n.
Cecil, William, 1st Baron Burghley 5, 6, 7, 9, 115, 266n., 489n.
Celestine V, Pope 499n.
Cercignani, Fausto 182n., 199n., 220n., 223n., 225n., 231n., 354n., 455n., 462n.
Chamberlain, John 14n.
Chamberlain's Men, the 10, 111, 120, 121n., 122n., 144, 515, 530, 532
Chambers, E.K. 5n., 14, 32n., 55, 112n., 114n., 116n., 120n., 122n., 123, 144, 145n., 146n., 185n., 188n., 189n., 196n., 264n., 312n., 348n., 364n., 385n., 395n., 419n., 454n., 458n., 461n., 466n., 472n., 474n., 476n., 481n., 491n., 493n., 502n., 504n., 514n.
Champion, Larry S. 192n.
Charles I 51, 52, 157, 488n.
Charles II 50, 51
Charles VI, King of France 137, 153, 174n., 175n., 191n., 268n., 488n., 489n.
Charlton, H.B. 117n.
Chase, Stanley Perkins xv
Chaucer, Geoffrey
    Knight's Tale, The 230n., 396n.
    Monk's Tale, The, 494n.
    Troilus and Criseyde 417n.
    Wife of Bath's Tale, The 232n.
Chester, Bishop of. See Burghill, John
Chettle, Henry 5n., 178n.
Chief Justice, Lord. See Gascoigne, Sir William
Cibber, Colley 44, 53

Cicero, Marcus Tullius 123
    Tusculan Disputations 164, 230n., 231n., 232n.
Clarence, George, Duke of (*Richard III*) 501n.
Clarence, Lionel, Duke of 8, 190n., 201n.
Clark, William George (Cambridge editor) 220n., 243n., 275n., 482–3n.,
Clegg, Cyndia Susan 17
Cleremont, Duke of (fictional, mentioned in Marlowe, *Edward II*) 424n.
Clifford, Margaret, Countess of Derby 9
Clotho. See Destinies
Cobham, Reginald, Lord (= John de Cobham, 3rd Baron?) 270n.
Coffin, John 168n.
Coghill, Nevill 232n., 396n.
Coint, Francis 270n., 272n., 525, 528
Coit, Charles Wheeler 157
Coke, Sir Edward 5n., 13
Colchester, William of, Abbot of Westminster 177n.
Coleridge, Henry Nelson 56, 360n.
Coleridge, Samuel Taylor 56, 63n., 88, 92, 110, 183n., 219n., 251n., 296n., 316n., 340n., 341n., 360n.
Collier, John Payne 243n., 319n., 383n., 494n.
Collins, Arthur 113n.
Copy of a Letter . . . about the present state and some proceedings of the Earl of Leicester (also entitled *Leicester's Commonwealth*). See Morgan, Thomas
Contention of Ajax and Ulysses, The. See Shirley, James
Cotgrave, John 91
Cottrell, Richard 98
Cox, Frank 102
Craftsman, The (periodical) 53, 54
Craig, Hardin 115n., 145n., 312n., 463n.
Craik, T.W. 468n., 504n.
Crane, Ralph 519
Cranmer, Thomas, Archbishop of Canterbury 499n.
Craven, Alan E. 214n., 268n., 286n., 294n., 303n., 304n., 368n., 379n., 386n., 391n., 430n., 431n., 434n., 436n., 447n., 449n., 457n., 501n., 519n., 533n., 536, 537, 537–8n., 538, 539

Créton, Jean 124, 152, 154–8, 177n., 226n., 308n., 322n., 324n., 326n., 357n., 358n., 387n., 394n., 413n., 429n., 432n., 491n., 492n., 498n., 499n., 501n., 504n.
Cromwell, Oliver 52
Cross Keys Theatre 120n.
Crouchback, Edmund, Earl of Lancaster 8
Cruikshank, Robert 94
Cumberland's British Theatre 93–4
Curtain Theatre 121

Dalai Lama, the 101
Dance of Death, The (Holbein) 84, 494n.
Daniel, P.A. 506n., 514n., 516n., 520, 523
Daniel, Samuel 232n.
  Complaint of Rosamond, The 141
  First Four Books of the Civil Wars, The
    33n., 71, 112–13, 118n., 124, 129n., 134n., 140–4, 152, 154, 156, 157, 174n., 178n., 217n., 246n., 247n., 248n., 256n., 269n., 274n., 281n., 291n., 297n., 303n., 304n., 307n., 308n., 315n., 325n., 335n., 341n., 347n., 348n., 356n., 357n., 371n., 388n., 390n., 394n., 400n., 401n., 414n., 415n., 416n., 418n., 420n., 422n., 425n., 428n., 429n., 430n., 431n., 434n., 444n., 458n., 459n., 460n., 468n., 474n., 475n., 476n., 481n., 482n., 483n., 487n., 488n., 491n., 493n., 494n., 498n., 499n., 500n., 501n., 526n.
Darcy, John, 5th Baron 279n.
d'Artois, Jenico 133, 460n., 468n., 469n., 471n.
David, King (Bible) 201n.
David, Richard 102n., 451n.
Davies, Thomas 54–5
Daviot, Gordon (Josephine Tey)
  Richard of Bordeaux 98
Davison, Peter 536n., 539
Davison, William 481–2n.
Day, John
  Isle of Gulls, The 91, 396n.
de Coucy, Philippe, Duchess of Ireland (wife of Robert de Vere) 491n.
de Witt, Johannes 121
Death (allegorical figure) 225n., 252n., 270n., 281n., 325n., 330n., 331n., 332n., 376n., 473n., 485n., 494n.
Dee, John 155

degradation, rituals of 35, 195n., 499n.
Dekker, Thomas 5n., 91, 178n.
  Honest Whore, The, Part 1 482n.
  Honest Whore, The, Part 2 258n.
  Shoemakers' Holiday, The 536n.
  Westward Ho (with Webster) 441n.
  Wonder of a Kingdom, The 358n.
Dent, R.W. 181n., 194n., 196n., 213n., 214n., 215n., 219n., 224n., 225n., 226n., 230n., 242n., 245n., 257n., 258n., 266n., 270n., 287n., 290n., 292n., 303n., 305n., 317n., 322n., 325n., 327n., 332n., 362n., 363n., 374n., 381n., 386n., 395n., 397n., 398n., 407n., 419n., 425n., 449n., 454n., 456n., 458n., 462n., 470n., 482n., 493n., 495n.
Despenser, Henry, Bishop of Norwich 296n.
Despenser, Sir Thomas, Baron (former Earl of Gloucester). See Spenser, 'Hugh'
Destinies (or Fates; classical mythology) 202n., 225n.
Deucalion (classical mythology), 493n.
Devereux, Robert, 2nd Earl of Essex 5n., 9–10, 11, 12, 14, 15, 16, 41n., 52, 121, 122n., 122, 236n., 487n., 515, 516n.
Digges, Leonard 342n.
Dillon, Janette 407n., 427n.
Diogenes 230n.
divine right of kings 1, 17–18, 30–1, 34, 35, 36, 40, 44, 49, 51, 61, 65–6, 69, 74, 81, 101, 102, 126, 139, 150, 151, 157, 161, 190n., 203n., 204n., 252n., 253n., 300n., 321n., 325n., 331n., 337n., 346n., 347n., 387n., 390n., 395n., 400n., 456n., 474n., 477n., 490n., 492–3n., 495n., 498n., 503n.
Doleman, R. (pseudonym) 10n.
Dolman, John (translator of Cicero) 164, 230n., 231n., 232n.
Donne, John 409n.
Dos Mariae (Mary's Dowry) 488n.
Douce, Francis 494n.
Dowden, Edward 95, 503n.
Dowling, Margaret 14n.
Drayton, Michael 5n., 178n., 487n.
Dryden, John 91, 431n.
Du Bartas, Guillaume de Salluste 123, 165, 245n., 487n., 488n.
Dudley, Craig 106n.

Dudley, Robert, 1st Earl of Leicester 5, 6, 7, 41n., 266n.
Duls, Louisa D. 24
Dyce, Alexander 448n.
Dyson, H.V.D. xv

Edmond Ironside, or War Hath Made All Friends 327n., 376n., 401n., 501n.
Edmund, Saint 488n.
Edward I 8, 176n., 246n., 315n.
Edward II 6, 159–60, 287n., 418n., 424n., 463n., 465n., 491n.
Edward III 10n., 71, 82, 83, 145, 149, 150, 159, 174n., 175n., 176n., 180n., 189n., 190n., 201n., 252n., 253n., 254n., 256n., 260n., 269n., 321n., 348n., 349n., 405n., 484n., 492n.
Edward IV 140, 489n.
Edward V (*Richard III*) 501n.
Edward VI 62, 490n.
Edward of Angoulême (elder brother of Richard II) 174n.
Edward of York, Earl of Rutland, Duke of Aumerle. See Aumerle, Duke of
Edward the Confessor, Saint 321n., 412n., 413n., 488n., 492n.
Edward, Prince of Wales (the Black Prince) 82, 145, 152n., 174n., 180n., 182n., 201n., 254n., 260n., 269n., 300n., 409n., 490n.
Edwards, Philip 35, 74n.
Eliot, John 165, 245n., 487n.
Elizabeth I 1, 5, 6–7, 8–9, 12, 13, 14, 15, 16, 17, 19, 38n., 55, 114, 122, 201n., 238n., 255n., 266n., 353n., 423n., 481n., 489n., 492n., 504n., 516
Elizabeth of York (daughter of Edward IV) 136
Ellis, Havelock 159
Elson, John James 144n.
Elyot, Sir Thomas 442n.
England's Parnassus. See Allot, Robert
Envy (allegorical figure) 202n.
Erasmus, Desiderius, of Rotterdam 63, 287n., 462n.
Erpingham, Sir Thomas 270n., 272n.
Essex, 2nd Earl of. See Devereux, Robert
Evans, G. Blakemore (*Riverside* editor) 271n., 462n., 506n., 514n., 522n.
Evans, Maurice 98, 99, 100
Eve (Genesis) 75–6, 369n.
Exeter, Bishop of. See Stafford, Edmund
Exeter, Duke of. See Holland, Sir John

Exton, Sir Nicholas 178n.
Exton, Sir Pierce of 5n., 178n., 458n., 459n., 460n., 472n., 475n., 481n., 483n., 500n., 505n.

Fabyan, Robert 138n., 140, 442n., 474n.
Famous Victories of Henry V, The 442n., 444n.
farming the realm 22, 27, 49, 54, 69, 148, 238n., 247n., 253n., 487n.
Farnham, Willard 494n.
Fastolfe, Sir John 177n.
Fates. See Destinies
Ferguson, W. Craig 536n.
Feuillerat, Albert 115n., 229n., 519, 520
Fiennes, Ralph 98
Finch, Jon 232n., 387n.
Findlater, Richard 100
First Part of the Life and Reign of King Henry IV, The. See Hayward, Sir John
Fitzalan, Richard, 4th Earl of Arundel 186n., 188n., 267n., 271n., 272n., 373n., 380n.
Fitzwater (or Fitzwalter), Walter, 4th Baron 381n.
Fitzwater (or Fitzwalter), Walter, 5th Baron 177n., 178n., 185n., 372n., 376n., 377n., 378n., 379n., 380n., 381n., 382n., 383n., 476n., 478n., 496n., 526, 528, 540
Fletcher, John 91
  Lovers' Progress, The (with Massinger) 311n., 501n.
  Mad Lover, The 471n.
  Noble Gentleman, The 320n.
Fletcher, Richard, Bishop of London 516
Foakes, R.A. 167
Ford, John,
  Perkin Warbeck 282n.
Forker, Charles R. 7, 28n., 35, 50n., 55, 56, 88, 91n., 92, 95, 96, 98, 123n., 159, 162, 194n., 286n., 352n., 359n., 360n., 361n., 399n., 431n., 474n., 489n., 494n., 500n., 502n., 503n.
Forman, Dr Simon 5, 146n., 188n.
Fortescue, Sir John 19
Fortuna (goddess) 37, 250n., 397n., 410n., 463n., 485n., 494n.
Foster, Donald 122, 509n., 516n.
Foxe, John 499n.
Friedman, Donald M. 67
Frijlinck, Wilhemina P. 116, 145n.

Froissart, Jean 124, 140, 143, 147n., 149, 152–4, 180n., 188n., 204n., 207n., 217n., 219n., 226n., 237n., 239n., 241n., 248n., 256n., 260n., 270n., 272n., 273n., 280n., 291n., 308n., 313n., 334–5n., 336n., 342n., 355n., 358n., 360n., 361n., 371n., 386n., 391n., 393n., 394n., 399–400n., 405n., 421n., 429n., 430n., 460n., 469n., 486n., 487n., 488n., 489n., 496n., 497n., 499n., 502n., 504n., 505n.

Galen 467n.
Garrick, David 92
Gascoigne, George 135
Gascoigne, Sir William, Lord Chief Justice 443n., 444n.
Gaunt, John of, Duke of Lancaster 128–9, 144, 145, 146, 147, 149, 150, 151, 153–4, 174–5n., 176n., 179n., 180n., 187n., 189n., 190n., 201n., 204n., 207n., 226n., 239n., 240n., 241n., 247n., 250n., 253n., 259n., 273n., 282n., 297n., 300n., 301n., 348n., 350n., 381n., 494n., 497–8n., 505n.
Gaveston, Piers 159, 161, 162, 465n., 491n.
Genius of England (allegorical figure in Daniel's *Civil Wars*) 143, 303n.
Gentleman, Francis 92
George I 52
George II 50
George, Saint 214n., 305n., 488n., 502n.
Gibson, Gail McMurray 485n.
Gielgud, Sir John 55, 98, 99, 100, 105
Gilbert, John, Bishop of Hereford, then of St David's 385n., 386n.
Gilbert, Miriam 73, 75, 102n.
Giles, David 98, 105, 196n., 232n., 387n.
Gilman, Ernest B. 399n., 490n.
Glendower, Owen 178n., 313n., 492n.
Globe Theatre (1st) 10, 15, 91, 121, 122, 531, 532
Globe Theatre (2nd) 121, 146n.
Globe Theatre (modern reconstructed) 344n.
Gloucester, 1st Duke of (6th son of Edward III). See Woodstock, Thomas of
Gloucester, Earl of. See Spenser, 'Hugh'
Gloucester, Humphrey, Duke of ('the Good', son of Henry IV) 147n., 176n., 416n. 501n.

Glover, John (Cambridge editor) 243n.
Glover, Robert 18, 20, 55
Golden Legend, The 486n.
Golding, Arthur 202n.,
Goodhall, James 92
Googe, Barnabe 351n.
Gorboduc. See Sackville, Thomas; Norton, Thomas
Gordon, Dillion 488n.
Gosson, Stephen 491n.
Grabes, Herbert 407n.
Grafton, Richard 140, 415n.
Graham-White, Anthony 518–19n.
Granville-Barker, Harley 96, 98
Green, Sir Henry, 117, 144, 146, 151, 176n., 177n., 238n., 283n., 288n., 289n., 301n., 309n., 331n., 487n., 491n., 493n., 500n.
Greene, Robert
    Friar Bacon and Friar Bungay, 246n.
    Looking Glass for London and England, A (with Lodge) 135, 524n.
    Spanish Masquerado, The 245n.
Greer, C.A. 114n., 115n., 506n.
Greg, W.W. 116n., 518n., 519n., 532n., 533, 536n., 537, 539
Grey, Lady Catherine 8, 9
Grey, Lady Jane 8
Grose, Francis 409n.
Guenelon (*Chanson de Roland*) 498n.
Guilpin, Everard 15, 91, 487n.
Guinness, Alec 98, 99, 100
Gurr, Andrew (Cambridge[2] editor) xv, 77, 80, 115n., 120n., 121, 175n., 178n., 182n., 184n., 189n., 194n., 203n., 206n., 210n., 212n., 213n., 220n., 233n., 234n., 238n., 239n., 241n., 242n., 244n., 245n., 249n., 250n., 251n., 255n., 256n., 260n., 266n., 267n., 274n., 281n., 285n., 286n., 292n., 294n., 303n., 305n., 325n., 336n., 344n., 348n., 349n., 356n., 359n., 364n., 367n., 370n., 372n., 373n., 377n., 390n., 396n., 399n., 408n., 410n., 423n., 430n., 434n., 447n., 449n., 455n., 458n., 463n., 467n., 474n., 491n., 492n., 493n., 503n., 506n., 508n., 515n., 522, 525

Hall, Arthur 491n.
Hall, Edward 33, 124, 136–8, 139, 143, 152, 153, 154, 155, 158, 179n., 180n., 187n., 195n., 207n., 208n., 242n.,

269n., 270n., 301n., 338n., 348n.,
352n., 384n., 394n., 395n., 402n.,
428n., 433n., 434n., 436n., 442n.,
443n., 446n., 447n., 460n., 474n.,
475n., 482n., 496n., 497n., 499n.,
502n.
Hall, John 496n.
Hall, Peter 98, 102
Hallam, Henry 503n.
Halliwell, James O. 373n., 487n.
Hands, Terry 98, 106
Hanmer, Sir Thomas 319n.
Harbage, Alfred xv, 3
Hardyng, John 158
Harris, Kathryn Montgomery 79, 80
Harrison, G.B. 114n., 236n., 487n.
Harrison, William 491n.
Harvey, Gabriel 298n.
Hasker, Richard E. 507n., 521, 522, 523
Hastings, Henry, 3rd Earl of
Huntingdon 9
Hatton, Sir Christopher 7
Hawkins, William (sea captain) 122
Hawkins, William (theatre critic) 100
Hayes, George 95
Hayne, Murray 101
Hayward, Sir John 12–14, 15, 91, 148n.
219n., 302n., 307n., 388n., 389n.,
400n., 430n., 459n., 482n., 486n.,
504n.
Hazlitt, William 88, 92
Hearne, Thomas 504n.
Heffner, Ray 14, 16
Helen of Troy (classical legend) 164,
408n.
Heninger, S.K. 73
Henry II 458n.
Henry IV. See Bolingbroke, Henry
Henry V 117, 130, 176n., 177n., 293n.,
302n., 348n., 442–3n., 444n., 445n.
Henry VI 6, 139n., 501n.
Henry VII 136, 282n., 459n., 500n.
Henry VIII 8
Henry of Monmouth (Prince Hal). See
Henry V
Herbert, George 91, 397n.
Hereford, Bishop of. See Gilbert, John
Herford, C.H. 159, 162, 240n., 305n.,
334n., 341n., 349n., 352n., 373n.,
375n., 379n., 407n., 429n., 432n.,
458n., 492n., 502n., 503n.
Herodotus 365n.
Heywood, Thomas 91, 194n.

*If You Know Not Me, You Know
Nobody, Part 1* 358n., 359n., 474n.,
501n.
*If You Know Not Me, You Know
Nobody, Part 2* 361n., 495n.
Hibbard, G.R. 123
Hill, Thomas 366n.
Hilliard, Nicholas 11
Hiller, Wendy 105
Hinman, Charlton 518n., 519n., 533,
536, 537, 539, 540, 540n., 541n.
History of King Richard the Second, The.
See Tate, Nahum
Hobson, Harold 91, 104
Hoby, Sir Edward 114–15
Hockey, Dorothy C. 61n.
Hodges, C. Walter 121, 122, 207n., 344n.
Holbein, Hans, the Younger 62, 84,
490n., 494n.
Holinshed, Raphael 17n., 21, 23n., 24n.,
25, 34, 85, 111, 124–35, 136, 137, 140,
143, 146, 148, 152, 153, 155, 156, 158,
174n., 175n., 176n., 177n., 178n.,
179n., 180n., 186n., 187n., 188n.,
190n., 191–2n., 204n., 207n., 208n.,
209n., 210n., 211n., 215n., 217n.,
220n., 224n., 226n., 235–6n., 237n.,
238n., 240n., 241n., 243n., 247n.,
253n., 256n., 259n., 262n., 263n.,
264n., 265n., 267n., 268n., 270n.,
271n., 272n., 273n., 274n., 279n.,
280n., 283n., 284n., 285n., 286n.,
287n., 288n., 289n., 291n., 293n.,
296n., 297n., 298n., 301n., 304n.,
306n., 307n., 309n., 310n., 311n.,
313n., 314n., 315n., 319n., 320n.,
321n., 322n., 324n., 326n., 334n.,
335n., 336n., 339n., 342n., 346n.,
349n., 350n., 355n., 357n., 358n.,
359n., 360n., 361n., 364n., 369n.,
372n., 373n., 374n., 375n., 376n.,
377n., 378n., 379n., 380n., 383n.,
384n., 385n., 386n., 387n., 388n.,
391n., 392n., 393n., 394n., 395n.,
396n., 397n., 399n., 400n., 401n.,
402n., 404n., 405n., 408n., 412n.,
413n., 414n., 415n., 421n., 424n.,
427n., 428n., 429n., 432n., 433n.,
434n., 435n., 436n., 440n., 441n.,
442n., 443n., 444n., 445n., 446n.,
447n., 448n., 457n., 458n., 459n.,
460n., 462n., 467n., 468n., 469n.,
471n., 472n., 473n., 474n., 475n.,

476n., 477n., 478n., 479n., 480n.,
481n., 483n., 484n., 485n., 487n.,
489n., 491n., 492n., 493n., 495n.,
496n., 497n., 498n., 499n., 500n.,
502n., 503n., 505n., 511n., 514, 516n.,
527, 528

Holland, Henry 2

Holland, Joan, Duchess of York (2nd
wife of Edmund of Langley) 175n.,
248n., 272n., 443n., 502n., 503n.

Holland, Sir John, Earl of Huntingdon,
Duke of Exeter 130–1, 271n., 314n.,
338n., 433n., 434n., 435n., 446n.,
457n., 476n., 477n., 479n., 496n.

Holland, Sir Thomas, 2nd Earl of Kent
177n.

Holland, Sir Thomas, 3rd Earl of Kent,
Duke of Surrey 125, 177n., 178n.,
207n., 227n., 314n., 376n., 380n.,
381n., 428n., 433n., 434n., 446n.,
476n., 478n., 496n., 514, 540

Homer 491n.

*Homilies (Certain Sermons . . . Appointed
to be Read in Churches)* 19, 150, 157,
203n., 247n., 287n., 347n., 388n.,
389n., 403n., 498n., 503n., 504n.

Honan, Park 430n.

Hooker, Richard 18

Howard, Alan 98, 106

Howard, Philip, 13th Earl of Arundel
271n.

Howard, Richard 106–7

Howard, Thomas, 14th Earl of Arundel
271n.

Howard-Hill, T.H. 519n.

Hudson, Henry N. 28n., 95, 112, 319n.

Hughes-Hallett, Lucy 106

Huizinga, Johan 432n.

Humphrey, Duke of Gloucester. See
Gloucester, Humphrey, Duke of

Humphreys, A.R. 442–3n., 444n.

Hunsdon, Lord (Lord Chamberlain). See
Carey, Henry

Hunter, G.K. 116n., 117, 513n.

Huntingdon, Earl of. See Hastings,
Henry; Holland, Sir John

Huth, Henry 533

Ibsen, Henrik Johan 58

Ingram, William 121n.

Innocent III, Pope (*King John*) 366n.

Insatiate Countess, The. See Marston, John

Interlude of the Four Elements, The, 221n.

Invidia (allegorical figure) 202n.

Ireland, Duchess of. See de Coucy, Philippe

Irons, Jeremy 98

Irving, Sir Henry 210n., 297n., 387n.,
440n.

Isabel of Valois, 2nd queen of Richard II
112, 141, 142, 143, 147, 152, 155n.,
157–8, 168, 174n., 191n., 264n., 274n.,
281n., 313n., 361n., 371n., 421n.,
424n., 430n., 432n., 491n., 500n.,
501n., 502n., 505n.

Isabel, queen of Edward II (daughter of
Philip IV of France) 159n., 161,
424n., 491n.

Isabella, Infanta of Spain (daughter of
Philip II) 9, 21

Isabelle of Castile, Duchess of York (1st
wife of Edmund of Langley) 428n.,
502n.

Iselin, Pierre 464n.

Isle of Dogs, The. See Nashe, Thomas

Isle of Gulls, The. See Day, John

Jack Straw, The Life and Death of 5, 489n.

Jackson, MacDonald P. 520

Jacobi, Derek 98, 105

Jaggard, William 395n., 508n., 515, 521,
522, 523, 540, 541

James I (James VI of Scotland) 8, 9, 21,
91, 121, 193n., 334n., 498n., 532

James II. See James, Duke of York

James VI, King of Scotland. See James I

James, Duke of York, afterwards James
II 51

James, Saint (Apostle, brother of John)
298n.

James, Saint (Epistler). See Bible, The

Jenkins, Elizabeth 353n., 423n., 482n.

Jensen, Howard 106–7

Jesse, Tree of 201n., 423n.

Jesus Christ 34, 36, 66, 73, 76–8, 95,
102, 137, 156, 188n., 201n., 247n.,
255n., 282n., 310n., 327n., 347n.,
348n., 353n., 369n. 390n., 394n.,
404n., 423n., 458n., 462n., 488n.,
495n., 498n., 499n., 503n.

Jewkes, Wilfred T. 512n.

Joan of Navarre (wife of John IV, Duke
of Brittany; 1st queen of Henry IV)
272n.

John II, King of France 490n.

John IV (John de Montfort), Duke of
Brittany 268n., 270n., 272n.

John, Ivor B. (Arden[1] editor) 159, 325n., 395n., 451n.

'John of Bordeaux' (or 'John of London'), false name of Richard II 499–500n.

John, King of England 458n., 482n., 494n.

John, Saint (Gospeller) 66

John, Saint, the Baptist 488n.

Johnson, Dr Samuel 92, 209n., 277n., 329n., 334n., 376n., 384n., 397n., 417n., 425n., 436n., 451n., 467–8n., 492n., 493n., 494n., 496n., 498n., 503n.

Johnson, Richard 'Song of a Beggar and a King' 451n.

Jones, John 514n.

Jonson, Ben 11n. *Catiline* 365n.

Jowett, John (*TxC* editor) 112n., 113n., 120n., 194n., 212n., 225n., 240n., 243n., 255n., 261n., 266n., 272n., 279n., 290n., 293n., 312n., 318n., 325n., 332n., 343n., 359n., 386n., 396n., 403n., 435n., 445n., 449n., 454n., 457n., 486n., 496n., 506n., 507n., 514n., 515n., 516n., 519n., 520, 523–4, 524n., 526, 528, 529

Judas Iscariot (Bible) 36, 76, 78, 156, 327n., 394n., 493n., 498n.

Julius Caesar 76n., 415n., 416n., 516n.

Jupiter (or Zeus; classical mythology) 214n., 345n., 355n.

Kantorowicz, E.H. 17, 331n.

Kean, Charles 93–4, 95, 96, 111, 428n.

Kean, Edmund 92, 93, 363n.

Keeling, William 122

Keightley, Thomas 210n., 266n.

Keller, Wolfgang 145n.

Kelly, H.A. 158n.

Kemble, John Philip 533

Kent, Earl of. See Holland, Sir Thomas

Kent, Jonathan 98, 485n.

Kiefer, Frederick 397n.

Kincaid, A.N. 115

'King Cophetua and the Beggar Maid' (ballad) 451n.

King Leir 292n., 446n., 480n.

King's Men, the 91, 121, 515, 531, 532

king's two bodies, theory of. See divine right of kings

King, J.E. 230n., 231n., 232n.

King, T.J. 174n.

Kipling, Gordon 157n.

Kirby, J.L. 178n.

Kittredge, G.L. 114n., 115, 189n., 221n., 246n., 249n., 254n., 256n., 258n., 265n., 267n., 316n., 403n., 405n., 440n., 469n.

Klinck, Dennis R. 252n.

Knack to Know a Knave, A 503n.

Knight, Charles 112, 523n.

Knollys, Sir Francis 5n.

Kyd, Thomas 58, 189n. *Jeronimo* 347n. *Spanish Tragedy, The* 175n., 198n., 215n.

Kyle, Barry 98, 464n.

Lachesis. See Destinies

Lamb, Charles 92, 100, 158

Lambarde, William 5, 14, 122

Lambert, Saint 199n., 485n.

Lambrechts, Guy 114n., 117n.

Lampe, David E. 485n.

Langley, Edmund of, 1st Duke of York 144, 147, 149, 150, 154, 175n., 180n., 187n., 201n., 241n., 250n., 259n., 263n., 264n., 282n., 283n., 285n., 286n., 289n., 291n., 296n., 297n., 298n., 300n., 304n., 309n., 349n., 361n., 385n., 414n., 427n., 432n., 433n., 446n., 469n., 495n., 496n., 497n., 502n., 503n., 538n.

Langley, Francis 121

Lanham, Richard A. 85

Lapoole (fictional character in *Woodstock*) 147

Law, Matthew, 506n. 531, 532, 541

Le Beau, Jean 124, 155

Le Botiller, James, 4th Earl of Ormonde 444n.

Lees, F.N. 117n.

Leicester's Commonwealth. See Morgan, Thomas

Leicester, 1st Earl of. See Dudley, Robert

Leiter, Samuel L. 99, 110n.

Life of Sir Thomas More. See Ro: Ba:

Littlewood, Joan 102

Livy (Titus Livius) 123, 365n.

Lloyd, William Watkiss 93

Lodge, Thomas 123 *Alarum against Usurers, An* 491n. *Looking Glass for London and England, A* (with Greene) 135, 524n.

Truth's Complaint over England 165,
246n., 249n., 361n., 487n., 495n.
Logan, George M. 113
London, Bishop of. See Fletcher, Richard
London, William 91
Long, William B. 116, 508n., 512n., 524
*Longer Thou Livest the More Fool Thou
Art, The*. See Wager, W.
Looking Glass of London and England, A.
See Greene, Robert; Lodge, Thomas
Lorichius, Reinhardus 488n.
Lothian, John M. 115n., 214n., 222n.,
228n., 450n., 455n., 482n.
Lucan (Marcus Annaeus Lucanus) 113,
141
Luce, Morton 159
Lupset, Thomas 462n.
Lydgate, John 415n., 494n.
Lyly, John 123, 164, 198n., 221n., 230n.,
231n., 232n., 233n., 255n., 374n., 450n.

McAvoy, William C. 488n.
McDonald, Russ 89
McGuire, Philip C. 80
McKellen, Ian, 98 100–2
McKenna, Virginia 415n.
MacLean, Sally-Beth 483n.
McLeod, R.R. 168, 512
McManaway, James G. 54–5, 517
McMillin, Scott, 407n. 410n., 483n.,
490n.
MacPherson, Alastair 110n.
McQueen, Jim 106n.
Machiavellianism 15, 43, 74, 131, 146n.,
161, 397n., 492n.
Macready, William Charles 93
Maguire, Laurie E. 506n.
Mahood, M.M.
Playing Bit Parts in Shakespeare 169,
283n., 307n., 308n., 379n., 380n.,
438n., 464n., 467n., 471n., 504n.
Shakespeare's Wordplay 88, 229,
236n., 241n., 366n., 399n., 487n.
Malcontent, The. See Marston, John
Malone, Edmond 213n., 271n., 316n.,
340n., 395n., 405n., 414n., 413n.
Manners, Francis, 6th Earl of Rutland
312n.
Maradan, Frank 106n.
March, Earl of. See Mortimer, Edmund;
Mortimer, Roger
Margaret of Anjou (queen of Henry VI)
295n.

Marie, daughter of Jean, Duc de Berri
(cousin of Charles VI) 488n.
Marius, Caius (Roman general) 296n.
Marlowe, Christopher 58, 189n.
Doctor Faustus 164, 202n., 406n.,
407n., 408n.
Edward II 100, 116, 117–18, 124, 135,
159–64, 201n., 230n., 240n., 243n.,
287n., 303n., 312n., 325n., 329n.,
351n., 352–3n., 359n., 379n., 399n.,
401n., 404n., 405n., 406n., 412n.,
418n., 419n., 424n., 426n., 445n.,
460n., 463n., 465n., 475n., 484n.,
491n., 494n., 500n.
Jew of Malta, The 164, 455n.
Tamburlaine, Part I 60, 159, 164,
254n., 494, 503
Tamburlaine, Part 2 159, 241n.,
Marprelate pamphlets 7
Marriage of Wit and Science, The 244n.
Mars (classical mythology) 245n., 300n.,
390n.
Marston, John
Insatiate Countess, The 424n.
Malcontent, The 397n.
Mary, Queen of England (Mary Tudor)
501n.
Mary, Queen of Scots (Mary Stuart)
7n., 8, 49n., 482n.
Mary, Saint (the Virgin) 235n., 488n.
Masefield, John 4
Massinger, Philip. See Fletcher, John
Master of the Revels. See Tilney, Sir
Edmund
Mathe (Richard II's greyhound) 504–5n.
Maudelyn, Richard 131, 433n., 505n.
Melchiori, Giorgio 255n.
Meres, Francis 91, 323n.
Merke, Thomas, Bishop of Carlisle 126,
128, 177n., 226n., 314n., 337n., 339n.,
344n., 358n., 372n., 391n., 414n.,
433n., 468n., 476n., 479n., 495n.,
497n., 498n.
Messina, Cedric 105
Meyrick, Sir Gilly 16, 121
Michel, Laurence 113n., 493n., 526n.
Milton, John
Lycidas 225n.
Paradise Lost 394n., 413n.
Miram Joseph, Sister 86n.
Mirror for Magistrates, The 124, 135,
138–9, 140, 153, 179n., 187n., 206n.,
207n., 218n., 238n., 249n., 255n.,

256n., 266n., 267n., 268n., 280n., 301–2n., 356n., 358n., 407n., 462n., 491n., 494n., 503n.

Mnouchkine, Ariane 108–9, 111

Monsarrat, Gilles 273n.

Montacute, John de, 3rd Earl of Salisbury 138, 177n., 178n., 306n., 314n., 322n., 324n., 337n., 339n., 344n., 358n., 433n., 435n., 460n., 468n., 476n., 477n., 489n., 492n., 493n., 514, 526, 538n.

Montacute, Sir William, 1st Earl of Salisbury (*Edward III*) 177n.

Montacute, Thomas de, 4th Earl of Salisbury 139n., 177n., 187n.

Montague, C.E. 96, 100, 474n.

Moot, John, Abbot of St Albans 391n., 498n.

More, Sir Thomas 115, 453n.

Morgan, Thomas (supposed author of *Copy of a Letter . . . (Leicester's Commonwealth)*) 6, 7n., 266

Morse, Ruth 28

Mortimer, Edmund, 5th Earl of March 8, 130, 159n., 190n., 241n., 501n.

Mortimer, Roger, 4th Earl of March 138, 190n., 349–50n.

Mortimer, Roger, of Chirke (Marlowe, *Edward II*) 351n.

Mortimer, Roger, of Wigmore, 1st Earl of March (Marlowe, *Edward II*) 159n., 161, 351n.

Mortimer, Sir Edmund (uncle of Edmund, 5th Earl of March) 190n.

Moses (Bible) 403n.

Moss, Roger 464n.

Mowat, Barbara A. 344n., 403n., 506n., 507n.

Mowbray, Thomas, 1st Duke of Norfolk 7, 127–8, 136, 137, 138, 139, 145, 176n., 178n., 179n., 186n., 187n., 191n., 192n., 196n., 207n., 208n., 215n., 217n., 218n., 220n., 372n., 382n., 383n., 384n., 385n., 487n., 495n., 496n.

Mowbray, Thomas, Earl of Norfolk (*2 Henry IV*) 176n., 384n.

Muir, Kenneth 115n., 154, 158, 165, 192n., 230n., 231n., 233n., 246n., 247n., 249n., 258n., 272n., 298n., 351n., 361n., 487n., 491n., 495n., 507n.

Naomi (Bible) 425n.

Nashe, Thomas 114n.

Christ's Tears over Jerusalem 330n.

Have With You to Saffron Walden 114n., 368n., 371n., 471n.

Isle of Dogs, The, 11n.

Piers Penniless, 471n.

Summer's Last Will and Testament, 231n.

Naylor, E.W. 465n.

Neale, J.E. 7n., 8, 21n.

Neoplatonism 410n.

Neptune (classical mythology) 247n.

Nestor (classical legend) 300n., 491n.

Neville, John 39n., 98, 100, 101, 415n.

Neville, Ralph, 1st Earl of Westmoreland (Earl Marshal) 279n., 391n., 446n., 477–8n., 498n.

Neville, Richard, 5th Earl of Salisbury (*2 Henry VI*) 177n.

Nevo, Ruth 43, 69

New Custom 221n.

Newbolt, Henry 497n.

Nichols, John 38n.

Nicoll, Allardyce 65

Nightingale, Benedict 106

Norberry, Sir John 270n., 272n.

Norfolk, 1st Duke of. See Mowbray, Thomas

Norfolk, Earl of. See Mowbray, Thomas

Northumberland, Earl of. See Percy, Sir Henry

Norton, Thomas
Gorboduc (with Sackville) 459n.

Norwich, Bishop of. See Despenser, Henry

Nowottny, Winifred 463n.

Oates, Titus 50

Obedience of a Christian Man, The. See Tyndale, William

O'Brien, Timothy 102n.

Ockham, William of 507n.

Olivier, Sir Laurence 100

Ormonde, 4th Earl of. See Le Botiller, James

Ovid (Publius Ovidius Naso) 123
Fasti 164, 230n., 365n.
Heroides 374n.
Metamorphoses 202n., 355n., 493n.

Oxford, 9th Earl of. See Vere, Sir Robert de

Oxford, 10th Earl of. See Vere, Sir Aubrey de

Page, Malcolm 70, 80, 83, 100, 102, 106
Palingenius, Marcellus Stellatus 351n.
Pallas (classical mythology) 202n.
Palmer, John 9, 16, 32n., 33n., 34
Palmer, Sir James 488n.
Parliament 16, 17n., 20, 23n., 34, 55,
    125, 127, 128, 284n., 288n., 289n.,
    334n., 350n., 360n., 372n., 373n.,
    375n., 380n., 385n., 387n., 390n.,
    392n., 393–4ns., 396n., 401n., 402n.,
    485n., 496n., 497n., 502n., 516n., 531,
    532
Parsons, Robert 6, 7, 10n., 21, 266n.
Partridge, A.C. 519n.
Pasco, Richard 75, 98, 102–4, 168n.
Patch, Howard R. 397n.
Pater, Walter 35, 55, 57, 96, 399n.
Patrick, Saint 258n.
Peacham, Henry 85
Peck, D.C. 7n., 266n.
Peele, George 375n.
    Arraignment of Paris, The 245n.
    Edward I 215n., 245n., 327n., 415n.
Pembroke's Company 11n.
Pennell, Nicholas 105n.
Penry, John 7
Percy, Sir Henry ('Hotspur') 113, 118,
    154, 176–7n., 279n., 291n., 293n.,
    294n., 342n., 378n., 413n., 443n.,
    445n., 476n., 496n., 538n.
Percy, Sir Henry, 1st Earl of
    Northumberland 118n., 130–1, 138,
    140, 154, 176n., 177n., 180n., 279n.,
    280n., 291n., 293n., 314n., 336n.,
    342n., 346n., 350n., 358n., 391n.,
    392n., 403n., 422n., 423n., 446n.,
    476n., 478n., 496n., 497n., 498n.,
    499n., 500n., 526., 527, 540
Percy, Sir Thomas, 1st Earl of Worcester
    126, 280–1n., 286n., 293n., 294n.,
    315n., 421n., 422n., 497n.
Percy, Thomas (*Reliques of Ancient
    English Poetry*) 451n., 487n.
Perrière, Guillaume de la 37
Petersson, Robert T, 115n. 348n.
Phaëton (classical mythology) 73, 76n.,
    80, 163, 355n., 356n., 491n.
Philip II, King of Spain 9
Phillipa of Lancaster, Queen of Portugal
    497n.
Phillips, Augustine 10, 122
Philopatris, John (pseudonymn) 7n.
Pickup, Ronald 98, 102

Pilate, Pontius (Bible) 25, 76, 77, 157,
    310n., 342n, 404n., 423n., 484n.,
    498n., 503n.
Pimlot, Steven 46n., 485n.
Pius V, Pope 9n.
Plantagenet, Richard, 3rd Duke of York
    (*3 Henry VI*) 501n.
Plantagenet, Richard, 4th Duke of York
    (*Richard III*) 501n.
Plato 230n.
Plutarch
    De Exilo 230n.
    De Garrulitate 198n.
    Parallel Lives 296n.
Poel, William 96, 98
Pollard, A.W. 219n., 235n., 261n., 268n.,
    282n., 318n., 364n., 379n., 382n.,
    419n., 422n., 435n., 453n., 463n.,
    485n., 486n., 506n., 507n., 508n., 518,
    519n., 520, 521, 522n., 528
Ponet, John, Bishop of Winchester 18
Pope, Alexander 53, 166, 181n., 194n.,
    205n., 217n., 283n., 287n., 313n.,
    318n., 368n., 391n., 393n., 414n.,
    438n., 444n., 456n., 466n.
Porter, Eric 102
Portugal, Queen of. See Phillipa of
    Lancaster
Proudfoot, Richard 168n., 188n., 197n.,
    212n., 214n., 222n., 225n., 227n.,
    230n., 255n., 257n., 280n., 293n.,
    294n., 304n., 305n., 318n., 334n.,
    338n., 350n., 367n., 396n., 414n.,
    451n., 458n., 462n., 493n., 494n.,
    503n., 507n.
Ptolemy (Claudius Ptolemaeus) 183n.,
    307n., 319n.
Purfoot, Thomas 532
Puritans 7, 8n., 9, 10, 21, 455n.
Puttenham, George 85

Quartermaine, Leon 99
Quayle, Anthony 98, 99
Queen's Men, the 483n.

Rabkin, Norman 27, 28n., 50
Rackin, Phyllis 27, 372–3n.
Raleigh, Sir Walter 5n., 41n., 178n., 487n.
Ramston, Sir Thomas 270n., 272n.
Ramus, Peter 455n.
Ranald, Margaret Loftus 35, 499n.
Rebhorn, Wayne A. 90
Redgrave, Michael 98, 99, 100

Reyher, Paul 269n., 351n., 494n.
Rhind-Tutt, Julian 108
Rich, John 50–1, 53, 54, 92
Richard I ('Coeur de Lion') 246n., 260n.
Richard II 5, 6, 8, 12, 14, 17n., 21, 24, 25,
    39, 114, 115, 116, 117, 127n., 129, 130,
    131–3, 135, 136, 137, 138, 139, 140,
    142n., 144, 146, 149, 150, 151, 152,
    153, 154, 155, 156, 159n., 162, 174n.,
    175n., 176n., 177n., 178n., 179n.,
    180n., 186n., 188n., 190n., 191n.,
    207n., 217n., 226n., 227n., 237n.,
    238n., 241n., 242n., 249n., 253n.,
    259n., 260n., 262n., 263n., 265n.,
    266n., 267n., 268n., 269n., 272n.,
    273n., 274n., 280n., 281n., 283n.,
    285n., 287n., 291n., 298n., 300n.,
    301n., 306n., 309n., 314n., 315n.,
    319n., 321n., 322n., 324n., 326n.,
    335n., 341n., 342n., 350n., 355n.,
    357n., 358n., 359n., 361n., 369n.,
    371n., 372n., 373n., 384n., 385n.,
    386n., 389n., 391n., 396n., 400n.,
    402n., 405n., 406n., 408n., 412n.,
    421n., 427n., 428n., 430n., 431n.,
    432n., 433n., 444n., 449n., 458n.,
    459n., 460n., 462n., 469n., 472n.,
    475n., 479n., 481n., 484n., 485n.,
    487n., 488n., 489n., 491n., 492n.,
    493n., 494n., 495n., 496n., 497n.,
    498n., 499n., 500n., 501n., 502n.,
    504n., 505n., 526, 531, 532, 538n.
Richard III 13, 115, 140, 501n.
Richard of Bordeaux. See Daviot, Gordon
Richard of Cirencester 135
Richard, Earl of Cambridge 440n.
Richardson, Ian 75, 98, 102–4, 168n.
Richardson, Sir Ralph 98
Ritson, Joseph 210n., 249n., 271n.
Rivers, 2nd Earl. See Woodville, Anthony
Ro: Ba: (*The Life of Sir Thomas More*)
    459–60n.
Roberts, John 54
Roberts, Josephine A. xv
Ross, Sir William 177n., 279n., 291n.,
    296n.
Rossiter, A.P. (editor of *Woodstock*) 57,
    59n., 117, 154, 192n., 247n., 253n.,
    255n., 259n., 289n., 490n., 494n., 500n.
Rowe, Nicholas 174n., 185n., 266n.,
    337n., 338n., 362n., 422n.
Rowlands, Richard 6, 7, 489n.
Russell, Stephen 106n.

Ruth (Bible) 425n.
Rutland, Earl of. See Aumerle, Duke of;
    Manners, Francis
Rutter, Carol Chillington 111
Sackville, Thomas
    Gorboduc (with Thomas Norton)
        459n.
    Induction to 'Buckingham' (*Mirror for
        Magistrates*) 462n.
St Albans, Abbot of. See Moot, John
Saintsbury, George 122, 159, 431n.,
    503n.
Salisbury, Earl of. See Montacute, John
    de; Montacute, Sir William;
    Montacute, Thomas de; Neville,
    Richard
Satan (Genesis) 369n.
Saul (Bible) 467n.
Saul, Nigel 174n., 176n., 190n., 191n.
    217n., 238n., 309n., 350n., 460n.,
    474n., 476n., 488n., 500n.
Saviolo, Vincentio 379n.
Scala Sancta (Church of St John
    Lateran) 453n.
Schaefer, George 100
Schlegel, A.W. von 92
Schell, Edgar 152
Schelling, F.E. 344n.
Schmidt, Alexander 453n.
Scofield, Paul 98, 100
Scott-Giles, C.W. 73, 189n., 196n.,
    202n., 491n.
Scroop (Scrope or Lescrope), Sir
    William, Earl of Wiltshire 117, 177n.,
    238n., 264n., 289n., 301n., 305n.,
    309n., 324n., 331n., 493n.
Scroop (Scrope), Richard, Archbishop of
    York 177n., 385n., 386n., 429n., 497n.
Scroop (Scrope), Lord Henry, of
    Masham 177n.
Scroop (Scrope), Sir Stephen, 2nd Baron
    Scrope of Masham 177n.
Scroope, Sir Thomas (*Woodstock*) 144,
    151, 177n., 487n.
Scroop (Scrope), Richard, 1st Baron
    Scrope of Bolton 177n.
Scroop (Scrope or Lescrope), Sir
    Stephen (son of Richard, 1st Baron
    Scrope of Bolton) 177n., 264n.,
    314n., 324n., 337n., 339n., 344n.,
    358n., 468n., 493n.
Seely, Sir Bennet 477n.
Senior, Michael 494n.

Seymour, Thomas, 4th Baron de Saint
  Maur 295–6n.
Shakespeare Allusion-Book 91
Shakespeare's England 364n. 366n.
Shakespeare Ladies Club 53
Shakespeare, William
  Plays and other works in the
    Shakespeare canon
    All's Well That Ends Well 276n.,
      333n., 441n., 468n.
    Antony and Cleopatra 4, 340n., 361n.
    As You Like It 123n., 258n., 413n.,
      463n., 466n., 495n.
    Comedy of Errors, The 57, 495n.
    Coriolanus 230n., 381n., 432n.
    Cymbeline 184n., 246n., 271n.,
      294n., 311n., 379n.
    Edward III 120n., 153, 177n.,
      213n., 245n., 255n., 260n., 271n.,
      316n., 348n., 454n., 493n.
    *First Part of the Contention
      (2 Henry VI)* 536n., 538n.
    Hamlet 3, 122, 126n., 180n., 185n.,
      221n., 222n., 225n., 236n., 250n.,
      255n., 265n., 275n., 276n., 277n.,
      294n., 295n., 303n., 307n., 325n.,
      329n., 361n., 363n., 371n., 374.,
      376n., 402n., 406n., 410n., 416n.,
      429n. 471n., 473n., 495n., 520
    Henry IV, Part 1 42, 90, 91, 111, 114n.,
      118, 119, 130, 144n., 159n., 169,
      176n., 177n., 178n., 190n., 229n.,
      236n., 244n., 280n., 281n., 293n.,
      294n., 295n., 297n., 299n., 302n.,
      304n., 312n., 315n., 319n., 336n.,
      344n., 348n., 349n., 352n., 376n.,
      379n., 408n., 412n., 413n., 416n.,
      422n., 423n., 438n., 441n., 443n.,
      444n., 445n., 446n., 468n., 478n.,
      483n., 492n., 515n., 538n., 541
    Henry IV, Part 2 24, 42, 74, 77, 91,
      105, 114n., 118, 119, 176n.,
      177n., 181n., 191n., 199n., 216n.,
      220n., 274n., 292n., 315n., 364n.,
      384n., 393n., 400n., 421n., 422n.,
      429n., 443n., 444n., 451n., 483n.,
      486n., 515n., 517, 536n., 541.
    Henry V 7, 74n., 118, 119, 156,
      176n., 177n., 184n., 214n., 221n.,
      242n., 245n., 272n., 326n., 341n.,
      385n., 417n., 426n., 440n., 457n.,
      464n., 468–9n., 481n., 501n.,
      512n., 541

    Henry VI, Part 1 3, 112, 116,
      120n., 137, 152, 159, 175n.,
      177n., 181n., 195n., 241n.,
      316n., 323n., 330n., 332n.,
      348n., 377n., 386n., 387n.,
      390n., 394n., 418n., 463n.,
      480n., 482n., 494n., 501n.
    Henry VI, Part 2 3, 52, 116, 117,
      120n., 137, 147n., 159, 175n.,
      177n., 178n., 187n., 189n., 201n.,
      208n., 250n., 258n., 305n., 312n.,
      317n., 354n., 374n., 381n., 387n.,
      390n., 416n., 426n., 459n., 475n.,
      493n., 494n., 495n., 528
    Henry VI, Part 3 3, 41, 112, 116,
      120n., 137, 139, 159, 168n.,
      175n., 176n., 183n., 197n., 271n.,
      276n., 320n., 327n., 332n., 355n.,
      387n., 390n., 401n., 403n., 412n.,
      423n., 449n., 460n., 488n., 494n.,
      495n., 500n., 501n., 541
    Henry VIII 58, 494n.
    Julius Caesar 4, 214n., 242n.,
      289n., 307n., 332n., 394n., 422n.,
      481–2n.
    King John 42, 112, 120n., 121n.,
      179n., 181n., 204n., 236n., 248n.,
      260n., 271n., 297n., 300n., 307n.,
      325n., 330n., 331n., 340n., 349n.,
      369n., 393n., 398n., 409n., 420n.,
      421n., 458n., 462n., 472n., 482n.,
      487n., 488n., 494n., 520n.
    King Lear 3, 67, 91, 92, 122, 208n.,
      224n., 228n., 241n., 247n., 255n.,
      257n., 268n., 283n., 295n., 316n.,
      317n., 354n., 393n., 405n., 412n.,
      420–1n., 432n., 436n., 439n.,
      459n., 463n., 467n.
    Love's Labour's Lost 57, 63, 112,
      190n., 298n., 305n., 327n., 381n.,
      409n., 451n., 455n.
    Macbeth 184n., 193n., 213n., 214n.,
      218n., 258n., 269n., 274n., 303n.,
      305n., 317n., 327n., 329n., 330n.,
      338n., 356n., 366n., 390n., 394n.,
      432n., 446n., 447n., 492n.
    Measure for Measure 409n., 446n.,
      452n., 454n., 455n., 458n.
    Merchant of Venice, The 121n.,
      258n., 272n., 275n., 276n., 330n.,
      393n., 432n., 454n., 463n., 503n.
    Merry Wives of Windsor, The 292n.,
      469n.

Midsummer Night's Dream, A 57,
112, 317n., 325n., 364n., 374n.,
384n., 410n., 482–3n.
Much Ado About Nothing 191n.,
259n., 363n., 417n. 426n., 515n.,
536n.
Othello 122, 219n., 236n., 272n.,
301n., 303n., 400n., 446n., 466n.,
480n.
Passionate Pilgrim, The 202n.,
459n.
Pericles 312n., 406n., 494n.
Rape of Lucrece, The 57, 141, 244n.,
430n., 459n.
Richard II
  adaptations of 50–3, 92–5,
    104–5, 108–11
  Aumerle
    name change of 68, 168
    Theobald and 52–3
    Wroughton and 92–3
  Bolingbroke,
    alternative views of 3, 17,
      23–4, 25–50, 309n.
    ambiguous characterization of
      3, 25–7, 29–30, 31, 32–3,
      34, 36, 40, 43–4, 50, 106,
      151, 236n., 273n., 298n.,
      309n., 311n., 313n., 341n.,
      374n., 383n., 385n., 482n.,
      492n.
    as man of destiny 23
    as player-king 3, 40, 42, 74,
      104, 431n.
    as pragmatist 3, 35, 39, 43,
      67, 68, 96
    as subordinate character 102
    associated with Cain and Abel
      77
    compassion and magnanimity
      of 42, 43–4, 133, 384n.,
      479n., 480n.
    expanded role of 103–5
    guilt of 3, 28, 43, 44, 56, 77,
      78, 119, 135, 140, 157, 161,
      479n.
    Lancastrian and Yorkist
      prejudices towards 23–4,
      498n.
    language of 57, 60–1, 67,
      68–9, 224–5n., 292n.,
      300n., 302n., 341n., 342n.,
      343n., 344n., 398n.

    motivation of 23, 31–2, 105,
      124–5, 129, 131–3, 137,
      143–4, 161, 273n., 298n.,
      301n., 303n., 304n., 341n.,
      346n., 383n., 385n., 492n.
    patriotism of 27, 69, 235n.
    relation of, to later histories
      77, 118, 119, 129–30, 176n.,
      211n., 236n., 280n., 295n.,
      304n., 336n., 349n., 384n.,
      387n., 412n., 413n., 422n.,
      443n., 481n., 483n.
    shifting identity of 44n., 68,
      75, 110, 168
    shrewdness of 23, 49
    Tate and 51
    York's description of 40–1,
      429–31ns.
  censorship of 4, 50–4, 165,
    204n., 271n., 387n., 453n.,
    458–9n., 504n., 508n., 513,
    516
  choric elements in 22, 40–1, 59,
    75, 105, 360n., 513n.
  conspiracy scenes in 41–3, 59,
    93, 131–3, 502n.
  deposition scene in 10n., 33–8,
    54, 56, 69, 125, 133, 134, 154,
    157, 161, 165–6, 392–412ns.,
    506–7, 510, 511, 513n.,
    515–17, 516n., 520, 522, 523,
    525, 532, 540–1
  early revivals of 53–5, 92, 93–5,
    121
  Flint Castle scene in 25–7, 32–3,
    109, 121, 336–60ns.
  formality and ritualism in 26,
    35, 42, 54–5, 58–60, 101, 105,
    109, 111, 123, 124, 160, 161,
    167, 179n., 180n., 181n.,
    185n., 190n., 195n., 196n.,
    197n., 198n., 199n., 207n.,
    208n., 209n., 212n., 215n.,
    216n., 217n., 222n., 223n.,
    248–9n., 264n., 294n., 299n.,
    331n., 336n., 341n., 344n.,
    346n., 350n., 351n., 357n.,
    358n., 373n., 375n., 386n.,
    395n., 399–401ns., 446n.,
    476n., 495n., 513
  garden and green world in 33,
    56, 58, 59, 69–70, 71, 76, 81,
    86, 109, 114n., 122, 123, 133,

135, 158, 161, 221n., 245n.,
246n., 305n., 307n., 360–1n.,
363n., 365n., 366n., 371n.,
389n., 423n., 483n., 491n.,
494–5n., 513n.
Gaunt
  as critic of Richard 47, 48, 54,
    100, 128, 131, 147, 149
  language of 56, 57–8, 59, 60,
    63, 66–8, 69, 70, 71, 76, 77,
    79, 82, 87, 254n.
  parting of, with son 40, 68–9,
    128
  passive obedience, belief in
    19, 27, 28–9, 128, 134–5,
    146, 150, 153
  praise of England of 4, 59, 60,
    63, 70, 82, 93, 134, 142,
    149, 158, 164–5, 245–8ns,
    487–8n., 488n.
  role of, played by Shakespeare
    122
  support of divine right 18
Gloucester's death in 4, 27–8,
  30, 33, 44, 47, 48–9, 76, 125,
  127, 145n., 146, 148, 153,
  187–8n., 191–2n., 194n.,
  200n., 204n., 219n., 220n.,
  221n., 223n., 224n., 253n.,
  255n., 256n., 319n., 373n.,
  374n., 375n., 377n., 380n.,
  383n., 384n., 485n.
Great Chain of Being in 34, 36,
  72, 80–1, 189n., 307n., 343n.,
  345n., 416n., 418n., 491n.
Groom 44, 104, 133, 134, 174n.,
  429n., 464n., 467n., 468n.,
  469n., 470n., 504n.
imagery and motifs in 64–5
  birth and death 82–3, 246n.,
    250n., 275n., 281n., 347n.,
    410n.
  blots and stains 71, 78, 223n.,
    247–8n., 323n., 327n.,
    345n., 414n., 450n.
  buckets and well 36, 61, 80,
    160n., 370n., 396–7n., 412n.
  crown and jewels 74, 229n.,
    246n., 252n., 274n.,
    329–30ns, 353n. 368n.,
    395–6n., 418n., 488n.
  earth and blood 44, 69–71, 78,
    80, 135, 142, 193n., 194n.,

198n., 200n., 201n., 212n.,
  232n., 255n., 308n., 316n.,
  328–9n., 341n., 347–8n.,
  349n., 390n., 401n., 415n.,
  483n., 493n.
elements 18, 79–81, 342n.,
  343n., 474n.
fortune, destiny and
  providence 23, 24, 29,
  40–1, 80, 81, 82, 130, 139,
  144, 160, 199n., 250n.,
  279n., 295n., 297n., 311n.,
  335n., 362n., 370n., 376n.,
  397n., 410n., 417n., 463n.,
  470n., 484n., 494n.
language 61, 65–9, 74,
  220–1n., 224–5n., 242n.,
  352n., 353n., 369n., 405n.
legal bonding 248n.
memento mori 70, 74, 76,
  82–3, 105, 110, 270n.,
  330n., 390n., 494n.
mirror 36, 38, 46, 61, 75, 79,
  104, 134, 135, 138, 152,
  164, 254n., 404n., 405n.,
  407n., 408n., 409n., 410n.,
  490n., 495n.
nature 70–1, 135, 245n.,
  291n., 307n., 311n., 317n.,
  319n., 325n., 343n.,
  347–8n., 360–1n., 364n.,
  366n., 367n., 416n., 435n.,
  423n., 435n., 483n.
perspectives 3, 61, 75, 79, 85,
  276n., 410n., 490n.
pilgrimage 77, 211n., 226n.,
  228n., 258n., 310n.
public vs. private 39, 41–3,
  190n., 200n., 248n., 274n.,
  309n., 352n., 427n., 428n.,
  460–1ns., 479n., 480n.
seasons 81, 142, 364n., 366n.,
  382n., 406n., 424n., 435n.,
  501n.
sun 26, 30, 71–4, 78, 79, 142,
  230n., 308n., 319n., 320n.,
  335n., 337n., 343n.,
  344–5n., 355n., 377n.,
  379n., 380n., 401n., 406n.,
  491n., 494n.
sweet and sour 79–80, 213n.,
  232n., 242n., 260n., 316n.,
  323n., 333n., 334n., 371n.,

404n., 416n., 454n., 455n., 465n., 480n.
symbolic twinship in 104, 110–11
time 77, 81–2, 225n., 226n., 256n., 262n., 465n., 466n., 467n.
vengeance 27, 49, 76, 134, 146, 153, 189n., 200n., 201n., 212n., 381n.
venom 78, 258n., 316n., 317n., 493n.
verticality 80–1, 105, 212n., 217n., 345n., 356–7n., 368n., 370n., 397n., 398n., 422n., 501n.
invented material in 133–6, 200n., 233n., 241n., 274n., 291n., 293n., 300n., 310n., 311n., 339n., 360n., 372n., 374n., 484n., 387n., 401n., 415n., 428n., 429n., 436n., 442n., 443n., 460n., 476n., 481n., 483n., 487n., 495n., 496n., 497n., 500n.
lamentation and tears in 56, 59, 75, 79, 110, 142, 147, 149, 157, 159, 200n., 212n., 222n., 224n., 234n., 276n., 277n., 278n., 316n., 322n., 332n., 352n., 354n., 359n., 363n., 371n., 404n., 406n., 410n., 417n., 420n., 425n., 426n., 428n., 432n., 466n., 490n., 499n., 500n., 501n., 513n.
medievalism vs. modernism in 3, 67, 106
monarchy, attitudes towards, in 17–23, 50, 147, 149–50, 269n., 288n., 302n., 329–30ns., 337n., 343n., 344n., 345n., 346n., 348n., 349–50n., 352–3n., 356–7n., 368n., 369n., 387n., 389n., 392n., 393–4n., 297n., 298n., 406n., 409n., 418n., 432n., 460–7ns., 488n.
Mowbray
  as crusader 77, 128, 384n.
  associated with Cain 76–7, 188–9n.
  patriotism of 69
  reminiscence of, in *Henry IV Part 2*, 119

speech of, contrasted with Bolingbroke's 57, 183n.
murder scene in 44–6, 141, 147, 460–75ns.
musical quality of 4, 55, 56, 57, 64–5, 95, 98, 161, 322n., 323n., 324n.
nobles and commons, sympathy for, in 22
Northumberland
  as Bolingbroke's agent 21, 28, 39, 47, 270n., 292n., 314n., 336n., 337n., 340n., 342n., 349n. 350n., 351n., 354n., 355n., 356n., 358n., 391n., 401n., 407n., 421n., 422n., 425n., 477–8n.
  as critic and prosecutor of Richard 21, 28, 54, 265n., 266n., 268n., 269n., 270–4ns., 401n., 402n., 404–7ns.
  fulsomeness of 29, 292n.
  later histories and 176n.
  plain speech of 59–60
  Theobald and 53
  treason of, forecast by Richard 39, 80, 82, 119, 140, 142, 422n., 423n.
  unceremoniousness of 26, 68, 337n., 341n., 346n., 351n., 404n., 421n.
popularity of, in non-English-speaking countries 109
proverbial elements in 60, 88–9, 158, 181n., 191n., 194n., 196n., 213n., 214n., 215n., 219n., 224n., 225n., 226n., 230n., 242n., 245n., 249n., 257n., 258n., 266n., 270n., 287n., 290n., 292n., 303n., 305n., 317n., 322n., 325n., 327n., 332n., 344n., 362n., 363n., 381n., 385n., 386n., 395n., 397n., 398n., 407n., 416n., 419n., 425n., 449n., 452n., 454n., 458n., 462n., 470n., 482n., 493n., 495n.
quarrel scenes in 27, 30, 49, 56, 58–9, 60, 65, 68, 70, 71, 93, 99, 105, 125, 127, 128, 136, 137, 179–99ns., 205n., 207–24ns., 372–3n., 374–85ns. 493n.

Queen
  as commentator on Richard's
    plight 33, 78, 275–8ns.,
    281n., 360–1n., 369n.,
    370n., 371n., 415n.,
    418–19ns.
  as emblem of sorrow 56, 61,
    82, 274n., 275n., 276n.,
    277n., 278n., 360n., 361n.,
    362n., 363n., 371n.,
    424–7ns.
  as evoker of sympathy 29, 48,
    274n., 360–3ns., 370n.,
    371n., 415n., 416n., 417n.,
    424–7ns.
  as refractor of emotional
    change 75
  biblical Fall and 33, 76, 78,
    369n.
  Henry IV, Part 1 and 119,
    416n.
  Tate and 51–2
  Theobald and 53
  Wroughton and 93
rhetoric and rhetorical figures in
  83–90, 112, 167, 182n., 195n.,
  198n., 201n., 212n., 228n.,
  245n., 249n., 251n., 261n.,
  299n., 317n., 337n., 340n.,
  343n., 344n., 348n., 362n.,
  375n., 387–8n., 391n., 408n.,
  425n., 427n., 439n., 452n.,
  455n., 466n., 488n.
rhyme in 57–8, 60, 92, 112, 166,
  175n., 181n., 183n., 194n.,
  195n., 196n., 199n., 206n.,
  212n., 219n., 220n., 224n.,
  225n., 226n., 242n., 243n.,
  244n., 251n., 256n., 258n.,
  263n., 264n., 268n., 278n.,
  286n., 287n., 305n., 312n.,
  322n., 323n., 328n., 332n.,
  333n., 334n., 354n., 360n.,
  368n., 369n., 371n., 391n.,
  394n., 398n., 412n., 413n.,
  414n., 424n., 426n., 432n.,
  435n., 451n., 453n., 454n.,
  455n., 456n., 457n., 464n.,
  468n., 471n., 473n., 474n.,
  477–8n., 482n., 483n., 492n.,
  502–3n., 503n., 527
Richard
  as martyr 3, 17, 24, 30,
    35–8, 40, 49, 102, 105,
    106, 110, 119, 134, 255n.,
    327n., 360n., 394n., 404n.,
    474n., 485n., 495n.,
    498–9n., 499n.
  as player-king 3, 17, 26, 30,
    32, 34–6, 38, 39, 40, 45–6,
    69, 74, 96, 104, 110, 125,
    147, 161, 323n., 324n.,
    329n., 330n., 334n., 335n.,
    353n., 354n., 372n., 395n.,
    397n., 409n., 410n., 413n.,
    415n., 460n., 463n., 466n.
  blurred guilt of 28, 43, 44,
    48–9, 134, 163, 223n.,
    251n., 402n., 461n., 465n.
  charm of 45, 99, 161
  doom-eagerness of 26, 30–1,
    126, 130, 134, 324n., 328n.,
    329n., 347n., 352n., 393n.,
    409n.
  identity crisis of 3, 17–18,
    30–1, 34–8, 43–4, 45–6, 64,
    67, 75, 96, 110, 151, 153–4,
    168, 275n., 331n., 346n.,
    399n., 405n., 406n., 407n.,
    409n., 410n., 464n., 490n.
  immaturity and youth of 24,
    47, 110, 147, 180n., 188n.,
    249n., 263n., 266n., 355n.,
    359n., 406n., 444n.
  Lancastrian and Yorkist
    prejudices towards 23–4,
    158, 498n.
  language of 3, 36, 39, 45–6,
    57, 58, 60–1, 66–7, 68, 69,
    86, 224–5n., 317n.,
    352–3n., 398n., 415n.,
    419n., 422n., 466n.
  later histories and 119, 220n.,
    280n., 302n., 315n., 336n.,
    384n., 416n., 422n., 429n.,
    444n., 476n., 481n.
  mixed responses to 3, 17,
    23–5, 26, 28, 29, 31–2, 33,
    35–8, 39–40, 44, 45–6, 47,
    48–9, 50, 104, 158, 188n.,
    189n., 190n., 217n., 236n.,
    261n., 264n., 310n., 345n.,
    393n., 395n.
  motivation of 27–8, 48–9, 105,
    106, 124–5, 127–8, 129, 130,
    186n., 191n., 194n., 204n.,

212n., 217n., 220n., 223n., 224n., 233n., 235n., 236n., 257n., 264n.

parting of, from Queen 39–40, 56, 59, 119, 125, 133, 141, 142, 157–8, 162, 281n., 415–27ns., 500–1n.

psychological complexity of, 1 31–2, 36–8, 45–6, 75, 104, 105, 106, 109–11, 135, 137, 147, 151, 180n., 328n., 331n., 334n., 352–3n., 395n., 399n., 401n., 409n., 463n., 464n., 466n.

sacredness of 1, 3, 17–18, 28, 30–1, 32, 34, 35, 36, 44, 48, 49, 66, 95, 98, 101, 102, 106, 134n., 139, 150, 161, 190n., 203–4n., 300n., 320–1n., 331n., 337n., 346n., 347n., 387n., 390n., 395n., 399n., 400n., 404n., 423n., 432n., 456n., 474n., 492–3n.

self-consciousness, narcissism and self-discovery of 3–4, 17, 26, 31, 34, 36–8, 39–40, 45–6, 61, 64, 69, 74, 75, 96, 104, 126–7, 135, 254n., 260n., 316n., 317n., 323n., 324n., 329n., 330n., 331n., 354n., 397n., 407n., 409–10n., 415n., 420n., 427n., 461n., 465n., 500n.

sentimentality of 26, 30, 31, 161, 212n., 222n., 224n.,316n., 354n., 404n., 420n., 426n., 470n.

soliloquy of 45–6, 64, 95, 105, 113, 141, 460–7ns.

Tate and 51–2, 111

Theobald and 52–3, 111

weakness of 24, 26, 27, 28, 29, 30, 31, 33, 39, 49, 66, 74, 78, 85, 92, 93, 95, 96, 99, 100, 102, 105, 126, 130, 198–9n., 217n., 265n., 337n., 340n., 345n., 351n., 356n., 370n., 394n., 418–9n.

Wroughton and 92–3, 111

structure of 28, 30, 33, 40, 43, 47, 48–50, 59, 65, 71–3, 80, 85, 88, 92, 96, 104, 138, 159–60, 179n., 200n., 207n., 233n., 273n., 274n., 275n., 284n., 291n., 306n., 307n., 309n., 314n., 336n., 360n., 370n., 372–3n., 376n., 379n., 384n., 385n., 389n., 393n., 396–7n., 411n., 415n., 421n., 427n., 428n., 442n., 448n., 451n., 458n., 470n., 476n., 482n., 484n., 492n., 495–6n., 512–13n., 528

style, plain and golden, in 61n., 63–4, 201n., 242n., 245n., 254n., 276n., 332n., 344n., 381n., 387–8n., 415n., 425n., 447n., 449n., 451n., 455n., 466n., 516n.

subordinate characters, function of, in 47–8, 92, 127–8, 178n., 199n., 200n., 227n., 239n., 270n., 274n., 293n., 309n., 339n., 344n., 360–1n., 363n., 373n., 379n., 391n., 401n., 421n., 428n., 438n., 439–40n., 443n., 558n., 464n., 468n., 473n., 475n., 492n., 496n.

topicality and 4, 6–16, 50–4, 122n., 165

versification and metre in 58, 100, 112, 166, 180n., 195n., 197n., 199n., 204n., 210n., 214n., 217n., 221n., 222n., 226n., 229n., 234n., 237n., 244n., 246n., 247n., 251n., 252n., 253n., 254n., 257n., 266n., 268n., 269n., 271n., 272n., 277n., 279n., 280n., 281n., 282n., 283–4n., 284n., 285n., 286n., 287n., 288n., 292n., 293n., 297n., 300n., 303n., 304n., 305n., 307n., 312n., 313n., 315n., 318n., 320–1n., 321n., 322n., 323n., 324n., 325n., 326n., 327n., 331n., 337n., 338n., 339n., 340n., 345n., 348n., 349n., 351n., 357n., 360n., 363n., 367n., 368n., 370n., 373n., 375n., 379n., 382n., 384n., 385n., 386n., 388n., 389n., 391n., 392n., 394n., 396n., 403n., 405n., 407n., 418n.,

419n., 422–3n., 430n., 431n.,
434n., 435n., 436n., 437n.,
438n., 441n., 443n., 445n.,
446n., 447n., 449n., 451n.,
453n., 457n., 459n., 461n.,
462n., 466n., 468n., 469n.,
470n., 471n., 472–3n., 473n.,
474n., 477n., 478n., 482n.,
486n., 502n., 518, 519, 527,
528, 538
wordplay in 4, 35, 39, 61, 63, 87,
88–9, 92, 112, 142, 162, 184n.,
193n., 196n., 197n., 200n.,
221n., 228–9n., 230n., 233n.,
234n., 235n., 236n., 240n.,
241n., 243n., 244n., 247n.,
248n., 250–1n., 252n., 254n.,
256n., 261n., 262n., 266n.,
268n., 269n., 274n., 277n.,
292n., 294n., 298n., 299n.,
301n., 317n., 321n., 324n.,
325n., 327n., 331n., 332n.,
338n., 343n., 346n., 347n.,
348n., 351n., 352n., 353n.,
354n., 356n., 366n., 368n.,
369n., 372n., 379n., 380n.,
381n., 394n., 395n., 398n.,
399n., 401n., 404n., 412n.,
417n., 419n., 422n., 423n.,
424n., 426n., 427n., 433n.,
435n., 450n., 452n., 455n.,
456n., 465n., 466n., 467n.,
468n., 471n., 474n., 482n.,
503n.
York
as critic of Bolingbroke and
Northumberland 23,
29–30, 299n., 300n., 303n.,
337n., 338n.
as critic of Richard 22, 48–9,
93, 243–4ns., 259–63ns.
as political reflector 40–1, 75,
261–3ns., 283n., 286n.,
287n., 309n., 432n.
as Richard's surrogate 29–30,
33, 59, 282–3ns., 285n.,
Aumerle and 41–3, 428n.,
433–4n., 437n.
characterization of 3, 40, 43,
47–8, 259n., 261n., 263n.,
264n., 282n., 283–4n.,
285n., 286n., 300n., 304n.,
304–5n., 309n., 337n.,

345n., 428n., 439n., 450n.,
452n., 502n.
comic elements in 48, 134,
299n., 429n., 438n.,
438–9n., 451n., 455n.,
503n.
conflicting loyalties of 29,
154, 286n., 287n., 303n.,
304n., 305n., 337n., 345n.,
428n., 432n., 503n.
description of Bolingbroke and
Richard 40–1, 56, 64, 91,
93–5, 98, 113, 119, 134, 141,
154, 427–33ns., 501–2n.
language of 58, 59, 63, 80, 81,
166, 285n., 286n., 299n.,
429n., 431n., 434n., 435n.,
437n., 438n., 439n., 452n.,
490n., 502–3n.
loss of identity 43, 304–5n.,
502n.
support of divine right 18,
48, 68, 78, 300n.
Tate and 51
Theobald and 53
Richard III 3, 44, 91, 102, 106,
112, 116, 120n., 122, 137, 139,
180n., 190n., 240n., 243n., 250n.
252n., 254n., 259n., 267n., 315n.,
329n., 334n., 350n., 380n., 385n.,
387n., 390n., 393n., 404n., 405n.,
412n., 415n., 421n., 435n., 457n.,
467n., 474n., 475n. 482n., 483n.,
494n., 501n., 515n., 541
Romeo and Juliet 1, 112, 121n.,
218n., 230n., 245n., 275n., 299n.,
311n., 316n., 317n., 328n., 348n.,
399n., 424n., 426n., 446n., 451n.,
455n., 471n.
Sir Thomas More, The Book of
415n., 453n., 503n., 519n., 520
Sonnets, The 57, 64, 220n., 345n.,
382n., 435n.
Taming of the Shrew, The 182n.,
231n., 344n., 384n., 416n., 424n.,
450, 465n.
Tempest, The 245n., 269n., 316n.,
343n., 369n., 398n., 420n.,
432n.
Timon of Athens 231n., 328n.
Titus Andronicus 1, 112, 181n.,
198n., 257n., 276n., 329n., 344n.,
394n., 416n., 520

Troilus and Cressida 67, 184n.,
198n., 282n., 300n., 332n., 384n.,
403n., 408n., 409n., 418n., 426n.,
454n., 491n.
Twelfth Night 251n., 299n., 363n.,
365n., 432n., 490n.
Two Gentlemen of Verona 230n.,
251n., 355n., 374n., 419n., 420n.,
423n., 466n., 471n.
Two Noble Kinsmen, The 364n.,
381n., 470n., 501n.
Venus and Adonis 57, 244n., 260n.,
376n., 424n., 459n.
Winter's Tale, The 215n., 374n.,
412n., 420n.
Shapiro, I.A. 115
Sharpe, Robert 122n.
Shaw, Fiona 98, 108, 110–11
Shaw, George Bernard 58
Shaw, Glen Byam 99
Shaw, Robert 11n.
Shelley, Percy Bysshe 479n.
Shelley, Sir Thomas, of Aylesbury 479n.
Shenar, Paul 443n.
Shewring, Margaret 50n., 54n., 96, 99,
102, 110, 357n., 480n.
Shirley, James
Contention of Ajax and Ulysses, The
256n.
Sicilian Usurper, The (adaptation of
Richard II). See Tate, Nahum
Sidney, Sir Philip 18, 189n., 282n., 426n.
Apology for Poetry, An 58, 63, 139, 244n.
Arcadia 140
Astrophil and Stella 420n.
Sidney, Sir Robert 113
Simmes, Valentine 515, 516, 517, 519n.,
530, 532, 533, 538
Simpson, Richard 6, 7, 489n.
Sisson, Charles J. 350n., 487n., 524n.
Sixtus V, Pope 503n.
Smidt, Kristian 24n., 48, 49, 192n.,
219n., 234n.
Smith, R.M. 134n.
Smith, Sir Thomas 18
'Song of a Beggar and a King'. See
Johnson, Richard
Spain (Castile), Queen of. See Catherine
of Lancaster
Spanish Armada 246n.
Spencer, Gabriel 11n.
Spenser, Edmund 189n., 231n.
Faerie Queene, The 140–1, 195n.,

340n., 417n., 430n., 450n.
Letter to Gabriel Harvey 298n.
View of the Present State of Ireland, A,
258n.
Spenser, 'Hugh', Lord (i.e. Sir Thomas
Despenser, Baron, former Earl of
Gloucester) 433n., 476–7n., 477n.,
478n., 514, 519, 526, 527
Spevack, Marvin 174n.
Sprague, Arthur Colby 92, 93n., 98,
178n.
Stafford, Edmund, Bishop of Exeter
289n.
Stanley, Ferdinando, Lord Strange, 5th
Earl of Derby 9
Staunton, Howard 240n.
Stavropoulos, Janet C. 150, 152n.
Steevens, George 286n., 297n., 384n.
Stirling, Brents 30, 32n., 346n.
Stow, John 140, 155, 156, 201n., 315n.,
358n., 415n., 442n., 443n., 496n.,
497n.
Straw, Jack 187n.
Stredder, James 102n., 104
Stuart, Lady Arabella 9
Stuart, Lady Margaret, Countess of
Lennox 9
Stuart, Mary. See Mary, Queen of Scots
Stubbs, William 19n.
Suchet, David 106
Surrey, Duke of. See Holland, Sir
Thomas
Sudbury, Simon, Archbishop of
Canterbury 489n.
Swan Theatre, 121, 122, 207n. 344n.
Swinburne, Algernon Charles 159,
502n., 503n.
Sylvester, Joshua 165, 245n., 246n.,
248n., 487n., 488n.

Talbert, Ernest William 18, 19n., 25,
355n., 385n., 407n., 498n., 506n.
Talbot, Sir John 386n.
Tarquin (Lucius Tarquinius Priscus)
365n.
Tate, Nahum 50–1, 92, 111
Taylor, Gary (Oxford editor) 194n.,
261n., 279n., 293n., 315n., 318n.,
325n., 359n., 386n., 435n., 459n.,
496n., 507n., 514n., 515n., 516n.,
519n., 520, 523–4, 524n., 526, 528,
529
Taylor, Paul 111n.

Teucer (classical mythology) 230n.
Tey, Josephine. See Daviot, Gordon
Theatre (Elizabethan playhouse) 120, 121, 122
Theobald, Lewis 52–3, 92, 111, 166, 185n., 211n., 217n., 226n., 253n., 261n., 348n., 399n., 454n., 457n., 492n., 493n.
Thorndike, Ashley H. 159
Threlfall, David 109
Tibetot, Milicent 177n.
Tillyard, E.M.W.
   Elizabethan World Picture, The 345n., 416n., 418n.
   Shakespeare's History Plays 136, 153, 154
Tilney, Sir Edmund, Master of the Revels 517
Timberlake, Philip W. 117
Time (allegorical figure) 256n., 262n., 485n.
Tobin, J.J.M. 114n.
Tomlinson, Michael 49–50
Tooker, William 492n.
Tourneur, Cyril
   Atheist's Tragedy, The 342n.
Tragedy of King Richard the II, The (adaptation of *Richard II*). See Theobald, Lewis
Traïson (*Chronique de la Traïson et Mort de Richart Deux Roy Dengleterre*) 124, 152, 154–8, 188n., 208n., 211n., 214n., 238n., 256n., 305n., 308n., 355n., 358n., 360n., 361n., 379n., 387n., 391n., 394n., 428n., 429n., 434n., 440n., 474n., 492n., 496–7n., 498n., 499n., 500–1n., 511n.
Tree, Sir Herbert Beerbohm 96, 98
Tresilian, Sir Robert 117, 138, 144, 145, 146
Trewin, J.C. 39n., 100, 415n.
Troilus and Cressida. See Dryden, John
Troublesome Reign of King John, The, Part 1 366n., 494n., 503n.; *Part 2*, 248n.
Trousdale, Marion 83–5
True Tragedy of Richard the Third, The 327n., 483n.
Tudor, Margaret (sister of Henry VIII) 8
Tudor, Mary. See Mary, Queen of England
Tyler, Wat 187n.
Tynan, Kenneth 100
Tyndale, William 193n., 419n.

Tyrant of Sicily, The (adaptation of *Richard II*). See Tate, Nahum
Tyrrel, James 501n.
Udall, Nicholas 287n.
Ure, Peter (Arden[2] editor) xv, 15, 144n., 155, 193n., 195n., 201n., 203n., 215n., 218n., 239n., 245n., 246n., 248n., 250n., 254n., 256n., 267n., 268n., 269n., 270n., 271n., 291n., 302n., 303n., 308n., 313n., 316n., 317n., 327n., 329n., 330n., 333n., 336n., 355n., 358n., 365n., 367n., 368n., 370n., 374n., 376n., 382n., 385n., 386n., 388n., 389n., 391n., 395n., 397n., 398m., 401n., 407n., 408n., 413n., 416n., 419n., 428n., 430n., 431n., 434n., 441n., 442n., 456n., 457n., 459n., 460n., 462n., 468n., 475n., 481n., 483n., 486n., 487n., 490n., 492n., 493n., 497n., 498n., 499n., 503n., 504n., 505n., 506n., 515n., 519, 522, 523

Venus (classical mythology) 491n.
Vere, Sir Aubrey de, 10th Earl of Oxford 514, 519, 526, 527
Vere, Sir Robert de, 9th Earl of Oxford, Duke of Ireland 6
Vergil, Polydore 136, 140, 415n.
Verity, A.W. 159, 208n., 332n., 388n., 396n., 419n., 441n., 466n., 474n., 503n.
Verstegan, Richard (pseudonymn) 7n.
Vickers, Brian xv, 86n., 431n.
Virtus (allegorical figure) 37, 397n.

Wager, W.
   Longer Thou Livest the More Fool Thou Art, The, 221n.
Walker, W.S. 454n.
Walkington, Thomas 9, 501n.
Waller, R.D 117n.
Walpole, Sir Robert 51, 53, 54
Walsingham, Sir Francis 7
Walsingham, Thomas 140, 158
Walton, J.K. 507n.
Wardle, Irving 44n.
Warner, David 98, 102
Warner, Deborah 98, 108, 110–11, 429n.
Wars of the Roses 1, 9, 140, 175n., 390n., 416n.
Warwick, 12th Earl of. See Beauchamp, Thomas

Waterton, Robert 270n., 272n.
Watt, A.F. 296n.
Webb, John 155, 504n.
Webster, Margaret 98, 99
Webster, John 91
  Duchess of Malfi, The 329n., 491n.
  Westward Ho (with Dekker) 441n.
  White Devil, The 282n., 397n.
Weeks, J.R. 117n.
Wells, Stanley (Oxford editor) xvi, 56,
  102n., 169, 181n., 185n., 191n., 218n.,
  227n., 232n., 240n., 241n., 248n.,
  252n., 256n., 257n., 261n., 264n.,
  268n., 315n., 316n., 328n., 335n.,
  341n., 344n., 345n., 352n., 355n.,
  363n., 380n., 382., 388n., 401n., 404n.,
  405n., 410n., 411n., 425n., 427n.,
  439n., 440n., 459n., 471n., 493n.
Wendell, Barrett 159
Wentworth, Peter 7, 8n., 21
Werstine, Paul 268n., 344n., 403n.,
  506n., 507n.
Westminster, Abbot of 131, 133,
  175–6n., 177n., 272n., 305n., 315n.,
  361n., 372n., 414n., 427n., 433n.,
  443n., 457n., 476n., 478n., 479n.
  496n., 505n., 514
Westmoreland, 1st Earl of. See Neville,
  Ralph
White, Anthony 101
White, Richard Grant 112, 290n.
White, William 531, 532
Whitgift, John, Archbishop of
  Canterbury 516
Whyte, Rowland 113
Wilde, Oscar 494n.
William I (the Conqueror) 415n.
William of Hatfield (son of Edward III)
  201n.
William of Windsor (son of Edward III)
  201n.
Williams, Benjamin 156
Williams, David 98
Williams, George Walton 120n., 174n.,
  181n., 198n., 210n., 220–1n., 235n.,
  240n., 249n., 255n., 258n., 271n.,
  284n., 295n., 310n., 338n., 339n.,
  344n., 349n., 356n., 421n., 423n.,
  425n., 430n., 484n., 485n., 486n.,
  493n., 504n., 509n., 512n.
Williams, Harcourt 98
Willoughby, Sir William 175n., 177n.,
  279n., 291n., 296n.

Wilson, John Dover (Cambridge[1] editor)
  xv, 58, 114n., 115n., 117n., 147n., 156,
  179n., 183n., 197n., 198n., 204n.,
  205n., 214n., 223n., 224n., 225n.,
  228n., 238n., 239n., 249n., 252n.,
  267n., 275n., 284n., 295n., 297n.,
  321n., 322n., 324n., 332n., 336n.,
  338n., 348n., 352n., 364n., 365n.,
  379n., 381n., 383n., 384n., 387n.,
  389n., 391n., 395n., 396n., 398n.,
  405n., 406n., 407n., 409n., 410n.,
  411n., 417n., 419n., 421n., 432n.,
  436n., 440n., 444n., 445n., 453n.,
  454n., 457n., 459n., 473n., 483n.,
  486n., 487n., 489n., 492n., 493n.,
  494n., 496n., 498n., 503n., 504n.,
  506n., 510n., 518, 521
Wilson, Mona 282n.
Wilson, Robert 5n., 178n.
Wilson, Thomas 85
Wilton Diptych 132, 321n., 488n.
Wiltshire, Earl of. See Scroop, Sir William
Winchester, Bishop of. See Beaufort,
  Henry; Ponet, John
Winter, William 95
Wise, Andrew 506n., 515, 516, 517, 530,
  532
Wither, George 72
Wolsey, Thomas, Cardinal 358n., 494n.
Woodman, William 443n., 464n., 499n.
Woodstock 5, 17, 116–18, 124, 128,
  144–52, 153, 155n., 174n., 176n.,
  178n., 180n., 182n., 184n., 186n.,
  187n., 188n., 200n., 201n., 203n.,
  205n., 206n., 207n., 219n., 220n.,
  238n., 241n., 243n., 247n., 248n.,
  249n., 250n., 253n., 255n., 256n.,
  259n., 260n., 263n., 266n., 267n.,
  269n., 275n., 285n., 286n., 289n.,
  301–2n., 305n., 307n., 323n., 325n.,
  326n., 347n., 349n., 386n., 408n.,
  487n., 490n., 491n., 494n., 500n.,
  512n., 514, 524, 529
Woodstock, Thomas of, 1st Duke of
  Gloucester 10n., 116, 127, 133, 138,
  144, 145, 146, 148, 149, 150–1, 154,
  176n., 185n., 186n., 187–8n., 189n.,
  191n., 192n., 196n., 200n., 201n.,
  202n., 204n., 206n., 212n., 221n.,
  223n., 224n., 238n., 250n., 251n.,
  253n., 255n., 256n., 259n., 261n.,
  263n., 267n., 268n., 285n., 289n.,
  319n., 355n., 372n., 373n., 374n.,

375n., 377n., 380n., 383n., 384n., 485n., 490n., 495n., 496n., 514, 529

Woodville (or Wydevill), Anthony, 2nd Earl Rivers (*Richard III*) 474n.

Worcester, 1st Earl of. See Percy, Sir Thomas

Wright, William Aldis (Cambridge editor) 220n., 243n., 275n., 482–3n.

Wroughton, Richard 92–3, 111, 362n.

Wylie, J.H. 479n.

Yeats, William Butler 4, 96

Yoder, Audrey 386n., 494n.

York, Archbishop of. See Scroop, Richard

York mystery cycle. See *Agony in the Garden, The*

York, 1st Duke of. See Langley, Edmund of

York, 2nd Duke of. See Aumerle, Edward of York

York, 3rd Duke of. See Plantagenet, Richard

York, 4th Duke of. See Plantagenet, Richard

Zeno 198n.

Zeus (classical mythology). See Jupiter

Zitner, Sheldon P. 42, 434n., 440n., 502n., 503n.